D0208074

Conservative Judaism
in America

Conservative Judaism in America

A BIOGRAPHICAL DICTIONARY AND SOURCEBOOK

Pamela S. Nadell

Marc Lee Raphael
SERIES EDITOR

Jewish Denominations in America

Greenwood Press

New York • Westport, Connecticut • London

Library of Congress Cataloging-in-Publication Data

Nadell, Pamela Susan.
　　Conservative Judaism in America : a biographical dictionary and
sourcebook / Pamela S. Nadell.
　　　　p.　cm. — (Jewish denominations in America)
　　Bibliography: p.
　　Includes index.
　　ISBN 0–313–24205–4 (lib. bdg. : alk. paper)
　　1. Conservative Judaism—United States.　2. Jews—United States—
Biography—Dictionaries.　3. Jewish Theological Seminary of
America.　4. Rabbinical Assembly.　5. United Synagogue of America.
I. Title.　II. Series.
BM750.N33　1988
296.8′342′0922—dc19
[B]　　　　　　　　　　　　　　　　　　　　　　87–31782

British Library Cataloguing in Publication Data is available.

Library of Congress Catalog Card Number: 87–31782
ISBN: 0–313–24205–4

First published in 1988

Greenwood Press, Inc.
88 Post Road West, Westport, Connecticut 06881

Printed in the United States of America

The paper used in this book complies with the
Permanent Paper Standard issued by the National
Information Standards Organization (Z39.48–1984).

10　9　8　7　6　5　4　3　2　1

For Ed

CONTENTS

PREFACE

Since its early years, the leaders of the Conservative movement have struggled to define those facets of the movement upon which all its members can agree.[1] In almost every case, the effort to formulate principles of unity has provoked dissension. Yet it is likely that there is accord on what Max Routtenberg, former executive vice-president of the Rabbinical Assembly (RA), the union of Conservative rabbis, wrote in 1960: "Much of the strength of our movement lies not in the central institutions but in the lives and careers of individual men . . . as they pour their energies and strength, their devotion and love, their idealism and their learning into the fabric of Jewish life."[2]

Surely one of the great strengths of Conservatism has been its leaders, its rabbis, both those who have spent their lives guiding local congregations and those who, standing at the helms of its central institutions—Conservatism's fountainhead, the Jewish Theological Seminary of America (established 1886); the Rabbinical Assembly (1901); and the congregational body, the United Synagogue of America (1913)—have set the policies and directions of the larger movement. Together these men have shaped Conservatism as an American religious movement.

Conservative Judaism in America: A Biographical Dictionary and Sourcebook provides the first extensive documentation of the lives and careers of the most important leaders in Conservatism's first century as well as a brief history of the movement and its central institutions. The bulk of this volume consists of biographical sketches of some 130 key Conservative leaders, the overwhelming majority of them rabbis. Each entry contains essential biographical data and provides an evaluation of the figure's most important contributions to the development of American Conservatism, its institutions, guiding policies, ideology, and/or literature. Each portrait concludes with a bibliography of the individual's major writings in chronological order followed by works he edited or translated and then by references about him arranged alphabetically. Following the preface, all names that are preceded by an asterisk (*) are cross-referenced in this volume, and biographical information can be found in the main body of the dictionary.

Surely one of the most difficult tasks in this project has been to decide just whom to include in the biographical dictionary. This is not an encyclopedic project covering the thousands of men and women who, in the past century, have devoted their energies to Conservatism in both its local and national settings. Instead, the biographical dictionary highlights those whose careers have best exemplified Routtenberg's premise that the strength of the movement lies in its men. (Please note that as a religious movement that originally accorded only a small portion of its work to women and whose leaders tend to come from the ranks of the professional rabbinate, the most significant Conservative leaders have, with very few exceptions—notably the officers of the National Women's League for Conservative Judaism and certain Seminary administrators—been male. Only one woman, Mathilde Roth Schechter, founding president of the National Women's League for Conservative Judaism, appears here. An updating of this work in 2035, fifty years after the Seminary began ordaining women as rabbis, will surely see women's names added to the roster of Conservatism's movers and shapers.)

The winnowing of the biographical dictionary from a lengthy list of Conservative rabbis and lay leaders began with the decision to focus upon Conservatism's professional leaders, those whose careers—as rabbis, administrators, officers, teachers, or scholars—have been spent within the movement. As a result, Conservatism's many important lay leaders, including influential members of the Seminary's Board of Directors and officers of the various lay organizations, with the exception of their founding presidents, have been omitted.

The exclusion of most lay leaders still left a long roster of men who dedicated their lives to Conservatism. After all, since 1894 the Seminary has ordained more than 1,200 rabbis, but not all significant Conservative leaders were its graduates. Membership in the RA topped 1,200 in the 1980s. The elimination of all rabbis ordained after 1962 on the grounds that at least a quarter of a century is essential for evaluation of one's place within the movement (the one exception, Paul Freedman, was the founding president of United Synagogue Youth) still left a lengthy list of candidates. Consequently, the following criteria were applied to the selection of names for the biographical dictionary. It must be added that there is considerable overlap among these categories and that limited space forced the inclusion of only the most prominent figures in each area.

Obviously, it was of paramount importance to discuss those men who headed Conservatism's national institutions. Their names, familiar to those both within and without the movement, stand for Conservative Judaism in America. They include the presidents and chancellors of the Seminary, Sabato Morais, Solomon Schechter, Cyrus Adler, Louis Finkelstein, Gerson Cohen, and Ismar Schorsch, as well as their colleagues, administrators like Max Arzt, Simon Greenberg, David Lieber, and Bernard Mandelbaum, who played pivotal roles in charting the course of the Seminary and its West Coast affiliate, the University of Judaism.

Similarly, although many of their names are not widely known outside the movement, the forty presidents of the RA, from founding president Henry Speaker to the current president, Kassel Abelson, appear, along with sketches of the RA's supervising directors, Wolfe Kelman, Jules Harlow, and Gilbert Epstein. Because presidents of the United Synagogue were lay leaders after 1927, only the biographical sketches of its chief executives—Seminary rabbis Samuel M. Cohen, Albert Gordon, Simon Greenberg (to illustrate but one of the many instances of overlap), Bernard Segal, and Benjamin Kreitman—appear.

In addition to these executives and officers in Conservatism's headquarters, others within these settings made substantial contributions to the movement. Since only a few of the hundreds of men and women who have taught at the Seminary since its first class was held in 1887 could be included, three criteria were applied in selecting faculty members for the biographical dictionary. These teachers had to have played important roles in the larger Conservative movement and/or stood out, by virtue of their personalities, presence, or lengthy tenure, for their influence in training generations of Conservative rabbis. A few, regularly named in celebrations of the great Seminary scholars of the past, won a place for their scholarship alone.[3] Faculty meeting these criteria included Alexander Kohut, who was pivotal in the Seminary's early years; the scholars appointed by Schechter—Louis Ginzberg, Alexander Marx, Israel Friedlaender, Israel Davidson, and Mordecai M. Kaplan—men who shaped the first generations of the Conservative rabbinate; the later luminaries, Saul Lieberman and Abraham Joshua Heschel; and the influential scholars, Boaz Cohen, Robert Gordis, H. L. Ginsberg, Seymour Siegel, Shalom Spiegel and David Weiss.

A number of the members of the RA gained prominence for their leadership as chairmen, secretaries, and/or authors of important *responsa* (legal opinions) for the various Conservative committees on Jewish law. They included Morris Adler, Aaron Blumenthal, Louis Epstein, Theodore Friedman, Julius Greenstone, Michael Higger, Isaac Klein, Max Routtenberg, and others.

Because fostering Jewish education from cradle to grave emerged as one of the primary missions of the movement, those individuals who played a major role in developing educational programs within the synagogue or in Conservatism's youth and camping movements are covered. Accordingly, the biographical dictionary incorporates entries on those who directed education for the United Synagogue, like Morton Siegel and Marvin Wiener, and those, like Abraham Burstein, Judah Goldin, and Alter Landesman, whose books, development of curricula, or leadership of the Seminary's Teachers Institute placed them in the forefront of the Jewish educators of their day.

Another category encompassed the architects of Conservatism's ideology and philosophy. Obviously, many of those already named, especially the leaders and faculty of the Seminary, played pivotal roles here. But others within the movement who helped formulate Conservative ideology—rabbis like Jacob Agus, Ben Zion Bokser, and Harold Schulweis—and whose influence is recognized by the inclusion of their writings in such works as the Rabbinical Assembly's series

Emet Ve-Emunah, Studies in Conservative Jewish Thought, merited inclusion. Furthermore, this category was expanded to include historians like Moshe Davis and Abraham Karp, whose scholarship has enhanced our understanding of the history of Conservatism, and early liturgists like Jacob Bosniak and Morris Silverman, whose prayer books guided Conservative congregations before the movement developed its own.

Many of the Conservative leaders already named—men like Morais, Greenberg, and Gordis—were influential not only for their contributions to the larger movement but, first and foremost, as pulpit rabbis. So much of the strength of the movement has lain in its men out in their congregations that it seemed essential to establish criteria to include those who were best known as congregational rabbis. Clearly, some pulpit rabbis—Solomon Goldman, Israel Goldstein, and Israel Levinthal immediately come to mind—had national reputations as leaders of American Jewish organizations and/or were known for their writings and volumes of sermons. But other Conservative rabbis, known perhaps within the movement but not generally without, merited a place in the biographical dictionary for single-handedly pioneering Conservative Judaism in its early decades in the hinterlands. Often standing at the helm of the only Conservative synagogue in their cities, Seminary rabbis like Herman Abramowitz of Montreal, Louis Feinberg of Cincinnati, Charles Eliezer Hillel Kauvar of Denver, Hyman Rabinowitz of Sioux City, Iowa, and Nathan Zelizer of Columbus, Ohio, maintained bastions of Conservatism in their communities. Others like Harry Epstein of Atlanta and Louis Swichkow of Milwaukee were not even Seminary graduates, but they gradually, and often in face of great opposition, led their formerly Orthodox congregations into the movement that came, to them, to express the best fusion of traditional Judaism and progressive Americanism. In the decades before the explosive growth of United Synagogue member congregations in the postwar suburbs, these men were Conservative Judaism across America.

Finally, the last category of those included in the biographical dictionary, the key figures of the Reconstructionist movement, has already provoked some concern from the Reconstructionist camp. The Jewish Denominations in America series consists of three volumes. Since the early leaders of Reconstructionism, most notably Mordecai Kaplan, Ira Eisenstein, Jack Cohen, Eugene Kohn, and Milton Steinberg, began within the Conservative movement and often remained there for the greater part of their careers, the pioneers of Reconstructionism cannot easily be separated from the history of Conservatism. Their inclusion in the biographical dictionary reveals that as the left wing of the Conservative movement they greatly enriched Conservatism by their challenges while they were gradually creating Reconstructionism as a separate religious movement. Their presence in this biographical dictionary in no way indicates that Reconstructionism remains subordinate to Conservatism, but rather that the youngest of the four denominations of American Judaism does not yet fill a volume of its own.

As Conservatism's premiere historian, Abraham J. Karp, has shown, Conservative Judaism is a coalition movement governed by consensus, the

product of both the ideological ferment in nineteenth-century Jewish life and the sociological realities of twentieth-century America. The former brought about the coalition of acculturated Orthodox and moderate Reform rabbis and laymen that founded the Seminary in 1886; the latter influenced the distinctive mission and program of the Conservative synagogue.[4]

A movement in the center, stemming the tide against Reform's radicalism while repudiating Orthodoxy's insularity, Conservative Judaism came to operate by consensus, hesitating from ideological and definitional pronouncements liable to alienate those who had embraced the precarious coalition that had sparked its formation. Instead, in different periods throughout its history, Conservative Judaism has stood for different things to its different constituencies—a stance, its critics charge, that reveals the movement's vagueness and weakness.

For its founders Conservatism was first and foremost a philosophy, a tendency, named for its determination to "conserve" traditional Judaism in the midst of an alluring American diaspora inhospitable to Jewish tradition. But it was never a monolithic school of thought. Instead it was and has continued to be characterized by tremendous variety and complexity, a diversity readily evident in the widely divergent philosophies and theologies put forward by its leading spokesmen.

Later, as a result of the efforts of its first generations of leaders and changes in the post–World War II American Jewish community, Conservative Judaism evolved into a movement, one which, according to Conservative rabbi and historian Herbert Rosenblum, "[m]ore than either of its sister movements . . . came to wrestle with American Jewry's central issues—liturgy, Jewish law, education, community organization, Jewish nationalism (and Zionism), and intellectual scholarship."[5] This agenda revealed the determination of its leaders, the men of the Conservative rabbinate, to make Conservatism a blend of "tradition and change," forging, according to historian Naomi Cohen, a synthesis of "progressivism and Americanism with a commitment to rabbinical Judaism."[6] In their congregations and especially in the movement's national institutions and organizations, its scholars and rabbis made decisions to guide their 800 plus congregations and 1.5 million members to live within the parameters fixed by their adaptations of Jewish tradition to the American setting.

Yet, one of Conservatism's fundamental principles has remained the individualism of its congregations. For many laity the movement extends no further than these synagogues. Each, led by rabbis and laymen and women, ultimately determines its own ritual practices and theological boundaries. Consequently, each defines for itself Conservative Judaism. Thus just as the movement does not embrace a monolithic theology, so too great diversity characterizes its congregations.

Moreover, another factor—the great discrepancy between the ideals and standards set by Conservative leaders and the actual practice of the great majority of their congregants—adds to the marked dichotomies of the movement. For Conservative Jews, Conservatism means to participate as much or as little as they like in the social, educational, and religious lives of their synagogues. For this laity Conservative Judaism promises High Holiday services, a place to celebrate familial rites of passage, Sisterhood variety shows, Men's Club breakfasts, and adult education forums. Their children go to its Hebrew schools and their teens to United Synagogue Youth conventions and Camp Ramah. But the consensus achieved by the movement's leaders on the critical issues of adapting Jewish tradition to America are, if known and heeded at all, considered guidelines, not dictates, for their lives outside the synagogue.

Therefore, Conservative Judaism remains today, as it was at its inception, a movement of great diversity and frequent disparity. A definition of Conservatism, drawn from the writings and teachings of its leaders, yields but one answer to the question that has plagued Conservative rabbis, scholars, and even some laity since the movement's inception: just what is Conservative Judaism? A definition based on the conduct of its congregations would yield a second. A definition drawn from the lives of those who identify as Conservative Jews would yield a third. A coalition movement, Conservatism is not a cohesive movement. Rather it is the sum of its many parts.

The essays in *Conservative Judaism in America*—based on printed sources since the archives of the Conservative movement, lacking funds for cataloguing, were unavailable at the time of my research—reflect this perception. Their subjects emerged from the concerns of the biographical dictionary and are thus reflective of Conservatism's elite, its leaders who wrestled with the central issues of American Jewish life. While no single essay presents a comprehensive history of the evolution of Conservative Judaism, together they constitute a history of Conservatism's movers and shapers, their chief concerns, and their achievements.

For example, the introductory essay explores the history of Conservatism through its most important tenet, the assertion that Conservative Judaism is a *halachic* movement. Insisting upon the maintenance of the body of Jewish law and tradition, known as *halachah*, the Conservative movement has consistently upheld the notion of the historical development of Judaism and that *halachah* was never fixed at any given point in the past. Conservative rabbis of the present, just like the sages of the past, are obligated to adjust *halachah*, through time-honored legal mechanisms, to make it viable for contemporary Jewry. After surveying Conservatism's origins in nineteenth-century European Jewish thought, the essay discusses the movement's various committees on Jewish law, their key challenges and decisions. It then evaluates their successes and failures in guiding Conservative laity to live within the boundaries of *halachah*. Finally, because one of the key distinctions between Reconstructionism and Conservatism is that the former is not a *halachic* movement, the introductory essay concludes with an overview of the ideology and institutions of Reconstructionism.

The concluding essays of the volume offer brief histories of the three chief organizations of Conservative Judaism—the Seminary, the Rabbinical Assembly, and the United Synagogue. The essay on the Seminary traces its development from a tiny school for the training of rabbis into the fountainhead of a movement that claims 1.5 million adherents. Its key themes are the emergence of the Seminary as a premier scholastic institution; its expansion beyond a rabbinical school into a university for training scholars, teachers, cantors, and communal servants for American Judaism; and its emergence as the dominant force in the Conservative movement. The essay on the Rabbinical Assembly (RA) traces its evolution from the Alumni Association of the Jewish Theological Seminary of America to ''the international organization of Conservative rabbis.'' It highlights the roles the RA played in ameliorating the poor status of the American rabbinate and in creating a literature to disseminate the Conservative point of view. The essay on the United Synagogue traces the circumstances that necessitated the founding of a third confederation of American synagogues and discusses both its expansion and its fashioning of the educational and youth programs designed to win the next generation to Conservative Judaism. Granted that there was and is much duplication of effort among the three central institutions of Conservatism—for example, all three bodies develop educational programs—these institutional histories provide one way of understanding the amorphous movement.

Conservative Judaism in American concludes with appendices listing the leaders of the most important Conservative and Reconstructionist associations. An extensive bibliography suggests areas for further research.

In the four years of researching and writing this volume, many Conservative leaders, colleagues, and friends shared their impressions of the Conservative movement with me. While I cannot list all of these, discussions with Debra Greenfeld Becker, Steven Diner, Robert Fierstien, Jeffrey Gurock, Wolfe Kelman, Norman Mirsky, Stanley Rabinowitz, Gershon and Shuly Rubin Schwartz, Morton Siegel, Saul Wachs, Jack Wertheimer, Marvin Wiener, and my colleagues in the American University History Department were especially valuable. Benjamin Kahn, Director of the American University Jewish Studies Program, president of the Seminary senior class of 1938, and a joy to work with, was ever willing to share his recollections of nearly a half century in the movement. American University generously provided travel funds and grants for course-release time. Librarians at the Seminary, Library of Congress, Ohio State University, and American University, and especially the librarians in charge of interlibrary loan services, Ohio State's Clara Goldschlager and American's Shirley Rosenstock, smoothed my research. Ruth Perry and Rhonda Arbeit of the United Synagogue were kind enough to make back copies of the *United Synagogue Review* available to me. Several people, including Rebecca Trachtenberg Alpert, David Altshuler, Mark Bauman, Hasia Diner, Jules Harlow, and Marjorie Wyler read and offered valuable comments upon portions of the manuscript. Jonathan D. Sarna was especially generous in sharing his time and his prodigious memory, and I am especially appreciative of his careful reading of the manuscript. The indefatigable Marc Lee Raphael, editor of *Jewish Denominations in America*, continued, as he had in the past, to teach me much by his careful editing and judicious comments. Cynthia Harris of Greenwood Press was an ever-patient and careful guide. And finally, my husband, Edward Farber, sustained, as always with patience and love, both this project and the author. I gratefully acknowledge their assistance.

Of course, responsibility for all errors remains mine as does the hope that in some small way this work will enhance the reader's understanding of Conservative Judaism in America.

NOTES

1. See, for example, Louis Finkelstein, "The Things That Unite Us" (1927) and Mordecai M. Kaplan, "Unity in Diversity in the Conservative Movement" (1947), reprinted in *Tradition and Change*, ed. Mordecai M. Waxman (New York, 1958), pp. 211–28, 333–36. A more recent attempt is that of David Novak, "The Distinctiveness of Conservative Judaism," *Judaism* 26, 3 (Summer 1977), pp. 305–8.

2. Max J. Routtenberg, "The Conservative Rabbinate" (1960), reprinted in his *Decades of Decision* (New York, 1973), p. 155.

3. See, for example, "Oral Festschrift in Tribute to Seminary Scholarship," *PRA 1986* vol. 48, pp. 145–220.

4. Abraham J. Karp, "A Century of Conservative Judaism in the United States," *AJYB* vol. 86 (New York, 1986), p. 3.

5. Herbert Rosenblum, *Conservative Judaism: A Contemporary History* (New York, 1983), p. 65.

6. Naomi Cohen, *Encounter with Emancipation: The German Jews in the United States, 1830–1914* (Philadelphia, 1984), p. 184.

ABBREVIATIONS

AJA	*American Jewish Archives*
AJYB	*American Jewish Year Book*
CJ	*Conservative Judaism*
EJ	*Encyclopedia Judaica*
JE	*The Jewish Exponent*
NYT	*New York Times*
PRA	*Proceedings of the Rabbinical Assembly*
Recorder	*United Synagogue Recorder*
Review	*United Synagogue Review*
WWAJ	*Who's Who in American Jewry*
WWWJ	*Who's Who in World Jewry*

Conservative Judaism
in America

INTRODUCTION

In an address given in 1965, Vice-Chancellor of the Jewish Theological Seminary of America Simon *Greenberg defined the essence of Conservative Judaism as its acceptance of the dichotomies inherent in American Jewish life:

One of the primary characteristics of the Conservative movement, which perhaps more than any other makes it the authentic bearer of the mainstream of the Jewish tradition, is its insistence upon embracing within itself both poles of the polarities that are ubiquitously inherent in all of human life generally, and in Jewish life in particular; the insistence upon the validity of the *Halakhah* and the need for taking the needs of modern American Jewish life into consideration; the place of centrality of Eretz Yisrael in Jewish life and thought, and the indispensable role of the Diaspora; the role of ritual in Jewish religion and the dominant place of the moral and ethical law; the ceaseless striving for unity in Jewish life and the acceptance of the diversity through which it expresses itself.[1]

Nowhere is Conservatism's grappling with contemporary realities, acquiescence to the imperative of moral law, and acceptance of diversity more sharply revealed than in the history of the movement's striving to adapt the body of Jewish tradition and law, known as *halachah*, to twentieth-century America. Conservative leaders—in the Seminary, the movement's rabbinical school and fountainhead; the Rabbinical Assembly, the international association of Conservative rabbis; and the United Synagogue of America, Conservatism's congregational union and lay organization—have wrestled with the central issues of American Jewish life, and forged a synthesis of progressive Americanism with rabbinical Judaism.

In *Tradition and Change*, the first collection of essays published by the RA presenting its view of Conservatism, the editor, Rabbi Mordecai *Waxman, wrote: "Conservative Judaism holds itself bound by the Jewish legal tradition, but asserts the right of its rabbinical body, acting as a whole, to interpret and to apply Jewish law." Since the days of the Seminary Alumni Association, the Conservative rabbinate has struggled to interpret and, when necessary, to adapt *halachah* to the unique circumstances of twentieth-century America. The men of the RA believed that if they could show that Jewish law was sufficiently flexible to meet head-on the changed conditions of life in the contemporary world, they would succeed in laying the foundations for American Jews' adherence to *halachah*. Their triumphs and disappointments in adjusting *halachah* led rabbi and future RA president Max *Routtenberg to claim on the eve of the sixtieth anniversary of the founding of the Seminary Alumni Association: "The problem of Jewish law and its applicability to life remains the 'grand obsession' of the Rabbinical Assembly."[2]

This "grand obsession" united the members of the RA, who, according to Routtenberg, "without exception, believe that the law can be adjusted." They based their conviction on the nineteenth-century ideology Positive-Historical Judaism, the forerunner of Conservatism in America. Briefly, this school of thought asserted that *halachah* was never fixed at any given point. Instead, the Historical School emphasized the evolving character of Jewish tradition and showed that the historic experience of the Jewish people was organic to that development. In its acceptance of contemporary conditions as a positive force shaping that tradition, the Historical School stressed that prior scholars and sages effected

tremendous, almost revolutionary changes . . . in adjusting the heritage to the lives of the people . . . [T]hrough the ages, the rabbinic authorities faced the demands of a changing society and met them courageously, modifying or adapting the law, and suspending it when necessary, and creating new laws when the circumstances so required.[3]

As the intellectual heirs to the Historical School, the Conservative rabbis were unable to accept the Reform movement's deliberate abrogation of Jewish law. Yet they considered Orthodoxy's determination to maintain a rigid, unadjusted *halachah* to be an equally grave abandonment of the evolutionary historical tradition of the Jewish people. On the one hand bound by *halachah* and on the other committed to the notion of historical change, the RA set about the business of "adjusting the heritage" to the modern world.[4]

The key forces of change affecting American Jews were Americanization and secularization. By the beginning of the twentieth century many American Jews, including large numbers of the recent immigrants from the towns and *shtetlakh* of Eastern Europe, already considered much of the *halachah* immaterial to their lives. Others would arrive at the same conclusion as they rushed to Americanize and to climb the social and economic ladders that led from the immigrant neighborhoods. The Jewish agencies of the past that had coerced conformity within the premodern communities did not survive the transplantation to America. In America, as in the European countries where Jews were also emancipated, Jews as individuals entertained, perhaps for the first time in Jewish history, the notion that adherence to Jewish law was optional and personally selective.

By the beginning of the twentieth century, the widespread abandonment of *halachah* by much of American Jewry was already evident. When the Seminary was founded in 1886, in the decade when the rush of East European Jewish immigration was just getting underway, it pledged itself to uphold *halachah*. Its constitution mandated "the preservation in America of the knowledge and practice of historical Judaism, as ordained in the Law of Moses (*Torah*), and expounded by the prophets (*Nevi'im*) and sages (*Hakhamim*) of Israel in Biblical and Talmudical writings." But by 1913, when the United Synagogue was founded, the great bulk of these immigrants had already landed, radically transforming the American Jewish community. Cognizant of the voluntary nature of Jewish affiliation in America and aware of American Jewry's cultural and religious diversity, the founders of the United Synagogue planned for their new association to appeal to the broadest possible spectrum. Because these men knew that the United Synagogue could not coerce members to conform to their understanding of Jewish law, they made no attempt to do so. The promise to be bound by *halachah* was, therefore, missing from its constitution.[5]

During the course of the twentieth century, as Americanization and secularization made ever greater inroads, American Jews—including many who affiliated with the Conservative movement—fashioned their own Jewish tradition, picking and choosing among the remnants of *halachah*, observing certain holidays and forgetting others, upholding certain rites and rituals, inventing new ones, and to a great extent ignoring others. This *halachic* anarchy, however, seriously undermined the tradition the Conservative rabbinate upheld. The solution, Conservative rabbis believed, was for them to take charge of shaping *halachah*, striking a balance between the forces of "tradition and change" so that Conservative Jews could and would volunteer to observe it. This delicate task became the "grand obsession" of the RA.

Although Conservative rabbis were unanimous in their belief that *halachah* could and must be adjusted, "[t]hey differ[ed] as to whether it should be done by interpretation or legislation, by enactment or abrogation." These differences over the nature and extent of this adjustment led to the evolution of the three wings of the movement. The seeds of the ideological divisions lay in the early years of the Seminary Alumni Association, when even the Philadelphia weekly *Jewish Exponent* could not help but remark upon the wide "variety of opinions" expressed at the association's annual conventions. By the time the RA formed its first Committee on Jewish Law in 1927, the wings had crystallized. The movement became a coalition of the right, left, and center divided by differing views on how to strike the correct balance between "tradition and change" in developing *halachah*. Those on the right favored the maintenance of tradition over any but the most essential changes. Those on the left, represented for many years by the Reconstructionists, demanded significant adaptations necessary to meet the radically changed world inhabited by an Americanized Jewry. And in the middle stood a large, but often less articulate, center, trying valiantly to balance the sometimes shaky coalition.[6]

Although Positive-Historical Judaism emphasized the ongoing evolutionary nature of *halachah*, it never established a clear formula for this process of change and development. Early leaders of the Seminary, especially President Solomon

*Schechter and Professor Israel *Friedlaender, taught that minor *halachic* changes could be effected without altering the essentially traditional nature of Judaism. The key was to legitimize the changes by reinterpreting the traditional texts to prove that the innovations were attuned to the basic spirit of Jewish law. The Seminary men also believed that *halachah* must reflect the will of the community, of "Catholic Israel" to borrow the phrase introduced by Schechter. Different views of the will of "Catholic Israel" and different opinions over the extent of change sanctioned by reinterpretation of the sources divided the wings of the movement.[7]

The mechanism the Conservative movement adopted for effecting the adjustment of *halachah* was the establishment of a series of committees on Jewish law. The first of these was organized in 1917 when the United Synagogue established its Committee for the Interpretation of Jewish Law, chaired by the Conservative movement's reigning *halachic* expert, Seminary professor Louis *Ginzberg. In his address to the United Synagogue convention a year later, Ginzberg emphasized that the committee was formed to correct the misperception "that in religious matters anyone, however ignorant, can judge for himself." Only experts, men trained in the workings of *halachah*, were qualified to take care of the "sorting, distributing, selecting, harmonizing, and completing," the great tradition that contemporary Jewry inherited from the past.[8]

Although the Committee for the Interpretation of Jewish Law consisted of five members, it was essentially a one-man operation run by Ginzberg. He wrote most of the committee's decisions, replying, as rabbis have done since the close of the Talmudic era (ca. sixth century C.E.), to inquiries about every aspect of Jewish life and practice. His overriding view of *halachah* was that no change should be promulgated without the consent of all sectors of Jewry. Nevertheless, like the *halachic* experts of the past, he was confronted with a wide range of issues raised by the historical problem of adapting tradition to the contemporary setting, in this case Jazz Age America. Ginzberg ruled on the permissibility of the sale of synagogues, of withholding a *get* (the Jewish bill of divorcement) until a civil court dissolved the marriage, and of using unfermented wine for ritual purposes during Prohibition. He explored the appropriate architecture of synagogue-centers and considered questions on *kashrut*, prayer, and *Shabbat*, areas of the tradition that would continue to engage his successors.[9]

Some within the United Synagogue soon began to grumble about the strictness of Ginzberg's rulings, especially his view on seating patterns in the synagogue. Traditional synagogues mandate the separation by partition of men and women in worship. While Ginzberg sanctioned the abolition of the medieval women's gallery as a relatively recent innovation, he believed that the long tradition of separating the sexes during prayer could not be dispensed with lightly. Yet many, if not most, United Synagogue congregations already allowed family pews. The United Synagogue sought to reassure its member congregations at its annual convention in 1922 that it could not and would not attempt to coerce compliance with the positions taken by its Committee for the Interpretation of Jewish Law.

It was impressed that the United Synagogue did not consider these decisions as final, that they were a summary of the Law on the questions and that it was a matter for the individual congregation to decide whether it wanted to obey. No committee could force a member to do a right thing, nor could any, by sanction, make proper a wrong.[10]

In the face of growing opposition, Ginzberg conceded the untenability of his task and stepped down. Lacking the prestige of a scholar of his caliber at its helm, the Committee for the Interpretation of Jewish Law foundered.

In the meantime *halachic* questions from rabbis and congregations struggling to live within the tradition continued to flow to the committee. By 1927 its inability to act forced the United Synagogue to relinquish authority over *halachah* for the Conservative movement. The Seminary, led by President Cyrus *Adler, refrained from entering the arena, passing the challenge to lead the movement in adjusting *halachah* to the contemporary environment to its alumni in the RA. To guide the way, the RA established a Committee on Jewish Law (1928–48) and charged it to include representatives reflective of the "various tendencies" of the RA. Of its ten members, four had to come from the right wing, "representing the more conservative tendency," and four were to belong to "the liberal tendency." Two additional members were then chosen by these eight. The committee began in a flourish of great enthusiasm. Max *Drob, its first chairman and president of the RA in 1928, reported that its creation marked "the first step towards the organization of an American *bet din hagadol* [supreme court of Jewish law] which will study the problems arising in our new environment and solve them in the spirit of our Torah."[11]

The Committee on Jewish Law included Louis *Epstein, Louis *Finkelstein, and Julius *Greenstone, and Chairman Drob from the right wing and Mordecai *Kaplan, Jacob *Kohn, Herman *Rubenovitz, and Solomon *Goldman from the left. They were joined by Harry S. Davidowitz and Morris Levine. The RA empowered the committee to act in "an advisory capacity to the members of the Assembly in matters of religious and legal procedure" and to receive and respond to questions from rabbis. It planned that unanimous decisions would become "the authoritative opinion[s] of the Rabbinical Assembly." In cases yielding minority and majority reports, the committee would furnish both to the inquirer, who was free, according to tradition, to follow either. Although Max Drob enthusiastically envisioned a grand future for the committee, he prophetically warned his colleagues: "Do not expect to solve all the problems of Jewry *al regel echat*, 'while standing on one foot.' It has taken years to crystallize the organization of such a Committee and you should not be disappointed if it takes sometime before the Committee accomplishes its mission."[12]

Drob was unwittingly right on target when he anticipated that the committee would struggle for "sometime"—in fact, for decades—in its efforts to make significant headway in solving the problems met by an Americanized Jewry trying to live within *halachah*. The committee began, however, with a flurry of promising activity. In 1929, it published its first two *responsa*, the traditional *halachic* documents in which rabbis answer the questions posed, in the *Pro-*

ceedings of the Rabbinical Assembly. But soon organizational difficulties got in the way. After the committee failed to deliver a report at the 1931 RA convention, the RA called for its reorganization. In February 1932 the Committee on Jewish Law began to function once again, this time with Julius Greenstone as chairman (1932–36). Now Boaz *Cohen, a member of the Seminary faculty, joined its ranks as secretary and later as chairman (1940–48). One of the committee's most influential members, he authored many of its decisions, *responsa* that were consonant with his belief "that there are limits to genuine interpretation and that we cannot attempt to remedy all evils." Cohen refrained from sanctioning the promulgation of new laws that could not be derived from traditional law. And he refused to abolish laws, such as the Biblical prohibition against shaving with a razor, that had become obsolete because of the willful neglect of the people.[13]

Enhancing the "conservative" leaning of this committee was the influence of Louis Ginzberg, who consented to assist the RA in establishing *bet din* (Jewish courts of law) throughout America. Although not officially a member of the committee, Ginzberg's influence extended far beyond this single project: the committee consulted him regularly, especially whenever any important question arose. Chairman Boaz Cohen acknowledged the committee's debt: "As in the time past, Professor Ginzberg has been ever gracious to us, giving us unstintingly of his boundless knowledge and permitting us to benefit by his rich understanding of American Jewish life." Ginzberg's influence decisively shifted the balance of the committee toward the right. As Eli Ginzberg explained of his father:

He never understood why Jewish theology and law should be restructured for men and women who did not know what the law was and who basically did not care. He was not so rigid as to believe that the law should not change, but felt that it had to be changed by scholars who knew and cared, for a community that respected their authority.

Even a subsequent reorganization of the committee in 1934 to enlarge its membership failed to stem the conservative tide.[14]

A wide variety of questions came before the committee. They dealt primarily with *kashrut*, synagogue customs, funeral practices, conversion, circumcision, and intermarriage. Relatively minor issues—whether or not a likeness of the deceased could be engraved on the tombstone, whether it was permitted to play cards in the annex of a synagogue, or whether congregants could install a piano intended for school programs in the sanctuary—were easily dispatched. Others, however, had greater import. The committee ruled that intermarried Jews could not join synagogues. Recognizing the difficulties of observing *kashrut* in a highly mobile American society, it determined that eating broiled fish in restaurants and hotels was permissible. To its dismay, many Conservative Jews took this as a blanket approval to their eating regularly in restaurants—as long as they limited their menu selections to fish. This led the committee to reformulate the permission to apply only to emergencies. But it was the agonizing debate over the plight of the *agunah* that became the key symbol for the RA's "grand obsession" with *halachah*.[15]

Already by 1929 the committee was exploring ways to solve "one of the most distressing and painful conditions" of Jewish life, the plight of the deserted wife, the *agunah*. Under Jewish law a woman whose husband's death cannot be established with certainty or whose husband refuses to grant her a *get* is prohibited from ever remarrying. She remains anchored by the Jewish laws of marriage to a husband who no longer lives with her. (*Halachah* imposes no comparable disability upon abandoned husbands.) For the next forty years the RA wrestled with various attempts to solve this serious inequity in *halachah*.[16]

In 1930 Louis Epstein, a member of the committee and its chairman from 1936 to 1940, presented to the RA "A Solution to the Agunah Problem." Epstein proposed the addition of an instrument to the *ketubah* (the Jewish marriage contract) that would provide in advance for the husband to authorize his wife to write her own *get* under the supervision of a *bet din* in such cases where he could not or would not do it himself. In 1935 Epstein's proposal was approved by the committee and adopted by the RA, which called for the establishment of a *bet din* to implement it.[17]

But what followed next paralyzed the committee. The Orthodox rabbinical association, the *Agudat ha-Rabbanim*, unleashed a vicious attack in the Yiddish press, "hysterical[ly] condemn[ing] the Conservative rabbinate for daring to invade a *halachic* realm over which they claimed to hold an exclusive monopoly." The invective stung the RA and pressured the committee to reconsider its support of Epstein's proposal. The committee decided to wait to implement the scheme until the RA solicited the cooperation of all other rabbinic bodies in America, Europe, and Palestine and until Professor Ginzberg issued a *responsum* on the legitimacy of the proposal. When it became evident that neither the *responsum* nor the desired cooperation were forthcoming, the committee repudiated Epstein's proposal, affirming that it was "not ready to lay down principles which would be in conflict with Orthodox practice."[18]

Despite the recalcitrance of the committee, the *agunah* controversy continued to exercise the RA at its 1940 convention. While the committee intended to form a *bet din* of three outstanding *halachic* experts, headed by Ginzberg, to determine the validity of Epstein's plan, the RA heard Rabbi David *Aronson review Epstein's book *Li-Shealat Ha-Agunah*, defending his proposal. Although Aronson sketched an alternative *halachic* solution to the *agunah's* dilemma, his anxiety over her plight led him to move that the committee circulate a questionnaire in the RA calling for a vote on Epstein's proposal. Once one hundred members of the RA agreed to abide by the plan, the RA could unofficially organize a *bet din* to implement it. The RA endorsed Aronson's motion, but once again the committee refused to cooperate, asserting this time that the RA lacked the jurisdiction necessary to introduce any measure that could potentially affect all of American Jewry.[19]

As America entered World War II, the committee turned its attention briefly away from the *agunah* to consider the *halachic* problems of the men in the armed forces. The wartime emergency brought several pragmatic interpretations of the tradition. The committee ruled that soldiers were obliged to adhere to Jewish dietary and Sabbath laws only insofar as possible, given the demands of their service. It allowed rabbis to celebrate marriages on days interdicted by Jewish law for men about to be shipped overseas. Unfortunately, the war also raised the specter that these marriages might end suddenly, leaving young brides grief-stricken *agunot* if their husbands' deaths could not be validated according to the tests of Jewish law. The potential problem was so serious that in 1942 Ginzberg drafted for the committee a document, not dissimilar to Epstein's, allowing a husband to authorize in advance agents to write his wife a *get* should he fail to return within two years of the conclusion of the war. With relief the RA endorsed Ginzberg's text and obligated RA members to present it to every couple that came before them for marriage and called upon the armed forces chaplains to discuss it with the men in their charge who were already married. But Ginzberg and the committee considered the proposal a temporary, wartime emergency measure. It was not meant to be a comprehensive solution to the *agunah* controversy. Consequently, at the war's end these special arrangements were allowed to lapse.[20]

In the immediate postwar years, members of the RA became increasingly critical of their committee and its reluctance to move forward in adjusting *halachah*. In 1947 the chairman of the committee, Boaz Cohen, rejoined:

We are not oblivious to the fact that a feeling exists among others that our Committee is inadequate to the task. This sentiment stems from a viewpoint toward Jewish Law not shared by the Committee, and originates in a difference in conception about the manner in which the Committee should exercise its office . . . We are content to measure our progress in inches for the time being.

Apparently, the committee was content with "progress in inches," most members sharing Cohen's conviction that any other course would "be perilous, if not fatal to the principles of the continuity of Jewish Law." But they were no longer attuned to the will of the majority of the RA rabbis. Since the inception of the committee in 1927, the RA had grown significantly in size and in stature. As it changed its name from the Rabbinical Assembly of the Jewish Theological Seminary of America to the Rabbinical Assembly of America in 1940, it began to assert its independence from the very influential and very traditional forces of the Seminary. No longer would the RA—which had now opened its ranks to outsiders—see itself as a subordinate alumni association. One reflection of its growing independence was the dissolution of the Committee on Jewish Law and the inauguration of the Committee on Jewish Law and Standards in 1948.[21]

Following Boaz Cohen's report at the 1947 convention, Rabbi Jacob *Agus—who although trained and ordained at institutions associated with American Orthodoxy left them behind when he joined the RA in 1945—proposed the reorganization of the committee. The next spring the RA held a special conference on "The *Halachah* and the Challenges of Modern Life." There Rabbi Michael

*Higger, a consultant to the committee who taught and lived at the Seminary, argued that although *halachic* experts distinguished among the various forms of authority—intepretation, reinterpretation, legislation, and abrogation—if the RA presumed one form of authority, it had the power to exercise all. Out of this conference came a resolution to devote an entire day at the 1948 convention to analyzing the three basic attitudes toward Jewish law within the RA. At the end of these discussions the RA would vote on the reorganization of its law committee.[22]

The 1948 convention in Chicago was a turning point. The symposium, "Towards a Philosophy of Conservative Judaism," with addresses by rabbis Theodore *Friedman, William *Greenfeld, and Isaac *Klein, dealt with *halachah*. The key question was whether or not the new law committee would be permitted to extend *halachah* once the limits of legitimate interpretation had been reached. Would the RA empower the committee to go beyond the boundaries of *halachah* to allow for adjustments or innovations in the tradition? Would the reorganized committee have the authority to abrogate laws which the people ignored or to amend ones—such as those mandating the inequality of women—which it viewed as ethically unjust? Could the committee address areas which the tradition had never even contemplated, such as adoption? Could the committee move away from *halachah*—such as when dealing with the intermarried—where "a strictly *halachic* solution would, if attempted, destroy rather than maintain and foster Jewish religious consciousness"? Would the RA allow the committee to consider factors—the highest moral and ethical standards—other than *halachah* in rendering its decisions?[23]

At the conclusion of the debate following the presentations, the RA voted on resolutions to redefine the composition, scope, and powers of the Committee on Jewish Law. Finally, the discussions centered on the crucial section of the set of resolutions formulated by Louis Epstein. Section five read: "The Committee shall be instructed to hold itself bound by the authority of Jewish law and within the frame of Jewish law to labor toward progress and growth of the Law to the end of adjusting it to present day religious needs and orientation, whether it be on the side of severity or leniency." This meant that at all times and in all cases the committee would be bound by *halachah*. The RA defeated the resolution, empowering its new Committee on Jewish Law and Standards with the authority to go beyond *halachah*.[24]

The new name, the Committee on Jewish Law and Standards (CJLS; 1948–70, reorganized 1972–   ), reflected both the extra-*halachic* powers of the CJLS and its anticipation that with its expanded authority, its decisions would succeed in "the raising of the standards of piety, understanding, and participation in Jewish life" among Conservative Jewry. The CJLS expanded its ranks to twenty-five members, who were to represent as far as possible the diverse views of the RA. But it deliberately excluded from membership Seminary faculty, unless they were also pulpit rabbis, because they did not share in the frontline experience of serving in congregations bound by its decisions. Detroit rabbi Morris *Adler became its first chairman (1948–51), and Michael Higger was appointed secretary and research fellow delegated to answer specific questions addressed to the CJLS. In order to extend its influence, the CJLS determined that in addition to answering questions, it could of its own accord initiate studies in areas of the law that it felt would be of practical use to rabbis and their congregations. As soon as the CJLS was formerly constituted, it authorized subcommittees on the Sabbath and on synagogue rituals to open such inquiries.[25]

The CJLS agreed to circulate among the RA minority and majority reports signed by those members of the CJLS subscribing to each opinion. Members of the RA were free to follow either *responsum*, even if the minority opinion bore only a single signature. However, in the event the CJLS made a unanimous recommendation, it became the official position of the RA, binding on all members. Yet because the RA historically supported the concept of *mara d'atra*, that each rabbi was the *halachic* expert for his community, the committee recognized from the first that it could "not apply sanctions against members who refuse[d] to accept even a unanimous decision of the Law Committee." Morris Adler declared that the CJLS would "introduce into our thinking this revolutionary fact—the impact of an entirely changed world both outer and inner." And he assured his colleagues that no longer would the RA halt, stopped squarely in its tracks between its "fear of the Orthodox and danger to Reform."[26]

The CJLS began boldly. The *agunah* problem immediately claimed attention. The RA charged the CJLS with implementing the measures for averting future *agunot* that had been developed for the wartime emergency. But before proceeding any further on that front, the CJLS turned its attention to what it perceived as one of the most critical problems of American Jewish religious life—the widespread violations of the commandment to honor the Sabbath day.[27]

The rabbis planned to campaign among Conservative Jewry to revitalize Sabbath observance. But first they found themselves confronted with the unique conditions of the American environment that in and of themselves caused Jews to violate the laws of *Shabbat*. Determined, unlike its predecessor, to recognize the impact of contemporary America, the CJLS acknowledged that contemporary circumstances required *halachic* adjustments of certain laws of *Shabbat*. The migration to the suburbs and the widespread use of the automobile mandated a rethinking of the traditional prohibition against travel on *Shabbat*. In 1932 the Committee on Jewish Law had refused to lift the ban on travel on *Shabbat*. By 1950, however, suburban sprawl made it increasingly impossible for many Jews to attend communal worship unless they drove to the synagogue. Realistically, the CJLS recognized that all too few Conservative Jews participated in *Shabbat* services—a situation the rabbis hoped to correct. But for those who did, many—especially the men of the RA—faced the dilemma of either traveling to the synagogue on *Shabbat*—or skipping services altogether. Having "learn[ed] to adjust our strategy to the realities of our time and place," the CJLS, in a *responsum*, jointly authored by Morris Adler, Jacob Agus, and Theodore Friedman, lifted the traditional prohibition against travel on *Shabbat* solely for the purpose of riding to the synagogue to join in communal worship.[28]

At the same time the CJLS also permitted the use of electricity, which had previously been interdicted as a proscribed form of fire, in order to enhance the observance of the Sabbath in the home. The rabbis tied these permissions to the Sabbath Revitalization Campaign, designed to encourage members of their congregations to recapture for themselves and their families the spirit of *Shabbat* as a day of rest, set apart from all others by the beauty of rituals observed in the home, reading of sacred literature, and participation in communal worship. The RA thus conserved tradition—the prohibition on travel on the Sabbath was retained—but allowed for change, adjustments in the Sabbath laws designed to enhance observance of the day of rest. The *responsum* revealed that the RA viewed *halachah* as a tool for enriching Jewish spiritual life. The RA planned that this would be the first of many such essential reinterpretations of *halachah*. As the CJLS charted out *halachic* alternatives for an Americanized Jewry, the rabbis envisioned Conservative Jews voluntarily assuming ever greater standards of observance.

As soon as the Conservative movement launched the Sabbath Revitalization Campaign, the CJLS, led by Chairman Theodore Friedman (1951–54), began to consider the status of women in Jewish law. This time the committee planned not only to address the "unfinished business of the *agunah* problem," but also to explore the questions of granting women the honor of *aliyot*—the privilege of reciting the blessings before and after the Torah reading—and of counting women in the *minyan*, the quorum of ten, traditionally men, necessary for Jewish worship.[29]

In 1951 the RA heard David Aronson elaborate his plan, which he had first raised in 1940, to solve the plight of the *agunah*. The following January the CJLS held a special conference in Atlantic City to consider the plan. Out of that conference emerged a comprehensive proposal to solve the *agunah* question. But the Seminary quickly moved to head off what it viewed as a radical act of the RA. Seminary chancellor Louis Finkelstein told the RA that the laws of marriage and divorce were too important for its rabbis to decide alone. Essentially, in matters of synagogue ritual the Seminary was willing to concede to the Rabbinical Assembly the authority to determine what would go on in the congregations. But when it came to the critical issues of personal status—issues with the potential to affect all Jews, not just Conservative Jews—the Seminary was not willing to concede authority to its alumni.[30]

Consequently, in 1953 the Seminary and the RA established the Joint Law Conference, governed by a Joint Steering Committee of ten members, co-chaired by Theodore Friedman representing the RA and Judah *Goldin representing the Seminary, as the only body within the Conservative movement empowered to deal with the laws of marriage and divorce. The conference established a national *bet din* to deal with these matters and was granted the authority to enact *takanot*, to legislate. This paved the way for the historic *takanah*, the additional clause formulated by Seminary professor Saul *Lieberman, Conservatism's leading *halachic* expert since Louis Ginzberg's death in 1953. Inserted into the *ketubah*, the Lieberman *takanah* made the *ketubah* a civilly binding contract that committed the bride and groom to abide by the recommendations of a *bet din* if their marriage ended in divorce. In the event that the husband was unwilling to issue a *get*, the civil courts could presumably enforce compliance with the terms of the *ketubah*. As the national *bet din* soon discovered, in many instances, the persuasive power of the threat of a successful lawsuit quickly brought a recalcitrant husband to end the marriage Jewishly as well as civilly.[31]

Once the *agunah* affair was out of its hands, the CJLS turned to other matters. With Arthur *Neulander as chairman (1954–59), the CJLS was reorganized into six subcommittees, charged with exploring the creative adaptation of *halachah*. The CJLS hoped that by finding *halachic* solutions to ongoing problems, such as the unequal status of Jewish women, it would succeed in enhancing the level of observance among Conservative Jewry in general. To assist its operations, Rabbi Max *Davidson undertook the arduous task of organizing and indexing the records of the various law committees to substantiate where progress had been made in the past and where the CJLS needed to head in the future.[32]

In general, however, much of the CJLS's time was taken up, as had been true of its predecessor, with the routine answering of questions on *kashrut*, synagogue ceremonies and rituals, circumcision, conversion, mixed marriages, and funeral rites. Many of these involved relatively minor matters. The CJLS prohibited construction work to continue on a synagogue on a holiday. It did not permit non-Jews to sing in synagogue choirs. But as before, some decisions held greater import. To aid isolated Jewish communities in following the laws of *kashrut*, it allowed for the kashering of frozen, properly slaughtered meat after it had been defrosted. The CJLS maintained the ruling against granting synagogue membership to intermarried couples. And it took a step toward granting women equality within the synagogue when in 1955 Rabbi Aaron *Blumenthal, one of its more liberal members, issued a *responsum* allowing women to have *aliyot*.[33]

Under Neulander's successors—CJLS chairmen Ben Zion *Bokser (1959–60 and 1963–65), Max Routtenberg (1960–63), and Israel Silverman (1965–66)— the CJLS remained preoccupied with the routine answering of questions. Because the *responsum* allowing travel to synagogue on the Sabbath had been interpreted by many Conservative Jews as a blanket permission for driving on the Sabbath, the CJLS reexamined the 1950 *responsum* and clarified its intention. But efforts to move forward on other important issues were stymied by the number of problems brought before the CJLS and its lack of personnel. Although the CJLS employed research consultants—among them, rabbis Michael Higger, Phillip Sigal, Marshall Meyer, and Edward Gershfield—lack of funds precluded hiring these men on more than a part-time basis. Yet, with more than 170 questions submitted in a single year, the CJLS spent most of its time responding to questions. That left little time to initiate the kinds of inquiries that had led to the *responsum* on the Sabbath in 1950. The CJLS could not coerce its members, who remained occupied with full-time congregational responsibilities, into finding time to write well-researched *responsa* on the many unresolved issues. The CJLS pleaded its limitations before the RA, but once again criticism over the slow process of adaptation of *halachah* to contemporary life surfaced. Many questions remained unresolved. What could the rabbis do about the widely ignored observance of the second day of festivals? Were sturgeon, swordfish, and gelatin kosher? What should the RA do to establish appropriate observances to memorialize the Holocaust and to commemorate the birth of the state of Israel? And with increasing urgency, how far could the committee go in granting equality to women within *halachah*?[34]

Certainly the greatest successes of the Committee on Jewish Law in the 1930s and 1940s and the CJLS in the 1950s and 1960s lay in setting standards for the synagogues and for the public gatherings of Conservative Jews. The law committees made decisions about synagogue membership, worship, rites, and rituals that to a large extent unified the congregations of the movement. Their decisions, and in some cases refusal to render a decision, allowed for innovations in congregational practices, such as the use of a microphone, organ, and mixed choirs; a triennial cycle of Torah reading; abbreviated prayer services; and the introduction of English prayers. Not all rulings, however, were on the side of lenient accommodation to the American environment. The CJLS discountenanced the *Shabbat* afternoon (*minchah*) Bar Mitzvah, preferred by some to facilitate Saturday night celebrations, and it set high standards for Bar and Bat Mitzvah and Confirmation.[35]

As "the collective rabbi of the Conservative movement," the Committee on Jewish Law and the CJLS responded to questions from the United Synagogue, Women's League, Federation of Jewish Men's Clubs, and the United Synagogue Youth Commission. The law committees accepted without endorsement some lenient, but customary, practices of Conservative congregations, such as mixed seating, as de facto congregational innovations. But in other cases the law committees set strict standards for the national bodies of the Conservative movement that at times exceeded the more lenient rulings of earlier *responsa*. For example, in 1964 the CJLS asked the United Synagogue Youth to schedule its conventions so as to avoid arrangements that would require USYers to travel on the Sabbath. Despite these acknowledged successes, fifteen years after the establishment of the CJLS, its chairman, Max Routtenberg, voiced the dissatisfaction, shared by many, over its failure to creatively extend *halachah*. He called for a law committee that would raise questions, not just answer them.[36]

Throughout the 1960s, as earlier, the key symbol of the RA's difficulty in balancing tradition and change in its view of *halachah* remained the *agunah*. Even though only one case of an *agunah* actually came before the RA in these years, Executive Vice-President Wolfe *Kelman reflected: "Many of us feel that the problem of the *agunah* is symbolic of our relationship to *halachah*. We are married to it. Some of us don't want to live with it, but we don't want to divorce it.'' Because the Lieberman *takanah* only applied to marriages solemnized by the RA *ketubah*, it was at best a partial solution to the problem. Moreover, the new *ketubah* had not gained widespread acceptance within the RA. Some rabbis refused to use it because it was an insufficient stopgap measure. Others failed to endorse it because they questioned its enforceability or the desirability of involving secular authorities in a religious matter. Regional branches of the RA were, when necessary, finding their own solutions to the plight of women whose husbands refused to grant *gittin*. A survey conducted in 1968 found that, when necessary, 30 percent of the Conservative rabbis would not require a *get* for a remarriage and that another 48 percent would advise women seeking remarriage who lacked *gittin* to turn to Reform rabbis to sanctify their marriages. The dichotomy was evident. Nearly 80 percent of the Conservative rabbinate utilized alternative solutions to the problem of the *agunah*, while the movement agonized over what to do.[37]

With the appointment of Rabbi (and later United Synagogue executive director) Benjamin *Kreitman as chairman (1966–72), the CJLS once again began to move forward, boldly enacting decisions that broke through many *halachic* logjams that had previously stymied its operations. Kreitman reorganized the CJLS. While it still considered unanimous decisions binding on RA members, the committee recognized that its authority in this matter was limited to ''moral persuasion.'' Now minority opinions voiced by one member or subscribed to by two in a written *responsum* carried ''official and equal standing with the majority'' opinion. The CJLS issued new and more lenient opinions on the playing of bingo in the synagogue and the eating of fish meals in non-kosher restaurants. It allowed for the use of a swimming pool as a *mikveh* (ritual bath) and permitted hitherto forbidden marriages between a *Kohen* and a convert. It reopened the question of the observance of the second day of festivals, making their celebration optional. In recognition of the establishment of the state of Israel, it allowed for weddings to take place on certain days previously interdicted by Jewish law. And the CJLS made advances in the laws of *kashrut*, ruling that gelatin, swordfish, and most hard cheeses were kosher.[38]

Most importantly, after forty years of debate, the CJLS resolved the *agunah* controversy. Recognizing that the Joint Law Conference had not achieved its original purpose in the revision of Jewish marriage law, the RA allowed the agreement with the Seminary to lapse. In 1968 it unanimously adopted a new proposal that added a conditional agreement, a *t'nai b'kiddushin*, to the marriage ceremony. This meant that the rabbis would have the authority to annul the marriage, if necessary, after a civil divorce had been granted, if the husband refused to issue a *get*. The power of annulment meant the rabbis would not have to look to the civil courts to support their authority, as was necessary with the Lieberman *takanah*. Still, this only applied to future marriages. In 1969 the *bet din* of the CJLS heard the case of a woman who had remained an *agunah* for eighteen years because of her recalcitrant ex-husband. Deciding that in extraordinary cases it could ''invoke the powers of annulment inherent in rabbinic authority," the *bet din* annulled the marriage and informed her rabbi that he could officiate at her remarriage. With these two decisions the RA ended the *agunah* controversy.[39]

Yet just when it seemed as if the most important stumbling blocks of the CJLS had been overcome, its activist phase under Kreitman unexpectedly came to a halt. Ostensibly the barrier to its continued progress was the standard necessary for conversion, but in reality the looming question was the validity of minority opinions subscribed to by only one or two of the twenty-five members of the CJLS. In December 1970 one member of the CJLS ruled that *tevilah* (immersion in a ritual bath) was not necessary for conversion. Most of the members of the CJLS had been hoping that a unanimous affirmative vote would make conversion with *tevilah* binding upon all RA rabbis. In response, sixteen members of the CJLS resigned in protest over the permissive administrative procedures which they believed paralyzed the CJLS. For the next two years a Special Committee for the Revitalization of the Law Committee, chaired by former RA presidents Robert *Gordis and Max Routtenberg, surveyed the general situation. In 1972 the Special Committee, Brown University Professor of Religious Studies Rabbi Jacob Neusner, and the CJLS, which had regrouped in the interim, all made proposals at the annual convention of the RA for the reconstitution of the CJLS. The proposal formulated by the CJLS won a majority of votes. It provided for the issuing of majority and minority *responsa*. When approved by four-fifths of the CJLS and ratified by the RA in convention, majority opinions would became Standards of Rabbinic Practice. In order for minority opinions to be made available to the RA membership as valid alternatives, they had to bear the signatures of at least three members of the CJLS. (That number was reportedly raised to six signatures in 1985.) But as before, the CJLS recognized that it had no sanctions, merely "moral persuasion," to implement its decisions. After an interim of two years, the CJLS was reconstituted in March 1972 under the chairmanship of RA president S. Gershon *Levi (1972–73).[40]

No sooner had the committee reformed when it was plunged directly into perhaps its most challenging issues—the demand for the ritual equality of women. Under the chairmanship of Seminary professor Seymour *Siegel (1973–80), the CJLS boldly moved ahead over the next decade to accord women equal rights within the synagogue. In 1970 the United Synagogue had asked the CJLS whether or not women could be counted in the *minyan*. Although the congregations did not yet clamor for change, a small group of Jewish feminists, organized by 1971 as *Ezrat Nashim*, had sparked the campaign for women's rights within Conservatism. The reconstituted CJLS perceived the issue of the *minyan* as an opportunity to initiate change, rather than—as so often in the past—reacting to it after the fact. In August 1973 the CJLS voted to permit women to count in a *minyan*. According to Siegel, this decision received more news coverage than any Jewish legal decision since the Middle Ages. Reported on the front page of the *New York Times*, it brought home to the laity the possibilities and promises of even greater changes. Before 1973, 6 percent of the RA rabbis allowed the practice. Two years later 47 percent of Conservative congregations counted women in their *minyanim*.[41]

Ritual equality within Conservative Judaism raised a host of *halachic* questions for the CJLS and the Conservative movement. Were all members of the *minyan* to wear ritual garb? The CJLS reaffirmed women's right to receive *aliyot*, a minority opinion established two decades before; did this mean that women could also read from the Torah? Women could sing in mixed choirs; could they also lead prayer? They counted in a *minyan*; could they now serve as witnesses? And if women were to be accorded full rights, could *halachah* be reinterpreted to grant equality in matters of leadership? Would the Seminary ordain women as rabbis? The CJLS's agenda over the next decade under Chairman Siegel and his successors, Ben Zion Bokser (1980–84) and Joel Roth (1984–   ), considered all of these matters. In 1983, after long, arduous, and often heated debate, the Seminary faculty, finding that ethical arguments and the absence of *halachic* counterarguments constituted a strong case for the ordination of women, voted to open the Rabbinical School to women. Two years later, Seminary chancellor Gerson *Cohen presided over the ordination of Amy Eilberg. And in 1987 his successor, Ismar *Schorsch, saw the graduation of the first women cantors.[42]

The enthusiastic response to the publicity surrounding the *minyan* decision led Conservative leaders to make more of the decisions of the CJLS available to Conservative laity. The RA published digests of actions taken on *kashrut*, on the role of women, and on *Shabbat* and festivals. In 1977 it issued an important volume of essays, *Conservative Judaism and Jewish Law*, edited by Seymour Siegel with Elliot Gertel, to dispel the notion that "there really is no philosophy of Jewish law in the Conservative movement." In 1979 the Seminary published *A Guide to Jewish Religious Practice* by former RA president Rabbi Isaac Klein, one of the leading members of the CJLS. Although in the foreword Chancellor Cohen wrote that it was not an "official creed or guide to Conservative Jewish practice." Klein's single volume summarized many of the *halachic* decisions that the RA law committees had taken in the past. These works and plans for future publications reflected the new confidence of the CJLS, rooted in its successes in taking the lead in fashioning *halachah* since its reorganization.[43]

The confidence grew not only from its decisions in matters pertaining to women, but also from other far-reaching decisions the CJLS made following its reorganization. Under Siegel it entered the new field of biomedical ethics, addressing the many questions raised by scientific and technological medical advances. In 1982 the CJLS unanimously adopted five papers dealing with the long-standing, and always sensitive, subject of congregational relations with intermarried couples. Recognizing that Jewish law called for efforts "to save for Judaism even the marginal members of [the] people and their descendants," the CJLS amplified an earlier decision allowing for some integration into the synagogue of intermarried families. The Jewish spouse could join a synagogue. In the hope of eventually converting the non-Jewish partner, the CJLS encouraged synagogues to welcome the non-Jewish spouse to join in educational and social events. If the couple agreed to raise the children as Jews, the children could participate fully in synagogue life. But because *halachah* has traditionally recognized that the child of a Jewish mother is Jewish, children of intermarried couples whose mothers were not Jewish would have to undergo ritual immersion prior to Bar or Bat Mitzvah. These examples show that in the 1980s, as in the past, for the RA the fundamental philosophy of Conservative Judaism remained as Robert Gordis defined it: "Growth is the law of life, and Law is the life of Judaism."[44]

Yet this promising activity could not hide the crucial question. To what extent did the RA's reinterpretations of *halachah* lead Conservative laity to live their lives in accordance with the dictates of Jewish law? In the non-hierarchical, non-coercive American Jewish community, the committees on Jewish law could not even command colleagues in the RA to follow their decisions. Obviously, the law committees exercised no coercive power whatsoever over the laity. By all accounts the 1950 Sabbath Revitalization Campaign was a failure. Writing in 1970 a new chapter to his major work, *Conservative Judaism*, the sociologist Marshall Sklare bluntly stated: "The fact is that there is not a Conservative synagogue in the country where most congregants practice the *mitzvoth* [commandments] according to the Conservative regimen." Seymour Siegel echoed Sklare's findings: "We have found, much to our chagrin, that many times we are legislating without a constituency."[45]

If, then, Conservative Jews by and large do not follow *halachah*, what has the RA's "grand obsession" meant? Were all these years of effort to adjust *halachah* to the American environment a waste of energy and display of futility on the part of the Conservative rabbinate? Sidney Schwarz, a Reconstructionist rabbi, seemed to think so, arguing in his dissertation that although adherence to *halachah* was the myth that united the Conservative movement:

the practice of the laity belied that entire elite myth structure . . . Many of the rabbis most intimately connected with the movement's *halachic* activity were unsure whether it had made any difference. Juxtaposing the CJLS decisions with the practice of the Conservative laity left one with the uneasy feeling that the tail had been wagging the dog all along.

But Conservative rabbi and historian Herbert Rosenblum suggested that the "large majority of Conservative leaders" took pride in the legislative accomplishments of the CJLS, seeing themselves, as the dean of contemporary Jewish historians, Salo W. Baron, observed, "true to the spirit of traditional Judaism," maintaining the validity of Jewish law while adapting it to the changing environment. Certainly, the movement's successes in insuring observance of the *mitzvot* in the synagogue and in the public gatherings of Conservative Jews, and the great interest, if not always enthusiasm, that met the pioneering decisions on women in the synagogue showed that Conservative laity were cognizant, if not generally observant, of the importance of *halachah*.[46]

Although the Conservative movement has had only limited success in fostering personal *halachic* observance among Conservative Jews, the RA's "grand obsession" with *halachah* was a key part in the evolution of Conservative Judaism as an Americanized Judaism. As Will Herberg showed in his classic *Protestant Catholic Jew*, the immigrants were not expected to change their religion when they landed in America, but they were expected to accommodate American patterns of religious life. The RA's struggle with *halachah* has been a part and extension of that process of accommodation. Because it is the inherent nature of *halachah* to regulate every aspect of the Jewish way of life, not just the religious sphere, the Conservative rabbis set for themselves the task of accommodating *halachah* to America. From the past the Conservative rabbis preserved loyalty to *halachah* and maintenance of the rabbinical prerogative of reinterpretation. But true to the present, they took for their agenda the key social and intellectual issues of the contemporary American scene. That agenda—mixed seating and organs in the synagogue, driving on the Sabbath, intermarriage, conversion, women's rights, biomedical ethics, and even the *agunah*—most eloquently showed the Conservative rabbis' determination to meet head-on the changed circumstances of Jewish life in America and their belief that with adaptation *halachah* remained a viable guide for Jewish life in America.[47]

RECONSTRUCTIONISM

Differing conceptions of *halachah* reveal but one of the distinctions between Conservative and Reconstructionist Judaism. Long before Reconstructionism emerged to become the fourth denomination of American Judaism, Mordecai M. Kaplan had articulated its philosophy, providing a rationale and program transcending denominational dividing lines to enrich American Jewish life. Yet more than half a century after Kaplan's initial writings, many American Jews have never heard of Reconstructionism; few know that it ranks with Orthodoxy, Conservatism, and Reform as one of the denominations of American Judaism. Even the Synagogue Council of America continues to deny its legitimacy. Created in 1926, this umbrella organization includes representatives from the rabbinical and congregational associations of the Orthodox, Conservative, and Reform movements. In 1986 its Orthodox delegates once again vetoed the membership application of the Federation of Reconstructionist Congregations and Havurot (FRCH), Reconstructionism's equivalent of a synagogal body.[48]

Yet as an ideology Reconstructionism powerfully reflects the realities of American Jewish life. Its philosophy and program constitute what sociologist Charles Liebman believes to be the folk religion or popular religious culture of American Jewry. Liebman argues that Orthodox, Conservative, and Reform Judaisms are "elitist ideologies" consisting of the rituals, beliefs, doctrines, and organizations formulated and shaped by their rabbinical leaders. But Reconstructionism most accurately explains the Jewish subculture in which many, if not most, of the elite's lay members participate. Thus, while American Jews barely recognize the term and although the movement has had limited success—in 1987 the FRCH had some 75,000 members in 55 affiliated bodies compared to the 1.5 million

Jews and more than 800 synagogues claimed by the Conservative movement—most American Jews are ideologically, though not consciously or formally, Reconstructionist.[49]

Reconstructionism's conceptual framework was the work of one of the giants of twentieth-century Jewish thought, Mordecai M. Kaplan. Born in Swenziany, Lithuania, in 1881 and ordained at the Seminary in 1902, in 1909 Kaplan became the head of the Seminary's newly established Teachers Institute (1909–46). A few months later he joined the faculty of the Rabbinical School as professor of homiletics (1910–47; professor of philosophies of religion, 1947–63). Joining the Seminary faculty marked a turning point in his life. As a writer, lecturer, administrator, and professor for more than fifty years at the Seminary, Kaplan became one of the polestars of the Conservative movement. Before his death in 1983 at the age of 102, the challenges he posed by his comprehensive reconstruction of Judaism had influenced virtually every aspect of organized Jewish life.

In 1934, at the age of fifty-three, Kaplan published his magnum opus, *Judaism as a Civilization*. Here he explored Judaism in terms of community, nationhood, organizational structure, theology, history, and culture. His Reconstructionist philosophy responded to the inner spiritual and cultural needs of twentieth-century American Jewry by offering modern Jews, who would soon be wrestling with the catastrophe of the Holocaust and the exhilaration of the rebirth of Israel, a bridge connecting the Jewish past and the American present. The point of departure for his Reconstructionism was the contemporary scene and present-day religious experience, not the dictates of the religious life and authority of the past. In formulating Reconstructionism, Kaplan drew upon both Jewish and American civilizations, turning for guidance to traditional and modern Jewish sources, including the Zionist Ahad Ha-Am, and to Western writers, including social scientist Emile Durkheim and the American philosophical pragmatist William James.[50]

His conception of Judaism as an "evolving religious civilization" was his solution to the contemporary question of Jewish identity. Judaism was a dynamic social process, a civilization encompassing land, language, arts, literature, history, mores, laws, folkways, social structure, ideals, and values. By "religious" Kaplan meant that the religious life in the synagogue and the home remained at the heart of this civilization. And by "evolving" he indicated that Judaism was not fixed, that it must consider the Jewish people and their needs and responses to changed circumstances. Because modern Jews, using tradition as a guide, must confront life's perplexities, diverse viewpoints and solutions would emerge.

Kaplan understood that the only way to overcome the fragmentation produced by this diversity was for American Jewry to form an organic community. Although he taught that the land of Israel was the spiritual homeland of the Jewish people and that outside it Judaism became a secondary civilization, he insisted upon forging creative life for Diaspora Jewry. The key to their creative survival lay in democratically organized local and national organic communities run neither by congregations nor federations but by representatives of the various Jewish organizations who would administer all communal property and employ communal functionaries. These organic communities would function as the instruments of Jewish life as a whole and meet all its needs.

Kaplan proposed a total revolution in Jewish theology by accepting naturalism, teaching that Judaism must be "reconstructed" from supernaturalism to naturalism. He rejected the notion of a supernatural God, redefining God as the Power in the universe that makes for salvation, the sum of the forces that help men and women make the most of their lives. For Judaism to survive the challenges of modernity there could be no miracles, no supernatural revelation. Rather than serving God, the purpose of human existence was to help create a society whose members would maintain what he called a sense of active moral responsibility contributing to the intellectual, moral, and spiritual progress of humankind.

Kaplan rejected not only the belief in God as a supernatural being but also authoritarianism and supernaturalism in every aspect of Jewish religious life and thought. Reconstructionist Judaism is not a *halachic* form of Judaism. Instead Kaplan replaced *halachah* with the concept of folkways. No longer could one understand the *mitzvot* (commandments) as laws or mystic symbols necessary to commune with God or to earn a portion in the world to come. But as folkways, the sacred texts, seasons, rites, rituals, and customs were vehicles of Judaism that answered human needs. They would remain the very stuff of Jewish life, the sources of its spirituality, but because they were no longer laws, they could be modified as required to meet the changed circumstances of contemporary life.

Kaplan's rejection of the concept of the Jews as the chosen people also grew out of his rejection of supernaturalism. Furthermore, he felt that the entire notion of chosenness was out of step with the ideals and democratic ethos of the dominant American society. It was especially these controversial theological reconstructions of fundamental Jewish beliefs on the nature of God, law, and the Jewish people that created for Kaplan grave tensions and left deep scars within the Conservative movement.

Following the publication of *Judaism as a Civilization*, Kaplan and his collaborator and son-in-law, Ira *Eisenstein, laid the seeds of Reconstructionist organizational life. For much of his life Kaplan proclaimed Reconstructionism to be a school of thought, denying that it was an independent movement in the hope that its ideology would eventually capture Conservatism. Instead, its program was to enrich the Jewish lives of all by intensifying Jewish life in the home, in the synagogue, and in Palestine; by emphasizing Jewish education, culture, and the arts; and by democratizing the Jewish community and raising its ethical and social conscience. While supporting this program, Eisenstein, however, continued to push, with eventual success, for the formation of Reconstructionism as the fourth denomination of contemporary Judaism.

Beginning in 1922, the organizational basis of Reconstructionism was the Society for the Advancement of Judaism (SAJ), the synagogue-center founded by Kaplan, which he and Eisenstein guided as "spiritual leaders." The SAJ and its journal, the *SAJ Review*, provided early forums for the exploration of Reconstructionism. While some students of Reconstructionist Judaism date the founding of the movement to the organization of the SAJ, others argue that the movement followed the publication of *Judaism as a Civilization* when new Reconstructionist endeavors began to delineate it from the other denominations of American Judaism.

To continue discussion of the questions raised by *Judaism as a Civilization*, Kaplan and his colleagues launched the *Reconstructionist* magazine (1935–   ), the successor to the *SAJ Review*. In 1940 the Jewish Reconstructionist Foundation was established to sustain the Reconstructionist Press and to coordinate Reconstructionist activities, which until then had been chiefly supported by the Friends of Reconstructionism, a group of generous members of the SAJ and of Rabbi Milton *Steinberg's Park Avenue Synagogue. The publication in the 1940s of several prayer books edited by Kaplan and his colleagues revealed the liturgical implications of Reconstructionist theology and provoked the ire of the Orthodox—and of some of his Seminary colleagues. In 1945 the Union of Orthodox Rabbis (*Agudat ha-Rabbanim*) burned the Reconstructionist *Sabbath Prayer Book* (1945) and excommunicated Kaplan for heresy.

Meanwhile, to further the dissemination of Reconstructionist thought, Kaplan encouraged the formation of small fellowships (*havurot*) whose members, while remaining affiliated with Reform or Conservative synagogues, would meet to study Reconstructionist literature. *Havurot* later came to refer to small, intimate communities—some, but not all, based in congregations—whose members gather together for worship, study, celebration, and support in a kind of extended family. In 1954 the handful of Reconstructionist groups organized the Reconstructionist Federation of Congregations (RFC). In 1961 when the RFC became the Federation of Reconstructionist Congregations and Havurot (FRCH), it took a further step toward denominational identity by declaring that its members no longer had to maintain affiliation with any of the other branches of American Judaism. Thus by the 1960s Reconstructionism was moving away from being a school of thought and clarifying its structure as a movement.

It was not, however, until 1968, several years after Kaplan retired from active teaching at the Seminary, that the Reconstructionist Rabbinical College (RRC), with Eisenstein as president (1968–81), was established in Philadelphia. Its curriculum—with each successive year devoted to a different phase of Jewish civilization and with emphasis upon practical rabbinics and knowledge of other religions—reflected Kaplan's theory of evolving Jewish civilization. Kaplan, then in his eighties, traveled to Philadelphia to teach its first students. In 1974 its first nine alumni formed the Reconstructionist Rabbinical Association. (Its forerunner, the Reconstructionist Rabbinical Fellowship, established in 1950, included Reform and Conservative rabbis.) By 1987 its members numbered 137. With an organizational structure parallel to the other denominations of American Judaism—a seminary, rabbinical conclave, and congregational body—the Reconstructionist movement had clearly become the fourth denomination of American Judaism.

While its future cannot be predicted, its recent growth is striking. Between 1980 and 1985 the number of FRCH affiliates doubled. Moreover, contemporary Reconstructionist leaders have not hesitated to follow in Kaplan's footsteps in tackling head-on the difficult issues of the day. In seeking answers to the challenges of contemporary Jewish life, they have confronted the rising rate of intermarriage in the American Jewish community. Reconstructionist rabbis may sanctify intermarriages but are encouraged to use a civil, not a religious, ceremony. They also encourage intermarried couples to join and affirm patrilineality, that the child of a Jewish father and a non-Jewish mother who is raised as a Jew is a Jew. Following Reconstructionism's long-standing position on the equality of women—Kaplan created the first Bat Mitzvah ceremony, and by the 1950s Reconstructionist congregations counted women in their *minyanim*—the RRC opened its admissions to women. The second woman ordained in America was its graduate, Sandy Eisenberg Sasso. Retaining Reconstructionism's historic commitment to social activism, the RRC has sponsored the Shalom Center to explore Jewish perspectives on preventing nuclear holocaust. There are plans, if funding permits, to build family camps, expand youth programming, and establish a stronger presence in Israel. These activities and strong public stances show the vitality of the Reconstructionist movement. They underlie its leaders' hopes that in the near future greater numbers of American Jews will come to recognize that, at heart, they too are Reconstructionists.

NOTES

1. Simon Greenberg, "In Honor of Louis Finkelstein," *PRA 1965* vol. 29, pp. 80–81.

2. Mordecai Waxman, ed., *Tradition and Change* (New York, 1958), p. 20; Max Routtenberg, "The Conservative Rabbinate," in his *Decades of Decision* (New York, 1973), p. 149.

3. Moshe Davis, *The Emergence of Conservative Judaism: The Historical School in Nineteenth-Century America* (Philadelphia, 1963), p. 13; Routtenberg, "The Jew Who Has Intermarried," *Decades*, pp. 71–72.

4. See Sidney Schwarz, "Law and Legitimacy: An Intellectual History of Conservative Judaism, 1902–1973" (Ph.D. diss., Temple University, 1982).

5. *Constitution and By-Laws of Jewish Theological Seminary Association* (New York, 1886); Herbert Rosenblum, *Conservative Judaism: A Contemporary History* (New York, 1983), pp. 113–14.

6. Routtenberg, "The Conservative Rabbinate," *Decades*, p. 149; *JE* 5 July 1912, p. 6.

7. Solomon Schechter, *Studies in Judaism*, vol. 1 (London and Philadelphia, 1896–1924), p. xviii.

8. Louis Ginzberg, "Presidential Address to the United Synagogue of America," (1918), JTS Library.

9. *Recorder* 1, 3 (July 1921), pp. 7–8; Abraham J. Karp, *A History of the United Synagogue of America, 1913–63* (New York, 1964), pp. 25–27.

10. "Impressions of the Convention," *Recorder* 2, 2 (April 1922), pp. 11, 13.

11. *PRA 1927* vol. 1, p. 11; Max Drob, "President's Message," *PRA 1928* vol. 2, p. 21.

12. Drob, President's Message," p. 21.

13. "Opinions Rendered by the Committee on Jewish Law," *PRA 1929* vol. 3, pp. 151–65; Boaz Cohen, "Canons of Interpretation of Jewish Law," *PRA 1935* vol. 5, pp. 170–87, esp. p. 185.

14. *PRA 1941* vol. 8, p. 38; Eli Ginzberg, "Address in Honor of Louis Ginzberg," *PRA 1964* vol. 28, p. 114.

15. "Report of the Committee on the Interpretation of the Jewish Law," *PRA 1929* vol. 3, pp. 57–59; *PRA 1934* vol. 4, pp. 100–03; *PRA 1940* vol. 7, p. 30; *PRA 1947* vol. 11, pp. 53–63.

16. *PRA 1929* vol. 3, pp. 57–59.

17. "Report of Committee on Jewish Law," *PRA 1935* vol. 5, pp. 167–69.

18. Max Arzt, "Conservative Judaism Comes of Age," *PRA 1975* vol. 37, pp. 332–33; "Report of the Special Committee on the Problem of the *Agunah*," *PRA 1936* vol. 5, pp. 333–35; *PRA 1938* vol. 5, p. 406.

19. Louis Epstein, *Li-Shealat Ha-Agunah* (New York, 1940); David Aronson, "Dr. Louis M. Epstein's 'The Agunah Question,' " *PRA 1940* vol. 7, pp. 301–11; "Report of the Committee on Jewish Law," *PRA 1941* vol. 8, p. 33.

20. "Report of the Committee on Jewish Law," *PRA 1942* vol. 8, pp. 143–45.

21. "Report of the Committee on Jewish Law," *PRA 1947* vol. 11, pp. 54–55.

22. *PRA 1947* vol. 11, p. 66; *PRA 1948* vol. 12, pp. 88–89; Michael Higger, "Authority to Interpret Jewish Laws," *CJ* 5, 4 (June 1949), pp. 20–22.

23. "Towards a Philosophy of Conservative Judaism," *PRA 1948* vol. 12, pp. 110–92.

24. "Statement and Resolutions Proposed by Rabbi Louis M. Epstein," *PRA 1948* vol. 12, pp. 167–74.

25. David Aronson, "President's Message: The Demands of the New Diaspora," *PRA 1949* vol. 13, pp. 136–38.

26. "Report of the Committee on Jewish Law and Standards," *PRA 1949* vol. 13, pp. 46–57; David Aronson, "President's Message: At Fifty for Counsel," *PRA 1950* vol. 14, pp. 98–99.

27. *PRA 1949* vol. 13, p. 86.

28. *PRA 1932* vol. 4, p. 236; "Responsum on the Sabbath," *PRA 1950* vol. 15, pp. 119–34.

29. "Report of the Committee on Jewish Law and Standards," *PRA 1951* vol. 15, pp. 40–42.

30. David Aronson, "*Kedat Moshe Ve'Yisrael*," *PRA 1951* vol. 15, pp. 120–40; "Report of the Committee on Jewish Law and Standards," *PRA 1952* vol. 16, pp. 48–53.

31. "Report of the Steering Committee of the Joint Law Conference, 1953–54," *PRA 1954* vol. 18, pp. 62–68.

32. "Report of the Committee on Jewish Law and Standards," *PRA 1957* vol. 21, pp. 27–28.

33. For a summary of the major decisions of the CJLS, see Benjamin Kreitman, "The

First Ten Years of the Committee on Law and Standards," *PRA 1958* vol. 22, pp. 68–80.

34. "Report of the Committee on Jewish Law and Standards," *PRA 1960* vol. 24, pp. 286–91; *PRA 1961* vol. 25, pp. 188–94; *PRA 1962* vol. 26, pp. 233–38.

35. "Report of the Committee on Jewish Law and Standards," *PRA 1963* vol. 27, pp. 221–29.

36. *PRA 1964* vol. 28, pp. 240–41.

37. *PRA 1960* vol. 24, p. 70; *PRA 1961* vol. 25, p. 191; William Greenfeld, "Future Prospects of the Bet Din," *PRA 1957* vol. 21, pp. 175–81; *PRA 1957* vol. 21, pp. 58–59; "Report of the Committee on Jewish Law and Standards," *PRA 1968* vol. 32, p. 215.

38. "Report of the Committee on Jewish Law and Standards," *PRA 1967* vol. 31, pp. 189–94; *PRA 1968* vol. 32, pp. 206–28; *PRA 1969* vol. 33, p. 200.

39. "*T'nai B'kiddushin*," *PRA 1968* vol. 32, pp. 229–40; *PRA 1969* vol. 33, p. 200.

40. *Beineinu*, 3, 1 (January 1973), pp. 45–51.

41. *PRA 1974* vol. 36, pp. 24–25; *PRA 1975* vol. 37, p. 125.

42. "Final Report of the Commission for the Study of the Ordination of Women as Rabbis," 30 January 1979, JTS Library.

43. Seymour Siegel and Elliot Gertel, eds., *Conservative Judaism and Jewish Law* (New York, 1977); Isaac Klein, *A Guide to Jewish Religious Practice* (New York, 1979), p. xxii.

44. "Forum on Bio-Medical Ethics," *CJ* 30, 2 (Winter 1976), pp. 10–39; *CJ* 35, 4 (Summer 1982), pp. 33–62; Gordis, quoted in Marc Lee Raphael, *Profiles in American Judaism* (San Francisco, 1984), p. 104.

45. Marshall Sklare, *Conservative Judaism* (1955; rev. 1972; reprint ed., Lanham, Md., 1985), p. 274; Seymour Siegel, "Conservative Judaism and Jewish Law," *PRA 1975* vol. 37, p. 125.

46. Schwarz, "Law and Legitimacy," p. 369; Baron quoted in Rosenblum, *Conservative Judaism*, pp. 126–27; *PRA 1975* vol. 37, p. 19.

47. Will Herberg, *Protestant—Catholic—Jew* (1955; rev. Garden City, N.Y., 1960), pp. 27, 191–92.

48. *Washington Jewish Week* 24 April 1986, p. 1.

49. Charles S. Liebman, "Reconstructionism in American Jewish Life," in *AJYB* vol. 71 (1970), reprinted in his *Aspects of the Religious Behavior of American Jews* (New York, 1974), pp. 189–285, esp. pp. 276–78. On Reconstructionism, see also Raphael, pp. 179–94; Rebecca T. Alpert and Jacob J. Staub, *Exploring Judaism: A Reconstructionist Approach* (New York, 1985).

50. Mordecai M. Kaplan, *Judaism as a Civilization* (New York, 1934). The bibliographies in the entries on Kaplan, Jack Cohen, Ira Eisenstein, Eugene Kohn, and Milton Steinberg indicate the major Reconstructionist writings.

A

ABELSON, KASSEL ELIJAH (1924–). Rabbi. The son of George and Laya Kasnowitz Abelson, Kassel Abelson was born in Brooklyn, New York, on June 28, 1924. He earned a B.A. from New York University in 1943 and was ordained in 1948—as his father had been in 1920—at the Seminary.

Abelson began his career as assistant rabbi at Beth El Synagogue, Minneapolis, Minnesota (1948–51). Beth El had been formed in 1922 when the members of the Young People's Synagogue of an older congregation decided to establish a modern, decorous service of their own. At Beth El, Abelson worked with its founding rabbi, the distinguished Conservative leader David *Aronson. Abelson organized Beth El's youth program, which became the nucleus of Conservatism's national organization, United Synagogue Youth.

Abelson next spent two years serving as a U.S. Air Force chaplain in Casablanca (1951–53) before returning to congregational life as rabbi of Shearith Israel Synagogue, Columbus, Georgia (1953–57). While in the South he also chaired the Committee on Adult Education established by the Southeastern Region of the United Synagogue in 1954.

In 1957 Abelson returned to Minneapolis and Beth El and since Aronson's retirement in 1959 has led the congregation (associate rabbi 1957–60, senior rabbi 1960–). Recognizing that the work of the Rabbinical Assembly's Committee on Jewish Law and Standards remained relatively unknown among Minneapolis Jewry, he joined with fellow Twin Cities Conservative rabbis in establishing a local *bet din* as the center of authority for the metropolitan Conservative community. In addition to meeting weekly, its members published digests of the committee's decisions in their synagogue bulletins, endorsed them, and joined together in statements before the state legislature and in the local press. His Jewish communal activities included the presidency of the Minnesota Rabbinical Association and membership on the Talmud Torah Board and Board of the Federation for Jewish Service. In civic affairs Abelson served on the

Executive Committee of the Urban Coalition and the Governor's Advisory Committee on the Family, and he represented Minnesota at the 1980 White House Conference on the Family. He also convened the Minnesota Interreligious Committee and was co-chairman of its Committee on Biomedical Ethics.

Abelson has played a leading role in the Rabbinical Assembly. One of his abiding interests has been the development of Jewish law. As a member of the Committee on Jewish Law and Standards, he believes that its work is at the heart of the Conservative movement, but that it must debate its work openly and disseminate its decisions widely. He has called for the training of rabbis to write *responsa* in new areas of concern, such as biomedical ethics and environmental issues. Among the *responsa* that he wrote for the committee was a paper recommending the inclusion of intermarried couples in many aspects of synagogue life. A member of the Rabbinical Assembly's Executive Council since 1982, in 1986 Abelson was elected president of the Rabbinical Assembly. He also served on its Joint Retirement Board and chaired its Future Planning Committee.

Abelson married Shirley Raskin in 1947; they had three children. After her death in 1984, he married Lois Segal.

Writings: "The Status of a Non-Jewish Spouse and Children of a Mixed Marriage in the Synagogue," *CJ* 35, 4 (Summer 1982), pp. 39–49; "The Rabbinical Assembly and the Development of Halakhah," *PRA 1983* vol. 45 (1984), pp. 77–83.

References: *PRA 1954* vol. 18 (1955), p. 201; *PRA 1967* vol. 31 (1967), pp. 224–25; Gilbert Rosenthal, *Contemporary Judaism: Patterns of Survival*, 2d ed. (New York, 1986), pp. 350–52.

ABRAMOWITZ, HERMAN (1880–1947). Rabbi. The son of Lazarus and Miriam Burros Abramowitz, Herman Abramowitz was born in Russia on February 28, 1880. He was brought to the United States in 1890. Abramowitz earned a B.A. from the City College of New York and was ordained at the Seminary in 1902. In 1907 he became the first student to earn a Doctor of Hebrew Letters at the Seminary.

In 1903 Abramowitz became rabbi at Shaar Hashomayim Congregation, Montreal, Canada (1903–47). Organized in 1846, Shaar Hashomayim, Canada's oldest Ashkenazi congregation, had deliberately chosen to emulate in name a prestigious congregation in Great Britain. Abramowitz's combination of traditional Judaism and executive ability enabled him to shape Shaar Hashomayim into one of the leading synagogues in the British Empire. He guided the congregation as it expanded its activities to include numerous auxiliaries and a daily Hebrew school. In 1922 its members dedicated a new synagogue in the Montreal suburb of Westmount with a community center capable of seating 2,000 people during the High Holidays.

Abramowitz was the leading Canadian rabbi of his era, taking an active part for nearly half a century in every segment of Canadian Jewish life. He directed the Montreal Federation of Jewish Philanthropies and the Montreal United Talmud Torahs; chaired the United Jewish Campaign for the Province of Quebec;

and sat on the Jewish School Commission, convened by the Quebec provincial government to study the issue of Jewish children's attendance at school. During World War I, Abramowitz was senior Jewish chaplain for the Canadian Army. Cooperating with the Jewish Colonization Association of Paris, he worked to establish schools and communal institutions in Jewish farming colonies in western Canada. And he helped found the Canadian Jewish Congress. It was largely his testimony that disproved the notorious blood libel accusation, spread by Plamondon of Quebec, in 1912.

An active member of the United Synagogue of America, Abramowitz was elected its president in 1926. This marked the first time that an American Jewish organization went outside the United States to choose its highest executive. As president (1926–27), he issued a call for an enrollment campaign of individuals in the United Synagogue and worked to raise the funds necessary to build the Yeshurun Synagogue Center in Jerusalem.

Abramowitz married Theresa Bockar in 1911; they had two children. He died on September 24, 1947, in Montreal.

Writings: Posthumously, *One Hundred Years of Spiritual Growth* (Montreal, 1948).

References: *EJ* vol. 2, col. 169; *NYT* 26 September 1947, p. 23; *Recorder* 6, 3 (June 1926), p. 7; 7, 1 (January 1927), p. 8; 8, 2 (April 1928), pp. 15–16; Stuart E. Rosenberg, *The Jewish Community in Canada*, vol. 1 (Toronto, 1970), pp. 127–29; *WWAJ* 1938–39, p. 6.

ADLER, CYRUS (1863–1940). Scholar, administrator, President of the Jewish Theological Seminary of America. The son of Samuel and Sarah Sulzberger Adler, Cyrus Adler was born in Van Buren, Arkansas, on September 13, 1863. Following his father's death in 1867, the family moved to Philadelphia.

Adler received his early education in the Hebrew Education Society school that met at the Philadelphia Sephardic congregation, Mikveh Israel. His close relationship with Mikveh Israel's minister-*hazzan* Sabato *Morais greatly shaped his religious traditionalism. Adler continued his secular education in the Philadelphia public schools and studied Hebrew literature privately with tutors, including Morais. He earned a B.A. from the University of Pennsylvania in 1883 and went to Johns Hopkins University, where in 1887 he became the first person to receive a Ph.D. in Semitics from an American university. Adler was immediately appointed to the teaching staff of the Johns Hopkins Semitics department and eventually promoted to associate professor (1884–93).

In 1889 he also joined the staff of the Smithsonian Institution, Washington, D.C. (1888–1908), after proposing that it include a section of oriental antiquities. Adler advanced from librarian to assistant secretary, one of the highest appointive political offices occupied to that time by an American Jew. He was largely responsible for the development of the Smithsonian's divisions of historic archaeology and historic religions. When he resigned in 1908, he retained the title Honorary Associate in Historic Archeology.

During this period of government service and teaching, Adler was also appointed a commissioner of the 1893 Chicago Columbian Exposition. His negotiations with governments and industrialists to participate in the exhibition led him to travel to North Africa and the Middle East, including Palestine.

A man of boundless energy and exceptional administrative talents, Adler had a remarkable ability to move easily among many different groups—scholars and businessmen, Jews and Christians. He established himself during his years of government service as a leader of American Jewry, the preeminent native-born Jew of his era. He was a leading member of the "Philadelphia Group" of scholars and intellectuals who were the great architects of many of the leading institutions of the American Jewish community.

Adler held the presidency of five major Jewish organizations at the same time. He was among the founders of the Jewish Publication Society of America (1888) and chairman of its numerous committees. He edited the first seven volumes of the *American Jewish Year Book* (1899–1905, the last two with Henrietta Szold), chaired the Board of Editors of the society's 1917 translation of the Bible, and was responsible for the establishment of its Hebrew press. He was a founder of the American Jewish Historical Society (1892) and for more than twenty years its president (1898–1922). One of the founders of the American Jewish Committee (1906), he represented the committee at the Paris Peace Conference and was elected president (1929–40). He was also a leader of the Joint Distribution Committee and was president of the Jewish Welfare Board. In Philadelphia, Adler was president of the short-lived Jewish Community of Philadelphia, or *Kehilah*, of Mikveh Israel, and of the Board of Trustees of the Free Library. He was also a founder of Gratz College.

Impressive as his organizational ability was, perhaps Adler's greatest contribution was his consistent effort to establish and to nurture all types of Jewish learning in America. Jewish education remained one of his priorities, for he was convinced that the future of American Jewry depended upon its cultural and intellectual creativity.

Adler was closely associated with the Seminary—and with the institutions of Conservative Judaism—from the opening of the school in 1887 to his death in 1940. In the early Seminary he was instructor in Biblical archaeology and advisor to his former teacher, Seminary president Morais. Adler considered his role in marshalling financial support to reorganize the moribund Seminary in 1901 and in bringing Solomon *Schechter to America as president of its faculty one of his major contributions to American Jewry.

The financial supporters of the Seminary persuaded Adler to stay on to help steer the reorganized Seminary. As president of the board of the new Seminary Corporation (1902–5), he divided his time between New York and Washington, administering fiscal affairs and overseeing the construction of the new Seminary, while Schechter built the faculty and curriculum. Adler resigned as president of the corporation after the Seminary moved from its old Lexington Avenue headquarters into the new building in Morningside Heights, and Schechter became president of the Seminary. But Adler continued to remain intimately involved with its affairs and with the growing Conservative movement.

At the same time a new project, the founding of Dropsie College in Philadelphia, a postgraduate institute for "Hebrew and Cognate Studies," occupied Adler's attention. His appointment in 1908 as founding president of Dropsie (1908–40) led him to resign his Smithsonian post in order to devote himself full time to American Jewish life, and especially to these two fledgling institutions (Dropsie and the Seminary) of Jewish higher learning. Adler assembled Dropsie's faculty, library, and physical plant, and, with Schechter, brought the British journal the *Jewish Quarterly Review* to the college. Together they edited the *Jewish Quarterly Review* (1910–15), and following Schechter's death in 1915, he continued to edit it alone (1916–40).

During these years, Adler was deeply concerned that "Schechter's Seminary" might falter, like the early Seminary, for lack of support. He therefore joined in the efforts launched by Schechter and Seminary alumnus Herman *Rubenovitz to form a union of Conservative forces in America. Adler's staunch opposition to the use of the word *Conservative*—a term he avoided all his life, even in his autobiography—led to naming the new union the United Synagogue of America. He served as one of its founding vice-presidents (1913–14).

When Schechter died in 1915, Adler became acting president (1916–24) of the Seminary. The temporary appointment became a permanent one in 1924 (1924–40). As president, Adler's chief concerns were administering the Seminary and bolstering its financial resources. Thanks to the generosity of Israel Unterberg, Louis S. Brush, and the Schiff family, his administration supervised the construction of the present Seminary campus. Its buildings then housed not only Seminary classrooms, offices, the Rabbinical School, and the Teachers Institute, but also an expanded Seminary College of Jewish Studies and the offices of the Rabbinical Assembly, United Synagogue, and American Jewish Historical Society. The Seminary Library became a separate corporation to allow those who could not support the Seminary on theological grounds to sustain this great collection. Adler also acquired the building for and established the Jewish Museum in 1931, before the full impact of the Depression forced retrenchment.

For a short time Adler was not only Seminary president, he was also president of the United Synagogue (1914–17), succeeding Schechter, who had resigned as founding president due to ill health. Adler led the United Synagogue in organizing its central office in the Seminary headquarters, planning textbooks, and recruiting new members. His proposal that the United Synagogue create an organ to deal with Jewish law led to the establishment of its Committee on the Interpretation of Jewish Law, chaired by Louis *Ginzberg. Adler, however, resigned his presidency in 1917 in opposition to the United Synagogue's support for and participation in the pro-Zionist American Jewish Congress.

Despite his many strengths as an administrator, Adler, as historian Herbert *Parzen observed, allowed for serious weaknesses in the curriculum of the Rabbinical School. Vacancies in the faculty occurred before the financial exigencies of the Depression, but they were left open because of ideological concerns. Although Adler championed academic freedom, as evidenced by his refusal to bend to pressure to muzzle or to dismiss the leader of the Seminary's left wing, Mordecai M. *Kaplan, he was unwilling to appoint new members of the faculty whose views differed from his own very traditional stance. He opposed ideological development of Conservative Judaism, understanding it to be "a general term . . . applied to those congregations which have departed somewhat in practice from the Orthodox, but not in any great extent in theory." (*Lectures, Selected Papers, Addresses*, p. 251). He conceived of Judaism as a divinely revealed religion, not subject to ideological innovation or even liturgical emendation. Consequently, when he did make new appointments to the faculty, among them Louis *Finkelstein and Simon *Greenberg, they shared Adler's commitment to this traditionalism. The result was that gradually the Seminary became isolated from its grass roots, the congregations led by Seminary-trained and ordained rabbis.

Adler's non-Zionism also led to tensions with the faculty and students. A staunch opponent of political Zionism and its plans to create a Jewish state, he nevertheless was a strong supporter of the physical rehabilitation of Palestine. He was thus intimately involved in shaping and building numerous institutions there, including the Haifa Technion and Hebrew University. Adler also played a leading role in creating the Jewish Agency, the international, non-governmental body that bridged the gulf between the Zionists and non-Zionists by providing a vehicle for world Jewish financial support of the land of Israel. He served as president of its Council and chairman of its Administrative Committee.

Adler did not produce book-length scholarly studies, but he did compile catalogues of Hebraica and Judaica collections. He also wrote numerous essays, addresses, and studies, many of them for the *American Jewish Year Book* and the early volumes of the *Publications of the American Jewish Historical Society*. Some of these were later collected in a single volume. He also wrote an auto-biography, *I Have Considered the Days* (1941). Adler was a gifted editor. In addition to his editorial work for the Jewish Publication Society and the *Jewish Quarterly Review*, he edited the articles on post-Biblical antiquities and Jews in America for *The Jewish Encyclopedia* (1901–6) and was a member of the editorial board of the *American Hebrew*.

Adler married Racie Friedenwald in 1905; they had one daughter. He died in Philadelphia on April 7, 1940.

Writings: *Lectures, Selected Papers, Addresses* (Philadelphia, 1933); *I Have Considered the Days* (Philadelphia, 1941); *Selected Letters of Cyrus Adler*, ed. Ira Robinson, 2 vols. (Philadelphia, 1985). Ed., *The Voice of America on Kishineff* (Philadelphia, 1904); *Jewish Theological Seminary of America: Semi-Centennial Volume* (New York, 1939). With Allan Ramsey, *Told in the Coffee House: Turkish Tales Collected and Done into English* (Washington, D.C., 1898); with I.M. Casanowicz, "Descriptive Catalogue of a Collection of Objects of Jewish Ceremonial Deposited in the U.S. National Museum by Hadji Ephraim Benguiat," *U.S. National Museum Annual Report* (Washington, D.C.,

1899); with I.M. Casanowicz, "The Collection of Jewish Ceremonial Objects in the U.S. National Museum," *U.S. National Museum Proceedings* (Washington, D.C., 1908).

References: David G. Dalin, "Cyrus Adler, Non-Zionism, and the Zionist Movement: A Study in Contradictions," *AJS Review* 10, 1 (Spring 1985), pp. 55–86; *EJ* vol. 2, cols. 272–74; *National Cyclopedia of American Biography* vol. 41 (New York, 1956), p. 16; Abraham A. Neuman, *Cyrus Adler: A Biographical Sketch* (Philadelphia, 1942); Herbert Parzen, *Architects of Conservative Judaism* (New York, 1964), pp. 79–127; Herbert Rosenblum, "The Founding of the United Synagogue of America, 1913" (Ph.D. diss., Brandeis University, 1970), pp. 142–97; Maxwell Whiteman, "The Philadelphia Group," in *Jewish Life in Philadelphia, 1830–1940*, ed. Murray Friedman (Philadelphia, 1983), pp. 163–64.

ADLER, MORRIS (1906–66). Rabbi, scholar. The son of Rabbi Joseph and Jennie Resnick Adler, Morris Adler was born in Slutsk, Russia, on March 30, 1906. He was brought to the United States in 1913 and educated in the New York City public schools. He received his B.S.S. from the City College of New York in 1928 and was ordained at the Seminary in 1935.

Prior to entering the Seminary, Adler spent a year as the spiritual leader of an Orthodox congregation in Saint Joseph, Missouri (1929–30). His experiences there convinced him that the rabbinate was his true calling. After ordination, he served Temple Emanu-El in Buffalo, New York (1935–38). In 1938 he was called to Congregation Shaarey Zedek, Detroit, Michigan. Except for his military chaplaincy in the Pacific and Japan during World War II, Adler served Shaarey Zedek until his death in 1966.

As rabbi of Shaarey Zedek, Adler, a man of patience, warmth, and wit, served Detroit's second oldest congregation and its largest Conservative synagogue. He loved the many lives the rabbinate enabled him to lead, but was disturbed by American Jews' ignorance of Jewish history and literature. Consequently, he became a pioneer in adult Jewish education and made his congregation his forum. His sermons highlighted the distinctiveness of the Jewish people and showed his congregants how to make Judaism function. A concealed recorder enabled his secretary to make verbatim transcriptions of his sermons. Two collections were published posthumously.

In 1962 Adler dedicated the synagogue's new $4.5 million building which served the congregation's 1,500 families. Shaarey Zedek rewarded its rabbi's efforts with life tenure (1954) and a sabbatical in Israel (1965).

Viewed by many as the leading spokesman of Detroit Jewry, Adler distinguished himself in public service. He believed that his dual heritage as an American and a Jew required that he bring the teachings of Judaism to bear on the social issues of his time, and he claimed that man's primary task was to live his life so that his presence made a difference in society. He was, therefore, active in the larger Detroit community. His understanding of other faiths led him to found the Detroit Round Table of Catholics, Protestants, and Jews. A close friend of United Auto Workers president Walter P. Reuther, Adler chaired the UAW Public Review Board (1957–66). He also served on the Michigan Fair Election Practices Commission, the Labor Management Citizens Commission, and the Governor's Commission on Higher Education (1963–66).

Within the Conservative movement, Adler chaired the Rabbinical Assembly's Committee on Jewish Law and Standards (1948–51). Its predecessor, the Committee on Jewish Law, had been reorganized in 1948 as the CJLS. Adler became its first chairman. The inclusion of standards in the title of the reorganized committee reflected both its extra-legal powers and the hope that these would lead to raising the standards of piety among Conservative Jewry. Adler was determined that in rendering its decisions the CJLS would now take into consideration the realities of the contemporary world. One of its first opinions, which he co-authored, was the historic 1950 *responsum* permitting automobile travel and the use of electricity to enhance Sabbath observance.

Adler's work with the B'nai B'rith Commission on Adult Jewish Education, which he chaired from 1963 to 1966, enabled him to continue his lifelong commitment to adult Jewish education. He wrote for its quarterly, *Jewish Heritage*, and helped edit the *Jewish Heritage Reader* (1965).

Believing that modern Jews had much to gain from a creative confrontation with the past, he worked to make traditional Jewish texts available to the general Jewish community. He edited *Great Passages from the Torah* (1947) and wrote the widely used *The World of the Talmud* (1958).

Adler married Goldie Kadish on June 12, 1929. They had one daughter. An emotionally disturbed young member of his congregation shot Adler at his pulpit on February 12, 1966. He died from his wounds on March 11, 1966. Michigan governor George Romney proclaimed the date of his funeral a public day of mourning.

Writings: *Great Passages from the Torah* (New York, 1947); *The World of the Talmud* (Washington, D.C., 1958; 2d ed. 1963). With Lily Edelman, eds., *Jewish Heritage Reader* (New York, 1965). Posthumously, Goldie Adler and Lily Edelman, eds., *May I Have a Word with You?* (n.p., 1967); Jacob Chinitz, ed., *The Voice Still Speaks: Message of the Torah for Contemporary Man* (New York, 1969).

References: *Detroit News* 13 February 1966, p. 1; 11 March 1966, p. 1; *EJ* vol. 2, cols. 83–84; T.V. LoCicero, *Murder in the Synagogue* (Englewood Cliffs, N.J., 1970); Adele Mondry, *Wyszkowo, A Shtetl on the Bug River* (New York, 1980); *NYT* 13 February 1966, p. 40; 12 March 1966, p. 27; *PRA 1949* vol. 13 (1950), pp. 148–52; *WWWJ* 1965, p. 13.

AGUS, JACOB BERNARD (1911–1986).   Rabbi, scholar. The son of Judah Leib and Bela Devorah Bereznitzky Agushewitz, Jacob Agus was born in Swislocz, Poland, on November 8, 1911. His family immigrated to the United States in 1927. Agus graduated from the Talmudic Academy in New York in 1929, earned an A.B. from Yeshiva University in 1933, and was ordained there in 1935.

Agus occupied several pulpits in his early rabbinical career. He first served as rabbi at Congregation Beth Abraham, Norfolk, Virginia (1934–36). While working toward a doctorate in modern Jewish thought at Harvard University (1939), he was rabbi of Temple Ashkenaz, Cambridge, Massachusetts (1936–40). In 1940 he moved to Agudas Achim North Shore Congregation, Chicago, Illinois (1940–42), where he completed his first work, *Modern Philosophies of Judaism* (1941), an analysis of the unorthodox approaches of Martin Buber, Mordecai M. *Kaplan, Franz Rosenzweig, and Hermann Cohen to the key themes of the conception of God and His relation to humanity.

In 1942 Agus became rabbi of Beth Abraham United Synagogue Center, Dayton, Ohio (1942–50). Founded in 1897, Beth Abraham merged in 1941 with Beth Jacob and the Dayton View Center to form the Beth Abraham United Synagogue Center. As the center's first rabbi, Agus helped unify the congregation by establishing a Hebrew school and supervising the construction of a new synagogue. While at Beth Abraham, Agus, who had been trained and ordained in institutions associated with American Orthodoxy, formally affiliated with the Conservative movement as a member of the Rabbinical Assembly (1945).

In 1950 he began a thirty-year career as founding rabbi of Beth El Congregation, Baltimore, Maryland. Agus led the congregation as it grew from ninety members to more than 1,100 families. He persuaded his congregants to introduce mixed seating and to allow for worshippers to drive to Sabbath services. He led an active program of adult Jewish education and introduced Bat Mitzvah. When he retired from the active rabbinate in 1980, he was elected rabbi emeritus.

Outside of Beth El, Agus was a powerful force in ecumenical and interracial relations in Baltimore. He advocated trialogue, open communication among Jewish, Christian, and Muslim groups. He was a founder of the Interfaith Roundtable of Baltimore's St. Mary's Seminary and Ecumenical Institute, and he also taught Judaic thought there. He was a board member of the predominantly black Morgan State University and of the Baltimore National Council on Christians and Jews.

Within a few short years of his association with Conservatism, Agus emerged as an influential member of the Rabbinical Assembly, particularly active in its *halachic* and theological projects. As a member of the Committee on Jewish Law and Standards, he chaired the subcommittee on the Sabbath and co-authored with Morris *Adler and Theodore *Friedman the groundbreaking ''*Responsum* on the Sabbath'' (1950) that allowed for Jews who would otherwise not attend synagogue to drive to worship and for the use of electricity to enhance Sabbath observance. The *responsum* included the call for the Sabbath Revitalization Program, a national campaign to encourage Sabbath observance and worship among Conservative laity. Agus chaired its commission of representatives from the Rabbinical Assembly, Women's League, United Synagogue, National Federation of Men's Clubs, and Young Peoples League (1950–53). His numerous other *responsa* included ''The *Mizvah* of *Keruv*'' (1982) on developing synagogue policy for intermarried couples and their children.

Agus led other important committees in the Rabbinical Assembly. He chaired the Prayer Book Committee (1952–56) that produced the first draft of the Rabbinical Assembly's *Weekday Prayer Book* (1961), the first prayer book published solely by the Rabbinical Assembly. He also chaired the RA's Conference in Memory of the Six Million (1963–64).

Most importantly, Agus was one of the chief critics of Conservatism's failure to articulate its ideology. He asserted that the principle of Catholic Israel, which "militates against any break with other sections of the Jewish people" and which lay at the heart of Conservatism, was no longer viable since the "masses of our people have already broken away from the ancient moorings of Jewish Law." He believed that the rabbinate, in accordance with the evolutionary nature of *halachah*, must review and reexamine the rituals of Jewish tradition and that they must issue *takanot* that would effect the changes necessary for Jewish law to meet the demands of the modern world. Agus formed and led the Rabbinical Assembly's Continuing Conference on Conservative Ideology (1956–63) in an effort to forge the ideological development that he sought. Although the conference failed to reach a consensus, his book, *The Meaning of Jewish History* (1963), was written partly in response to its work.

A prolific writer of numerous books and articles chiefly on the themes of Jewish law and thought, Agus, a modern rationalist, became one of the leading individual spokesmen of Conservative ideology. *The Evolution of Jewish Thought* (1959) traced the development of Jewish thought from antiquity to the modern period to demonstrate that the sources of the various contemporary ideologies grew out of the great diversity of Jewish thought in the past. *Jewish Identity in an Age of Ideologies* (1978) explored the challenges posed to Judaism and the Jewish people and the responses of key Jewish thinkers to the great modern intellectual movements of racism, Zionism, socialism, liberalism, and nationalism. Agus also compiled several collections of his previously published essays, including *Dialogue and Tradition* (1971), noted especially for his responses to the historian Arnold Toynbee, and *The Jewish Quest* (1983), articles on theological, *halachic*, and ecumenical themes.

Agus was editorial consultant to the *Encyclopedia Britannica* for Judaism and Jewish history (1956–68), and he served on the editorial boards of several journals, including the *Journal of Ecumenical Studies, Judaism*, and the *Jewish Quarterly Review*. He was a professor of modern Jewish thought at several Philadelphia schools, including Temple University (1968–71), Dropsie College, and the Reconstructionist Rabbinical College.

Agus married Miriam Shore in 1940; they had four children. He died in Baltimore on September 26, 1986.

Writings: *Modern Philosophies of Judaism* (New York, 1941); *Banner of Jerusalem* (New York, 1946), reprinted as *High Priest of Rebirth: The Life, Times and Thought of Abraham Isaac Kuk* (New York, 1972); "Studies in Philosophy of Kabala," in *Sefer Hashana, 5707* (New York, 1947); "Laws as Standards—The Way of Takkanot," (1950), reprinted in *Conservative Judaism and Jewish Law*, ed. Seymour Siegel with Elliot Gertel

(New York, 1977), pp. 28–45; "Report of the Prayer Book Committee," *PRA 1953* vol. 17 (1954), pp. 95–99; *Guideposts in Modern Judaism* (New York, 1954); "Theoretical Evaluation of Jewish Law: Evaluating Jewish Law," *PRA 1958* vol. 22 (1959), pp. 81–89; *The Evolution of Jewish Thought* (New York, 1959); *The Meaning of Jewish History*, 2 vols. (New York, 1963); *The Vision and the Way* (New York, 1966); *Dialogue and Tradition* (New York, 1971); "Halakhah in the Conservative Movement," *PRA 1975* vol. 37 (1976), pp. 102–17; *Jewish Identity in an Age of Ideologies* (New York, 1978); "The *Mizvah* of Keruv," *CJ* 35, 4 (Summer 1982), pp. 33–38; *The Jewish Quest: Essays on Basic Concepts of Jewish Theology* (New York, 1983). With Morris Adler and Theodore Friedman, "Responsum on the Sabbath," *PRA 1950* vol. 14 (1951), pp. 112–37.

References: *American Jewish Biographies*, pp. 4–5; *PRA 1948* vol. 12 (1949), pp. 152–54; *WWAJ* 1980, p. 7; *WWWJ* 1955, p. 13.

ALSTAT, PHILIP R. (1894–1976). Rabbi. The son of Mendel and Fannie Reis Alstat, Philip Alstat was born in Vexna, Lithuania, on July 15, 1894, and brought to the United States in 1898. He earned a B.A. from City College of New York in 1912 and was ordained at the Seminary in 1920.

Alstat served several congregations: Temple Sons of Israel, White Plains, New York (1920–21); Temple Beth Elohim, Bronx, New York (1921–25); Temple Adath Israel, Grand Concourse, Bronx, New York (1925–30); and Temple B'nai Israel-Sheerith Judah, Washington Heights, New York City (1933–55?). Alstat also served as chaplain at the Manhattan House of Correction (also known as the Tombs, 1953–74), at the Jewish Memorial and Sydenham hospitals, and at the Williams Memorial Residence.

In an early address to the Rabbinical Assembly, Alstat bemoaned the low esteem in which the rabbinate was held, noting that at that time few Rabbinical Assembly rabbis encouraged their sons to follow in their footsteps. For the last four decades of his life, Alstat lived in the dormitory of the Seminary, serving as unofficial rabbi to several generations of students.

Alstat wrote more than 1,500 weekly columns, "Strange to Relate," for the *Jewish Week*.

He died on November 29, 1976, in New York City.

Writings: "Observations on the Status of the Rabbinate," *PRA 1929* vol. 3 (1930), pp. 115–18.

References: *NYT* 30 November 1976, p. 42; *WWWJ 1955*, p. 19.

ARONSON, DAVID (1894–). Rabbi, author. The son of Yekutiel Zalman and Yetta Kudritzen Aronson, David Aronson was born in Vitebsk, Russia, on August 1, 1894. He immigrated to the United States in 1906. Aronson earned a B.A. from New York University in 1916 and was ordained at the Seminary in 1919.

A rabbinical student during World War I, Aronson served as U.S. Army chaplain at Camp Upton, Long Island, New York (1917–19). After his ordination, he held rabbinic posts in Salt Lake City, Utah (1920–21) and Duluth, Minnesota (1922–24).

In 1924 Aronson was called to Beth El Synagogue, Minneapolis, Minnesota. Beth El had been formed when the members of the Young People's Synagogue of an older congregation decided to establish a modern, decorous service of their own. In 1922 these 150 families began planning to build a synagogue, and in 1924 they invited Aronson to lead the congregation. Aronson guided Beth El for more than a quarter of a century (1924–59). He attracted new members, and by 1945 Beth El included 376 families, making it the second largest Conservative congregation in the Twin Cities. At the same time Aronson took an active role in Minneapolis Jewish and civic affairs, serving as the associate editor of the *American Jewish World* (1931–59) and on the governor's Human Rights Commission (1943–59). In 1959 Aronson, who had previously taught at the Seminary (1944–45) and at the University of Judaism (1950), retired from Beth El to become a professor of rabbinics at the University of Judaism.

Aronson was a leading member of the Rabbinical Assembly. As its president (1948–50), he recognized that the establishment of the state of Israel had important implications for Conservative Jewish observance. He called for the abolition of the second day of festivals, observed by Jews in the Diaspora, to standardize Jewish observance worldwide and to symbolize the unity of the Diaspora with Israel. Recognizing the partisan nature of religious life in the new state, he also proposed the organization of a movement of Conservative Zionists to give Conservatism a voice in the new state.

A trailblazer in the shaping of Conservative thought who demanded the adjustment of Jewish law to modern times, Aronson pioneered, long before the Conservative movement accepted them, certain innovative interpretations of *halachah*. Twenty-five years after he suggested the abolition of the second day of festivals, its observance became optional for Conservative synagogues. In 1951 Aronson proposed to solve the long-standing *agunah* problem by allowing a Jewish court to initiate a divorce. But his colleagues deemed that solution too radical at the time. A member of the Committee on Jewish Law and Standards, he also explored the possibility of setting up regional Jewish courts, and as chair of the RA's Membership Committee (1944–45), he streamlined the processing of membership applications from non-Seminary graduates.

The National Academy for Adult Jewish Studies published Aronson's *The Jewish Way of Life*, a basic text on the key principles, practices, and social ideas of Judaism intended for adult study groups.

Aronson married Bertha Friedman in 1927; they have two children.

Writings: "President's Message—The Demands of the New Diaspora," *PRA 1949* vol. 13 (1950), pp. 124–42; "At Fifty for Counsel—President's Message," *PRA 1950* vol. 14 (1951), pp. 91–105; *The Jewish Way of Life* (New York, 1946; rev. 1957); "The Authority of Halakhah and the Halakhah of Our Authority," *PRA 1978* vol. 40 (1979), pp. 42–56.

References: Albert I. Gordon, *Jews in Transition* (Minneapolis, 1949), pp. 162–63; *PRA 1945* vol. 9 (1949), p. 35; *PRA 1946* vol. 10 (1947), pp. 212–14; *WWAJ* 1980, p. 15.

ARZT, MAX (1897–1975). Rabbi, scholar, and administrator. The son of Hyman and Anna Grossbach Arzt, Max Arzt was born in Stanislav, Poland, on March 20, 1897. He was brought to the United States in 1900. Educated in New York City at the Rabbi Jacob Joseph School and Rabbi Isaac Elchanan Yeshivah, Arzt earned a B.S. from the City College of New York in 1918, was ordained at the Seminary in 1921, and earned a Doctor of Hebrew Letters there in 1934.

Arzt emerged as one of the leading figures in the Conservative movement, leaving a distinguished career in the pulpit in mid-life in order to return to the Seminary to guide its expansion and the growth of the Conservative movement. At the same time he earned a reputation as a leading scholar in the field of Jewish liturgy.

From 1921 to 1924, Arzt served Temple Raphael, Stamford, Connecticut. In 1924 he became the spiritual leader of Temple Israel, Scranton, Pennsylvania. He helped shape Temple Israel into one of the leading Conservative congregations in Pennsylvania, using the synagogue as a laboratory for innovative educational programming. In Scranton he also served as president of the Council of Social Agencies. As a member of the Commission on Public Relief and Assistance for the Commonwealth of Pennsylvania, he helped abolish the poor boards and establish the state's Department of Public Assistance Relief.

In 1939, in response to Louis *Finkelstein's call, Arzt returned to the Seminary to set up the Department of Field Service and Activities. As its director, he worked unstintingly on behalf of the Seminary campaigns, developing a broad base among the laity for the support of the national organizations of the Conservative movement. He thus laid the groundwork for the laity's identification with Conservatism as a national movement. In 1951 he became vice-chancellor of the Seminary. Arzt also taught practical theology in the Rabbinical School, becoming the Israel Goldstein Professor of Practical Theology in 1962.

Seminary duties did not prevent him from undertaking other public responsibilities. Arzt served as a U.S. delegate to the North Atlantic Treaty Organization Congress (1959) and was a charter member of the advisory council of the International Movement for Atlantic Union.

His writings suggest that he was particularly concerned with the disunity of American Jewry and the divisiveness caused by the fragmentation of the American Jewish community into competing organizations. This concern was reflected in his attempts to reconcile the wings within his own movement. As president of the Rabbinical Assembly (1939–40), Arzt recognized that rabbis shared part of the blame for the chaotic character of American Jewish life. He admitted that Conservative Judaism had not defined its positions more clearly in order to avoid the sharp lines of distinction that bred intolerance. Yet, as a member of the Joint Prayer Book Commission of the Rabbinical Assembly and United Synagogue, which he chaired from 1947 to 1952, he defended the liturgical changes made in the *Sabbath and Festival Prayer Book*, calling them "intellectually honest."

Similarly, in an attempt to resolve the Rabbinical Assembly's conflict over the *agunah* problem, Arzt first proposed the amendment incorporated in the Conservative *ketubah* as the "Lieberman clause." Composed by Seminary professor Saul *Lieberman, this amendment empowered either the husband or wife, as signators of this *ketubah*, to invoke the authority of the *bet din* of the Rabbinical Assembly and the Seminary to dissolve their marriage in Jewish law if the marriage had already been dissolved in civil law.

Arzt's penchant for practical jokes and his humor were much appreciated by his colleagues, congregants, and friends. His announcement at an early Rabbinical Assembly convention that a special meeting of all rabbis satisfied with their positions would take place in a phone booth became one of the classic jokes of the Conservative rabbinate.

Arzt hoped to make the two most familiar books in Jewish life, the Bible and the prayer book, vehicles for a greater understanding of the basic teachings of Judaism. At the time of his death, he was one of the editors preparing the new English translation of the Bible for the Jewish Publication Society. His book-length commentaries on the Sabbath and High Holiday liturgies showed that the *Siddur* and the *Mahzor* highlighted "the beliefs about God, man, and the universe which are distinctive of historic Judaism."

Arzt married Esther Podolsky in 1922. Their two sons, Raphael and David, their son-in-law, and a grandson were all ordained at the Seminary. Arzt died on August 31, 1975, at Lake Mohegan, New York.

Writings: "Presidential Address," *PRA 1940* vol. 7 (1941), pp. 69–86; *Justice and Mercy: Commentary on the Liturgy of the New Year and the Day of Atonement* (New York, 1963). Posthumously, *Joy and Remembrance: Commentary on the Sabbath Eve Liturgy* (New York, 1979).

References: *EJ* vol. 3, col. 670; *NYT* 1 September 1975, p. 18; *PRA 1949* vol. 13 (1950), p. 32; *PRA 1976* vol. 38 (1977), pp. 253–56; Marshall Sklare, *Conservative Judaism* (1955; rev. 1972; reprint ed., Lanham, Md., 1985), p. 127; *WWWJ* 1965, p. 35.

B

BERMAN, MYRON (1928–   ). Rabbi, historian. The son of Martin and Rose Modell Berman, Myron Berman was born on April 2, 1928, in New York City. Educated in the New York City public schools, Berman earned his B.S.S. from the City College of New York in 1949, was ordained at the Seminary in 1953, and received his Ph.D. from Columbia University in 1963.

After ordination, Berman entered the U.S. Air Force as a chaplain (1953–55). After pursuing graduate studies at Columbia University, he served as associate rabbi at Temple Beth El, Cedarhurst, New York (1958–65). Working there with Beth El's senior rabbi, Edward *Sandrow, Berman organized the Hebrew High School and the Adult School of Jewish Studies of the Five Towns. In 1965 Berman accepted a call to the pulpit of Temple Beth-El, Richmond, Virginia.

In Richmond Berman worked extensively in the field of Jewish education. He directed and expanded the religious school, integrating the Sunday and weekday elementary programs to meet the minimum standards set by the United Synagogue. He created a High School Department and arranged with the Richmond Board of Education for Beth-El students to earn public school credits for their work in Hebrew. Determined to maintain similarly high standards for Beth-El's adult education program, Berman invited distinguished leaders of the American Jewish and Israeli communities to the congregation's lecture series. Under his leadership, Beth-El's membership approached 800 families, making it the largest of Richmond's synagogues.

Berman was the first rabbi to head the Richmond Area Clergy Association. As president of its 600–member board during the civil rights unrest of 1969–1970, he created a biracial committee to raise funds for day-care centers. For this work he received the city's medallion for interfaith activities in 1970. In 1977 he received the Brotherhood Award of the National Conference of Christians and Jews.

In *Richmond's Jewry, 1769–1976* (1979), Berman argued that an agrarian economy, geographic isolation, the predominance of the race issue, and religious fundamentalism distinguished southern Jewish history from that of other American Jewish communities. In *The Attitude of American Jewry Towards East European Jewish Immigration, 1881–1914* (1980), which was his doctoral dissertation, he showed that while American Jews aided Jewish immigrants in the 1880s and 1890s, they at first acquiesced to the restrictive immigration legislation enacted in those years. After the Kishinev pogrom, however, American Jews became more favorably disposed to East European Jewish immigration, and they determined to fight nativism.

Berman married Ruth Solat in 1954; they have two children.

Writings: *Richmond's Jewry, 1769–1976: Shabbat in Shockoe* (Charlottesville, Va., 1979); *The Attitude of American Jewry Towards East European Jewish Immigration, 1881–1914* (New York, 1980).

References: *Temple Beth-El Golden Jubilee, 1931–1981* (Richmond, Va., 1982).

BLUMENTHAL, AARON H. (1908–82). The son of Abraham and Bessie Jacobowitz Blumenthal, Aaron Blumenthal was born in Montreal, Canada, on February 7, 1908. He earned a B.A. from McGill University in 1928 and was ordained at the Seminary in 1932.

Early in his career Blumenthal led several congregations: Beth Israel Center, St. Albans, Long Island (1932–36); Jewish Center, Bayshore, Long Island (1936–37); and Temple Beth-El, Houston, Texas (1937–43). But chaplaincy duty on Staten Island during World War II (1943–46) brought him back to New York City.

In 1946 Blumenthal joined the exodus to suburban Westchester County when he became rabbi of Congregation Emanuel, Mount Vernon, New York (1946–73). He built the congregation where none had been before and used this pulpit as his springboard for testing his ideas on education, social justice, and especially *halachah*. A dedicated teacher, he experimented at Emanuel with holding adult education classes in lieu of the traditional Friday night sermon. His first book, *If I Am Not for Myself* (1973), a study of the ancient rabbi Hillel written for the United Synagogue, grew out of a course he taught on rabbinic Judaism in the Emanuel high school. A passionate supporter of the civil rights movement, he spoke out on busing despite personal threats and organized and chaired the Mount Vernon Community Tensions Seminar (1962–66), an interracial group that strove to keep peace during the difficult decade of the sixties.

From the security of his position at Emanuel, Blumenthal emerged as a leading member of the Rabbinical Assembly. He constituted the one-man Committee on Regions (1953) organized to coordinate the expansion of the Rabbinical Assembly. He chaired the Chaplaincy Availability Board (1955–57) and later led the Chaplaincy Commission of the Jewish Welfare Board. In 1956 he was elected president of the 650–member Rabbinical Assembly (1956–58). An outspoken critic of the Rabbinical Assembly's failure to develop a program for Conservative

Judaism and of the very traditional stance of the Seminary, he worked to strengthen the organization and to establish its publications program on a sound basis.

But perhaps his greatest contributions were as a member of the Committee on Jewish Law and Standards (1948–82). Believing that Jewish religious life had to exist within the framework of *halachah*, he championed the readjustment of *halachah* to modern times and especially fought for the amelioration of the status of women in Jewish law. Among his *responsa* was ''An *Aliyah* for Women'' (1955), presented in 1954 as a minority opinion permitting women to be called for *aliyot*. He also supported the counting of women in the *minyan* and their ordination as rabbis. Another opinion, *''Yom Tov Sheni Shel Goluyot''* (1964), called for experimentation to revitalize the second day of festivals and was unanimously adopted by the committee as a ''binding decision'' of the Rabbinical Assembly. Blumenthal also fought within the committee for the right to articulate and to preserve minority opinions.

Many of his writings, including several *responsa* and selections from columns he wrote for the *Emanuel Bulletin* (1946–73), *Jewish Post and Opinion* (1973–78), and Houston's *Jewish-Herald Voice* (1975–81) were posthumously collected in *And Bring Them Closer to Torah* (1986).

Blumenthal married Jane Spitzer in 1937; they had four children. Their son David was ordained at the Seminary in 1964. Blumenthal died in Florida on June 13, 1982.

Writings: ''Committee on Regions,'' *PRA 1954* vol. 18 (1955), pp. 122–30; ''The Status of the Rabbinical Assembly in the Conservative Movement,'' *PRA 1955* vol. 19 (1956), pp. 126–40; ''Presidential Report,'' *PRA 1957* vol. 21 (1958), pp. 37–56; ''Presidential Address,'' *PRA 1958* vol. 22 (1959), pp. 43–67; ''The *Shulchan Arukh* After 400 Years,'' *PRA 1968* vol. 32 (1968), pp. 48–55; *If I Am Not for Myself: The Story of Hillel* (New York, 1973). Posthumously, *And Bring Them Closer to Torah: The Life and Work of Rabbi Aaron H. Blumenthal*, ed. David R. Blumenthal (Hoboken, N.J., 1986).

References: *PRA 1953* vol. 17 (1954), p. 139; *PRA 1954* vol. 18 (1955), pp. 31–34; *PRA 1983* vol. 45 (1984), pp. 191–93; *WWWJ* 1965, p. 107.

BOHNEN, ELI AARON (1909–). Rabbi. The son of Max Jacob and Nellie Elka Brill Bohnen, Eli Bohnen was born in Toronto, Canada, on September 16, 1909. Educated at the Harbord Collegiate Institute of Toronto, he earned a B.A. from the University of Toronto in 1931. Following his graduation he immigrated to the United States, was ordained at the Seminary in 1935, and earned a Doctor of Hebrew Letters there in 1953.

Holding that a rabbi's task was to make Judaism relevant to contemporary Jews, Bohnen began his career as assistant rabbi at Congregation Adath Jeshurun, Philadelphia, Pennsylvania (1935–39). Led by Rabbi Max *Klein, Adath Jeshurun had been one of the founding members of the United Synagogue. In 1939 Bohnen left Philadelphia to become rabbi of Temple Emanu-El, Buffalo, New York (1939–48). His service there was interrupted by the United States's entrance

into World War II. He left his pulpit to serve as assistant division chaplain with
the rank of major in the U.S. Army (1943–46). An advisor on displaced persons,
Bohnen entered Dachau with the U.S. forces. His work with Jewish refugees
shaped his future ministry.

Although he returned to Buffalo following his tour of duty, in 1948 Bohnen
moved to Providence, Rhode Island, to succeed Israel *Goldman as rabbi of
Temple Emanu-El (1948–73). Founded in 1924 by lay leaders with the assistance
of the United Synagogue's director, Samuel *Cohen, Emanu-El had become a
leading Conservative congregation of some 500 families under Goldman's direction. Bohnen led Emanu-El as it confronted the postwar membership boom;
directed it to conform to the major postwar trends within the Conservative
movement; and continued, as he had done in the past, to use his sermons to
"advertise education." In his first decade at Emanu-El, he oversaw the construction of the school auditorium building and new synagogue. He worked,
despite initial resistance, to replace the Sunday school with the three-day-a-week
Hebrew school as the norm for the congregation's children. By 1956 enrollment
in the Hebrew school had tripled. Bohnen discovered that with Emanu-El's
children receiving a more intensive Jewish education, many more parents were
challenged to join his adult study classes. He also helped to establish the synagogue's museum of ceremonial objects and to improve the library. By 1960
the congregation numbered 1,126 families. When Bohnen retired in 1973, he
was elected rabbi emeritus.

In addition to his congregational responsibilities, Bohnen was a leader among
Rhode Island Jewry, serving as president of the Rhode Island Board of Rabbis;
as chairman of the Rhode Island Israel Bonds Campaign; and as a member of
the boards of the United Fund, Council of Community Services, Community
Workshop, Jewish Federation of Rhode Island, Jewish Community Center, and
Providence Hebrew Day School. He was also a member of the Special Committee
of the State of Rhode Island on the Jurisprudence of the Future.

A member of the Rabbinical Assembly's Committee on Jewish Law and
Standards (CJLS), Bohnen argued that for some Jews *halachah* had become an
idol to be worshipped and that contemporary values must be considered in ·
interpreting Jewish law. He wrote several *responsa* for the CJLS and chaired its
subcommittee on the issues of personal status. He also served as secretary of
the Rabbinical Assembly and chairman of its Ethics Committee, Joint Placement
Commission (1962–63), and Chaplaincy Study Committee (1964–66). As president of the Rabbinical Assembly (1966–68) during the difficult crises of the Six
Day War, Vietnam War, and urban riots, Bohnen sensed the plight of Rabbinical
Assembly chaplains caught up in the moral dilemma posed by the bombing of
civilian targets. At the same time, he decried tensions within the American
Jewish community, claiming that the breach with Orthodoxy was "of their
making, not ours," and called for interdenominational cooperation.

Bohnen married Eleanor Rosenthal in 1939; they have two children.

Writings: "Something About My Ministry," *PRA 1949* vol. 13 (1950), pp. 157–62; "Converts of Questionable Status," *PRA 1966* vol. 30 (1967), pp. 105–8; "Presidential Address," *PRA 1967* vol. 31 (1967), pp. 1–9; *PRA 1968* vol. 32 (1968), pp. 1–6.

References: *Temple Emanu-El: The First Fifty Years, 1924–1975* (Providence, R.I., n.d.), pp. 58–93; *WWWJ* 1965, p. 110.

BOKSER, BEN ZION (1907–84). Rabbi, author. The son of Elie Morris and Gittel Katz Bokser, Ben Zion Bokser was born on July 4, 1907, in Lubomi, Poland. He immigrated to the United States in 1920 and was educated at the Talmudical Academy High School. He earned a B.A. from the City College of New York in 1928, was ordained at the Seminary in 1931, and earned a Ph.D. from Columbia University in 1935.

After serving briefly as rabbi at Congregation Kehillath Israel in the Bronx (1931–32) and in Vancouver, British Columbia (1932–33), in 1935 Bokser became rabbi at the Forest Hills Jewish Center, a leading Conservative congregation in Queens, New York. Bokser remained at Forest Hills for more than fifty years, except for a brief hiatus as a chaplain in the U.S. Army during World War II (1944–46). A champion of social justice, in the early 1970s he took a courageous stand, over the opposition of many of his congregants, in favor of building the Forest Hills Co-op, a housing project for the working poor, in the midst of the Jewish community.

Bokser's influence in the Conservative movement extended beyond Forest Hills. He remained closely involved with the Seminary as program editor of its radio show, "The Eternal Light" (1952–65); a lecturer on homiletics; and member of the Conference on Science, Philosophy, and Religion. Active in the Rabbinical Assembly, he led its mission to Israel in 1949 and later chaired its Committee on Israel and Zionism. As a member and chairman (1959–60, 1963–65, 1980–84) of the RA's Committee on Jewish Law and Standards, Bokser disapproved of the ruling that allowed Jews to ride to synagogue on the Sabbath and wrote the 1963 *responsum*, unanimously adopted by the committee, opposing the performance of circumcision on any day other than the eighth (except, of course, on medical or other *halachically* recognized grounds).

Because he opposed the liturgical changes made in the *Sabbath and Festival Prayer Book* of the Rabbinical Assembly and United Synagogue (1946), he published *The Prayer Book: Weekday, Sabbath, and Festival* (1957) and *The High Holy Day Prayer Book* (1959). Here he retained the classical Hebrew liturgy (with a single exception in the former), but allowed for the reinterpretation of many of the traditional prayers in English translations.

A prolific author, Bokser was drawn to the great rabbinic scholars of the past. Beginning with his first book, *Pharisaic Judaism in Transition* (1935), a study of the first-century master Rabbi Eliezer ben Hyrcannus, he set out to illuminate the lives and works of the sages in the context of their historical settings. He followed this with *The Legacy of Maimonides* (1950) on the medieval philosopher and legalist and with *From the World of the Cabbalah* (1954) on the towering scholar and spiritual leader of the sixteenth century, Rabbi Judah Loew of Prague. Perhaps his greatest contribution, however, lay in his study and translation of some of the most important writings of the religious mystic, the first Ashkenazic chief rabbi of modern Israel, *Abraham Isaac Kook* (1978). Bokser continued his exploration of mysticisim in *The Jewish Mystical Tradition* (1981), a survey of the mystical strain of Judaism from its Biblical origins to the writings of Kook.

He also wrote popular works addressed to wider Jewish and Christian audiences. *The Wisdom of the Talmud* (1951) introduced the great body of Jewish law. *Judaism and the Christian Predicament* (1967) argued that Jewish-Christian tensions would remain unresolved until Christianity adopted a policy of religious co-existence and refrained from trying to convert Jews. *Jews, Judaism, and the State of Israel* (1973) was drawn from his lectures before a largely Christian audience at Vanderbilt University.

In addition to teaching at the Seminary, Bokser was also adjunct professor of political science and religious studies at Queens College and co-founder and director of its Center for the Study of Ethics and Public Policy.

He married Kallia Halpern in 1940; they had two children. Their son, Baruch, was ordained at the Seminary. Bokser died on January 30, 1984, in New York City.

Writings: *Pharisaic Judaism in Transition: Rabbi Eliezer the Great and Jewish Reconstruction after the War with Rome* (1935; reprint ed., New York, 1973); *The Legacy of Maimonides* (New York, 1950; rev. 1962); *The Wisdom of the Talmud* (New York, 1951); *From the World of the Cabbalah: The Philosophy of Rabbi Judah Loew of Prague* (New York, 1954); *Judaism and Modern Man* (New York, 1957); *The Gifts of Life and Love* (New York, 1958; rev. 1975); *Judaism: Profile of a Faith* (New York, 1963); *Judaism and the Christian Predicament* (New York, 1967); *Jews, Judaism, and the State of Israel* (New York, 1973); *Abraham Isaac Kook: The Lights of Penitence, the Moral Principles, Lights of Holiness, Essays, Letters, and Poems* (Ramsey, N.J., 1978); *The Jewish Mystical Tradition* (New York, 1981); *Origins of the Seder* (Berkeley, Calif., 1984). Ed. and trans., *Selihot Service* (New York, 1955); *The Prayer Book: Weekday, Sabbath, and Festival* (New York, 1957); *The High Holy Day Prayer Book* (New York, 1959).

References: *American Jewish Biographies*, p. 41; *CJ* 13, 4 (Summer 1959), p. 53; Robert Gordis, "Reinterpretation—Its Canons and Limits," *CJ* 13, 4 (Summer 1959), pp. 21–26; *EJ* vol. 4, col. 1184; *NYT* 2 February 1984, p. B5; *PRA 1954* vol. 18 (1955), pp. 55–58; *PRA 1960* vol. 24 (1960), pp. 286–91; *PRA 1964* vol. 28 (1964), pp. 238–43, 273–74; *PRA 1984* vol. 46 (1985), pp. 141–43; *WWWJ* 1965, p. 110.

BOSNIAK, JACOB (1887–1963). Rabbi, liturgist. The son of Abraham Leib and Bessie Golub Bosniak. Jacob Bosniak was born in Gorodetz, Russia, on December 1, 1887. He was brought to the United States in 1903 and completed his rabbinical studies at Rabbi Isaac Elchanan Yeshivah in 1907. He received a B.S. from New York University in 1914, was ordained at the Seminary in 1917, and earned a Doctor of Hebrew Letters from the Seminary in 1933.

Bosniak's first congregation was Shearith Israel in Dallas, Texas (1916–20). Building there upon the groundwork laid by his predecessor, Louis *Epstein, Bosniak strengthened the Hebrew school, started a Young People's Group, raised funds for a new synagogue, and led Shearith Israel to affiliate with the United Synagogue.

In 1921 Bosniak became rabbi of the Ocean Parkway Jewish Center of the First Congregation of Kensington, Tiphereth Israel in the Flatbush section of Brooklyn (1921–49). Founded in 1911 as the successor to Congregation Tiphereth Israel, Ocean Parkway Jewish Center expanded under Bosniak's direction. He spearheaded a drive to acquire adjoining buildings to serve as a schoolhouse and meeting rooms, but the synagogue was still not large enough. In 1924 the center embarked upon an ambitious building program to build a new synagogue-center at a cost of $450,000. Within two years, membership of the Ocean Parkway Jewish Center climbed to 460 families involved in the center's wide range of activities.

An effective preacher, Bosniak's sermons indicated that he saw the modern rabbi grappling with the same problems that had plagued Ezekiel: indifference to faith, disloyalty to Jewish institutions, despair of national restoration of Israel, influence of a strange culture and environment, and misconceptions about the relationships between God, man, and Israel. But he believed that faith and the synagogue, combined with intelligence and reason, would sustain Jewish life in the America that he termed a beacon of light and a haven of refuge for the world.

Sensing that a uniform prayer book with modern English translations would strengthen the worship of his congregation, Bosniak published several prayer books that were widely used in Conservative synagogues. *Prayers of Israel* (1925; 3rd rev. ed. 1937) included English translations of the prayers for *Shabbat* and the Three Festivals, English hymns, responsive readings, and instructions to the prayers in English.

Within the Rabbinical Assembly, Bosniak chaired the Rabbinic Ethics Committee (1945–48), which prepared a code of ethics for the rabbis. He also served as president of the Brooklyn Board of Rabbis (1938–40) and as a judge and a member of the Board of Directors of the Jewish Conciliation Board of America (1945–63).

Congregational and communal duties prevented Bosniak from fulfilling his desire to continue Jewish scholarship. Consequently, when he retired from Ocean Parkway in 1949 and was elected rabbi emeritus, he once again turned to classical Jewish texts and published a critical edition of *The Commentary of David Kimhi on the Fifth Book of the Psalms* (1954).

Bosniak married Susan Halpin on June 29, 1919. They had two daughters. He died in Brooklyn, New York, on August 25, 1963.

Writings: *Interpreting Jewish Life: The Sermons and Addresses of Jacob Bosniak* (New York, 1944); *The Commentary of David Kimhi on the Fifth Book of Psalms CVII-CL* (New York, 1954). Ed., *Prayers of Israel*, 2 vols. (New York, 1925; 3d rev. ed. 1937); *Anthology of Prayer* (New York, 1958).

References: Samuel P. Abelow, *History of Brooklyn Jewry* (Brooklyn, 1937), pp. 91–96; *Golden Book of Congregation Shearith Israel* (Dallas, Tex., 1944); *NYT* 26 August 1963, p. 27; *PRA 1946* vol. 10 (1947), p. 319; *PRA 1947* vol. 11 (1948), p. 77; *WWWJ* 1955, p. 99.

BURSTEIN, ABRAHAM (1893–1966). Rabbi, editor, author. The son of Simon Phineas and Pauline Cary Berman Burstein, Abraham Burstein was born on October 25, 1893, in Cleveland, Ohio. He earned an A.B. from Columbia University in 1913 and was ordained at the Seminary in 1917.

During World War I, Burstein represented the Jewish Welfare Board in France and served as chief of the U.S. Graves Registration Bureau. He then introduced Conservatism to congregations in Chattanooga, Tennessee (1918–19); New Haven, Connecticut (Congregation B'nai Jacob, 1919–21); and Taunton, Massachusetts (1921–23). In 1923 Burstein was called to the pulpit of the Inwood Hebrew Congregation, New York City (1923–25), and he later served as rabbi at B'nai Israel Community Center, Bay Ridge, Brooklyn. Following his congregational experiences, he turned to the chaplaincy, serving as chaplain of the Jewish Theatrical Guild of America (1924–66?) and of the New York Department of Correction (1935–66).

Burstein was also an officer in a number of Jewish organizations, including secretary of the Rabbinical Assembly (1926–28) and of the Synagogue Council of America (1926–29), executive secretary of the Jewish Academy of Arts and Sciences (1934?), and president of the National Council of Jewish Prison Chaplains (1953–?).

Burstein's greatest contributions to Jewish life in America were his literary endeavors. He was a leading figure in the Anglo-Jewish press, editing or serving as literary editor for numerous Jewish publications, including the *Jewish Child* (1915), *Jewish Independent* (1917), *United Synagogue Recorder* (1924–29), *Jewish Forum* (1924–29), *Rabbinical Assembly Newsletter* (1925–28), *Jewish Examiner* (1929–35), *Jewish Review* (1932), *Young Judean* (1935), and *Jewish Mail* (1951–?). For more than twenty years he was managing editor of the *Jewish Outlook* (1936–57).

He also edited numerous books. In an effort to counter the tendency to center sermons around book reviews or political issues that had no Jewish basis, Burstein collected fifty-four sermons, based on the weekly *Shabbat* Torah readings and written by Reform, Conservative, and Orthodox rabbis, in *The Books of Moses* (1932).

A prolific author, Burstein wrote more than a dozen books of fiction and nonfiction of Jewish interest. He pioneered in the new field of Jewish juvenile literature. His first book, *The Ghetto Messenger* (1928), was a short-story collection for children, and he wrote a series of children's biographies of the great Jewish men of the past, including Maimonides, Rashi, Judah Halevi, Saadia Gaon, and the Gaon of Vilna. His second book, *Unpastoral Lyrics* (1930), was a collection of his light verse, much of which had previously appeared in leading American publications.

Burstein married Stella Cohn in 1920; they had four children. He died on October 3, 1966, in New York City.

Writings: *The Ghetto Messenger* (1928; reprint ed., New York, 1971); *Unpastoral Lyrics* (New York, 1930); *The Boy of Cordova: An Incident in the Youth of Maimonides* (New York, 1935); *Religious Parties in Israel: Their History, Methods, and Perils* (New York, 1936); *The Boy Called Rashi* (New York, 1940); *Judah Halevi in Granada* (New York, 1941); *The Boy of Wilna* (New York, 1941); *West of the Nile: A Story of Saadia Gaon* (New York, 1942); *Maxims for the Midrash* (New York, 1945); *Laws Concerning Religion in the United States* (New York, 1950; 2d ed. 1966); *Manual for Jewish Prison Chaplains* (New York, 1953); *Adventure on Manhattan Island* (New York, 1957). Ed., *The Books of Moses: Sermons by American Rabbis* (New York, 1932); *The Worlds of Norman Salit* (New York, 1966). Trans., *Symphonic Poems* (New York, 1936); *A Jewish Child's Garden of Verses* (New York, 1940).

References: Abraham J. Karp, "Abraham Burstein," *PRA 1967* vol. 32 (1967), pp. 169–72; *NYT* 4 October 1966, p. 47; *WWAJ* 1938–39, p. 151; *WWWJ* 1955, p. 114; Nahum Zilberberg, *The George Street Synagogue of Congregation B'nai Jacob* (New Haven, Conn., 1961).

C

CHANOVER, HYMAN (1920–   ). Rabbi, educator, author. The son of Abraham Isaac and Anna Certner Chanover, Hyman Chanover was born in Makow, Poland, on April 19, 1920. He was brought to the United States a year later. He earned a diploma at the Teachers Institute of Yeshiva University in 1939, a B.A. at Yeshiva College in 1941, was ordained at the Seminary in 1945, and earned an Ed.D. at New York University in 1971.

Chanover began his career as a pulpit rabbi at Congregation Ahavath Israel, Oak Lane, Philadelphia (1946–52). Already he viewed his "role in the rabbinate as one of a teacher," and he led Ahavath Israel to a United Synagogue Solomon Schechter Award for outstanding achievement in Jewish education (1951). He continued his career in the pulpit at Temple Israel, Albany, New York (1952–54), but soon decided to leave the congregational rabbinate to devote his energies full time to Jewish education.

Since then Chanover has worked unceasingly in the field of Jewish education, striving always to raise standards and to intensify the curriculum. For nearly a quarter of a century he was associated with the American Association of Jewish Education. From 1955 to 1964 he directed its personnel services and was executive secretary, and later a permanent member, of its National Board of License. He subsequently directed its Department of Community Planning (1964–70) and its National Curriculum Research Institute (1970–77). A consultant to the National Institute of Education, he also conducted planning studies for the boards of Jewish education and federations of Jewish philanthropies of New York, Baltimore, Greater Miami, Houston, and Hartford, Connecticut. Chanover edited *Our Teachers* (1958–63), wrote extensively on all aspects of Jewish education, and was adjunct professor of education at New York University's Graduate School (1974–77). When he retired from the American Association of Jewish Education, he became the executive vice-president of the Baltimore Board of Jewish Education (1977–   ) and Isaac C. Rosenthal Professor of Jewish Education at Baltimore Hebrew College.

While much of Chanover's educational work crossed denominational boundaries, he made a major contribution to Conservative Jewish education. He was a member of the United Synagogue's Commission on Jewish Education (1949–61) in the years in which the Conservative movement made the three-day-a-week congregational Hebrew school the norm for elementary education. Chanover played a major role in developing the wide variety of materials that the Commission published to meet the demands of the congregational schools. For educators he wrote curricula, syllabi, and teachers' guides. For the classroom he wrote textbooks, prayer books, and story books. He was also associate editor of the Commission's magazine, *The Synagogue School* (1949–61), chairman of its Foundation School Committee (1952–62), and honorary vice-president of his synagogue, Congregation Beth David, Lynbrook, New York.

Chanover was also a member of the National Council of the Boy Scouts of America (1941–47), of the Executive Committee of the National Council for Jewish Education, vice-president of the National Ethnic Studies Assembly (1972–75), and secretary of the Association for Multiethnic Programs (1974–77).

Chanover married Alice S. Fischer in 1944; they have two sons.

Writings: *Happy Hanukah Everybody* (New York, 1954); *Planning for Threes and Eights in the Hebrew School* (New York, 1954); *My Book of Prayers*, 2 vols. (New York, 1959); *Intensifying the Primary Program: A Working Syllabus for the Sixes and Sevens* (New York, 1962); *Teaching the Haggadah* (New York, 1964); *A Haggadah for the School* (New York, 1964); *History of the National Board of License for Teachers and Supervisory Personnel in American Jewish Schools* (New York, 1982). Co-author, with Alice Chanover, *Pesah is Coming* (New York, 1956); *Pesah is Here* (New York, 1956); with Evelyn Zusman, *A Book of Prayers for Junior Congregations* (New York, 1959); with F. Gelbart, L. Leshefsky, and A. Rosenberg, *A Curriculum Guide for the Kindergarten* (New York, 1960); with Eugene Borowitz and Harry Gersh, *When a Jew Celebrates* (New York, 1971); with Eugene Borowitz and Seymour Rossel, *When a Jew Prays* (New York, 1973); with Seymour Rossel and Chaim Stern, *When a Jew Seeks Wisdom* (New York, 1975).

References: *WWAJ* 1980, p. 75.

CHIEL, ARTHUR ABRAHAM (1920–83).   Rabbi, historian. The son of Solomon and Freida Chiel, Arthur Chiel was born in Taylor, Pennsylvania, on December 16, 1920. Educated in the local schools, he earned a B.A. at Yeshiva University in 1943 and was ordained in 1946 at the Jewish Institute of Religion.

Chiel's early years in the rabbinate demonstrated his organizational and administrative gifts. In 1944, while still a student, he became the religious director of New York's 92nd Street YMHA (1944–49). In 1949 he became director of the B'nai B'rith Hillel Foundation at the University of Manitoba (1949–57). Within three years, he had organized both the university's Department of Judaic Studies, where he taught as assistant professor, and a new Conservative congregation, Rosh Pina, Winnipeg (1952–57), which he led as rabbi. He also formalized his affiliation with the Conservative movement by joining the Rabbinical Assembly in 1949.

When Chiel left Winnipeg, he became rabbi of the Genesis Hebrew Center, Tuckahoe, New York (1957–62). In 1962 he became rabbi of Congregation B'nai Jacob, Woodbridge, Connecticut (1962–83), one of the leading synagogues in the New Haven area. Founded in 1912, B'nai Jacob, known for many years as the George Street Synagogue, had previously been led by Seminary rabbis Abraham *Burstein, Louis *Greenberg, and Stanley *Rabinowitz. When Chiel became its rabbi—a post he held until his death—the congregation had just moved to its new synagogue-center in Woodbridge. He also helped found the Ezra Academy, served on the New Haven Commission on Equal Opportunity (1965), wrote a column in the New Haven *Jewish Ledger*, and was president of the Connecticut Valley Region of the Rabbinical Assembly (1973–75).

Within the larger Conservative movement, Chiel was program editor for the Seminary's "Eternal Light" television program (1957–62), lectured at the Cantor's Institute, was secretary of the *bet din* of the Rabbinical Assembly and the Seminary, and earned a Doctor of Hebrew Letters at the Seminary (1962). In 1964 he led the first United Synagogue Youth Pilgrimage to Eastern Europe. He also edited the magazine *Conservative Judaism* (1979–80) and the festschrift published in honor of the Rabbinical Assembly's executive vice-president Wolfe *Kelman and translated and wrote the introduction and commentary to the Rabbinical Assembly's *Megillat Hanukkah* (1980).

Despite the demands of the congregational rabbinate and his role elsewhere in the Conservative movement, Chiel remained an active scholar. He wrote widely on Jewish topics from the Biblical to the contemporary eras, but his major works concerned the history of North American Jewry. Searching for answers to his students' questions about their local Jewish history led him to write *Jewish Experiences in Early Manitoba* (1955). *The Jews in Manitoba* (1961) was his doctoral dissertation. Always Chiel strove to set local Jewish history against the background of the larger historical panorama.

Chiel married Kinneret Dirnfield in 1944; they had four children. He died in Hyannis, Massachusetts, on August 27, 1983.

Writings: *Jewish Experiences in Early Manitoba* (Winnipeg, 1955); *The Jews in Manitoba* (Toronto, 1961); *Guide to Sidrot and Haftarot* (New York, 1971); *Pathways through the Torah* (New York, 1975). Ed., *Perspectives on Jews and Judaism: Essays in Honor of Wolfe Kelman* (New York, 1978); *Megillat Hanukkah* (New York, 1980).

References: *PRA 1984* vol. 46, pp. 146–48; Jonathan D. Sarna, "Necrology: Arthur A. Chiel (1920–1983)," *American Jewish History* 73, 3 (March 1984), pp. 324–26; *WWAJ 1980*, p. 78.

COHEN, ARMOND E. (1909–   ). Rabbi. The son of Samuel C. and Rebecca Lipkowitz Cohen, Armond E. Cohen was born in Canton, Ohio, on June 5, 1909. He earned a B.A. from New York University in 1931 and was ordained at the Seminary in 1934.

Following his ordination, Cohen became rabbi of the Cleveland Jewish Center, later Park Synagogue, Cleveland, Ohio (1934–   ). Founded by Polish Jewish immigrants as the Orthodox Congregation Anshe Emeth in 1869, Anshe Emeth was renamed the Cleveland Jewish Center when it built a new synagogue-center in the Glenville area in 1920. With sports facilities and an auditorium unequaled elsewhere in a neighborhood that contained, within a square mile, a major segment of Cleveland Jewry, the Cleveland Jewish Center became one of the leading congregations of the city. Under Rabbi Solomon *Goldman it also moved, despite strenuous opposition, into the ranks of the Conservative movement. Returning to the community in which he had been raised, Cohen followed Harry Dawidowitz as its rabbi.

The stability of Cleveland's leading congregations stemmed in part from the long tenure of their senior rabbis. Cohen's career at the Cleveland Jewish Center was no exception. Although membership had declined slightly to some 800 families when he arrived, fresh from the Seminary, in the midst of the Depression, the center continued to prosper. Cohen created activities and programs for the entire family, and he led the congregation as it joined Cleveland Jewry in re-locating to Cleveland Heights. In 1951 the congregation dedicated the Park Synagogue there and since then it has been known by that name. Cohen helped found Park Synagogue's Hebrew and high schools, nursery and preschools, and day camp. With its wide range of youth activities, special clubs for adults, and adult education classes, Park Synagogue grew under Cohen's leadership to some 2,000 families, declining, however, in the 1970s as the congregants and their families aged.

Cohen was a staunch advocate of interdenominational cooperation and a leader in Ohio Jewish communal affairs. He worked for community causes that tran-scended denominational differences, namely Zionism and the welfare of the Jewish community. A dedicated Zionist, he was president of the Cleveland branches of the Jewish National Fund (1938–40) and of the Zionist Organization of America (ZOA; 1940–42). As president of the ZOA of Ohio (1945–50), he sat on the ZOA's National Executive Committee and was elected honorary vice-president. He was also a member of the Board of Trustees of the Jewish Community Federation of Cleveland.

In civic affairs Cohen was a member of the Advisory Council of the Bureau of Employment Services for the State of Ohio (1938–75); public representative, appointed by the governor, of the Unemployment Compensation Committee of Ohio; and a trustee of the Council of World Affairs. He was also a member of the Board of Governors of Hebrew University and in 1983 was honored by the National Conference of Christians and Jews and named National Humanitarian of the Year.

In the Conservative movement Cohen was an early advocate of pastoral psy-chiatry. He served as a consultant to the Department of Religio-Psychiatry and was a visiting professor of Pastoral Psychiatry at the Seminary (1969–74). As chairman of the Rabbinical Assembly's Committee on Marriage and the Family

(1958–60), he called for the organization of a marriage counseling service, co-sponsored by the RA and the Seminary, and established under the auspices of the Joint Law Conference. He was also a member of the Board of Overseers of the Seminary and the RA's Executive Council (1950–58). He handled the delicate and demanding job of chairing the Joint Placement Commission (1960–61) as it moved to bring High Holiday placements under its jurisdiction.

In addition to preparing several texts for adult education classes, Cohen published *All God's Children*, a collection of open letters on Jewish-Christian relations and Jewish beliefs and rituals that had previously appeared anonymously in the weekly bulletin of the Cleveland Jewish Center. He also taught at the American Foundation of Religion and Health, New York City (1965–75), and served on its Board of Directors.

Cohen married Anne Lederman in 1934; they have three children.

Writings: *Outline of Jewish History* (n.p., 1938); *Survey of Medieval Hebrew Literature* (n.p., 1940); *Selected Readings in Zionism* (n.p., 1943); "Toward Cooperation in Synagogue Life," *PRA 1943* vol. 8 (1947), pp. 238–49; *All God's Children: A Jew Speaks* (New York, 1945); "Report of the Joint Placement Commission," *PRA 1961* vol. 25 (1961), pp. 185–87.

References: *PRA 1959* vol. 23, (1960), pp. 110–11; Lloyd P. Gartner, *History of the Jews of Cleveland* (Cleveland, 1978); Sidney Z. Vincent and Judah Rubinstein, *Merging Traditions: Jewish Life in Cleveland* (Cleveland, 1978); *WWAJ* 1980, p. 80; *WWWJ* 1965, p. 155.

COHEN, BOAZ (1899–1968). Rabbi, scholar. The son of Jacob (and ?) Cohen, Boaz (Benjamin) Cohen was born on February 26, 1899, in Bridgeport, Connecticut. Educated in the Bridgeport public schools, he earned a B.A. at the City College of New York, was ordained at the Seminary in 1924, and earned a Ph.D. at Columbia University.

Cohen remained at the Seminary for his entire career. In 1925 he became assistant librarian, joining Alexander *Marx in the Seminary library. A year later he was appointed instructor in Talmud in the Rabbinical Department, where he worked closely with his former teacher Louis *Ginzberg. Cohen later wrote appreciations of and collected the bibliographies of both Marx (1928) and Ginzberg (1945) and of his father-in-law, Seminary professor Israel *Friedlaender (1936). Cohen held both Seminary appointments for more than forty years, teaching and influencing several generations of the Conservative rabbinate.

Perhaps his greatest contribution to Conservatism was as the unofficial head of the *bet din* of the Rabbinical Assembly's Committee on Jewish Law, its recognized authority on rabbinic law. As secretary (1932–40) and as chairman (1940–48) of the Committee on Jewish Law and then as chairman of the *bet din* established by the Joint Law Conference of the Rabbinical Assembly and the Seminary in the 1950s, Cohen wrote thousands of opinions responding to the numerous questions raised by rabbis and their congregants about living within the parameters of *halachah* in contemporary America. His *responsa* ranged over the wide field of Jewish law and touched upon such subjects as adoption and conversion, wedding and funeral rites, synagogue practices, *kashrut*, and the authority of the Conservative rabbinate.

His opinions reflected his belief "that there are limits to genuine interpretation and that we cannot attempt to remedy all evils." He would neither countenance the abolition of laws that had become obsolete because of the willful neglect of the people nor sanction deliberate attempts to promulgate new laws that could not be derived from traditional law. He believed that *halachah* possessed absolute authority. Once the limits of legitimate interpretation by extant *halachic* canons were reached, the rabbis could go no further extending the law. Yet Cohen always maintained that creative interpretation could render *halachah* relevant.

He was especially concerned that no decision of the Committee on Jewish Law should shatter the unity of the Jewish people. Therefore, while he considered liberal interpretations on many matters affecting Conservative rabbis in their congregations, Cohen refused to allow the Committee on Jewish Law to render decisions that had the potential to affect all of the Jewish people. Thus, even though he led the committee as it wrestled with the plight of the *agunah*, he was unwilling to support any *halachic* solution that won the approval only of the Conservative rabbinate.

Cohen's scholarly love was the study of law, not just of Jewish law, but also of Roman, Canon, Islamic, and American law. His special interest in the interrelations of the various legal systems and in understanding where, how, and why they differed led him to write *Jewish and Roman Law* (1966). His studies convinced him that since legal order was the foundation of all societies, Jewish law was the basis of Jewish life.

A man of great erudition, with knowledge of Greek, Roman, Babylonian, and Assyrian literatures, Cohen was one of the first American-educated scholars to make significant contributions to the scientific study of rabbinic literature. A master of the short specialized study, he collected several of his papers on the principles and applications of Jewish law in *Law and Tradition in Judaism* (1959). His great bibliographic skill remains evident in the standard reference work *Kunteres ha-Teshuvot* (1930), an annotated bibliography of the rabbinic *responsa* of the Middle Ages that was one of the first attempts to classify *responsa* literature. His methodical mind produced the invaluable index to Louis Ginzberg's monumental *The Legends of the Jews*.

Cohen married Maryla Friedlaender; they had one son. He later married Blanche Stein. Cohen died in New York City on December 11, 1968.

Writings: *Professor Alexander Marx* (New York, 1928); *Kunteres ha-Teshuvot (An Annotated Bibliography of the Rabbinic Responsa of the Middle Ages)* (New York, 1930); "Canons of Interpretation of Jewish Law," *PRA 1935* vol. 5 (1939), pp. 170–87; *Israel Friedlaender: A Bibliography of His Writings* (New York, 1936); "Report of the Committee on Jewish Law," *PRA 1941* vol. 8 (1947), pp. 35–38; *Bibliography of the Writings of Professor Louis Ginzberg* (New York, 1945); *PRA 1946* vol. 10 (1947), pp. 41–51; *PRA 1947* vol. 11 (1948), pp. 53–63; "The Function of a Law Committee," *CJ* 3, 3

(May 1947), pp. 1–5; "Towards a Philosophy of Jewish Law," *CJ* 6, 1 (October 1949), pp. 1–31; "Report of the Committee on Jewish Law," *PRA 1947* vol. 11, pp. 54–55; *Law and Tradition in Judaism* (New York, 1959); *Jewish and Roman Law: A Comparative Study*, 2 vols. (New York, 1966); index to Louis Ginzberg, *Legends of the Jews* (Philadelphia, 1938).

References: *EJ* vol. 5, col. 667; Simon Greenberg, *Foundations of a Faith* (New York, 1967), pp. 90–112; *NYT* 18 December 1956, p. 31; *NYT* 12 December 1968, p. 47; *PRA 1969* vol. 33 (1969), pp. 173–75; *Recorder* 6, 3 (June-July 1924), p. 14.

COHEN, GERSON DAVID (1924–). Chancellor of the Jewish Theological Seminary of America. The son of Meyer and Nehama Goldin Cohen, Gerson Cohen was born in New York City on August 26, 1924. He earned a Bachelor of Hebrew Letters at the Seminary (1943) and a B.A. at the City College of New York (1944), was ordained at the Seminary (1948), and earned a Ph.D. at Columbia University (1958).

Cohen served as librarian (1950–57) and taught Jewish history and literature at the Seminary (lecturer, 1953–60; assistant professor, 1960–63). At the same time he was a lecturer at Columbia University (1950–60). In 1963 he became associate professor of Jewish history at Columbia, and in 1967 he succeeded the master historian Salo Wittmayer Baron as professor of Jewish history and director of the Columbia University Center of Israel and Jewish Studies (1967–70).

When Louis *Finkelstein invited Cohen to return to the Seminary full time as Jacob H. Schiff Professor of Jewish History, he accepted the position (1970–), in part for the opportunities it afforded his teaching. Within two years Cohen succeeded Finkelstein as president of the faculty and chancellor of the Seminary (1972–86). His appointment was in keeping with the Seminary's tradition of having a distinguished scholar of Jewish studies at its helm. Moreover, as the second chancellor trained within Seminary walls, Cohen's election confirmed the Seminary's tradition of producing its own leaders.

Cohen's historical studies convinced him that a great institution of learning lay at the heart of every creative Jewish community of the past. He conceived of the Seminary as the heir to the eminent Jewish academies of Palestine, Babylonia, and medieval and modern Europe, the paramount contemporary academy at the core of a vital American Jewry. Following the path charted by his predecessors, Cohen affirmed that the Seminary, a school dedicated to native American Torah scholarship, Zionism, *halachah*, and Hebraism, was the heart of the Conservative movement.

Building upon the work of Finkelstein, who had taken the Seminary far beyond its original purpose of training rabbis and teachers, Cohen modeled the Seminary on the university, making it an educational center for training all Jews, both professional leaders and laity. Maintaining that a rabbinical school alone was insufficient to guarantee a vibrant American Jewry, he strengthened the undergraduate College of Jewish Studies and reorganized the Seminary graduate and professional schools. The restructured curricula and joint programs with Columbia University established different tracks for training scholars, educators, social workers, public servants, cantors, and pulpit rabbis.

By moving the training of all non-rabbinic professionals to the graduate schools, Cohen was able to revamp the Rabbinical School, the hub of the Seminary, to make it what he believed it should be, a training ground for the preeminent Jewish professional leader, the congregational rabbi. The school's revised curriculum stressed professional training and emphasized the all-important role of the congregational rabbi as educator. Whereas in the past rabbinical students entered the Seminary with a strong foundation in the classical texts of Judaism, Rabbinical School admissions were now broadened to open them to those who, having discovered Judaism only in their college years, had little formal preparation. A year of study in Israel at Neve Schechter, once optional, became mandatory for rabbinical students.

Without question, the most striking change in the Rabbinical School during Cohen's tenure was the admission of women. During 1977–78 Cohen, who had initially opposed the ordination of women, presided over the Seminary's Commission for the Study of the Ordination of Women as Rabbis. The findings of the commission, which concluded by a vote of eleven to three that ethical arguments and the absence of *halachic* counterarguments constituted a strong case for the ordination of women, induced him to become a passionate advocate for women in the rabbinate. However, the Seminary Senate refused to act on the proposal to admit women to the Rabbinical School, largely because of the opposition of the Talmud faculty. In October 1983—after the death of one of the proposal's staunchest opponents, Talmud professor Saul *Lieberman—the Seminary Senate voted to admit women as candidates for rabbinic ordination. Because Cohen had already opened Rabbinical School classes to all Seminary students, in May 1985 Amy Eilberg completed its curriculum and became the first woman ordained as a Conservative rabbi.

As chancellor, Cohen worked to renovate the school's physical plant to create a center for the Seminary community and to revitalize its Morningside Heights neighborhood. With the dedication of the Mathilde Schechter Residence Hall in 1976, the Seminary offered students housing in three dormitories and cooperative apartments within three blocks of the campus. Successful legal battles to clear land and to raise funds led to the dedication of a spacious new library in 1983. For the first time since a tragic fire destroyed the old library in 1966, the entire Seminary collection was brought together under one roof. What a few years before seemed like an enclave in the midst of a dying neighborhood was transformed into a vital community for assembly, study, and prayer. Nowhere was this more evident than in the wide participation in the Seminary's two *Shabbat* services, one a traditional service held in the Seminary synagogue and the other an egalitarian service that included the participation of women.

Naturally, under Cohen the Seminary remained a center for scholarship. He made several new appointments to the faculty, including that of Judith Hauptman, the first woman to join the Talmud faculty. The roster of Jewish Theological

Seminary of America publications and Cohen's efforts to raise funds to develop by computer a Talmudic concordance confirmed the Seminary's continuing leadership in classical Jewish studies.

As chancellor, Cohen not only headed a school, he stood at the helm of the Conservative movement. Unlike earlier leaders of the Seminary, he dispensed with any hesitancy over the use of the word *Conservative* as a denominational label. Cohen understood that in the past the Jewish people had never been unified. In fact, he asserted, contemporary Jewry, united over the state of Israel, exhibited an historically unprecedented degree of unity. Given the diversity that characterized Jewries and Judaisms of the past, Cohen charged his colleagues to take pride in the accomplishments of the Conservative movement and to accept the fact that it had been decisively repudiated by Orthodoxy. Instead of Conservative rabbis abdicating their leadership of American Jewry by deferring to Orthodox dominance over the public institutions the two shared, Cohen urged the creation of separate Conservative structures *(kashrut* boards, ritual baths, day schools) and the training of Conservative functionaries *(mohalim* [ritual circumcisers] and *shochatim* [ritual slaughterers]). He also called for greater links between the Conservative and Reform movements in the area of social action.

Cohen hoped that his championing of Conservatism would lead to the rectification of what he saw as its most conspicuous weakness, its failure to develop a broad base of knowledgeable and observant laity. By rebutting the movement's critics, he hoped to generate a new fervor among the laity to embrace Conservatism's goals ''to build a community committed to the principles of Jewish law and classical Jewish values.'' (''Present State,'' *Judaism*, 26 [1977], p. 269).

Cohen was also in the forefront of the movement to protect the rights of the non-Orthodox in Israel. He met privately with Israeli prime minister Menachem Begin to protest efforts to further limit the rights of non-Orthodox Jews by revising the Law of Return. He encouraged the establishment of the *Masorti* movement to promote Conservative Judaism in Israel, and established the Foundation for Conservative Judaism in Israel to raise funds for its development. To extend the Conservative presence in Israel, the Seminary established Midreshet Yerushalyaim (1978), a year-long institute for undergraduate and graduate students engaged in the intensive study of Jewish classical texts.

Cohen wrote numerous articles. His critical edition of Abraham Ibn Daud's *Sefer ha-Qabbalah* (1967) is considered a model for editions of medieval Jewish historiography. He also edited the proceedings of the American Academy of Jewish Research (1969–72) and was a member of the boards of directors of, among others, the Alliance Israelite Universelle, Conference on Jewish Social Studies, Leo Baeck Institute, and the U.S. Holocaust Memorial Council.

Ill health forced Cohen's resignation as chancellor in 1986. In 1948 he married historian Naomi Wiener, author of *Encounter With Emancipation* (1984); they have two children.

Writings: *Sefer ha-Qabbalah: A Critical Edition with an Introduction and an Annotated Translation of Abraham Ibn Daud's Book of Tradition* (New York, 1967); *Re-*

construction of Gaonic History (New York, 1972); "Jews in the Changing Urban Environment: Reactions to Dr. Eli Ginzberg," *PRA 1973* vol. 35 (1974), pp. 35–38; "History of Judaism," *Encyclopedia Britannica*, 15th ed. (Chicago, 1974); "Major Trends in Modern German Jewish History," *Leo Baeck Institute Yearbook*, vol. 20 (New York, 1975); "The Maturation of Conservative Judaism in America," *PRA 1975* vol. 37 (1976), pp. 71–83; "The Present State of Conservative Judaism," *Judaism* 26, 3 (Summer 1977), pp. 268–74; "The Conservative Jewish Mission in Our Tenth Decade," *PRA 1977* vol. 39 (1978), pp. 37–43; "Chancellor's Address," *PRA 1978* vol. 40 (1979), pp. 139–46; "The State of the Seminary Today," *PRA 1980* vol. 42 (1981), pp. 25–30; "On the Eightieth Anniversary of Solomon Schechter's Arrival in the United States," *PRA 1982* vol. 44 (1983), pp. 57–68; "Abraham Joshua Heschel: The Interpreter of Classical Jewish Thought," *PRA 1983* vol. 45 (1984), pp. 105–11; "The End of an Era," *PRA 1984* vol. 46 (1985), pp. 86–92; "Conservative Judaism in Our Time," *PRA 1985* vol. 47 (1985), pp. 29–38.

References: *American Jewish Biographies*, p. 69; Michael Berenbaum, "Will There Be One Jewish People by the Year 2000?" *Washington Jewish Week* 27 March 1986, p. 1; *EJ* vol. 16, col. 1266; *NYT* 13 June 1985, p. II3; Herbert Rosenblum, *Conservative Judaism: A Contemporary History* (New York, 1983), pp. 133–35; *WWAJ* 1980, p. 82.

COHEN, JACK JOSEPH (1919–   ). Rabbi, educator. The son of Isidor and Helen Grossman Cohen, Jack Cohen was born on March 21, 1919, in Brooklyn, New York. He earned a B.A. at Brooklyn College and a Bachelor of Hebrew Letters at the Seminary in 1940. He was ordained at the Seminary in 1943, studied at Hebrew University, Jerusalem (1947–48), and earned a Ph.D. at Columbia University in 1959.

Cohen's first position was as educational director of the Cleveland Jewish Center, later the Park Synagogue, in Cleveland, Ohio (1943–45). There he worked with the center's rabbi, Armond *Cohen, to broaden the Hebrew school program and to develop a Hebrew high school. In 1945 Cohen returned to New York as director of the Jewish Reconstructionist Foundation (1945–52). Founded in 1940, the foundation developed and disseminated Reconstructionist literature and coordinated the activities and institutions of the growing movement. Cohen expanded its activities, establishing new fellowships, publishing several books and pamphlets, and creating new organizations, including a young people's group. He was also associate editor of the *Reconstructionist* magazine.

In 1952 Cohen moved to the Society for the Advancement of Judaism (SAJ), an egalitarian congregation founded by Mordecai M. *Kaplan in New York City in 1922 to "advance Judaism as a modern religious civilization." Cohen first served the model Reconstructionist synagogue-center as educational director (1952–54), working with its spiritual leader, Ira *Eisenstein. When Eisenstein left SAJ for Chicago, Cohen was elected rabbi (1954–61). At SAJ Cohen developed experimental elementary and high schools, adult educational activities, its youth division, and organized a communal Hebrew high school. He also pioneered a special year-long course of weekly study for Bar and Bat Mitzvah teenagers and their parents.

At the same time Cohen remained active in the larger Conservative movement. He taught philosophies of religion (1955–61) and philosophy of education (1960–61) and was a research fellow at the Seminary. He was also a member of the Executive Council and vice-chairman of the Placement Commission of the Rabbinical Assembly. As chairman of the United Synagogue Commission on Jewish Education (1960–61), he was also a member of its Educators Assembly and editor of the magazine, *The Synagogue School*.

Outside of the Conservative movement Cohen was a member of the Executive Council of the National Council for Jewish Education, the National Committee of the Labor Zionist Organization of America, and the National Board of the Religion and Labor Foundation.

In 1961 he left New York to settle in Israel and to direct the B'nai B'rith Hillel Foundation at Hebrew University, Jerusalem (1961–84). Opposing Reform and Conservative efforts to transplant the divisions of the American Jewish community to Israel, Cohen nevertheless believed in fostering all expressions of religious pluralism. He also worked to improve Arab-Jewish relations in the university community and to encourage interdisciplinary contacts among the faculty.

His books, several of them published by the Reconstructionist Foundation, helped to disseminate Reconstructionist ideology. In *The Case for Religious Naturalism* (1958) Cohen argued that the central task confronting American Judaism was the creation of a community to sustain it that would reckon with cultural pluralism and the folk basis of the Jewish religion. He conceived of creating the building blocks of that community by fashioning organizations, such as Jewish schools, to cut across denominational lines. In *Jewish Education in a Democratic Society* (1964) he discussed his general theory of Jewish education and offered a practical program for its implementation. In his other literary activities he remained a member of the editorial board of the *Reconstructionist*, chaired its Israel Editorial Board, and was a member of the editorial board of *Petachim*.

Cohen married Rhoda Levine in 1945; they have three children.

Writings: *The Case for Religious Naturalism: A Philosophy for the Modern Jew* (New York, 1958); *The Dilemma of Religion in Public Education* (New York, 1959); *Jewish Education in a Democratic Society* (New York, 1964); "Conservative Rabbis and Israeli Life: A Mini-Symposium," *CJ* 31, 3 (Spring 1977), pp. 55–56. With Rebecca Imber, *The Creative Audience* (New York, 1954).

Reference: *WWWJ* 1965, p. 160.

COHEN, MORTIMER JOSEPH (1894–1972). Rabbi, author. The son of Joseph and Rachel Harriet Levine Cohen, Cohen was born on March 1, 1894, in New York City. Educated at public schools in Charleston, South Carolina, and New York City, Cohen earned a B.S. from the City College of New York in 1915, was ordained at the Seminary in 1919, and earned a Ph.D. from Dropsie College in 1935.

In 1919 Cohen became rabbi of Beth Sholom, a new congregation in the Logan section of Philadelphia founded by members who had seceded from established Orthodox and Conservative congregations. Under Cohen's leadership, the congregation adopted the Conservative model and its activities grew. In 1922 Beth Sholom dedicated its first building.

One of Cohen's gifts was his ability to cope successfully with the geographic mobility of American Jewry. In the late 1940s it became apparent that Logan was losing its Jewish population. Cohen persuaded the congregation that if it was to survive, it would have to extend itself to the new Jewish communities. In 1952 a school and center were completed in suburban Elkins Park. Services were conducted alternately at each site.

The suburban school and center brought in many new members who wanted the synagogue to relocate to Elkins Park. Hoping to capture the imagination of the Jewish community in order to raise funds for the new building, the congregation commissioned Frank Lloyd Wright to design the synagogue. Wright adopted Cohen's vision of the synagogue as Mount Sinai symbolizing the union between God and man, and he credited Cohen as co-designer on the architectural plans. When completed in 1959, the building's exterior represented Mount Sinai and its interior, the cupped hands of God. The American Institute of Architects recognized the synagogue as one of the great architectural achievements of the time, and a model of Beth Sholom appears in the Museum of the Diaspora in Tel Aviv as the prototype of the modern synagogue. Cohen considered his contribution to American synagogue architecture the major achievement of his career.

Cohen became rabbi emeritus in 1964 but continued to serve Beth Sholom until his retirement in 1969. At that time the congregation that had started with 25 families in 1919 included more than a 1,000 families.

In addition to his synagogue activities, Cohen was president of the National Jewish Welfare Board (1960–69), president of the Jewish Book Council of America (1950–54), founding editor of *In Jewish Bookland* (1944–50), and president of the Philadelphia Board of Rabbis and United Synagogue Branch.

Cohen's writings are diverse. The author of numerous pamphlets and articles, Cohen also contributed chapters on Jewish subjects to several books, wrote a number of plays, and composed four oratorios with Beth Sholom's music director, Gedaliah Rabinowitz. He also published his doctoral dissertation, *Jacob Emden: A Man of Controversy* (1937). Here he placed the feud between Jacob Emden and Jonathan Eibeschuetz against the political, social, and economic background of the eighteenth century. He argued that their controversy reflected fundamental differences in the psychological makeup of the two men. In *Beth Sholom Synagogue: A Description and Interpretation* (1959), Cohen described the signs and symbols of the award-winning synagogue design. His *Pathways Through the Bible* (1946), adaptations of the Biblical narratives for adolescents, achieved international acceptance and was translated into Spanish and Portuguese.

In 1925 Cohen married Helen Kalikman, who wrote *Together They Built A Mountain* (1974), an account of the collaboration of Cohen and Wright. They had two daughters. Cohen died in Philadelphia on January 27, 1972.

Writings: *Jacob Emden: A Man of Controversy* (Philadelphia, 1937); *Pathways Through the Bible* (Philadelphia, 1946; 2d ed., 1956); *Beth Sholom Synagogue: A Description and Interpretation* (Elkins Park, Pa., 1959).

References: *The Beth Sholom Story, 1919–1969* (Elkins Park, Pa., 1969); Helen Cohen and Patricia Talbot Davis, *Together They Built a Mountain* (Lititz, Pa., 1974); *EJ* vol. 5, col. 683; *Jewish Book Annual* vol. 30 (1972), pp. 59–61; *National Cyclopedia of American Biography*, vol. 56 (1975), p. 312; *NYT* 29 January 1972, p. 32; *Philadelphia Inquirer* 28 January 1972, p. 14.

COHEN, SAMUEL MEIR (1886–1945). Rabbi, administrator. The son of Rachmiel and Ida Duscoff Cohen, Samuel Cohen was born in Slutzk, Russia, in July 1886 and brought to America as a child. He earned a B.S. from Columbia University in 1910 and was ordained at the Seminary in 1912.

In 1913 Cohen became rabbi at Congregation Keneseth Israel, Kansas City, Missouri. An Orthodox synagogue, Keneseth Israel had adopted some Conservative patterns in the worship service prior to Cohen's arrival. Cohen continued to direct the synagogue along Conservative lines, modernizing the Hebrew school and inaugurating a Sunday school. His failure, however, to persuade Keneseth Israel to affiliate with the United Synagogue caused the congregation to splinter in 1915. Cohen then became rabbi of its Conservative offshoot, Beth Sholom, which in 1924 reunited with Keneseth Israel as a single Conservative congregation.

In 1917 Cohen accepted an appointment as the first supervising director, later executive director, of the United Synagogue of America (1917–44). Under his direction the United Synagogue expanded its membership and activities, laying the groundwork for the development of this organization. When Cohen retired at the end of 1944, the United Synagogue had grown from 40 member congregations to more than 200, had divided into regional branches, and included auxiliaries (the Women's League, the Young People's League, and the National Federation of Men's Clubs). Traveling throughout the country, Cohen personally helped establish more than 150 congregations on behalf of the United Synagogue, promoting the concept of the synagogue-center as an integrated institution providing worship and fellowship for all elements of the Jewish community. His report on his visit to Palestine in 1924 led to the United Synagogue's most ambitious project of its early years—the building of a modern synagogue-center, the Yeshurun Synagogue, in Jerusalem.

During Cohen's tenure, the United Synagogue began to disseminate the Conservative viewpoint via a diverse publication program that included educational texts; the first of the Conservative prayer books, *The Festival Prayer Book* (1927); and magazines, the *United Synagogue Recorder, The Synagogue Center*, the *Outlook* of the Women's League, and *The Torch* of the Men's Clubs. In 1923

Cohen initiated the first Jewish religious radio programs with scripts based on Biblical themes.

An author of several books on Jewish youth, Cohen married Goldie L(?); they had one son. He died on August 29, 1945, in New York City.

Writings: *The Men's Club: A Manual* (New York, 1930); *The Progressive Jewish School* (New York, 1932); *Jewish Child Guidance* (New York, 1935); *Guiding Jewish Youth* (New York, 1939).

References: *The Herald of the United Synagogue Recorder* 1, 2 (May 1925), pp. 4–5; Abraham J. Karp, *A History of the United Synagogue of America, 1913–1963* (New York, 1964), pp. 54, 59, 67–68, 70; *NYT* 30 August 1945, p. 21; Joseph P. Schultz, "The Consensus of 'Civil Judaism': The Religious Life of Kansas City Jewry" in *Mid-America's Promise: A Profile of Kansas City Jewry*, ed. Joseph P. Schultz (Kansas City, 1982), pp. 19–20; *WWAJ* 1938–39, p. 184.

COHEN, SEYMOUR J. (1922–   ). Rabbi. The son of Philip J. and Rose Cohen Cohen, Seymour J. Cohen was born in New York City on January 30, 1922. He earned a B.S. at City College of New York in 1942, was ordained at the Seminary in 1946, and earned a Ph.D. in economics at the University of Pittsburgh in 1953.

Following ordination, Cohen spent a fellowship year (1946–47) studying at Hebrew University in Jerusalem and working with Holocaust survivors in Italy and France. His experiences cemented his unwavering commitment to Israel and world Jewry, concerns that he brought to each of the three congregations he subsequently served. Cohen was rabbi of Patchogue Jewish Community Center, Patchogue, New York (1947–51); B'nai Israel, Pittsburgh, Pennsylvania (1951–61); and Anshe Emet Synagogue, Chicago, Illinois (1961–   ). In each he emerged as a strong and innovative leader, closely concerned with both the physical and spiritual affairs of his congregations.

In Chicago Cohen followed Reconstructionist spiritual leader Ira *Eisenstein as rabbi of Anshe Emet Synagogue. Founded on Chicago's north side in 1873, Anshe Emet had previously been led by the distinguished orator Solomon *Goldman. Cohen instituted changes designed to strengthen the congregation's identification with Conservatism. He introduced the Conservative *Sabbath and Festival Prayer Book* of the Rabbinical Assembly and United Synagogue of America (1946), restored the observance of the second day of festivals, strove for greater lay participation, and offered the women of Anshe Emet new opportunities to participate in its religious life. He became a moving force behind the renovation of the synagogue and the expansion of its building to include an art gallery and new library.

In each of his pulpits, education, especially adult education, emerged as one of the priorities of his ministry. By integrating the administrations of Anshe Emet's Hebrew and day schools, Cohen helped strengthen both. In the 1980s the day school enrollment reached its largest registration ever, spurring the construction of a new wing. Cohen led his congregants in founding a Conservative

Hebrew high school. His innovative programs in adult education included the establishment of an annual professor-in-residence scholar. In 1971, at the end of his first decade at Anshe Emet, its distinction in education won it the United Synagogue's Solomon Schechter awards for adult education, the creative arts, and libraries.

Cohen was a leader in local and national Jewish communal affairs. In Pittsburgh he chaired the United Jewish Fund campaign (1957) and was one of the founders of the College of Jewish Studies. In Chicago he was president of the Board of Rabbis (1967–69) and is a director of the Jewish United Fund (1971–). As chairman of the American Jewish Conference on Soviet Jewry (1965), he was one of the first Jewish leaders to visit the Soviet Union to report on the plight of its Jews. He was also national chairman of the Zionist Organization of America's Rabbinic Council (1976).

Cohen was especially interested in furthering Jewish-Christian relations. As president of the Synagogue Council of America (1965–67), the coordinating agency of the Orthodox, Conservative, and Reform rabbinical and congregational organizations, he led the Jewish delegation to the first worldwide Jewish-Christian consultation in Geneva, Switzerland (1965). He also taught human relations at the University of Pittsburgh (1954–57), was a fellow of the Herbert H. Lehmann Institute of Ethics (1958), and a visiting professor of Judaism at St. Mary of the Lake Seminary, Mundelein, Illinois (1968–76).

Long concerned with social-welfare problems and civic affairs, Cohen was founding co-chairman of the Interreligious Committee Against Poverty and a moving force in the first National Conference on Race held in Chicago in 1963. He brought his concerns close to home by encouraging Anshe Emet to open its classrooms and playground to neighborhood Spanish-speaking children. He also served, at the request of the governor of Illinois, on the Gannon/Proctor Commission on the Status of Women in Illinois (1982–84) and is a member of the Illinois Committee to Commemorate the United States Constitution (1986–).

After serving the Rabbinical Assembly as convention chairman (1960), treasurer, and vice-president, Cohen became its president (1980–82). He brought his training in economics, his study of job satisfaction and occupational sociology, and his experience teaching labor relations to his leadership of the RA. Believing that the organization had trade-union responsibilities, Cohen charged his administration with revamping the RA's nominations procedures, improving the Joint Retirement Board, and augmenting the kinds of assistance given to rabbis negotiating contracts. Cohen also chaired the RA's Blue Ribbon Task Force on Retirement and Insurance (1980).

He frequently traveled as a representative of the Conservative movement. Cohen led the first Conservative rabbinic mission to the Histadrut, Israel's Federation of Labor (1964); headed the first Eternal Light Vigil for Soviet Jewry in Washington, D.C. (1965); and joined fellow rabbis in a mission to Egypt (1978) to meet with scholars, religious figures, and President Anwar Sadat in the hope of facilitating the peace-making process.

Cohen edited and translated several Hebrew classics and published two collections of sermons. *A Time to Speak* (1968) followed the order of the weekly Torah reading; *Form, Fire, and Ashes* (1978) included sermons on the themes of the holidays and festivals.

Cohen married Naomi Greenberg in 1946; they have three children.

Writings: *A Time to Speak* (New York, 1968); *Form, Fire, and Ashes* (New York, 1978); "Acceptance Address," *PRA 1980* vol. 42 (1981), pp. 37–43; "Presidential Address," *PRA 1981* vol. 43 (1982); "Presidential Address," *PRA 1982* vol. 44 (1983), pp. 31–46; *Affirming Life* (New York, 1986). Ed. and trans., *Orchot Tzaddikim: The Ways of the Righteous* (Jerusalem and New York, 1969; 2d ed. 1982); *Sefer Hayashar: The Book of the Righteous* (New York, 1973); *Iggeret Ha-Kodesh: The Holy Letter* (New York, 1976).

References: *The Anshe Emet Synagogue, 1873–1973* (Chicago, n.d), pp. 35–45; *PRA 1978* vol. 40 (1979), p. 2.

D

DAVIDSON, ISRAEL (1870–1939). Scholar. The son of David Wolf and Rebecca Cohen Movshovitz, Alter Movshovitz—he later took the name Israel Davidson—was born on May 27, 1870, in Yanova, Lithuania. At a young age Davidson became an orphan and went to live with his uncle and aunt in Grodno. There he received a traditional Jewish education. After study at both the Yanova and Slobodka *yeshivot*, he was ordained rabbi. In 1888 Davidson immigrated to New York City. There he worked at odd jobs while studying English and preparing for his college entrance examinations. Davidson graduated from the City College of New York in 1895 and earned a Ph.D. at Columbia University in 1902.

For a time he was a chaplain at Sing Sing prison (1899–1905) and a member of the Social Workers Organization. In 1905 Davidson joined the Seminary faculty as instructor in medieval Hebrew literature and was promoted to professor in 1916. His appointment completed the core of faculty assembled by Seminary president Solomon *Schechter, whose members, including Israel *Friedlaender, Louis *Ginzberg, Mordecai M. *Kaplan, and Alexander *Marx, trained the first generations of Conservative rabbis in America.

Davidson tried to instill in his students his love for scholarship and to impress upon them the need not to let the demands of the contemporary rabbinate absorb them to the exclusion of scholarship. In addition to teaching rabbinical students, Davidson also lectured in the Seminary's evening extension courses, served briefly as assistant librarian, and was secretary to the faculty and registrar. Although he twice considered leaving the Seminary to become chief of the Smithsonian's Oriental Department, Davidson remained at the Seminary for his entire career except for the semester he was invited to Jerusalem (1926) to lecture at the newly established Hebrew University. In addition to his responsibilities at the Seminary, for some years he was also principal of the Hebrew School of the Hebrew Orphans Asylum (1909–1917).

Davidson's scholarly contributions to the study of medieval Hebrew literature, especially its liturgy and poetry, included works in English and Hebrew. His first major publication in English was *Parody in Jewish Literature* (1907). His magnum opus, a labor of love conducted over twenty years in the rich library compiled by his colleague Alexander Marx, was *Ozar ha-Shirah ve-ha-Piyyut (Thesaurus of Medieval Hebrew Poetry)* (1924–38). Here Davidson listed in alphabetical order the initial words of 35,000 poems and prayers culled from printed and manuscript sources covering the corpus of Jewish literature from the post-Biblical period to the advent of the *Haskalah* (Jewish Enlightenment). Each entry contains information on the type and structure of the poem, its author, publication, translation, and commentary. Davidson was awarded the first Bialik Prize (1936) for this monumental reference work.

Among his other valuable contributions were critical editions of several medieval Hebrew works: Joseph ibn Zabara, *Sefer Sha'ashu'im* (1914); Solomon ibn Gabirol, *Mahberet mi-Shirei Kodesh* (1923), fifty poems of the eleventh-century Spanish-Hebrew poet Ibn Gabirol with English translations by Israel Zangwill; and *Ginzei Schechter* (vol. 3, 1928), poems from the Cairo *genizah*. Davidson's critical editions of several works of the tenth-century Babylonian sage Saadiah Gaon, including *Saadia's Polemic against Hiwi al-Balkhi* (1915), demonstrated that the program for the Jewish intellectual renaissance of the Spanish Golden Age was found in his works. Waiting one Sabbath afternoon for his students to arrive for their customary tea, Davidson discovered in a palimpsest of a Greek translation of the Torah the name *Yannai* in the Hebrew written underneath. His subsequent publication of *Mahzor Yannai* (1919) uncovered a critical work of this fifth- or sixth-century poet, a native of Palestine, that until then had been lost to moderns. Davidson's *Ozar ha-Meshalim ve-ha-Pitgamim*, a treasury of medieval Jewish parables and maxims, was published posthumously (1957).

Davidson married Carrie Dreyfuss in 1906; they had two daughters. He died on June 27, 1939, in Great Neck, New York.

Writings: *Parody in Jewish Literature* (1907; reprint ed., New York, 1967); *Ozar ha-Shirah ve-ha-Piyyut (Thesaurus of Medieval Hebrew Poetry)*, 4 vols. and supplement (New York, 1924–38). Ed., Joseph ben Meir ibn Zabara, *Sefer Sha'ashu'im* (with English introduction, New York, 1914; with Hebrew introduction, New York, 1925); *Saadia's Polemic against Hiwi al-Balkhi* (New York, 1915); *Mahzor Yannai* (New York, 1919); Solomon ibn Gabirol, *Mahberet mi-Shirei Kodesh*, with English translations by Israel Zangwill (New York, 1923); *Ginzei Schechter*, vol. 3 (New York, 1928); Salmon ben Yeruhim, *Sefer Milhamot Adonai* (New York, 1934). Posthumously, *Ozar ha-Meshalim ve-ha-Pitgamim* (New York, 1957).

References: Gerson D. Cohen, "The End of an Era," *PRA 1984* vol. 46 (1985), pp. 88–89; Carrie Davidson, *Out of Endless Yearnings* (New York, 1946); *EJ* vol. 5, cols. 1364–65; *NYT* 28 June 1939, p. 21; Shalom Spiegel, "A Monument of Jewish Scholarship," *Menorah Journal* 22 (Spring 1934), pp. 69–72.

DAVIDSON, MAX DAVID (1899–1977). Rabbi. The son of Charles and Bessie Stern Davidson, Max Davidson was born in Newark, New Jersey, on March 8, 1899. Educated in the Newark public schools, he earned a B.A. from New York University in 1919 and was ordained at the Seminary in 1922.

Davidson first served Congregation Beth El, Asbury Park, New Jersey (1922–28). In 1928 he became rabbi at Temple Beth Mordecai, Perth Amboy, New Jersey. Founded in 1895, Beth Mordecai, which had previously been led by rabbis Elias *Solomon and Eugene *Kohn, was already an established Conservative congregation. Davidson enjoyed a long career at Beth Mordecai and was elected rabbi emeritus following his retirement. Known as a leader in the Perth Amboy community, Davidson was also drama critic for the *Asbury Park Press* (1924–38). A freemason, he was grand chaplain of the Masons of New Jersey (1928) and grand patron of the Order of the Golden Chain (1933–34) and author of its ritual.

Among the most dedicated members of the Rabbinical Assembly, Davidson worked assiduously on its behalf, leading many of its most important committees and holding all of its major offices. His concern for due process and his reverence for freedom of conscience and diversity won him the respect of his colleagues and propelled him to leadership. As vice-chairman of the RA's Membership Committee (1944–45), he streamlined the procedures for admitting rabbis not ordained at the Seminary to the RA, paving the way for its expansion in the postwar period as the professional association of Conservative rabbis. Next, as chairman of the Joint Placement Commission (1945–47), he was busy finding congregational pulpits for demobilized military chaplains. As chairman of the Ethics Committee (1948–50), he oversaw the RA's adoption of its Code of Professional Conduct.

As RA treasurer (1947–48), vice-president (1948–50), and president (1950–52), Davidson's primary concern was first and foremost the welfare of his colleagues. A firm leader who could be counted upon to be a fair arbiter of disputes, he worried over the "frightening fact" of the toll of congregational life upon the rabbinate. After his presidency, Davidson became comptroller of the RA. A member of the Committee on Jewish Law and Standards, he undertook the massive project of gathering its scattered decisions and correspondence from its founding in 1927 to 1955 and indexing and digesting the nine volumes he compiled. He also subsequently chaired the Joint Prayerbook Commission of the Rabbinical Assembly and United Synagogue, following its reconstitution in 1971.

In addition to his time-consuming Rabbinical Assembly activities and his congregational work, Davidson recruited rabbis during World War II for the chaplaincy as a member of the Division of Religious Activities of the National Jewish Welfare Board. He subsequently chaired the division (1950–53), which had handled chaplaincy affairs for the three rabbinical groups and U.S. armed forces since its creation in 1942. He was also president of the United Synagogue of New Jersey (1937–39) and of the Synagogue Council of America (1959–61), an organization he had been instrumental in creating, and was a frequent contributor to *Commentary*.

Davidson married Margaret Kussy in 1927; they had two daughters. He died on September 9, 1977, in Perth Amboy, New Jersey.

Writings: "President's Message," *PRA 1952* vol. 16 (1953), pp. 109–118.

References: William C. McGinnis, *History of Perth Amboy, New Jersey, 1651–1958* vol. 1 (Perth Amboy, N.J., 1958), p. 146; *NYT* 11 September 1977, p. 36; *PRA 1945* vol. 9 (1949), pp. 35–36; *PRA 1946* vol. 10 (1947), pp. 316–17; *PRA 1950* vol. 14 (1951), pp. 30–31; *PRA 1978* vol. 40 (1979), pp. 195–98; *WWWJ 1965*, p. 152.

DAVIS, MOSHE (1916–   ).   Rabbi, educator, historian, editor. The son of William and Ida Schenker Davis, Moshe Davis was born in Brooklyn, New York, on June 12, 1916. He earned a B.A. from Columbia University in 1936, a degree in Jewish pedagogy from the Teachers Institute in 1937, and was ordained at the Seminary in 1942. In 1945 he became the first American to earn a Ph.D. from Hebrew University, Jerusalem.

Davis began his career at the Seminary as a lecturer in American Jewish history and registrar (1942–46). Already his organizational gifts and great energy were evident, and he became assistant to the dean of the Teachers Institute (1944–46). As dean of the Teachers Institute (1946–50), he was the guiding light behind the early Camp Ramah movement (1947). He also implemented Mordecai M. *Kaplan's plans for the creation of the Leadership Training Fellowship (1946), a national Conservative high school designed to prepare promising teenagers for professional careers as Hebrew teachers, rabbis, and leaders of Conservative Judaism and the American Jewish community. Davis also helped formulate the ideology and blueprints of the three-day-a-week Conservative congregational school that was then becoming the educational norm for the movement. Promoted to provost of the Seminary in 1950 (1950–59), he was also assistant professor of American Jewish history (1952–55); associate professor (1956–59); director of its American Jewish History Center (1950–63); and the first program editor of the Seminary's NBC television and radio shows, "Frontiers of Faith" (1951–53) and "The Eternal Light" (1942–52).

In 1959 Davis left New York to become visiting professor (1959–63) at Hebrew University, Jerusalem, where he founded the Institute of Contemporary Jewry. In this, the first institute of its kind—a postgraduate center for the study of the demographic, economic, social, and cultural life of Jewish communities everywhere—Davis essentially created a new discipline, contemporary Jewish studies. As the founding head (1959–   ) and principal director of its affairs (1959–73), he has shaped the institute to reflect his "four corners" approach of scholarship, training, pedagogy, and public education. Always emphasizing the practical work of educating the individuals and organizations responsible for contemporary Jewish life, he has supervised the institute's studies, publications, and conferences.

Davis was also project director and general editor of the America-Holy Land Studies Program. This joint project of the American Jewish Historical Society and the institute furthers the understanding of the special nature of the contemporary relationship between Israel and the United States by creating "a corridor between American history and Jewish history," exploring Americans' historic interest in the Holy Land. The program's publications have included archival guides to the wealth of materials in the field and America and the Holy Land, a seventy-two volume reprint series of early relevant works for which Davis was advisory editor (Arno Press, 1977).

Promoted to associate professor (1963–65) of Hebrew University, in 1965 he was appointed to the Stephen S. Wise Chair of American Jewish History and Institutions (1965–84, emeritus since 1984). In celebration of the twenty-fifth anniversary of the founding of the Institute of Contemporary Jewry and to mark his retirement as founding head, Hebrew University published *Contemporary Jewry: Studies in Honor of Moshe Davis*, which included an interview and bibliography listing more than 200 of his publications.

During these years Davis continued to maintain his close ties to the Seminary. As co-director of the Seminary's American Jewish History Center, he edited its four-volume Regional History Series of American Jewish communities (1963–78), and he is research professor of American Jewish history at the Seminary's Student Center in Jerusalem (1964–   ).

While Davis believed that "there must be a clear primacy of Israel in Jewish life," he worked to bring the best of Israel to the Diaspora communities and to increase the understanding among Israelis of Diaspora Jewries. He secured the patronage of Israel's third president, Zalman Shazar, for the Study Circle on World Jewry. Meeting since 1965 in the home of Israel's president, a tradition continued by Shazar's successors, the study circle was directed by Davis (1965–83), and he edited the thirteen-volume Publications of Study Circle on Diaspora Jewry in the Home of the President of Israel (1967–84). He is also chair of the President's Continuing International Seminar on World Jewry and the State of Israel (1973–   ). Both projects bring together community leaders and scholars from Israel and the Diaspora to explore the key questions of contemporary Jewish life. Davis was also academic chairman of the International Center for University Teaching of Jewish Civilization, founded in 1974 under the auspices of Israel's president and the chairman of the Zionist Executive. Recognizing the tremendous growth in Jewish studies in Diaspora universities and colleges, the International Center gathers data on Jewish studies programs, prepares curricula in various fields of Jewish studies, and translates important Israeli works for non–Hebrew-speaking students.

Davis was also honorary vice-president of the American Jewish Historical Society and a member of the advisory board of the *Jewish Journal of Sociology*, the publications committee of the Jewish Publication Society of America, and the executive committees of the Hebrew Arts Foundation, National Council for Jewish Education, and World Hebrew Union. He was also a national officer of the *Histadrut Ivrit* of America and helped establish the *Histadrut Hanoar Ha'Ivri*, the Hebrew Arts Foundation, and the Hebrew-speaking camps *Massad*.

His scholarly work was on American Jewry. Davis's numerous publications often appeared in both English and Hebrew and dealt largely with Jewish religious and communal life. His pioneering study, *The Emergence of Conservative Judaism* (1963), analyzed the nineteenth-century origins of the Conservative movement and the key ideas of the men of the Historical School, the founders of the Seminary.

Davis married Lottie Keiser in 1939; they have two children.

Writings: "Ladder of Jewish Education," *CJ* 5, 4 (June 1949), pp. 6–9; "Jewish Religious Life and Institutions in America," in *The Jews: Their History, Culture, and Religion*, ed. Louis Finkelstein (New York, 1949; rev. 1971); *The Shaping of American Judaism* (in Hebrew, New York, 1951); *The Emergence of Conservative Judaism* (Philadelphia, 1963); *From Dependence to Mutuality: The American Jewish Community and World Jewry* (in Hebrew, Jerusalem, 1970); *University Teaching of Jewish Civilization* (Jerusalem, 1979). Ed., *Mordecai M. Kaplan Jubilee Volume*, 2 vols. (New York, 1953); *Israel: Its Role in Civilization* (New York, 1956); *The Yom Kippur War: Israel and the Jewish People* (Jerusalem, 1974); *World Jewry and the State of Israel* (New York, 1977); *With Eyes Toward Zion: Scholars Colloquium on America-Holy Land Studies*, 2 vols. (New York, 1977, 1986). Ed. with Isidore S. Meyer, *The Writing of American Jewish History* (New York, 1957).

References: *EJ* vol. 5, cols. 1369–70; Walter Ruby, "Scholar Studies America-Holy Land Connection," *Long Island Jewish World*, 3–9 February 1984, pp. 10ff.; Geoffrey Wigoder, ed., *Contemporary Jewry: Studies in Honor of Moshe Davis* (Jerusalem, 1984); *WWAJ* 1980, p. 95; *WWWJ* 1965, p. 186.

DRESNER, SAMUEL H. (1923–   ). Rabbi, author. The son of Julius and Maude Handmacher Dresner, Samuel Dresner was born on November 7, 1923, in Chicago, Illinois. He earned a B.A. at the University of Cincinnati in 1945 and also studied at Hebrew Union College. He then joined his teacher and mentor Abraham Joshua *Heschel at the Seminary, where Dresner was ordained in 1951 and earned a Doctor of Hebrew Letters in 1954.

Dresner's career included the congregational rabbinate, public affairs, and scholarship. He saw the pulpit as a place where he could both touch individual lives and deal with the pressing issues of the day; in turn, he found his scholarship and writing informed by his life as a congregational rabbi. Dresner served four congregations: Har Zion, Philadelphia, Pennsylvania (associate rabbi, 1954–57), during which time he also directed the Hillel Foundation at the City College of New York (1954–57); Beth El, Springfield, Massachusetts (1957–69); North Suburban Synagogue Beth El, Highland Park, Illinois (1969–77); and Congregation Moriah, Deerfield, Illinois (1977–84).

For ten years Dresner edited the Rabbinical Assembly journal *Conservative Judaism* (1955–64). Launched in 1945, this forum for discussion and research was to help crystallize the development of Conservative philosophy. Because of poor circulation and high expenses, the project was abandoned in 1952. In 1955

Dresner and a small group of colleagues revived it. Despite inadequate financial and collegial support, Dresner almost single-handedly kept it alive over the next decade, writing numerous articles for it. Many, growing out of his primary field of scholarship, Hasidism, explicated Hasidic tales of the past to show that they could speak to contemporary Jewry and the crises of modern life.

Elsewhere in the Conservative movement, Dresner was a member of the Board of Visitors of the Jewish Theological Seminary, the United Synagogue Commission on Jewish Education, and the National Ramah Commission. He was nevertheless openly critical of the Conservative rabbinate. He decried what he saw as the central myths of the rabbis, namely that things were not so bad and that if they just preached better sermons or planned better programs, things would change and Conservative Jews would become more observant. He called for raising the standards and expectations of the Conservative movement to establish a code of Jewish living for its people, to renew Sabbath observance, and to inaugurate an adult Leadership Training Fellowship.

A participant in Jewish public affairs with special concern for the family and education and a leader in Jewish funeral reform, Dresner chaired the Committee of Federations and Welfare Funds and co-chaired the Committee on Funeral Practices of the Synagogue Council of America. He also served on the National Council of the Joint Distribution Committee, Advisory Council of the National Jewish Welfare Board, National Commission for Jewish Education, and Board of Governors of the American Association for Jewish Education. His involvement in public civic affairs accelerated in the 1960s during the civil rights struggle, when he led the Massachusetts Human Relations Commission.

A prolific author of numerous books and hundreds of articles, Dresner's writings paralleled his tripartite career in the pulpit, public affairs, and scholarship. The spiritual concerns of his congregants sparked several of his books. For example, *The Sabbath* (1970) addressed the issue of how to enhance the quality of life; *The Jewish Dietary Laws* (1959) explained how to hallow the everyday; *Prayer, Humility, and Compassion* (1957) explored relations between the Divine, the self, and others; and *Between the Generations* (1971) dealt with reconciling parents and children in contemporary families. He addressed Jewish public affairs, especially the struggle for power within the Jewish community, in *Agenda for American Jews: Federation and Synagogue* (1976), published by the United Synagogue. And he expressed his concern about atomic warfare in *God, Man, and Atomic War* (1964). *The Jew in American Life*, a collection of studies on the American Jewish community, was chosen by the United States Information Agency as one of seventy-five books published in 1963 to be included in the International White House Library and distributed to over one hundred heads of state.

But Dresner's scholarly studies of Hasidism, especially its leadership, remain his most important works. Believing that the problem of leadership was among the crucial issues of the twentieth century, he decided to explore religious leadership of the past. In *The Zaddik* (1960) he studied the Hasidic masters who were both at the centers of their communities and intimately bound up with God. He then went on to write a biography of one of the greatest of these masters, *Levi Yitzhak of Berditchev* (1974). In describing Levi Yitzhak's encounters with God and man, his prayer, his compassion, and his yearning for messianic redemption, Dresner preserved a glimmer of the light that had once shone in a world that is no more. Dresner also edited and translated some of the writings of his beloved teacher Heschel (*I Asked for Wonder*, 1983).

In later years, as congregational life demanded less time, he has also taught at Spertus College, Chicago (1977–   ) and Hebrew University, Jerusalem (1985).

Dresner married Ruth Rapp in 1951; they have four daughters.

Writings: *Prayer, Humility, and Compassion* (New York, 1957); *The Jewish Dietary Laws* (New York, 1959); *Three Paths of God and Man* (New York, 1960); *The Zaddik* (New York, 1960); *The Jew in American Life* (New York, 1963); *God, Man, and Atomic War* (New York, 1964); "Open Forum: Renewal," *CJ* 19, 4 (Summer 1965), pp. 53–69; *The Sabbath* (New York, 1970); *Between the Generations* (Connecticut, 1971); *Levi Yitzhak of Berditchev: Portrait of a Hasidic Master* (New York, 1974); *Agenda for American Jews: Federation and Synagogue* (New York, 1976); *Judaism: The Way of Sanctification* (New York, 1978). Ed. and trans., *I Asked for Wonder* (New York, 1983).

DROB, MAX (1887–1959). Rabbi. The son of Judah Idel and Etta Schwartz Drob, Max Drob was born on September 23, 1887, in Mlawa, Poland. He was brought to the United States in 1895 and educated in Pittsburgh. Drob earned a B.A. from Columbia University in 1908 and was ordained at the Seminary in 1911.

Drob served numerous congregations including Adath Yeshurun, Syracuse, New York (1911–13), Congregation Beth El, Buffalo, New York (1913–19), and Washington Heights Congregation, New York City (1919–27). After briefly holding a pulpit in Philadelphia (1927–29), Drob was called to the Concourse Center of Israel, Bronx, New York, where he remained, becoming rabbi emeritus in 1947. In serving several congregations, Drob was typical of the Conservative rabbinate in its first decades. A survey of the members of the Rabbinical Assembly conducted in 1929 found that the average RA rabbi remained with a congregation for less than five years.

In New York Drob was president of the New York Board of Rabbis (1933–34), a founder of the Bronx Council of Rabbis, and a member of the commission established by New York State to supervise the enforcement of the laws of *kashrut*. He also served as chaplain at Manhattan State Hospital on Ward's Island (1936–56).

Drob represented the so-called right wing within the Rabbinical Assembly. He affirmed that the Judaism he professed was "not of my making or of my choosing." While he knew that the observance of Judaism in America was not scrupulous, he could not accept any change in the tenets or practices of what he called Traditional Judaism. He affirmed divine revelation and demanded strict adherence to *halachah*, holding that an outmoded law could be abandoned only if accepted rules of interpretation made it amenable to revision. He held that the Traditional Judaism of the Seminary differed from the Orthodox Judaism of Eastern Europe only in method. In America this Traditional Judaism could be promulgated in synagogues that were outwardly beautiful, where decorum prevailed, and where rabbis with secular education preached in English.

As president of the Rabbinical Assembly from 1925 to 1928, Drob oversaw the increasing professionalization of the Conservative rabbinate. His administration confronted the material issues of pensions, rabbinic placement, the development of regional branches, a written constitution, publication of the convention proceedings, and the organization of the Committee on Jewish Law.

A member of the board of the Seminary, Drob was national chairman of its 1923–1924 million dollar endowment fund campaign. One of the founders of the United Synagogue, Drob chaired its Religious Observance Committee as it worked to enable modern American Jews to observe *halachah*. Under Drob's guidance, the Religious Observance Committee published a directory of kosher restaurants, opened Students Houses, and arranged for the sale of a kosher wrapped bread.

Drob married Dorothy Littenberg in 1921; they had four children. He died in Wingdale, New York, on June 4, 1959.

Writings: "President's Message," *PRA 1927* vol. 1 (1928), pp. 19–24; "President's Message," *PRA 1928* vol. 2 (1929), pp. 17–24; "A Reaffirmation of Traditional Judaism," *PRA 1929* vol. 3 (1930), pp. 43–50.

References: *EJ* vol. 6, col. 231; *NYT* 5 June 1959, p. 27; *PRA 1929* vol. 3 (1930), pp. 116–118; *Recorder* 1, 1 (July 1920), p. 3; 4, 2 (October 1923), p. 6; 5, 2 (April 1925), p. 15; 5, 3 (July 1925), p. 16; *WWWJ* 1955, p. 165.

E

EICHLER, MENAHEM MAX (1870–1927). Rabbi, lawyer. Born in Zemplen-Butka, Hungary, on December 27, 1870, Menahem Max Eichler was educated at the gymnasium, at various *yeshivot*, and at the Teachers Seminary of Budapest. In 1892 he immigrated to the United States. In 1899 he earned a B.A. from the City College of New York and was ordained at the Seminary.

From 1899 to 1905 Eichler served Congregation Beth Israel in Philadelphia. There, in June 1901, graduates and former students of the Seminary gathered at Eichler's home to discuss the impending collapse of the financially strapped Jewish Theological Seminary. Their meeting culminated in the founding of the Alumni Association of the Jewish Theological Seminary of America, the forerunner of the Rabbinical Assembly. Eichler was its second president (1904–7). He also sat on the financial committee that planned the Jewish Theological Seminary's million dollar campaign.

In 1905 Eichler moved to Boston to become rabbi of Congregation Ohabei Shalom, where he served until 1913. After earning an L.L.B. from Boston University in 1914, he divided his time between his law practice and numerous Jewish communal organizations. He was a founder and president of the Central Jewish Organization of Boston, director of the Federated Jewish Charities of Boston, and director of the Zionist Bureau of New England (1918–20). In 1920 he returned to the rabbinate, succeeding Rabbi Max *Drob at Temple Beth El, Buffalo, New York. Eichler served there until his death.

He married Sophie Simpson in 1900; they had three daughters. Eichler died on May 11, 1927, in Buffalo, New York.

Writings: *What Makes Life Worth Living* (Philadelphia, 1904); *Jewish Home Prayers* (Boston, 1913).

References: *Buffalo Evening News* 12 May 1927, p. 46; *The Jewish Exponent* 16 July 1920, p. 7; Jewish Theological Seminary, *Students' Annual* vol. 2 (1915), pp. 17–

18; *PRA 1927* vol. 1 (1928), pp. 89–90; *Recorder* 7, 3 (July 1927), pp. 3, 5; Max Routtenberg, *Decades of Decision* (New York, 1973), p. 118.

EISENSTEIN, IRA (1906–   ). Rabbi, author. The son of Isaac and Sadie Luxenberg Eisenstein, Ira Eisenstein was born on November 26, 1906, in New York City. Educated in the New York City public schools, he earned a B.A. from Columbia College in 1927, was ordained at the Seminary in 1931, and earned a Ph.D. from Columbia University in 1941.

Eisenstein followed in the footsteps of his teacher and father-in-law, Mordecai M. *Kaplan, as a leader in the Reconstructionist movement. A year before his ordination he became executive director of the Society for the Advancement of Judaism (SAJ; 1930–31), an egalitarian congregation Kaplan founded in New York City in 1922 to ''advance Judaism as a modern religious civilization.'' Eisenstein served SAJ as assistant leader (1931–33); associate leader (1933–45); and, following Kaplan's retirement in 1945, as spiritual leader (1945–54) of the model Reconstructionist synagogue-center.

In 1954 Eisenstein left SAJ to develop a Reconstructionist base at Anshe Emet Synagogue in Chicago (1954–59), where he succeeded the distinguished orator Solomon *Goldman. Eisenstein led Anshe Emet as it inaugurated an ambitious youth program, organized an adult school of Jewish education, and began rehabilitating the synagogue.

Four years later he returned to New York to work full time for the Reconstructionist movement as president of the Jewish Reconstructionist Foundation (1959–70), the organization established in 1940 to carry on the Reconstructionist program. Eisenstein was also editor of its biweekly magazine, *The Reconstructionist*, and director of the Reconstructionist Federation of Congregations (later the Federation of Reconstructionist Congregations and Havurot) founded in 1955. Although Kaplan had deliberately refrained from creating a fourth denomination of American Judaism, Eisenstein led a growing faction calling for the transformation of Reconstructionism from a ''school of thought'' into a ''wing'' of American Judaism. Following Kaplan's appointment as professor emeritus at the Seminary, the founder of Reconstructionism sanctioned the movement toward independence. The opening of the Reconstructionist Rabbinical College in Philadelphia in 1968 with Eisenstein as president (1968–81) finalized the establishment of Reconstructionism as the fourth branch of American Judaism.

Although most widely known as a leader of Reconstructionism, Eisenstein was influential within the Conservative movement prior to the split in 1968. He taught homiletics at the Seminary and was president of the Rabbinical Assembly (1952–54). Believing that the Jewish people must learn to live with Judaism's diversity, he coordinated the first meeting ever held among the presidents of the Reform, Conservative, and Orthodox rabbinical associations but failed to gain consensus for cooperation on common projects. As chairman of the RA's Social Justice Committee (1947–49), he reorganized and expanded it into a joint commission of the Rabbinical Assembly and United Synagogue.

Eisenstein wrote numerous articles and several books, primarily about the quality of Jewish life and contemporary problems, which explored these subjects from a Reconstructionist viewpoint. He called for the creation of self-sustaining, egalitarian Jewish communities modeled on the traditional Jewish communal organization, the *kehilah*, as viable alternatives to the "over-organized chaos" of the American Jewish community. Many of his works popularized Kaplan's ideas to bring them to a wider audience. He based *Creative Judaism* (1936) on Kaplan's *Judaism as a Civilization* (1934) and *What We Mean by Religion* (1938) on Kaplan's *The Meaning of God in Modern Jewish Religion* (1937). Working with Kaplan and Eugene *Kohn among others, Eisenstein co-edited several prayer books, making a lasting contribution to the liturgy of the Reconstructionist movement.

In 1934 Eisenstein married musicologist Judith Kaplan, author of *Heritage of Music: The Music of the Jewish People* (1972). The Eisensteins co-authored several cantatas on Jewish themes. They have two daughters.

Writings: *Creative Judaism* (New York, 1936; rev. 1953); *What We Mean By Religion* (New York, 1938; rev. 1958); *The Ethics of Tolerance Applied to Religious Groups in America* (New York, 1941); "President's Message," *PRA 1953* vol. 17 (1954), pp. 139–50; "President's Message," *PRA 1954* vol. 18 (1955), pp. 147–57; *Judaism under Freedom* (New York, 1956); *Reconstructing Judaism: An Autobiography* (New York, 1986). Ed., *Varieties of Jewish Belief* (New York, 1966). Cantatas, with Judith Kaplan Eisenstein, *Our Bialik* (New York, 1945) and *Seven Golden Buttons* (New York, 1947). Co-ed., with Mordecai M. Kaplan and Eugene Kohn, *The New Haggadah* (New York, 1942; rev. 1978); with Mordecai M. Kaplan, Eugene Kohn, and Milton Steinberg, *Sabbath Prayer Book* (New York, 1945); with Mordecai M. Kaplan and Eugene Kohn, *High Holiday Prayer Book*, 2 vols. (New York, 1948); with Eugene Kohn, *Mordecai M. Kaplan: An Evaluation* (New York, 1952).

References: *American Jewish Biographies*, pp. 89–90; *The Anshe Emet Synagogue, 1873–1973* (Chicago, n.d.), pp. 34–35; Richard Libowitz, "The Writings of Ira Eisenstein," in *Shiv'im: Essays and Studies in Honor of Ira Eisenstein*, ed. Ronald A. Brauner (Philadelphia and New York, 1977), pp. 287–306; *PRA 1948* vol. 12 (1949), p. 46; *PRA 1949* vol. 13 (1950), p. 85; *PRA 1954* vol. 18 (1955), pp. 234–39; Marc Lee Raphael, *Profiles in American Judaism* (San Francisco, 1984), pp. 189–92; *WWAJ* 1980, p. 108; *WWWJ* 1965, p. 214.

EPSTEIN, GILBERT M. (1927–   ). Rabbi, administrator. The son of Louis and Selma Rosenbaum Epstein, Gilbert Epstein was born in New York City on October 6, 1927. He earned a B.A. at Yeshiva University in 1948 and was ordained at the Seminary in 1952.

Epstein began his career as a congregational rabbi. He was assistant rabbi of Congregation Sons of Israel, Woodmere, New York (1952–55). He then led Congregation Beth Emet, Hewlett, New York (1955–61), and the Conservative Synagogue of Fifth Avenue, New York City (1961–65). Deeply involved in Israel and the Zionist movement, he led young Zionists on tours of Israel and directed at Kfar Silver the first American teen summer camp in Israel (1962–64).

In 1965 Epstein joined the staff of the Rabbinical Assembly as director of community services and director of the Joint Commission on Rabbinic Placement. He thus relieved Rabbinical Assembly executive vice-president Wolfe *Kelman of many of the placement responsibilities that he had carried since becoming the "rabbi of the rabbis" in 1951. Epstein handled with dedication and grace the sensitive and often trying tasks of matching rabbis and congregations. Most of his work as placement director took place after the great expansion in Conservative congregational affiliations had ended, narrowing the possibilities for pulpit rabbis to change congregations. During the era of explosive growth, especially in the decade following the end of World War II, Epstein's predecessors found themselves juggling the requests in any given year of as many as 150 rabbis seeking the new opportunities and challenges promised by a change in pulpit. But by the 1970s, as Epstein observed, even though the Rabbinical Assembly numbered more than 1,000 rabbis, there were far fewer opportunities for change and consequently fewer requests to move; in 1978 he coordinated but fifty-eight placements. Yet these changes often involved rabbis and their families in crises over unresolvable conflicts between the rabbis and their congregations. Epstein won the esteem of his colleagues for his handling of these difficult situations and for sustaining their morale throughout.

As a representative of the Rabbinical Assembly, Epstein was active in the work of the Conference of Presidents of Major American Jewish Organizations, the Synagogue Council of America, the National Conference on Soviet Jewry, and the New York Board of Rabbis. He was also a member of the Board of Directors of the Jewish National Fund and the Rabbinic Cabinet of Israel Bonds and the United Jewish Appeal.

Epstein married Bernice Glabman in 1960.

Writings: "A Perspective on the Community," *Beineinu* 3, 1 (January 1973), pp. 1–6; "Response," *PRA 1975* vol. 37 (1976), pp. 90–93.

References: Wolfe Kelman, "A Tribute to Rabbi Gilbert Epstein," *PRA 1975* vol. 37 (1976), pp. 84–89; *PRA 1979* vol. 41 (1979), p 16.

EPSTEIN, HARRY (1903–). Rabbi. The son of Ephraim and Hannah Israelovitz Epstein, Harry Epstein was born on April 1, 1903, in Plunge, Lithuania, and brought to Chicago in 1909. Educated in the Chicago public schools, at Beth HaMidrash LaRabonim, New York's Rabbi Isaac Elchanan Theological Seminary, and the University of Chicago, Epstein returned to Lithuania in 1922 to attend the Slobodka Yeshivah. In 1924 he was one of ten students chosen to go to Hebron, Palestine, to help establish a branch of the yeshivah there. During his two years in Palestine, Epstein received *semichah* from several prominent rabbis, including Abraham Isaac Kook. He then spent a year (1925–1926) touring the United States and Canada with his uncle, *Rosh Yeshivah* Moshe Mordecai Epstein, to raise funds for the Hebron school. Epstein completed his education, earning a B.A. and M.A. at Emory University (1929–32) and a Ph.D. at the University of Illinois School of Law (1952).

Epstein began his career in the pulpit of Congregation B'nai Emunah, Tulsa, Oklahoma (1926–27), and a year later he was elected rabbi of Congregation Ahavath Achim, Atlanta, Georgia (1927–82). Established in 1887, the congregation had before his arrival been striving to reconcile the tensions between those desirous of modernization and those preferring the maintenance of traditional ways. Epstein struck a balance between the two groups by very gradually, and after consultation with lay leaders, introducing changes in the synagogue. He slowly transformed the services, promoting order and decorum, introducing responsive English readings and English sermons, and allowing for mixed seating. He started Friday night services at eight to attract younger members and held Bat Mitzvah ceremonies. He upgraded the synagogue's educational system by demanding a more strenuous curriculum, raised the standards necessary for Bar Mitzvah, and established the synagogue bulletin and brotherhood.

Under Epstein, Ahavath Achim evolved away from modern Orthodoxy toward Conservatism, which he came to believe embraced modern traditionalism. Therefore, in 1952 he led the congregation to formalize this identification by joining the United Synagogue of America. Ahavath Achim became the largest Conservative congregation in the South. After its affiliation, the congregation established the Harry H. Epstein/Solomon Schechter Day School and, as Atlanta Jewry moved to new neighborhoods in the northern part of the city, built a new building there. As a Conservative rabbi, Epstein joined the Rabbinical Assembly and was president of its Southeastern Region (1964). Upon his retirement in 1982, he was elected rabbi emeritus.

Epstein was a leader in Atlanta Jewish and communal affairs. A dedicated Zionist, he chaired the Georgia Palestine Emergency Campaign (1929) and the state division of the Jewish National Fund (1943, 1946). He was a founder and honorary chairman of Atlanta Men's ORT, a part-time chaplain at local military installations during World War II, and a member of the boards of trustees of the Atlanta Jewish Community Council, the Hebrew Orphans Home, and the Bureau of Jewish Education. He served as an arbiter in Jewish legal cases, was active in the Atlanta Federation of Jewish Charities, helped found the Emory University Hillel (1947), and was co-chair, along with Atlanta Reform rabbi Jacob Rothschild, of the Jewish Welfare Fund "Unity Campaign of 1950." His civic activities included chairing the Emergency Relief Committee of the Atlanta Community Chest (1931) and serving on the Atlanta Community Relations Committee. Some of his early addresses and sermons were published in *Judaism and Progress* (1935).

Epstein married Reva Chashesman in 1929; they have two daughters.

Writing: *Judaism and Progress: Sermons and Addresses* (New York, 1935).

Reference: Mark K. Bauman, "Harry Hyman Epstein and the Rabbinate As the Conduit for Change" (unpublished paper, Atlanta Junior College).

EPSTEIN, LOUIS M. (1887–1949). Rabbi, scholar. The son of Rabbi Ezriel and Rebecca Mehler Epstein, Louis Epstein was born in Onixt, Lithuania, on October 19, 1887. When his father left Lithuania for an American pulpit, the adolescent Epstein remained behind to study at the *yeshivah* of Slobodka. In 1904 Epstein joined his family in the United States. He earned his B.S. at Columbia University in 1911, was ordained at the Seminary in 1913, and earned a Doctor of Hebrew Letters there in 1921.

In his first congregation, Shearith Israel, Dallas, Texas (1913–15), Epstein laid the foundations for a Conservative program in the synagogue. Despite objections, he initiated late Friday night services, organized a women's auxiliary, started a Sunday school, and established a teacher-training program for the young women of the congregation.

Despite his apparent success in Dallas, Epstein began to doubt his calling to the American rabbinate. Raised in the piety of the European *yeshivot* and desirous of the life of the scholar, he found himself troubled by the clash with modern American Jewish life. These doubts grew to disillusionment during his tenure at B'nai Israel Synagogue, Toledo, Ohio (1915–18).

In 1918 Epstein left the Midwest for Roxbury, Massachusetts, and the pulpit of Beth Hamedrosh Hagadol. There at last he found himself comfortable with the demands of the life of a congregational rabbi. In 1925 he became rabbi of Congregation Kehillath Israel, Brookline, Massachusetts, where he remained until his death, becoming rabbi emeritus in 1947.

A leading member of the Rabbinical Assembly, Epstein served as its president from 1922 to 1925. He led the RA as it worked to standardize rabbinic placement and to raise the status of the rabbinate. During his administration, his colleagues endowed the Solomon *Schechter Chair in Theology at the Seminary.

Epstein was also a member of the RA's Committee on Jewish Law (1927–40) and served as its chairman (1936–1940). There he helped frame various proposals, the best known being his method of solving the *agunah* problem published in his *Li She'elat ha-Agunah* (1940). In 1930 and again in 1935, Epstein proposed to the Rabbinical Assembly that it append to the marriage contract a document in which the husband would authorize his wife to act as his agent to write her own *get* under rabbinic supervision. At first the RA accepted this innovation, but the proposal was subsequently abandoned because of the vehement opposition of the Orthodox rabbinate and of some members of the Seminary faculty.

Epstein realized that opposition to the *agunah* proposal had stymied the initiative of the Committee on Jewish Law. Therefore, in 1948 he drafted one of the proposals that led to the reorganization of the committee as the Committee on Jewish Law and Standards.

Epstein chose *halachah* as his field of study, seeing within Jewish law "the essence of Judaism as well as its most faithful record." In his works on Jewish marriage law he drew upon diverse sources, including materials from other nations, to illuminate the development of the Jewish laws and customs. In *The*

Jewish Marriage Contract (1927), he analyzed the rights and privileges accorded Jewish women by the *ketubah*. In *Sex Laws and Customs in Judaism* (1948), he portrayed the evolution of Jewish standards of sexual conduct and modesty from preexilic to post-Talmudic times.

Epstein married Minnie Hannah Winer in 1914. He died in New York City on March 22, 1949.

Writings: *The Jewish Marriage Contract: A Study in the Status of the Woman in Jewish Law* (1927; reprint ed., New York, 1973); *A Solution to the Agunah Problem* (New York, 1936); *Li She'elat ha-Agunah* (in Hebrew, New York, 1940); *Marriage Laws in the Bible and Talmud* (Cambridge, Mass., 1942); *Sex Laws and Customs in Judaism* (1948; reprint ed., New York, 1967).

References: *EJ* vol. 6, col. 834; *Golden Book of Congregation Shearith Israel* (Dallas, 1934); Abraham A. Neuman, "In Memory of Dr. Louis M. Epstein" *CJ* 5, 3 (April 1949), pp. 1–5; *PRA 1948* vol. 12 (1949), pp. 165–74; *PRA 1949* vol. 13 (1950), pp. 444–48; *Recorder* 3, 4 (October 1923), p. 13; 4, 4 (October 1924), p. 11; *WWAJ* 1938–39, p. 242.

F

FEINBERG, LOUIS (1887–1949). Rabbi. The son of Mordecai and Chaye Chasa Feinberg, Louis Feinberg was born in Rossieny, Lithuania, on March 25, 1887. He was brought to the United States in 1893. Educated in the Philadelphia public schools and at Yeshivah Mishkan Israel, Feinberg earned an A.B. from the University of Pennsylvania in 1915 and was ordained at the Seminary in 1916.

From 1916 to 1918 Feinberg served Congregation Ohel Jacob in Philadelphia, Pennsylvania. In 1918 he was called to the pulpit of Adath Israel, Cincinnati, Ohio, where he remained until his death. Feinberg's gentleness, personal piety, and sense of humor suited him to the rabbinate. Under his guidance, Adath Israel flourished as a traditional synagogue in a city better known for its prestigious Reform congregations and the leadership of Hebrew Union College. In Cincinnati Feinberg served on the Board of Governors of the United Jewish Social Agencies, the Jewish Community Council, and the Bureau of Jewish Education.

Founder of the Menorah Society at the University of Pennsylvania and editor of *Our Jewish Youth*, Feinberg also wrote short stories for the Anglo-Jewish press under the pseudonym Yishuvnik. A collection of his essays and sermons, *The Spiritual Foundations of Judaism* (1951), appeared posthumously. They demonstrate his love of the Jewish people, delight in the religious and spiritual life, and his fascination with *halachah*.

Feinberg married Rosa Rauneker in 1920; they had three children. He died in Cincinnati on February 19, 1949.

Writing: Posthumously, *The Spiritual Foundations of Judaism and Other Essays, Selected Addresses, and Writings* (Cincinnati, 1951).

References: *PRA 1949* vol. 13 (1950), pp. 440–43; *WWAJ* 1938–39, p. 258.

FINKELSTEIN, LOUIS (1895–). Chancellor of the Jewish Theological Seminary of America. The son of Simon and Hannah Brager Finkelstein, Louis Finkelstein was born in Cincinnati, Ohio, on June 14, 1895. In 1902, when his father accepted a call to the pulpit of Congregation Oheb Shalom, the family moved to the Brownsville section of Brooklyn. There, under the supervision of his father, he continued his classical Jewish education. Finkelstein earned an A.B. from the City College of New York in 1915, a Ph.D. from Columbia University in 1918, and was ordained at the Seminary in 1919. In 1923 he became the first graduate of the Seminary awarded *hatarat horaah*, classical rabbinic ordination, from Seminary professor Louis *Ginzberg.

Finkelstein began his career in the pulpit of Congregation Kehillath Israel, then one of the only congregations serving the nearly half-million Jews in the Bronx led by a Seminary rabbi (1919–31). Finkelstein guided Kehillath Israel as it, like other congregations in the 1920s, joined in the heyday of synagogue-center building. Kehillath Israel's new community center, dedicated in 1924, included a 1,000–seat synagogue and a school for 600 students. Under Finkelstein, the congregation also developed programs, including a Friday evening lecture forum, and auxiliaries, including a sisterhood and a Young People's League, typical of contemporary urban Conservative synagogues.

While gaining invaluable practical experience in the rabbinate, Finkelstein began his career at the Seminary. In 1920 he joined the Seminary faculty as instructor in Talmud (1920–24). He then became Solomon Schechter Lecturer in Theology (1924–30). Promoted to associate professor (1930) and then professor (1931), in 1931 Finkelstein left the congregational rabbinate to devote all his energies to the Conservative movement. Guided by the Seminary's president Cyrus *Adler, he began to assume increasing administrative responsibilities, becoming assistant to the president (1934–37) and then provost (1937–40). After Adler's death, Finkelstein became president of the Seminary (1940–51). In 1951, following an administrative reorganization necessitated by his expansion of the Seminary's programs and activities in the preceding decade, Finkelstein was elevated to the newly created post of chancellor (1951–72).

As leader of the Seminary, Finkelstein commanded it to respond concretely to the crises emanating from a Europe dominated by Hitler. Hitler's campaign against Jewish learning had, by the time Finkelstein assumed the reins of leadership, destroyed the leading rabbinical seminaries of Central and Eastern Europe. As the extent of the Nazi persecution of the Jews unfolded, it became evident that the massacre of 6 million European Jews left American Jewry, by default, the central Jewish community in the world. Finkelstein envisioned the Seminary playing a preeminent role, directing American Jewry as it responded to the challenges of its new position. He believed that not only must the Seminary produce large numbers of rabbis and teachers for American and even for world Judaism, but that it must also enter fields of service normally outside the purview of a theological school to meet the spiritual crisis of world Judaism. The result of Finkelstein's sweeping vision was the reassertion of the Seminary as the fountainhead of the Conservative movement.

Finkelstein recognized that the Seminary had to develop a sound fiscal policy in order to fulfill his long-range goals. His idea was to target Seminary rabbis out in the field and their congregants as untapped reservoirs of income and strength for the development of the movement. In 1937 the Seminary had some 2,000 contributors who donated $23,000 annually. By fiscal year 1943–44, thanks largely to the efforts of the Seminary's campaign director, Max *Arzt, whom Finkelstein appointed, the Seminary was raising $300,000 a year. As the number of synagogues affiliated with the movement doubled in the years 1949 through 1963, the funds raised for the annual joint campaigns of the Seminary, Rabbinical Assembly, and United Synagogue increased proportionately.

The greater revenues enabled Finkelstein to institute his expansion program, transforming the Seminary from a small rabbinical school into a major multidimensional institution, nationally prominent in Jewish and interfaith affairs. For Finkelstein the essential commandment of Judaism was that only through study would all Jews, not just the scholars, achieve the understanding necessary to apply the norms of Torah to life in a world constantly in flux. Because the primacy of study lay at the heart of his vision of Judaism, the center of Conservatism had to be a school, namely the Seminary. By virtue of Finkelstein's personality, the prestige of its faculty, and its control over the movement's purse strings, the Seminary under Finkelstein triumphed as the dominant power in the Conservative movement.

Finkelstein's administration expanded the Seminary's student programs, adding a cantorial school (the Cantors Institute-Seminary College of Jewish Music [1952]) and initiating, in 1953, the Seminary's joint college program between Columbia University and the Seminary College of Jewish Studies (since 1986 the Albert A. List College of Jewish Studies). Envisioning the development of university Jewish studies programs long before their proliferation, Finkelstein made the Seminary a center for the graduate training of scholars in such areas as Talmud and Jewish history. To extend the Seminary's influence in youth education, the Leadership Training Fellowship (1946), Ramah camps (1947), and Prozdor high school (1951) were established during his administration. To reach out to Jews far from the Seminary's New York headquarters, Finkelstein's administration built two additional campuses, the University of Judaism in Los Angeles to serve a burgeoning West Coast Jewry and, in Jerusalem, the American Student Center at Neve Schechter (1961), where all rabbinical and cantorial students spend a year in study.

Of course, at the heart of the Seminary remained the Rabbinical School and its faculty. Recognizing that rabbis in America needed skills beyond their traditional knowledge of Talmud and Codes, Finkelstein's administration revamped the rabbinical curriculum by adding courses in pastoral psychiatry (1953). His appointments of luminaries Saul *Lieberman (Talmudist) and Abraham Joshua *Heschel (theologian) to the faculty reflected his own traditional leanings and determination to counterbalance the persuasive influence of Professor Mordecai M. *Kaplan's Reconstructionist thought upon the students. As before, the Seminary remained a bastion of Jewish scholarship. New centers for research established during Finkelstein's tenure, including the Schocken Institute for Jewish

Research in Jerusalem (1961) and the Melton Research Center for Jewish Education (1960), enhanced its scholarly reputation.

But under Finkelstein the Seminary was to become more than a school. It was to emerge as a center for Jewish cultural life and interreligious affairs. In 1947 the Seminary's Museum of Jewish Ceremonial Objects moved to the Warburg mansion on Fifth Avenue and became the Jewish Museum of art and artifacts. The "Eternal Light" (1944) weekly radio program and "Frontiers of Faith" (1951) television series depicted the richness of Jewish tradition and won wide recognition for its sponsor, the Seminary. Because Finkelstein believed that Judaism was a moral force in the world with a unique perspective to share, he established the Institute for Religious and Social Studies, originally founded in 1938 as the Seminary Institute of Interdenominational Studies, to bring together clergy of different faiths for theological exploration. To bridge the chasm between science and religion, in 1940 he inaugurated the Conference on Science, Philosophy, and Religion in Their Relation to the Democratic Way of Life. Finkelstein served as its president and co-edited several volumes of its papers.

These extraordinary achievements enhanced the chancellor's prestige at the same time that synagogue affiliations made Conservatism the largest denomination of American Judaism. Finkelstein thus became one of the most widely known Jewish religious leaders of his day. In 1951 he was featured on the cover of *Time* magazine. He served four United States presidents: advising Franklin D. Roosevelt on Jewish affairs (1940–45), praying at the inauguration of Dwight D. Eisenhower, joining the American delegation to the installation of Pope Paul VI at the request of John F. Kennedy (1963), and preaching to Richard M. Nixon at the White House.

Finkelstein's national standing and his centralization of the forces of Conservatism at the Seminary made him more powerful than any single individual in the movement since Solomon *Schechter. As a result, he exerted a large measure of control over the policies of all of Conservatism's constituent agencies, partly because earlier he had played leading roles in both the United Synagogue, as a member of its Executive Committee (1932–40), and the Rabbinical Assembly, as secretary of its Placement Committee and president (1928–30). During his tenure as Rabbinical Assembly president, the Committee on Jewish Law met for the first time, and Finkelstein successfully resisted his colleagues' calls, in the midst of the Depression, to limit their ranks. Throughout his long career Finkelstein continued to hold great sway over the Rabbinical Assembly. Time and again its members found themselves, despite initially opposing him, swayed to accept his point of view on such matters as the proliferation of the Seminary's activities and the convocation of the Joint Law Conference (1953–68), which effectively ceded to the Seminary control over the Jewish laws of marriage and divorce for the entire movement.

An esteemed scholar, Finkelstein wrote and edited nearly one hundred books on Judaism, religion, sociology, culture, and ethics. During the early years of his career, he distinguished himself for his insights into the history and classical literature of Judaism. His first published work, *Jewish Self-Government in the Middle Ages* (1924), is considered a classic treatment of the subject. His doctoral thesis was a new edition of *The Commentary of David Kimhi on Isaiah* (1926). These were followed by *Akiba: Scholar, Saint, and Martyr* (1936), a biography of the second-century rabbi and martyr, and a work on the economic and social background of the ancient Jewish religious sect, *The Pharisees* (1938). Despite pressing administrative demands, Finkelstein continued his scholarship. He edited a major, three-volume study, *The Jews: Their History, Culture, and Religion* (1949), as well as *American Spiritual Autobiographies* (1948) and *Social Responsibility in an Age of Revolution* (1971). After retiring from the Seminary in 1972, he turned to a critical edition of the *Sifra*, a fourth-century commentary on the Biblical book of Leviticus; the third and fourth volumes of the projected six-volume series appeared in 1985.

Finkelstein married Carmel Bentwich in 1922; they have three children.

Writings: *Jewish Self-Government in the Middle Ages* (New York, 1924); "The Presidential Message: Traditional Law and Modern Life," *PRA 1929* vol. 3 (1930), pp. 18–30; "Presidential Address: The Present and Future of Traditional Judaism in America," *PRA 1930* vol. 4 (1933), pp. 9–19; *Akiba: Scholar, Saint, and Martyr* (New York, 1936); *Tradition in the Making* (New York, 1937); *The Pharisees* (Philadelphia, 1938); *The Religions of Democracy* (New York, 1941); *Faith for Today* (Garden City, N.Y., 1941); "The Seminary Expansion Program," *PRA 1944* vol. 8 (1947), pp. 303–05; *New Light from the Prophets* (London, 1969); *Pharisaism in the Making* (New York, 1972); "The Underlying Concepts of Conservative Judaism," *CJ* 26, 4 (Summer 1972), pp. 2–12. Ed., *The Commentary of David Kimhi on Isaiah* (New York, 1926); *Rab Saadia Gaon: Studies in His Honor* (New York, 1944); *American Spiritual Autobiographies: Fifteen Self-Portraits* (New York, 1948); *The Jews: Their History, Culture, and Religion*, 3 vols. (Philadelphia, 1949); *Social Responsibility in an Age of Revolution* (New York, 1971).

References: *A Bibliography of the Writings of Louis Finkelstein* (New York, 1977); *Current Biography* (1952), pp. 191–93; *EJ* vol. 6, cols. 1293–95; *NYT* 1 September 1985, p. 57; Herbert Parzen, *Architects of Conservative Judaism* (New York, 1964), pp. 207–18; *Recorder* 3, 3 (July 1923), p. 3; 5, 1 (January 1925), p. 30; "A Trumpet for All Israel," *Time* 15 October 1951, pp. 52–58.

FREEDMAN, PAUL M. (1934–). Rabbi, administrator. Paul Freedman was born in Middletown, Connecticut, on December 30, 1934.

In 1951 he was elected founding president of United Synagogue Youth (USY; 1951–53). Conservative leaders had for some time been concerned about the defection of post-Bar and Bat Mitzvah youth from the synagogue. Consequently, the United Synagogue set out to create a new national youth movement to succeed its Junior Young People's League, which had never had a large following. Under the direction of United Synagogue staff member Morton *Siegel, USY held its founding convention in December 1951 in New York City. Its 500 delegates, representing USY's sixty-eight charter members, elected Freedman president.

In 1956(?) Freedman earned a B.S. from New York University. He then spent several years in Israel, studying at Hebrew University in Jerusalem (1958–60) while working as coordinator of the National Mental Health Rehabilitation Team of the Health Ministry. He was ordained at the Seminary in 1970.

In 1960 Freedman joined the staff of the United Synagogue as director of special activities for the Department of Youth Activities. His early responsibilities included direction of USY activities in Israel, including the establishment of its Israel region, and the organization of *Atid*, a youth movement established in 1961 for college-age men and women, most of whom were USY graduates. Freedman served as the department's assistant director (1960–67) and is now director (1967–   ). He is responsible not only for guiding and developing programming for the 20,000 members of USY but also for overseeing the 10,000–member, preteenage youth movement, *Kadima,* established in 1968. Under Freedman's direction, USY has continued to sponsor new programs, including *kinnusim* and encampments, and opened Camp USY in Glen Spey, New York. Purchased with funds raised by USYers, Camp USY was a summer camp for youth ineligible to attend Conservatism's premier summer camping movement, Camp Ramah, because they did not meet its Hebrew and Jewish educational requirements. Under Freedman's direction, USY also launched its East European pilgrimage; *Nativ*, a year-long program in Israel in partnership with *Noar VeHalutz* and Hebrew University of Jerusalem; and a Hebrew language *ulpan* on Kibbutz Ain Tzurim. For many years Freedman led the USY summer Israel pilgrimages, each summer guiding hundreds of teens on a tour of Israel that incorporated study, worship, and such special events as work on an archaeological site. He also coordinated the Conservative movement's settlement committee which supported the first Conservative kibbutz in Israel, Kibbutz Hannaton.

Freedman married Nina Schiff in 1958; they have three sons.

References: *Review* 13, 3 (Autumn 1960), p. 21; 20, 3 (October 1967), p. 20; 20, 4 (January 1968), p. 11; 21, 1 (April 1968), p. 14; 21, 4 (January 1969), pp. 14, 31; 23, 2 (Summer 1970), p. 19; 31, 1 (Fall 1978), p. 11; 32, 1 (Fall 1979), p. 8.

FRIEDLAENDER, ISRAEL (1876–1920). Scholar, communal leader. The son of Pinchas and Gittel Friedlaender, Israel Friedlaender was born in Wlodwa, Poland, on September 8, 1876. In his fourth year his family moved to the Warsaw suburb of Praga, where he was educated in a traditional *cheder*, tutored in modern Hebrew and the curriculum of the Russian gymnasium, and ordained at the age of sixteen. For a time he flirted with Hasidism, but in 1892 Friedlaender moved to Berlin to attend the university and the Hildesheimer Rabbinical Seminary. He earned his doctorate in 1901 at the University of Strassburg, where his teacher was the Semiticist Theodor Noeldeke. Friedlaender then remained in Strassburg for another two years researching *genizah* fragments and Moslem historiography and teaching Arabic philology and Jewish philosophy at the university.

In 1903 Seminary president Solomon *Schechter invited him to join the rabbinical faculty as Sabato Morais Professor of Biblical Literature and Exegesis. Friedlaender's primary training, in what was then called oriental studies, was as a medievalist and Arabist. However, since the German university curriculum did not distinguish between ancient and medieval Semitic studies, Schechter considered him for the post as professor of Bible. Friedlaender taught Biblical literature, history of the canon, and medieval Jewish philosophy at the Seminary (1903–20) and Jewish history at the Teachers Institute (1910–20).

Beloved and respected by his students, he offered extracurricular classes in Arabic language and modern Hebrew literature, dispensed financial aid as chairman of the Student Loan Fund, and first proposed building a dormitory at the Morningside Heights campus to save his students the wearying subway commute. He welcomed the future rabbis to his home and aided them, whenever possible, in securing positions. Considered at one time Schechter's likely successor at the Seminary and nominated for the founding presidency of Dropsie College, Friedlaender was disappointed to lose both appointments to Cyrus *Adler.

As a scholar, Friedlaender regarded himself as an orientalist and medievalist rather than a Biblical expert. Although he had promised Schechter to turn to Biblical studies, Friedlaender continued to prefer his original fields of scholarship. His studies of, among others, Maimonides, messianism, folk culture, philology, and the political status of medieval Jewry in Islamic lands were models of scientific research.

Friedlaender should not, however, be classified as a narrow specialist. Instead, much of his writing applied his knowledge of the past to the present. Excited by the broad range of Jewish history, he wrote scholarly and popular articles that searched for historical lessons that could speak to an American Jewry struggling with the present. To that end he introduced and translated Simon Dubnow's *History of the Jews in Russia and Poland* (1916–20) because it explained the cultural background of the East European immigrants to the dominant American Jewish leadership. Similarly, his Biblical studies responded to contemporary circumstances as he revealed the ideological bent of the then reigning Wellhausen School of Higher Criticism of the Bible. He also used Biblical ideas to promote cultural Zionism and to defend Jewish ceremonial law. A number of his essays were collected in *Past and Present* (1919).

Friedlaender was one of the early architects of Conservative Judaism. Committed to Historical Judaism (the antecedent of American Conservatism) prior to his immigration, he helped articulate the ideology of the Conservative movement. In 1917 he delivered a series of public lectures on the "Aspects of Historical Judaism" at the bastion of New York Reform Judaism, Temple Emanuel. Here he presented Conservatism as the contemporary expression of the three intertwined ideas rooted at the heart of Jewish religious culture: God, Torah, and Israel, or monotheism, ceremonialism, and Jewish nationalism. He also showed how Conservatism differed from Reform in its incorporation of the ceremonial and national components that Reform deemphasized or dismissed.

Similarly, he stressed that Conservatism was distinguished from Orthodoxy by its historical approach, which recognized that Judaism had in the past and would continue in the present and future to develop and change in response to external forces.

Unlike many of his professorial colleagues, Friedlaender was devoted to Jewish communal affairs, often at the expense of his scholarly work. He emerged as an intellectual force and social engineer of early twentieth-century American Jewry, as he labored tirelessly on behalf of Jewish religion, education, Zionism, and the East European immigrants. Essentially, his social thought revolved around the single issue of the perils of emancipation and its consequences of fragmentation, assimilation, and materialism. Because he recognized the dangers posed to Jewish survival by American freedom, he preached to American Jewry the spirit of Jewish renewal, expressed in the writings of the East European historian Simon Dubnow and the cultural Zionist Ahad Ha-Am, whose works he had earlier translated for German Jewry. Friedlaender advocated for American Jewry "constructive Americanization." He knew that wholesale adoption of American attitudes and behaviors would cause the immigrants to succumb to assimilation and American materialism. He believed that American Jewry must preserve its communal life and traditional culture within the context of American citizenship. As a result, he labored, often with great frustration, for numerous organizations that he hoped could aid the immigrants, foster Jewish communal structure, unite the fragmented segments of American Jewry, and educate his brethren.

One of the founders of the New York *Kehillah*, Friedlaender considered it a solution to the chaotic organization of Jewish life in America. He remained a member of its Executive Committee and chairman of its Bureau of Jewish Education even when such activity clashed with what Schechter viewed as the best interests of the Seminary and the Teachers Institute. As a member of the Board of Directors of the Educational Alliance, the Lower East Side immigrant settlement house, Friedlaender advocated restructuring the alliance to reflect the East European cultural milieu of Jewish music, art, language, values, and religious observance; and he wanted to see the Russian Jews whom it served guide the agency. Concerned with all facets of Jewish education, Friedlaender, a member of the governing board of the Intercollegiate Menorah Society, lectured widely on college campuses and contributed articles to its journal. In 1912 he also helped establish, with Mordecai M. *Kaplan, the Young Israel movement.

A Zionist, Friedlaender contributed to the Hebrew renaissance by writing for the Hebrew press, and he attended the Zionist congresses while in Europe. Naturally then, he joined the fledgling Federation of American Zionists (FAZ) when he arrived in New York. He chaired the Zionist Council of New York (1905), headed FAZ's educational program (1906), drafted a Zionist manual, organized the Zionist youth organization, Young Judea (1909), was active in the Intercollegiate Zionist Organization, and chaired the Executive Committee of FAZ (1910–11). When World War I broke out in 1914, American Zionist leader Louis Brandeis organized the Provisional Executive Committee for General Zionist Affairs and named Friedlaender recording secretary and archivist. Friedlaender represented the United Synagogue at the pro-Zionist American Jewish Congress; worked to persuade the American Jewish Committee, of which he was a member by virtue of his role in the Educational Alliance, to cooperate with the congress; and was secretary of the short-lived Achavah Club, a group of intellectuals dedicated to the renascence of Jewish national life. Perhaps his greatest influence as a Zionist, however, lay in his transmission of the ideas of cultural and spiritual Zionism of Ahad Ha-Am to his students at the Seminary and Teachers Institute. He thus profoundly influenced the first generation of Conservative rabbis in America, which became staunch supporters of American Zionism.

Distressed by the ravages of World War I and its aftermath, Friedlaender worked unceasingly for the relief of the beleaguered Jewries of Palestine and Eastern Europe. He was determined to play a personal role in dispensing aid to those Jews whose lives had been shattered, but he was forced to resign his appointment to a Red Cross Palestine relief mission in 1918 when ugly rumors surfaced alleging that he had pro-German sympathies. Instead, in 1920 he traveled, as chairman of the Joint Distribution Committee's Committee on Russia, to Eastern Europe to dispense funds. That journey brought him to the pogrom-ridden Ukraine, where he was murdered near the town of Yarmolinetz on July 5, 1920.

Friedlaender married Lilian Ruth Bentwich in 1905; they had six children.

Writings: *Der Sprachgebrauch des Maimonides: Ein lexikalischer und grammatischer Beitrag zur Kenntnis des Mittelarabishcen* (Frankfurt am Main, 1902); "The Problem of Judaism in America: A Lecture," *Jewish Comment* 28 (1908), pp. 193–95, 204–05; 29 (1909), pp. 219–220, 223; *The Heterodoxies of the Shiites According to Ibn Hazm: Introduction, Translation, and Commentary* (New Haven, 1909); *The Jews of Russia and Poland: A Bird's-Eye View of Their History and Culture* (New York and London, 1915); "The Americanization of the Jewish Immigrant, "*Survey* 38 (May 5, 1917), pp. 103–08; *Past and Present: A Collection of Jewish Essays* (1919; reprint ed., New York, 1961). Trans., Simon Dubnow, *History of the Jews in Russia and Poland: from the Earliest Times until the Present Day*, 3 vols. (Philadelphia, 1916–20).

References: Boaz Cohen, *Israel Friedlaender: A Bibliography of His Writings with an Appreciation* (New York, 1936); Herbert Parzen, *Architects of Conservative Judaism* (New York, 1964), pp. 155–88; Baila Round Shargel, *Practical Dreamer: Israel Friedlaender and the Shaping of American Judaism* (New York, 1985).

FRIEDMAN, THEODORE (1908–   ). Rabbi, author. The son of Harry and Anna Kapit Friedman, Theodore Friedman was born in Stamford, Connecticut, on January 5, 1908. He earned a B.A. from the City College of New York in 1929, was ordained at the Seminary in 1931, and earned a Ph.D. from Columbia University in 1952.

Friedman first served as rabbi at congregations Beth El, North Bergen, New Jersey (1931–42), and Beth David, Buffalo, New York (1942–44). He then led the Jackson Heights Jewish Center, Jackson Heights, Long Island (1944–54), where he organized a Hebrew high school. In 1954 Friedman became rabbi of Congregation Beth El, South Orange, New Jersey (1954–70). An authority in the field of Jewish education and a member of the Board of Governors of the National Academy of Adult Jewish Studies, he organized an innovative adult education program at Beth El based on a four-year curriculum that he designed. Following his retirement in 1970, he was elected rabbi emeritus.

Friedman played a leading role in guiding the Rabbinical Assembly as it expanded in new directions in the post-World War II period. In 1948 he presented at the RA's annual convention one of the key position papers, "Towards a Philosophy of Conservative Judaism," which led to the reorganization of the RA's Committee on Jewish Law into the Committee on Jewish Law and Standards (CJLS). Here he effectively argued for going beyond *halachah* in addressing the many problems of Jewish life. As a member of the CJLS Friedman co-authored with Morris *Adler and Jacob *Agus the *responsum* on the Sabbath permitting the use of electricity and allowing congregants to drive to synagogue for communal *Shabbat* worship. As its chairman (1951–54), he agreed to share with the Seminary the responsibility for solving the long-standing crisis of the *agunah*, the deserted woman prohibited by Jewish law from remarriage. This led to the establishment of a Joint Law Conference of the Rabbinical Assembly and the Seminary as the Conservative movement's sole authority for adjudicating matters involving the Jewish laws of marriage and divorce. Friedman co-chaired its Steering Committee and was secretary of its national *bet din*. As vice-president of the Rabbinical Assembly (1960–62), he led the committee that revised the constitution. As RA president (1962–64), he tried to build bridges with the other Jewish denominations and called upon his fellow rabbis to speak from their pulpits to encourage their congregants to embrace the causes of civil rights and Soviet Jewry.

Friedman also chaired the RA's Hebrew Culture Committee (1944–46) and was president of the Long Island Region of the Rabbinical Assembly (1947). In addition to his work on behalf of the Rabbinical Assembly, he taught homiletics at the Seminary, was a member of the Jewish Book Council of America, and was managing editor of the journal *Judaism*.

Friedman edited for the National Academy of Adult Jewish Studies *What is Conservative Judaism?* (n.d.), a mimeographed anthology of the writings of the leading exponents of Conservative Judaism that was one of the earliest attempts to articulate Conservatism's ideology. He co-edited with Robert *Gordis *Jewish Life in America* (1955), an expansion of the special issue *Judaism* published in 1954 to celebrate the tercentenary of American Jewry. Friedman also wrote *Judgment and Destiny* (1965), a selection of his sermons published to mark the tenth anniversary of his rabbinate at Beth El, and *Letters to Jewish College Students* (1965), a collection of his monthly letters to his congregants' college students, discussing the doctrines and practices of Judaism and their relevance to the contemporary world.

Following his retirement from Beth El, Friedman moved to Jerusalem. He continued, however, to voice his opinions in his column, "Letter from Jerusalem," in the Rabbinical Assembly quarterly, *Conservative Judaism*.

He married Ruth Braunhut in 1931; they had three children. In 1974 Friedman married Florence Brandt.

Writings: "Towards a Philosophy of Conservative Judaism," *PRA 1948* vol. 12 (1949), pp. 112–20; "President's Address," *PRA 1963* vol. 27 (1963), pp. 155–62; "Presidential Address," *PRA 1964* vol. 28 (1964), pp. 96–107; *Judgment and Destiny: Sermons for the Modern Jew* (New York, 1965); *Letters to Jewish College Students* (New York, 1965). Ed., *What is Conservative Judaism?* (New York, n.d.). Co-ed., with Robert Gordis, *Jewish Life in America* (New York, 1955). With Morris Adler and Jacob Agus, "Responsum on the Sabbath," *PRA 1950* vol. 14 (1951), pp. 112–37.

References: *PRA 1954* vol. 18 (1955), pp. 62–68; *PRA 1960* vol. 24 (1960), pp. 43–48; *PRA 1961* vol. 25 (1961), p. 86; Marshall Sklare, *Conservative Judaism* (1955; rev. 1972; reprint ed., Lanham, Md., 1985), pp. 233–34; *WWWJ* 1965, p. 288.

G

GEFFEN, JOEL SYLVAN (1902–). Rabbi. The son of Tobias and Hene Rabinowitz Geffen, Joel Geffen was born in Kovno, Lithuania, on August 7, 1902, and brought to the United States in 1903. Reared in Atlanta, Georgia, Geffen earned a B.A. from Emory University in 1922 and was ordained at the Seminary in 1926.

In his senior year of rabbinical school Geffen was called to Harrisburg, Pennsylvania, to become rabbi of its first Conservative congregation, Temple Beth El, founded in 1926. Within two years he had built its membership to 200 families. Using his apartment as the congregation's headquarters until the synagogue was completed in 1928, he organized an afternoon Hebrew school, Sabbath school, sisterhood, brotherhood, and youth groups. In 1929 Geffen moved to Troy, New York, where he became the founding rabbi of another Temple Beth El. Troy's Beth El became a model Conservative congregation with Geffen leading the way in creating intercongregational youth groups and introducing adult education programs. He also organized and supervised a community Talmud Torah.

In 1944 Geffen returned to the Seminary to serve as director of the Department of Field Activities and Community Education, a position he held until his retirement in 1984. His congregational experiences with laity of all ages assisted him in his goal of furthering Conservative Judaism among the various constituencies of the movement. Geffen worked with the youth, serving as an executive member of the national Leadership Training Fellowship and founding Camp Ramah in the Berkshires in Wingdale, New York.

As spiritual advisor to the National Federation of Jewish Men's Clubs from 1944 to 1984, Geffen guided that organization's development during its early years of significant growth. He edited its quarterly magazine, *The Torch* (1950–1975), and contributed regularly to its newsletter, *Torchlight*. He also worked on behalf of the United Synagogue and was director of its New York Metropolitan

Region (1953–1965). He was also an advisor to the Board of Overseers of the Seminary.

Interested in contemporary Jewish history, Geffen wrote articles for the *American Jewish Historical Quarterly* and served as a member of the American Academy of Jewish Research. He co-edited *Roads to Jewish Survival* (1967), a selection of articles from the first twenty-five years of *The Torch*.

Geffen married Sylvia Mintz in 1926; they have two daughters.

Writing: Ed., with Milton Berger and M. David Hoffman, *Roads to Jewish Survival* (New York, 1967).

References: *Fiftieth Anniversary: Temple Beth El, 1926–1976* (Harrisburg, Pa., n.d.); *WWAJ* 1980, p. 153; *WWWJ* 1965, p. 298.

GELB, MAX (1907–   ). Rabbi. The son of Solomon and Bessie Isakowitz Gelb, Max Gelb was born in Austria on March 7, 1907, and was brought to the United States in 1914. Educated at the Yeshivah Rabbi Chaim Berlin and Rabbi Isaac Elchanan Yeshivah, he earned a B.A. from the City College of New York in 1929 and was ordained at the Seminary in 1932.

Gelb succeeded fellow Seminary graduate Rabbi Alexander Burnstein as rabbi of Temple Beth El, Harrisburg, Pennsylvania (1933–39). He found the congregation beset by serious financial problems, brought on by the Depression, that jeopardized mortgage payments on its new synagogue. A declining membership and the failure of most of the congregation's auxiliaries, with the exception of the Sisterhood, added to the low morale he found at Beth El. Despite his inexperience in practical rabbinics, Gelb plunged in to strengthen the basic functions of the temple. By 1935, with the congregation's financial outlook secured, Gelb moved to initiate new activities. He strengthened the curriculum of the Sunday school to make it a preparatory program for the three-day-a-week Hebrew school that he had just launched. The new enthusiasm generated by the Hebrew school led to increased membership and the addition of a junior congregation, a Young Judea Club, adult education classes, and a Young People's League to the roster of congregational activities.

In 1939 Gelb left Harrisburg to return to the New York metropolitan area as rabbi of Temple Israel Center, White Plains, New York. Initially, he found many of his plans hampered by a very small building that simply did not have the space for the programs he felt the congregation should sponsor. Yet despite space limitations, within a decade of his coming to Temple Israel Center it had grown fourfold to 450 families. In a thoughtful discussion of his first ten years at Temple Israel Center, Gelb highlighted concerns shared by many of his colleagues in the pulpit. Rapid growth forced him to spend much time fund-raising and planning for a new synagogue. Not surprisingly, given the burdens of the building program, he found many of his congregants overly concerned with synagogue finances and increasing membership. He had to battle to get their approval for a budget sufficient to hire the personnel to staff the religious and cultural activities he deemed essential to the mission of any synagogue. Gelb was troubled by the strong Christian environment of White Plains, a situation common to many new suburban Jewish communities and which he sensed lured Jewish youth, and by the congregation's emphasis upon secular and social activities. Throughout his career at Temple Israel Center Gelb continued to stress programs with strong Judaic content. He was elected rabbi emeritus after more than thirty years of service.

A leader in Westchester County Jewish communal affairs, Gelb was president of the White Plains Region of the Zionist Organization of America (1940–42) and vice-president (1952–54) and president (1954) of the Westchester Council of Rabbis. But his most important contributions to Westchester Jewry lay in his work in pioneering day school education. In 1950 he joined with Orthodox colleagues to establish the first day school in Westchester County. Increasingly uncomfortable with its Orthodox leaders' single-handed rule over the philosophy and curriculum of the school, Gelb initiated, in 1965, the establishment of the first Conservative day school in Westchester County. Despite the opposition of some of his congregants, who feared the day school would compete with their afternoon Hebrew school, the Solomon Schechter Day School of Westchester County opened in the fall of 1966 with twenty-two students in two classes. By 1974, with Gelb as dean (1966–   ), the school had grown to nine grades, had its own building and included a staff of twenty-four.

In the Conservative movement Gelb was a member of the Executive Committee of the Rabbinical Assembly (1945–48) and the Joint Placement Commission (1954). He edited *Understanding Conservative Judaism* (1978), a collection of essays by Robert *Gordis that appeared as the second volume in the Rabbinical Assembly series, Studies in Conservative Jewish Thought.

Married in 1940, Gelb and his wife, Leah, have two sons.

Writings: "The Rabbi in a Small Community," *PRA 1949* vol. 13 (1950), pp. 178–83; "The Day School: Making It an Effective Enterprise," *PRA 1974* vol. 36 (1975), pp. 114–21. Ed., Robert Gordis, *Understanding Conservative Judaism* (New York, 1978).

References: *Fiftieth Anniversary: Temple Beth El, 1926–1976* (Harrisburg, Pa., n.d.), pp. 11–18; *WWWJ* 1955, p. 240.

GINSBERG, HAROLD LOUIS (1903–   ). Scholar. Harold Louis Ginsberg was born on December 6, 1903, in Montreal, Canada. Educated at the University of London, he earned both a B.A. (1927) and a Ph.D. (1930) there.

In 1936 Ginsberg, who had just arrived in the United States from Palestine, joined the faculty of the Seminary as lecturer in Bible (1936–41). He later became the Sabato Morais Professor in Biblical History and Literature (1941–   ). Although Ginsberg did not play a leading role within the larger Conservative movement, by virtue of his long tenure as a teacher and scholar at the Seminary he influenced several generations of Conservative rabbis.

As a scholar, Ginsberg was a renowned Semiticist and master of the historical-critical method of studying Biblical texts. He went beyond textual and linguistic explication to illuminate the historical contexts in which Biblical books as diverse as Daniel and Ecclesiastes were written. A pioneer in the interpretation of Ugaritic texts and their relationship to Biblical literature, he explored the subjects of Biblical religion and Aramaic linguistics. Ginsberg was also one of the editors of the Jewish Publication Society's new translation of the Bible (*Tanakh*, 1985), its first since 1917, and was editor-in-chief of the translation of the Prophets (*Prophets*, 1978). He also edited the Bible division of the *Encyclopedia Judaica* (1972) and was a fellow of the American Academy for Jewish Research (vice-president, 1969–70), honorary president of the American Society of Biblical Literature (1969), and a member of the Israel Academy for the Hebrew Language.

Writings: *The Legend of King Keret: A Canaanite Epic of the Bronze Age* (New Haven, Conn., 1946); *Studies in Daniel* (New York, 1948); *Studies in Koheleth* (New York, 1950); *Commentary on Ecclesiastes* (Jerusalem and Tel Aviv, 1961). Ed., *Kitvei Ugarit* (Jerusalem, 1938); *Rashi Anniversary Volume* (New York and Philadelphia, 1941); *The Five Megilloth and the Book of Jonah* (Philadelphia, 1974); *The Prophets* (Philadelphia, 1978).

References: *EJ* vol. 7, col. 580; David Lieber, "Yehezkel Kaufman in Retrospect: A Tribute to H.L. Ginsberg," *PRA 1986* vol. 48 (1986), p. 167.

GINZBERG, LOUIS (1873–1953).   Scholar. The son of Isaac and Zippe Jaffe Ginzberg, Louis Ginzberg was born on November 28, 1873, in Kovno, Russia, into an influential Lithuanian family of students, scholars, and saints that counted among its ancestors the Vilna Gaon (Elijah ben Solomon Zalman), whose life and work greatly influenced his great-grandnephew. Ginzberg received his early education with private tutors in the towns of Klin and Neustadt. At the age of eleven he undertook advanced Talmudic studies at the *yeshivot* of Telz and Slobodka (1883–87). He then continued his studies in Vilna with his uncle, Arye Leib Rashkos, who introduced him to the study of the Palestinian Talmud. In ill health, the fourteen-year-old Ginzberg joined his parents in their new home in Amsterdam to convalesce. Because Amsterdam did not offer opportunities to continue his classical Jewish education, and because his illness had been brought on by the rigors of his life as a student in Lithuania, Ginzberg went to Germany to pursue a modern education and Judaic studies.

In 1889 he settled in Frankfurt-am-Main where he completed in two years the regular eight-year gymnasium course preparatory to entering the university. While continuing to read classical Jewish literature on his own, Ginzberg studied first mathematics and then Semitics at the University of Berlin. At the University of Strassburg his teacher was the renowned Semitics scholar Theodore Noeldeke. Ginzberg earned a doctorate in 1898 at the University of Heidelberg for *Die Haggada bei den Kirchenvarten* (1899). In this work he began his ambitious search through patristic literature for the lost legends of Jewish origins preserved only in early Christian texts. Ginzberg thus combined classical Jewish scholarship with the scientific methods of study pioneered by the *Wissenschaft des Judentums* school of thought. His future publications would make him one of its greatest exponents.

After completing his doctorate, Ginzberg returned to his family in Amsterdam, where he pursued postgraduate studies at the University of Amsterdam (1898–99). During this year he made one last visit to Lithuania, where he received *semichah*. Unable to find a university teaching post in Europe, he began considering immigration to America.

In 1899, when the chair in Talmud at Hebrew Union College in Cincinnati became vacant, Ginzberg was promised the post. Although the usually perfunctory approval of the Board of Governors had not yet been secured, HUC president Isaac Mayer Wise urged him to come to America immediately in order to acquire greater fluency in English before the start of the term. When Ginzberg landed in New York, he learned to his surprise that the appointment had been cancelled, in part because Wise, having heard rumors that Ginzberg was a proponent of the Wellhausen theory of Biblical criticism, refused to continue to back the appointment.

A new project promised sustenance. Ginzberg was invited to join the staff of the *Jewish Encyclopedia* as editor of the department of rabbinical literature (1900–1902). He wrote some 450 articles for the *Encyclopedia*, many of which remain classical statements. Three of these—"Allegorical Interpretation of Scripture," "The Cabbala: History and System," and "Codification of Jewish Law"—were later collected in *On Jewish Law and Lore* (1955). At the same time Ginzberg was persuaded by the Jewish Publication Society to prepare *The Legends of the Jews*. Although he promised Henrietta Szold, editor for the society, one volume to be delivered in 1903, *Legends* (1909–38) became one of his life's great works. With an index by his Seminary colleague Boaz *Cohen, it grew to seven volumes. Here Ginzberg combined hundreds of legends, maxims, and parables culled from a lifetime of research in *midrash*, the Apocrypha, Hellenistic literature, and early Christian texts into a continuous narrative of the patriarchs of the people of Israel, its heroes, and its prophets. He produced perhaps the most lucid and learned compilation of *agadah* of the Bible ever written.

In 1902 the new president of the Jewish Theological Seminary of America, Solomon *Schechter, invited Ginzberg to become professor of Talmud and the first member of the faculty of the newly reorganized Seminary. Ginzberg resigned from the *Encyclopedia* and held this post until his death (1902–53). With Schechter, who at one time considered the Talmud professor his likely successor, Ginzberg played a leading role in shaping the Seminary. In Ginzberg's first year at the Seminary, he and Schechter taught all of the courses except homiletics. The following summer the two traveled to Europe in search of additional faculty. There Ginzberg wooed and won for the Seminary Israel *Friedlaender as professor of Biblical literature and exegesis. From the beginning Ginzberg shared with Schechter the vision that the Seminary must expand its programs to train not only rabbis but also teachers and scholars for American Jewry. When Cyrus

*Adler became acting president and then president of the Seminary after Schechter's death, Ginzberg continued to exert considerable influence in its affairs. He was acting president during Adler's absence at the Paris Peace Conference and was instrumental in persuading the Seminary to add Louis *Finkelstein, H. L. *Ginsberg, Saul *Lieberman, and Shalom *Spiegel to its faculty.

In addition to his teaching, two concerns of Ginzberg's left their imprint upon the several generations of his students—his dismay over his role in training a rabbinate which, driven by the demands of congregational life, had so little time for study and his disputes with Mordecai M. *Kaplan. Ginzberg's clashes with his Seminary colleague Kaplan were well known within and without the Seminary community. They reached a climactic point in 1945 when Ginzberg and his colleagues Saul Lieberman and Seminary librarian Alexander *Marx denounced Kaplan for the publication of the *Reconstructionist Prayer Book*.

Clearly, Ginzberg's influence in the Conservative movement extended far beyond the Seminary walls. For more than fifty years Ginzberg was the reigning *halachic* expert of Conservative Judaism. He taught some 650 Conservative rabbis, who carried his views of the nature of Judaism out into their congregations and communities. Moreover, he participated both openly and behind the scenes as an advisor in the practical affairs of the Conservative movement. He thus became one of the principal architects of Conservatism.

Ginzberg's scholarly expertise lay in his knowledge of the unfolding history of *halachah*, the aggregate of Jewish teachings, which he understood as a growing organism, developing and adapting in response to the external economic, social, and political circumstances of Jewish life. He saw as his chief purpose to demonstrate that the development of *halachah* in the past was not just the work of the scholars isolated in their houses of study but rather a realistic reflection of their lives and times. But he subscribed to this evolution as a theory of the past, of history, and refused, in general, to apply his historical view of Jewish law to the contemporary world. Furthermore, he discouraged his students, the Conservative rabbinate, from employing the implications of his research for modern religious life. He believed that the overwhelming majority of his students were insufficiently expert to promulgate change. And he was skeptical of making changes that both unobservant Conservative laity and Orthodox rabbis would refuse to follow. The Conservative rabbinate's deep personal respect for Ginzberg and his scholarship led them for the greater part of his life to abide by his views and to refrain from adjusting *halachah*. Only after he retired from active teaching at the Seminary in 1948 did the Rabbinical Assembly reorganize its Committee on Jewish Law to become the Committee on Jewish Law and Standards. Its bold statements on travel and the use of electricity on the Sabbath violated Ginzberg's sanction against contemporary *halachic* development.

Ginzberg ventured into public life in the Conservative movement, particularly during the early years of Cyrus Adler's administration (1916–22). He was acting president of the United Synagogue of America (1917–18), which he had helped to found in order to win greater support for the Seminary. As chairman of its

Committee on the Interpretation of Jewish Law, established in 1917, he wrote several *responsa*, including one allowing for the use of grape juice for ritual celebrations in lieu of wine as a means of solving the scandalous problem of rabbis, pseudo-rabbis, and bootleggers trafficking in wine during Prohibition. But he refrained from sanctioning the family pews that were becoming the norm in Conservative congregations. In the face of growing opposition, especially to this latter ruling, Ginzberg conceded the untenability of his task and stepped down.

In 1927 the responsibility for interpreting *halachah* for the Conservative movement passed from the United Synagogue to the Rabbinical Assembly, which established the Committee on Jewish Law. Although not formally a member of the committee, Ginzberg remained influential behind the scenes and was consulted whenever important questions arose. As the committee wrestled with Louis *Epstein's proposal to solve the plight of the *agunah*, Ginzberg's reluctance to endorse Epstein's plan unless all sectors of world Jewry subscribed to it led the committee to repudiate the proposal. And yet Ginzberg was sensitive to the urgency of the problem. Fearing that World War II would create hundreds of *agunot*, he drafted a wartime emergency document for the Law Committee allowing husbands to take steps in advance of their military service to prevent their wives from becoming *agunot*.

Ginzberg was also a founder (1919–20) and president until 1947 of the American Academy of Jewish Research, established to stimulate Jewish learning and to set standards for Jewish scholarship. He spent the academic year 1928–29 as the first professor of *halachah* at Hebrew University in Jerusalem and in 1934 was a member of the Hartog Commission, whose recommendations led to important changes in the administration of the university.

His scholarship dealt mainly with the origins of *agadah*, *halachah*, and the literature of the *geonim*, and his studies illuminated rabbinic literature. His writings on the growth and development of the Talmud developed the idea that the differences between the Palestinian and Babylonian Talmuds reflected the contrasting cultures and economic systems in which they developed. He researched the Cairo *genizah*, culling from it fragments of the Jerusalem Talmud, *midrashim*, *geonic* literature, and ancient Karaite texts. In *Geonica* (1909), a study of the documents of the *genizah*, he opened up a new chapter in the history of the hitherto obscure period of the *geonim*. His introductions and commentaries to various texts are important studies in obscure and difficult problems of Talmudic and rabbinic literature. They explore historical questions and highlight the emergence and development of various customs and institutions.

Ginzberg's fame carried beyond the world of Jewish scholarship. He was one of sixty scholars granted an honorary degree by Harvard University in celebration of its tercentennial. The award not only recognized that he was the foremost Jewish scholar of his age, but that the study of rabbinic literature had become a major humanistic discipline.

From 1903 to 1908 Ginzberg had what he termed an "extraordinary friend-ship" with his student, translator, and editorial assistant, Henrietta Szold; in 1909, he married Adele Katzenstein. They had two children. Ginzberg died in New York City on November 11, 1953.

Writings: *Die Haggada bei den Kirchenvarten* (Heidelberg, 1899); *Geonica*, 2 vols. (New York, 1909); *Yerushalmi Fragments from the Genizah (Seride ha-Yerushalmi min ha-Genizah asher be-Mitsrayim)* (New York, 1909); *The Legends of the Jews* 7 vols. (Philadelphia, 1909–38); *Studies in the Origins of the Mishnah* (New York, 1920); *Eine Bekannte Juedische Sekte* (New York, 1922); *Excerpts of Midrash and Agadah* (New York, 1925); *Students, Scholars, and Saints* (Philadelphia, 1928); *Genizah Studies*, 3 vols. (New York, 1928–29); *Commentaries and Innovations in the Yerushalmi (Perushim vehidushim bi-Yerushalmi*, 3 vols. (New York, 1941–61). Posthumously, *On Jewish Law and Lore* (Philadelphia, 1955); *Legends of the Bible* (New York, 1956); *An Unknown Jewish Sect* (New York, 1976).

References: Boaz Cohen, *Bibliography of the Writings of Professor Louis Ginzberg* (New York, 1945); Joan Dash, *Summoned to Jerusalem: The Life of Henrietta Szold* (New York, 1979), pp. 47–100; David Druck, *Reb Levi Ginzberg* (New York, 1933); *EJ* vol. 7, cols. 584–85; Eli Ginzberg, "Address in Honor of Louis Ginzberg," *PRA 1964* vol. 28 (1965), pp. 109–19; Eli Ginzberg, *Keeper of the Law: Louis Ginzberg* (Philadelphia, 1966); *Louis Ginzberg Jubilee Volume* (New York, 1945); Henry H. Mayer, "What Price Conservatism?: Louis Ginzberg and Hebrew Union College, *AJA* 10, 2 (October 1958), pp. 145–50; Herbert Parzen, *Architects of Conservative Judaism* (New York, 1964), pp. 128–54; Herbert Rosenblum, "The Founding of the United Synagogue of America, 1913" (Ph.D.diss. Brandeis University, 1970), pp. 144, 245–46; Marshall Sklare, *Conservative Judaism* (1955; rev. 1972; reprint ed., Lanham, Md., 1985), p. 171; *Recorder* 1, 3 (July 1921), pp. 7–8.

GOLDFEDER, FISHEL (1912–81). Rabbi. The son of Edward M. and Ida Mandell Goldfeder, Fishel Goldfeder was born on November 5, 1912, in Pitts-burgh, Pennsylvania, and educated at the Yeshivah Torah Vodaath in Brooklyn. In the 1930s he left America to study in Lithuania at the Mir Yeshivah, but he returned to the United States in 1938, fleeing the increasing anti-Semitism. He earned a B.A. at New York University and was ordained at the Seminary in 1944.

Goldfeder began his career in the pulpit substituting at Kadimah Synagogue, Springfield, Massachusetts, for Isaac *Klein, who was serving as a military chaplain during World War II. In 1945 Goldfeder became assistant rabbi at Adath Israel Congregation, Cincinnati, Ohio. Goldfeder led the congregation from 1949, when its senior rabbi, Louis *Feinberg, died, until his retirement in 1980.

Founded by Polish Jews in 1853, Adath Israel was for many years the leading non-Reform synagogue in Cincinnati. Many of its practices were Orthodox, and in 1923 the congregation had amended its constitution to prohibit family pews. Nevertheless, for much of the twentieth century Seminary rabbis had led the congregation, and it was affiliated with the United Synagogue. As Adath Israel grew under Goldfeder's guidance in the 1950s, younger congregants demanded mixed seating, one of the chief distinguishing characteristics of the Conservative synagogue. With their rabbi's support, the Board of Trustees and the congregation voted to allow for optional mixed seating. Enraged over this willful violation of Orthodox practice, a faction in the synagogue sued the congregation for violating its constitution stipulating worship "according to the Orthodox forms adopted by Polish Jews."

An entire issue of *Conservative Judaism* (Fall 1956) was devoted to a discussion of the case. Here Goldfeder articulated his view of the Conservative synagogue as one comprised of members who had deliberately left Orthodox houses of worship to move away from such strict interpretations of the law. In his eyes Adath Israel already was a Conservative synagogue. It had instituted other ritual changes—confirmation for girls, women addressing the congregation, and a microphone at services—without vehement opposition. Moreover, the synagogue did not have a *mechizah* separating men and women in worship. Although a court of arbitration ruled that the religious questions involved were outside its jurisdiction, it did affirm that the congregation by majority vote could alter the synagogue seating pattern. The dissatisfied Orthodox minority left Adath Israel, which, with Goldfeder's leadership, now moved squarely into the Conservative camp.

In the 1960s Goldfeder, who believed that "a rabbi's life is his people's life," supervised Adath Israel's relocation from Avondale to Amberley. By the time he was elected rabbi emeritus in 1980, the congregation of 1,000 members had become one of the largest in Cincinnati.

In his thirty-five years in Cincinnati, Goldfeder played a leading role in numerous Jewish educational, philanthropic, and communal endeavors. He helped found the Yavneh Day School, Chofetz Chaim Day School, Jewish Culture and Art Series, and the first city-wide Jewish Youth Council. He served as president of the Board of Rabbis and the Zionist Federation. He chaired the Soviet Jewish Committee and the Southern Ohio Region of Israel Bonds and was co-chair of the Jewish Welfare Fund (1973–74). He also served on the National Advisory Council of the United Jewish Appeal, Israel Bonds National Rabbinic Cabinet, and the Executive Committee of the Jewish Community Relations Council. In the Rabbinical Assembly, he was a member of the Executive Committee and the Committee on Jewish Law and Standards.

In 1945 Goldfeder married Ruth Kramer; they had three children. He died on February 21, 1981, in Jerusalem.

References: *American Israelite* 6 November 1980, p. 21; 26 February 1981, p. 1ff.; *Cincinnati Enquirer* 23 February 1981, p. D1; *CJ* 11, 1 (Fall 1956); Isaac Klein, *The Anguish and Ecstasy of a Jewish Chaplain* (New York, 1974), p. 29; *PRA 1981* vol. 43 (1982), pp. 94–97; Jonathan D. Sarna, "Synagogue Seating in America," in *The History of the Synagogue in America*, ed. Jack Wertheimer (New York, 1987).

GOLDIN, JUDAH (1914–   ). Rabbi, educator, author. The son of Gerson David and Rachel Robkin Goldin, Judah Goldin was born on September 14, 1914, in New York City. He earned a B.S. from the City College of New York in 1934, a Bachelor of Hebrew Letters from the Seminary College of Jewish Studies in 1934, was ordained at the Seminary in 1938, and earned a Doctor of Hebrew Letters there in 1943.

Goldin was instructor of religious foundations at the University of Illinois (1939–43), lecturer and visiting associate professor of Jewish literature and history at Duke University (1943–45), and associate professor of religion at the University of Iowa (1946–52). As dean of the Seminary's Teachers Institute and associate professor of *agadah* in the College of Jewish Studies (1952–58), he chaired the Leadership Training Fellowship, a national Conservative high school founded in 1946 to prepare promising teenagers for professional careers as Hebrew teachers, rabbis, and leaders of Conservative Judaism and the American Jewish community. He also co-chaired with Theodore *Friedman the Joint Law Conference of the Seminary and Rabbinical Assembly. In 1958 Goldin left the Seminary to become professor of classical Judaica at Yale University (1958–73), where he also edited the Yale Judaica Series. From 1973 until his retirement, he was professor of post-Biblical Hebrew literature at the University of Pennsylvania.

Goldin's scholarly research explored rabbinic Judaism, especially its *midrashic* literature, and he provided graceful translations—often the first in English—of important classical rabbinic texts. These works were enhanced by skillful interpretations of the text—in essence Goldin's commentaries on commentaries—based upon scholarly readings of variant manuscripts and his understanding of comparative literatures, grammar, and philology.

Goldin married Grace Avis Aaronson in 1938; they have two children.

Writings: Ed., *The Jewish Expression* (New Haven, 1976); *The Munich Mekilta* (Copenhagen and Baltimore, 1980). Ed. and trans., *The Fathers According to Rabbi Nathan* (New Haven, 1955); *The Living Talmud: The Wisdom of the Fathers* (Chicago, 1957); *The Song at the Sea* (New Haven, 1971). Trans., Shalom Spiegel, *The Last Trial* (New York, 1967).

References: *CJ* 26, 2 (Winter 1972), pp. 89–90; *WWAJ* 1980, p. 173.

GOLDMAN, ISRAEL (1904–79). Rabbi, educator. The son of Morris and Anna Rosen Goldman, Israel Goldman was born in Poland on February 13, 1904. He earned a B.A. from the City College of New York in 1924, was ordained at the Seminary in 1926, and earned a Doctor of Hebrew Letters there in 1937.

In 1924 the executive director of the United Synagogue, Samuel *Cohen, laid the groundwork for the establishment of Temple Emanu-El, a Conservative synagogue founded to serve the growing Jewish community on the east side of Providence, Rhode Island. As a senior rabbinical student, Goldman conducted the congregation's first High Holiday services and was engaged as rabbi following his ordination (1926–48). He quickly introduced Conservative programming—late Friday evening services, Confirmation, and Bat Mitzvah—and later resolved an internal dispute to permit the playing of an organ at *Yizkor* and High Holiday services. The congregants dedicated their synagogue in 1927 and under Goldman's direction made plans to expand it to allow for its growing membership, which reached 493 families by 1945.

Goldman's interest in Jewish education was evident from the outset. He organized a Sunday school, Hebrew school, and Parent-Teachers Association and established an Annual Jewish Education Day at Temple Emanu-El. Determined to meet the educational needs of the adult members of the congregation as well, he established the Institute of Jewish Studies, which sponsored such distinguished lecturers as Mordecai M. *Kaplan and Abram Sachar, enrolling 350 students in 1941.

The success of the institute brought Goldman a national reputation in the Conservative movement as a leader in adult Jewish education. In 1938 he analyzed for his colleagues in the Rabbinical Assembly the recent development of adult education in America and its influence upon the field of adult Jewish education. He believed adult educators needed "to educate the whole Jew," to make Jewish education a lifelong process, to introduce Jewish thought via the classic texts of Jewish tradition, to inculcate a sense of the "worthwhileness of Jewish life," and to develop the individual's kinship with the Jewish community. To coordinate the adult education activities of the Conservative movement and to achieve these goals, Goldman proposed the establishment of the National Academy for Adult Jewish Studies, which was organized in 1941 under the auspices of the Seminary. Goldman was appointed its first director (1941–51). The academy published syllabi and textbooks such as Simon *Greenberg's *The Ideals of the Jewish Prayer Book.* With the National Federation of Jewish Men's Clubs, it took the lead in reviving the traditional summer adult study session, the *kallah*, holding the first one at the Seminary in 1944. Later institutes were held "away from home" at campsites—Tel Noar Lodge, Hampstead, New Hampshire, and Camp Wohelo in the Blue Mountains—which offered the possibility of combining traditional group-living arrangements with the study program.

As president of the Rabbinical Assembly (1946–48), Goldman was the chief executive of an organization that included some 400 men in the immediate postwar years. He recognized that the Conservative movement was on the verge of significant numerical and geographic expansion and that it was necessary to strengthen the organizational structure of the RA to meet these challenges. He therefore recommended the establishment of regional branches and long-range planning to insure that the annual conventions would meet throughout the country. He also anticipated the future growth of Conservatism beyond the confines of North America to South America and even to Palestine. Confronting the growing Jewish-center movement, he pressed for the expansion of all Conservative synagogues into synagogue-centers that would educate young and old and offer social and recreational facilities. Recognizing that the Rabbinical Assembly had to respond more forcefully to the basic social questions of the day—world peace, race relations, and civil rights—he pushed for the reorganization and expansion of the Social Justice Commission.

Goldman's activities on the national scene in the Conservative movement in the 1940s created tension within his congregation. While he felt that he was not only the spiritual leader of Emanu-El but also teacher and leader of all Jews with whom he came into contact, many of the lay leaders of the synagogue felt that the congregation should be his first priority. In 1947 Goldman and the board of the synagogue hammered out a statement of principles on lay and rabbinical duties that harmonized the views of Goldman and the lay leadership. Nevertheless, in 1948, despite efforts to persuade him to remain, Goldman left Emanu-El for the greater challenges posed by the larger Jewish community of Baltimore, Maryland, and its Chizuk Amuno Congregation.

As rabbi of Chizuk Amuno, founded in 1871, Goldman paved the way for its successful relocation to the Baltimore suburb of Pikesville, supervising the construction of its new synagogue there and tripling its membership. A leader in civil rights, he was a member (1951–56) and vice-chairman (1956–69) of the Maryland Commission on Interracial Relations and headed its study of intergroup relations. Its condemnation of discrimination in Baltimore public accommodations led to the passage of civil rights legislation. His participation in a protest against segregation at an amusement park led to his arrest in July 1963, an event Goldman considered the most dramatic of his life. Chizuk Amuno congregants championed their rabbi's civil rights endeavors and supported his efforts to strengthen interfaith relations. They also shared his lifelong commitment to Zionism. Goldman was president of both the Providence and Baltimore districts of the Zionist Organization of America and a member of its national Administrative Committee. When Goldman retired in 1976, Emanu-El named him rabbi emeritus.

Goldman wrote *The Life and Times of Rabbi David ibn Abi Zimra* (1970), a study of Sephardic Jewry in the Ottomon Empire following its expulsion from Spain in 1492. His *Lifelong Learning Among Jews* grew out of his work in adult education.

He married Mildred Gandal, former secretary to Louis *Finkelstein, in 1943; they had two daughters. Goldman died in Baltimore on February 9, 1979.

Writings: "Objectives in Adult Jewish Education," *PRA 1938* vol. 5 (1939), pp. 435–60; "The Rabbinical Assembly of America in the Contemporary World: Presidential Message," *PRA 1947* vol. 11 (1948), pp. 140–60; "New Demands on the Rabbinate and the Laity: President's Message," *PRA 1948* vol. 12 (1949), pp. 83–104; *The Life and Times of Rabbi David ibn Abi Zimra* (New York, 1970); *Lifelong Learning Among Jews: Adult Education in Judaism from Biblical Times to the Twentieth Century* (New York, 1975).

References: *Baltimore Evening Sun* 10 February 1979, p. 18; Simon Noveck and Lily Edelman, "The Laymen's Institute: An Adventure in Jewish Living," reprinted in

Roads to Jewish Survival, ed. Milton Berger, Joel Geffen, and M. David Hoffman (New York, 1967), pp. 270–72; *PRA 1980* vol. 42 (1981), pp. 240–41; *Review* 16, 2 (Summer 1963), p. 1; *Temple Emanu-El: The First Fifty Years, 1924–1975* (Providence, R.I., 1975); *WWWJ* 1965, p. 334.

GOLDMAN, SOLOMON (1893–1953). Rabbi, communal leader, scholar. The son of Abraham Abba and Jeanette Grossman Goldman, Solomon Goldman was born in Kozin, Russian Poland, on August 19, 1893. He was brought to the United States in 1902 and educated at the Rabbi Isaac Elchanan Yeshiva. Goldman earned a B.A. from New York University in 1917, was ordained at the Seminary in 1918, and earned a Doctor of Hebrew Letters there in 1936.

After serving B'nai Israel Congregation, Brooklyn, New York (1917–18), Goldman became rabbi at B'nai Jeshuran, Cleveland, Ohio (1918–22). Frustrated by his inability to mold B'nai Jeshuran into a synagogue-center, Goldman left the congregation in 1922 to become rabbi at the Cleveland Jewish Center (1922–29).

Founded by Polish Jewish immigrants as the Orthodox Congregation Anshe Emeth in 1869, Anshe Emeth was renamed the Cleveland Jewish Center when it built a new synagogue-center in the Glenville area in 1920. Goldman followed Seminary graduate Samuel Benjamin as its rabbi. With sports facilities and an auditorium unequaled elsewhere in a neighborhood that contained, within a square mile, a major proportion of Cleveland Jewry, the Cleveland Jewish Center became one of the leading congregations of the city. Goldman's fervor and oratorical skills attracted large crowds for late Friday night services. A man of great vitality, he instituted a Sunday lecture series, administered a large Hebrew school, and implemented ritual reforms indicative of the Conservative movement, including seating men and women together during worship. The introduction of mixed seating led to a stormy battle as an Orthodox contingent tried to block the congregation's move toward Conservatism. In 1927 they sued Goldman in civil court, charging that mixed seating violated the synagogue by-laws stipulating an Orthodox congregation. The court sided with Goldman, and when he left Cleveland in 1929, partly over the scars of the battle, the Cleveland Jewish Center was firmly in the Conservative camp.

Goldman moved to Chicago to become rabbi at Anshe Emet Synagogue (1929–53). He proceeded to revive this sixty-year-old congregation, which had only seventy-five members in 1929. Goldman instituted late Friday night services, raised funds in the middle of the Depression for a new educational building, and inaugurated the Anshe Emet Forum of outstanding lectures. By 1935 the congregation had grown to 1,100 families, and in 1946 it opened the Anshe Emet Day School. Goldman served Anshe Emet until his death, the synagogue benefiting from his superior administrative and organizational abilities, his eminence as an orator, and his leadership of its adult education program.

Within the Conservative movement Goldman pleaded for the strengthening of the United Synagogue and for the full partnership of the Conservative rabbinate and congregations in the leadership of the movement. A member of the Board of Trustees of the Seminary, Goldman believed that rabbinic students needed better preparation for the diverse responsibilities of the pulpit, and he successfully lobbied to change the administration of the Seminary's rabbinical school so that a board of faculty, alumni, and laymen were involved in curricular decisions.

A committed Zionist, Goldman worked to popularize Zionism in America. As president of the Zionist Organization of America (ZOA; 1938–40), he raised funds for immigration to Palestine and restructured the ZOA's cumbersome bureaucracy to attract members and competent leaders. Goldman was also active in numerous Jewish relief and Hebrew cultural organizations. He was president of the *Histadrut Ivrit* (1936–38), and he helped establish the National Hillel Foundation of B'nai B'rith.

In his essays Goldman viewed Judaism as inseparable from the Jewish people, and he believed that the land of Israel and the Hebrew language bound this people into a nation. These beliefs enabled Goldman to fuse Zionism with a passionate commitment to Diaspora Jewry. In *The Jew and His Universe* (1936), Goldman viewed Maimonides, not as an Aristotelian, but as a Jew who saw the world as the unfolding of God's creative will. In his magnum opus, *The Book of Human Destiny* (1948–56), Goldman, a distinguished Bible scholar, began a commentary and translation of the Torah, utilizing traditional and non-traditional sources, that demonstrated the relevance of the Torah for contemporary life. He also edited and translated several volumes of Hebrew literature.

Goldman married Alice Lipkowitz in 1918; they had two daughters. He died in Chicago on May 14, 1953.

Writings: *A Rabbi Takes Stock* (New York, 1931); *The Jew and the Universe* (New York, 1936); *The Golden Chain* (New York, 1937); *Crisis and Decision* (New York, 1938); *The Book of Human Destiny*, 3 vols. (New York, 1948–56). Ed., H.N. Bialik, *Agadot Sheloshah v'Arba'ah* (New York, 1941); Moses ben Maimon, *Igeret Teman* (New York, 1950).

References: *The Anshe Emet Synagogue, 1873–1973* (Chicago, n.d.); *Chicago Daily Tribune* 15 May 1953, p. 12; *CJ* 11, 4 (Summer 1957), pp. 42–44; *EJ* vol. 7, col. 722; Lloyd P. Gartner, *History of the Jews in Cleveland* (Cleveland, 1978), pp. 170, 276–77; *NYT* 15 May 1953, p. 24; *PRA 1946* vol. 10 (1947), pp. 211, 214–15; *Recorder* 5, 3 (July 1925), pp. 20–22; Sidney Z. Vincent and Judah Rubinstein, *Merging Traditions: Jewish Life in Cleveland* (Cleveland, 1978), pp. 6–8; Jacob L. Weinstein, *Solomon Goldman: A Rabbi's Rabbi* (New York, 1973).

GOLDSTEIN, ISRAEL (1896–1986). Rabbi, communal leader. The son of David and Fannie Silver Goldstein, Israel Goldstein was born on June 18, 1896, in Philadelphia. Educated in the Philadelphia public schools, at Yeshivah Mishkan Israel, and at Gratz College, Goldstein also spent part of his childhood in a traditional *cheder* outside of Riga. He earned a B.A. at the University of Pennsylvania in 1914, was ordained at the Seminary in 1918, and earned a Doctor of Hebrew Letters from the Seminary in 1927.

Newly ordained, Goldstein was persuaded by Cyrus *Adler to accept the challenge of the rabbinate at B'nai Jeshurun in New York City. Founded in 1825, B'nai Jeshurun had been troubled by an apathetic membership and a frequent change in spiritual leaders. Goldstein, however, revitalized the congregation. He immediately introduced late Friday night services followed by a lecture, added *Yizkor* services on the last days of festivals, and instituted special High Holiday services for youth. He expanded the education program, adding weekday Hebrew classes, a high school department, and a junior congregation, and acquired a building to house them. In 1921 he launched the B'nai Jeshurun Center directed by Louis *Levitsky. The community center's new building was dedicated in 1928. Goldstein's numerous Zionist activities and communal responsibilities often took him away from his pastoral duties. Nevertheless, B'nai Jeshurun supported his endeavors and emerged as a leading fund-raiser for Israel during his tenure. Goldstein served B'nai Jeshurun for forty-two years, retiring at the end of 1960 to fulfill his dream of *aliyah*. But as rabbi emeritus, he returned annually to his congregation to preach at the High Holidays.

Gifted with oratorical and organizational skills, Goldstein was an indefatigable communal leader. President of his first Zionist organization at the age of ten, he demonstrated at that young age his extraordinary dedication to building up Israel and to laying the foundations for its support within the American Jewish community. As president of the Jewish National Fund (1933–43), Goldstein reorganized its administration and developed new fund-raising techniques. As vice-president (1934–43) and then as president of the Zionist Organization of America (ZOA; 1943–45), he worked to secure the support of American political and American Jewish leadership for the 1942 Biltmore Program calling for the establishment of a Jewish commonwealth in Palestine and to double ZOA membership. In 1946 he helped found the National Confederation of General Zionists, a center group counterbalancing the right and left wings of the Zionist movement, and served as its president (1946–61). He was chairman of the United Jewish Appeal and co-chairman of the United Palestine Appeal (1947–48). Elected treasurer of the Jewish Agency in 1948 and given a sabbatical by B'nai Jeshurun, Goldstein spent the following year in Israel administering the budget for absorption and immigration, education, and youth work. As world chairman of the Keren Hayesod-United Israel Appeal (1961–71), he traveled throughout the world raising funds to finance immigration and settlement programs. Only in 1971 did Goldstein retire from Zionist public service.

Goldstein's Zionist activities did not preclude his leadership in numerous other Jewish and interfaith public organizations. In the Conservative movement Goldstein served as the first president of the Young People's League (1921–25), the United Synagogue's initial endeavor to organize Jewish youth in the service of Judaism, and he was the first chairman of the Rabbinical Assembly's Committee on Social Justice (1931–35). He decried the lack of organization of American Jewry despite its plethora of organizations, and he encouraged both the RA and the Synagogue Council of America, during his tenure as its president (1943–

45), to assume the leadership he felt rabbis should exercise in American Jewish life.

In 1928 Goldstein helped found the National Conference of Christians and Jews. In *Jewish Justice and Conciliation* (1981), he wrote a history of the Jewish Conciliation Board, a voluntary arbitration tribunal that heard cases in Yiddish and which he had headed (1930–68). Recognizing that the Jews were the one major American religious group that had not sponsored a university, in 1946 Goldstein helped launch Brandeis University by acquiring the campus in Waltham, Massachusetts. As president of the American Jewish Congress (1951–58), he supported civil rights and school desegregation and opposed McCarthyism. As chairman of the Western Hemisphere Executive of the World Jewish Congress (1949–60), he worked to facilitate Jewish claims against Germany.

Goldstein published widely. Numerous volumes of his sermons and addresses appeared. He also completed histories of B'nai Jeshurun and of the founding of Brandeis University as well as several volumes of memoirs. These writings reveal that he was drawn to the rabbinate as the best way to serve God, Israel, Torah, America, and humanity; that his *aliyah* reflected his belief that only in Israel could a Jewish life be fully lived; and that he saw the synagogue and Jewish education as the cornerstones of a healthy and creative Jewish community.

Two *feschriften* were dedicated to Goldstein, and a chair in practical theology at the Seminary and a synagogue at Hebrew University bear his name.

In 1918 Goldstein married Bertha Markowitz, a leader of Pioneer Women. They had two children. He died in Tel Aviv on April 11, 1986.

Writings: *A Century of Judaism in New York: B'nai Jeshurun 1825–1925* (New York, 1930); *Toward a Solution* (New York, 1940); *Shana b'Yisrael* (Jerusalem, 1950); *Brandeis University: Chapter of its Founding* (New York, 1951); *American Jewry Comes of Age: Tercentenary Addresses* (New York, 1955); *Transition Years: New York-Jerusalem, 1960–62* (Jerusalem, 1962); *Israel at Home and Abroad (1962–1972)* (Jerusalem, 1973); *Jewish Justice and Conciliation* (New York, 1981); *To Serve My People* (New York, 1983); *My World as a Jew: The Memoirs of Israel Goldstein*, 2 vols. (New York, 1984).

References: *EJ* vol. 7, col. 747; Harry Schneiderman, *Two Generations in Perspective: Notable Events and Trends, 1896–1956* (New York, 1957); *Silver Jubilee Celebration of the Ministry of Rabbi Israel Goldstein to Congregation B'nai Jeshurun* (New York, 1944); *Studies in the History of Zionism* (Jerusalem, 1976); *WWAJ*, p. 179; *WWWJ* 1965, p. 342.

GOODBLATT, MORRIS SOLOMON (1901–78). Rabbi. The son of Abraham and Rebecca Lichtenstein Goodblatt, Morris Goodblatt was born in Mlawa, Russian Poland, on September 18, 1901. He immigrated to the United States in 1912. Educated in the New York City public schools, the Rabbi Jacob Joseph School, and the Mizrachi Teachers Institute, he earned a B.A. from City College of New York in 1924, was ordained at the Seminary in 1927, and earned a Doctor of Hebrew Letters there in 1944.

Goodblatt served as rabbi at Congregation Beth Am Israel, Philadelphia, Pennsylvania, from its founding in 1927. For more than fifty years he guided the development and growth of the synagogue, taking great pride in its school, which sent a dozen of its graduates on to the Seminary's Rabbinical School, and smoothing the way for the synagogue's relocation as Philadelphia Jewry moved to the suburbs. He became rabbi emeritus in 1968. Active in local Jewish affairs, Goodblatt was president of the Jewish National Fund Council of Philadelphia (1930) and of the Board of Rabbis of Greater Philadelphia (1944–45).

In 1960 Goodblatt helped found, as a member and former president of the Philadelphia Region of the Rabbinical Assembly, the Academy for Judaism. To release area RA rabbis from the time-consuming task of individually tutoring prospective converts, the academy undertook the instruction of proselytes and set standards and guidelines for conversion. In addition to his responsibilities as dean and director of the academy (1960–78), Goodblatt taught classes in the fundamentals of Judaism, personally guiding hundreds of converts.

During the 1940s Goodblatt co-chaired with Alter *Landesman the United Synagogue Commission on Jewish Education. Established in 1940 as a joint commission of the United Synagogue and Rabbinical Assembly, it served as the Conservative movement's central agency for elementary Jewish education. The commission strove to coordinate and to standardize congregational curricula by publishing educational materials and developing "The Objectives and Standards for the Congregational Schools." Goodblatt headed the publication committee for its monthly bulletin, *The Jewish School and Democracy*, and in 1945 was instrumental in securing the services of his classmate Abraham *Millgram as the commission's educational director.

As chairman of the Rabbinical Assembly's Special Committee on Ritual Survey (1946–48), Goodblatt compiled a detailed picture of the rites and practices— worship services, Bar and Bat Mitzvah ceremonies, Confirmation celebrations, use of organs, funeral customs, and other observances—in the Conservative synagogue. He also chaired the RA's Membership Committee (1953–64) as it dealt with the time-consuming task of evaluating the increasing number of applications for admission from non-Seminary graduates. He was also a member of the RA's Committee on Jewish Law and Standards.

Goodblatt wrote *Jewish Life in Turkey in the Sixteenth Century* (1952), a study of the resettlement of Sephardic Jewry in the Ottomon Empire following the expulsions from Spain and Portugal at the end of the fifteenth century.

He married Doris Rappoport in 1934; they had two sons. Goodblatt died in Philadelphia on March 20, 1978.

Writings: "Report of the Commission on Jewish Education," *PRA 1943* vol. 8 (1947), pp. 253–55; *PRA 1946* vol. 10 (1947), pp. 318–20; "Synagogue Ritual Survey," *PRA 1948* vol. 12 (1949), pp. 105–9; *Jewish Life in Turkey in the Sixteenth Century: As Reflected in the Legal Writings of Samuel De Medina* (New York, 1952); "Preparing the Convert," *PRA 1973* vol. 35 (1974), pp. 91–95.

References: *Philadelphia Inquirer* 22 March 1978, p. 8E; *Recorder* 7, 3 (July 1927), p. 15; *WWWJ* 1955, p. 278.

GOODMAN, ARNOLD M. (1928–   ). Rabbi. The son of Louis A. and Jeanne Masin Goodman, Arnold Goodman was born in Brooklyn, New York, on June 27, 1928. He earned a B.S. at the City College of New York in 1948 and was ordained at the Seminary in 1952. After earning a J.D. at DePaul University in 1962, Goodman was admitted to the bar associations of both Illinois (1962) and Israel (1972).

Goodman served as a chaplain in the U.S. Army at Fort Sheridan, Illinois (1952–54). In 1954 he became the first full-time rabbi of Congregation Rodfei Sholom-Oir Chodosh, Chicago, Illinois (1954–65). Founded in 1952, the congregation grew during Goodman's tenure from 250 to 700 families. While serving as the congregation's spiritual leader, Goodman was also its Hebrew and Sunday school principal and a member of the St. Louis Park Human Relations Committee (1960–62).

In 1966 he left Rodfei Sholom-Oir Chodosh for the pulpit of Adath Jeshurun Congregation, Minneapolis, Minnesota (1966–82). Founded in 1884 by Russian and Rumanian immigrants, Adath Jeshurun, a leading midwestern Conservative congregation, had been led by Seminary rabbis C. David *Matt and Albert *Gordon. Goodman guided his new congregants to experiment with *kallot* as a means of creating community within the 1,100–family congregation. Adath Jeshurun's award-winning *kallah* program, recognized for distinction with a United Synagogue Solomon Schechter award, prompted the building in 1974 of its Kallah Retreat Center in Minnetonka, a western suburb of Minneapolis. The center not only housed congregational *Shabbat kallot* but it also served as the site of the Adath Jeshurun weekday *gan hayeled* (nursery school).

Goodman led the congregation to a second Solomon Schechter award for its *Chevra Kavod Hamet* (society for the honor of the dead). Determined to restore tradition to Jewish funeral practices, in 1975 Goodman called for Adath Jeshurun to form its own burial society to conduct funerals according to the dictates of Jewish law. The congregation enthusiastically endorsed the plan. Its 125–member *Chevra* became the subject of an ABC television documentary, "A Plain Pine Box," and a book Goodman wrote with the same title (1981).

In 1982 Goodman left Minneapolis to become rabbi of Ahavath Achim, Atlanta, Georgia (1982–   ), the second largest Conservative congregation in the United States. There he succeeded Harry H. *Epstein, who in fifty-four years of service had led the congregation from modern Orthodoxy into Conservatism.

Outside of his congregations, Goodman emerged as a leading member of the Rabbinical Assembly. He was a member of its Committee on Jewish Law and Standards (1962–64) and, after serving as Rabbinical Assembly vice-president (1980–82), was elected president (1982–84). Goodman, who actively supported the ordination of women as rabbis, found his administration charged by the issue of the admission of women to the ranks of the Rabbinical Assembly. At both the 1983 and 1984 conventions the Rabbinical Assembly considered and narrowly defeated proposals to admit Beverly Magidson, a rabbi ordained at the Reform movement's Hebrew Union College-Jewish Institute of Religion, to its ranks. As president, Goodman also took steps to grapple with the ever-present problem of stress in the rabbinate by creating a new Committee on the Rabbinic Family and instituting a parallel women's convention for the wives of Rabbinical Assembly members. He also reactivated the Rabbinical Assembly's Social Action Committee and charged it to consider the issue of nuclear freeze. Since completing his term as president, he has chaired the Rabbinical Assembly's Personnel Committee (1984–) and served on the Joint Retirement Board (1984–).

Goodman married Rae Parnes in 1949; they have three children.

Writings: *A Plain Pine Box* (New York, 1981); *PRA 1982* vol. 44 (1983), pp. 92–97; "Presidential Address," *PRA 1983* vol. 45 (1984), pp. 22–35; *PRA 1984* vol. 46 (1985), pp. 37–42.

Reference: *Review* 24, 2 (Summer 1974), p. 2.

GORDIS, ROBERT (1908–). Rabbi, Biblical scholar, author. The son of Hyman and Lizzie Engel Gordis, Robert Gordis was born on February 6, 1908, in Brooklyn, New York. Educated in the New York City public schools and at Rabbi Isaac Elchanan Yeshiva, he earned a B.A. from the City College of New York in 1926, a Ph.D. from Dropsie College, Philadelphia, in 1929, and was ordained at the Seminary in 1932.

After teaching at the Hebrew Teachers Training School for Girls (1926–28) and Yeshiva College (1929–30), Gordis joined the Seminary faculty as a lecturer in the College of Jewish Studies (1931–36). In 1937 he was appointed to the Seminary's Rabbinical School, overcoming a long-standing unwritten rule to hire only European-trained faculty to teach the great classical texts at the Seminary. In 1940 he was promoted to professor of Biblical exegesis and was subsequently appointed professor of Bible (1961–) and Meyer and Fannie Rapaport Professor of Bible and Philosophies of Religion (1974–). At the same time that he was a member of the Seminary faculty, Gordis also taught religion at Columbia University (1948–57), was professor of religion at Temple University (1967–74), was the first Jew to teach as visiting professor of Old Testament at the renowned (Protestant) Union Theological Seminary (1953–54), and was visiting professor of Bible at Hebrew University, Jerusalem (1970–71).

Believing that the challenges of the pulpit continually stimulated and informed his teaching and scholarship, Gordis was also rabbi of Temple Beth-El, Rockaway Park, New York, during these years (1931–68). Promoting intensive Jewish education was clearly his priority in his ministry, and his congregants appreciated his gifts as a preacher and teacher. In 1937 he and his wife inaugurated Temple Beth-El's adult education program, which they led together for the next thirty-seven years, teaching and influencing hundreds of congregants. In 1950 Gordis founded one of the first Conservative Jewish day schools, the Temple Beth-El

Day School, renamed the Robert Gordis Day School in honor of his retirement and election as rabbi emeritus in 1968.

One of the leading architects of Conservative Judaism, Gordis strove to crystallize and articulate its philosophy, to secure a solid foundation for its continued development, and to build a committed laity. In 1945 the National Academy of Adult Jewish Studies published his *Conservative Judaism: An American Philosophy*, one of the first attempts to explain the Conservative movement to the laity. Here he described its intellectual origins and showed that "in its pragmatic approach and its distrust of abstract theory, [Conservative Judaism] is characteristically American in spirit." He argued that Conservatism was "the modern interpretation of traditional Judaism" because it allowed for "reinterpretation" of that tradition in light of the realities of contemporary Jewish life. Gordis understood that the tradition grew by the accretion of new values, institutions, and laws. As the leading spokesman within the Conservative movement for the centrist position, he emphasized the necessity of both recognizing the binding authority of Jewish law and understanding its dynamic process of ongoing development. And he held that the rules of reinterpretation mandated that it be based upon historical development and maintain continuity with the past. He defended Solomon *Schechter's concept that changes in the tradition were legitimate if they emanated from the "collective conscience of Catholic Israel," but he redefined "Catholic Israel" to include only those who revere the authority of Jewish law and are concerned with its observance. This redefinition enabled the Conservative movement to continue to interpret Jewish law for the modern age in an era when the behavior of "Catholic Israel," as defined by Schechter, would otherwise have mandated abandonment of much of Jewish law.

Gordis held a number of important offices within the Conservative movement. He chaired the Rabbinical Assembly's Committee on Social Justice (1935–37) and represented the RA as delegate and as president (1948–49) of the Synagogue Council of America. As president of the Rabbinical Assembly (1944–46), he recognized that the Expansion Program of the Seminary highlighted three critical problems of Conservatism—the need to develop a philosophy and literature, to strengthen its weak organizational structure, and to bolster its programs of Jewish education. Gordis led the way in tackling these problems.

His administration began an active program of publication as the first step in developing a philosophy and literature for the movement. It founded the journal *Conservative Judaism* (1945–   ) as the RA's "forum of discussion and research for the crystallization of our philosophy" and issued pronouncements on key issues of the day—"Religious Observance in the Public Schools" and "The Goals and Objectives of Jewish Education." As chairman of the Joint Prayer Book Commission, he defended the liturgical changes made in the *Sabbath and Festival Prayer Book* published by the Rabbinical Assembly and the United Synagogue of America (1946). He also proposed that the RA create an ongoing conference on theology and philosophy and agitated, for many years unsuccessfully, for the publication of a guide to Jewish law to crystallize and to explain the ritual and ethical commandments of Conservative practice. And he chaired the Commission on the Philosophy of Conservative Judaism (1985–88), which published the *Statement of Principles of Conservative Judaism* (1988), the first such document ever to appear in the history of the movement.

Among the most significant accomplishments of his presidency was the establishment of the first pension plan for Conservative rabbis, a project that had been planned for nearly two decades and that went a long way toward strengthening the Rabbinical Assembly as an organization. In addition, Gordis advocated expanding the ranks of the RA to include greater numbers of non–Seminary-trained rabbis. And finally, he was a staunch proponent of more intensive Jewish education, calling for the afternoon Hebrew school to become the minimum program for Jewish education in the Conservative movement and for the creation of Conservative Jewish day schools.

After Gordis completed his term as Rabbinical Assembly president, he remained an active member of the RA's Committee on Jewish Law and Standards (CJLS). In 1970 he chaired the Special Committee on the Revitalization of the Law Committee, formed in the wake of the resignation of the majority of the members of the CJLS. Elsewhere in the Conservative movement, he was a member of the National Administrative Council of the United Synagogue and the Board of Governors of the National Academy of Adult Jewish Studies. A confirmed Zionist and chairman of the National Education Committee of the Zionist Organization of America, Gordis called for the creation of the Movement for the Reaffirmation of Conservative Zionism. MERCAZ works for the recognition of equal rights for all interpretations of Judaism in the state of Israel.

Outside the Conservative movement, Gordis's interests extended to church-state, interracial, and civic affairs. He was a member of the Council on Religious Freedom of the National Conference of Christians and Jews and the Board of Directors of the Institute of Church and State of Villanova University; honorary trustee of the Council for Religious and International Affairs; and a member of the Board of Directors of the John LaFarge Institute, an organization dedicated to interracial justice. He was also a member of the National Council of the Boy Scouts of America and honorary commissioner for life of the National Hillel Commission of B'nai B'rith. During a sabbatical from Temple Beth-El and the Seminary he served as the only Jewish consultant to the Center for Study of Democratic Institutions, Santa Barbara, California (1960–61).

In addition to this extraordinarily active career of service, Gordis wrote more than twenty books on Biblical scholarship, Conservative Judaism, the relationship of Judaism to contemporary problems, and the status of Judaism in the modern world. The following highlights just suggest the range of Gordis's scholarship and writings. His Biblical scholarship explored wisdom literature, especially the books of Ecclesiastes and Job; the forms of rhetoric and Biblical poetry; and aspects of the preservation of the Biblical text. *The Book of Job: Commentary, New Translation, and Special Studies* (1978) was the culmination of a lifetime of study of that text. *Understanding Conservative Judaism* (1978), a collection of essays written over several decades on the key issues of Conservatism, was published by the Rabbinical Assembly as the second volume in its series Studies in Contemporary Jewish Thought. *Love and Sex* (1978), part of a growing Jewish literature on contemporary marriage and human sexuality, written for the Women's League of Conservative Judaism, won a National Jewish Book Award.

Gordis was also one of the founders of *Judaism* (1950–   ), a quarterly published by the American Jewish Congress as a forum for the expression of all Jewish points of view on the "philosophy, ethics, and religion of Judaism as a factor in the contemporary world." He chaired its editorial board (1950–69) and since 1969 has served as editor.

Gordis married Fannie Jacobson in 1928; they have three sons.

Writings: *Conservative Judaism: An American Philosophy* (New York, 1945); "The Tasks Before Us: A Preface to Our Journal," *CJ* 1, 1 (January 1945), pp. 1–8; "New Vistas for Conservative Judaism," *PRA 1946* vol. 10 (1947), pp. 58–84; *Koheleth: The Man and His World* (New York, 1951); *Judaism for the Modern Age* (New York, 1955); "Reinterpretation—Its Canons and Limits," *CJ* 13, 4 (Summer 1959), pp. 21–26; *A Faith for Moderns* (New York, 1960); *The Root and the Branch: Judaism and the Free Society* (Chicago, 1962); "A Program for Conservative Judaism," *Review* 16, 4 (Winter 1964), pp. 18ff; *The Book of God and Man: A Study of Job* (Chicago, 1965); *Judaism in a Christian World* (New York, 1966); *Sex and the Family in Jewish Tradition* (New York, 1967); *Leave a Little to God* (New York, 1967); *Poets, Prophets, and Sages: Essays in Biblical Translation* (Indiana, 1971); *The Biblical Text in the Making* (New York, 1971); *The Song of Songs and Lamentations: A Study, Modern Translation, and Commentary*, 2 vols. (1954, 1958; rev., 1 vol., New York, 1974); *The Word and the Book: Studies in Biblical Language and Literature* (New York, 1976); *The Book of Job: Commentary, New Translation, and Special Studies* (1978); *Love and Sex: A Modern Jewish Perspective* (New York, 1978); *Understanding Conservative Judaism* (New York, 1978). Ed., *Sabbath and Festival Prayer Book* (New York, 1946).

References: *American Jewish Biographies*, p. 141; *CJ* 32, 2 (Winter 1979), pp. 104–5; *CJ* 33, 2 (Winter 1980), pp. 92–93; *EJ* vol. 7, col. 789; Salomon Faber, "Robert Gordis: A Tribute on the Occasion of His Seventy-fifth Birthday," *Jewish Book Annual* vol. 40 (1982–83), pp. 139–44; *WWAJ* 1980, p. 185.

GORDON, ALBERT ISAAC (1903–68). Rabbi, author. The son of Hyman Samuel and Martha Rosenzweig Gordon, Albert Gordon was born in Cleveland, Ohio, on May 11, 1903. Educated in the Cleveland public schools, Gordon earned an A.B. from New York University in 1927, was ordained at the Seminary in 1929, and earned a Ph.D. from the University of Minnesota in 1949.

Gordon first served as rabbi at Temple Israel, Washington Heights, New York City, and at Congregation Keneseth Israel-Beth Sholom in Kansas City, Missouri. In 1930 he moved to Minneapolis, Minnesota, to become rabbi of Adath Jeshurun Synagogue (1930–46). Founded in 1884 by Russian and Rumanian Jewish immigrants, Adath Jeshurun had no English-speaking rabbis until it invited Seminary graduate C. David *Matt in 1911. When Gordon arrived in 1930, he found the congregation in the midst of change. Although its younger members wished to retain many customs, they were no longer as traditional as their parents. With the backing of those members desirous of some change, Gordon moved to modernize the service. He also held study classes, organized the sisterhood and men's clubs, inaugurated a public issues forum, and started numerous youth activities. These programs attracted new members, and the congregation grew from 85 to 410 families, which enabled it to pay off its debts.

In addition to his congregational responsibilities in Minneapolis, Gordon conducted a weekly radio broadcast for ten years, was involved in labor arbitration (1934–46), and was a representative to the War Labor Board (1943–47). He was also instrumental in founding Mount Sinai Hospital and the Minneapolis Round Table of Christians and Jews and was president of the Minneapolis Federation for Jewish Service.

In November 1946 Gordon was appointed executive director of the United Synagogue (1946–49). He began to reorganize and expand this branch of the Conservative movement to enhance the participation of the laity, to make the United Synagogue its voice within Conservatism, and to give its members a sense of belonging to a national movement. After working to smooth over frictions among the various branches of the United Synagogue, the Rabbinical Assembly, and the Seminary, Gordon set out to expand its programs. Among the first steps of his administration was the establishment of the Cantor's Assembly in 1947, later followed by the first conference of Conservative synagogue administrators. Among the most important projects initiated was the founding of the first Camp Ramah under the auspices of the Chicago Council of the United Synagogue. In order to develop the United Synagogue, Gordon traveled extensively throughout the United States helping to establish new congregations, and he launched a publications program of synagogue aids. This work inaugurated an era of tremendous expansion in the United Synagogue, which grew from 293 member congregations in 1947 to 365, organized into seventeen regions, just two years later. Gordon, however, envisioned an organization that was more than a service agency to member congregations. He believed that to strengthen the United Synagogue, it was necessary to clarify Conservative ideology. This led to the launching of a Committee on the Philosophy of Conservative Judaism. Its failure and other frustrations spurred Gordon to resign in order to return to the pulpit full time.

In 1950 Gordon became rabbi of Temple Emanuel, Newton Center, Massachusetts (1950–68). Under his direction, the synagogue, founded in 1935, expanded tremendously, growing from 250 to 1,300 families. In 1950 Temple Emanuel had 300 children enrolled in a Sunday school, but only some 85 children attended Hebrew school. By 1958, of the more than 1,000 children in its school, 900 studied in the four-day-a-week Hebrew school, which had already gained a national reputation for excellence. The growth required the synagogue to add a community hall and sixteen-room school. Gordon also developed innovative youth and senior citizens programs and a special class for the parents of Bar and Bat Mitzvah children. In 1953, in recognition of his outstanding accomplishments, the congregation awarded their rabbi life tenure. Gordon also taught at Andover-Newton Theological School (1952–68) and was instructor in sociology at Boston University (1960–68), president of the New England Region of the Rabbinical Assembly, and a member of the Federal Mediation and Conciliation Service (1949–68).

A sociologist by training as well as a rabbi, Gordon wrote four major sociological studies. In *Jews in Transition* (1949) he described the accommodation of the East European Jewish immigrants to Minneapolis and documented that their struggle for acceptance as Americans led to a marked cultural loss of traditional rituals and religious practices. His next work, *Jews in Suburbia* (1959), was based to a great extent on observations gathered in his travels across the United States for the United Synagogue. In *Intermarriage* (1964) he predicted, based on a national survey of 150 intermarried couples, that all forms of intermarriage would increase as religious and ethnic distinctions among Americans waned in the relatively open American society. For his final work, *The Nature of Conversion* (1967), Gordon interviewed forty-five men and women—including Jews by choice and some who left Judaism—to elucidate the factors motivating their conversions. In addition to these studies, he wrote several booklets for the United Synagogue.

Gordon married Dorothy Etta Davis in 1929; they had two children. He died in Boston on November 5, 1968.

Writings: *How to Celebrate the Jewish Holy Days* (New York, 1946–47); ''The United Synagogue: A Vision for the Future,'' *PRA 1947* (1948) vol. 11, pp. 356–62; *In Times of Sorrow* (New York, 1948); *Bride and Groom* (New York, 1948); *Jews in Transition* (Minneapolis, 1949); *Jews in Suburbia* (Boston, 1959); *Intermarriage: Interfaith, Interethnic, and Interracial* (Boston, 1964); *The Nature of Conversion* (Boston, 1967).

References: Abraham J. Karp, *A History of the United Synagogue of America, 1913–1963* (New York, 1964), pp. 74–83; *National Cyclopedia of American Biography* vol. 55 (1974), pp. 447–48; *NYT* 7 November 1968, p. 47; *News of the United Synagogue of America* (December 1946); *PRA 1947* vol. 11 (1948), pp. 130–31, 138; *PRA 1949* vol. 13 (1950), pp. 107–09; *PRA 1956* vol. 20 (1957), pp. 176–77; *PRA 1969* vol. 33 (1969), pp. 176–77; Joseph P. Schultz, ''The Consensus of 'Civil Judaism': The Religious Life of Kansas City Jewry,'' in *Mid-America's Promise: A Profile of Kansas City Jewry*, ed. Joseph P. Schultz (Kansas City, 1982), p. 21; Marshall Sklare, *Conservative Judaism* (1955; rev. 1972; reprint ed., Lanham, Md., 1985), pp. 219–22.

GREENBERG, LOUIS (1894–1946). Rabbi, author. Born on November 1, 1893, in New Constantine, Russia, Louis Greenberg completed a traditional Talmudic education before immigrating to New York in 1913. There he supported himself by teaching Hebrew, Jewish history, and Bible in advanced Hebrew schools while acquiring an American education. He earned a B.A. from the City College of New York in 1924; was ordained at the Seminary in 1926, having completed the rabbinic course in three years; and in 1940 earned a Ph.D. from Yale University.

Greenberg first served as rabbi at Congregation Beth El, New Rochelle, New York (1926–28). Founded in 1909 as the Hebrew Institute, the congregation was meeting in rented quarters. Greenberg helped the congregants complete their fund-raising drive and dedicated Beth El's first synagogue in 1927.

In 1928 he left New Rochelle for B'nai Jacob Congregation, New Haven, Connecticut (1928–46). This congregation, which had been established in 1912, had already instituted mixed seating, late Friday night services, and a mixed choir. Greenberg carried these ritual innovations further, introducing an organ and permitting the mixed choir to perform on High Holidays. To meet the needs of the growing congregation, he expanded the school program and oversaw the extension of the synagogue. Active in communal, religious, and interfaith affairs, he was a leader in local Jewish organizations, including the Zionist Organization of America, and was a member of the New Haven Council of Churches and Round Table of Christians and Jews.

Greenberg's rabbinical duties at B'nai Jacob allowed him sufficient time to complete his doctorate at Yale University and to write a major historical study, *The Jews in Russia: The Struggle for Emancipation* (1944–51). It explored the rise and development of the movement for civil rights carried on by Russian Jewry in the nineteenth century, surveyed the parochial attitudes of the Russian tsars toward their Jewish subjects, and traced the rise of the *Haskalah* movement.

Greenberg married Bessie Rutberg; they had one daughter. He died in Lebanon, Connecticut, on February 7, 1946.

Writing: *The Jews in Russia: The Struggle for Emancipation*, 2 vols. (1944–51; reprint ed., New Haven, Conn., 1965, 1976).

References: *AJYB* vol. 48 (1946–47), p. 490; Stanley Irving Batkin, *Let Them Make Me a Sanctuary* (New York, 1978); *B'nai Jacob: One Hundred Years, 1882–1982* (Woodbridge, Conn., n.d.), pp. 11–12; *New Haven Journal-Courier* 8 February 1946, p. 1; *NYT* 8 February 1946, p. 19; *PRA 1946* vol. 10 (1947), pp. 243–46; Nahum Zilberberg, *The George Street Synagogue of Congregation B'nai Jacob* (New Haven, Conn., 1961).

GREENBERG, SIDNEY (1917–). Rabbi, author. The son of Morris and Sadie Armel Greenberg, Sidney Greenberg was born in Brooklyn, New York, on September 27, 1917. Educated at the Hirsh Laib Berlin Yeshivah in East New York, he earned a B.A. from Yeshiva University in 1938, was ordained at the Seminary in 1942, and earned a Doctor of Hebrew Letters there in 1947.

Greenberg has the distinction of having led but one congregation—Temple Sinai, located originally in Philadelphia and later in Dresher, Pennsylvania— and Temple Sinai has the distinction of having had but one rabbi since its founding in 1942. With Greenberg's guidance, Temple Sinai became one of the leading Conservative synagogues in Philadelphia, receiving several Solomon Schechter awards for innovative programming in the Conservative movement. Temple Sinai's Board of Directors was among the first in the movement to require both

regular attendance at Sabbath services and participation in some program of
Jewish study for all board members. Greenberg's commitment to women's equality led to according ritual equality to women in the synagogue. A Zionist, in
1968 he inaugurated Temple Sinai's annual pilgrimage to Israel. Believing that
the mission of the synagogue is making the Jewish family more Jewish, he
founded the Temple Sinai Family Council. Composed of representatives of the
synagogue's auxiliaries—Sisterhood, Men's Club, youth groups, and school—
the council planned programs involving the entire family. His pastoral duties in
counseling mourners inspired his first book, *A Treasury of Comfort* (1954), to
soften the grief and offer the bereaved the courage and faith to carry on with
their lives.

In addition to his congregational activities, Greenberg wrote a weekly column
for the *Philadelphia Inquirer* (1978–82) and Philadelphia's *Jewish Exponent*
(1982–   ). Here he mastered the art of "reduc[ing] a good idea to 700 nice
concrete words," and he collected the best of these in *Say Yes to Life* (1982).
He also served on the editorial boards of *The Jewish Digest* and *The Reconstructionist*, the executive boards of the United Synagogue of America, Technion,
and Bonds for Israel, and chaired the Committee of 1,000 for Soviet Jewry. In
the Rabbinical Assembly he was a member of the Executive Committee (1950–
53) and president of the Philadelphia Region (1953–55).

A masterful preacher, noted for his encyclopedic command of Jewish and
general sources and the ability to relate their teachings to the problems of contemporary men and women, Greenberg published several volumes of sermons.
A graceful liturgist, he edited and translated a number of prayer books, including
several services for children and youth. He also compiled several anthologies,
including *Light from Jewish Lamps* (1960; rev. 1986), a collection of modern
writers' statements on Jewish deeds, doctrines, and destinies. He also taught
homiletics, both at the Seminary and at the Reconstructionist Rabbinical College.

Greenberg married Hilda Weiss in 1942; they have three daughters.

Writings: *Adding Life to Our Years* (New York, 1959); "Raising Standards for
Synagogue Leadership," *Review* 13, 3 (Autumn 1960), pp. 8–9; *Finding Ourselves* (New
York, 1964); "Making the Jewish Family More Jewish," *Beineinu* 3, 2 (May 1973),
p. 64; *Say Yes to Life* (New York, 1982); *Lessons for Living* (New York, 1985). Ed., *A
Treasury of Comfort* (New York, 1954; rev. 1974); *Light from Jewish Lamps: A Modern
Treasury of Jewish Thoughts* (New York, 1960; rev. 1986); *A Treasury of the Art of
Living* (Hartford, Conn., 1963); *Likrat Shabbat* (Bridgeport, Conn., 1973). Co-ed., with
Abraham Rothberg, *The Bar Mitzvah Companion* (New York, 1959); with Morris Sil-
verman, *Our Prayer Book* (Hartford, Conn., 1961); with S. Allan Sugarman, *Sabbath
and Festival Services for Children* (Hartford, Conn., 1970); with Jonathan Levine, *The
New Mahzor* (Bridgeport, Conn., 1977).

Reference: *WWWJ* 1965, p. 365.

GREENBERG, SIMON (1901–   ). Rabbi, educator, administrator. The son
of Morris and Bessie Chaidenko Greenberg, Simon Greenberg was born in
Horoshen, Russia, on January 8, 1901. Brought to the United States in 1905,

he was educated in the public schools and Talmud Torah in Woodridge, New York. He graduated from the Teachers Institute in 1919, attended the University of Minnesota (1920–21), and earned a B.A. from the City College of New York in 1922. Greenberg then studied in Jerusalem at the American School for Oriental Research and was the first American student at Hebrew University (1924–25). Ordained at the Seminary in 1925, he earned a Ph.D. from Dropsie College, Philadelphia, in 1932.

Greenberg served as rabbi at Har Zion Temple, Philadelphia, Pennsylvania (1925–46). Organized in the Wynnefield section of Philadelphia in 1922, Har Zion erected its synagogue in 1924. Benefiting from Greenberg's gifted and superior spritual leadership, the congregation became a model synagogue-center and the "religious standard-bearer" of the Conservative movement. Once early financial difficulties were overcome, he turned his energies to organizing a variety of activities—a nursery, kindergarten, youth groups, adult study circles, Men's Club Adult Institute, Young People's League, "Har Zion Bulletin," and others—designed to entice congregants of all ages. The many activities required extended facilities, and in 1941 the congregation dedicated its expanded synagogue and new school building. Under Greenberg's leadership Har Zion was noted for its outstanding support of Zionist and Hebrew cultural organizations and the Seminary. Consequently, a survey of its congregants' home religious practices, conducted in the 1950s, which revealed a shockingly low observance of *kashrut* and *Shabbat*, provoked painful questions about the success of Conservatism's ideology and aims.

A leader in Philadelphia's civic and Jewish communal affairs, Greenberg was a founder and director of the Philadelphia Psychiatric Hospital (1937–39), president of the Philadelphia branch of the Zionist Organization of America (1940–43) and chairman of its national education committee (1943–45), and a founder of Akiba Day School.

In 1931, while continuing at Har Zion, Greenberg was invited by Cyrus *Adler to teach education at the Seminary. Groomed by Adler and Louis *Ginzberg for leadership, he eventually held major positions in all the national organizations of the Conservative movement.

As president of the Rabbinical Assembly (1937–39), Greenberg presided over its 300 members. To unite this large and growing body, his administration inaugurated the *Rabbinical Assembly Bulletin*. Recognizing that cooperation among the national organizations of the movement was essential to its growth, Greenberg worked closely with Louis *Finkelstein and Max *Arzt to link the fund-raising efforts of the Seminary to those of the United Synagogue and Rabbinical Assembly. This cooperation resulted in the development of the Joint Campaign for Conservative Judaism, which paved the way for the growth of all its national agencies. His administration also issued the RA's first "Pronouncement on Zionism," and it managed for the first time in seven years to publish a volume of the *Proceedings of the Rabbinical Assembly*. Greenberg was also the first president of the Rabbinical Assembly to greet officially his Reform brethren, the Central Conference of American Rabbis.

In 1946 Greenberg left Har Zion, where he was succeeded by David Goldstein, to work full time toward strengthening the national institutions of Conservatism. In addition to his responsibilities as professor of education at the Seminary (1932– 68), Greenberg became professor of homiletics (1946–), provost (1946–52), and vice-chancellor and president of the faculties (1950–). Recognizing that it was imperative for the Conservative movement to establish a strong presence in the growing Jewish community on the West Coast, he helped found the University of Judaism, serving as its president (1948–63) and chancellor (1963– 68), and after 1968 as its chancellor emeritus.

As executive director of the United Synagogue (1950–53), Greenberg initiated several projects of long-range importance. He worked with the Rabbinical Assembly to launch the Sabbath Revitalization Campaign. The United Synagogue's Commission on Jewish Education expanded its publication program and explored the possibility of developing a network of Ramah camps. United Synagogue Youth was chartered, and the United Synagogue took over the National Academy for Adult Jewish Studies. Greenberg also paved the way for the adoption of the "Guide to Standards for Congregational Life," and he committed the United Synagogue to building a *penimiah* in Jerusalem, a residence hall for scholars and students. This was the first project the United Synagogue had sponsored in Israel since it built the Yeshurun Synagogue in the 1920s.

Greenberg is perhaps best known among Conservative laity for his work as an educator. Along with Moshe *Davis and others, he formulated the ideology and blueprints for Jewish education in the Conservative synagogue that included Hebrew, history, Bible, and the indoctrination of Jewish values and ethics. He incorporated these ideas in the *Ha-rishon* series of textbooks, published by the United Synagogue's Joint Commission on Jewish Education. For adult study circles, Greenberg wrote for the National Academy for Adult Jewish Studies *The Ideals of the Jewish Prayer Book*, a modern reinterpretation of the sacred Hebrew liturgy designed to offer an alternative to meaningless, rote congregational prayer. In his pamphlet *The Conservative Movement in Judaism* he dealt with Conservatism's four cardinal principles—scientific study of the past, understanding of Judaism as a Torah-centered civilization embracing all areas of life, commitment to the unity of the Jewish people, and an acknowledgment of diversity of practice among its congregations that does not mar the essential unity of the movement.

One of the most articulate spokesman for Conservative Judaism and a student of the interaction of Jewish and American ideals, Greenberg reluctantly accepted the fact that Conservatism had become but one of the denominations of modern Judaism. He did not favor an official authoritative program for the movement, arguing that each rabbi should define this for himself. In his collection of essays *Foundations of Faith* (1967), a "modern *Guide for the Perplexed*," he offered general principles for adapting Jewish law to the contemporary world. Yet, because he believed in the primacy and centrality of divine revelation, he stressed the binding nature of Jewish law, even of commandments inexplicable in twentieth-century terms.

A Zionist who in an early period had been attracted to the religious Mizrachi political party and who was a member of the Executive Committee of the World Zionist Organization (1963–68), he worked to establish the distinctive Conservative viewpoint in Israel, organizing, developing, and helping to finance Israel programs for the Seminary. This led in 1984 to his appointment as the first executive director of the Foundation for Conservative (*Masorti*) Judaism in Israel (1984–).

In 1925 Greenberg married Betty Davis; they have three children.

Writings: "President's Message," *PRA 1938* vol. 5 (1939), pp. 422–31; "President's Message," *PRA 1939* vol. 5 (1940), pp. 20–36; *Living as a Jew Today* (New York, 1940); *The Ideals of the Jewish Prayer Book* (New York, 1940); *Ha-rishon Series: Five Texts for the First Two Years of Hebrew Studies* (1940; reprint ed., New York, 1954); "Educational Content in Terms of Contemporary Needs: Elementary Jewish Schools," *PRA 1943* vol. 8 (1947), pp. 182–90; *The First Year in the Hebrew School: A Teacher's Guide* (New York, 1946); *The Conservative Movement in Judaism: An Introduction* (New York, 1955); "Some Guiding Principles for a Conservative Approach to Judaism," *PRA 1957* vol. 21 (1958), pp. 69–124; *Foundations of Faith* (New York, 1967); "And He Writes Her a Bill of Divorcement," *CJ* 29, 3 (Spring 1970), pp. 75–141; *The Ethical in the Jewish and American Heritage* (New York, 1977); *A Jewish Philosophy and Pattern of Life* (New York, 1981).

References: *EJ* vol. 7, col. 906; *The Har Zion Temple, 1924–1949* (Philadelphia, 1949); Abraham J. Karp, *A History of the United Synagogue of America, 1913–1963* (New York, 1964), pp. 83–90; Abraham E. Millgram, "Implementing a Program of Intensive Jewish Education in the Congregational School," *CJ* 5, 4 (June 1949), pp. 1–9; *PRA 1981* vol. 43 (1982), pp. 6–7; Marshall Sklare, *Conservative Judaism* (1955; rev. 1972, reprint ed., 1985), pp. 144, 274–75; *WWAJ* 1980, p. 192.

GREENFELD, WILLIAM P. (1906–60). Rabbi. The son of Hayim and Sarah Greenfeld, William Greenfeld was born in the Ukraine on May 8, 1906, and brought to the United States in 1907. Educated in the Boston public schools, he earned an A.B. at Harvard in 1928 and was ordained at the Seminary in 1932.

Greenfeld first led Congregation Beth El, Waterbury, Connecticut (1932–46). Founded in 1924, Beth El under Greenfeld grew from 65 to 240 families and established a men's club. Active in local and even international Jewish affairs, Greenfeld helped organize the Jewish Federation Appeal of Waterbury, served on the Administrative Council of the Zionist Organization of America, and was a delegate to the World Jewish Congress (1936) and the World Zionist Congress (1939).

In 1946 Greenfeld became rabbi of Beth-El Zedeck, Indianapolis, Indiana (1946–60), the only Conservative congregation in Indianapolis and one of the leading Conservative congregations in the Midwest. Founded when two congregations, Beth El and Ohev Zedeck, merged in 1927, Beth-El Zedeck had earlier been led by Seminary rabbis Milton *Steinberg (1928–33), Elias Charry (1933–42), and Israel Chodos (1942–46). Greenfeld supervised the construction of its new synagogue (1958) and oversaw the congregation's expansion from 375 to nearly 1,000 families. More importantly, Greenfeld, who hoped for a synthesis of Reconstructionism and Conservatism, was influential in guiding Beth-El Zedeck toward Reconstructionism. He introduced ritual changes consonant with its ideology, such as abolishing the hierarchy of Cohen, Levi, and Israelite Torah honors; introducing Bat Mitzvah; granting women *aliyot*; and allowing for the counting of women in the *minyan* some two decades before this became Conservatism's policy. Active in 1955 in the organization of the Federation of Reconstructionist Congregations and Havurot, Greenfeld led Beth-El Zedeck to join the fledgling Reconstructionist body while maintaining its affiliation with Conservatism's United Synagogue. In Indianapolis he was also active in local Jewish and civic affairs, including the American Civil Liberties Union and the National Association for the Advancement of Colored People.

One of his great loves was the study of the Talmud. Not surprisingly, he was especially sensitive to the dilemmas faced by rabbis out in the field trying to mete out decisions consonant with Jewish law and concerned with the Rabbinical Assembly's role in making that law viable for contemporary Jews. At its convention in 1948, Greenfeld delivered one of the three major addresses in the symposium, "Towards a Philosophy of Conservative Judaism," which led to the formation of the new Committee on Jewish Law and Standards. He was its co-chair (1957–58) and a leader in Conservatism's Sabbath Revitalization Campaign (1951). He was also secretary of the Rabbinical Assembly (1951).

Greenfeld married Buzya Bluma Gedrich in 1932; they had one daughter. He died in Indianapolis on October 21, 1960.

Writings: "How Can Religion Make the Home and Family Life More Effective," *PRA 1940* vol. 7 (1941), pp. 190–96; "Towards a Philosophy of Conservative Judaism," *PRA 1948* vol. 12 (1949), pp. 121–28; "The Revitalization of the Sabbath," *PRA 1951* vol. 15 (1952), pp. 112–13; "Future Prospects of the Beth Din," *PRA 1957* vol. 21 (1958), pp. 175–81.

GREENSTONE, JULIUS HILLEL (1873–1955). Rabbi, educator, author. The son of Pesah David and Leah Puskelinsky Grunstein, Julius Greenstone was born in Mariampol, Lithuania, on April 25 (23?), 1873. He immigrated to the United States in 1894. Educated in Russia in the *cheder* and in the Talmudical College, Greenstone earned a B.A. from the City College of New York and was ordained at the Seminary in 1900. He earned another B.A. (1902) and a Ph.D. from the University of Pennsylvania in 1905.

After serving briefly at Congregation Mikveh Israel, Philadelphia (1900–1902), Greenstone joined the faculty of Gratz College in Philadelphia. There he taught religion and education (1905–33) and served as principal (1933–48) and as principal emeritus (1948–55).

Greenstone was one of the early leaders of Conservatism. In 1901 he helped found the Alumni Association of the Jewish Theological Seminary of America, the forerunner of the Rabbinical Assembly. As early as 1904, he proposed to the association that it establish a *bet din* to determine religious matters and to handle controversies. An active member of the RA's Committee on Jewish Law from its beginnings in 1927 until his death, Greenstone chaired the committee (1932–36) as it struggled to define the scope of its powers and as it began to debate the *agunah* issue.

As an educator, Greenstone worked with the United Synagogue to improve the quality of Jewish education. In 1914 Greenstone and Mordecai M. *Kaplan surveyed congregational schools for the United Synagogue, and Greenstone subsequently chaired its Education Committee (1920–25) as it began producing textbooks for those schools.

Greenstone was among the first American Jews to write books of popular Jewish scholarship in English. *The Religion of Israel* (1902), a textbook for religious instruction based on "conservative principles," was subsequently rewritten and expanded into *The Jewish Religion* (1920). *The Messiah Idea in Jewish History* (1906) traced the concept of messianism in Jewish literature. Greenstone's commentaries on Numbers and Proverbs appeared in the series Holy Scriptures with Commentary published by the Jewish Publication Society. In addition to his substantial contributions to the *Jewish Encyclopedia*, Greenstone wrote for some twenty years a popular, though scholarly, column, "About Men and Things," for the Philadelphia weekly, *Jewish Exponent*. Some of these essays were collected in *Jewish Feasts and Fasts* (1945).

Greenstone married Carrie E. Amram. He subsequently married Ray Steinhardt Abeles in 1916; they had three daughters. Greenstone died in Philadelphia on March 7, 1955.

Writings: *The Religion of Israel* (1902; reprint ed., Philadelphia, 1929); *The Messiah Idea in Jewish History* (1906; reprint ed., Philadelphia, 1943); *The Jewish Religion* (Philadelphia, 1920); "Reminiscences of Old Seminary Days," *Recorder* 6, 4 (October 1926), pp. 9–10; *The Book of Numbers with Commentary* (Philadelphia, 1939); *Jewish Feasts and Fasts* (New York, 1945); *The Book of Proverbs with Commentary* (Philadelphia, 1950).

References: *AJYB* vol. 6 (1904–5), p. 106; *EJ* vol. 7, cols. 911–12; *Philadelphia Inquirer* 8 March 1955, p. 33; Herbert Rosenblum, "The Founding of the United Synagogue of America, 1913" (Ph.D. diss., Brandeis University, 1970), p. 240; Max Routtenberg, *Decades of Decision* (New York, 1973), p. 135; *WWWJ* 1955, p. 295.

GUTSTEIN, MORRIS AARON (1905–86). Rabbi, author. The son of Naftali and Sarah Pearl Taubes, Morris Gutstein was born on February 26, 1905, in Ottynia, Galicia. He earned a B.S. from New York University in 1929, was ordained at the Seminary in 1932, and earned a Ph.D. from Webster University in 1939. In 1948 he earned a Doctor of Hebrew Letters from the Seminary and in 1974 a certificate in psychotherapy from the Chicago Medical School.

After serving as rabbi at Temple Beth El, Long Beach, New York (1929–32), Gutstein became rabbi at the Touro Synagogue of Congregation Yeshuat Yisrael in Newport, Rhode Island (1932–43), the oldest extant synagogue in America. In the colonial era the Touro Synagogue had had a distinguished history. In 1790 its congregants congratulated George Washington upon his election to the presidency. His response confirmed that the U.S. Constitution "to bigotry gives no sanction." But the Revolutionary War had ruined Newport's trade and already its residents were abandoning the city. By 1822 not a single Jew remained, and the synagogue was closed. For the next half-century it remained shuttered, but the building was maintained by bequests from the Touro family, whose patriarch, Isaac Touro, had been the synagogue's first *hazzan*.

In 1883 the synagogue was reopened. As East European Jewish immigrants once again built a Jewish community in Newport, the congregation was revived, and the Touro Synagogue declared a national historic shrine. As rabbi, Gutstein presided over Touro Synagogue's celebrations of the Rhode Island Tercentenary (1936) and the Newport Tercentenary (1939), as well as the festivities commemorating the fiftieth anniversary of the reopening of the synagogue.

In Newport Gutstein began to write Jewish communal historical studies. These histories often had a contemporary interest. *The Story of the Jews of Newport* (1936), a history of the community primarily in the colonial era, was written as the Touro Synagogue's literary contribution to the Rhode Island Tercentenary. Gutstein wrote *Aaron Lopez and Judah Touro* (1939) to counter agitation against harboring refugees from Nazism by presenting examples of two immigrants who enriched the United States.

In 1943 Gutstein left Rhode Island for Chicago. He led several congregations there: Humboldt Boulevard Temple (1943–47); Congregation Shaare Tikvah (1947–71), where he was elected rabbi emeritus in 1971; Congregation Etz Chaim, Flossmoor, Illinois (1971–75), where he was elected rabbi emeritus in 1975; and the North Sheridan Hebrew Congregation Adas Israel (1976–?). In his sermons Gutstein stressed that Conservative Judaism was "not really a new movement" but rather a stage in the "process of the traditional evolution of Judaism" from antiquity to the twentieth century.

In Chicago Gutstein continued his work in American Jewish history, turning now to write about Chicago Jewry in *A Priceless Heritage* (1953). Gutstein was also associate professor of American Jewish history at Chicago's College of Jewish Studies, later the Spertus College of Judaica, and in 1969 he became director of the Chicago Jewish Archives. He was also secretary of the Chicago Rabbinical Association (1945–46), chairman of its Executive Committee (1947–52), and a member of the Executive Committee of the Zionist Organization of Chicago (1946–56).

Gutstein married Goldie Leah Nussbaum in 1929; they had two sons. He died in Chicago in 1986.

Writings: *The Touro Family in Newport* (Newport, R.I., 1935); *The Story of the Jews of Newport: Two and a Half Centuries of Judaism, 1658–1908* (New York, 1936);

Aaron Lopez and Judah Touro: A Refugee and a Son of a Refugee (New York, 1939); *A Priceless Heritage: The Epic Growth of Nineteenth-Century Chicago Jewry* (New York, 1953); *To Bigotry No Sanction, 1658–1958* (New York, 1958); *Frontiers of Faith: Sermonic Discourses on the Weekly Biblical Readings* (New York, 1967); *Profiles of Freedom: Essays in American Jewish History* (New York, 1967); *The Dignity of Man* (New York, 1971); *Faith and Form: An Exhibition* (Chicago, 1976). Co-ed., *The Holy Scriptures: A Jewish Family Bible* (1955). Ed. and trans., *Passover Haggadah* (New York, 1966); *Yom Kippur Eve Service* (1969).

References: *EJ* vol. 12, cols. 1042–43; *WWAJ* 1980, p. 202.

H

HADAS, GERSHON (1896–1980). Rabbi. The son of David and Gitel Draizin Hadas, Gershon Hadas was born in Volkovisk, Poland, on July 9, 1896, and brought to the United States in 1900. Raised in an enlightened and pious home in Atlanta, Georgia, Hadas earned a B.A. from Columbia University in 1918 and was ordained at the Seminary in 1922.

Hadas began his rabbinic career at the First Hebrew Congregation, Peekskill, New York (1922–25), and at Sons of Israel Congregation, New Britain, Connecticut (1925–29). In 1929 he became rabbi of Congregation Keneseth Israel-Beth Shalom (Beth Sholom), Kansas City, Missouri, a Conservative congregation whose former rabbis included Samuel M. *Cohen and Albert *Gordon. The original congregation, Keneseth Israel, had splintered in 1915 when a number of members, angered over Keneseth Israel's refusal to affiliate with the United Synagogue, formed Beth Shalom. The two congregations reunited in 1924, but when Hadas arrived five years later, he found the congregation fragmented by serious differences and burdened by substantial debt. Hadas battled throughout the Depression to unite the congregation and to pay off the deficit. His urbanity and culture, combined with fund-raising and organizational skills, made him the ideal leader of this midwestern congregation, which offered Kansas City Jewry an alternative to the Reform stronghold, Congregation B'nai Jehudah.

Hadas built Keneseth Israel-Beth Shalom into a synagogue-center modeled on the Reconstructionist ideology of his teacher Mordecai M. *Kaplan. He initiated a variety of social, cultural, and athletic programs designed to appeal to all segments of Kansas City Jewry. For the youth he established a Young Peoples' League, a Boy Scout troop, and a summer recreational program. For the adults, he developed Confirmation and graduation ceremonies, graced by cantatas and noted for their pageantry, and he established a synagogue museum of ceremonial objects. These activities and the aesthetic appeal of Keneseth Israel-Beth Shalom revitalized and united the congregation and attracted new members.

Hadas employed the Reconstructionist concept of Jewish folkways to meet the needs of both the traditional and more liberal segments of his congregation. At the same time that he maintained traditional daily, Sabbath, and holiday services, Hadas used the Reconstructionist *Haggadah* at the annual congregational *seder*.

A leader among Kansas City Jewry, Hadas played a major role in the founding of the Jewish Federation of Kansas City in 1933. He was active among the General Zionists and was one of several Kansas City Zionists who helped enlighten Eddie Jacobson, President Truman's former business partner, about Zionism, so that Jacobson could in turn present Zionism to Truman. Hadas was also contributing editor to the *Kansas City Jewish Chronicle* and head of the Guardian Society for Jewish Children. And he cooperated with other local rabbis in joint ventures, such as prayer services, helping to offset the pull of denominationalism in Kansas City.

In 1961 Hadas retired as senior rabbi of Congregation Beth Shalom, as it was now called. In his thirty-two-year career at Beth Shalom, he had made the congregation one of the leading Conservative congregations of the Midwest, as evidenced by the strong ties its laity had to national Conservative institutions such as the Seminary and Camp Ramah.

Although primarily a congregational rabbi, Hadas made a lasting contribution to Conservatism in liturgy. Chairman of the Daily Prayer Book Committee of the Rabbinical Assembly (1957–61), Hadas built upon the work of rabbis Jacob *Agus and Jack *Riemer in editing and translating the *Daily Prayer Book* (1961). During the 1960s he chaired the RA's Prayer Book Committee and also published a translation of the Book of Psalms.

Hadas married Anne Isenberg in 1924; they had two children. He died on December 11, 1980, in Kansas City, Missouri.

Writings: Trans., *The Book of Psalms: For the Modern Reader* (New York, 1964).

References: Carla L. Klausner, "The Zionist Spectrum," in *Mid-America's Promise: A Profile of Kansas City Jewry*, ed. Joseph P. Schultz (Kansas City, 1982), pp. 111, 115; Joseph P. Schultz, "The Consensus of 'Civil Judaism': The Religious Life of Kansas City Jewry," in *Mid-America's Promise*, pp. 21–27; *WWWJ* 1955, p. 309.

HAILPERIN, HERMAN (1899–1973). Rabbi, author. The son of Baer and Sarah Gutkin Hailperin, Herman Hailperin was born in Newark, New Jersey, on April 6, 1899. He earned a B.A. from New York University in 1919, was ordained at the Seminary in 1922, and earned a Ph.D. from the University of Pittsburgh in 1933.

In 1922 Hailperin became rabbi at Tree of Life Congregation, Pittsburgh, Pennsylvania, founded in the 1860s. He worked to transform Tree of Life into a Conservative synagogue-center. In addition to establishing several auxiliaries, such as a young folk's group which invited university faculty to speak, he moved the reading of the *megillah* on Purim to a late evening service. The congregation applauded Hailperin's efforts and elected him rabbi for life.

Hailperin introduced other innovations at Tree of Life typical of left-wing Conservative congregations. These included the playing of an organ at worship services and the abolition of the second day observance of festivals. This latter decision contravened the 1963 *responsum* of the Rabbinical Assembly's Committee on Jewish Law and Standards, in which the Committee unanimously called for a decade of experimentation to revitalize the observance of *Yom Tov Sheni*. In abrogating second day observance, Hailperin, who claimed that he had grappled with this problem for forty years, seriously challenged the authority of the Rabbinical Assembly. Until then the RA had held that unanimous decisions of the CJLS were binding on all members. The RA's choices in this test case were either to reprimand Hailperin, a former member of its Executive Committee and the Committee on Jewish Law and Standards, or to abandon this policy. The RA chose to abandon the policy of binding decisions.

A leader sensitive to the joys and sorrows of his congregants, Hailperin became rabbi emeritus of Tree of Life Congregation in 1968. In addition to his congregational responsibilities, he taught Jewish history at the University of Pittsburgh (1926–27, 1942–45) and at Duquesne University (1937–41).

A scholar who specialized in medieval thought and theology, Hailperin published *A Rabbi Teaches* (1939), several addresses commemorating the octocentennial of Maimonides' birth. In *Rashi and the Christian Scholars* (1963) he analyzed the cross-cultural influence of Rashi's Biblical commentary on medieval Christian scholars, especially the Franciscan Nicolaus de Lyra. In his final work, *The Three Great Religions*, he explored the cultural and theological interconnections among Judaism, Christianity, and Islam.

Hailperin married Harriet Silverman in 1922; they had two children. After her death, he married Celia Moss. Hailperin died on January 9, 1973, in Pittsburgh.

Writings: *A Rabbi Teaches: A Collection of Addresses and Sermons* (New York, 1939); *Rashi and the Christian Scholars* (Pittsburgh, 1963). Posthumously, *The Three Great Religions: Their Theological and Cultural Affinities* (Pittsburgh, 1978).

References: *NYT* 10 January 1973, p. 44; *PRA 1973* vol. 35 (1974), pp. 117–20; *Recorder* 4, 2 (April 1924), p. 15; 5, 2 (April 1925), p. 21; Phillip Sigal and Abraham J. Ehrlich, "A Responsum on Yom Tov Sheni Shel Galuyot," *CJ* 24, 2 (Winter 1970), p. 31; *WWWJ* 1965, p. 388.

HALPERN, HARRY (1899–1981). Rabbi. The son of David and Dora Seratchek Halpern, Harry Halpern was born on February 4, 1899, in New York City. Educated in the New York City public schools and at the Talmudical School of Brooklyn, he earned a B.A. from the City College of New York in 1919. He then studied at the Rabbi Isaac Elchanan Yeshiva (1919–22) and was ordained rabbi. While serving as rabbi at the Jewish Communal Center of Flatbush (1919–29), he pursued legal studies, earning an LL.B. (1925) and a J.D. (1926) at Brooklyn Law School. Halpern once again turned to rabbinical studies, this time at the Seminary, where he was ordained in 1929 and earned a Doctor of Hebrew Letters in 1951.

Following his graduation from the Seminary, Halpern became rabbi of the East Midwood Jewish Center in Brooklyn (1929–77). Organized in 1924, East Midwood was by 1929 one of the more elegant synagogue-centers in Brooklyn, boasting a million dollar structure and an annual budget of $55,000. It hosted numerous fraternal lodges, family circles, philanthropic societies, and Boy Scout troops. Noted for his rapier wit, Halpern taught and preached to his congregants not what they wished to hear, but what he believed they needed to learn, hammering away at Jewish indifference, complacency, and mediocrity. An advocate of intensive Jewish day school education long before it became fashionable, Halpern founded and taught for twenty-five years in the Rabbi Harry Halpern Day School that met at East Midwood.

A leader among New York Jewry in Jewish and civic affairs, he was a founder and benefactor of the Yeshivah of Flatbush, a co-educational school organized in 1922 with 22 students; by 1936 it had grown to 370 pupils. Halpern chaired its Board of Education and English Department. He was president of the Brooklyn Region of the Zionist Organization of America (1947–49) and a member of the National Executive (1954–56). He sat on the Board of Directors of the Pride of Judea Mental Health Center and of the Rabbinic Cabinet of the United Jewish Appeal of Greater New York. He was also a founder and life trustee of the Commission on Synagogue Relations of the Federation of Jewish Philanthropies and was also president of the largest board of rabbis in America, the New York Board of Rabbis (1961). A member of the Kings County Advisory Council of the New York State Commission Against Discrimination, he served on the Human Rights Commission (1967–78) and was a member of the executive committees of the Brooklyn Red Cross, Brooklyn Cancer Society, and New York Division of the National Conference of Christians and Jews.

Halpern worked assiduously on behalf of the Conservative movement. He was instrumental in organizing the Metropolitan New York Region of the Rabbinical Assembly in 1950. One of its first tasks was to arrange the celebration of the RA's jubilee convention with a city-wide rally held in Carnegie Hall. As president of the Rabbinical Assembly (1954–56), his administration resumed the publication of the temporarily discontinued quarterly *Conservative Judaism;* continued work on the *Weekday Prayer Book;* saw through the publication of the Rabbinical Assembly *ketubah*, which included the emendations of Seminary professor Saul *Lieberman; and established a Committee on Tenure and Related Matters. Halpern unsuccessfully pursued contacts with the Orthodox Rabbinical Council of America to see if the two bodies could agree upon the establishment of a national *bet din.* As chairman of the Joint Commission on Social Action of the Rabbinical Assembly and United Synagogue (1956–61), he worked to revitalize that body and strongly opposed federal aid to private and parochial schools.

Closely involved in the activities of the Seminary, Halpern chaired the Rabbinic Cabinet (1951–53), founded in 1951 by several rabbis to assist the Seminary with fund-raising. He served on the Seminary's Board of Directors (1951–53) and was national co-chairman of the Seminary Planning Commission. One of the founders of the Seminary's pastoral counseling program, he taught pastoral psychiatry and homiletics at the Seminary.

To commemorate his forty-fifth anniversary at the East Midwood Jewish Center, Halpern published *From Where I Stand* (1974), a collection of 160 columns that he had written over the years for the weekly synagogue bulletin.

He married Mollie Singer in 1941. Following her death, he married Jean Rosenhaus. Halpern had one daughter by his first wife. He died in New Haven, Connecticut, on June 10, 1981.

Writings: "President's Address," *PRA 1955* vol. 19 (1956), pp. 115–25; *PRA 1956* vol. 20 ((1957), pp. 71–81; *From Where I Stand* (New York, 1974).

References: Samuel Abelow, *History of Brooklyn Jewry* (Brooklyn, 1937), pp. 86–91, 138–40; *AJYB* vol. 83 (1983), p. 356; Deborah Dash Moore, *At Home in America: Second Generation New York Jews* (New York, 1981), pp. 135, 137, 141, 143; *NYT* 21 June 1981, p. D15; *PRA 1952* vol. 16 (1953), p. 88; *PRA 1954* vol. 18 (1955), pp. 129–30; *PRA 1959* vol. 23, pp. 22–23; *PRA 1982* vol. 44, pp. 155–57; *Recorder* 9, 3 (July 1929), p. 13; *WWWJ* 1965, p. 391.

HARLOW, JULES (1931–   ). Rabbi, liturgist, administrator. The son of Henry and Lena Lipman Harlow, Jules Harlow was born on June 28, 1931, in Sioux City, Iowa. In 1952 he earned a B.A. at Morningside College, Sioux City, and in 1959 was ordained at the Seminary.

Fresh out of the Seminary, Harlow joined the staff of the Rabbinical Assembly as associate director (1959–65), assisting RA executive vice-president Wolfe *Kelman in what until then had been a one-man office in charge of all affairs— placement, conventions, committees, and publications—for the 650–member RA. Preferring the demands of the Rabbinical Assembly headquarters to life as a congregational rabbi, Harlow spent his entire career within this center of the Conservative movement.

Among his first projects at the Rabbinical Assembly was the *Weekday Prayer Book*. By the time Harlow joined the RA, it had come to recognize, thanks to the enormous success of the 1946 *Sabbath and Festival Prayer Book* of the Rabbinical Assembly and the United Synagogue, how one prayer book used in the vast majority of Conservative synagogues could lead Conservative laity to identify with the national Conservative movement. Because the Rabbinical Assembly had been working on its second liturgical project, a weekday prayer book, for more than a decade, Harlow's first task was to get it to press, and he was appointed secretary of the RA's Prayer Book Committee. Two years later, the *Weekday Prayer Book* (1961), edited by Gershon *Hadas, appeared. Since then Harlow has emerged as the chief liturgist of the Conservative movement.

Convinced that classic texts require fresh translations to open them to succeeding generations, Harlow, as RA director of publications (1965–), has played a major role as editor and translator of nearly all the prayer books published by the Rabbinical Assembly for more than a quarter of a century. Among these are *Yearnings* (1968) and *Yearnings II* (1974), supplementary readings and meditations for the Days of Awe. His keen aesthetic sense shaped the landmark *Mahzor for Rosh Hashanah and Yom Kippur* (1972). Here the use of purple ink not only highlights special *Shabbat* readings and instructions to the congregation but also reminds worshippers of the High Holiday theme of God the King. The *Mahzor* is graced by Harlow's moving mourners' prayer: interspersed among the lines of the *kaddish* are the names of seventeen Nazi death camps. The number seventeen, deliberately one less than the eighteen of *chai*, the Hebrew word for life, signifies that after the Holocaust life can never be complete. Perhaps Harlow's most ambitious project, however—eleven years in the making—was the prayer book *Siddur Sim Shalom* (1985), the first comprehensive Conservative prayer book combining weekday, Sabbath, and festival services as well as personal meditations, in a single volume.

Harlow's prayer books, especially *Siddur Sim Shalom*, reveal a command of and sensitivity to the traditional and contemporary sources of Jewish creativity, which he weaves together in the liturgies. They also confirm his vision that the participation of women, remembrance of the Holocaust, and the reality of the state of Israel belong in modern Jewish worship. He thus has established the Rabbinical Assembly as one of the leaders of American Jewish liturgical creativity.

Although best known as a liturgist, Harlow was involved in numerous other literary projects within the Conservative movement. He was managing editor of the *United Synagogue Review* (1959–61), editor of the *Proceedings of the Rabbinical Assembly* (co-editor, 1959; editor, 1960–), and managing editor (1962–64) and associate editor (1964–80) of *Conservative Judaism*, the Rabbinical Assembly's chief forum for research and discussion of Conservative ideology. He also edited and translated *A Rabbi's Manual* (1965), revising Isidore *Signer's 1952 *Rabbinical Assembly Manual*. This Conservative officiants' guide to the services, prayers, and benedictions of congregational life includes ceremonies for the common life-cycle events and even a celebration for the burning of a synagogue mortgage. Harlow also served on the committee that edited and translated the Rabbinical Assembly's *Passover Haggadah: The Feast of Freedom* (1982).

Among his early posts at the Rabbinical Assembly was that of administrative secretary of the Committee on Jewish Law and Standards (1959–65). Cognizant of the many problems in the workings of the committee that within a decade would cause it to disband, Harlow nevertheless continued to concern himself closely with its affairs, even after he was no longer officially its secretary.

Outside of the Rabbinical Assembly, he edited several children's textbooks and translated Hebrew short stories, including some of the work of Nobel laureate Shmuel Yosef Agnon.

Harlow married Shayna Chasman in 1959; they have two children.

Writings: "On Editing a Prayer Book," *CJ* 36, 1 (Fall 1971), pp. 61–69; "New Dimensions in Liturgy," *PRA 1973* vol. 35 (1974), pp. 1–10. Ed., *Lessons from Our Living Past* (New York, 1972); *Stories from Our Living Past* (New York, 1974); *Exploring Our Living Past* (New York, 1979). Ed. and trans., *A Rabbi's Manual* (New York, 1965); *Yearnings* (New York, 1968); *Mahzor for Rosh Hashanah and Yom Kippur* (New York, 1972); *Yearnings II* (New York, 1974); *The Bond of Life* (New York, 1975); *Siddur Sim Shalom* (New York, 1985). Trans., S.Y. Agnon, "From Lodging to Lodging," "To Father's House," in *Twenty-One Stories*, ed. Nahum N. Glatzer (New York, 1970).

References: Aaron H. Blumenthal, "The Open Forum," *CJ* 26, 2 (Winter 1972), p. 69; Shira Dicker, "New Conservative Siddur," *Washington Jewish Week* 5 December 1985, pp. 18–19; *Review* 12, 3 (Autumn 1959), p. 20.

HERTZ, JOSEPH HERMAN (1872–1946). Chief Rabbi of the United Hebrew Congregations of the British Empire. The son of Simon and Esther Fanny Moskowitz Hertz, Joseph Hertz was born on September 25, 1872, in Rebrin, Slovakia. In 1884 he immigrated to America. He earned a B.A. from the City College of New York in 1891 and a Ph.D. from Columbia University in 1894. In 1894 Hertz became the first graduate of the Jewish Theological Seminary of America.

Hertz first served Congregation Adath Yeshurun, Syracuse, New York (1894–98). In 1898 he became rabbi of Witwatersrand Old Hebrew Congregation, the principal synagogue of Johannesburg, South Africa. Expelled from the Transvaal Republic for his "uitlander" sympathies in 1899, Hertz rejoined his congregation in 1901. In 1911 he returned to the United States as rabbi of Congregation Orach Chayim, New York City. In 1913 Hertz succeeded Hermann Adler as chief rabbi of the United Hebrew Congregations of the British Empire.

As chief rabbi, Hertz championed the interests of the East European immigrants who had become a majority in the Anglo-Jewish community. He denounced Russian persecution of the Jews and opposed the newly founded Liberal Jewish movement. A staunch Zionist, he was consulted by the British government prior to the publication of the Balfour Declaration. During 1920–21 Hertz visited forty-two different communities on three continents in a pastoral tour of the Jewish communities of the British Empire. His last years were spent fighting the Nazi menace and denouncing the policies of the Mandatory government in Palestine.

In providing a popular interpretation in English of the classic texts of Judaism, Hertz filled a great gap in Jewish literature. *A Book of Jewish Thoughts*, originally issued in 1917 to Jewish members of the armed forces, went through twenty-two editions and was translated into seven languages. His most lasting contribution, however, was the publication of *The Pentateuch and the Haftorahs* (1929–36). It contains each week's Torah and Haftorah readings, their cantillation, translation, and an English homiletic commentary Hertz based largely upon classical rabbinic sources. Commonly known as the Hertz Bible, it remains the standard text for the Torah service in most Conservative and Orthodox congregations.

Hertz married Rose Freed in 1904; they had six children. He died in London on January 14, 1946.

Writings: *The Ethical System of James Martineau* (New York, 1894); *A Book of Jewish Thoughts* (London, 1917); *Affirmations of Judaism* (London, 1927); *Sermons, Addresses, and Studies*, 3 vols. (London, 1938); *Early and Late: Addresses, Messages, and Prayers* (Hindhead, Surrey, 1943); *The Authorized Daily Prayer Book of the United Hebrew Congregations of the British Empire* (London, 1942–45; rev. 1949). Ed., *The Pentateuch and the Haftorahs* (1929–36; 2d ed. London, 1968).

References: *Dictionary of National Biography 1941–1950* (London, 1959), pp. 379–80; *EJ* vol. 8, col. 397; Isidore Epstein, ed., *Joseph Herman Hertz, 1872–1946 in Memoriam* (London, 1947); Isidore Epstein, Ephraim Levine, and Cecil Roth, *Essays in Honour of the Very Rev. Dr. Joseph Herman Hertz* (London, 1942); Elias Solomon, "Chief Rabbi Joseph Herman Hertz" *CJ* 2, 4 (June 1946), pp. 29–39.

HERTZBERG, ARTHUR (1921–   ). Rabbi, author, historian. The son of Zvi Elimelech and Anna Alstadt Hertzberg, Arthur Hertzberg was born on June 9, 1921, in Lubaczow, Poland, into a prominent Hasidic family. He was brought to the United States in 1926. Educated at Baltimore City College, a high school, he also pursued at the same time intensive Talmudic studies, preparing to follow in the family's rabbinical tradition. But the lure of modernity drew Hertzberg to the Conservative rabbinate, which offered the promise of blending the tradition of Jewish heritage with the challenges of the contemporary world. Hertzberg earned a B.A. at Johns Hopkins University in 1940, was ordained at the Seminary in 1943, and earned a Ph.D. from Columbia University in 1966.

He began his career as director of the B'nai B'rith Hillel Foundation in Amherst, Massachusetts, which served area colleges, including Amherst and the University of Massachusetts (1943–44). After a year Hertzberg moved to the congregational pulpit as rabbi of Ahavath Israel, Oak Lane, Philadelphia (1944–47), and then of West End Synagogue, Nashville, Tennessee (1947–56). In 1951 he volunteered for chaplaincy duty with the U.S. Air Force (1951–53) and was stationed in England.

He returned briefly to Nashville after his discharge, but soon moved east to become rabbi of Temple Emanu-El, Englewood, New Jersey (1956–85), a congregation of some 600 families. Here Hertzberg, one of American Jewry's most articulate and provocative thinkers and writers, established his reputation as a stirring speaker and advocate of liberal, and often unpopular, causes. As early as 1963 he warned against the dangers of the growing American involvement in Southeast Asia. He railed against the complacency of the disinterested segment of his congregants, whom he called the "silent two-thirds," members of the synagogue who only participated in its life on High Holidays. He warned the Rabbinical Assembly of the coming crisis in the synagogue: "Our religious institutions are committing suicide by internal dissension in an age when they ought to be pulling themselves together against erosion and against evaporation, which constitute the gravest crisis in the history of Judaism in the last two millenia" ("The Jewish People" *Beineinu* 2, 1 [January 1972], p. 54). Yet he did not hesitate to wage a "towering fight" against building the lavish Englewood Jewish Community Center, even though his stance split his congregation.

Hertzberg was an equally sharp critic of the modern rabbi, the "institutional executive," who had become an "entertainer" in the synagogue, and he called upon his rabbinical colleagues to return to the tradition of rabbis as creative scholars. His own life mirrored this conviction. He earned his doctorate in history at Columbia University while at Temple Emanu-El. Drawn to academic life, Hertzberg also began university teaching, first as a lecturer and later as an adjunct professor of history at Columbia University (1961–), and then as a visiting professor of Jewish studies at Rutgers University (1966–68), of religion at Princeton University (1968–69), and of history at Hebrew University, Jerusalem (1970–71). He also taught at the Seminary. In 1985 he retired from congregational life to become a professor of religion at Dartmouth College (1985–).

Hertzberg spoke and wrote on the key issues of contemporary American Jewry, Israel, public policy, and interfaith activities from the platform of several organizations. In the Rabbinical Assembly he chaired the Commission on International Affairs, was vice-chairman of the Executive Committee and a member of the Prayer Book Commission. He chaired the Social Action Commission of the Synagogue Council of America and was founder and first president of the International Jewish Committee on Interreligious Consultations. As president of the American Jewish Congress (1972–78), one of American Jewry's foremost community relations agencies, he called for it to recognize that Jews were both "universalists and particularists" and that the Jewish community had to champion social justice for all without neglecting the quality of Jewish life. He is also vice-president of the World Jewish Congress (1975–). Although he served on the Board of Governors of the Jewish Agency for Israel and the Executive of the World Zionist Organization (1969–78), Hertzberg, an ardent Zionist, did not hesitate to attack Israeli policies, including its treatment of the poor, slum-dwelling activist "Black Panthers" and the construction of Israeli settlements on the West Bank. He was also the president of the Conference on Jewish Social Studies (1967–72) and founded and is president of the American Jewish Policy Foundation (1978–).

In addition to being a prolific writer for a wide variety of Israeli, American, and American-Jewish periodicals, including a regular column for the *National Catholic Reporter*, Hertzberg edited and wrote several full-length works. The widely used *The Zionist Idea* (1959), an anthology of the writings of the early theoreticians of the Zionist movement, includes Hertzberg's masterful introductory essay on the intellectual history of Zionism. In *The French Enlightenment and the Jews* (1968), he traced both the roots of Jewish emancipation and modern anti-Semitism to the French Enlightenment. *Being Jewish in America* (1979) collected his most important articles. He also edited *Judaism* (1961), a selection of classical Jewish literature illustrative of the key themes of Jewish life for Braziller's Great Religions of Modern Man series and was a member of the editorial boards of *Midstream* and *Jewish Social Studies.*

Hertzberg married Phyllis Cannon in 1950; they have two daughters.

Writings: *Religion in Crisis* (New York, 1949); *Essays on Jewish Life and Thought* (New York, 1959); *The French Enlightenment and the Jews* (New York, 1968); "The Jewish People, The Land and the Synagogue," *Beineinu* 2, 1 (January 1972), pp. 51–56; *Being Jewish in America* (New York, 1979). Ed., *The Zionist Idea* (New York, 1959); *Judaism* (New York, 1961). With Martin E. Marty and Joseph N. Moody, *The Outbursts That Await Us: Three Essays on Religion and Culture in the United States* (New York, 1963).

References: *American Jewish Biographies*, pp. 170–71; John Murray Cuddihy, *No Offense: Civil Religion and Protestant Taste* (New York, 1978), pp. 101–55; *Current Biography Yearbook* (1975), pp. 191–93; *EJ* vol. 8, cols. 398–99; Estelle Gilson, "Arthur Hertzberg: Writer, Scholar, Polemicist, Rabbi," *Present Tense* 7, 4 (Summer 1980), pp. 33–38; *WWAJ* 1980, p. 216.

HESCHEL, ABRAHAM JOSHUA (1907–72). Scholar, theologian. A scion of several of the great Hasidic dynasties of Eastern Europe, Abraham Joshua Heschel, the son of Moshe Mordecai and Reisel Perlow Heschel, was born in Warsaw in 1907. After completing a traditional Jewish education, including the study of Jewish mystical literature, and spending two years studying in Vilna, Heschel earned a doctorate at the University of Berlin (1933). There he also studied and taught Talmud at the Hochschule fuer die Wissenschaft des Judentums.

In 1937 the philosopher Martin Buber invited Heschel to replace him as director of the Juedisches Lehrhaus, Frankfurt-am-Main. Heschel also taught at the Mittelstelle fuer juedische Erwachsenenbildung (Central Office for Adult Jewish Education). The Central Office oversaw Jewish education after the Nazis prohibited Jews from attending German educational institutions. A year later Heschel was deported to Poland, where he taught briefly at the Warsaw Institute of Jewish Studies. Six weeks before the Nazi invasion of Poland in 1939 he fled to England, where he established in London the Institute for Jewish Learning. In 1940 he immigrated to America to join the faculty of the Reform rabbinical seminary, Hebrew Union College in Cincinnati. As assistant professor (1940–43) and then as associate professor of philosophy and rabbinics (1943–45), Heschel appreciated the role of the college in the life of American Jewry but found that its interpretation of Judaism was not in full accord with his own. In particular, he urged the Reform rabbinate to give up its prejudice against *halachah*. Consequently, in 1945 he resigned his appointment at the college to join the faculty of the Seminary.

Although Heschel was not in the fullest sense identified with Conservatism as a movement, as professor of Jewish ethics and mysticism at the Seminary he exerted a profound influence upon its students and alumni (1945–72). Heschel was a charismatic teacher whose personal traditionalism—derived from a unique synthesis of Hasidic, mystical, and philosophic components—was a major influence upon his students. He continually sought to convey to them the sense of awe and wonder that were prerequisites to approaching holiness, God, and Torah. He believed that a spark lay hidden in each Jew and that his mission was to help ignite its flame by his teaching. His students reciprocated his devotion with esteem and affection for their teacher, whose wide-ranging mind stimulated their explorations of Talmudics, metaphysics, and the mysteries of God's concern for creation. At the same time that he taught at the Seminary, Heschel won the distinction of being the first Jewish scholar appointed to the faculty of the (Protestant) Union Theological Seminary in New York (1965–66).

Heschel combined his pietistic East European background with his West European scholarly training in his lifeworks as a scholar of religious thought, studying the classical sources of Jewish tradition, and as a theologian, developing his own philosophy of Judaism. Superbly trained in the techniques and methods of scholarship and gifted with an amazing grasp of languages, Heschel wrote more than a score of books in German, Yiddish, English, and Hebrew. His literary career began with a book of Yiddish poems, *Der Shem Hameforash, Mentsch, Lieder* (1933), and his lyrical style was always evident in his writing. He wrote books and monographs on a wide range of topics—Biblical prophecy, medieval philosophy, the lives of medieval philosophers, Jewish mysticism, rabbinic theology, East European Jewry, prayer, the state of Israel, applied religious ethics, Hasidism, and the nature of man. *Sabbath: Its Meaning for Modern Man* (1951) was published in conjunction with the Conservative movement's Sabbath Revitalization Campaign.

Heschel made outstanding scholarly contributions to four distinct fields of Jewish learning: Biblical thought, rabbinic thought, medieval philosophic thought, and Hasidic and mystical thought. His most important work in the field of Biblical studies was *Die Prophetie* (1936; Eng. ed., 1962). Here he analyzed prophetic consciousness, explaining that in the prophetic religion God not only commanded, but He was also moved by what happened in the world. Human actions, failures, and successes thus both affected human history and, according to Heschel, the very life of God.

In the field of rabbinic thought, his magnum opus was a two-volume Hebrew work, *Torah min Hashamayim b'Aspeklarya shel Hadorot (The Doctrine of Divine Revelation in the Light of the Generations,* 1962–65). In this he explored the concept of *Torah min ha-Shamayim,* the doctrine of divine revelation, which modern Biblical and historical criticism and contemporary skepticism have sharply challenged. Heschel's studies of voluminous rabbinic writings led him to conclude that while some ancient sages believed in the idea of a preexistent Torah in heaven transmitted by Moses to the Israelites, other rabbis held a rationalist approach, limiting the miraculous and seeing the Bible as the result of Divine/human cooperation and interpretation.

Heschel's studies of medieval Jewish philosophers, especially his biography of Moses Maimonides, led him to conclude that the great medieval scholars had recognized that there were limits beyond which the intellect could not penetrate Divine mysteries. Heschel was one of the few scholars to bring critical tools to the study of the history of Hasidism. Because Heschel was familiar with Hasidism as a living phenomenon, his student Samuel *Dresner concluded that his teacher was best able to analyze the movement. Heschel wrote several biographical studies of the circle of men around the founder of Hasidism, Israel Baal Shem Tov, including one of his last completed works, *Kotzker* (1973), a study of the Hasidic master Menachem Mendel of Kotzk.

Applying insights from all epochs of the Jewish past and drawing upon his extraordinary command of the sources of Jewish tradition, Heschel endeavored to develop for his contemporaries an authentic theology. He strove to penetrate and to illuminate the reality underlying religion, the living and dynamic relationship between man, Torah, and God. Yet at the same time Heschel understood the limits of this rational analysis. His philosophy is found chiefly in his great works, *Man Is Not Alone* (1951) and *God in Search of Man* (1955). In formulating a Jewish theology directly related to the moral issues of the day, Heschel became one of the most influential modern philosophers of religion, recognized widely in both Jewish and Christian circles.

Heschel's philosophy, called Depth Theology, went below the surface phenomena of modern doubt and rootlessness to illumine the Living God, not as a philosophical abstraction or psychological projection but as the Most Moved Mover, the God of pathos who stands in a dynamic and reciprocal relationship to creation, who is overwhelmingly real and shatteringly present. Heschel's theology explored the ongoing encounter between man and God, showing it to be an arduously difficult dialogue in which God remained a constant partner in man's work in the world. Heschel hoped that his theology would evoke in moderns a sympathetic understanding of and participation in the religious dimension of life.

The philosopher's leadership in the field of social action flowed naturally from his religious vision. He knew from his personal past that the silent man was an accessory to injustice. Denouncing racism as "man's gravest threat to man," he achieved national prominence in the civil rights movement by marching with Martin Luther King, Jr., in Selma, Alabama, in 1965. He announced publicly and early his opposition to the Vietnam War, was one of the founders of Clergy and Laity Concerned About Vietnam, and boldly encouraged those who resisted the military draft on grounds of conscience. His voicing of his concern for Soviet Jewry brought the issue to the forefront of American Jewry's agenda. In each of these mass movements, Heschel, a charismatic figure, stood out as a moral statesman deeply concerned with the key issues of his day.

Heschel was also a leader in ecumenical affairs. His meetings in 1964 with Pope Paul VI influenced the Second Vatican Council to make a strong statement on the Jews. Reeling from the insensitivity of so many Christian leaders to the dangers to Israel that precipitated the 1967 Six Day War, Heschel wrote *Israel: An Echo of Eternity* (1969) to explain to a wide audience the unique relationship between the state of Israel and the Jewish people.

In 1946 Heschel married Sylvia Straus; they had one daughter. He died in New York City on December 23, 1972.

Writings: *Der Shem Hameforash, Mentsch, Lieder* (Warsaw, 1933); *Maimonides: Eine Biographie* (Berlin, 1935; Eng. trans., New York, 1982); *Die Prophetie* (Cracow, 1936; Eng. trans., New York and Evanston, 1962); *Don Jizchak Abravanel* (Berlin, 1937); *Der Mizrah-Eiropeisher Yid* (New York, 1946); *The Earth Is the Lord's* (New York, 1950); *Sabbath: Its Meaning for Modern Man* (New York, 1951); *Man Is Not Alone: A Philosophy of Religion* (New York, 1951); *Man's Quest for God: Studies in Prayer and Symbolism* (New York, 1954); *God in Search of Man: A Philosophy of Judaism* (New York, 1955); *Between God and Man: An Interpretation of Judaism from the Writings of Abraham J. Heschel*, ed. Fritz A. Rothschild (New York, 1959); *Torah min Hashamayim b'Aspeklarya shel Hadorot*, 2 vols. (New York, 1962–65); *Who is Man?* (Stanford, Calif., 1965); *The Insecurity of Freedom* (New York, 1966); *Israel: An Echo of Eternity* (New York, 1969). Posthumously, *A Passion for Truth* (New York, 1973); *Kotzker: A Struggle in Integrity* (New York, 1973); *The Wisdom of Heschel* (New York, 1975); *I Asked for Wonder* (New York, 1983); *The Circle of the Baal Shem Tov: Studies in Hasidism*, ed. Samuel H. Dresner (Chicago, 1985).

References: Samuel Dresner, "Introduction of Dr. Abraham Joshua Heschel," *PRA 1968* vol. 32 (1968), pp. 86–90; *EJ* vol. 8, col. 425–27; "Abraham Joshua Heschel: A Yahrzeit Tribute," *CJ* 28, 1 (Fall 1973); Susannah Heschel, "My Father: Abraham Joshua Heschel," *Present Tense* 14, 3 (March/April 1987), pp. 48–51; *NYT* 24 December 1972, p. 40.

HIGGER, MICHAEL (1898–1952). Rabbi, scholar. The son of David and Gittel Rabinowitz Higger, Michael Higger was born in Rogovo, Lithuania, on January 6, 1898. He immigrated to the United States in 1915. Educated in the *yeshivot* of Telz and Kovno, Lithuania, Higger earned an A.B. from New York University in 1922, a Ph.D. from Columbia University in 1926, and was ordained at the Seminary in 1926.

Higger, who never married, lived and taught at the Jewish Theological Seminary, devoting his life to editing and publishing rabbinic texts with variant readings. A disciple of Seminary professor Louis *Ginzberg, Higger was a consultant to the Rabbinical Assembly's Committee on Jewish Law and secretary and research fellow to its successor, the Committee on Jewish Law and Standards. Charged with responding directly to the specific questions of Jewish law and practice addressed to the committees, Higger was responsible for many of their decisions. Willing to interpret *halachah*, he nevertheless remained a traditionalist who refused to abrogate it or to take steps that he deemed not consonant with traditional methods of interpretation. Higger thus helped set the hesitant tone of the first Committee on Jewish Law, which considered proposals such as Louis *Epstein's solution to the *agunah* problem too radical a departure from Jewish tradition.

One of the most prolific writers among the graduates of the Seminary, Higger first published, with introductions, notes, and variant readings, critical editions of several minor tractates of the Talmud. His most exhaustive work was the ten-volume *Otzar Ha-Beraitot* (1938–49), a critical collection of all the *beraitot* and other non-*Mishnaic*, tannaitic statements found in the printed and manuscript editions of the Babylonian and Jerusalem Talmuds. In addition, Higger wrote numerous articles and *The Jewish Utopia* (1932), a reconstruction of the rabbinic ideal society.

Higger died in New York City on November 22, 1952.

Writings: *Intention in Talmudic Law* (New York, 1927); *The Jewish Utopia* (Baltimore, Md., 1932); "Criteria for Interpreting Jewish Law," *CJ* 3, 3 (May 1947), pp. 5–9. In Hebrew: *Aggadot Ha-Tannaim* (New York, 1929); *Masektot Zeirot* (New York, 1929); *Sheva Masektot Ketanot* (New York, 1930); *Masektot Semachot* (New York, 1931); *Hilchut VeAgadut* (New York, 1933); *Masketot Derek Eretz* (New York, 1935); *Masektot Kallah* (New York, 1937); *Otzar Ha-Beraitot*, 10 vols. (New York, 1938–49).

References: *EJ* vol. 8, cols. 469–470; Joshua Modlinger, *Michael Higger: Idealist, Systematizer of the Talmud, and Progressive-Traditionalist Interpreter of Its Laws* (New York, 1947); *NYT* 24 November 1952, p. 23; *PRA 1937* vol. 5 (1939), p. 383; *PRA 1949* vol. 13 (1950), pp. 47–48; *WWAJ* 1938–39, p. 439.

HOFFMAN, CHARLES ISAIAH (1864–1945). Lawyer, rabbi, and journalist. The son of Moses and Hannah Kaufman Hoffman, Charles Hoffman was born in Philadelphia on January 3, 1864. Educated at the University of Pennsylvania, he earned a B.A. in 1884, L.L.B. in 1886, and M.A. in 1887.

In 1886 Hoffman established a law practice in Philadelphia. During his fifteen years as a lawyer he remained active in Jewish affairs. He helped found and was the first editor and publisher of the *Jewish Exponent*, a Philadelphia Anglo-Jewish weekly that was sympathetic to Jewish immigration and Zionism. He also worked with the Association for Jewish Immigrants and the Baron de Hirsch Fund to help settle immigrants in agricultural colonies in New Jersey, and he served as president of Beth Israel Congregation.

While visiting England, Hoffman met Solomon *Schechter. Schechter persuaded him to abandon the legal profession and to prepare for the rabbinate. In 1900 Hoffman began his studies with Schechter at Cambridge University. In 1902 he returned to the United States, following Schechter to the Seminary, and in 1904 he was ordained.

Hoffman first served the Indianapolis Hebrew Congregation where he helped establish the school and acquire a building (1904–5). But troubles with the congregation's lay leaders and lack of funds despite increased membership helped persuade Hoffman to accept a call to Oheb Shalom Congregation, Newark (later South Orange), New Jersey in 1906. There he remained, serving as rabbi emeritus after 1940, until his death.

Hoffman shaped Oheb Shalom along the lines advocated by his teacher and mentor, Schechter. He arranged the service, modernized the school, created adult study groups, and founded youth clubs and a Zionist organization. In 1911 Hoffman dedicated its new building, designed to house all these activities. He also influenced a number of future leaders of the Conservative movement, including Leon *Lang, who served at Oheb Shalom with Hoffman.

One of the founders of the Alumni Association of the Jewish Theological Seminary of America, the forerunner of the Rabbinical Assembly, Hoffman served as its president from 1907 to 1912. During his tenure the Seminary Alumni Prize for the best student essay on a rabbinical subject was established. As president, Hoffman also proposed that the alumni endow a chair in Jewish jurisprudence at the Seminary.

His efforts to build a lay following for the Seminary paved the way for the creation of the United Synagogue. Hoffman served as secretary to the United Synagogue for more than twenty-five years, as editor of the *United Synagogue Recorder* from 1921 to its demise in 1929, and as director of a nationwide network of United Synagogue branches that assisted small Jewish communities by providing for their religious needs. Hoffman had hoped that the United Synagogue would enrich both Conservative Judaism and America. An ardent Zionist, he was nevertheless disturbed by the subordination of religion to Zionism in the United Synagogue, and consequently he resigned as secretary in 1943.

Hoffman's weekly column in the *Jewish Exponent*, "Men and Things," and his editorials in the *United Synagogue Recorder* evidenced his belief that Judaism rested on the principles of unity, integrity, and the completeness of Torah; the unity and integrity of Israel; and the development of Torah to apply to contemporary problems.

In 1893 Hoffman married Fanny Binswanger, who was president of the Women's League of the United Synagogue of America (1919–28). They had five children. Hoffman died on June 7, 1945, in New York City.

Writing: "Essential Principles of Traditional Judaism," *Recorder* 7, 4 (October 1927), p. 12.

References: *AJYB* 48 (1946), p. 491; *EJ* vol. 8, col. 808; *JE* 12 June 1908, p. 8ff.; 14 July 1911, p. 8ff.; M. David Hoffman, "Charles Isaiah Hoffman: One Hundredth Anniversary (1864–1964)," *American Jewish Historical Quarterly* vol. 55 (1965–66), pp. 212–34; *NYT* 8 June 1945, p. 19; Herbert Rosenblum, "The Founding of the United Synagogue of America" (Ph.D. diss. Brandeis University, 1970), pp. 144, 240–41.

K

KADUSHIN, MAX (1895–1980). Rabbi, scholar, educator. The son of Solomon Phineas and Rebecca Mazel Kadushin, Max Kadushin was born in Minsk, Russia, on December 6, 1895, and brought to Seattle, Washington, in 1897. Educated in the Seattle public schools, he earned a B.A. from New York University in 1916, was ordained at the Seminary in 1920, and earned a Doctor of Hebrew Letters there in 1932.

In 1921, following a year of independent study, Kadushin was invited by Congregation B'nai Israel, Washington Heights, New York City to become the rabbi of its newly constructed synagogue-center. In 1926 he left B'nai Israel and New York for Chicago, partly in order to pursue his rabbinic career independent of the powerful influence of his teacher, Mordecai M. *Kaplan.

In Chicago Kadushin became rabbi of Humboldt Boulevard Temple (1926–31), a congregation composed of pious Hungarian immigrants. There Kadushin, who at that time considered himself a Reconstructionist, helped found the Midwest Council of the Society for the Advancement of Judaism. Although he considered the rabbinate at Humboldt Boulevard Temple the happiest of his career, his scholarly inclinations drew him to the university. In 1931 he left Chicago to became rabbi at the Hillel Foundation of the University of Wisconsin (1931–42). Kadushin thrived intellectually on his contact with the faculty and the brightest students, but he failed to establish successful relationships with his other constituencies, the general Jewish student body and the local Jewish community. This led to tensions with the headquarters of the National Hillel Foundation and to his resignation in 1942.

Kadushin then accepted the invitation of Alexander Dushkin of the Jewish Education Committee of New York to direct the Hebrew High School of Greater New York, later known as the Marshaliah Hebrew High School (1942–52). Initially, this supplementary school, with eighteen branches and more than 500 students, thrived under Kadushin's direction. It became a forum for the development of a series of experimental texts based on his study of rabbinic thought, and many of its students went on to attend the Teachers Institute of the Seminary. But after Dushkin left the Jewish Education Committee in 1949, the school began to decline due to financial problems, demographic changes, and frictions between Kadushin and the committee, all of which led to his resignation in 1952.

During the next eight years Kadushin occupied several positions. He was forced to return to the pulpit, and although he excelled in teaching and preaching, he disliked the organizational and fund-raising responsibilities expected of the pulpit rabbi, particularly in the post-World War II period of synagogue growth and expansion. Kadushin served as rabbi at the Bay Shore Jewish Center, Long Island, for a year (1953–54?) and at Synagogue Adath Israel, Riverdale, Bronx, for four years (1954–58?). In 1958 he became dean and professor of *Midrash* and homiletics at the Academy for Higher Jewish Learning, an interdenominational rabbinical seminary that briefly existed in New York City in the 1950s. Finally, in 1960 the appointment he had hoped for materialized when he was invited to become visiting professor in ethics and rabbinic thought at the Seminary (1960–80).

Kadushin's major scholarly contribution was his disproof of the long-held notion that rabbinic thought in the Talmud was disorganized and chaotic. His work explained the unique character of the rabbinic mind. By explicating *agadic* literature, he discerned the organizing principles of rabbinic theology. In *Organic Thinking* (1938) he demonstrated that rabbinic thinking presented an organic system whose theology included four fundamental value-concepts—God's loving kindness, God's justice, Torah, and Israel. These concepts and a host of sub-concepts interlaced with one another to form a complex system of rabbinic theology that was organic, not hierarchical, in nature. Kadushin recognized that these value-concepts were concretized in action via *halachah*, which regulated daily behavior, and via rabbinic teachings, which explicated the *agadah*. This organic system of concepts enabled the Jews to live together by uniting the Jewish people in a common mode of thought and action. The organic complex thus became the group mind of the Jewish people.

Kadushin's subsequent work explored these value-concepts in specific texts, such as the liturgy of the prayer book (*Worship and Ethics*, 1964). In *A Conceptual Approach to the Mekilta* (1969) he extended his analysis to focus upon particular subconcepts and to show how rabbinic concepts differed from, but were related to, their Biblical antecedents.

Although Kadushin had considered himself a Reconstructionist early in his career, his study of rabbinic thought led him to search out the fundamental concepts of Judaism that resisted arbitrary change and caused his break with Kaplan. Kadushin then became a leader of the right wing of the Conservative movement.

In 1923 he married Dr. Evelyn Garfiel, a psychologist, who taught at the universities of Chicago and Wisconsin and wrote *The Service of the Heart* (1958), a commentary on the prayer book. They had two sons. Kadushin died on July 23, 1980, in New York City.

Writings: *The Theology of Seder Eliahu* (New York, 1932); *Organic Thinking* (New York, 1938); *The Rabbinic Mind* (New York, 1952); *Worship and Ethics* (Evanston, Ill., 1964); *A Conceptual Approach to the Mekilta* (New York, 1969).

References: *EJ* vol. 10, cols. 668–69; Judah Goldin, "The Thinking of the Rabbis," *Judaism* vol. 5 (1956), pp. 3–12; *Recorder* 2, 4 (October 1922), p. 11; Theodore Steinberg, "Max Kadushin: An Appreciation," *CJ* 35, 4 (Summer 1982), pp. 3–16; Theodore Steinberg, "Max Kadushin, Scholar of Rabbinic Judaism: A Study of his Life, Work, and Theory of Valuational Thought" (Ph.D diss., New York University, 1980); *WWWJ* 1965, p. 463.

KAPLAN, MORDECAI MENAHEM (1881–1983). Rabbi, educator, founder of the Reconstructionist movement. The son of Israel and Anna Kowarsky Kaplan, Mordecai M. Kaplan was born on June 11, 1881, in Swenziany, Lithuania. In childhood he was called Mottel and for a time Maurice, Max, and Mark. In 1888 his father immigrated to New York. After a sojourn in Paris, Anna and the children joined him in New York's Lower East Side (1889).

Kaplan studied classical Jewish texts with his father, was tutored by the unorthodox Biblical scholar Arnold Ehrlich, and attended the Machzike Talmud Torah and Yeshivah Etz Chaim. A few months before his Bar Mitzvah, he enrolled in the Jewish Theological Seminary. He earned a B.A. at the City College of New York in 1900. In 1902 he was ordained at the Seminary. Having studied philosophy and sociology—two subjects that would greatly inform his thought—he also earned an M.A. at Columbia University (1902).

After another year of study, Kaplan began his career at New York's distinguished Orthodox synagogue, Congregation Kehillath Jeshurun (1903–9). His main responsibilities were to preach an English sermon once a month and to organize a five-day-a-week afternoon congregational school, the first in the United States. At the same time he continued his leading role in the Jewish Endeavor Society. Founded in 1901 by the early students and first rabbis of the Seminary, the Endeavorers organized in immigrant neighborhoods "young people's synagogues" that retained the traditional prayer book and separation of men and women but allowed for English prayers, translations, and sermons. These later became the models for the Young Israel movement, the backbone of the English-speaking, modern Orthodox synagogue, which Kaplan co-founded with Israel *Friedlaender.

At Kehillath Jeshurun, Kaplan's title was "minister," not rabbi, reflecting that Seminary ordination did not confer *semichah*, the classical formula for rabbinic ordination. Subsequently, while on his honeymoon in Europe in 1908, he received *semichah* from Rabbi Isaac Jacob Reines of Lida, Russia, the founding head of the Zionist religious Mizrachi movement. Nevertheless, Kaplan found himself increasingly unhappy in the Orthodox pulpit. For a time he contemplated abandoning the rabbinate altogether and turning, as some other early Seminary rabbis did, to law or to business. Not surprisingly then, in 1909, when Seminary president Solomon *Schechter offered him the opportunity to head the newly established Teachers Institute, he eagerly accepted the post.

The appointment marked a major turning point in Kaplan's life. As he ceased to be primarily a pulpit rabbi, he turned his attention to the elaboration of his own philosophy, a task essential to his work as an educator. Kaplan emerged as one of the giants of twentieth-century Jewish thought. He influenced virtually every aspect of organized American Jewish life. As a writer, lecturer, administrator, and professor for more than fifty years at the Jewish Theological Seminary, he was one of the polestars of the Conservative movement. A creator and organizer, he conceived of and founded numerous Jewish institutions. But perhaps his greatest achievements lay in the challenge that he posed to American Jewry by his comprehensive reconstruction of Judaism and in his fashioning of the Reconstructionist movement, which eventually became the fourth denomination of American Judaism.

Schechter had established teachers courses at the Seminary soon after his arrival in America, but because they met in the evenings far from the centers of Jewish life, they failed to attract enough students. Another effort to make the Seminary a center for Jewish teacher training succeeded when, with a gift from Jacob Schiff, the Teachers Institute was established. As its principal (1909–31) and dean (1931–46), Kaplan decisively shaped the institute and played a leading role in the professionalization of American Jewish education. He was responsible for bringing into the field of Jewish education many people who later became its foremost leaders. He structured the curriculum to reflect what he understood to be the chief aims and objectives of Jewish education: to develop in the rising generation a desire and ability to participate in Jewish life, to nurture an understanding of and appreciation for Hebrew language and literature, and to inculcate conduct rooted in Jewish patterns of ethical and religious behavior. Within a decade he raised the Teachers Institute's standards and attracted outstanding Hebraists to teach at its New York East Village site. Almost all those who held significant positions in Jewish education in the first half of the twentieth century were at one time Kaplan's students at the Teachers Institute.

Shortly after he took over the helm of the Teachers Institute, Seminary professor of homiletics Joseph M. Asher died, and Kaplan was invited to succeed him in the Rabbinical Department. As professor of homiletics and *midrash* (1910–47) and professor of philosophies of religion (1947–63), he taught Seminary rabbinical candidates for more than five decades, guiding generations of Conservative rabbis. A thought-provoking, demanding, and creative teacher, Kaplan believed teaching afforded him a sacred opportunity, and he inspired hundreds of disciples to carry his message forward. No matter what the formal subject— homiletics, *midrash*, or philosophy—his classes examined the fundamental questions of contemporary Jewish life and explored ways of meeting the challenges modern thought and the American environment posed to traditional Jewish beliefs and practices.

Kaplan's administrative and teaching responsibilities did not preclude his active participation in Jewish communal and educational affairs outside the Seminary. He was among the founders of the New York *Kehillah* and, as a member of its Bureau of Jewish Education, conducted its historic survey of Jewish education in New York. The crystallization of his thought on the synagogue-center was influenced by his membership on the Board of Directors of the 92nd Street YMHA (Young Men's Hebrew Association). He was particularly active in the Intercollegiate Menorah Society and supported new educational ventures, including the School for Jewish Communal Work and the Central Jewish Institute.

Kaplan's first opportunity to test some of his new ideas on the nature of contemporary Jewish life and communal organization came in 1915 when he was invited to help found a new synagogue on New York's Upper West Side. By this time Kaplan envisioned American Jewry gathering together in synagogue-centers for worship, fellowship, study, social service, and recreation. He organized the Jewish Center as the first such synagogue-center. Its million-dollar building, completed in 1917, included a sanctuary for worship and facilities for sports and social activities. It was meant to become, with Kaplan as rabbi (1918–22), the center of life for its community.

In 1920 Kaplan published "A Program for the Reconstruction of Judaism" in *The Menorah Journal*. The article, which contained the seeds of his philosophy of Reconstructionism, alienated a number of the more traditional members of the Jewish Center, who felt that they could no longer support him. Even though Kaplan received a vote of support, he decided to leave the center. In 1922 he and a group of center members founded, a block away, the Society for the Advancement of Judaism (SAJ), a religious fellowship for Jewish men and women who wanted Judaism to exert an ethical influence in their everyday lives. With Kaplan as "spiritual leader" (1922–44), the SAJ became a synagogue-center par excellence and his laboratory for implementing his philosophy of Reconstructionism.

Some of Kaplan's innovations at SAJ were highly successful and widely imitated. He created new rituals, holding the first Bat Mitzvah ceremony, for his daughter Judith, in 1922. Believing that teaching Torah was a vital part of a rabbi's duties, he used the SAJ to test his ideas on adult education, making group study integral to the lives of its members.

The SAJ was also his forum for liturgical experimentation. In his first years there, Kaplan, determined to drop outmoded forms, changed the text of the *Kol Nidre* prayer but retained the traditional haunting melody that signaled to one and all the arrival of Yom Kippur. Eventually, he and several colleagues, including SAJ "associate leader" Ira *Eisenstein (his son-in-law) and Rabbi Eugene *Kohn, recast the traditional prayer books and services to reflect Reconstructionist theology. For example, *The New Haggadah for the Pesah Seder* (1941) omitted the ten plagues, changed the language that referred to the chosenness of the Jewish people, and added passages on Moses that did not appear in the traditional text. The SAJ thus became the nucleus of the burgeoning Reconstructionist movement.

In 1934, at the age of fifty-three, Kaplan published his magnum opus, *Judaism as a Civilization*. Here for the first time in book form he set forth a complete account of his philosophy of Reconstructionism, a philosophy that Kaplan had formulated and refined over the course of two decades in articles in *The Menorah Journal* and *S.A.J. Review*. To continue discussion of the questions raised by *Judaism as a Civilization*, he and his colleagues launched the *Reconstructionist* magazine (1935–) with Kaplan as chairman of its editorial board (1935–59). In 1940 the Jewish Reconstructionist Foundation was established to carry on the Reconstructionist publications program and to coordinate Reconstructionist activities, which until then had been chiefly sustained by SAJ. These two events, the creation of an ongoing intellectual forum and the setting up of an organizational superstructure, formalized the Reconstructionist movement.

For most of his life, Kaplan resisted the temptation to establish Reconstructionism as a separate denomination, preferring that it remain a school of thought affecting all types of Jews. In 1955 a congregational body, the Reconstructionist Federation of Congregations, later the Federation of Reconstructionist Congregations and Havurot, was organized. It was not, however, until 1968, several years after Kaplan retired from active teaching at the Seminary, that the Reconstructionist Rabbinical College opened its doors in Philadelphia. Its curriculum— with each successive year devoted to a different phase of Jewish civilization— reflected Kaplan's theory of evolving Jewish civilization. Kaplan, then in his eighties, traveled to Philadelphia to teach its first students. With an organizational structure parallel to the other denominations of American Judaism—the Reconstructionist Rabbinical Association, made up of graduates of its Seminary (its forerunner, the Reconstructionist Rabbinical Fellowship, established in 1950, included Reform and Conservative rabbis), a congregational union, and a seminary—the movement had become what Kaplan had avoided most of his life, the fourth denomination of American Judaism.

But before the split between the Conservative and Reconstructionist movements occurred, Kaplan, the spiritual and intellectual guide to generations of Conservative rabbis and teachers, immeasurably enriched the content and programs of Conservatism and its institutions. In 1910 he rallied the Seminary Alumni Association to work for the founding of the United Synagogue of America, and for several terms he served as one of its vice-presidents. As the first chairman of its Educational Committee, he and Julius *Greenstone surveyed members' congregational schools and began the long process of upgrading their standards and curricula.

When Kaplan realized that the United Synagogue would not espouse the homogeneity among its affiliates that he desired, he became disgruntled with the organization and gathered together a group of like-minded rabbis, including Herman *Rubenovitz and Jacob *Kohn, into the Society for Jewish Renascence (1919–20). In some ways a prototype of later Reconstructionist fellowships, it stood outside the main channels of the Conservative movement. Its members planned to meet regularly, not to found another party in Judaism, but to revitalize Judaism within and without the synagogue to make it consonant with contemporary Jewish life.

Kaplan was also a leader in the Rabbinical Assembly. In fact, his untitled address to the Seminary alumni in 1909 was his first public discussion of his new perspective on Judaism. He was the first candidate for the RA presidency to run in opposition to the wishes of the until-then dominant leadership. Bitterly opposed, he won by a scant majority, becoming the first member of its left wing to serve as president (1932–33). He thus paved the way for others in the left wing, including Eugene Kohn and Ira Eisenstein, to lead the RA. As president, Kaplan proposed that the RA undertake an unprecedented range of projects in liturgy, adult education, social justice, and philosophy. After the Depression, many of these moved to the forefront of the RA agenda. Kaplan thus set in motion the process of transforming the Rabbinical Assembly into one of the guiding lights of the Conservative movement.

As dean of the Teachers Institute, he also conceived of the Leadership Training Fellowship. Established in 1946, this national high school fostered the development of future rabbis, teachers, and leaders of American, and especially of Conservative, Jewry from within the ranks of the Conservative movement. Kaplan planned that congregational rabbis would work, in conjunction with the Teachers Institute and the Seminary College of Jewish Studies, with a select group of teens, raising up disciples and preparing them to enter the Seminary and the Teachers Institute. That same year Moshe *Davis became dean of the Teachers Institute, freeing Kaplan to design the blueprint for the University of Judaism, the Los Angeles affiliate of the Seminary and the first center for higher Jewish studies on the West Coast.

Kaplan's controversial ideas also pushed the Seminary to affirm that it stood for academic freedom. Many of the Jewish Center members whom Kaplan alienated in the early 1920s were financial backers of the Seminary. Although Seminary president Cyrus *Adler knew that the school would lose support if he did not muzzle or remove Kaplan from the faculty, his administration and faculty supported the principle of academic freedom.

Kaplan offered guiding principles for the Conservative movement. For him the operative principle of Conservatism was ''unity in diversity.'' In an address to the United Synagogue in 1947, he articulated the four underlying principles upon which, he believed, the movement's three wings agreed: the centrality of the land of Israel for Diaspora Jewry; the primacy of religion in Jewish life; the maximum degree of Jewish culture and customs, including the use of Hebrew, in the synagogue and personal life; and the commitment to the scientific approach to Jewish scholarship. He understood that these constituted a framework within which the right, center, and left wings of the Conservative movement functioned.

Clearly, Kaplan's thinking and action were affected by the strenuous opposition that he faced within the Conservative movement, especially from among some of his Seminary colleagues. Although for a time Kaplan considered moving to the Reform Hebrew Union College in Cincinnati, and although Stephen Wise tried to woo him away to head the non-denominational seminary, the Jewish Institute of Religion, established in 1922, Kaplan decided to remain at the Seminary. The tensions, however, that had led him to consider moving did not abate. The *Sabbath Prayer Book* (1945), which Kaplan edited with Kohn, Eisenstein, and Milton *Steinberg, was burned shortly after publication by the *Agudas Harabbanim*, and this Union of Orthodox Rabbis also excommunicated Kaplan. In an open letter in the Hebrew weekly *Hadoar*, three of Kaplan's colleagues, Seminary professors Louis *Ginzberg, Alexander *Marx, and Saul *Lieberman, joined in the vituperative denunciation of the man and his work. Nevertheless, Kaplan remained steadfast, working within the confines of Conservatism for the greater part of his long life and continually challenging it to cope realistically with the unprecedented circumstances of twentieth-century Jewish life.

Kaplan's Reconstructionist philosophy explored Judaism in terms of community, nationhood, organizational structure, theology, history, and culture. It responded to the inner spiritual and cultural needs of twentieth-century American Jewry, a community formed in the trials of mass migration, forged by the catastrophe of the Holocaust, and exhilarated by the rebirth of Israel. He offered his modernistic philosophy of Reconstructionism as a bridge connecting the Jewish past and the American present. The point of departure for his Reconstructionism was the contemporary scene and present-day religious experience, not the dictates of the religious life and authority of the past. Not surprisingly then, in formulating Reconstructionism, Kaplan drew upon both Jewish and American civilizations, turning for guidance to traditional and modern Jewish sources, including the Zionist Ahad Ha-Am, and to Western writers, including social scientist Emile Durkheim and the American philosophical pragmatist William James.

His conception of Judaism as an "evolving religious civilization" was his solution to the contemporary question of Jewish identity. Judaism was a dynamic social process, a civilization encompassing land, language, arts, literature, history, mores, laws, folkways, social structure, ideals, and values. By "religious" Kaplan meant that the religious life in the synagogue and the home remained at the heart of this civilization. And by "evolving" he indicated that Judaism was not fixed, that it must consider the Jewish people, their needs, and responses to changed circumstances. Because each Jew, using tradition as a guide, must solve life's perplexities on his or her own, diverse viewpoints would emerge.

He understood that the only way to overcome the fragmentation of Jewish life in America that this diversity produced was for Jews to form an organic community. Although he taught that the land of Israel was the spiritual homeland of the Jewish people and that outside it Judaism became a secondary civilization, he insisted upon forging creative life for Diaspora Jewry. The key to their creative survival lay in democratically organized, local and national organic communities, run neither by congregations nor federations but by representatives of the various Jewish organizations who would administer all communal property and employ communal functionaries. These organic communities would function as the instruments of Jewish life as a whole and meet all its needs.

Kaplan proposed a total revolution in Jewish theology by accepting naturalism, teaching that Judaism must be "reconstructed" from supernaturalism to naturalism. He rejected the notion of a supernatural God, redefining God as the Power in the universe that makes for salvation, the sum of the forces that help men and women make the most of their lives. For Judaism to survive the challenges of modernity there could be no miracles, no supernatural revelation. Rather than serving God, the purpose of human existence was to help create a society whose members would maintain what he called a sense of active moral responsibility, contributing to the intellectual, moral, and spiritual progress of mankind.

Kaplan rejected not only the belief in God as a supernatural being, but also authoritarianism and supernaturalism in every aspect of Jewish religious life and thought. He replaced Jewish law with the concept of folkways. No longer could one understand the *mitzvot* as laws or mystic symbols necessary to commune with God or to earn a portion in the world to come. But as folkways, the sacred texts, seasons, rites, rituals, and customs were vehicles of Judaism that answered human needs. They would remain the very stuff of Jewish life, the sources of its spirituality; but because they were no longer laws, they could be modified as required to meet the changed circumstances of contemporary life.

Kaplan's rejection of the concept of the Jews as the chosen people also grew out of his rejection of supernaturalism. Furthermore, he felt that the entire notion of chosenness was out of step with the ideals and democratic ethos of the dominant American society. It was especially these controversial theological reconstructions of fundamental Jewish beliefs on the nature of God, law, and the Jewish people that created for Kaplan grave tensions and left deep scars within the Conservative movement.

A prolific author, Kaplan wrote widely for scholarly and lay audiences about Reconstructionism. Two of his works, *Judaism as a Civilization* and *The Future of the American Jew* (1949) have already won their places as classics.

He married Lena Rubin in 1908; they had four daughters. After Lena's death, he married Rivka (?) in 1951. In the 1930s Kaplan lived for a brief period in Palestine when he was a visiting professor at Hebrew University in Jerusalem. At the age of ninety-five, he made *aliyah*. He died on November 11, 1983, in Riverdale, New York, at the age of 102, having lived longer than any other major Jewish personality of modern times.

Writings: *A New Approach to the Problem of Judaism* (New York, 1924); "President's Message (1933)," *PRA 1939* vol. 6 (1940), pp. 177–202; *Judaism as a Civilization* (New York, 1934); *Judaism in Transition* (New York, 1936); *The Meaning of God in Modern Jewish Religion* (New York, 1936); *The Future of the American Jew* (New York, 1949); *Know How to Answer: A Guide to Reconstructionism* (New York, 1951); "Response," *PRA 1951* vol. 15 (1952), pp. 211–19; *A New Zionism* (New York, 1955; 2d ed., 1959); *Questions Jews Ask* (New York, 1956; rev. 1966); *Basic Values in Jewish Religion* (New York, 1957); *Judaism Without Supernaturalism* (New York, 1958); "Unity in Diversity in the Conservative Movement," in *Tradition and Change*, ed. Mordecai Waxman (New York, 1958), pp. 211–28; *The Greater Judaism in the Making* (New York, 1960); *Higher Jewish Education and the Future of the American Jew* (Los Angeles, 1963); *The Purpose and Meaning of Jewish Existence* (Philadelphia, 1964); *Not So Random Thoughts* (New York, 1966); *The Religion of Ethical Nationhood* (New York, 1970). Ed., *The Jewish Reconstructionist Papers* (New York, 1936). Co-ed., with Eugene Kohn and Ira Eisenstein, *The New Haggadah for the Pesah Seder* (New York, 1941; rev. 1942), and *High Holiday Prayer Book*, 2 vols. (New York, 1948); with Eugene Kohn, Ira Eisenstein, and Milton Steinberg, *Sabbath Prayer Book* (New York, 1945); with Jack J. Cohen, Eugene Kohn, and Ludwig Nadelmann, *The Festival Prayer Book* (New York, 1958); with Jack Cohen, Ira Eisenstein, Eugene Kohn, and Ludwig Nadelmann, *The Daily Prayer Book* (New York, 1963). Ed. and trans., S. D. Luzzatto, *Mesillat Yesharim* (New York, 1937). Posthumously, *Dynamic Judaism: The Essential Writings of Mordecai M. Kaplan*, ed. Emanuel S. Goldsmith and M. Scult (New York, 1985).

References: "Special Issue: Mordecai M. Kaplan on His Centennial," *CJ* 34, 4 (March-April 1981), pp. 1–41; *EJ* vol. 10, cols. 751–53; Arthur A. Goren, *New York Jews and the Quest for Community: The Kehillah Experiment, 1908–1922* (New York and London, 1970); Richard Libowitz, *Mordecai M. Kaplan and the Development of Reconstructionism* (New York and Toronto, 1983); Charles Liebman, "Reconstructionism in American Jewish Life," *AJYB* vol. 71 (1970), pp. 3–99; *Mordecai M. Kaplan Jubilee Volume* (New York, 1953); Herbert Parzen, *Architects of Conservative Judaism* (New York, 1964), pp. 189–206; Herman H. and Mignon L. Rubenovitz, *The Waking Heart* (Cambridge, Mass., 1967), pp. 58–69; Mel Scult, "Mordecai M. Kaplan: Challenges and Conflicts in the Twenties," *American Jewish Historical Quarterly* 66 (March 1977), pp. 401–16; Mel Scult, "The Teachers Institute and the Foundations of Jewish Education in America," *AJA* 38, 1 (April 1986), pp. 57–84.

KARP, ABRAHAM JOSEPH (1921–   ). Rabbi, historian. The son of Aaron and Rachel Schor Karp, Abraham Karp was born on April 5, 1921, in Indura (Amdur), Poland, and brought to the United States in 1930. He earned a diploma at the Teachers Institute of Yeshiva University in 1939, a B.A. at Yeshiva University in 1942, and was ordained at the Seminary in 1945.

While working toward a Master of Hebrew Letters at the Seminary (1948), Karp began a brief career as an administrator. He was assistant director of the Seminary College of Jewish Studies (1945) and director of the Metropolitan New York Region of the United Synagogue (1946–47). In 1948 he left organizational work for the congregational rabbinate as rabbi of Temple Israel, Swampscott, Massachusetts (1948–51). He next worked with the senior rabbi, Gershon *Hadas, at Kansas City's Congregation Keneseth Israel-Beth Shalom (1951–56).

In 1956 Karp moved to his own pulpit, following Stuart *Rosenberg as rabbi of Temple Beth El, Rochester, New York (1956–72). Beth El was founded in 1915 when several of the younger and more affluent members of its parent synagogue, the Leopold Street Beth El, one of the founding congregations of the United Synagogue, moved to a newer neighborhood where they established their own synagogue. Although in its early years the congregation had leaned toward Reform, Rabbi Jacob *Minkin led Temple Beth El squarely into the Conservative camp. In addition to the usual rabbinical duties and working with Beth El's Sisterhood, Men's Club, school, and youth organizations, Karp also conducted a weekly radio program, "From a Rabbi's Study."

At the same time he continued to serve the larger Conservative movement. Karp was active in the Rabbinical Assembly as a member of the Rabbinical Cabinet, Executive Council, *Conservative Judaism*'s editorial board, and the Joint Prayer Book Commission of the Rabbinical Assembly and United Synagogue. He was also president of the Midwest Region of the Rabbinical Assembly (1955).

During his years in the pulpit, Karp was also establishing a solid reputation as a scholar of American Jewish history. He was drawn to academic life, teaching first as a visiting professor at Dartmouth College (1967), the Seminary (1967–71, 1976), and Hebrew University, Jerusalem (1970, 1979). In 1972 he decided to retire from congregational life to devote himself full time to scholarly research and teaching as a professor of history and religious studies at the University of Rochester, where he was appointed Philip S. Bernstein Professor of Jewish Studies in 1975.

Karp's numerous articles and books range over the course of American Jewish history and include a study of Jewish philanthropy, *To Give Life: The UJA in the Shaping of the American Jewish Community* (1981), and a synthesis of American Jewish history, *Haven and Home* (1984). However, he retained a particular interest in the religious history of American Jews, and especially of Conservative Judaism, and has been one of the few scholars of American Jewry to explore this topic. He edited *Conservative Judaism: The Legacy of Solomon Schechter* (1963), an anthology of short statements made by leading exponents of Conservatism. *A History of the United Synagogue of America, 1913–1963* (1964) commemorated the fiftieth anniversary of the founding of Conservatism's congregational union with a survey of its evolution and growth. Karp has continued to explore the origins of the Conservative movement and to study its leadership in articles written especially for *Conservative Judaism, Proceedings of the Rabbinical Assembly*, and *American Jewish Archives*. He also wrote *The Jewish Way of Life and Thought* (1962; rev. 1980), meditations and readings from classical Jewish literature on the "vitality, meaning, and message" of Judaism.

In his other scholarly activities he was chairman of the Publications Committee of the American Jewish Historical Society (1963–69); president of the society (1972–75); and editor of *The Jewish Experience in America* (5 vols., 1969), a collection of articles that had previously appeared in *Publications of the American Jewish Historical Society*. He is also a corresponding member of Hebrew University's Institute of Contemporary Jewry and a member of the Publications

Committee of the Jewish Publication Society of America (1970–   ) and the board of the National Foundation for Jewish Culture.

Karp married Deborah Burstein in 1945; they have two sons.

Writings: *New York Chooses a Chief Rabbi* (New York, 1955); *The Jewish Way of Life and Thought* (New York, 1962; rev: 1981); "Preaching Schechter," *PRA 1963* vol. 27 (1963), pp. 21–46; *A History of the United Synagogue of America, 1913–1963* (New York, 1964); "The Origins of Conservative Judaism," *CJ* 19, 4 (Summer 1965), pp. 33–48; *To Give Life: The UJA in the Shaping of the American Jewish Community* (New York, 1981); "The Conservative Rabbi," *AJA* vol. 25, 2 (November 1983), pp. 188–262; *Haven and Home: A History of the Jews in America* (New York, 1984); "A Century of Conservative Judaism in the United States," *AJYB* vol. 86 (New York, 1986), pp. 3–61. Ed., *Conservative Judaism: The Legacy of Solomon Schechter* (1963; reprint ed., New York, 1975); *The Jewish Experience in America*, 5 vols. (New York, 1969); *Beginnings—Early American Judaica* (Philadelphia, 1975); *The Golden Door to America: A Jewish Immigration Reader* (New York, 1976). Trans., *Five from the Holocaust* (Rochester, N.Y., 1974).

References: *EJ* vol. 10, col. 802; Stuart E. Rosenberg, *The Jewish Community in Rochester, 1843–1925* (New York, 1954), pp. 178–80; *WWAJ* 1980, p. 249: *WWWJ* 1965, p. 482.

KAUVAR, CHARLES ELIEZER HILLEL (1879–1971). Rabbi, educator. The son of Solomon Salkind and Rose de Waltoff Kauvar, Charles Kauvar was born in Vilna, Lithuania, on August 14, 1879. He was brought to New York in 1891. Educated in the New York City public schools, Kauvar earned a B.A. from the City College of New York in 1900, was ordained at the Seminary in 1902, and earned a Doctor of Hebrew Letters there in 1909.

In 1902 Kauvar was elected rabbi of Congregation Beth Ha-Medrosh Hagodol, Denver, Colorado. He spent his entire career there and was elected rabbi for life in 1919. Kauvar transformed Beth Ha-Medrosh Hagodol from a sixty-member congregation in 1902 into a model synagogue-center whose new structure, completed in 1929, included a 1,500–seat auditorium, ballroom, library, school, and adjacent community center. He retired as rabbi emeritus in 1952.

Dedicated to traditional Judaism and Zionism, Kauvar defined his role in Denver as communal religious leader, pastor, and administrator. He founded a number of local organizations including the Denver Hebrew School (1905); the Jewish Consumptive Relief Society (1904), which later became the American Medical Center; and the Central Jewish Council (president, 1912–20), modeled on the traditional Jewish communal organization, the *kehilah*. An ardent Zionist, Kauvar founded the Denver chapter of Mizrachi (1911). He also served as president of the Denver Jewish Welfare Board (1914–25).

An early leader in the Conservative movement, Kauvar helped found the United Synagogue of America and served as its first vice-president (1912–14). As a member of the Rabbinical Assembly, Kauvar was the first president of its Midwest Region (1923). But ultimately he objected to many of the ritual and doctrinal changes advocated by Conservatism. Believing that Conservative Judaism was a form of Traditional Judaism, not a distinctive branch of Judaism, in 1958 Kauvar and Beth Ha-Medrosh Hagodol severed ties with the organizations that he had helped to create.

In 1920 Kauvar joined the faculty at the University of Denver as professor of rabbinic literature. He taught there until 1966, laying the foundations for the University of Denver's Jewish Studies program. Kauvar wrote a number of works based on his lectures at the university.

Kauvar married Belle G. Bluestone (1887–1930) in 1909; they had three children. After her death, he married Sara Sperber Gross (1895–1974) in 1937. Kauvar died on August 23, 1971, in Denver.

Writings: *Pirke Aboth Comments* (Philadelphia, 1929); *What is Judaism* (1933); *Religion, the Hope of the World* (Denver, 1949); *Torah Comments* (1952).

References: Michael Wayne Rubinoff, "Rabbi Charles Eliezer Hillel Kauvar of Denver: The Life of a Rabbi in the American West" (Ph.D. diss., University of Denver, 1978); *WWWJ* 1955, p. 392.

KELMAN, WOLFE (1923–). Rabbi, Executive Vice-President of the Rabbinical Assembly. The son of Hersh Leib and Mirl Fish Kelman, Wolfe Kelman was born on November 27, 1923, in Vienna, Austria. In his youth his family moved to Toronto, Canada, where he was educated in the public schools. Prior to completing his undergraduate studies, Kelman served in the Royal Canadian Air Force (1943–45). He earned a B.A. from the University of Toronto in 1946 and then immigrated to the United States to attend the Seminary, where he was ordained in 1950.

In 1951 Kelman was engaged in field work in Washington, D.C., on behalf of the Seminary when he received an invitation to succeed Max *Routtenberg as the chief executive of the Rabbinical Assembly (1951–). For more than thirty-five years, first as executive secretary, then as executive director, and finally as executive vice-president (1955–), Kelman has been the rabbi of the rabbis.

His primary responsibility for many years was as director of the Joint Placement Commission (1951–66). Kelman was uniquely qualified for this time-consuming and delicate task. As a rabbinical student he had directed High Holiday student placements (1949–50) and designed the students' system for pooling and redistributing their earnings based on need and seniority. Rabbinic placement required extraordinary energy in the 1950s and 1960s, the years of great expansion and growth in the Conservative movement. In but one twelve-month period (1952–53), Kelman handled more than eighty placements. His task was complicated by the paradox of the Conservative movement at that time—fewer rabbis than congregations, the reluctance of most rabbis to serve in remote areas, and an insufficient number of promotional positions, especially in the metropolitan congregations to which most of his colleagues aspired. By the time Gilbert *Epstein relieved Kelman of day-to-day placement responsibilities in 1965, Kelman had assisted some 1,500 rabbis and rabbinical students in finding pulpits.

His concern for his colleagues did not begin and end with rabbinic placement. Kelman remained their consultant and confidant, the director-general of rabbi-congregational relationships. He served as the watchman for rabbis negotiating to renew their contracts and as the liaison between the Placement Commission and synagogue boards in working out amicable separation and pension plans. His pioneering work in these matters and in leading the Rabbinical Assembly to adhere to strict organizational discipline helped professionalize and win dignity for the entire American rabbinate.

Kelman guided the Rabbinical Assembly as it grew rapidly in size, achievements, and stature within the Conservative movement and among American Jewry. As its head, he shaped the Rabbinical Assembly into an organization "profoundly concerned with fashioning contemporary Jewish life in this country," and he emerged as one of the chief statesmen of the Conservative movement.

When he first took office, the Rabbinical Assembly included some 300 rabbis serving primarily metropolitan congregations. Thirty-five years later it numbered more than 1,200 members in a dozen countries. The character of the Rabbinical Assembly changed significantly in this period. First, an increasing number of rabbis trained at rabbinical schools other than the Seminary applied for admission. Then large numbers of its members left the pulpit for alternative careers, and the Reconstructionists seceded to form their own denomination of American Judaism. And finally the Rabbinical Assembly wrestled with the issue of women rabbis and voted in 1985 to admit them. Kelman's optimism, flexibility, and fair-mindedness guided the association through these often wrenching developments. He always insisted on the autonomy and freedom of the rabbinate to speak its conscience and made certain that both the right and left wings within the Rabbinical Assembly were granted the opportunity to speak and to be heard.

He was largely responsible for orchestrating the many projects of the Rabbinical Assembly. He supervised its publications program, including the *Weekday Prayer Book* (1961), the journal *Conservative Judaism*, and the *Proceedings* of its annual conventions, before Jules *Harlow joined the RA as director of publications. Kelman coordinated the numerous meetings of the many RA committees, supervised the development of its regions, and was closely involved with the affairs of its very important Committee on Jewish Law and Standards and *bet din*. A champion of social justice, he helped push the social justice program that the Rabbinical Assembly had espoused since the 1930s into a new activist phase that saw Conservative rabbis championing civil rights, not only from their pulpits, but also on the picket lines and in marches.

Kelman was a vociferous defender of the Conservative movement and its success in the face of studies that showed the movement failing to replenish itself from its own ranks. The perspective of his office in the Seminary headquarters and the length of his service at the heart of the movement afforded him a clear understanding of Conservatism's many real accomplishments. His annual addresses to his colleagues served as reminders of their achievements and were meant to forestall the "pervasive public malaise" that dwelt on the problems of the present and the weaknesses of Conservatism. He often managed to turn these problems on their heads, observing, for example, during the trials of the 1960s youth rebellion that its challenges to institutional synagogues reflected not the rabbis' failures but actually the beginning of their successes.

Kelman's travels fostered the Rabbinical Assembly's growing international recognition. He was visiting rabbi of the West London Synagogue of British Jews (Upper Berkeley Street Synagogue, 1957–58). In 1963 he spent five months in Jerusalem engaged in a study of Judaism in Israel for the American Jewish Committee. In 1968 he visited the Soviet Union, Prague, and Bucharest to encourage their Jewish communities. In 1977 with Stanley *Rabinowitz and Saul *Teplitz he met with Israeli prime minister Menachem Begin to protest the "Who Is a Jew" legislation.

Kelman also served the Conservative movement outside of the Rabbinical Assembly. He taught homiletics (1967–73) and history (1973–   ) at the Seminary, was a member of the national Leadership Training Fellowship faculty, and chaired the academic board of the Melton Research Center for Jewish Education (1969–71). Elsewhere, he was president of the Hebrew Arts Foundation, a member of the governing council of the World Jewish Congress, chairman of its Cultural Commission, and co-chairman of its International Religious Affairs Commission. He was also a member of the Board of Directors of the Hebrew Immigrant Aid Society and president of the Committee of Neighbors Concerned with the Elderly, Their Rights, and Needs.

In 1952 Kelman married Jacqueline Miriam Levy, daughter of the noted Reform rabbi Felix Levy; they have three children.

Writings: "Report of the Executive Secretary," *PRA 1952* vol. 16 (1953), pp. 29–35; *PRA 1953* vol. 17 (1954) pp. 19–25; "Report of the Executive Director," *PRA 1955* vol. 19 (1956), pp. 19–23; "Report of the Executive Vice-President," *PRA 1960* vol. 24 (1960), pp. 70–80; *PRA 1965* vol. 29 (1965), pp. 1–17; "Judaism in Israel," *CJ* 19, 2 (Winter 1965), pp. 1–19; "Introspective Overview," *PRA 1969* vol. 33 (1969), pp. 1–8; "The American Synagogue: Present and Prospects," *CJ* 26, 1 (Fall 1971), pp. 3–24; "The American Synagogue: From Supermarket to Boutique," *PRA 1975* vol. 37 (1976), pp. 14–29; "Defeatism, Triumphalism or *Gevurah*?," *PRA 1980* vol. 42 (1981), pp. 13–24.

References: *American Jewish Biographies*, pp. 208–9; Gerson D. Cohen, "Wolfe Kelman—A Personal Tribute," in *Perspectives on Jews and Judaism: Essays in Honor of Wolfe Kelman*, ed. Arthur A. Chiel (New York, 1978), pp. 1–6. *WWAJ* 1980, p. 258.

KLEIN, ISAAC (1905–79). Rabbi, scholar. The son of Samuel and Ella Hershkowitz Klein, Isaac Klein was born in Ruthenia, Hungary, on September 5, 1905. In 1921 he and his family immigrated to the United States to join his father, who had arrived before World War I. Klein earned a B.A. from the City College of New York in 1931. Although he began his rabbinical studies at the Rabbi Isaac Elchanan Yeshiva, Klein was ordained at the Seminary in 1934.

From 1934 to 1953 Klein served as rabbi at Kadimah Congregation in Springfield, Massachusetts. There he continued his studies, earning a Ph.D. from
Harvard. And after continued study with Seminary professor Louis *Ginzberg,
he also became one of the few Seminary graduates to receive full ordination
(*hatarat horaah*).

During World War II, Klein served as a chaplain in the U.S. Army (1942–
46). His memoir, *The Anguish and the Ecstasy of a Jewish Chaplain*, describes
his experiences as a Jew in France in the wake of D-Day and his efforts to
organize relief for the Jews who had survived in Nazi-occupied Europe. On
leave from Kadimah Congregation during 1949–50, Klein served as a religious
advisor to the High Commissioner of Germany helping to reorganize Jewish
communities in Germany and to reestablish their communal institutions.

In 1953 Klein moved to the pulpit of Temple Emanu-El, Buffalo, New York.
He continued as rabbi after the synagogue merged with Temple Beth David to
become Temple Shaarey Zedek in 1968. As a congregational rabbi, Klein derived
great satisfaction from his teaching, but he repeatedly warned that the most
significant challenge facing Conservative Judaism was its inability to develop
sufficient numbers of congregants who observed Jewish law. Klein retired from
Shaarey Zedek in 1972, spending his winters in California where he taught
Jewish law at the University of Judaism.

Klein was one of the outstanding leaders of the right wing of the Conservative
movement. Not willing to sanction adjustments of *halachah* merely for the sake
of convenience, he nevertheless differed from Orthodoxy in his recognition of
the historical factors that affected the evolution of Jewish law. He was president
of the Rabbinical Assembly (1958–60) and a leading member of its Committee
on Jewish Law and Standards (CJLS) from its reorganization in 1948 until his
death. An authority on *halachah*, he authored many of the committee's most
important *responsa*, including those on the problems of abortion, autopsy, questions of medical ethics, *halizah*, and the marriage of a *kohen* and a convert.
Klein was also a member of the national *bet din* of the Conservative movement
and served as an associate professor of Jewish law at the Seminary.

In addition to his *responsa*, Klein published several works. In his magnum
opus, *A Guide to Jewish Religious Practice*, he set forth a modern code for
Jewish living in the twentieth century that incorporated many of the decisions
of the CJLS. A collection of his sermons, *Spiritual Legacies*, was published
posthumously.

Klein married Henriette Levine in 1932; they had three daughters. He died in
Los Angeles, California, on January 23, 1979.

Writings: *The Ten Commandments in a Changing World* (New York, 1944); "Towards a Philosophy of Conservative Judaism" *PRA 1948* vol. 12 (1949), pp. 129–38;
"Science and Some Ethical Issues—The Jewish View," *CJ* 13, 4 (Summer 1959), pp. 35–
47; "Abortion and the Jewish Tradition," *CJ* 24, 3 (Spring 1970), pp. 26–33; *The Anguish
and the Ecstasy of a Jewish Chaplain* (New York, 1974); *Responsa and Studies in
Halachah* (New York, 1975); *A Guide to Jewish Religious Practice* (New York, 1979).

Trans., *Code of Maimonides*, Book XII (1951), Book VII (1972), Book IV (1973) (New Haven, Conn.). Posthumously, *Spiritual Legacies: Sermons* (New York, 1981).

References: Herman Dicker, *Piety and Perseverance: Jews from the Carpathian Mountains* (New York, 1981); *EJ* vol. 10, col. 1100; *PRA 1979* vol. 41 (1979), pp. 262–65; *WWWJ* 1965, p. 508.

KLEIN, MAX DAVID (1885–1973). Rabbi. The son of Leopold and Sara Friedman Klein, Max Klein was born in New York City in 1885. Educated in the New York City public schools and the Talmud Torah School, he earned a B.A. from New York University in 1908 and was ordained at the Seminary in 1911.

As a senior rabbinical student, Klein led High Holiday services at Congregation Adath Jeshurun. Founded in 1859, Adath Jeshurun was one of the oldest synagogues in Philadelphia, Pennsylvania. After his ordination, Klein served as rabbi at Adath Jeshurun for more than fifty years. In 1913 he persuaded the congregation to become one of the founding members of the United Synagogue of America. During the next decades he worked to transform it into a Conservative synagogue-center. Building a new school and enlarging the synagogue in the 1920s attracted new members and led to expanded programming including a Young People's Congregation. To celebrate his forty years of service at Adath Jeshurun, Klein wrote, edited, and gracefully translated the prayer book *Seder Avodah for Sabbath, Festivals, and Weekdays* (1951). He followed that with *Seder Avodah for Rosh Hashannah and Yom Kippur* (1960), just prior to his retirement in 1961, when he was elected rabbi emeritus.

A leader in Philadelphia Jewish communal affairs, Klein helped found the Allied Jewish Appeal. He was a founder, first president, and later honorary president of the Philadelphia Board of Rabbis. An ardent Zionist, he was president of the Philadelphia Zionist Organization, national vice-president of the United Palestine Appeal, and chairman of the World Zionist Organization. As president of the Philadelphia branch of the United Synagogue, he worked to raise funds to open a Jewish students' house at the University of Pennsylvania in 1924.

One of the early leaders of Conservative Judaism, Klein was president of the Seminary Alumni Association (1916–22) longer than any other rabbi. He worked to strengthen the association internally, calling for greater harmony among the diverse wings of the association, and externally, demanding that representatives of the Seminary Alumni be included on national Jewish boards equally with representatives from other rabbinical bodies. He called for the establishment of a publication program and most significantly led the Seminary Alumni Association to adopt its new name, the Rabbinical Assembly of the Jewish Theological Seminary of America. Throughout his career Klein remained an active member of the RA, chairing several committees, including Rabbinical Ethics (1930–31) and its Seminary Campaign (1944–46). In 1950 he edited the "Code of Professional Conduct of the Rabbinical Assembly."

Klein died on December 4, 1973, in Jenkintown, Pennsylvania.

Writings: *Hymns of Praise and Prayer* (Philadelphia, 1926); *Seder Avodah for Sabbath, Festivals, and Weekdays* (Philadelphia, 1951); *Seder Avodah for Rosh Hashannah and Yom Kippur* (Philadelphia, 1960).

References: *The Jewish Exponent* 9 June 1911, p. 9; 29 June 1917, p. 9; 6 July 1917, p. 2; 28 June 1918, p. 2; 20 June 1919, p. 10; 14 December 1973, p. 92; Abraham J. Karp, *A History of the United Synagogue of America, 1913–1963* (New York, 1964), p. 50; *PRA 1974* vol. 36 (1975): 202; *PRA 1975* vol. 37 (1976): 308; *Recorder* 8, 2 (April 1928), p. 15.

KOGEN, DAVID CHAIM (1919–   ). Rabbi, educator, administrator. The son of Meyer and Esther Reiter Kogen, David Kogen was born on September 19, 1919, in Rutki, Poland, and brought to the United States in 1928. He earned an A.B. from the University of Chicago in 1942 and was ordained at the Seminary in 1946.

Kogen began his career as rabbi at Congregation Beth Israel, Vancouver, British Columbia (1946–55), where he was also director of the B'nai B'rith Hillel Foundation at the University of British Columbia (1946–55). In the course of a decade in Canada, Kogen emerged as a leader in several Vancouver communal organizations, including the Institute for Church and Social Service Workers, the Red Cross, and the Jewish Family Welfare Bureau.

After ten years in Canada, Kogen returned to New York City. At the same time that he was visiting rabbi at Park Avenue Synagogue (1956–57), rabbi at Temple Ansche Chesed (1957–58), and president of the Hebrew Arts Foundation (1956–58), he moved away from the congregational rabbinate, turning to a career in administration in the chief organizations of the Conservative movement. Kogen was director of community activities for the United Synagogue (1955–58) and a member of its Committee on Congregational Standards. Then, having already served both on the Executive Council and the Membership Committee of the Rabbinical Assembly, he was asked to replace RA executive vice-president Wolfe *Kelman during Kelman's sabbatical (1957–58). At the end of that year, during which he represented the Rabbinical Assembly in both Washington and Albany in debates on key legislation affecting Jewish religious life, Kogen joined the Seminary as assistant to the chancellor (1958–66). The Israel Goldstein Assistant Professor in Practical Theology, Kogen eventually became the Seminary's administrative vice-chancellor (1966–   ).

In more than a quarter of a century at the Seminary Kogen has had numerous responsibilities. He was registrar of the Rabbinical Department, director and instructor in liturgy in the Cantors Institute-Seminary College of Jewish Music, liaison to the Rabbinical Assembly's Executive Council, and Seminary representative on the Joint Placement Commission, Chaplaincy Availability Board, and Joint Retirement Board. He directed the Seminary's Graduate School and the Institute for Advanced Studies in the Humanities, chaired the Department of Professional Skills, and taught a practical rabbinics course designed to prepare rabbinical candidates to celebrate rites of passage, raise funds, and manage budgets. He also served on the boards of directors of the United Synagogue, National Ramah Commission, and the Institute for Religious and Social Studies.

Kogen married Dena Rosenblum in 1947; they have four sons.

References: *PRA 1958* vol. 22 (1959), pp. 56–57; *WWAJ* 1980, p. 267; *WWWJ* 1965, p. 517.

KOHN, EUGENE (1887–1977). Rabbi, liturgist. The son of Siegfried and Bertha Kussy Kohn, Eugene Kohn was born in Newark, New Jersey, on January 26, 1887. He earned a B.A. from New York University in 1907 and was ordained at the Seminary in 1912.

Kohn served numerous congregations, including Congregation Chizuk Amuno, Baltimore, Maryland (1912–18); Beth Mordecai, Perth Amboy, New Jersey (1921–23); Congregation Beth-El, the pioneer Conservative congregation in Milwaukee, Wisconsin (1923–26); Congregation Anshe Emeth, Youngstown, Ohio (1926–29); Temple Emanu-El, Bayonne, New Jersey (1929–34); and Beth Israel Center, St. Albans, New York (1936–37). In addition, Kohn also served on the staff of Young Judea. The many positions suggest that Kohn was not entirely successful as a congregational rabbi. However, he left his mark on American Judaism as one of the foremost exponents of Reconstructionism.

A disciple of Mordecai M. *Kaplan, Kohn was associated with the Reconstructionist movement from its inception. He played an important role in its development as the first editor of its magazine, *Reconstructionist* (1938–63), editor of the Reconstructionist press, and as an administrator and ideologist. Kohn believed that whereas past generations had expected prayer to influence favorably the conditions of life, modern Jews expected it to arouse religious emotion and to inspire ethical behavior. This change in attitude demanded modification of the prayer books. He played a leading role in editing several liturgical works published by the Reconstructionist Foundation, including *Shir Hadash* (1939), a book of readings and prayers; *The New Haggadah for the Pesah Seder* (1941; rev. 1942); the *Sabbath Prayer Book* (1945); and the *High Holiday Prayer Book* (1948).

Kohn also wrote a number of books of religious philosophy. In the *Future of Judaism in America* (1934), he argued that many of the traditions observed by Jews in the ghetto period were obsolete in the twentieth century. Although modern Judaism still revolved around the traditional themes of God, Israel and Torah, these concepts required reinterpretation if they were to function in modern life. In addition to this call for the reconstruction of Jewish ideology, Kohn proposed a reorganization of Jewish social and institutional life to modify those institutions, namely the home, school, and the synagogue, which had sustained Jews in the past. In *Religious Humanism* (1953) he set forth his philosophy of religion and of Reconstructionism.

As president of the Rabbinical Assembly (1935–37), Kohn pushed for the implementation of his ideas within the Conservative movement. He called for an evaluation of the organization of Jewish communal life, the development of techniques for implementing social action, and the redefinition of ethical concepts to effect the reconstruction of society in accordance with ethical criteria.

In 1915 Kohn married Mildred Jaine; they had four children. Kohn died in New York City on April 1, 1977.

Writings: *The Future of Judaism in America* (New Rochelle, N.Y., 1934); "President's Message" *PRA 1936* vol. 5 (1939), pp. 252–66; "President's Message" *PRA 1937* vol. 5 (1939), pp. 358–67; *Religious Humanism: A Jewish Interpretation* (New York, 1953). Ed., *American Jewry: The Tercentenary and After: 1694–1954* (New York, 1955); *Good to Be a Jew* (New York, 1959); *Shir Hadash* (New York, 1939). Co-ed., with Mordecai M. Kaplan and Ira Eisenstein, *The New Haggadah for the Pesah Seder* (New York, 1941; rev. 1942); *High Holiday Prayer Book* (New York, 1948); with Mordecai M. Kaplan, Ira Eisenstein, and Milton Steinberg, *Sabbath Prayer Book* (New York, 1945); with Mordecai M. Kaplan, Jack Cohen, and Ludwig Nadelmann, *The Festival Prayer Book* (New York, 1958); with Mordecai M. Kaplan, Jack Cohen, Ira Eisenstein, and Ludwig Nadelmann, *The Daily Prayer Book* (New York, 1963).

References: *EJ* vol. 10, col. 1144; *NYT* 2 April 1977, p. 22; *PRA 1940* vol. 7 (1941), p. 180; *Reconstructionist* vol. 43 (May 1977), pp. 5–6; *Recorder* 4, 1 (January 1924), p. 14; *WWAJ* 1938–39, pp. 551–52.

KOHN, JACOB (1881–1968). Rabbi, educator. The son of Siegfried and Bertha Kussy Kohn, Jacob Kohn was born in Newark, New Jersey, on September 15, 1881. Educated in the Newark public schools, he earned a Ph.D. from New York University in 1902, was ordained at the Seminary in 1907, and earned a Doctor of Hebrew Letters there in 1917.

Kohn first served Congregation Adath Jeshuron, Syracuse, New York (1908–11). He then led Congregation Ansche Chesed, a fashionable, upper-middle-class congregation in New York City (1911–31). At this early date Ansche Chesed had already adopted practices—ushers to insure decorum, family pews, a choir, and an organ—that later came to be associated with many Conservative congregations. Kohn's thoughtful, philosophically oriented sermons influenced Seminary rabbinical students who attended his services in order to compare his style of preaching with that of their homiletics professor Mordecai M. *Kaplan, and Kohn personally guided men such as Milton *Steinberg to the rabbinate.

In 1931, at the age of fifty, Kohn left New York to lay the groundwork for Conservative Judaism in Los Angeles at Sinai Temple (1931–57). There Kohn, a soft-spoken rabbi who espoused theological radicalism, was esteemed for defending the workingman's right to organize. Despite Kohn's reputation as a leader of Los Angeles Jewry, a staunch Zionist, and a theological scholar of national reknown, he was unable to attract new and younger members to Sinai Temple. As he aged, the membership of Sinai Temple aged and was not replaced until Kohn's successor, Rabbi Israel Chodos, moved the congregation to the more fashionable Wilshire Boulevard. In 1957 Kohn became rabbi emeritus of Sinai Temple following his retirement.

Kohn had a distinguished career as a leader within the Conservative movement. He was president of the Alumni Association of the Jewish Theological Seminary, the forerunner of the Rabbinical Assembly (1912–14). A founder of the United Synagogue, Kohn was its first recording secretary, and he served briefly as its president in 1931. Kohn opposed Cyrus *Adler's efforts to prevent the United Synagogue from evolving into a third denomination within American Judaism. Therefore, in 1919 he joined the Society for Jewish Renascence, founded by Mordecai M. *Kaplan, and in 1922 organized the Conference of Conservative Rabbis. Both organizations proposed to formulate new Conservative platforms. Kohn also helped found the West Coast branch of the Seminary, the University of Judaism, in 1948. He served as dean of its Graduate School and associate professor of philosophy.

Long insistent that the Conservative movement needed to publish its own prayer books, Kohn proposed liturgical amendments to render worship consonant with the outlook of twentieth-century Jewry. In 1927 he helped edit the *Festival Prayer Book*, published by the United Synagogue of America. This prayer book appeared in two editions, one with the traditional text intact and one in which Kohn introduced liturgical emendations for use in certain Conservative congregations. Kohn was also a member of the commission that prepared *The Sabbath and Festival Prayer Book* of the Rabbinical Assembly and the United Synagogue of America (1946).

In 1932 the Women's League published Kohn's *Modern Problems of Jewish Parents*, which advocated the early development of a strong Jewish identification to prevent intermarriage. Kohn later published two theological studies concerned with evolution, the nature of God, and the problem of evil.

Kohn married Augusta Hirsch in 1908; they had four children. Kohn died in Los Angeles on September 10, 1968.

Writings: *Modern Problems of Jewish Parents* (New York, 1932); *The Moral Life of Man: Its Philosophical Foundations* (New York, 1956); *Evolution as Revelation* (New York, 1963).

References: *AJYB 1969* vol. 70 (1969), p. 522; Simon Noveck, *Milton Steinberg, Portrait of a Rabbi* (New York, 1978), pp. 15–16; *PRA 1960* vol. 24 (1960), pp. 266–68; *PRA 1969* vol. 33 (1969), pp. 182–83; *PRA 1973* vol. 35 (1974), p. 41; Herbert Rosenblum, "The Founding of the United Synagogue of America" (Ph.D. diss., Brandeis University, 1970), pp. 144, 174–75, 247, 252; Herman H. and Mignon L. Rubenovitz, *The Waking Heart* (Cambridge, Mass., 1967), p. 58; Max Vorspan and Lloyd P. Gartner, *History of the Jews of Los Angeles* (San Marino, Calif., 1970), pp. 211, 215, 260; *WWWJ* 1965, p. 408.

KOHUT, ALEXANDER (1842–94). Rabbi, scholar. The son of Jacob and (?) Kohut, Alexander Kohut was born in Felegyhaza, Hungary, on April 22, 1842. Family poverty prevented him from beginning his elementary education until the age of nine. Educated in Kecskemet, he progressed rapidly through the elementary and gymnasium courses while taking classical Jewish studies. Kohut then went on to study in Budapest. He earned a Ph.D. in oriental languages at the University of Leipzig in 1864 and was ordained at the Jewish Theological Seminary of Breslau in 1867. There, one of his teachers was Zacharias Frankel, the father of Positive-Historical Judaism, the European ideological predecessor of American Conservatism.

For nearly two decades Kohut served as a rabbi in Hungary, first in Stuhlweissenburg (1867–72); then in Fuenfkirchen (1872–80), where he was chief rabbi; and last at Grosswardein (1880–84). Widely known for his preaching, he emerged during these years as a leader among Hungarian Jewry. While in Stuhlweissenburg, he became the first Jew named county superintendent of schools in Hungary. He was elected secretary of the Congress of Jewish Notables, held in Budapest in 1868. In 1885 Prime Minister Koloman von Tisza, deeply impressed by his oratory, appointed him representative of the Jews to parliament. But Kohut's immigration to the United States that May to succeed Dr. Adolph Huebsch as rabbi of Congregation Ahavath Chesed, New York City, prevented him from taking the appointment.

Established in 1846, Ahavath Chesed (later called the Central Synagogue) had already introduced many reforms. Huebsch had arranged an abridged German-Hebrew prayer book for the congregation, allowed mixed seating, and varied the traditional order of the weekly Torah readings. The congregation had also eliminated celebration of Purim, Chanukah, and the second day of festivals. Through his teaching and preaching Kohut called upon his new congregants to return to greater traditionalism. Yet at the same time he approved their family pews and abbreviated prayer services—he even prepared a new edition of Huebsch's prayer book—as innovations essential to draw modern Jews to services. Kohut thus remained true to the spirit of the Historical School which emphasized the evolving character of Jewish tradition and recognized the historic experiences of the Jewish people as organic to its development.

Kohut's defense of traditionalism almost immediately brought him into debate with the champions of Reform Judaism. Kohut believed that the future of American Jewry—its continuance or disappearance as a Jewish community—depended upon its acceptance of the authority of Torah and the rabbinic tradition. Kohut took the themes of the imperative of Jewish law and the chain of rabbinic authority, articulated in the Mishnaic text *Pirke Avot*, as the subjects of his first sermons from the pulpit of Ahavath Chesed (published as *Ethics of the Fathers*, 1885). Kaufman Kohler, then rabbi of New York's Temple Beth El and later president of the Reform Hebrew Union College, saw Kohut's defense of traditionalism as a challenge to American Reform. Kohler's rebuttal from his pulpit and in the Jewish press, published as *Backward or Forward* (1885), transformed the rabbis' sermons into a debate between the proponents and opponents of Reform Judaism.

The debate became a turning point in the development of the Conservative and Reform movements. It marked Kohut, within a few short months of his landing in New York, as an articulate defender and the chief ideologue of the

Historical School in America. Linked by his education at the Jewish Theological Seminary of Breslau to the leaders of the European Positive-Historical School, Kohut thus bridged the European and American schools of historical Judaism. His formulation of the Historical School's ideology, as Moshe *Davis has shown, helped unify the disparate forces of the American Historical School into the group that founded the Jewish Theological Seminary of America. Of no less importance, the debate pushed the Reformers to call the Pittsburgh Conference of 1885 to crystallize their ideology. Its radical program, the Pittsburgh Platform, drafted by Kohler, became the banner of Reform Judaism in America.

Kohut played a principal role in the founding of the Jewish Theological Seminary of America in 1886. Having been in America for only a short time, he lacked the credentials to lead an American school. But when the radicalism of the Reform movement, capped by the Pittsburgh Platform, compelled the establishment of a second rabbinical school in America, one dedicated to traditionalism, Kohut joined Sabato *Morais in guiding its development. He helped raise funds for the Seminary, persuading his own Ahavath Chesed to enlist in the Seminary Association at the same time that it remained a member of the Reform Union of American Hebrew Congregations. Kohut joined the faculty, teaching *midrash* and Talmudic methodology. But his greatest contribution was his influence in modeling the Seminary curriculum and educational philosophy on that of his alma mater, the Jewish Theological Seminary of Breslau. Along with Bernard Drachman, the Seminary's first faculty member, who was also a graduate of the Breslau school, Kohut convinced Seminary leaders to pattern the curriculum after Breslau's seven-year program. The New York school thus not only stressed Talmud and Codes, the traditional subjects of the East European *yeshivot*, but also Bible, Jewish history, philosophy, *midrash*, and homiletics. One hundred years later this curriculum—with the additions of modern Hebrew literature and pastoral psychology—remains the basic curriculum of the Seminary.

Kohut's bequest to the development of Conservatism includes another contribution. He was among the first leaders of the Seminary to use the term *Conservative Judaism*. In articles in the *American Hebrew* and in addresses at the Seminary, he expressed the hope that the spirit of Conservative Judaism would prevail there. Yet he firmly resisted a denominational label for the school and fought against the title (the Orthodox Seminary) proposed by Morais. Instead Kohut hoped—much like subsequent leaders—that all elements of American Jewry would unite behind the Seminary.

Long before his immigration to the United States, Kohut established himself as a scholar of the first rank. He wrote on such diverse topics as the social and political relations of the Jews in Rome, the Parsic origins of the Jewish angelology and demonology, the Talmud and Parseeism, the Book of Tobit, Second Isaiah, mythology, and Yemenite *midrashim*. His magnum opus, conceived in his early teens, was the *Arukh Ha-Shalem* (1878–92), a lexicon of Talmudic terms. Although in form it was a new edition of the twelfth-century Talmudic dictionary of Nathan ben Jehiel of Rome, in fact it was a path-finding contribution in which Kohut offered etymologies and new sources drawn from his wide knowledge of oriental and classical languages.

Kohut and his first wife, Julia, had eight children. After she died in 1886, Kohut married Rebekah Bettelheim in 1887. Kohut died on May 25, 1894, in New York City.

Writings: *Uber die judische Angelologie und Dämonologie in ihrer Abhangigkeit vom Parsimus* (Leipzig, 1866); *Kritische Beleuchtung der persischen Pentateuch* (Leipzig and Heidelberg, 1871); *Arukh Ha-Shalem*, 8 vols. (Vienna, 1878–92); *The Ethics of the Fathers*, ed. Barnett A. Elzas (1885; 2d ed. 1920). Ed., Nathanel Ibn Yeshaya, *Light of Shade and Lamp of Wisdom* (New York, 1894). Trans., *Prayers for the Divine Services of Congregation Ahavath Chesed*, ed. A. Huebsch (New York, 1889).

References: *EJ* vol. 10, cols. 1149–52; Moshe Davis, *The Emergence of Conservative Judaism* (New York, 1963); Ismar Elbogen, in *AJYB* vol. 44 (1942), pp. 73–80; *Jewish Encyclopedia* 7, pp. 537–38. George Alexander Kohut, *The Alexander Kohut Memorial Foundation* (Vienna, 1928); *Concerning Alexander Kohut: A Tentative Bibliography* (Budapest, 1927); *Morituri: A Reminiscence of My Father* (New York, 1907); Rebekah Bettelheim Kohut, *My Portion: An Autobiography* (1925; reprint ed., New York, 1975).

KREITMAN, BENJAMIN ZVI (1919–   ). Rabbi, administrator. The son of Jacob and Anna Grabower Kreitman, Benjamin Kreitman was born in Warsaw, Poland, on December 25, 1920, and brought to the United States in 1924. He earned a B.A. from Yeshiva University in 1940 and was ordained at the Seminary in the fall of 1942 in a special convocation ceremony. In order to meet the wartime emergency call for chaplains, the Seminary accelerated the ordination of rabbinical candidates.

Kreitman immediately joined the U.S. armed forces as Navy chaplain (1943–46). After the war he began a thirty-year career as a congregational rabbi. First he was assistant rabbi at Kehillath Israel, Brookline, Massachusetts (1947–48), working with Rabbi Judah *Nadich. After a year Kreitman moved to his own pulpit as rabbi at Beth El Synagogue, New London, Connecticut (1948–52). There he took the lead in developing adult education programs.

In 1952 he returned to New York to the Brooklyn Jewish Center. As associate rabbi (1952–54) and as rabbi (1954–68), Kreitman worked with the senior rabbi, master preacher Israel *Levinthal, in this model Conservative urban synagogue-center of more than a thousand families. Kreitman continued to develop innovative programs in adult education for the Brooklyn Jewish Center, including the Mishnah Fellowship, Great Books Seminar, and Great Jewish Books Seminar. In 1968 he moved to the pulpit of Shaare Torah Synagogue in the Flatbush section of Brooklyn (1968–76) and was elected rabbi emeritus in 1976.

Kreitman's numerous Jewish communal and civic posts included president of the Small Business Operations Corporation (1962–65) and of the Brooklyn Jewish Community Council (1970–73), chairman of the Brooklyn Borough Human Rights Commission (1960–67), and he was the only non-medical member of the

New York City Board of Health. He also taught Judaica at Brooklyn College (1974) and Codes at the Seminary (1975).

During these years Kreitman emerged as an influential member of the Rabbinical Assembly. He was vice-chairman of its Metropolitan Region and chairman of the Brooklyn Region. But most importantly, he was chairman of the Rabbinical Assembly's Committee on Jewish Law and Standards (CJLS; 1966–72). Believing that Jewish law "must concern itself with and accommodate itself to the needs of the day," he led the CJLS in a period of great creativity to make bold decisions, breaking through many *halachic* logjams that had previously stymied the committee. During his tenure the committee recognized developments in the laws of *kashrut*, allowed for the abolition of the widely ignored second day of festivals, and ended the long-standing debate over the *agunah*, relieving the plight of the abandoned wife. But in 1970 the activist phase of the committee unexpectedly came to a halt when a majority of its members resigned in protest over administrative procedures. The crisis precipitated its reorganization two years later.

In 1976 Kreitman left the congregational rabbinate to succeed Rabbi Bernard *Segal as executive vice-president of the United Synagogue. In his inaugural address he called for an end to timidity, claiming it was time for the United Synagogue to recognize that Conservatism had grown from a "tendency" into a "movement." Kreitman's pulpit career had revealed the changing character of the Conservative synagogue. No longer were Conservative congregations primarily child-centered institutions. Instead, an increasing portion of their activities involved senior citizens, adult education, and pastoral counseling. Kreitman determined, therefore, to lead the United Synagogue in developing new programs and publications for the contemporary Conservative synagogue.

He was also influential in the Conservative movement's thrust to establish Conservatism securely in the state of Israel. With Kreitman as a consultant, the World Council of Synagogues was transformed from primarily an agency of the United Synagogue into an organization representing all branches of the Conservative movement. Its reorganization paved the way for the World Council to join the World Zionist Organization. Kreitman co-authored with the Rabbinical Assembly's Wolfe *Kelman and the Seminary's Simon *Greenberg the World Council's preamble promoting the expression of religious pluralism in Israel. Kreitman also confirmed the United Synagogue's stance, emphasized in the last years of Segal's administration, of promoting the immigration of Conservative Jews to Israel. In order to encourage Conservative Jewish immigration, the United Synagogue maintained an *aliyah* desk in its New York headquarters and an absorption desk in Israel.

Kreitman married Joyce Krimsky in 1956; they have two children.

Writings: "The First Ten Years of the Committee on Law and Standards: Creative *Halachah* and the Conservative Movement," *PRA 1958* vol. 22 (1959), pp. 68–80; "Report of the Committee on Jewish Law and Standards," *PRA 1967* vol. 31 (1967), pp. 189–94; *PRA 1968* vol. 32 (1968), pp. 206–18; *PRA 1970* vol. 34 (1971), pp. 191–

99; "From 'Tendency' to 'Movement'," *Review* 28, 3 (Winter 1976), pp. 8ff; "From the Executive Vice-president," *Review* 29, 2 (Fall 1976), pp. 2ff.

References: Herbert Rosenblum, *Conservative Judaism* (New York, 1983), pp. 53–55; *WWAJ* 1980, p. 276; *WWWJ* 1965, p. 531.

KUSHNER, HAROLD (1935–   ). Rabbi, author. The son of Julius and Sarah Hartman Kushner, Harold Kushner was born on April 3, 1935, in Brooklyn, New York. He received his early Jewish education at the Brooklyn Jewish Center, earned a B.A. from Columbia University in 1955, was ordained at the Seminary in 1960, and earned a Doctor of Hebrew Letters there in 1972.

After beginning his career as U.S. Army chaplain at Fort Sill, Oklahoma (1960–62), Kushner served as assistant rabbi to Mordecai *Waxman at Temple Israel, Great Neck, New York (1962–66). Since 1966 he has led Temple Israel, Natick, Massachusetts, where he has experimented with creative liturgy. Convinced that "the rabbi has become a caregiver first and a teacher second" and that rabbis teach by the way they care for people, he has found counseling congregants in times of crisis the most important aspect of his ministry.

In the Conservative movement Kushner was president of the New England Region of the Rabbinical Assembly (1972–74), and he edited the journal *Conservative Judaism* (1980–84). He also served on the editorial committee that prepared the Rabbinical Assembly's prayer books *Likrat Shabbat* (1973) and *Mahzor Hadash* (1977).

Kushner earned a national reputation for his best seller, *When Bad Things Happen to Good People* (1981), a popular theology that sold two million copies. Here he reflected on the death of his fourteen-year-old son and expressed the view that all that happened in the world was not part of the grand design of God's plan. Nevertheless, Kushner defended the importance of religion which serves to strengthen the individual and provide solace amidst the tragedies of life. Because Kushner found great strength in the congregational rabbinate, which kept him connected to other people, he chose to remain in the pulpit despite his literary fame. He continued, however, to write. *When All You Ever Wanted Isn't Enough* (1986) was inspired by his turning fifty and his reflections over his changing goals and aspirations.

Kushner married Suzette Estrada in 1960; they had two children.

Writings: *When Children Ask About God* (New York, 1971); *Commanded to Live* (Bridgeport, Conn., 1973); *CJ* 29, 2 (Winter 1975), p. 52; *When Bad Things Happen to Good People* (New York, 1981); "The Hunger for the Sacred," *PRA 1982* vol. 44 (1983), pp. 22–30; *When All You Ever Wanted Isn't Enough* (New York, 1986).

References: *CJ* 26, 2 (Winter 1972), pp. 88–89; *CJ* 37, 1 (Fall 1983), pp. 71–73.

L

LANDESMAN, ALTER (1895–1980?).   The son of S. Levi and Zelaha Schmuelson Landesman, Alter Landesman was born in Lithuania on December 5, 1895, and immigrated to the United States in 1906. He earned a B.A. at Western Reserve University in 1917, was ordained at the Seminary in 1922, and earned a Doctor of Hebrew Letters there in 1948.

Following his ordination, Landesman was appointed superintendent (later executive director) of the Hebrew Education Society of Brooklyn (1922–62). Established in 1899 by the Baron de Hirsch Fund and modeled on the Educational Alliance of Manhattan's Lower East Side, the Hebrew Education Society was originally an educational and social center fostering the acculturation of immigrants. But under Landesman's direction it was transformed into a community center serving Brownsville Jewry, which for a time was the largest Jewish community in New York. The society provided the neighborhood with a host of educational, recreational, and social services, and it served as a meeting site for numerous clubs and groups.

As executive director of this important community institution, Landesman was naturally involved in a variety of Brownsville activities. He was the founding president of the Brownsville Neighborhood Council, established in 1938 by representatives of local civic, social, and business organizations to deal jointly with communal affairs affecting housing, health, recreation, and social services. Landesman also helped guide the development of Young Israel of Brownsville and East Flatbush. As a pioneer in the Jewish center movement, he served as president of the Metropolitan Association of Jewish Center Workers (1942) and vice-president of the National Association of Jewish Center Workers. His intimate knowledge of Brownsville Jewry led him to write *Brownsville* (1969), a history of this community.

In the Conservative movement Landesman was an early leader in the development of its educational programs. For nearly a quarter of a century he chaired the chief educational body of the United Synagogue (chair, Committee on Jewish Education, 1925?–40; co-chair, Joint Commission on Jewish Education, 1940–47). Landesman also wrote the United Synagogue's first *Curriculum for Jewish Religious Schools* (1922). This consisted of four separate curricula: for the school meeting daily, for the three-day-a-week school, for the Sunday school, and a special two-year course for children beginning their schooling at age eleven. Landesman also was active in the Rabbinical Assembly, serving as corresponding secretary (1927–30) and heading the board that edited the first two volumes of its *Proceedings* (1927–28).

Landesman died in 1980(?).

Writings: *Curriculum for Jewish Religious Schools* (New York, 1922); *Brownsville: The Birth, Development, and Passing of a Jewish Community in New York* (New York, 1969; 2d ed. 1971); *A History of New Lots, Brooklyn to 1887* (Port Washington, N.Y., 1977).

References: Abraham J. Karp, *A History of the United Synagogue of America, 1913–1963* (New York, 1964), p. 42; *PRA 1981* vol. 43 (1982), pp. 113–14; *WWWJ 1978*, p. 517.

LANG, LEON S. (1898–1956). Rabbi. The son of David and Annie Suwalki Lang, Leon Lang was born in Rishon LeZion, Palestine, on May 9, 1898. Brought to America in 1898, Lang was educated in the Chicago public schools. He went back to Palestine as a youth and was educated at Tel Aviv's Gymnazia Herzlia. Returning to the United States, he earned a B.S. from Columbia University in 1927, was ordained at the Seminary in the same year, and earned a Ph.D. from Dropsie College in 1950.

As associate rabbi of Congregation Oheb Shalom, Newark, New Jersey (1927–39?), Lang was chiefly responsible for Oheb Shalom's growing South Orange satellite. An authority on family relations, he directed the Institute on Marriage and Jewish Family Living in Newark (1935–40). This work convinced Lang that one of the most important functions of the rabbinate, one all too frequently slighted, was counseling.

In 1939 Lang moved to Philadelphia to become rabbi at the Germantown Jewish Center. In 1942 he became spiritual director of Philadelphia's Congregation Beth El. In Philadelphia Lang worked in the field of Jewish education. He chaired the Philadelphia Jewish Committee on Religion and the Public Schools (1942–52) and the Curriculum Committee of the Philadelphia Board of Education of the United Synagogue. He also completed *A Curriculum for the Congregational School* (1950) for which he earned his doctorate.

Lang played an active role in the chaplaincy. In 1949 he was one of four clergymen sent by the U.S. Department of Defense to tour Germany and Austria to evaluate de-Nazification and the conditions of the Jews remaining in the displaced persons camps. In 1953 he toured the Chaplains Corps in Korea, Japan, and the Pacific islands. Lang also served as chief Jewish chaplain to the Philadelphia Civilian Defense, and he chaired the Rabbinical Assembly's Chaplaincy Availability Board (1950–53).

As president of the Rabbinical Assembly (1940–42), Lang called for the creation of a commission to publish a prayer book to reflect the practice in Conservative congregations, and he worked to fill the need for Jewish chaplains created by the U.S. entrance into World War II. Lang also edited the *Proceedings of the Rabbinical Assembly* (1930–32), and he was the founding editor of the Rabbinical Assembly journal *Conservative Judaism* (1944–52).

Lang married Rebecca Greenspan in 1922; they had four children. He died on April 25, 1956, in West Philadelphia, Pennsylvania.

Writings: "Presidential Message" *PRA 1941* vol. 8 (1947) pp. 3–25; "Presidential Message," *PRA 1942* vol. 8 (1947), pp. 56–63; "Personal Guidance by the Rabbi" *PRA 1946* vol. 10 (1947), pp. 17–22; "Notes on a Tour through Germany," *CJ* 6,1 (October 1949), pp. 68–73; *A Curriculum for the Congregational School* (Philadelphia, 1950); *Jewish Values in Family Relationships* (New York, 1951); *The Sabbath and Jewish Family Living* (New York, 1953).

References: *NYT* 27 April 1956, p. 27; *WWWJ* 1955, p. 430.

LEVI, SAMUEL GERSHON (1908–   ). Rabbi. The son of Paul and Minnie Fleishman Levi, S. Gershon Levi was born on June 13, 1908, in Toronto, Canada. He earned a B.A. from the University of Toronto in 1929 and was ordained at the Seminary in 1933.

Following his ordination, Levi returned to Canada as educational director of Montreal's leading Conservative congregation, Shaar Hashomayim (1936–41), then led by Rabbi Herman *Abramowitz. Levi left the synagogue during World War II to serve as the senior Jewish chaplain in the Canadian armed forces (1941–46). Posted to England with the rank of major, he shared responsibility with the U.S. Army's senior Jewish chaplain, Rabbi Judah *Nadich, for planning and conducting the religious services held prior to the D-Day invasion.

After the war, Levi settled in the United States as rabbi of the Jamaica Jewish Center, Jamaica, New York (1947–72). There he worked to upgrade the curriculum and standards of the weekday Hebrew school and the adult education programs. After twenty-five years of service, he was elected rabbi emeritus.

In addition to congregational responsibilities, Levi directed Camp Ramah in the Poconos (1951) and was a member of the Queens Council of the New York State Commission Against Discrimination. But he devoted much of his efforts outside his congregation to the Rabbinical Assembly. He was a member of the Executive Council and chairman of its Ethics Committee. As treasurer (1957–65), he brought order to its fiscal affairs and fixed a system of graduated dues. During his tenure as editor of *Conservative Judaism* (1965–69), the journal doubled its circulation, thanks to Levi's promotion of this important forum of Jewish thought. As vice-president (1968–70) and then as president of the Rabbinical Assembly (1970–72), he sensed that the RA was at a crossroads. He led its seventy-first convention, the first ever held in Israel, and called for greater support for the Conservative movement there. His administration also weathered the temporary disbandment of the Committee on Jewish Law and Standards. Levi drafted one of several schemes proposed for its reorganization. When the committee regrouped in 1972, he briefly assumed its chair (1972–73).

After Levi retired from congregational life, he settled in Jerusalem. There he translated and/or edited several works, including *Barnett Janner* (1984), a biography of the Lithuanian immigrant who served in Parliament for forty years and was president of the Board of Deputies of British Jewry.

In 1932 Levi married Shonie Biegelsen, chairwoman of the Education and Reading Committee of the National Women's League (1948–60) and co-author with Sylvia R. Kaplan of its *Guide for the Jewish Homemaker* (1959; rev. 1964). The Levis have two children.

Writings: "The President's Reports," *Beineinu* 3, 1 (January 1973), pp. 26–32. Ed., Elsie Janner, *Barnett Janner: A Personal Portrait* (London, 1984). Ed. and trans., Gedalia Alon, *The Jews in Their Land in the Talmudic Age, 70–640 C.E.* (Jerusalem, 1980). Trans., Hayyim Hazaz, *The Gates of Bronze* (Philadelphia, 1975).

References: *PRA 1969* vol. 33 (1969), p. 50; *WWWJ* 1965, p. 450.

LEVINTHAL, ISRAEL HERBERT (1888–1982). Rabbi. The son of Rabbi Bernard and Minna Kleinberg Levinthal, Israel Levinthal was born in Vilna, Lithuania, on February 12, 1888, the descendant of twelve generations of rabbis. He was brought to the United States in 1891 and raised in Philadelphia, where his father founded the *Agudat ha-Rabbanim*, the Union of Orthodox Rabbis, in 1902. Levinthal earned a B.A. from Columbia University in 1909, was ordained at the Seminary in 1910, and earned a Doctor of Hebrew Letters from the Seminary in 1920.

Levinthal's first congregation was Temple B'nai Shalom in Brooklyn (1910–15). Disturbed by the pressure to solicit members and to clear the debt on the synagogue's mortgage, Levinthal began to study law as an alternative career. He earned a J.D. from New York University in 1914, but ultimately decided that the practice of law was not spiritually fulfilling.

In 1915 Levinthal accepted a call from Brooklyn's Petach Tikvah. There he laid the foundations for a Conservative synagogue, introducing late Friday night services, directing youth clubs, administering a daily Hebrew school, and supervising numerous affiliated organizations. Meeting resistance to his notion of the synagogue as a synagogue-center and to his involvement in Zionist and communal activities outside the synagogue, Levinthal left Petach Tikvah in 1919 to become the the the first rabbi of the newly formed Brooklyn Jewish Center.

Levinthal's remarkable career at the Brooklyn Jewish Center mirrored the emergence and decline of the urban Conservative synagogue. Levinthal built the Brooklyn Jewish Center into an outstanding model of the synagogue-center advocated by Mordecai M. *Kaplan. Levinthal dedicated the center's structure in 1922. It included a pool and gym, an auditorium, and a two-story synagogue. By 1925 the center had 1,000 families and it housed, in addition to services and a school, a variety of auxiliary organizations and adult education programs. Levinthal persuaded the center to adopt the Conservative model, introducing mixed seating and the *Sabbath and Festival Prayer Book* of the Rabbinical Assembly and United Synagogue (1946). Although he hesitated to deviate from the traditional liturgy, he recognized the importance of the Friday night service in restoring the Sabbath to the center of Jewish consciousness. To meet the liturgical need posed by the innovation of that service, Levinthal published with composer Rabbi Israel Goldfarb the service *Song, and Praise for Sabbath Eve* (1920), which was used for decades in hundreds of congregations in addition to the Brooklyn Jewish Center. As urban neighborhoods changed in the 1960s, urban synagogues faced the migration of their congregants to the suburbs. While many synagogues successfully relocated, Levinthal tried to preserve the center, despite a sharp curtailment of activities that included the abandonment of the Hebrew school and the cancellation of late Friday night services in 1973.

Levinthal was recognized as a leader in the Conservative movement and among Brooklyn Jewry. While he was president of the Rabbinical Assembly (1930–32), his administration dealt with the material problems of the rabbinate in the first years of the Depression, the growing organization of the Rabbinical Assembly, and the omnipresent attempt to formulate a philosophy for Conservative Judaism. From 1932 to 1935 Levinthal chaired the United Synagogue campaign for the Synagogue Center in Jerusalem, laying the cornerstone of the Yeshurun Synagogue in 1934. In Brooklyn he was a founder and first president of the Brooklyn Board of Rabbis (1929–31), the Brooklyn Zionist Region (1933–35), and the Brooklyn Jewish Community Council (1940–44).

An exceptionally gifted preacher, Levinthal excelled in the traditional exposition of Biblical and rabbinical texts. Considered one of the masters of the classical Jewish sermon in this century, he called his preaching the most important work of his ministry. Believing that a sermon was not a Jewish sermon unless it was based upon the teaching and interpretation of the classic sources of Jewish literature, Levinthal turned to rabbinic texts, especially the *midrash*, in preparing his sermons. His numerous volumes of sermons highlight such themes as the basic tenets of Judaism *(Judaism—An Analysis and an Interpretation* [1935]), the turmoil of the war years *(A New World Is Born* [1943]), and the denominations of American Judaism *(Point of View* [1958]). Levinthal had a unique ability to derive from the same text messages directed to radically different generations. As visiting professor of homiletics at the Seminary (1947–62), he shared this gift with a generation of rabbis.

Levinthal married May Rahel Bogdanoff in 1908; they had two children. In 1939 his daughter, Helen Levinthal Lyons, was the first woman in the United States to complete the full rabbinic course leading to ordination at the Jewish Institute of Religion. She was, however, denied ordination. Levinthal died on October 31, 1982, in New Rochelle, New York.

Writings: *The Jewish Law of Agency* (New York, 1920); *Steering or Drifting—Which?: Sermons and Discourses* (New York, 1928); *PRA 1931* vol. 4 (1933), pp. 122–

35; *PRA 1932* vol. 4 (1933), pp. 243–51; *Judaism—An Analysis and an Interpretation* (New York and London, 1935); *A New World Is Born* (New York and London, 1943); *Point of View: An Analysis of American Judaism* (London and New York, 1958); *Judaism Speaks to the Modern World* (London, 1963); *The Message of Israel: Sermons, Addresses, Memoirs* (New York, 1973); *CJ* 29, 2 (Winter 1975), pp. 57–62.

References: Elliot B. Gertel, "The Sermons and Other Writings of Rabbi Israel H. Levinthal," (unpublished paper); Simon Greenberg, "Rabbi Israel H. Levinthal," (unpublished address, 1983); Deborah Dash Moore, *At Home in America: Second Generation New York Jews* (New York, 1981), pp. 129–47; *NYT* 4 November 1982, p. B19; *Recorder* 5, 3 (July 1925), p. 23; *Recorder* 8, 2 (April 1928), p. 15; *WWAJ* 1980, p. 302.

LEVITSKY, LOUIS MOSES (1897–1975). Rabbi, educator. The son of Samuel and Frieda Wolowick Levitsky, Louis Levitsky was born in Kremenchug, Russia, on January 4, 1897. Brought to Canada as a child, Levitsky was educated in the Montreal public schools and the Montreal Hebrew School. He immigrated to the United States in 1916. Levitsky earned a B.A. from City College of New York in 1920, was ordained at the Seminary in 1923, and earned a Doctor of Hebrew Letters there in 1933. While a student at the Seminary, Levitsky directed the newly founded B'nai Jeshurun Center in New York City (1921–23).

Levitsky's first pulpit was at Temple Israel, Wilkes-Barre, Pennsylvania (1922–40). There he experimented with a variety of innovative adult education projects that established his reputation as a leader in the field. These included circles devoted to text study, a Jewish Women's Institute open to Jewish and non-Jewish women, and an interfaith Institute on Religion.

In 1940 Levitsky left Wilkes-Barre to succeed Charles I. *Hoffman as rabbi of Oheb Shalom Congregation, Newark, New Jersey. Levitsky made adult education a priority at Oheb Shalom, establishing a university of adult Jewish studies in the congregation. He remained there until his death, becoming rabbi emeritus in 1973.

Levitsky found the role of a rabbi in a large Jewish community quite different from the demands he had known as rabbi in a small Jewish community. In Wilkes-Barre Levitsky was responsible to the Jewish community outside his congregation. But in Newark he discovered that he was not obligated to participate in all Jewish activities outside the synagogue. Consequently, he was able to devote his energies to the institutions of Conservative Judaism. Levitsky directed the Seminary School of Jewish Studies and the Women's Institute of the Seminary (1940–65). He also chaired the Board of Trustees of the Seminary (1947–53) and the Board of Governors of the National Academy of Adult Jewish Studies (1961–63).

As president of the Rabbinical Assembly (1942–44), Levitsky presided over the organization when one-third of its membership was serving in the armed forces. He called repeatedly for greater coordination of the activities of the Seminary, the Rabbinical Assembly, and the United Synagogue, noting especially that the popularity of the RA chaplains in the armed forces promised the future growth of Conservative Judaism. He laid the foundations for contacts with the Jewish communities of South America. As chairman of the Army and Navy Activities Committee (1946–48), Levitsky worked to bring the Committee on Army and Navy Activities of the National Jewish Welfare Board under rabbinic control. He also carried the difficult burden of chairing the RA Placement Commission (1950).

In addition to numerous addresses to the Rabbinical Assembly, Levitsky wrote *Story of an Awakened Community* (1934) and *A Jew Looks at America* (1939), which explored the relationship of religion to democracy and of Judaism to Americanism.

Levitsky married Anna Levy in 1919; they had one daughter. Levitsky died on June 14, 1975, in East Orange, New Jersey.

Writings: *Story of an Awakened Community* (?, 1934); "Report of Adult Education Program in Temple Israel, Wilkes-Barre, Pa," *PRA 1936* vol. 5 (1939), pp. 461–63; "An Experiment in Jewish-Christian Relationships," *PRA 1939* vol. 6 (1940), pp. 41– 47; *A Jew Looks at America* (New York, 1939); "President's Address," *PRA 1943* vol. 8 (1947), pp. 169–81; "Spiritual Leadership in the Post-War World," *PRA 1944* vol. 8 (1947), pp. 281–97; "Salient Features of My Rabbinate in a City over 50,000 Jews," *PRA 1949* vol. 13 (1950), pp. 143–50.

References: *EJ* vol. 11, col. 150; *NYT* 15 June 1975, p. 51; *Recorder* 3, 3 (July 1923), pp. 3ff.; *WWWJ* 1955, p. 459

LIEBER, DAVID LEO (1925–). Rabbi, President of the University of Judaism. The son of Max and Gussie Jarmush Lieber, David Lieber was born on February 20, 1925, in Stryj, Poland, and brought to the United States in 1927. In 1944 he earned a B.A. at the City College of New York and a Bachelor of Hebrew Letters at the Seminary. He was ordained at the Seminary in 1948 and earned a Doctor of Hebrew Letters there in 1951.

Lieber had a brief career as a congregational rabbi at Sinai Temple, Los Angeles (1950–54), where he worked with Senior Rabbi Jacob *Kohn. Then, from 1954 to 1956 he directed the B'nai B'rith Hillel in Seattle, Washington.

Lieber was one of the guiding lights in the development and growth of the University of Judaism. Established in Los Angeles in 1947 as the West Coast affiliate of the Seminary, the University of Judaism was the city's first institute for advanced Jewish study. Lieber was dean of students (1956–63), Samuel A. Fryer Professor of Biblical Literature and Thought (1963–), and president (1963–). He has thus played a major role in transforming UJ from its small beginnings as a teachers college and school for adult Jewish study into a large institution with four degree-granting schools, including an undergraduate liberal arts college and a graduate school named in his honor. He has overseen the university's acquisition and building of the Mulholland Drive campus, which enabled the expansion of its programs, including summer classes for educators and college students desiring intensive Jewish studies, as well as the creation of a Masters of Business Administration degree program (whose courses in fund-raising, public relations, and Judaica prepare graduates specifically for careers in Jewish organizations), a postgraduate scholars program, a lengthy list of continuing education classes in Judaica and the arts, and the Wagner Human Services Paraprofessional Program, which trains volunteers in social, communication, and counseling skills for service to the Jewish community. With these diverse offerings the University of Judaism strives, under Lieber's guidance, to meet the many intellectual and social needs of West Coast Jewry.

Elsewhere in the Conservative movement Lieber served on the Executive Council of the Rabbinical Assembly and the editorial board of *Conservative Judaism* (1968–70) and is vice-chancellor of the Jewish Theological Seminary (1973–). Drawing upon his experience as head counselor at the second Camp Ramah in Maine in 1947, he directed Camp Ramah in California. In the greater Los Angeles area he is vice-chairman of the American Jewish Committee (1972–), a board member of the Jewish Federation Council (1980–), and a member of the Department of Near Eastern Languages at the University of California, Los Angeles (1957–).

Lieber married Esther Kobre in 1945; they have four children.

Writings: "Modern Trends in Bible and Study," *CJ* 20, 2 (Winter 1966), pp. 37–46; "The Melton Materials," *CJ* 23, 3 (Spring 1969), pp. 68–73; "The Conservative Congregational School: Prospects for the Future," *CJ* 27, 4 (Summer 1973), pp. 24–34.

References: *Direction: A Publication of the University of Judaism* 17, 3 (Spring 1986); *WWAJ* 1980, p. 307.

LIEBERMAN, SAUL (1898–1983). Rabbi, scholar. Saul Lieberman was born on May 28, 1898, in Motol, Belorussia. A child prodigy gifted with an extraordinary memory, Lieberman studied at the Yeshivah of Malch and then at the Slobodka Yeshivah in Lithuania, where he was ordained in 1916. His intellectual quests soon took him beyond the world of the *yeshivah*. In the 1920s he attended the University of Kiev, where he studied medicine and learned Latin. Then, after a short stay in Palestine, he continued his studies in France. In 1928 Lieberman settled in Jerusalem, where he studied Talmudic philology, Syriac, and Greek language and literature at Hebrew University. He earned an M.A. there in 1931 and was appointed university lecturer in Talmud the same year (1931–36). In Palestine Lieberman also taught at the Mizrachi Teachers Seminary and was dean of the Harry Fischel Institute (1935–40).

In 1940 Lieberman immigrated to the United States to join the faculty of the Seminary as professor of Palestinian Literature and Institutions (1940–53). He subsequently became dean of the Rabbinical School (1948), rector (1958), and professor of Talmud (1954–83).

Lieberman was the model of the disciplined scholar. He believed that his time belonged to the study of the Talmud and he considered teaching his relaxation from his regimen of research and writing. Because he begrudged time away from scholarship, Lieberman would often have his rabbinical students schedule their dreaded Talmud exams near midnight so that he could complete an evening's work before stopping for the few minutes it took the student to reveal what he had mastered.

Lieberman's strength as a scholar of rabbinics derived from his encyclopedic mastery of the whole of Talmudic and rabbinic literature and his wide-ranging reading of ancient Graeco-Roman, Jewish, and Christian literatures for the light they shed on rabbinic works. This powerful combination made him one of the leading practitioners of critical research of rabbinic sources. His critical editions of rabbinic texts and commentaries remain monumental contributions to the field.

One of Lieberman's chief areas of investigation was textual criticism of ancient sources. His first major work, *Al Hayerushalmi* (1929), discussed the various sources of mistakes in the transmission of the Palestinian Talmud and offered important variant readings for the treatise *Sotah*. In his work on the Talmud of Caesarea *(Talmudiah shel Keisariyah*, [1931]), Lieberman revealed himself to be a literary historian of keen insight. He demonstrated that the Palestinian Talmud was not the product of a single school at Tiberias, as had generally been assumed, for several tractates were composed in Caesarea in the mid-fourth century. Perhaps Lieberman's greatest contribution was his critical work on the Tosefta, the collections of Jewish oral traditions of the first and second centuries which supplement the second-century code of Jewish law, the Mishnah. In his magnum opus, the ten-volume *Tosefta Kifshutah* (1955–79), Lieberman offered extensive commentaries, philological and historical materials, wide-ranging bibliographical references, and explanatory allusions to the Mishnah. Lieberman's English works, among them *Greek in Jewish Palestine* (1942), *Hellenism in Jewish Palestine* (1950), and the essays in *Texts and Studies* (1974), afford the English reader new views of the life, institutions, beliefs, and literature of Jewish Palestine in the rabbinic period.

At the core of his thinking was a revolutionary view of rabbinic literature. While the traditional *yeshivah* curriculum emphasized study of the Mishnah and the Babylonian Talmud, Lieberman recognized that the Mishnah and Tosefta are basically the same literature. He understood that critical study of rabbinics requires one to pay equal attention to all its literary sources, the Tosefta and the Mishnah, the Palestinian and Babylonian Talmuds, to set the entire corpus of rabbinic literature in its proper context.

Despite his expertise in rabbinics, Lieberman rarely ventured into contemporary rabbinical affairs. In the 1950s, however, he did become involved in the Conservative movement's efforts to resolve the plight of the *agunah*, the woman anchored by the Jewish laws of marriage and divorce to a husband who no longer lives with her. Lieberman explored, unsuccessfully, with Orthodox Rabbi Joseph B. Soloveitchik ("the Rav"), the possibility of establishing a national *bet din* to handle divorces. In 1953 Lieberman composed for the Rabbinical Assembly a *takanah*, a special clause to be inserted into its *ketubah*. The Lieberman *takanah*, as it came to be known, was subsequently upheld in the New York State courts and empowered a Jewish court of law to turn to secular judicial authorities to compel a recalcitrant husband to grant his wife a religious divorce.

Lieberman served his fellow scholars as president of the American Academy for Jewish Research and was a member of the Israeli Academy of Humanities and the Sciences. He won several prizes for his writings: the Bialik Prize (1956), the Israel Prize (1971, the first non-Israeli to win this), and the Harvey Prize of the Israel Institute of Technology (1976).

Lieberman married Judith Berlin, dean of the Shulamith School for Girls, the first Jewish day school for girls in the United States. They had no children. Lieberman died in his sleep on March 23, 1983, aboard a plane bound for Israel.

Writings: *Al Hayerushalmi* (Jerusalem, 1929); *Talmudiah shel Keisariyah* (Jerusalem, 1931); *Hayerushalmi Kifshuto* (Jerusalem, 1934); *Tosefet Rishonim*, 4 vols. (Jerusalem, 1938–39); *Shekiin* (Jerusalem, 1939); *Greek in Jewish Palestine* (New York, 1942); *Hellenism in Jewish Palestine* (New York, 1950); *Tosefta Kifshutah*, 10 vols. (New York, 1955–79); *Tosefta*, 3 vols. (New York, 1955–73); *Sifrei Zutta* (New York, 1968); *Texts and Studies* (New York, 1974). Ed., *Hilkhot Hayerushalmi: The Halakhah of the Palestinian Talmud of Moses ben Maimon* (New York, 1947); *Salo Wittmayer Baron Jubilee Volumes*, 3 vols. (Jerusalem, 1974).

References: Gilbert Epstein, "Response," *PRA 1975* vol. 37 (1976), p. 90; *EJ* vol. 11, cols. 218–20; Norman Lamm, "Unity and Integrity," *Washington Jewish Week* 27 March 1986, pp. 20–21; Alexander Marx, "Dr. Lieberman's Contribution to Jewish Scholarship," *PRA 1948* vol. 12 (1949), pp. 259–71; *NYT* 24 March 1983, p. B10; Phillip Sigal, "The Scholarship of Saul Lieberman: Reflections on His First Yahrzeit," *Judaism* 33, 2 (Spring 1984), pp. 135–45; Dov Zlotnick, "Professor Saul Lieberman," *PRA 1983* vol. 45 (1984), pp. 202–07.

M

MALEV, WILLIAM S. (1898–1973). Rabbi. The son of Sholom and Musya Radeloff Malev, William Malev was born on August 4, 1898, in Homel, Russia. He immigrated to Brooklyn in 1908. He graduated from the Teachers Institute in 1918 and earned a B.A. at the City College of New York in 1919. Drawn initially to the study of English literature, Malev was persuaded by Mordecai M. *Kaplan to enter the rabbinate and was ordained at the Seminary in 1925.

As rabbi at Concourse Center of Israel, Bronx, New York (1925–1927?), Malev expanded the activities of this synagogue-center to include a late Friday night lecture series on Jewish religious subjects and a weekday evening forum on Jewish secular topics. Drawing upon his pedagogical training and his prior experience as president of the Jewish Teachers Association (1921–22), he then addressed the center's educational program, reorganizing the Hebrew school, creating a girls' Confirmation class and a post-Bar Mitzvah class, and organizing extracurricular activities. He also established the Central Council, the ruling body of the center composed of delegates from its various clubs and groups.

Malev next served briefly as rabbi at Kingsbridge Heights Jewish Center, Bronx, New York (1927–28?). Then for nearly twenty years he led the Jamaica Jewish Center, Jamaica, New York (1928–46). In 1946 he left that leading Conservative synagogue-center for the challenges of pioneering Conservative Judaism in Houston, Texas, at Congregation Beth Yeshurun (1946–73). Malev left his mark on the congregation and on all aspects of Jewish life in the Southwest. He helped fuse the two congregations that had merged to form Beth Yeshurun into one of the great synagogues of the Southwest. He continued, as before, to work tirelessly on behalf of intensive Jewish education, championing higher standards and the requisite expanded budget. He took the lead in establishing the first day school in the Southwest. A staunch Zionist, he lectured throughout the Southwest on behalf of the Zionist Organization of America. He was also president of the Texas Kallah of Rabbis.

Malev was a religious force in the larger community and a leader in interfaith and interracial affairs. He was president of the Houston Ministerial Association and wrote a weekly column for the *Houston Post*. He also taught Hebrew at the University of Houston.

Primarily a congregational rabbi, Malev led the Rabbinical Assembly's short-lived Committee on College Youth (1945–46), established to encourage contact between RA members and the future generation of American Jewish leaders.

He married Bella Gershon in 1928; they had two children. Malev died in Houston, Texas, on July 14, 1973.

Writings: "The Jew and the Negro: The Jew of the South in the Conflict on Segregation," *CJ* 13, 1 (Fall 1958), pp. 35–46; *Living Creatively* (Houston, Tex., 1972).

References: *PRA 1946* vol. 10 (1947), pp. 321–22; *PRA 1974* vol. 36 (1975), pp. 206–09; *Recorder* 5, 3 (July 1925), pp. 9, 22.

MANDELBAUM, BERNARD (1922–   ). Rabbi, educator, administrator. The son of Jacob and Ida Cohen Mandelbaum, Bernard Mandelbaum was born on January 12, 1922, in Brooklyn, New York. He earned a B.A. at Columbia University in 1942, was ordained at the Seminary in 1946, and earned a Doctor of Hebrew Letters there in 1953.

Mandelbaum spent the greater part of his twenty-seven years at the Seminary as an administrator and educator, involved in almost every Seminary program. In addition to being Seminary professor of homiletics and reader in *midrash* on the faculty of the Rabbinical School, he held numerous administrative posts, including registrar (1946–50), dean of students (1951–59), provost (1959–66), and president (1966–73). Among his principal responsibilities were program editor of "The Eternal Light," the award-winning NBC radio and television shows; administrator of the Seminary's Israel activities, including the American Student Center in Jerusalem and the Schocken Institute for Jewish Research; and director of the Rabbinical School's Department of Religion and Psychiatry. With Louis *Finkelstein he co-directed the Institute for Religious and Social Studies. He also directed the World Brotherhood program and co-chaired the Leadership Training Fellowship, sponsored by the Teachers Institute and the Seminary College of Jewish Studies to select and to nurture within the ranks of the Conservative movement the future lay and professional leaders of American Jewry.

Outside of the Seminary, Mandelbaum served briefly as rabbi of the Bayswater Jewish Center, Far Rockaway, New York (1951–53). He was also a member of the Executive Committee of the *Histadrut Ivrit*, the New York City Commission on Human Rights, the New York City Youth Board, and the Advisory Committee on the Arts of the John F. Kennedy Center for the Performing Arts.

After becoming president emeritus of the Seminary in 1973, Mandelbaum served as president of the America-Israel Cultural Foundation (1973–77) and as executive vice-president of the Synagogue Council of America, an umbrella organization founded in 1926 by the rabbinical and congregational arms of the

Orthodox, Conservative, and Reform movements. Mandelbaum was also director of research of its Institute for Jewish Policy Planning and Research.

His first work of scholarship was a critical edition of the *Pesikta* of Rab Kahana, a Palestinian *midrash* of the sixth century. Mandelbaum also edited several collections of essays, chiefly on the subjects of ethics and the interpretation of Judaism. He used the themes of the Seminary's annual High Holiday messages, which he co-authored for many years with Victor M. Ratner, as the framework for *Choose Life* (1968). He also wrote, for the United Synagogue adult study series, the pamphlet *The Maturing of the Conservative Movement* (1968), which dealt with the theoretical underpinnings of Conservatism, and *The Wisdom of Solomon Schechter* (1963), which examined the life, thought, and critical influence of the second president of the Seminary on the development of Conservatism.

Mandelbaum married Judith Werber in 1945; they have five children.

Writings: *Assignment in Israel* (New York, 1960); *The Wisdom of Solomon Schechter* (New York, 1963); *The Maturing of the Conservative Movement* (New York, 1968); *To Live with Meaning* (New York, 1973; rev. 1980); *Add Life to Your Years* (Boston, 1974); *Art and Judaism: Conversation between Yaacov Agam and Bernard Mandelbaum* (New York, 1981). Ed., *Pesikta de Rav Kahana: A Critical Edition* (New York, 1962); *From the Sermons of Rabbi Milton Steinberg*, 2 vols. (New York, 1954–63). With Victor M. Ratner, *Choose Life* (New York, 1968).

References: *EJ* vol. 16, col. 1401; *WWWJ* 1965, p. 630.

MARGOLIS, ELIAS (1880–1946). Rabbi. The son of Isaac and Hinde Bernstein Margolis, Elias Margolis was born on July 15, 1880 (1879?) in Merecz, Lithuania, and brought to the United States in 1885. Educated in the New York City public schools and at the Felix Adler Ethical Culture School, Margolis earned an A.B. from the University of Cincinnati in 1900, was ordained at Hebrew Union College (HUC), Cincinnati, in 1901, and earned a Ph.D from Columbia University in 1915.

After graduating from the Reform rabbinical seminary (HUC), Margolis served as rabbi at Congregation Re'im Ahuvim, Stockton, California (1901–03), and at Temple Emanu-El, Pueblo, Colorado (1903–05). He then moved to New York City and temporarily left the rabbinate to serve as assistant manager of the Baron de Hirsch Fund (1905–08) and assistant director of the Industrial Removal Office (1908–10).

Margolis returned to the pulpit in 1910, serving Congregation Peni-El, New York City (1910–13), and Congregation Sheerith Judah, New York City (1913–16). In 1916 Margolis helped organize Congregation Emanu-El, Mt. Vernon, New York, serving as rabbi (1916–46) and as honorary chaplain of the Mt. Vernon Police Department (1934–46) until his death.

Having left Reform Judaism for Conservatism, Margolis determined to play a leading role in the development of Conservative Judaism. He chaired the $500,000 campaign for the United Synagogue (1928–29). An active member of the Rabbinical Assembly, he worked to transform it into a professional association. Margolis was one of the incorporators of the RA in 1929 and edited the published proceedings for that year. He served as treasurer (1928–30), chaired the newly organized Palestine Committee (1931–32) and the committee that developed the plans for a pension fund (1943–44). In 1933 Margolis became the first rabbi elected president of the Rabbinical Assembly (1933–35) who had not graduated from the Seminary. As president, he tried to cope with an unsatisfactory placement system and the employment problems caused by the Depression. Margolis also served as president of the Synagogue Council of America (1936).

Margolis married Esther Molly Jacobson in 1910; they had four children. He died on November 26, 1946.

Writings: "The Influence of the Conservative Movement on American Judaism," *PRA 1929* vol. 3 (1930), pp. 105–14; "The President's Message," *PRA 1934* vol. 5 (1939), pp. 64–68.

References: *AJYB* vol. 5 (1903–04), p. 79; *NYT* 27 November 1946, p. 25; *PRA 1944* vol. 8 (1945), pp. 329–40; *Recorder* 8, 4 (October 1928), p. 4; *WWAJ* 1938–39, pp. 707–08.

MARX, ALEXANDER (1878–1953). Scholar, librarian. The son of George and Gertrude Simon Marx, Alexander Marx was born on January 29, 1878, in Elberfeld, Germany. He received excellent secular and Jewish educations, studying rabbinic literature and the works of the *Wissenschaft des Judentums* scholars and graduating from the Kneiphof Gymnasium in Koenigsberg in 1895. Marx continued his education in Berlin at the Rabbiner-Seminar and at the university, studying Semitics and working closely with the outstanding Jewish bibliographer Moritz Steinschneider. After a year of service in a Prussian artillery regiment, he went on to earn a Ph.D. at the University of Koenigsberg in 1903.

In the summer of 1903 Seminary president Solomon *Schechter and Professor Louis *Ginzberg journeyed to Europe in search of additional faculty for the rabbinical school. Schechter invited Marx to come to America as professor of Jewish history (he was later the Jacob H. Schiff Professor of History) and as Seminary librarian (1903–53).

Marx was a distinguished historian. Generations of students learned from the highly detailed lectures in his five-year course in Jewish history that began in the Hellenistic period and ended in the 1600s, for after that, according to Marx, everything in Jewish life was "current events." Teaching his students to be scholars and believing that they could learn to be rabbis on their own, he emphasized that Jewish civilization had developed in symbiosis with the dominant societies.

Marx's great legacy to the Seminary, to American Jewry, and to Jewish scholarship went beyond the classroom. He transformed the modest library that he found when he arrived at the Seminary into one of the largest and most valuable collections of Judaica ever owned by Jews, a library of unrivaled importance for scholars all over the world. Established in the early days of the old Seminary, the original library was intended primarily for the use of the faculty and students. But Marx envisioned a great library. With the generosity of Seminary supporter Judge Mayer Sulzberger, who early in his life had realized that a first-class library was essential to the development of Jewish scholarship in America, Marx set out to transform the Seminary library into the major American repository of Judaica.

Shortly after Marx arrived in New York, Sulzberger donated 7,500 books and 750 manuscripts to the Seminary. This magnanimous gift, which doubled the library's holdings and included many rare volumes, laid the foundation for Marx's vision of what the library should become. For fifty years, thanks in large measure to the continued generosity of Sulzberger and to the support of patrons Mortimer L. Schiff and Reform rabbi and scholar Hyman Enelow, Marx pursued that vision. He brought to the task his phenomenal memory, his gift for languages, his great skill as a bibliographer, his expertise in paleography, and his extraordinary ability to determine a manuscript's age just by looking at it.

Marx amassed a great collection of Judaica in Hebrew and all other relevant languages for the Seminary library by constantly seeking new acquisitions, greater funds, and more staff. The library's rapid growth from 5,250 books and 3 manuscripts in 1903 to 100,000 books and 7,000 manuscripts three decades later prompted several reorganizations of its existing space and ultimately its removal in 1930 to the new Seminary campus. In addition, Marx arranged for several exhibitions of manuscripts and rare editions. When he died in 1953, the Seminary library contained 165,000 books and over 9,000 Hebrew, Samaritan, Aramaic, and Yiddish manuscripts. It had become Marx's contribution to Jewish scholarship in America.

Outside the Seminary, Marx was a member of the Publication Committee of the Jewish Publication Society of America, vice-president of the American Jewish Historical Society, and president of the American Academy for Jewish Research (1931–33) and of the Alexander Kohut Memorial Foundation. He was elected in 1926 to the Medieval Academy of America. As a member of the Executive Council of the United Synagogue, he proposed that it publish a directory of kosher hotels and restaurants in the United States.

Marx was a master of the short, scholarly essay. His numerous articles and monographs, written in several languages and for various journals, ranged widely over problems in Jewish history and literature. He explored aspects of Talmudic, geonic, and medieval Jewish life in essays on, among others, Maimonides, the expulsion of the Jews from Spain, the Jews of Cochin, and Hebrew liturgy. He also published numerous bibliographical essays; short biographical sketches of his teachers, friends, and colleagues; and critical editions of Hebrew manuscripts. His work was distinguished by meticulous attention to the facts and rigorous textual criticism. Many of his essays were reprinted and later collected in two volumes, *Studies in Jewish History and Booklore* (1944) and *Essays in Jewish Biography* (1947).

But perhaps his most important work was the pioneering *History of the Jewish People* (1927), written with Dropsie College professor Max L. Margolis. This tour de force, emphasizing Jewish economic and social life, communal organization, and legal status, compressed into one carefully researched volume forty centuries of Jewish history.

Marx married Hanna Hoffman in 1905; they had two children. He died on December 26, 1953, in New York City.

Writings: *Biblical Manuscripts and Books in the Library of the Jewish Theological Seminary* (New York, 1913); "The Library of the Jewish Theological Seminary of America," in *Jewish Theological Seminary: Semi-Centennial Volume,* ed. Cyrus Adler (New York, 1939), pp. 87–120; *Studies in Jewish History and Booklore* (New York, 1944); *Essays in Jewish Biography* (Philadelphia, 1947); *Bibliographical Studies and Notes on Rare Books and Manuscripts in the Library of the Jewish Theological Seminary of America* (New York, 1977). With Max L. Margolis, *A History of the Jewish People* (Philadelphia, 1927). Ed., with H. Malter, *Steinschneider, Gesammelte Schriften* (Berlin, 1925); with S. Baron, *Jewish Studies in Memory of George Alexander Kohut* (New York, 1935).

References: *Alexander Marx Jubilee Volume,* 2 vols. (New York, 1950); Boaz Cohen, *Professor Alexander Marx* (New York, 1928); *EJ* vol. 11, col. 1069; Simon Greenberg, "A Tribute to Professor Alexander Marx," *CJ* 4, 2 (Fall 1948), pp. 2–4; A.S. Halkin, in *AJYB* vol. 56 (1955), pp. 580–88; *NYT* 27 December 1953, p. 60; *WWAJ* 1938–39, p. 715.

MATT, CALMAN DAVID (1887–1951).

Rabbi, poet. The son of Isaac and Sarah Zlata Sorinkes Matt, C. David Matt was born in Kovno, Russia, on June 24, 1887, and brought to Philadelphia in 1890. Educated in the Philadelphia public schools, at Yeshiva Mishkan Israel, and at Gratz College, Matt earned an A.B. from the University of Pennsylvania in 1909 and was ordained at the Seminary in 1913.

Matt became the first English-speaking rabbi of Adath Jeshurun, Minneapolis, Minnesota (1912–27). There he worked to direct this Orthodox congregation, founded in 1884, toward Conservatism. Matt established auxiliary organizations, conducted Hebrew classes, reorganized the Sunday school, and developed the plans for a new structure. After he left Minneapolis, Matt served as rabbi at Beth David, Buffalo, New York (1927–29), and at the West Philadelphia Jewish Community Center (1929–51).

In each community Matt was active in Jewish civic and Zionist affairs. In Minneapolis he directed the Talmud Torah and the Jewish Welfare Board. In Philadelphia he was president of the Philadelphia Board of Rabbis and the Philadelphia branch of the Rabbinical Assembly.

A gifted poet, Matt sought to transmit the spirit of Judaism in his verse. Many of his poems were paeans to the leaders of Conservative Judaism. His well-known "A Rabbi Died," dedicated to the memory of Louis *Epstein, Louis *Feinberg, and Moses Hyamson, became his own epitaph. Among Matt's frequent contributions to the Anglo-Jewish press was the column "Sermonettes."

Matt married Lena Friedman in 1913; they had five children. He died on December 3, 1951, in Philadelphia.

Writings: *The Collected Poems of Rabbi C. David Matt*, ed. Milton Nevins (Philadelphia, 1953).

References: Albert Gordon, *Jews in Transition* (Minneapolis, 1949), pp. 153–54; *NYT* 4 December 1951, p. 33; *WWAJ* 1938–39, p. 718.

MEYER, MARSHALL THEODORE (1930–). The son of Isaac and Anna Silbertstein Meyer, Marshall Meyer was born in New York City on March 25, 1930. He earned an A.B. at Dartmouth College in 1952 and was ordained at the Seminary in 1958.

Meyer began his career as secretary of the Rabbinical Assembly's Committee on Jewish Law and Standards (1958–59). But within a year of his ordination he found himself the head of the fledgling South American Conservative movement. In 1959, shortly after the formal establishment of the World Council of Synagogues, North American Conservative leaders traveled to Buenos Aires to consult with Latin American synagogue leaders on problems of religious life. As a result of their meeting, Conservatism's leaders decided to send Meyer as their emissary to Argentina. He was to help lead Argentina's 200,000 Jews— and eventually all of Latin American Jewry—toward Conservatism. During the next quarter of a century, Meyer transplanted the leading institutions of Conservative Judaism to South America and was thus largely responsible for the emergence of Conservatism as a religious movement among South American Jewry.

Although he was initially associated with the leading Buenos Aires synagogue, Congregacion Israelita de la Republica Argentina (assistant rabbi, 1959–62), in 1962 Meyer became, as a result of a schism in the congregation, the founding rabbi of Buenos Aires' largest Conservative synagogue, Communidad Bet El (1962–84). Within two years its numerous activities for all members of the congregation and the large attendance at its services necessitated the appointment of Gerald Zelizer as assistant rabbi.

Soon other Latin American synagogues began to emulate the Conservative patterns introduced at Bet El, especially the popular late Friday night service, a service practically unknown to Latin American Jewry prior to Meyer's arrival. To unite his congregants in worship, Meyer published Hebrew/Spanish editions of the *siddur* (1965) and the Ashkenazic and Sephardic High Holiday prayer books (1967), the first such prayer books published in Spanish since the expulsion of the Jews from Spain in 1492. To encourage adult education in the synagogue, he also had contemporary Jewish works translated into Spanish, including writings of his teacher Abraham Joshua *Heschel. Meyer's work paved the way for other Seminary-trained rabbis, including Abraham Morhaim, Michael Leipziger, and Manuel Kamenetzky, to follow in leading modern Conservative congregations in Latin America.

Keenly aware that Conservatism's future in South America depended upon winning over the youth, one of Meyer's first projects was to transplant Camp Ramah to the Southern Hemisphere. In 1960 he founded and directed the first Camp Ramah in Latin America, located 300 miles south of Buenos Aires, near the town of Mar del Plata. Launched with forty-eight children, it soon drew thousands of children from Argentina, Peru, Bolivia, Chile, Uruguay, and Brazil.

Next, in 1962, with the help of the World Council of Synagogues, whose Latin American office Meyer directed, he founded the Seminario Rabinico Latino-Americano, a preparatory school for the training of modern, native-born, Spanish-speaking rabbis. Although its first class had just four students, within three years its student body numbered twenty-three. Its students, who study simultaneously at the University of Buenos Aires, prepare to undertake advanced studies at the Seminary leading to rabbinic ordination.

Meyer found Argentina to be a country organized into ethnic enclaves, whose Jewish community was isolated from participation in the general life of the community. He worked to open bridges between Argentinian Jewry and other religious and ethnic groups by dealing with such issues as anti-Semitism and fostering interreligious dialogue. He was a member of the Argentine Association of Family Planning and the Executive Commission of the Argentine Institute of Mental Health, and was vice-president of the United Jewish Appeal of Argentina.

Meyer won an international reputation for his work on behalf of Argentinian Jewry and those who disappeared during the military junta's reign of terror (1976–83). He denounced the human rights violations from his pulpit, was a founding member of the Permanent Assembly for Human Rights and the Jewish Committee on Human Rights (1981), and—at risk to his own life—visited prisoners, including the publisher Jacobo Timmerman, in jail. He also sharply criticized the central body of Argentine Jewry for failing to decry the human rights violations or to use its leverage with world Jewry to condemn this, the darkest period of Argentine history.

In 1984 Meyer left Argentina to became rabbi of B'nai Jeshurun, one of New York's oldest congregations, and special consul to the chancellor of the Seminary.

Meyer married Naomi Friedman in 1955; they have three children.

References: Yehoshua Aizenberg, "Isidoro Goes to Camp," *Review* 15, 2 (Summer 1962), pp. 14–15; Aviva Cantor, "My Children Are Disappeared: An Argentine Mother's Story," *Lilith* 15 (Summer 1986), pp. 17–21; *EJ* vol. 3, col. 422; Abraham J. Karp, *A History of the United Synagogue of America, 1913–1963* (New York, 1964), pp. 95–96; *PRA 1959* vol. 23 (1960), p. 119; *PRA 1960* vol. 24 (1960), p. 181; *PRA 1980* vol. 42 (1981), pp. 23, 26; *Review* 25, 4 (Winter 1973), p. 15; Seymour Siegel, "Argentina Revisited," *CJ* 19, 1 (Fall 1964), pp. 25–32; *WWWJ* 1978, p. 613.

MILLGRAM, ABRAHAM EZRA (1901–). Rabbi, educator. The son of Israel and Mollie Kreis Millgram, Abraham Millgram was born on February 1, 1901, in Russia. He immigrated to the United States in 1913. Educated in the New York City public schools, he graduated from the Teachers Institute in 1923, earned a B.S. from the City College of New York in 1924, was ordained at the Seminary in 1927, and earned a Ph.D. from Dropsie College, Philadelphia, in 1944.

Millgram first served as rabbi at Temple Beth Shalom, Wilmington, Delaware (1927–30), founded in 1922 as a Conservative congregation to offer an alternative to Wilmington's established Orthodox and Reform synagogues. The congregants welcomed their third rabbi in four years, sharing his youthful enthusiasm and conviction regarding the importance of programming for synagogue youth. When he left Wilmington three years later for the greater challenges offered by Philadelphia's larger Jewish community, Beth Shalom housed several junior clubs and a Young People's League and had incorporated Zionism into the school curriculum.

Millgram next served as rabbi at Beth Israel, Philadelphia, Pennsylvania (1930–40), a congregation established as the Polish Synagogue in 1840. There he edited, at the request of his congregants, the *Beth Israel Hymnal* (1937), a prayer book containing supplementary hymns, responsive readings, and a memorial service. In 1940, aware that the neighborhood around Beth Israel had changed radically, causing members of the congregation to move, Millgram accepted an appointment to head the new Hillel Foundation of the University of Minnesota (1940–45). Within five years Millgram raised funds to purchase a building and established a wide variety of programs, including a Hebrew-speaking club and weekly *Shabbat* services.

Millgram's greatest contribution to Conservatism was as an educator. He was the first educational director of the United Synagogue's Commission on Jewish Education (1945–61), established in 1940 as a joint endeavor of the Rabbinical Assembly and the United Synagogue to be the movement's central agency for elementary Jewish education. When he retired in 1961, the commission had dramatically improved the educational program of the congregational school. Under Millgram's direction it published "The Objectives and Standards for the Congregational School," a *Curriculum Outline*, syllabi, a variety of textbooks, and the magazine *The Synagogue School*; sponsored educational conferences; developed a teacher-training program for nursery and kindergarten teachers; established a teacher placement bureau; and formulated guiding principles to govern the relationships between congregational schools and central bureaus of Jewish education. Recognizing that the commission had to educate both children and their parents, Millgram wrote a guide for the Jewish student's parents and the *Handbook for Congregational School Board Member* to acquaint the board with its roles and those of the rabbi, educational director, and United Synagogue Commission on Jewish Education. He also organized the Jewish Educators Assembly in an effort to improve the training and status of Hebrew teachers. Following his retirement, he taught as assistant professor at the Teachers Institute (1960–63) and was vice-president of the National Council for Jewish Education.

Millgram edited an *Anthology of Medieval Hebrew Literature*, a representative sampling of the varieties of Jewish literature covering the eighth through the eighteenth centuries intended for the beginning student. He also edited *Great Jewish Ideas*, a volume of essays on Israel, Torah, faith, and modern life, for the B'nai B'rith Great Books series.

A dedicated Zionist, he organized and was president of the League for Labor Zionism, chaired the Philadelphia–New York Region of the Poalei Zion (1946–47), chaired the Histadrut Campaign in the Twin Cities (1941–45), and finally settled in Jerusalem in 1963. There he continued his scholarly activities, writing his most important work, *Jewish Worship* (1971), a comprehensive historical overview of the organization, contents, and evolution of Jewish worship and the prayer book. During periodic visits to the United States he has served as an educational consultant to Jewish communities such as that of Kansas City.

Millgram married Ida Tulchinsky in 1930; they have one son.

Writings: "Report of the United Synagogue Commission on Jewish Education," *PRA 1947* vol. 11 (1948), pp. 87–93; *PRA 1948* vol. 12 (1949), pp. 49–51; "Implementing a Program of Intensive Jewish Education in the Congregational School," *CJ* 5, 4 (June 1949), pp. 1–9; *PRA 1949* vol. 13 (1950), pp. 72–73; *PRA 1950* vol. 14 (1951), pp. 55–56; *Handbook for Congregational School Board Member* (New York, 1953); *Jewish Worship* (Philadelphia, 1971). Ed., *Beth Israel Hymnal* (Philadelphia, 1937); *Sabbath, the Delight* (Philadelphia, 1944); *An Anthology of Medieval Hebrew Literature* (1935; reprint ed., Philadelphia, 1961); *Great Jewish Ideas* (Washington, D.C., 1964); *Concepts that Distinguish Judaism* (Washington, D.C., 1985).

References: Benjamin Kahn, "Interview with Ezra Millgram on Hillel," (interviewer's transcript, n.d.); Abraham J. Karp, *A History of the United Synagogue of America, 1913–1963* (New York, 1964), pp. 77–78; *Recorder* 7, 3 (July 1927), p. 15; Joseph P. Schultz, "The Consensus of 'Civil Judaism': The Religious Life of Kansas City Jewry," in *Mid-America's Promise: A Profile of Kansas City Jewry*, ed. Joseph P. Schultz (Kansas City, 1982), p. 71; *Temple Beth Shalom: Fifty Year Historical Record, 1922–72* (Wilmington, Del., 1972); *WWWJ* 1965, p. 670.

MINKIN, JACOB SAMUEL (1885–1962). Rabbi, author. The son of Leib and Rachel Leah Friedman Minkin, Jacob Minkin was born in Scwieciany, Russian Poland, on October 1, 1885 (1883?). He immigrated to the United States in 1904. Educated in the *cheder*, *yeshivah*, and at the gymnasium in Prague, Minkin earned a B.A. from Columbia University in 1908, was ordained at the Seminary in 1910, and earned a Doctor of Hebrew Letters there in 1935.

Encouraged by Solomon *Schechter to take a pulpit in a small city so that he would find time to write, Minkin became the rabbi of Congregation Anshe Sholom, Hamilton, Canada (1910–17). In Hamilton Minkin was active in the field of Jewish education. He organized an English evening school for Jewish immigrants at the synagogue. The Hamilton Board of Education subsequently assumed responsibility for the school and appointed Minkin superintendent of the Hamilton Night Schools in 1914.

In 1919 Minkin accepted a call from Temple Beth El, Rochester, New York. Beth El was founded in 1915 when several of the younger and more affluent members of its parent synagogue, the Leopold Street Beth El, one of the founding congregations of the United Synagogue, moved to a new neighborhood where they established their own synagogue. Although the new congregation initially leaned toward Reform, Minkin led Temple Beth El squarely into the Conservative movement. He established a school and adult education classes. But his traditional stance on ritual matters, such as his refusal to allow the use of an organ or to schedule weddings on days interdicted by Jewish law, led to discord with the congregation. In 1929 Minkin left Rochester to accept a position at Inwood Hebrew Congregation, New York City (1929–33).

In 1933 Minkin determined to devote greater time to his scholarship, so he accepted a part-time appointment as Jewish chaplain at Fordham Hospital in New York City, where he remained for the next twenty-five years. Minkin had continued his literary endeavors during his years in the pulpit. He regularly contributed articles to several periodicals, and he wrote a syndicated column, "News of the Jewish World," that appeared in over fifty newspapers (1922–30). But the end of his congregational responsibilities enabled him to write longer, scholarly studies. Interested in the lives, personalities, and creativity of Jewish men of the past, Minkin wrote studies of Herod, Don Isaac Abarbanel, Maimonides, and a fictional account of Uriel da Costa. His *Romance of Hassidism* (1935), one of the first books on Hassidism in English, was a history of the movement told through the biographies of its outstanding leaders.

Minkin married Fanny R. Rabinowitz in 1911. He died in Tel Aviv, Israel, on March 13, 1962.

Writings: *The Romance of Hassidism* (New York, 1935); *Herod: A Biography* (New York, 1936); *Abarbanel and the Expulsion of the Jews from Spain* (New York, 1938); *The World of Moses Maimonides* (New York and London, 1957). Posthumously, *The Shaping of the Modern Mind: The Life and Thought of the Great Jewish Philosophers* (New York and London, 1963); *Gabriel da Costa* (South Brunswick, N.J., 1969).

References: *JTS Students' Annual* vol. II (1915), pp. 25–26; Fanny R. Minkin, "Jacob Minkin: An Appreciation," in Jacob Minkin, *The Shaping of the Modern Mind*, pp. 9–35; Stuart E. Rosenberg, *The Jewish Community in Rochester, 1843–1925* (New York, 1954), pp. 178–80; *WWWJ* 1955, p. 529.

MORAIS, SABATO (1823–97). Minister-*hazzan*, President of the Jewish Theological Seminary of America. The son of Samuel and Buonina Wolf Morais, Sabato Morais was born in Livorno, Italy, on April 13, 1823, and educated there.

In 1846 Morais moved to London to become the Hebrew master of the orphanage of the Sephardic Bevis Marks Congregation (1846–51). Five years later he immigrated to America to succeed Isaac Leeser as minister-*hazzan* of the Philadelphia Sephardic Congregation, Mikveh Israel (1851–97).

Founded in 1771, Mikveh Israel was the oldest synagogue in Philadelphia and one of the oldest congregations in America. Morais introduced programs that would later become the hallmarks of twentieth-century synagogues. He developed Mikveh Israel's educational activities to include weekly adult education classes and a supplementary school. He persuaded his congregants to grant him a personal discretionary fund for distributions to the needy. As Mikveh Israel's spiritual leader, he also influenced future leaders of American and Conservative Jewry, including Cyrus *Adler.

Morais' tenure at Mikveh Israel, the longest of any nineteenth-century American Jewish congregational leader, was not without its difficulties. He worked to unite the distinctive and often divisive Sephardic and Ashkenazic elements within the congregation. His public stance against slavery led to tensions that resulted in short-lived attempts to muzzle his preaching. Nevertheless, despite these difficulties and numerous offers to lead other congregations, Morais remained Mikveh Israel's spiritual leader for nearly half a century, holding this distinguished synagogue as a bastion against the sweeping tide of nineteenth-century Reform.

Like many other early American Jewish religious leaders, Morais was involved in almost every aspect of American Jewish life. He was a principal member of the "Philadelphia Group" of scholars and intellectuals who shaped not only the Philadelphia Jewish community, but also the larger American Jewish community. Morais played an essential role, as either founder or supporter, of nearly every Philadelphia Jewish philanthrophy and institution.

His views on the larger national and Jewish communal issues of his day became widely known. His protests against Christian language in government proclamations marked him as a bold champion of a very broad interpretation of the separation of church and state. His staunch support of immigrants and open immigration started with his single-handed organization of a work program for impoverished German Jewish immigrants before the Civil War and extended to include opposition to the Oriental Exclusion Act (1882) and support for material assistance to the growing Russian Jewish immigration. His concept of social justice brought him to the forefront, much to the dismay of the wealthy manufacturers, of the efforts to settle the disastrous cloakmakers strike of 1890 with justice for the workers. Morais worked tirelessly for American Jewish unity and, hoping to unite all American synagogues in worship, he was even willing to relinquish the familiar Sephardic *minhag* (prayer service) in favor of a uniform Ashkenazic ritual.

From 1867 to 1873 Morais was a professor of Bible and Biblical literature at the short-lived Maimonides College, one of the early attempts to create an institution of higher Jewish learning in America. In 1886 he rallied many of the same men involved in that earlier experiment to found the Jewish Theological Seminary Association, the sponsor and supporter of the Jewish Theological Seminary of America. The founders of the Seminary shared with Morais opposition to the radical turn the Reform movement had taken, especially in the Pittsburgh Platform. Although Morais himself had earlier supported Isaac Mayer Wise and the Cincinnati rabbinical school, Hebrew Union College, Morais was essentially a traditionalist. The growing radical tide of the Reform movement pushed him to gather together other like-minded Jewish leaders who shared his concern to "preserve historical Judaism" against Reform, to form "an institution for training young Israelites to the ministry on principles thoroughly conservative [sic]." Morais became the founding president of the Seminary (1886–97).

As president of the Advisory Board of Ministers, as the Seminary faculty was then called, he organized the faculty and taught Bible and Biblical exegesis when the Seminary began offering classes in 1887 in New York's Shearith Israel. Morais oversaw the Seminary's acquisition of and move to its first building on Lexington Avenue, which housed the students' classrooms, dormitory, and dining hall. Although he originally conceived of the school as "The Orthodox Seminary," he yielded to Alexander *Kohut's conception of modeling it on the rabbinical seminary in Breslau, training candidates educated in both Jewish and secular studies. Consequently, most students in the early Seminary attended City College classes in the mornings. Hebrew instruction and Seminary classes met in the afternoon and evenings. Morais refused to abandon Mikveh Israel to fulfill his new duties, preferring instead to commute weekly from Philadelphia to New York.

Morais considered the Oral Law binding, but he did not see the *Shulchan Aruch* as the final authority. He could conceive of changes in Jewish custom and law, provided they were made by rabbis faithful to the tradition. During his presidency the early Seminary did not openly espouse the label Conservative.

Morais loved Jewish music and contributed to Jewish scholarship in the area of Sephardic studies by translating a number of Italian-Hebrew works into English. He also promoted the revival of Hebrew, published a commentary on the Book of Esther, and produced the first draft of the translation of Jeremiah for the Jewish Publication Society's 1917 edition of the Bible.

Morais married Clara Esther Weil in 1855; they had seven children. He died in Philadelphia on November 11, 1897.

Writings: *Italian-Hebrew Literature*, ed. Julius H. Greenstone (New York, 1926).

References: Moshe Davis, *The Emergence of Conservative Judaism* (New York, 1963); *EJ* vol. 12, cols. 294–95; Julius H. Greenstone, "Reminiscences of Old Seminary Days," *Recorder* 6, 4 (October 1926), pp. 9–10; *National Cyclopedia of American Biography*, vol. 10 (New York, 1900), p. 170; Herbert Parzen, *Architects of Conservative Judaism* (New York, 1964), pp. 18–25; Marc Lee Raphael, *Profiles in American Judaism* (San Francisco, 1984), pp. 84–85; Herbert Rosenblum, *Conservative Judaism: A Contemporary History* (New York, 1983), pp. 13–15; Maxwell Whiteman, "The Philadelphia Group," in *Jewish Life in Philadelphia, 1830–1940*, ed. Murray Friedman, pp. 163–64.

N

NADICH, JUDAH (1912–). Rabbi, author. The son of Isaac and Lena Nathanson Nadich, Judah Nadich was born on May 13, 1912, in Baltimore, Maryland. Educated at the Rabbi Isaac Elchanan Yeshiva, he earned a B.A. from the City College of New York in 1932, was ordained at the Seminary in 1936, and earned a Doctor of Hebrew Letters there in 1953.

Nadich began his career as rabbi at Temple Beth David, Buffalo, New York (1936–40). He was then co-rabbi with Solomon *Goldman at Anshe Emet Synagogue, Chicago, Illinois (1940–42).

During World War II he was the senior Jewish chaplain (with the rank of lieutenant colonel) in the U.S. Army (1942–46). Posted to the European theater of operations, he was appointed Special Advisor on Jewish Activities to the theater commander, a new post General Dwight D. Eisenhower created after the first death camps were captured. As special advisor, Nadich toured the displaced persons camps of Germany and Austria, an experience he recounted in *Eisenhower and the Jews* (1953). Following his retirement from active duty in 1946, he continued to work for the welfare of chaplains and their men as president of the Association of Jewish Chaplains of the Armed Forces (1971–73) and later as chairman of the Commission on Jewish Chaplaincy of the Jewish Welfare Board. In 1971 and again in 1974 he was invited by the Department of Defense to visit chaplains in Southeast Asia and Germany and to conduct services there.

Drawing upon his wartime activities, Nadich went on extensive lecture tours for the United Jewish Appeal and Joint Distribution Committee across the United States and South Africa in 1946 and 1947. In 1947 he returned to the United States, succeeding Louis *Epstein as rabbi of Congregation Kehillath Israel, Brookline, Massachusetts (1947–57). In 1957 he returned to New York, following Simon *Noveck as rabbi at Park Avenue Synagogue. Among his projects there was the development of a four-year, integrated curriculum for adult studies in Jewish history, literature, and thought. His congregants understood a rabbi's need to retreat regularly for study and scholarship, and they allowed him the time necessary to write *Jewish Legends of the Second Commonwealth* (1983). In this invaluable contribution to the body of rabbinic literature available to the English reader, Nadich selected from rabbinic sources the non-legal materials— the traditions and folklore—about Jewish life and personalities in the land of Israel in the Second Commonwealth (539 B.C.E. to 70 C.E.). *Jewish Legends* also served as the basis for ten episodes of "The Eternal Light Summer Series," the Seminary's NBC radio program.

Nadich's many Jewish communal and civic activities included service on the boards of directors of the National Jewish Welfare Board, the Federation of Jewish Philanthropies of New York, the 92nd Street YM-YWHA, and the Schocken Library and Research Institute in Jerusalem. He was also vice-president of the Jewish Braille Institute, a member of the Committee on Religious Affairs of the Federation of Jewish Philanthropies, and special advisor to the chairman of the United States Holocaust Memorial Council.

In the Rabbinical Assembly Nadich led the Zionist Actions Committee in the years just prior to the birth of the state of Israel. He also handled the delicate responsibilities of chairing the Joint Placement Commission (1964–66) and the RA's Commission on Community Service (1968–70). The latter was formed in 1968 following the abrogation of the RA's prevailing system for the procurement of military chaplains. Its experiment in assigning two-year "equivalency" community service positions to all recent Seminary graduates prior to their election as full members of the Rabbinical Assembly was abandoned in the wake of vigorous opposition from the graduating classes of 1968 and 1969.

During Nadich's term as president of the 1,100–member Rabbinical Assembly (1972–74), the long-awaited Rabbinical Assembly High Holiday *Mahzor* appeared and the revitalized Committee on Jewish Law and Standards began its historic period of ground-breaking decisions according women ritual equality in the synagogue. Nadich also revitalized the Committee on Liturgical Publications and called for increased support for the Conservative movement in Israel. To bridge the differences with the Reform and Orthodox rabbinates, he proposed the holding of overlapping conventions so that the leaders of the major rabbinic organizations could meet on a regular basis. And he called for the Rabbinical Assembly to go on record as ready to accept women as members a decade before the RA actually made that decision. Nadich continued to remain active in the leadership of the Rabbinical Assembly following his presidency. In 1980 he wrote for the RA's self-study Blue Ribbon Committee the report on placement procedures and salary negotiations.

Nadich was also associate editor of *Reconstructionist* magazine, president of the Jewish Book Council of America (1969–73), and vice-president of the Jewish Braille Institute and of the Hebrew weekly *Hadoar*.

In 1947 he married Martha Hadassah Ribalow, who was executive secretary of the Rabbinical Assembly prior to their marriage. They have three daughters.

Writings: *Eisenhower and the Jews* (New York, 1953); "Report of the Commission on Community Service," *PRA 1969* vol. 33 (1969), pp. 196–98; *PRA 1970* vol. 34 (1971), pp. 186–87; "Presidential Address," *PRA 1973* vol. 35 (1974), pp. 11–19; *PRA 1974* vol. 36 (1975) pp. 20–31; "Adult Education," *PRA 1975* vol. 37 (1976), pp. 127–35; *Jewish Legends of the Second Commonwealth* (Philadelphia, 1983). Ed. and trans., Menachem Ribalow, *The Flowering of Modern Hebrew Literature* (New York, 1959).

Reference: *WWAJ* 1980, p. 351.

NEULANDER, ARTHUR H. (1896–   ). Rabbi, author. The son of Jerome and Bertha Kohn Neulander, Arthur Neulander was born in Epesjes, Hungary, on May 7, 1896, and brought to the United States in 1903. He earned a B.A. from New York University in 1918 and was ordained at the Seminary in 1921.

Neulander was the rabbi of several congregations: Temple Gates of Prayer, Flushing, New York (1922–25); Society for the Advancement of Judaism, New York (1925–26); Temple Beth-El, Camden, New Jersey (1926–27); Temple Beth Israel, Richmond Hill, New York (1928–53), and Bayswater Jewish Center, Far Rockaway, New York (1953–1968) until his retirement.

In the Rabbinical Assembly Neulander served for many years on the Executive Committee, and he edited the *Proceedings of the Rabbinical Assembly* (1941–44). A member of the Committee on Jewish Law and Standards (CJLS), he wrote one of its pioneering *responsa* on the Sabbath permitting the use of electricity "in consonance with the spirit of the Sabbath." As chairman of the CJLS (1954–59), Neulander restructured the committee, appointing six subcommittees in areas such as family status and the status of women in the synagogue. The members of these subcommittees were to become experts in a particular field of Jewish law. This expertise would enable them to go beyond the routine answering of questions directed to the CJLS, to develop new standards of conduct for modern Jewry. These changes led to the *responsum* permitting *aliyot* for women in 1955 and to the reopening of the study of the *agunah* problem in 1959.

Neulander also chaired the Committee on Textbook Publications for the United Synagogue Commission on Jewish Education (1946–47) and the Joint Placement Commission. An officer in the Long Island branch of the Zionist Organization of America, he was instrumental in raising money to purchase the land now known as Neve Ilan in Israel. When some 20,000 Jews fled Hungary in the wake of the 1956 uprising against the Communist regime, Neulander was asked by the U.S. government to escort the refugees, who included many rabbis and Jewish leaders, to the United States.

Neulander wrote *What Is in the Prayer Book*, published by the United Synagogue.

He married Grace Goodfriend in 1926; they have four children.

Writings: "*Responsum* on the Sabbath," *PRA 1950* vol. 14 (1951), pp. 165–71; *What Is in the Prayer Book* (New York, n.d.).

References: *PRA 1947* vol. 11 (1948), p. 89; *PRA 1955* vol. 19 (1956), pp. 31–33; *PRA 1959* vol. 23 (1960), pp. 114–21.

NEUMAN, ABRAHAM AARON (1890–1970). Rabbi, educator, historian. The son of Max and Rachel Rose Neuman, Abraham Neuman was born in Brezan, Austria, on September 23, 1890. He was brought to the United States in 1898. Neuman earned a B.S. from Columbia University in 1909, was ordained at the Seminary in 1912, and earned a Doctor of Hebrew Letters there in 1914.

An instructor in history at the Teachers Institute (1912–13), Neuman joined the faculty of Dropsie College for Hebrew and Cognate Learning (now Annenberg Research Institute) in Philadelphia in 1913. He advanced from instructor to associate professor in 1923 and to full professor and secretary of the faculty in 1934. In 1941 he succeeded Cyrus *Adler as president of Dropsie. As president (1941–66), Neuman organized new departments in Jewish philosophy and Hebrew literature, history of Semitic civilization, comparative religion, and Assyriology. He inaugurated the School of Education and the Institute for Israel and the Middle East (1948). In addition to expanding the curriculum, he worked to raise academic standards at the college.

While Neuman's chief interest as an historian was the social history of medieval Spanish Jewry (*The Jews in Spain* [1942]), his scholarly writings reflected great breadth. They included essays on the evolution of Judaism ("Judaism Among the Great Religions of the Modern World" [1946]) and the critical issues and contributions of contemporary American Jewry. Many of these were collected in *Landmarks and Goals* (1953), which commemorated his tenth anniversary as president of Dropsie. Neuman also wrote *Cyrus Adler: A Biographical Sketch* (1942), about the third president of the Seminary. Neuman's scholarly activities included serving as editor-in-chief of *The World History of the Jewish People*; editing, with Solomon Zeitlin, the *Jewish Quarterly Review* (1940–66), published by Dropsie College; and working on an English translation of the Apocrypha and the Pseudepigrapha.

In addition to his educational and scholarly interests, Neuman remained closely involved with the affairs of the Conservative movement. He held two pulpits in Philadelphia, Congregation B'nai Jeshurun (1919–27) and Congregation Mikveh Israel (1927–43), which was one of the founding congregations of the United Synagogue. He was president of the Board of Jewish Ministers of Philadelphia, a member of the Executive Council of the United Synagogue, and president of its Philadelphia branch. He also chaired the United Synagogue's Palestine Committee as it dedicated itself to building the Yeshurun Synagogue, a modern synagogue-center, in Jerusalem. And he was an early advocate for the development of a placement system for Conservative rabbis.

Neuman married Gladys Reed in 1919; they had one son. Divorced from his first wife, Neuman married Elsie Gans Guggenheim in 1944. He died in Philadelphia on November 20, 1970.

Writings: *Cyrus Adler: A Biographical Sketch* (Philadelphia, 1942); *The Jews in Spain: Their Social, Political, and Cultural Life During the Middle Ages*, 2 vols. (Philadelphia, 1942); *Landmarks and Goals* (Philadelphia, 1953). Ed., with S. Zeitlin, *Saadia Studies* (Philadelphia, 1943).

References: Meir Ben-Horin, Bernard D. Weinryb, and Solomon Zeitlin, eds., *Studies and Essays in Honor of Abraham A. Neuman* (Leiden and Philadelphia, 1962); *National Cyclopedia of American Biography*, vol. 55, p. 415; *Recorder* 2, 2 (April 1922), p. 13.

NOVECK, SIMON (1914–). Rabbi, author. The son of Samuel and Helen Matzkel Noveck, Simon Noveck was born in Atlanta, Georgia, on July 9, 1914. He earned a B.A. from Yeshiva College in 1936, was ordained at the Seminary in 1941, and earned a Ph.D. from Columbia University in 1955.

Noveck served several congregations. He was rabbi at the Baldwin Jewish Center, Long Island (1940–44); acting rabbi at Temple Beth-El, Cedarhurst, Long Island (1944–46); and rabbi at Congregation B'nai Israel, Freeport, Long Island (1946–49). In 1949 he became assistant rabbi of New York's Park Avenue Synagogue (1949–50), then led by the well-known author and Reconstructionist ideologue Milton *Steinberg. Following Steinberg's death, Noveck became rabbi at Park Avenue (1950–57).

By this time Noveck had already established himself as a leader in the field of adult Jewish education and was also directing the National Academy for Adult Jewish Studies (1952–57), which had moved its headquarters from the Seminary to the United Synagogue. As director of the National Academy, he was responsible for creating curricular materials and new adult education programs and for sending lecturers on Judaism to Conservative congregations across North America. Noveck brought his interest in adult education programming home to his congregation, leading Park Avenue to sponsor a lecture series, Judaism and Psychiatry, on the psychological values inherent in the Jewish way of life. He subsequently edited the lectures for publication by the National Academy (*Judaism and Psychiatry* [1956]).

In 1957 Noveck left Park Avenue to become the full-time director of the three-year-old B'nai B'rith Department of Adult Jewish Education. He recognized that the contemporary trend in adult education was reading the great classical books of Western thought. To move adult Jewish education in the same direction, he edited the five-volume B'nai B'rith Great Books Series (1959–63), a selection of the classical sources of ancient, medieval, and modern Jewish religious thought for the adult education audience.

In 1961 Noveck returned to the pulpit, succeeding Morris *Silverman as rabbi at Emanuel Synagogue (1961–69), the first Conservative synagogue founded in Hartford, Connecticut (1919). Under Noveck's direction its 955 families planned to build a new sanctuary and additional classrooms.

Noveck's other literary activities included editing four volumes of essays for the B'nai B'rith series History of the Jewish People (1985) and writing a biography of Milton Steinberg, an important contribution to the small number of biographies of leading American rabbis. He also taught political science at the City College of New York (1944–48) and modern Jewish history at the Seminary College of Jewish Studies (1945–50).

Noveck and his wife, Doris, have two daughters.

Writings: *Adult Education in the Modern Synagogue* (New York, 1953); *Laymen's Institute: An Adventure in Jewish Living* (New York, 1954); "New Trends in Adult Jewish Education, *PRA 1954* vol. 18 (1955), pp. 201–3; *Milton Steinberg: Portrait of a Rabbi* (New York, 1977); "Adult Jewish Education Reconsidered," *PRA 1980* vol. 42 (1981), pp. 183–89. Ed., *Judaism and Psychiatry* (New York, 1956); *Great Jewish Personalities in Ancient and Medieval Times* (Washington, D.C., 1959); *Great Jewish Personalities in Modern Times* (Washington, D.C., 1960); *Contemporary Jewish Thought: A Reader* (Washington, D.C., 1963); *Great Jewish Thinkers of the Twentieth Century* (Washington, D.C., 1963); *Creators of the Jewish Experience: In the Modern World* (Washington, D.C., 1985).

References: Abraham J. Karp, *A History of the United Synagogue of America, 1913–1963* (New York, 1964), p. 92; Morris Silverman, *Hartford Jews, 1659–1970* (Hartford, Conn., 1970), p. 98; *WWWJ* 1955, p. 558.

P

PARZEN, HERBERT (1896–1985). Rabbi, historian. The son of Charles and Molly Dobczinski Parzen, Herbert Parzen was born in Lodz, Poland, on December 23, 1896, and immigrated to the United States in 1909. He earned a B.A. from the University of Michigan in 1919 and was ordained at the Seminary in 1926.

After serving as rabbi at Temple Aaron, St. Paul, Minnesota (1926–28), Parzen accepted a call to Temple Ahavai Shalom, Portland, Oregon (1928–31?), founded in 1868 by Prussian and Polish Jewish immigrants who preferred establishing their own synagogue to joining the existing congregation run by immigrants from southern Germany. Serious financial difficulties in the 1920s had hindered Ahavai Shalom's efforts to keep any rabbi for more than a few years, and its membership had declined from a high of 277 members in 1923 to 169 by 1928. When Parzen arrived in 1928, a bequest had remedied the congregation's financial situation, and he managed to stem the tide of declining membership despite the difficulties of the early years of the Depression. A committed Zionist, he also headed the Portland chapter of the Zionist Organization of America (1939–41).

Parzen returned to the East Coast in 1942, serving as rabbi at Temple B'nai Israel, Freeport, Long Island (1942–44), chaplain at the House of Detention for Women in New York City (1945–79), and lecturer in Jewish history and literature at the Theodore Herzl Institute in New York City (1970–83). During these years he put his editorial skills to work on behalf of the Conservative movement, editing the bimonthly, in-house newsletter *Rabbinical Assembly Bulletin* in the early 1950s, directing the United Synagogue publications programs, and editing the *News of the United Synagogue* (1950–54). His most important contribution, however, was a series of articles written for the early issues of *Conservative Judaism*, which he later worked into the first history of Conservatism, *Architects of Conservative Judaism* (1964). This work offers profiles of the early leaders of the Conservative movement—Solomon *Schechter, Cyrus *Adler, Louis

*Ginzberg, Israel *Friedlaender, and Mordecai M. *Kaplan—as well as their forerunners Isaac Leeser and Sabato *Morais. Parzen was also for a time executive director of the Jewish Reconstructionist Foundation (1954–59?), organized in 1940 to disseminate Reconstructionist literature and to coordinate the activities and institutions of its growing movement.

His other writings focused on aspects of Zionism and include *The Hebrew University, 1925–35*, an account of a controversial and critical investigation in 1933 into the academic and administrative affairs of Hebrew University.

Parzen married Sylvia Goldsmith in 1923; they had no children. He died in 1985 in Southfield, Michigan.

Writings: *A Short History of Zionism* (New York, 1962); *Architects of Conservative Judaism* (New York, 1964); *The Hebrew University, 1925–1935* (New York, 1974); *Review* 7, 5 (April 1954), p. 7.

References: William Toll, *The Making of an Ethnic Middle Class: Portland Jewry Over Four Generations* (Albany, N.Y., 1982), pp. 138, 175–78.

PRESSMAN, JACOB (1919–   ). Rabbi. The son of Solomon and Dora Levin Pressman, Jacob Pressman was born on October 26, 1919, in Philadelphia, Pennsylvania. He earned a B.A. from the University of Pennsylvania in 1940 and was ordained at the Seminary in 1945.

Pressman began his career as rabbi at Forest Hills Jewish Center (1944–46), temporarily replacing Rabbi Ben Zion *Bokser, who served as a chaplain during World War II. Pressman helped plan and raise funds for the relocation of the center. At the same time he was also director of youth activities for the United Synagogue.

In 1946 Pressman moved to California to become associate rabbi of Sinai Temple, Los Angeles (1946–50). There he worked with the senior rabbi, Jacob *Kohn, to help motivate the congregation to relocate. He also supervised Sinai Temple's satellite school and introduced its community *seder*.

In 1950 Pressman became rabbi of the Olympic Jewish Center, Los Angeles (1950–85). Founded in 1935, it was renamed Temple Beth Am in 1957. In thirty-five years as Beth Am's spiritual leader, Pressman planned and raised funds for a new synagogue, school, and Beth Am Manor, an adjacent low-rent senior citizens' housing project. He expanded the congregation's educational programs to include a nursery school; elementary and secondary day schools, later named the Rabbi Jacob Pressman Academy; a summer camp; and a full adult education program. With his guidance Beth Am also sponsored Israel Expo West, an exhibition that drew more than 50,000 participants. When he retired in 1985, he was elected rabbi emeritus.

Pressman was a leader in the development of the Conservative movement on the West Coast. He was president of the Western Region of the Rabbinical Assembly and chairman of the 1979 annual RA convention, held in Los Angeles. He pioneered in the founding of every major Conservative educational institution created in the Los Angeles area, including Camp Ramah at Ojai, the Los Angeles

Hebrew High School, and the University of Judaism, the West Coast branch of the Seminary. He also served as the university's first registrar and later as special assistant to the president.

Outside of the Conservative movement, he was active in Los Angeles Jewish communal affairs. Pressman was president of the Board of Rabbis of Los Angeles and a member of the Executive Council of the Los Angeles Federation. Chairman of the Israel Bonds campaign for the region, he was also a member of the national rabbinic cabinets of the United Jewish Appeal and Israel Bonds. He was chairman of the Los Angeles Zionist Youth Commission and a founder of the Brandeis-Bardin Camp Institute. His civic activities included membership in the National Safety Council, and he was also founding president of the Beverly Hills Maple Center, a full-service counseling center (1972–75).

Pressman married Marjorie Steinberg in 1942; they have three children.

References: Abraham J. Karp, *A History of the United Synagogue, 1913–1963* (New York, 1964), p. 71; *The Pressman Chronicles in the Jubilee Year of Temple Beth Am, 1935–1985* (Los Angeles, 1985); *WWAJ* 1980, p. 380.

PUTTERMAN, DAVID J. (1900–1979). Cantor. David J. Putterman was born in New York City on August 29, 1900. He studied cantorial arts privately in Europe and the United States, and before his eighteenth birthday became cantor of Temple Israel, Washington Heights, New York (1918–32).

Putterman was a distinguished cantor and gifted composer of synagogue music, acclaimed for his sincerity and piety in leading worship and for his commitment to enriching liturgical music. After leaving Temple Israel, he became cantor at New York's Park Avenue Synagogue (1933–76; cantor emeritus 1976–79), arriving at the same time as Park Avenue's new rabbi, Milton *Steinberg. Steinberg accorded the cantor great freedom in setting the musical arrangements. Putterman not only introduced new melodies to the congregation, he also commissioned new works for the Sabbath eve from such leading composers as Leonard Bernstein and Kurt Weill. He thus played a major role in revitalizing Park Avenue's Sabbath and holiday services and contributed to the growth of the congregation.

But Putterman's vision extended beyond his own synagogue. Determined to raise the standards, scope, and direction of the American cantorate, he emerged as one of the leading forces in the professionalization of the cantorate in the Conservative movement. In 1947 he assumed the directorship of the United Synagogue's new Department of Music. By this time Putterman's radio broadcasts, concerts, records, and solos on the Seminary-sponsored NBC radio program, "The Eternal Light," had won him a national reputation as one of the foremost American authorities on synagogue music. As director of the Department of Music, he provided guidance and information on synagogue music to Conservative congregations, assisted cantors with their problems, and worked to raise the standards of the cantorate.

One of his first projects at the United Synagogue was the establishment of the Cantors Assembly in 1947. For over a decade Putterman served as its executive vice-president (1947–59). Modeling itself on the Rabbinical Assembly, the Cantors Assembly took over the placement work that had earlier been conducted under United Synagogue auspices by the Cantorial Placement Bureau. In an era before cantors were professionally trained in the United States, the Cantors Assembly auditioned and interviewed men to test their musical skills and Jewish knowledge, and if they were found satisfactory, to assist with their placement in Conservative congregations. With fifty founding members, the Cantors Assembly immediately set about providing retirement benefits and planning publications to standardize congregational singing in Conservative synagogues.

In 1948, with Putterman's guidance, the Cantors Assembly embarked on its most ambitious undertaking, the creation of the Cantors Institute at the Seminary, a school for the professional training of cantors to serve the growing congregations of the Conservative movement. With the destruction of the Jewish communities of Europe, the informal settings in which most cantors, including Putterman, had prepared for their careers no longer existed. Moreover, by this time the role of the cantor in the Conservative synagogue had evolved from one of a performer whose beautiful voice was to inspire other worshippers to an integral member of the synagogue's professional staff, in charge of all music and many educational aspects of the congregation. The decision to establish the Cantors Institute and the Seminary College of Jewish Music reflected this transition and the need to provide for the professional education of Conservative cantors. Prompted also by the fact that the Reform Hebrew Union College was already making plans to establish its own cantorial school, the Cantors Assembly pledged itself to raise $25,000 to establish the Cantors Institute and Seminary College of Jewish Music. In 1952 they began conducting classes at the Seminary. Two years later Putterman became the first fellow of the Cantors Institute (1954). For more than twenty-five years he taught traditional and modern liturgical melodies and inspired its students.

Putterman married Amy B. Racoosin; they had two sons. Following her death, he married Rea Cohen Racoosin. He died in New York City on October 10, 1979.

Writings: *Synagogue Music by Contemporary Composers* (New York, 1947); "Greetings," *PRA 1948* vol. 12 (1949), pp. 81–82; *Mismor L'David* (New York, 1979).

References: *AJYB* vol. 81 (1981), p. 373; *News of the United Synagogue* 2, 7 (February 1947), p. 1; *NYT* 12 October 1979, p. B4; Simon Noveck, *Milton Steinberg: Portrait of a Rabbi* (New York, 1978), pp. 59–60; *Review* 4, 3 (November 1948), p. 1; 5, 4 (February 1952), p. 6; Marjorie Wyler, "Cantors Institute: The First Twenty-Five Years," *Review* 32, 1 (Fall 1979), p. 6.

R

RABINOWITZ, HYMAN REUVEN (1893–   ).   Rabbi. The son of Jacob and Devorah Fogel Rabinowitz, Hyman Rabinowitz was born on January 30, 1893, in Srednick, Lithuania, and brought to the United States in 1904. He earned a B.A. at Columbia University in 1916 and was ordained at the Seminary in 1925.

Rabinowitz was one of the early pioneers of Conservative Judaism in the West. He served one congregation, Shaare Zion Synagogue, Sioux City, Iowa (1925–59). In 1914 with the assistance of Denver rabbi Charles Eliezer Hillel *Kauvar, a group of Sioux City Jews formed a branch of the United Synagogue of America. In the following years the group disbanded, in part because they lacked a synagogue. They reorganized in 1925 and founded Shaare Zion Synagogue, hired Rabinowitz as rabbi, and began planning to build a synagogue. Rabinowitz immediately organized the programs characteristic of burgeoning Conservative synagogues—late Friday evening services, a junior congregation, a sisterhood, and study circles. Within two years the congregation had raised the necessary funds to build its synagogue.

Rabinowitz was involved in every aspect of the lives of his congregants and the congregation. In his thirty-four years in Sioux City, he officiated at 325 weddings, named 625 infants, and conducted 348 funerals. He led the way in establishing the congregation's Sunday school, library, and United Synagogue Youth chapter. When he retired in 1959, the congregants elected him rabbi emeritus.

Rabinowitz then settled in Jerusalem where he devoted himself to the study of Jewish classical texts and wrote, in Hebrew, two studies of outstanding preachers. *Deyoknaot shel Darshanim* (1967) evaluated the works of gifted preachers of the past, set them in the context of their eras, and showed how they cultivated relevant insights out of the Torah. *Bene Binah* (1972) used the same techniques, but it analyzed the preaching styles of contemporary masters and included essays on a number of his Rabbinical Assembly colleagues.

Rabinowitz married Gittel Vogel in 1925; they have one daughter.

Writings: *Deyoknaot shel Darshanim* (Jerusalem, 1967); *Bene Binah* (Jerusalem, 1972).

References: *CJ* 23, 1 (Fall 1968), pp. 86–88; *CJ* 27, 4 (Summer 1973), p. 96; *Recorder* 5, 3 (July 1925), p. 9; 6, 2 (March 1926), p. 25; Bernard Shuman, *A History of the Sioux City Jewish Community* (Sioux City, Iowa, 1969), pp. 47–56.

RABINOWITZ, STANLEY (1917–). Rabbi. The son of Jacob Meyer and Rose Zeichik Rabinowitz, Stanley Rabinowitz was born on June 8, 1917, in Duluth, Minnesota. He earned a B.A. at the State University of Iowa in 1939 and was ordained at the Seminary in 1943.

Rabinowitz began his career as director of the Midwest office of the Seminary and the Council of Conservative Synagogues of Chicago, traveling as an intinerant rabbi from community to community to fill in for men serving overseas (1943–45). He subsequently became director of field services for the United Synagogue and was its acting executive director (1946) between the retirement of its first executive, Samuel M. *Cohen, and the appointment of Albert *Gordon.

In 1947 Rabinowitz moved to the congregational rabbinate, serving three distinguished Conservative congregations in a forty-year career in the pulpit. He followed Louis *Greenberg as rabbi of B'nai Jacob Congregation, New Haven, Connecticut (1947–53). He then moved to the important Minneapolis congregation, Adath Jeshurun Synagogue (1953–60). In 1960 he was called to the pulpit of the leading Conservative synagogue in the nation's capital, Adas Israel Congregation, Washington, D.C. (1960–86). Adas Israel was founded in 1876 when several members left the classical Reform synagogue, Washington Hebrew Congregation, because they objected to the playing of an organ at services. Rabinowitz remained at Adas Israel for the rest of his career.

Believing that the ''challenge of the synagogue today is to create institutions which bestow identity,'' Rabinowitz introduced in each of the congregations he served programs designed to enhance Jewish identity for the different constituencies of the congregation. He fought, sometimes over strenuous opposition, to establish a nursery school, the *gan hayeled*, and to found or to improve the three-day-a-week Hebrew school. A staunch champion of women's rights to ritual equality in Judaism, he introduced the Bat Mitzvah ceremony in each congregation and persuaded Adas Israel to count women in the *minyan* before the Rabbinical Assembly's Committee on Jewish Law and Standards voted in favor of this groundbreaking measure. He also inaugurated at Adas Israel the adult B'not Mitzvah service for women who had not earlier had the opportunity of becoming Bat Mitzvah and vitalized the liturgical life of his congregants by offering them a choice of services—an informal *havurah*, an Orthodox *minyan*, a singles service, as well as the regular large formal service in the main sanctuary—on any given *Shabbat*. Recognizing the limitations of the three-day-a-week Hebrew school in the urban synagogue, Rabinowitz led Adas Israel to establish a summer camp, Tel Shalom, as an alternative educational model for the children of the congregation. When he retired from the pulpit in 1986, Adas Israel elected him rabbi emeritus.

Rabinowitz emerged as one of the leading members of the Rabbinical Assembly. In the 1950s he chaired the Committee on Synagogue Standards, which formulated a guide to standards, which among other areas, governed rabbi-congregational relations, and which was ratified by the United Synagogue. As secretary and then as vice-president (1974–76) and president (1976–78) of the Rabbinical Assembly, he was especially concerned with Zionism and Israel, and their relation to Conservative Jewry. During his presidency the Rabbinical Assembly entered as an equal partner in the World Council of Synagogues. This paved the way for the affiliation of the World Council with the World Zionist Organization, which at last gave the Conservative movement political representation in Zionist affairs. As president, Rabinowitz joined a delegation of Conservative leaders that traveled to Egypt to meet with religious and political leaders and he also joined with Reform rabbinical colleagues in protesting to Israeli Prime Minister Menachem Begin a proposed amendment to the Law of Return that would automatically invalidate the conversions of Jews converted under non-Orthodox auspices who immigrated to Israel. His experiences convinced him that only a strong political presence of the Conservative movement in Israel could defend the rights of non-Orthodox Jews there and in the Diaspora. Consequently, he became the founding president of the Movement for the Reaffirmation of Conservative Zionism (MERCAZ; 1977–85), established to provide a springboard from which Conservative ideology would enter the World Zionist Organization and protect the special interests of Conservative Zionists. Rabinowitz also worked to strengthen the internal affairs of the Rabbinical Assembly, creating the Financial Management Committee charged with protecting the assets and pension program of the Rabbinical Assembly.

As president of the Rabbinical Assembly, Rabinowitz was considered a leading candidate for the chair of the Conference of Presidents of Major Jewish Organizations. His candidacy depended upon the Rabbinical Assembly's amending its constitution to allow a president to serve a third one-year term if he was already nominated to the chair of the conference. The Rabbinical Assembly passed the amendment, making it possible for a future RA president to assume the leadership of this important Jewish organization. Nevertheless, political considerations, which led the conference to delay its nominations meeting until after the Rabbinical Assembly had met, prevented Rabinowitz from succeeding to the post. After Rabinowitz concluded his term as president, he spearheaded the Rabbinical Assembly's Blue Ribbon Committee, a self-study project which on the occasion of the RA's eightieth anniversary reported on its prospects for the future. It explored both the traditional ''trade union'' concerns of the Rabbinical Assembly—placement, salary negotiations, retirement, and rabbinical status—

and the larger substantive issues of Conservatism—ideology, Zionism, and the publications program.

Rabinowitz also chaired the United Jewish Appeal's Rabbinical Cabinet (1979) and traveled twice to Rumania, in 1972 and again in 1979, to give support and encouragement to its Chief Rabbi Moses Rosen.

He married Anita Lifson in 1945; they have three children.

Writings: "Report of the Committee on Synagogue Standards," *PRA 1952* vol. 16 (1953), pp. 97–99; "What Do We Want Our Synagogue to Be?" *Beineinu* vol. 3, 2, (May 1973), pp. 48–49; "The Rabbinate: Its Changing Role," *PRA 1974* vol. 36 (1975), pp. 168–73; "The Changing Rabbinate: A Search for Definition," *PRA 1975* vol. 37 (1976), pp. 51–60; "President's Address," *PRA 1977* vol. 39 (1978), pp. 13–24; "President's Address," *PRA 1978* vol. 40 (1979), pp. 1–14; "Romanian Rhapsody," *CJ* vol. 33, 3 (Spring 1980), pp. 57–62.

References: Michael Berenbaum, "Stanley Rabinowitz Reflects on Five Decades of Leadership," *Washington Jewish Week* 26 June 1986, p. 3; *B'nai Jacob: One Hundred Years, 1882–1982* (Woodbridge, Conn., n.d.), p. 13; *WWAJ* 1980, p. 383; *WWWJ* 1978, p. 705.

ROSENBAUM, SAMUEL (1919–   ). Cantor, administrator. The son of Isidore and Bertha Kogen Rosenbaum, Samuel Rosenbaum was born in New York City on June 11, 1919. Rosenbaum was educated at the Hebrew School of Williamsburg, the Hebrew High School of New York's Jewish Education Association, and the Herzliah Teachers Academy, and earned a B.A. from New York University in 1940. During these years, he studied music privately to prepare for the cantorate and later continued his training with cantors Jacob Beimel and Adolph Katchko.

Rosenbaum began his career as a cantor at the Queens Jewish Center, Queens Village, New York (1940–42). His tenure there was interrupted by military service in the U.S. Army during World War II (1942–46). When he completed his tour of duty, he became cantor of Temple Beth El, Rochester, New York (1946–   ). His innovative work there in musical programming led to awards from the Cantors Assembly (1965) and the United Synagogue (Solomon Schechter Award in Synagogue Activity Programming, 1965).

As president of the Cantors Assembly (1956–59), the Conservative cantors' association organized in 1947, and then as its executive director (1959–   ), Rosenbaum has led the organization to provide greater service to the professional Conservative cantorate. As the Cantors Assembly grew to become the largest organization of cantors in the world, its members extended their traditional role as performers in the synagogue to involvement in a wide range of congregational activities, especially educational programming. Rosenbaum, who was a fellow of the Seminary's Cantors Institute (1960), worked with the school to place its graduates. He also serves as managing editor of the Cantors Assembly's *Journal of Synagogue Music* (1970–   ).

As a composer, Rosenbaum has made a lasting contribution to the development of American Jewish liturgical music. In collaboration with other leading composers, he has written some thirty solo and choral works for performance, many of them originally commissioned by Conservative and Reform congregations. The oratorio *Yizkor: In Memory of the Six Million* (1973), written with Sholom Secunda and performed on ABC-TV's "Directions," was nominated for an Emmy award. Rosenbaum is also the author of several books of Jewish music and the texts *To Live as a Jew* (1969), for high school and adult education students on the Jewish life cycle, and *A Guide to Haftarah Chanting* (1973), a new method for teaching Biblical cantillation. He has also written and narrated several holiday recordings.

Rosenbaum married Ina C. Levi; they have three children.

Writings: *Sabbath and Festival Songs for the Young Singer* (New York, 1959); *To Live as a Jew* (New York, 1969); *A Guide to Haftarah Chanting* (New York, 1973); *Four Holiday Recordings* (Rochester, N.Y., 1981). With Issacher Miron, *Sing a Song of Israel* (New York, 1962); with Sholom Secunda, *Oneg Shabbat* (New York, 1964); with Charles Davidson, *A Singing of Angels* (New York, 1967); with Lazar Weiner, *The Last Judgment* (New York, 1967); with Sholom Secunda, *Yizkor: In Memory of the Six Million* (New York, 1973).

Reference: *ASCAP Biographical Dictionary*, 4th ed. (New York, 1980), p. 430.

ROSENBERG, STUART E. (1922–). Rabbi, author. The son of Hyman and Kate Weissman Rosenberg, Stuart Rosenberg was born on July 5, 1922, in New York City. He received his elementary education at the Yeshivah of Flatbush and graduated from James Madison High School. He earned a B.A. from Brooklyn College and graduated from the Herzliah Teachers Seminary in 1942, was ordained at the Seminary in 1945, and earned a Ph.D. at Columbia University in 1953.

Rosenberg began his career as rabbi of Temple Beth El, Rochester, New York (1946–56). Beth El was founded in 1915, when several of the younger and more affluent members of its parent synagogue, the Leopold Street Beth El, one of the founding congregations of the United Synagogue, moved to a new neighborhood where they established their own synagogue. Although in its early years the congregation had leaned toward Reform, Rabbi Jacob *Minkin led Temple Beth El squarely into the Conservative camp. Rosenberg brought leading members of the Seminary faculty to Rochester for Beth El's annual Institutes of Judaism.

While at Beth El, Rosenberg also pursued his doctorate, writing a model Jewish communal history, *The Jewish Community in Rochester, 1843–1925* (1954). With his Rochester Reform colleague Rabbi Philip S. Bernstein, he co-chaired the city's first Israel Bonds Campaign (1951). Rosenberg was also a lecturer in religion at the University of Rochester (1951–56) and at the Colgate-Rochester Divinity School. A Zionist who made his first trip to Israel in 1949, he was president of the Rochester district (1948–50) and vice-president of the Western New York Region (1950–52) of the Zionist Organization of America.

In 1956 Rosenberg left Rochester to become senior rabbi of Beth Tzedec Congregation, Toronto, Canada (1956–73). Two synagogues, Beth Ha-Midrash Ha-Gadol and Goel Tzedec, established as Orthodox congregations in downtown Toronto in the 1880s, had for some time been losing members who moved to affluent Forest Hill Village. In the 1950s the congregations agreed to merge into Beth Tzedec to afford it the ability to relocate and to build a new edifice. In 1955 the 2,000 families of Beth Tzedec Congregation dedicated their sumptuous synagogue, which boasted a 3,600–seat sanctuary, lavish catering facilities, and a large congregational school.

Rosenberg was drawn to Beth Tzedec by what he described as its members' strong ethnic identity and their willingness to allow him to shape their magnificent synagogue into a true house of study. He founded the monthly Beth Tzedec Institutes of Religion and Ethics. Modeled on similar institutes launched at the Seminary by Louis *Finkelstein, they fostered Jewish-Christian dialogue. To make Jewish studies a lifelong commitment for his congregants, Rosenberg created the Great Weekends with Great Jews series, bringing world Jewish notables, politicians, and scholars to Toronto. He also founded Beth Tzedec's day school, now the United Synagogue Day School of Toronto, launched Beth Tzedec's Jewish Museum, and in a daring move acquired its major collection.

Rosenberg's many achievements were not without their price. In *The Real Jewish World: A Rabbi's Second Thoughts* (1984), a personal history and commentary on contemporary Jewish life and thought, he wrote a perceptive portrait of the dilemmas of the congregational rabbi. Because the Seminary trained Conservative rabbis to be scholars, Rosenberg saw that the principal malaise of life as a congregational rabbi was that it consigned the rabbi to serving "pinch Judaism." Critical of the lavish and flamboyant celebrations of contemporary Jewry, which he knew bore little resemblance to the great Jewish traditions of the past, he was also frustrated by congregational politics. In 1972, when a new group within the synagogue wanted to wrest control from the reigning power bloc of Beth Tzedec's Board of Directors, it did not hesitate to manufacture issues, hold sit-ins, and pay for media coverage. Although Rosenberg did not elaborate on how he came to leave Beth Tzedec after nearly two decades of distinguished and creative leadership, presumably this election played a role in creating the difficulties that caused his departure in 1973.

Rosenberg was an early and ardent champion of Soviet Jewish emigration and a staunch opponent of the Jewish establishment's policy of quiet diplomacy as the principal means of securing the rights of Soviet Jews. He visited the Soviet Union in 1961, meeting with Yehudah Leib Levin, chief rabbi of Moscow, to see the situation firsthand. Rosenberg came away convinced that Soviet Jews were eager for emigration. As chairman of the 1966 Rabbinical Assembly convention in Toronto, he insisted that the RA devote an entire day to Soviet Jewry and was midwife to its pioneering resolution calling for Soviet Jewry's right to emigrate. He subsequently helped orchestrate a similarly strong statement for the Reform movement's Central Conference of American Rabbis.

Elsewhere in the Conservative movement, Rosenberg chaired the Central Canada Region of the Rabbinical Assembly, was a member of the Rabbinical Cabinet, and led an RA committee on the history of the Conservative movement. A chair in history was established in his honor at the Seminary.

He also taught at the Graduate Ecumenical Institute of Canada, the University of Toronto, the Toronto School of Theology, and San Diego State University. Active in Jewish academic organizations and an advocate of Jewish studies in Canadian universities, he was national president and founder of the Canadian Foundation for Jewish Culture, vice-president of the National Foundation for Jewish Culture, national executive vice-president of the Canadian Friends of Tel Aviv University (1977–80), and is a member of the Board of Governors of Tel Aviv University (1977–). He was chairman and founder of the Ontario Committee for Government Aid to Jewish Day Schools and chairman of the United Jewish Appeal of Metro Toronto (1966–67).

After leaving Beth Tzedec, writing and civic activities occupied Rosenberg. He is chair for the Government of Ontario's Funeral Services Review Board (1977–) and is a member of the Liquor License Appeal Tribunal (1982–). In 1982 he returned to congregational life as rabbi of Beth Torah Congregation, Toronto (1982–).

Rosenberg's writings are characterized by great diversity, but all deal with the key themes of contemporary Jewish life and identity. They also include a novel, *When the Bough Breaks* (1976), and a sociological study, *The New Jewish Identity in America* (1985). The latter synthesizes his earlier works, *America is Different* (1964) and *The Search for Jewish Identity in America* (1965), arguing that the "new and prideful ethnic identity" of American Jewry proves that via selective accommodation to America, Jews have learned how to live successfully within two cultures. Rosenberg also wrote the weekly syndicated column, "Lines of Life."

He married Hadassa Agassi in 1944; they have three daughters.

Writings: *The Jewish Community in Rochester* (New York, 1954); *Man Is Free* (New York, 1957); *A Time to Speak* (New York, 1960); *Bridge to Brotherhood: Judaism's Dialogue with Christianity* (New York, 1961); *The Bible Is for You* (New York, 1961); *America Is Different* (New York, 1964); *The Search for Jewish Identity in America* (New York, 1965); *Judaism* (Glen Rock, N.J., 1966); *The Jewish Community in Canada*, 2 vols. (Toronto, 1971); *To Understand Jews* (London, 1973); *When the Bough Breaks* (New York, 1976); *The Real Jewish World: A Rabbi's Second Thoughts* (New York, 1984); *The New Jewish Identity in America* (New York, 1985); *Christian and Jew: The Eternal Bond* (New York, 1985). Ed., *A Humane Society* (Toronto, 1962).

References: *Canadian Who's Who* 1983, p. 6048; *EJ* vol. 14, cols. 279–80; *PRA 1974* vol. 36 (1975), pp. 228–30; *WWWJ* 1965, p. 794.

ROUTTENBERG, MAX JONAH (1909–   ). Rabbi. The son of Harry David and Dora Garmaise Routtenberg, Max Routtenberg was born on March 22, 1909, in Montreal, Canada. He attended McGill University in Montreal (1925–27), earned a B.S. from New York University in 1930, was ordained at the Seminary in 1932, and earned a Doctor of Hebrew Letters there in 1949.

Routtenberg considered his first pulpit at Kesher Zion Synagogue, Reading, Pennsylvania (1932–48), "the laboratory where I learned how to be a rabbi." In the process he helped establish Conservative Judaism in eastern Pennsylvania, creating a modern Hebrew school and adult education institute at Kesher Zion. He also played a leading role in Jewish communal affairs as president of the Reading Zionist District (1938–42) and chairman of the United Jewish Appeal of Berks County (1947). During World War II Routtenberg left Kesher Zion to serve as senior chaplain of the U.S. Army's United Kingdom Base (1942–45).

Although he returned to Kesher Zion following his tour of duty, in 1949 Routtenberg left the pulpit rabbinate temporarily to serve the Conservative movement from within its New York national headquarters. As executive vice-president of the Rabbinical Assembly (1949–51), he served the Rabbinical Assembly at a time when it was struggling to fill the demand for pulpit rabbis. Consequently, most of his duties involved placement work; efforts to develop standards for rabbinic-congregational contracts; and the completion, after many years of false starts, of the RA's Code of Professional Conduct. In 1951 Routtenberg was elevated to the post of executive vice-president of the Seminary (1951–54) and dean of the newly established Cantors Institute and Seminary College of Jewish Music (1951–54). He was also a lecturer on education and synagogue administration at the Teachers Institute (1950–52).

In 1954 Routtenberg decided to return to congregational life as rabbi of Temple B'nai Sholom, Rockville Centre, Long Island (1954–72). His determination to enhance the adult education programs of the congregation led to the creation of the Institute for Adult Jewish Studies, the Women's Institute, a Judaica library, and the Lecture Forum. With Routtenberg's innovative leadership, extensive adult education programming, and a wide range of youth activities, B'nai Sholom emerged as a leading suburban congregation.

Routtenberg's administrative and leadership qualities were widely recognized by his colleagues, who continued to award him, both before and after his stint as a professional administrator, important positions of leadership within the national organizations of the Conservative movement. As secretary of the Prayer Book Commission in 1942, he compiled a survey on synagogue rituals to guide the commission in its preparation of a prayer book for the movement.

As chairman of the Committee on Jewish Law and Standards (CJLS; 1960–63), Routtenberg continued to search for a solution to the difficult *agunah* controversy that had plagued the Rabbinical Assembly for decades. Viewing the CJLS as the "collective rabbi of the Conservative movement," he believed in holding the constituent agencies of the Conservative movement to higher standards in the observance of Jewish law. Therefore, while the CJLS had a decade earlier made provision for worshippers to travel to synagogue on *Shabbat*, Routtenberg urged the United Synagogue Youth to make certain that its conventions did not cause participants to violate the Sabbath prohibition against travel. After the conclusion of his term as chairman, Routtenberg continued to make important contributions to the CJLS. He evidenced its more open stance toward intermarried couples when he wrote a majority opinion allowing for synagogue membership, albeit without honors, of the Jewish spouse who had intermarried, in the hope of winning over the entire family to Judaism and persuading the non-Jewish spouse to convert.

As president of the Rabbinical Assembly (1964–66), he led the RA to join the Conference of Presidents of Major Jewish Organizations and to work toward a new formulation of the relationship of Conservative Judaism with the state of Israel. He remained concerned with organizational problems within the Conservative movement, particularly the operations of the Liaison Committee, the top policy-making body in Conservative Judaism.

After completing his term as president, Routtenberg led some of the most important committees in the Rabbinical Assembly. He chaired the Rabbinical Assembly's Committee on Chaplaincy (1967–68) as it dealt with difficulties arising when the Seminary students, prompted in part by opposition to American involvement in the Vietnam War, voted to reject the system of compulsory procurement of chaplains for the U.S. armed forces. In 1970 Routtenberg co-chaired the Special Committee on the Revitalization of the Law Committee, established in the wake of the resignation of the majority of the members of the committee. He also chaired the RA's Publications Committee (1972–82) and Liturgical Committee (1982–   ) as they worked to prepare a new Sabbath and festival prayer book, *ketubah*, and *Haggadah* (1979), and the committee that revised the Rabbinical Assembly constitution in 1977.

Routtenberg was also chairman of the National Academy of Adult Jewish Studies (1955–60) and a member of the Liaison Committee of the Seminary, United Synagogue, and Rabbinical Assembly; the Joint Law Conference of the Seminary and the Rabbinical Assembly; the Joint Placement Commission; and the National Faculty Leaders Training Fellowship of the National Academy of Adult Jewish Studies. As a member of the United Synagogue's Committee on Synagogue Standards, he worked to eliminate bingo games as a means of fund-raising for Conservative synagogues. He also served as program editor of the Seminary's NBC-TV program, "The Eternal Light," and of ABC-TV's "Directions."

Routtenberg remained one of Conservatism's sharpest but most loyal critics, working from within to strengthen the movement organizationally, to cultivate a committed laity, and to find solutions to the weaknesses that he so readily perceived. He was particularly aware that the external successes of Conservatism failed to mask serious internal problems. He believed that the creation of the popular late Friday night services had contributed to the decline in the observance of the Sabbath as a day of religious observance. He was keenly aware of the extraordinary demands Conservative congregations placed upon their rabbis and of the loneliness and frustration inherent in this calling. He sensed the disparity between the success of the Conservative congregational school, when viewed from the point of view of its exponential development, and its failure in achieving its goals of graduating committed, educated Jews. And Routtenberg understood that the "spiritual malaise" that he observed in the Rabbinical Assembly in 1960 was caused not only by its failure to articulate Conservative ideology and to adjust Jewish law but also by the tension between the RA and the Seminary.

Outside of the Conservative movement, Routtenberg was a member of the Commission on the Jewish Chaplaincy of the National Jewish Welfare Board, the Delegates Council of the Synagogue Council of America, the Internal Affairs Commission of the New York Board of Rabbis, and, since 1980, has been on the Board of Directors of the Radius Institute.

Routtenberg wrote *Seedtime and Harvest* (1969), meditations on the holidays, on synagogue rites and rituals, and on the problems of contemporary Jewish life; *Decades of Decision* (1973), a collection of essays and addresses written over two decades dealing with the synagogue in American life, Jewish law, and Conservative Judaism; and *One in a Minyan* (1977), a collection of short stories on Jewish themes. He also edited with Leonard S. Kravitz, professor at the Reform movement's Hebrew Union College, and Gilbert Klaperman, past president of the Orthodox Rabbinical Council of America, a prayer book for Jewish military personnel, incorporating the Reform, Conservative, and Orthodox liturgies in one volume.

Routtenberg married Lilly Soloway in 1931; they have three children.

Writings: "Report of the Prayer Book Commission," *PRA 1942* vol. 8 (1947), pp. 146–59; "Report of the Executive Vice-President," *PRA 1949* vol. 13 (1950), pp. 27–39; *PRA 1950* vol. 14 (1951), pp. 29–39; "Report of the Committee on Jewish Law and Standards," *PRA 1961* vol. 25 (1961), pp. 188–94; *PRA 1963* vol. 27 (1963), pp. 221–29; "The President's Message," *PRA 1965* vol. 29 (1965), pp. 18–26; "Report of the Committee on the Chaplaincy," *PRA 1968* vol. 32 (1968), pp. 201–05; *Seedtime and Harvest* (New York, 1969); *Decades of Decision* (New York, 1973); *One in a Minyan and Other Stories* (New York, 1977).

References: *CJ* 33, 1 (Fall 1979), pp. 94–95; Marshall Sklare, *Conservative Judaism* (1955; rev. 1972; reprint ed., Lanham, Md., 1985), p. 262; *WWWJ* 1965, p. 811.

RUBENOVITZ, HERMAN HARRY (1883–1966). Rabbi, author. The son of Isaac and Feiga Feinstein Rubenovitz, Herman Rubenovitz was born in Kovno, Lithuania, on December 2, 1883. He was brought to Pittsburgh, Pennsylvania, in 1890. He earned a B.A. from the City College of New York in 1905 and was ordained at the Seminary in 1908.

In 1908 Rubenovitz became rabbi at Congregation Adath Jeshurun, Louisville, Kentucky. In 1910 he moved to Boston to become rabbi at Mishkan Tefila. One of the oldest congregations in Boston, Mishkan Tefila had been founded by

German immigrants in 1858. Rubenovitz spent the rest of his career there, transforming Mishkan Tefila into a Conservative congregation and laying the foundations for Conservative Judaism in a Boston that until then had been split between the Orthodox and Reform camps. In 1947 when he retired from Mishkan Tefila, he became rabbi emeritus.

An early pioneer of Conservative Judaism, Rubenovitz was instrumental in its organizational growth. While in Louisville, he recognized that the few and scattered Conservative congregations needed to band together to combat their isolation and to work together to strengthen Conservatism. At the same time Seminary president Solomon *Schechter was also working on a similar project. In 1910 Rubenovitz presented a plan for "a union of conservative forces in America" to the Seminary Alumni Association. The Seminary alumni then joined with Schechter in founding in 1913 the United Synagogue of America, the union of Conservative synagogues. Rubenovitz also organized the first northeast branch of the Jewish Theological Seminary in 1914, and he served on the Seminary's Board of Trustees (1944–45).

In 1920, discontented with the stasis in the United Synagogue, in particular its failure to revise the prayer book and to harmonize Jewish law with the contemporary world, Rubenovitz joined with Mordecai M. *Kaplan to found the Society for Jewish Renascence, the forerunner of the Reconstructionist movement. Rubenovitz edited for a time (1921–24) the society's chief publication, *The Jewish Center: A Magazine of Progressive Judaism.*

An ardent Zionist from his youth, he presided over the Zionist Council of Greater Boston (1912–15) and the New England Board of the Jewish National Fund (1935–38). Active also in Jewish education, he was president of the Jewish Educational Society of Boston (1913–18) and initiator of the plan to create a training school for Jewish teachers there. He also founded and presided over the Rabbinical Association of Greater Boston (1935–50), which evolved into the Massachusetts Board of Rabbis.

Rubenovitz co-authored an autobiography, *The Waking Heart*, with his wife, Mignon Levin Rubenovitz, whom he married in 1915. He died in 1966.

Writing: With Mignon Levin Rubenovitz, *The Waking Heart* (Cambridge, Mass., 1967).

References: *EJ*, vol. 14, col. 368; Abraham J. Karp, *A History of the United Synagogue of America, 1913–1963* (New York, 1964), p. 9; *WWWJ* 1955, p. 643.

S

SALIT, NORMAN (1896–1960). Rabbi, lawyer. The son of Michael and Rachel Ethel Altschul Salit, Norman Salit was born in Brooklyn, New York, on June 8, 1896. Educated in the New York City public schools, Salit earned a B.A. from the City College of New York in 1916, a J.D. from New York University in 1919, and was ordained at the Seminary in 1920.

A gifted speaker who won oration prizes during his academic career, Salit was especially suited to both the rabbinate and the practice of law. He began his rabbinical career as assistant rabbi at Congregation Beth Israel Anshei Emes, Brooklyn (1917). In 1918 he was rabbi at Congregation Etz Chaim, Oil City, Pennsylvania, and at the same time he represented the Jewish Welfare Board in Kansas at Fort Riley and Camp Funston. He then became rabbi at Temple Adath Israel, Bronx, New York (1919–24). As rabbi at Congregation Shaaray Tefila, Far Rockaway, New York (1924–29) Salit oversaw the building of its new synagogue-center and directed a large program of activities, including a daily Hebrew school, adult education classes, and daily and Sabbath services. His congregants prided themselves on the fact that their Sabbath morning services were even better attended than their popular late Friday night services.

Salit left the pulpit in 1929 to pursue law full time. In addition to his private legal practice, he was associate counsel for the New York State office of the Home Owners' Loan Corporation (1934–37); a member of the arbitration commission of the City Court of Queens County, New York; and chairman of the Legislation and Law Reform Committee of the Queens County Bar Association (1933–37). Salit was an unsuccessful candidate on the Democratic ticket in 1947 for presiding supervisor of Nassau County and in 1949 for Children's Court judge.

Legal work did not prevent Salit from remaining deeply involved in the affairs of the Jewish community, in particular of Conservative Judaism. He was active in the Rabbinical Assembly throughout his career. He served as its secretary

(1923–24), chaired the committee that wrote its new constitution in 1928, and served as unpaid legal counsel for the RA (1951–60). Chairman of the RA's Committee on Scouting, he was also a member of the National Council of the Boy Scouts of America.

During World War II Salit accepted Louis *Finkelstein's invitation to head the Wartime Emergency Commission for Conservative Judaism (1944–46), which coordinated the activities of the Chaplaincy Availability Board, the Seminary, the Placement Committee, the Rabbinical Assembly, and the United Synagogue. As executive director, he worked to solve the numerous problems created by the sudden departure of many congregational rabbis for the armed forces' chaplaincy.

After the war, Salit chaired the RA's Zionist Revaluation Committee (1949–50), which reexamined the relationship of Conservatism to the newly established state of Israel. This committee suggested numerous ways of fostering the Conservative point of view in Israel and even proposed the establishment of a separate Conservative Zionist organization. Salit followed this work with a ten-week tour to study Jewish religious life in Europe and Israel, from which he concluded that there was an urgent need for more American rabbis in Israel. He was also a member of the Seminary's Board of Overseers.

Salit's numerous offices in communal organizations included president of the Long Island division of the American Jewish Congress; secretary, treasurer, and vice-president of the New York Board of Jewish Ministers, now the New York Board of Rabbis (1924–29); president of the Long Island region of the United Synagogue of America (1927); president of the American Pro-Falasha Committee (1931); president of the Long Island Council for Palestine (1932); and director of the Freedom Foundation.

As president of the Synagogue Council of America (1953–55), Salit appeared with President Eisenhower, Bishop Fulton Sheen, and Norman Vincent Peale on the "Back to God" television program. In 1954 under his direction the council disseminated a tercentenary service in honor of the three-hundredth anniversary of Jewish settlement in America. In 1953 Salit was one of nine religious leaders, and the only Jew, invited by the West German government to visit Germany to study anti-Semitism. As the first American Jewish leader to be invited to Germany in twenty years, he was seriously disappointed to find that anti-Semitism remained deeply rooted there.

Salit married Ruth Levy in 1928; they had two children. He died on July 21, 1960, in New York City.

Writings: Posthumously, *The Worlds of Norman Salit: Sermons, Papers, Addresses*, ed. Abraham Burstein (New York, 1966).

References: *Current Biography* 1955, pp. 527–29; *NYT* 22 July 1960, p. 23; *PRA 1928* vol. 2 (1929), p. 12; *PRA 1945* vol. 9 (1949), pp. 13–14; *PRA 1950* vol. 14 (1951), pp. 222–31; *PRA 1961* vol. 25 (1961), pp. 165–66; *Recorder* 8, 2 (April 1928), p. 16; *WWWJ* 1955, p. 654.

SANDROW, EDWARD T. (1906–75). Rabbi, communal leader. The son of Nahum and Molly Cohen Sandrow, Edward Sandrow was born in Philadelphia, Pennsylvania, on December 23, 1906. He earned a B.A. from the University of Pennsylvania in 1929, was ordained at the Seminary in 1933, and earned a Doctor of Hebrew Letters there in 1952.

Sandrow first served as rabbi at Ahavai Shalom, Portland, Oregon (1933–37). In 1868 Prussian and Polish Jewish immigrants founded Ahavai Shalom, preferring to organize their own congregation rather than join the existing synagogue established by Jewish immigrants from southern Germany. Sandrow succeeded Rabbi Herbert *Parzen, who had already introduced many Conservative practices to the congregation. Despite the Depression, Ahavai Shalom managed to continue many of the activities and programs it inaugurated in the 1920s. Its membership, however, had fallen from a high of 277 families in 1923 to 152 by 1935, and one of Sandrow's primary responsibilities was therefore attracting new members. While in Portland, he was also an active supporter of the communal Hebrew school.

In 1937 Sandrow became rabbi of Temple Beth El, Cedarhurst, New York (1937–71). He was a pioneer of Conservative Judaism both in the congregation and in the larger community known as the Five Towns of Long Island. Sandrow worked to raise standards, maintain decorum at services, and institute a three-day-a-week Hebrew school. With the assistance of Beth El's associate rabbi Myron *Berman, he founded the Hebrew High School and Adult School of Jewish Studies of the Five Towns. Except for his World War II service as a chaplain in the U.S. Army (1942–46), Sandrow remained at Beth El for the rest of his career. In 1971 he was elected rabbi emeritus following his retirement.

Sandrow was a leader in Jewish and communal affairs in the Five Towns. He was chairman of the Board of Education of the Brandeis School (1963–72), Lawrence, New York; chairman of the South Shore Division of the United Jewish Appeal-Federation of Jewish Philanthropies; member of the Executive Board of the Long Island Jewish Community Services; president of the Jewish Community Council; a director of the Five Towns Community Chest; and a member of the executive committees of the Nassau County Mental Health Association and the Five Towns Community Council. In the larger Jewish community he was president of the New York Board of Rabbis (1966–68), chairman of its Council of Past Presidents, and dean of its Chaplaincy School. He chaired the Jewish Welfare Board Commission on Jewish Chaplaincy and was vice-president of the Jewish Chaplains Association. He was also a member of the Board of Governors of the American Association for Jewish Education, the Board of Directors of the Jewish Telegraphic Agency, the Board of Directors of American Friends of Hebrew University, and the Board of Governors of Hebrew University. His general civic activities included membership on the New York State Commission Against Discrimination in Housing and the New York Commission to the White House Conference on Children and Youth (1960).

Sandrow chaired several of the most important and most active committees of the Rabbinical Assembly. As chairman of the Zionist Actions Committee (1946–47), he called in those early years for developing curricula on Zionism for the congregational schools and for organizing Conservative synagogues in Palestine, a call that he reiterated some fifteen years later when he was president of the Rabbinical Assembly. He chaired the RA's Commission on the Seminary Campaign (1948–49), providing members with information and co-ordinating rabbinic fund-raising activities. He led the Joint Placement Commission (1951–54) when it finally established a policy for reckoning with seniority in placement. As RA president (1960–62), he called for the Rabbinical Assembly to "take the *lead* in *leading* the Conservative movement" [original emphasis] and recognized that the RA had to strengthen its organization in order to act with greater independence and autonomy. Accordingly, he formed the Administrative Committee to advise the president and help him deal with the growing scope and activities of the 750–member organization. He called for control over the *ad hoc* regions that had sprung up within the RA and for acquisition of adequate office facilities for the association. He worked to establish closer relations with the Seminary and initiated a revision of the *Rabbinical Assembly Manual* (1965). At the conclusion of his presidency, Sandrow remained active in the affairs of the assembly, heading the *Klal Yisrael* Committee and assuming in 1972 the chairmanship of the Joint Prayer Book Commission and the Committee on Liturgical Publications.

In addition to his work on behalf of the Rabbinical Assembly and his many communal and congregational responsibilities, Sandrow was a teaching fellow at New York University (1948–52), visiting professor of homiletics at the Seminary (1954–56, 1962–63), a fellow of its Lehmann Institute of Ethics, and a member of its Board of Directors. He was among the first in the Conservative movement to recognize the importance of training future rabbis in the techniques of modern psychiatry. He insisted that the Seminary add courses in pastoral psychiatry to its rabbinic program. To honor his pioneering efforts, his congregation and friends established the Seminary's Edward T. Sandrow Chair in Pastoral Psychiatry. A staff member of the Morris Bernstein Counseling Center and a visiting professor in Pastoral Psychology, Sandrow was also special counsel to the chancellor of the Seminary after his retirement from Beth El.

Sandrow's Zionism included love of the Hebrew language and promotion of its literature in America. He served on the editorial board of *Hadoar* and was a member of the *Histadrut Ivrith* Cultural Exchange Committee.

He married Miriam Slavin in 1933; they had one daughter. Sandrow died in Cedarhurst, New York, on December 16, 1975.

Writings: "Report of the Zionist Actions Committee," *PRA 1947* vol. 11 (1948), pp. 82–86; "Status of the Seminary Campaign," *PRA 1949* vol. 13 (1950), pp. 216–20; "Report of the Placement Commission," *PRA 1954* vol. 18 (1955), pp. 95–97; "President's Report," *PRA 1961* vol. 25 (1961), pp. 83–103; *PRA 1962* vol. 26 (1963), pp. 130–39.

References: *AJYB* vol. 77 (1977), p. 599; *PRA 1976* vol. 38 (1977), pp. 291–94; William Toll, *The Making of an Ethnic Middle Class: Portland Jewry over Four Generations* (Albany, N.Y., 1982), pp. 174–78; *WWWJ* 1965, p. 833.

SCHECHTER, MATHILDE ROTH (1859–1924). Founding President of the National Women's League of the United Synagogue. Mathilde Roth was born on December 16, 1857, in Guttentag, Germany. Her father died when she was very young, so she was educated in the Jewish orphans home in Breslau. There she proved to be a gifted student and was encouraged to advance her education in art, languages, and literature and to enter a teachers seminary. Forced by circumstances to support herself, Roth took a position in Hungary, gave lectures on art, taught German literature, and in 1885 went to England to study and to be a tutor in the home of Michael Friedlaender, principal of Jews' College. It was in the library of the college that she met Solomon *Schechter. They were married in 1887.

After her marriage, Mathilde Schechter subordinated her early interests to those of her husband. She accompanied him to Cambridge University when he was called to serve as a lecturer in rabbinics (1890–1902) and there gave birth to their three children, a son and two daughters. In Cambridge and in their subsequent home in New York, she proved herself a gracious hostess, who made the Schechter homes centers of Jewish intellectual life and abodes for scholars and students.

When Solomon Schechter was called to the United States to lead the reorganized Jewish Theological Seminary of America (1902), his wife and family naturally followed. In America, she complemented his work by laying the foundations for Conservative Judaism among American women. In his inaugural address at the founding of the United Synagogue, Solomon Schechter, who became its first president, called for women to assume a share in its activities and responsibility for some of its work. After her husband's death, Mathilde Schechter founded the National Women's League of the United Synagogue (later the Women's League for Conservative Judaism) in 1918. As founding president (1918–19), she drafted the blueprint for its future work as the coordinating body of Conservative synagogue sisterhoods.

She led the Women's League to set an agenda that included service to the home, synagogue, and community with special concern for youth and adult education, the blind, and the welfare of the students at the Seminary. Her primary interest was in enriching the quality of Jewish religious life in the home and the synagogue. She personally promoted projects to achieve these ends, including the printing of cards with the blessings for the Friday evening home rituals, the publication of *Friday Night Stories*, and the compilation of liturgical melodies, which she edited with Louis M. Isaacs. Mathilde Schechter was especially concerned about the living circumstances of the Seminary students. She persuaded the Women's League to undertake as one of its first projects the opening of a

Students' House (1918) to offer room, kosher board, and a homelike atmosphere to young Seminary students far from their own homes.

In addition to her activities on behalf of Conservatism, Mathilde Schechter founded and taught at the Columbia Religious and Industrial School for Jewish Girls and assisted Henrietta Szold in creating Hadassah. She served as its national chairwoman of education.

She died in New York City on August 27, 1924.

References: National Women's League of the United Synagogue of America, *They Dared to Dream: A History of the National Women's League, 1918–1968* (New York, 1967); Mel Scult, "The *Baale Boste* Reconsidered: The Life of Mathilde Roth Schechter (M.R.S.)," *Modern Judaism* 7, 1 (February 1987), pp. 1–27; Elfrida Solis-Cohen et al., "Mathilde Roth Schechter: A Biographical Sketch," *Recorder* 4, 4 (October 1924), pp. 5–7; Henrietta Szold, "The Lineaments of Mathilde Roth Schechter," *Recorder* 5, 1 (January 1925), pp. 10–11.

SCHECHTER, SOLOMON (1847–1915). Scholar, President of the Jewish Theological Seminary of America. Scion of a Hasidic family, Schechter migrated both physically and intellectually away from his East European past to Austria, Germany, and then to England, to the scholarly world of the university and the critical study of Judaism. Entranced by the possibilities and promises of the burgeoning American Jewish community, he determined to bring his view of Judaism to American Jewry. Schechter's legacy—reverence for the Jewish past, its holiness, fervor, and mysticism, married to Jewish scientific scholarship—became the hallmark of the Jewish Theological Seminary of America.

The son of Isaac and Chaya Rachel Schechter, Solomon Schechter was born in Focsani, Rumania, on December 7, 1847(?). After early study with his father, he attended *yeshivah* and studied for a time in the rabbinical school in Lemberg before returning to Focsani for several years. In 1874 he left his home to attend the Vienna Rabbinical Seminary (*Bet Ha-Midrash*, 1874–79), where he was first exposed to the Science of Judaism and its methods of research of the Jewish past and where he received classical rabbinical ordination (*hatarat horaah*). He moved to Germany in 1879 to study at the Berlin Hochschule für die Wissenschaft des Judentums and at the University of Berlin (1879–82).

After three years in Berlin, Schechter immigrated to London, drawn by the opportunities to tutor Claude Goldsmid Montefiore in rabbinics and to study the wealth of Hebrew manuscripts in the British Museum and Oxford's Bodleian Library. He spent the next eight years in London (1882–90), primarily engaged in scholarly research but also serving as a lecturer and then as reader in rabbinics at the London seminary, Jews' College. Schechter's first scholarly publications of critical editions of ancient Hebrew texts appeared in this period. The publication of *Abot de-Rabbi Nathan* (1887) enhanced his growing stature as a scholar of prominence and led to his appointment first as university lecturer (1890–94) and then as reader (1894–1902) in Talmudics at Cambridge University.

While at Cambridge, Schechter made his monumental contribution to twentieth-century Jewish scholarship—the redemption of the Cairo *genizah*, an extraordinary archive of old Hebrew and rabbinic texts languishing in the Ezra Synagogue in Fostat (Old Cairo), Egypt. Schechter traveled to Cairo in 1896–97 to bring its treasure—over 100,000 manuscripts and manuscript fragments—to Cambridge University. The find revolutionized the study of medieval Mediterranean Jewry. Among the manuscripts was the Hebrew original of the Book of Ben Sira, which Schechter published with Charles Taylor, the master of St. John's College, who had made his trip possible (*The Wisdom of Ben Sira*, 1899). As Schechter was leaving Cairo, the congregation presented him with a parting gift—the ark of the old synagogue—which he later placed in the Seminary synagogue.

Schechter completed two other scholarly editions at Cambridge, *Midrash Haggadol* (1902) and *Saadyana: Fragments of Saadya in the Genizah* (1903), and he began classifying the *genizah* collection. He also served as curator of the oriental division of the Cambridge library and was appointed Goldsmid Professor of Hebrew at London University.

He was unique among the scholars of *Wissenschaft* in that he addressed much of his writing to the masses. A number of his studies, essays, and addresses, promulgating his view of the evolving nature of Jewish tradition, appeared in this period. These writings, including his series "Epistles to the Jews" in the London *Jewish Chronicle* (1900–1901), marked him as a champion of Jewish traditionalism and demonstrated his talent for speaking to both scholars and laity.

Schechter's scholarship and fame were well known in America. Both Seminary founding president Sabato *Morais and Joseph Blumenthal, president of the Seminary Association, tried to bring him to the school as early as 1890. Subsequent efforts to woo Schechter to the United States led to an invitation to deliver a series of lectures on "The Aspects of Rabbinic Theology" at Gratz College in Philadelphia in 1895. This trip cemented Schechter's close relations with future financial leaders of the Seminary, including Judge Mayer Sulzberger, and drew several students, among them Charles Isaiah *Hoffman, to Cambridge to study rabbinics with him.

After Morais' death in 1897, another attempt to secure Schechter, this time as the president of the faculty, was launched. Although Schechter agreed to accept the post in the summer of 1899, it took the leaders of the Seminary, headed by Cyrus *Adler and Louis Marshall, another two years to accomplish the financial reorganization necessary to make Schechter's appointment a reality. Eager for disciples to carry his vision of Judaism to American Jewry and for a strong Jewish environment for his new family, Schechter decided to abandon the world of the university for the challenges of transforming the Seminary into the outstanding American center of Jewish scholarship. He arrived in New York in the spring of 1902 and became, by virtue of his new position, a leading figure in American Jewish life.

Schechter envisioned building a great Jewish academy in America with resources for research and scholarship, not merely a rabbinical school. The emblem he chose for the revitalized Seminary, the burning bush, and motto, "And the bush was not consumed," symbolized his view, bred in the Science of Judaism, of the enduring and evolutionary character of Jewish tradition.

He began by organizing the Rabbinical School. Schechter believed that the Seminary should educate rabbis to return to their traditional function as students and teachers of Torah, dedicated to creative study and serious scholarship. But he also conceived of an American rabbinate that combined Jewish learning and loyalties with a critical approach to Western culture. In order to allow for the essential, intensive rabbinical studies he planned, he shaped the Rabbinical School as a postgraduate institution, requiring all students to have completed a liberal college education (or its equivalent) prior to admission. He hoped thus to avoid the problem, evident in the early Seminary and at London's Jews' College, of students carrying a double burden of secular and rabbinical studies.

Schechter revamped the rabbinical curriculum, based largely on his own experiences in Vienna, to include the study of Jewish humanities—philosophy, modern Hebrew, history, and homiletics—as well as the traditional rabbinical subjects of Talmud and Codes. He assembled a diverse, and often fractious, but distinguished faculty, including Louis *Ginzberg (Talmud), Alexander *Marx (history), Israel *Friedlaender (Bible), Joseph Mayor Asher (homiletics), Israel *Davidson (Hebrew literature), and Mordecai M. *Kaplan (homiletics). Together they attracted large numbers of students and transformed the Seminary into one of the centers of the Jewish intellectual renaissance in America.

While Schechter was organizing the faculty and curriculum, the Seminary Board of Directors, headed by President Cyrus *Adler, was completing the construction of the new Seminary in Morningside Heights. In 1903 the school moved from its old Lexington Avenue site to its new headquarters. In 1905 Adler resigned his post and Schechter became president of the Seminary (president of the faculty, 1902–5; of the Seminary, 1905–15). Now all fiscal and administrative affairs as well as curricular and pedagogical matters were his responsibility.

As president of the Seminary, Schechter expanded its activities and established its great library. From the beginning he was concerned with the problems of religious education. He considered the supplementary school (Talmud Torah) an essential adjunct of the synagogue and pleaded for adult education. Acutely aware of the need for Hebrew teacher training, he initiated and taught educators' courses prior to the establishment in 1909, thanks to a gift from Jacob Schiff, of the Teachers Institute, the Seminary's vehicle for crusading for adequate educational programs and the production of essential educational materials for American Jewry.

Believing that the Seminary must be more than a rabbinical school and scholarly enclave, Schechter fashioned the school as the chief exponent of his view of Jewish religious life and thought. His understanding of Jewish tradition was rooted in the nineteenth-century German Historical School, shaped by, among others, Zacharias Frankel, the founding head of the first modern rabbinical seminary in Central Europe, the Juedisch-Theologisches Seminar in Breslau. Frankel's response to the challenges posed by Jewish emancipation was to teach "positive-historical Judaism." Defining Judaism as a creative living organism, the Historical School emphasized the evolving character of Jewish tradition, the historic experience of the Jewish people as organic to its development, and the acceptance of the external forces of modernity as a positive factor in the growth of that tradition. Schechter thus linked the Jewish Theological Seminary of America, founded in 1886 by the leaders of the American Historical School, to the European world of Jewish scholarship and thought.

As the fountainhead of the Conservative movement, Schechter's Seminary tried to lead American Jews to remain loyal to *halachah*, to revere the Jewish past and its traditions of holiness and mysticism, to honor the centrality of Torah and the synagogue, to instill a sense of unity with *klal yisrael* (the Jewish people), and to evidence a commitment to Zionism. Schechter stressed that affirmative adaptation to the environment was in accord with the historic Jewish experience and the authority of Jewish law. He understood that Judaism in the past had been kept on course not by curators of the tradition, but rather by teachers actively shaping that tradition as they confronted the contemporary world. Motivated by the principle of selective emphasis, which was always at work in Jewish history, these teachers led the corporate body, the Jewish people, to define and to emphasize those aspects of Judaism relevant to their particular eras. Schechter thus allowed for the possibility of change when consecrated by general use, or in his words, by "Catholic Israel."

The notion of Catholic Israel was among Schechter's most enduring legacies to the Conservative movement. It reflected his concern for Jewish unity. He believed that what sustained Jewish life throughout the ages was its ability to interpret its sacred texts to meet changing historical circumstances. And he understood that the center of authority for the interpretation of tradition rested, not with any corporate priesthood or rabbinate, but rather with "the collective conscience of Catholic Israel as embodied in the Universal Synagogue." (*Studies in Judaism*, Series One, p. xviii). Unwilling to sanction the establishment of a new ecclesiastical hierarchy to redefine Judaism, Schechter thus did allow for general custom to shape Jewish practice.

The concept of the authority of Catholic Israel as indicative of the unity of the Jewish people became one of the key tenets of Conservatism in America. Schechter, in fact, spurned the denominational label for the Seminary, believing instead, as Cyrus *Adler observed, in a "vision of creating a theological center which should be all things to all men, reconciling all parties and appealing to all sections of the community." (*Lectures, Selected Papers, Addresses* [Philadelphia, 1933], p. 101.) But as American Jewry moved further and further away from *halachic* observance, the legacy of Catholic Israel increasingly came to trouble Conservative leaders. These men, notably Robert *Gordis, eventually wrestled with and redefined for the movement Schechter's original concept.

Schechter's presidency was not without its difficulties. The small group of affluent Seminary directors, who had originally supported the school for its possibility of Americanizing the "downtown" immigrants, were increasingly disappointed by his failure to win grass-roots support for the Seminary. These Reform, anti-Zionist directors became further alienated after Schechter's open espousal of Zionism in 1906. At the same time other projects—the founding of the American Jewish Committee in 1906, Dropsie College in 1908, and the New York *Kehillah* in 1909, siphoned off their enthusiasm and financial aid. Sensing an urgent need to extend his base of support, Schechter began to seriously consider what he had hoped to avoid, founding a third federation of synagogues to support the Seminary and its policies.

Schechter's dream when he arrived in America in 1902 was to transform the Seminary into an institution that would unify the diverse elements of the American Jewish community. But after an initial honeymoon period in which both the forces of Reform on the left and those of Orthodoxy on the right welcomed him, he increasingly found himself and his Seminary under attack. By 1909 he realized the impossibility of his original vision. Meanwhile, Seminary-trained rabbis in their pulpits, finding themselves isolated, called for a union of Conservative congregations for mutual support. The Seminary alumni and Schechter thus moved to transform the Conservative tendency, which the Seminary represented, into a congregational union, the United Synagogue of America.

As the founding president of the United Synagogue (1913–14), Schechter imagined it would be his greatest bequest to American Jewry. To appeal to a wide spectrum of congregations and to preserve the idea of *klal yisrael*, the United Synagogue excluded from membership only those congregations that used the *Union Prayer Book* and that worshipped with uncovered heads. These criteria excluded synagogues affiliated with the Reform movement, whose abrogation of Jewish law in the 1885 Pittsburgh Platform was diametrically opposed to Schechter's philosophy of Judaism. Although negative parameters defined the United Synagogue, Schechter hoped that the greater ties of Seminary-trained rabbis, teachers, and preachers would bind its members.

Outside of the Seminary Schechter was involved in several important Jewish scholarly projects. He was a member of the Board of Translators of the 1917 Jewish Publication Society edition of the Bible and of the editorial board of the *Jewish Encyclopedia* (1901–06). With Cyrus Adler he was co-editor of the *Jewish Quarterly Review*, which he helped bring from England to Dropsie College. Although the demands of the Seminary limited Schechter's scholarship, he continued to write numerous important articles and addresses, messages to American Jewry, that were later collected into several books.

In his youth in Focsani, Schechter entered an arranged marriage, which ended a year later in divorce. In 1887 in London, he married Mathilde Roth; they had three children. Schechter died in New York on November 19, 1915.

Writings: *Studies in Judaism*, 3 vols. (London and Philadelphia, 1896–1924); *Some Aspects of Rabbinic Theology* (New York, 1909); *Seminary Addresses and Other Papers* (Cincinnati, 1915); *Selected Writings*, ed. Norman Bentwich (Oxford, n.d.). Ed., *Abot de-Rabbi Nathan* (London, 1887); *Agadat Shir Hashirim* (Cambridge, 1896); *Midrash Haggadol* (Cambridge, 1902); *Saadyana* (Cambridge, 1903). Ed. and trans., *Documents of Jewish Sectaries*, 2 vols. (Cambridge, 1910). Ed., with S. Singer, *Talmudical Fragments in the Bodleian Library* (Cambridge, 1896); with Charles Taylor, *The Wisdom of Ben Sira* (Cambridge, 1899).

References: Jacob Agus, "Halakhah in the Conservative Movement," *PRA 1975* vol. 37 (1976), pp. 102–17; Max Arzt, "The Legacy of Solomon Schechter," *CJ* 11, 2 (Winter 1957), pp. 5–12; Norman Bentwich, *Solomon Schechter: A Biography* (Philadelphia, 1940); Moshe Davis, *The Emergence of Conservative Judaism* (New York, 1963); Robert E. Fierstein, "Solomon Schechter and the Zionist Movement," *CJ* 29, 3 (Spring 1975), pp. 3–13; Charles Isaiah Hoffman, "Memories of Solomon Schechter," in *The Jewish Theological Seminary of America: Semi-Centennial Volume*, ed. Cyrus Adler (New York, 1939), pp. 49–64; Abraham J. Karp, *A History of the United Synagogue of America, 1913–1963* (New York, 1964), pp. 8–13, 16; Abraham J. Karp, "Preaching Schechter," *PRA 1963* vol. 27 (1963), pp. 21–46; Bernard Mandelbaum, "The Heritage of Solomon Schechter," *PRA 1963* vol. 27 (1963), pp. 1–20; Bernard Mandelbaum, "Solomon Schechter: The Man and His Vision," *CJ* 26, 2 (Winter 1972), pp. 47–54; *NYT* 10 November 1915, p. 13; Herbert Parzen, *Architects of Conservative Judaism* (New York, 1964), pp. 26–78; Herbert Rosenblum, *Conservative Judaism: A Contemporary History* (New York, 1983), pp. 15–23, 79–80.

SCHORSCH, ISMAR (1935–   ). Chancellor of the Jewish Theological Seminary of America. The son of Emil and Fanny Rothschild Schorsch, Ismar Schorsch was born on November 3, 1935, in Hanover, Germany. Shortly after his father's synagogue was destroyed in *Kristallnacht*, the massive German pogrom against the Jews (November 1938), the family fled to England with the help of the office of the chief rabbi of the British Empire, Joseph H. *Hertz. In 1940 they immigrated to the United States. Raised in Pottstown, Pennsylvania, where his father was the rabbi of the Conservative synagogue, Congregation Mercy and Truth, Schorsch earned a B.A. at Ursinus College in 1957 and was ordained at the Seminary in 1962. After serving as a chaplain in the U.S. Army (1962–64) with a tour of duty in Korea, he earned a Ph.D. from Columbia University in 1969.

In 1964, while completing his graduate studies, Schorsch began teaching at the Seminary (instructor, 1967–68; assistant professor, 1968–70; associate professor, 1970–76; professor, 1976–   ). In 1980 he became the Rabbi Herman Abramowitz Professor of Jewish History. Following Chancellor Gerson D. *Cohen's reorganization of the Seminary's professional and graduate programs, Schorsch became the first dean of its Graduate School (1975–79). In 1980 he became provost (1980–84), the Seminary's chief academic officer. In 1986, after Cohen announced his intention to resign, Schorsch, a gifted scholar and proven administrator, was elevated to the post of chancellor and president of the faculties (1986–   ).

As chancellor, Schorsch faces the challenges of sustaining the Seminary, resolving its financial crisis, recruiting new faculty, and maintaining its commitment to scholarship. Because more than a school, the Seminary is the fountainhead of Conservative Judaism, he is also the titular leader of the Conservative movement and its 1.5 million members. An evaluation of Schorsch's first year at the Seminary's helm suggests that his agenda for the movement will remain much the same as that of his predecessor. He has worked to keep open the lines of communication among the various Conservative constituencies, especially to the Union for Traditional Conservative Judaism, a group of right-wing Conservative rabbis and laity organized in opposition to the movement's decision to ordain women as rabbis and which has periodically considered secession. Forging a commitment to belief and practice among Conservative laity, especially among lay leaders, and strengthening Conservatism in Israel have remained pivotal concerns. Schorsch's decision to allow the awarding of the diploma of *hazzan* to women, certifying women as Conservative cantors, continued the liberalization of Conservative Judaism in the sphere of women's rights.

Considering himself a staunch centrist in the Conservative movement's ideological wars and comfortable with rabbis in both the traditional and liberal wings of the movement, Schorsch, who favored the movement's decision to ordain women, opposes any change in its stance against patrilineal descent, that is, recognizing the child of a Jewish father and a non-Jewish mother as a Jew. He envisions Conservatism as distinct from the extremes of Orthodoxy's fundamentalism and Reform's abrogation of Jewish law. In his view Conservative Judaism is based on the pillars of critical scholarship, loyalty to tradition, and acceptance of the outside world as a legitimate source of wisdom and experience.

A scholar of modern Jewish history, Schorsch wrote *Jewish Reactions to German Anti-Semitism, 1870–1914* (1972), a study of Germany Jewry's responses to anti-Semitism during the Second Reich and, in particular, of the work of its most important defense agency, the Centralverein Deutscher staatsbürger judischen Glaubens. A member of the Board of Directors of the Leo Baeck Institute since 1976, he was elected its president in 1985.

Married in 1960, Schorsch and his wife, Sally, have three children.

Writings: *Jewish Reactions to German Anti-Semitism, 1870–1914* (New York, 1972); "The Dynamics of Jewish Creativity," *CJ* 18, 3 (Spring 1974), pp. 13–20; "Historical Reflections on the Holocaust," *CJ* 31, 1–2 (Fall-Winter 1976/77), pp. 26–33; "Emancipation and the Crisis of Religious Authority: The Emergence of the Modern Rabbinate," in *Revolution and Evolution: 1848 in German-Jewish History*, ed. Werner E. Mosse et al. (Tubingen, 1981), pp. 205–48; "The Holocaust and Jewish Survival: Address," *Midstream* 27 (January 1981), pp. 38–42; "Zacharias Frankel and the European Origins of Conservative Judaism," *Judaism* 30, 3 (Summer 1981), pp. 344–54; "Rabbi Emil Schorsch," *PRA 1982* vol. 44 (1983), pp. 164–68; *Thoughts From 3080: Selected Addresses and Writings* (New York, n.d.). Ed., trans., and introduced, Heinrich Graetz, *Structure of Jewish History and other Essays* (New York, 1975).

References: *NYT* 4 March 1986, p. B4; Walter Ruby, "Schorsch: Seminary Is 'Pluralism in Action,' " *Washington Jewish Week* 8 January 1987, p. 7.

SCHULWEIS, HAROLD (1925–   ). Rabbi. The son of Maurice J. and Helen Rezak Schulweis, Harold Schulweis was born in New York City on April 14, 1925. He earned a B.A. at Yeshiva College in 1945, was ordained at the Seminary in 1950, and earned a Th.D. at the Pacific School of Religion, Berkeley, California, in 1972.

In his three pulpits, Temple Emanuel, Park Chester, New York (1950–52); Temple Beth Abraham, Oakland, California (1952–70); and Valley Beth Shalom, Encino, California (1970–   ), Schulweis has demonstrated his sensitivity to the struggles of contemporary life. He considers his primary tasks to be humanizing the synagogue and making congregational affiliation meaningful. One of his solutions to these problems was the *havurah* program that he created, first at Temple Beth Abraham and then at Valley Beth Shalom. Composed of a *minyan* of families, each *havurah* meets monthly in members' homes for study and celebration. Envisioning these *havurot* as a surrogate for the extended family, Schulweis has found their members joining together at holidays and in times of joy and sadness, celebrating the dedication of a new home, and sustaining a house of mourning. They have thus become the close-knit Jewish communities of his original vision. Within a few short years his Valley Beth Shalom congregants have formed dozens of *havurot*.

In addition to pioneering the *havurah* movement, Schulweis laid the foundations for several new synagogue auxiliaries at Valley Beth Shalom. Believing that the synagogue must offer its members more than a sanctuary for occasional prayer, he established paraprofessional counseling and senior citizens centers. He also formed a pararabbinic class, instructing congregants in Jewish theology and ritual to prepare them to guide others in Jewish ceremonies.

Schulweis' creativity has extended beyond the synagogue. He was founding chairman of the Institute for Righteous Acts—Documentation and Study Center on Rescuers of Jews in the Nazi Era, located at the Magnes Museum in Oakland, and of the Foundation to Sustain the Righteous Christians (1986–   ), a philanthropy to raise funds and to create a network of social support for needy Christians who rescued Jews during the Holocaust. A staunch social activist recognized by the United Synagogue for his contributions, he has also emerged as a leader in the call for unity, reconciliation, and recognition of the legitimacy of diversity within American Jewish life.

Schulweis has taught philosophy at the City College of New York and at the University of Judaism, the West Coast affiliate of the Seminary (1970–   ), where he occupies the Earl Warren Chair of Ethics in Human Relations. He also teaches theology at Hebrew Union College, Los Angeles (1971–   ).

Strongly influenced by Seminary professors Mordecai M. *Kaplan and Abraham Joshua *Heschel, Schulweis wrote *Evil and the Morality of God* (1984), a concise history of theodicy, the justification of God's ways that includes his personal exploration of the problem of the existence of evil in a world designed by a benevolent God. Widely known for his essays on synagogue organization and American Judaism, Schulweis wrote many of them as contributing editor to *Reconstructionist* (1970–), *Sh'ma* (1974–), and *Moment* (1974–) magazines.

He married Malkah Savod; they have three children.

Writings: "Bias Against Man," *PRA 1963* vol. 27 (1963), pp. 84–95; "Restructuring the Synagogue," *CJ* 27, 4 (Summer 1973), pp. 13–23; *Evil and the Morality of God* (New York, 1984). Co-ed., *Approaches to the Philosophy of Religion* (Englewood Cliffs, N.J., 1954).

Reference: *American Jewish Biographies*, pp. 391–92.

SEGAL, BERNARD (1907–84). Rabbi, administrator. The son of Eli and Gittel Zucker Segal, Bernard Segal was born in Lipno, Poland, on November 15, 1907, and immigrated to the United States in 1922. He earned a B.S. from Columbia University in 1931, was ordained at the Seminary in 1933, and earned a Doctor of Hebrew Letters there in 1950.

Segal first served as rabbi at the Patchogue Jewish Center on Long Island (1933–34) and then at Queens Jewish Center (1934–40). He was the first Jewish chaplain in the United States called to active duty in World War II. Following his discharge in 1945, he remained a lieutenant colonel in the Army reserves and was founding president of the Association of Jewish Chaplains of the Army and Navy of the United States (1945–47).

Over the course of three decades Segal held leading positions in all the major institutions of the Conservative movement, leaving his imprint on the development of Conservative Judaism as it expanded in new directions in the postwar era. During the war he chaired the Chaplaincy Availability Board (1943–46) and co-chaired with Norman *Salit the Conservative movement's Wartime Emergency Commission (1944–45). In 1945 he became the first executive director of the Rabbinical Assembly (1945–47) and director of the Joint Placement Commission of the Rabbinical Assembly and the Seminary. Two years later he was appointed executive vice-president of the Rabbinical Assembly (1947–49). His duties still included placement work, the general administration of the Rabbinical Assembly, and the installation of many of his colleagues who found new pulpits in the postwar era. As executive vice-president, Segal keenly sensed the changes underway in the Conservative movement and saw the unique opportunities its expansion opened for the rabbinate.

In 1949 he moved from the Rabbinical Assembly to the Seminary as assistant to the president (1949–51) and then as executive vice-president (1951–53). Recognizing the dire need for qualified Jewish educators, he encouraged Seminary students to pursue careers in Jewish education. At the same time he also directed the National Ramah Commission (1950–54).

In 1953 Segal become executive director of the United Synagogue of America (1953–70; executive vice-president, 1970–76). His administration was characterized by the vigor and initiative that his immediate predecessors, Albert *Gordon and Simon *Greenberg, brought to the United Synagogue in the postwar era. Immediately Segal began strengthening the organization, creating new departments and hiring more full-time personnel. He encouraged the United Synagogue to increase educational opportunities for all members of the synagogue, developing curricula for congregational schools, publishing a great variety of educational materials, founding numerous Solomon Schechter day schools, establishing the Burning Bush Press as the imprint of the National Academy of Adult Jewish Studies, and distributing the *El Am Talmud*. By 1970 the tremendous expansion in the United Synagogue activities necessitated an internal reorganization, and Segal was named executive vice-president.

Segal strove throughout his career to foster unity within the Conservative movement. He understood that the adoption of standards for synagogue practice would go a long way toward unifying the hundreds of United Synagogue member congregations. In ratifying these standards, the United Synagogue highlighted the public adherence to Jewish law and ritual that became a hallmark of Conservatism. Working to build bridges to the other institutions of the Conservative movement, he led the United Synagogue to join with the Rabbinical Assembly and National Women's League in creating the Commission on Social Action in 1954. Segal also envisioned bridges to world Jewry, a vision that enabled Conservative Judaism to gain international stature. In 1957 he and a handful of colleagues founded the World Council of Synagogues to implement the program of Conservative Judaism in Israel and Jewish communities throughout the world. He also guided the United Synagogue to membership in several umbrella organizations of American and world Jewry.

In addition to his work on behalf of Conservatism, Segal was also a member of the Board of Directors of the Committee on Religion in American Life (1954–56), the New York City Mayor's Commission on Housing (1954–58) and the New York Association for Middle Income Housing (1960–68).

Segal married Hattie Clark in 1934; they had two children. In 1977, after he retired from a lifetime of public service to Conservative Judaism, he settled in Jerusalem, Israel. He died there on June 4, 1984.

Writings: "The Rabbinical Assembly—Expanding Its Organizational Structure," *PRA 1947* vol. 11 (1948), pp. 363–70; "Our Goal is Unity, Not Uniformity," *Review* 11, 1 (Winter 1958), pp. 9–10.

References: Abraham J. Karp, *A History of the United Synagogue of America, 1913–1963* (New York, 1964), pp. 90–104; *News of the United Synagogue of America* 2, 3 (April 1946), p. 3; 3, 4 (January 1948), p. 4; *NYT* 6 June 1984, p. D25; *Review* 23, 4 (Winter 1971), p. 3; 24, 1 (Spring 1971), pp. 10–11; *Washington Jewish Week* 14 June 1984, p. 32; *WWWJ* 1965, p. 869.

SHAPIRO, ALEXANDER M. (1929–). The son of Sol J. and Gertrude Sussman Shapiro, Alexander Shapiro was born in Brooklyn, New York, on November 29, 1929. In 1950 he earned a B.A. from Brooklyn College and a

Bachelor of Hebrew Letters from the Seminary. He was ordained at the Seminary in 1955 and earned a Ph.D. from Dropsie University in 1970.

Shapiro was rabbi of Congregation Beth Tikvah, Philadelphia, Pennsylvania (1957–68). He then briefly served as co-rabbi at Philadelphia's Germantown Jewish Center (1968–69). After teaching at Temple University (1969–70)) and at Ben Gurion University (1970–72), he returned to the pulpit as rabbi of Oheb Shalom Congregation, South Orange, New Jersey (1972–   ).

Oheb Shalom was established in Newark, New Jersey, around 1860. Its founders, distressed over the growing Reform tendency of their parent congregation, B'nai Jeshurun, seceded to form a new synagogue. In the twentieth century Oheb Shalom, led by Seminary graduates Charles I. *Hoffman and Louis *Levitsky, had moved squarely into the Conservative camp. Not only had Hoffman and Levitsky led Oheb Shalom—each with a tenure of thirty-five years—but both rabbis had also been presidents of the Rabbinical Assembly. Shapiro, who envisioned the congregation as "an oasis of holiness in the midst of a segmented and secularized world," followed in their footsteps in the congregation, the community, and the Rabbinical Assembly. In the community he also served as a board member of the Jewish Federation of Metropolitan New Jersey (1972–76), the Solomon Schechter School (1973–81), and the Jewish Family Services (1973–76).

In the Rabbinical Assembly Shapiro first served as president of its Northern New Jersey Region (1976–78). Acutely sensitive to the demands the rabbinate made on rabbis and their families and especially to the isolation so many rabbis decried, he inaugurated a program designed to explore these issues. Shapiro then quickly moved into national leadership of the Rabbinical Assembly as treasurer (1980–82) and vice-president (1982–84).

As Rabbinical Assembly president (1984–86), he was involved in some of the most critical issues of contemporary Jewish life—women's rights, denominational polarization, and Conservative ideology. Shapiro presided over the Rabbinical Assembly as it, after a lengthy battle, opened its ranks to women in 1985 when it accepted as members the first woman ordained at the Seminary, Amy Eilberg, and rabbis Beverly Magidson and Jan Kaufman, who had been ordained outside the Seminary. Sensitive to the growing polarization among the denominations of American Judaism, Shapiro sought out opportunities for interdenominational dialogue. He became the first Conservative rabbi to address the annual convention of the Orthodox Rabbinical Council of America. There he reactivated a proposal, first raised many years before, for the establishment of a national bet din to deal with matters of personal status, especially conversion. Aware of the many ideological issues raised by the ordination of women as Conservative rabbis and of the fear of many in the Conservative movement's right wing that they were being written out of the movement, Shapiro joined with Seminary chancellor Gerson *Cohen in establishing a committee—the latest in a string of many—to articulate Conservative ideology. At the same time

Shapiro remained concerned with the traditional trade union aspects of the Rabbinical Assembly, especially its members' salaries and their health care.

Long involved in activist movements, Shapiro joined during the 1960s in the antiwar and civil rights movements, traveling to Birmingham, Alabama, with eighteen fellow Rabbinical Assembly rabbis to support Martin Luther King, Jr., in protests there. In 1985, as Rabbinical Assembly president, he was arrested in a civil demonstration in front of the Soviet Consulate in New York City.

Shapiro married Ruth Goldenberg in 1952; they have four children.

Writings: "Goals for Synagogue Life," *Review* 30, 1 (Summer 1977), pp. 12–13; "Trustbuilding Initiatives in the Rabbinic Community: Rationale and Report," *CJ* 33, 1 (Fall 1979), pp. 3–5; "Inaugural Address," *PRA 1984* vol. 46 (1985), pp. 76–85; "The Future of Black-Jewish Relations," *PRA 1985* vol. 47 (1985), pp. 15–21; "President's Report," *PRA 1985* vol. 47 (1985), pp. 21–28. Ed., with Burton I. Cohen, *Studies in Jewish Education and Judaica in Honor of Louis Newman* (New York, 1984).

References: "Our Leaders Speak Together: A Moment Interview," *Moment* 11, 4 (April 1986), pp. 34–42; *Washington Jewish Week* 23 May 1985, p. 1.

SHUCHAT, WILFRED G. (1920–). The son of Meyer and Beatrice Godel Shuchat, Wilfred Shuchat was born on June 9, 1920, in Montreal, Canada. He earned a B.A. from McGill University in 1941 and was ordained at the Seminary in 1945.

Shuchat briefly served as rabbi at two congregations, Sons of Israel, Albany, New York (1944–45), and Temple Beth El, Buffalo, New York (1945–46), before returning in 1946 to his native Montreal as assistant rabbi of Shaar Hashomayim Congregation. Organized in 1846, Shaar Hashomayim, Canada's oldest Ashkenazic congregation, was located in Montreal's Westmount suburb. Led by the distinguished Canadian rabbi Herman *Abramowitz, it was among the outstanding congregations of the British Empire. When Abramowitz died in 1947, Shuchat, a "product" of the congregation, became its rabbi (1948–).

While Shuchat continued programs established by his predecessor, he also introduced new ideas. He persuaded his congregants to endow a lectureship and to support *Shabbat Yahad*, an Israeli venture he established during his sabbatical year in Jerusalem in 1973. Working with Israeli rabbi and professor Pinchas Peli, Shuchat designed *Shabbat Yahad* to cross denominational boundaries to bring together Orthodox, Conservative, and Reform Jews for *Shabbat* celebration and dialogue. Some of his other endeavors were less successful: for example, many of his congregants opposed his plans to establish a congregational day school as too separatist.

Outside of Shaar Hashomayim, Shuchat has been a leader in the larger Canadian Jewish community and especially in adult Jewish education. He was the initiator and chairman of the Religious Welfare Committee of the Canadian Jewish Congress. In 1947, along with Rabbi Charles Bender, he founded and later was president of the Board of Jewish Ministers of Greater Montreal. As president, Shuchat led the board in establishing the Jewish Chaplaincy Committee, the Synagogue Council of Montreal, a weekly radio program, and a weekly column in the *Montreal Star*. He was program chairman for the Pavilion of Judaism at Montreal's Expo '67, and co-founder and honorary chaplain of the De Sola Club. He also served as the first Jewish chaplain in the Royal Canadian Reserve.

Like his teacher Abramowitz, Shuchat stands with the right wing of the Rabbinical Assembly, believing that the only difference between Conservatism and Orthodoxy is Conservatism's "acceptance of a human element in the Bible and projecting the authority of the rabbinic tradition as a historical development." As a member of the Committee on Jewish Law and Standards, he wrote numerous *responsa*. In 1964 he dissented from the majority opinion allowing intermarried couples conditional synagogue membership. Shuchat argued that denial of synagogue membership was one of the few concrete sanctions that the Jewish community could exercise against intermarried couples, and he was convinced that the threat of synagogue expulsion had prevented members of his own congregation from intermarrying. He also justified the retention of the Diaspora observance of the second day of festivals as a "permanent reminder of the spiritual superiority of *Eretz Yisrael* in Jewish life." If a change in the Jewish calendar were to occur, he believed it must emanate from Israeli rabbis.

Shuchat resigned from the Committee on Jewish Law and Standards during its 1971 crisis. After the committee regrouped, he refused to rejoin, frustrated by its inability to reach consensus on essential questions of religious policy. That inability, he feared, meant that Conservatism was becoming "a reform movement." Shuchat denied the committee the authority to legislate in matters affecting relations with other Jews. As a member of the Seminary's Commission on the Ordination of Women, Shuchat wrote a dissenting opinion. He ultimately joined several of his colleagues in the Conservative movement's right wing in founding the Union for Traditional Conservative Judaism, established partly in opposition to the Jewish Theological Seminary's decision to ordain women as rabbis. Shuchat was its first vice-president.

Shuchat married Miriam Sochet in 1954; they have four children.

Writings: "The Intermarried Jew and Synagogue Membership," *PRA 1964* vol. 28 (1964), pp. 249–54; "Response to a *Responsum*," *CJ* 24, 2 (Winter 1970), pp. 33–45; *Beineinu* 3, 1 (January 1973), pp. 48–49; "The Rabbi and His Family, "*PRA 1975* vol. 37 (1976), pp. 177–81; "Towards a Philosophy of Conservative Judaism," *PRA 1980* vol. 42 (1981), pp. 78–93.

References: *EJ* vol. 14, col. 1474; Stuart Rosenberg, *The Jewish Community in Canada*, 2 vols. (Toronto, 1970), pp. 127–29, 142; Stuart Rosenberg, *The Real Jewish World: A Rabbi's Second Thoughts* (New York, 1984), pp. 316–17; *WWWJ* 1965, p. 898.

SIEGEL, MORTON K. (1924–). Educator. The son of Samuel William and Esther Sackin Siegel, Morton K. Siegel was born on December 5, 1924, in New York City. He graduated from the Teachers Institute of Yeshiva University in 1943 and earned a B.A. at Yeshiva College in 1945 and a Ph.D. at Columbia University in 1952.

Siegel began his career as education director of the Laurelton Jewish Center, Queens, New York (1945–53). In 1949 he joined the staff of the United Synagogue as placement director for the Department of Education (1949–53) and soon assumed responsibility for directing the Department of Youth Activities (1951–64). Conservative leaders had for some time been concerned about the defection of post-Bar and Bat Mitzvah youth from the synagogue. Consequently, in 1951 Simon *Greenberg, then executive director of the United Synagogue, charged the Department of Youth Activities with creating a teenage youth movement to succeed the foundering Junior Young People's League. Siegel emerged as the chief architect of United Synagogue Youth (USY), established in 1951 for teens aged thirteen to seventeen. Within a few short years under his guidance, USY became an enormously successful youth movement and a training ground for future rabbis, Hebrew teachers, synagogue officers, and sisterhood presidents.

USY's rapid growth led Siegel to leave the Laurelton Jewish Center to work full time for the United Synagogue. In his thirteen years as director of its youth activities, USY grew from 500 to 24,000 members. Siegel inspired the creation of its very successful summer programs, the Israel Pilgrimage, which he led for many years, and USY-on-Wheels, begun in 1961, a summer bus tour across America, highlights of which include visits to places of Jewish interest and Jewish religious observance. Building upon the success of USY, in 1961 the United Synagogue also launched the college youth group, Atid; USY founding president, Paul *Freedman, then assistant director to Siegel in the Department of Youth Activities, took charge of guiding its development.

In 1964 Siegel became director of the United Synagogue's Department of Education and the Commission on Jewish Education (1964–), succeeding Walter I. Ackerman, who moved to the University of Judaism to become dean of its Teachers Institute. Both the department, which is a division of the United Synagogue, and the commission, which includes representatives from other Conservative movement organizations, remain concerned with all facets of Conservative Jewish education. Under Siegel's direction, the department and commission continue to set standards for all the religious schools of the Conservative movement, including its 725 afternoon schools, Solomon Schechter day schools, and congregational nursery and high schools. The department and commission have also developed guidelines for family, parent, and adult education programs and adopted a code of personnel practices for principals and educational directors. They publish curricular materials, a wide variety of texts, and teachers' guides. Siegel wrote several of these and also edited the educational publications *In Your Hands* and *Your Child*. The agencies also supervise the Conservative movement's regional education commissions, consult with affiliated schools, maintain "The Eternal Light" library of films produced by the Seminary, organize new day schools, and sponsor educational conferences and teacher-training courses in the United States and Israel.

In addition to these responsibilities, Siegel was a founding member and the first secretary of the Jewish Educators Assembly (1951), the professional association of Conservative educators. He also taught at New York University (1972–75)

Siegel married Pearl Fox in 1949; they have four children.

Writings: *Convert, Genuine Jew?* (New York, n.d.); *Curriculum for the Afternoon Jewish School: History/Community Section* (New York, n.d.); *Handbook for the Adult Education Committee* (New York, n.d.); *Manual for the School Board Member* (New York, n.d.); *Manual for the Teacher of Parents of Jewish Adolescents* (New York, n.d.); *Solomon Schechter Day School Manual* (New York, n.d.); *A Syllabus on Zionism: Roots* (New York, n.d.); *Covenant, Not Compromise* (New York, 1987); *Mitzvah, Tzedek, and "Love"* (New York, 1987).

References: Helen Mintz, "The Youth Challenge," *Review* 15, 4 (Winter 1963), pp. 10–13; *Review* 17, 2 (Summer 1964), p. 22; "United Synagogue Supplement," *Washington Jewish Week* 25 September 1986, p. 3; *WWAJ* 1980, p. 458.

SIEGEL, SEYMOUR (1927–1988). Rabbi, scholar. The son of David and Jeanette Morris Siegel, Seymour Siegel was born in Chicago, Illinois, on September 12, 1927. He earned a B.A. at the University of Chicago in 1947, was ordained at the Seminary in 1951, and earned a Doctor of Hebrew Letters there in 1958.

After completing his education, Siegel joined the Seminary faculty (1958–) as lecturer in theology and registrar of the Rabbinical School's Post-Graduate Department. He later became the Ralph *Simon Professor of Theology and Ethics. His teaching of the philosophy of Conservative Judaism, Holocaust theologies, and Jewish ethics reflected both his particular scholarly interests and his concern with contemporary moral affairs. Siegel also taught Talmud at the Seminario Rabinico in Buenos Aires (summers, 1962–64) and Jewish studies at the City College of New York (1971–73).

In the Conservative movement his abiding interests were the development of *halachah* and the exploration of the philosophy of Conservatism. As chairman of the Rabbinical Assembly's Committee on Jewish Law and Standards (1973–80), Siegel led it in an activist period as it dealt with long-standing matters relating to *kashrut*, conversion, and, most visibly, the status of women in the synagogue. A staunch advocate of the right of women to participate fully in the life of the synagogue and a champion of the ordination of women as rabbis, he widely publicized the CJLS's groundbreaking 1973 decision permitting the inclusion of women in the *minyan*. His exploration of Conservative philosophy led him to articulate the principles which he believed guided the CJLS in its work, namely the beliefs in the Living God of Israel, in the revealed Torah, and in the continuation of revelation through the Oral Law. Yet he also admitted with candor that all too often the rabbis legislated without a constituency.

Siegel applied these principles to his own leading work in the field of Jewish ethics, especially to his studies of biomedical ethics. In *responsa* written for his fellow rabbis and in articles in *Conservative Judaism*, the Jewish press, and other forums, he examined from the perspectives of Jewish law and tradition the difficult issues raised by the ability of modern medical technologies to help create and to sustain life. Siegel brought a religious perspective to the debates over the life and death questions concerning the implications of genetic engineering and the rights of patients and their families to refuse drastic life-prolonging treatments. His leading reputation in this new and critical field led to his appointments as delegate to the United Nations World Population Year Conference (1974), humanities fellow at the Medical College of Pennsylvania (1980–81), adjunct scholar of the Heritage Foundation (1980), member of the President's Commission for the Study of Ethical Problems in Medicine and Bio-Medical and Behavioral Research (1982), member of the editorial board of the *Encyclopedia of Bio-Medical Ethics*, and member of the Conference on Science, Philosophy, and Religion.

Siegel's studies of ethics, law, and philosophy led him to conclude that Conservative Judaism has indeed developed a distinctive ideology. To dispel the self-deprecating, but often repeated, notion that there is no philosophy of Conservatism, he edited and introduced two volumes in the Rabbinical Assembly series *Emet Ve-Emunah*: Studies in Conservative Jewish Thought. In the first, *Conservative Judaism and Jewish Law* (1977), with Elliot Gertel, Siegel gathered together scattered writings by some of the best thinkers of the movement, among them Louis *Ginzberg, Louis *Finkelstein, Robert *Gordis, and Mordecai M. *Kaplan, to show both the common denominators and the wide range of Conservatism's views toward *halachah*. Siegel's introduction outlined the basic unifying themes of Conservative ideology. This work also made available for the first time to a broad audience a number of important *responsa* of the CJLS, including those on abortion, wine, and women in the synagogue. They showed that Conservatism's historical approach allowed for the reinterpretation of *halachah* to reflect the unique circumstances of the contemporary world. In *God in the Teachings of Conservative Judaism* (1985), Siegel and Gertel again collected essays by Conservative luminaries, here exploring responses to the age-old philosophical questions of the knowledge of the existence of the Divinity and the persistence of evil in the Creator's world.

Siegel's interest in the philosophy of Conservative Judaism led him to political conservatism. Although he had supported liberal Democratic Party policies, he became disillusioned in the 1960s with what he saw as the Democratic "accommodationist philosophy" toward radical and left-wing governments which, he was convinced, was antithetical to Jewish interests. His conservative leanings led him to support the Vietnam War and to serve as an advisor to several Republican Party politicians, among them Richard Nixon and Gerald Ford. Siegel thus emerged as one of the first Jewish communal leaders to urge American Jewry to shift away from its long-standing allegiance to the Democratic Party toward the Republican right. In 1980 he helped found the American Jewish Forum to support conservative stances in foreign and domestic policies. In 1982

President Ronald Reagan appointed him executive director of the United States Holocaust Memorial Council (1982–85), the newly formed federal agency charged with constructing on the Mall in Washington, D.C., a museum and memorial to the martyrs.

He died on February 24, 1988, in New York City.

Writings: "Vietnam Journal," *CJ* 24, 1 (Fall 1969), pp. 30–40; "Ethics and the Halakhah," *CJ* 25, 3 (Spring 1971), pp. 33–40; "Conservative Judaism and Jewish Law," *PRA 1975* vol. 37 (1976), pp. 118–26; *The Jewish Dietary Laws: Contemporary Issues in Jewish Ethics* (New York, 1980); "Approaches to Halakhah in the Conservative Movement," *PRA 1980* vol. 42 (1981), pp. 398–403. Ed., with Elliot Gertel, *Conservative Judaism and Jewish Law* (New York, 1977); *God in the Teachings of Conservative Judaism* (New York, 1985).

Reference: *American Jewish Biographies*, pp. 404–5.

SIGNER, ISADOR (1900–1953). The son of Abraham Joseph and Malka Israelovitch Signer, Isador Signer was born on January 29, 1900, in Neamtz, Rumania. Brought to Canada as an infant, he was educated in the Montreal public schools. In 1917 he immigrated to the United States where, in 1924, he earned a B.A. from the City College of New York and was ordained at the Seminary.

After serving briefly as rabbi at Temple B'nai B'rith, Somerville, Massachusetts (1924–26), and at B'rith Sholom Community Center, Bethlehem, Pennsylvania (1926–27), Signer became rabbi at Temple Beth-El, Manhattan Beach, Brooklyn (1927–53). Founded in 1919, Temple Beth-El was the first synagogue established in what had previously been primarily a summer resort. The congregants dedicated the synagogue in 1924. When Signer arrived three years later, he organized a men's club and several youth organizations, including a Young Folks League and daughterhood; planned for the building of a meeting and schoolhouse adjoining the synagogue; and allowed *Shabbat* morning Bat Mitzvah ceremonies. He also served as a chaplain at the Brighton-Manhattan Post of the Jewish War Veterans, at the Bill Brown Post of the American Legion, and during World War II at the Veterans Hospital in Brooklyn (1943–45). In addition to his congregational and chaplaincy duties, he taught Bible at the Women's Institute of the Seminary.

Following the publication of the *Sabbath and Festival Prayer Book* in 1946, the Rabbinical Assembly embarked upon an ambitious publication program. Signer, who had edited the *Proceedings of the Rabbinical Assembly* (1932–39), undertook the preparation of the *Rabbinical Assembly Manual*. Published in 1952, the *Manual* offered prayers, services, and ceremonies to guide the rabbi. Its inclusion of a Bat Mitzvah ceremony reflected innovations in Conservative practice. Its ceremonies for affixing a *mezuzah* and consecrating a home revealed the numerous ministerial responsibilities of the Conservative rabbi. Its ceremony for the admission of proselytes acknowledged that marriage prompted most conversions. And its mortgage retirement ceremony reflected the maturity of many Conservative congregations which were about to pay off the loans they had incurred during the heyday of synagogue-center building in the 1920s.

Signer married Elka Rothstein in 1924; they had two children. He died on January 8, 1953, in Manhattan Beach, Brooklyn.

Writing: Ed., *Rabbinical Assembly Manual* (Philadelphia, 1952).

References: Samuel P. Abelow, *History of Brooklyn Jewry* (Brooklyn, 1937), pp. 62–65; *NYT* 9 January 1953, p. 21; *PRA 1946* vol. 10 (1947), p. 63; *Recorder* 4, 3 (June-July 1924), p. 14; *WWAJ* 1938–39, p. 988.

SILVERMAN, MORRIS (1894–1972). Rabbi, liturgist. The son of Simon and Lena Friedland Silverman, Morris Silverman was born in Newburgh, New York, on November 19, 1894. He earned a B.A. from Ohio State University in 1916, was ordained at the Seminary in 1922, and earned a Doctor of Hebrew Letters there in 1952.

As a student Silverman served Mount Sinai Temple (1917–20) in Brooklyn, and Temple Israel, later Gates of Israel Congregation, Washington Heights, New York (1920–23). In three short years he tripled Temple Israel's membership to 300, organized a Hebrew school and a variety of clubs, and settled the congregation in its first synagogue.

In 1923 Silverman left New York to become rabbi at Emanuel Synagogue, Hartford, Connecticut (1923–61). Founded in 1919, Emanuel Synagogue thrived under his leadership. He oversaw construction of the new synagogue in 1926 and of a new school and social hall in 1956. His outstanding youth work was considered among the most successful in the Conservative movement. In the late 1940s Emanuel's Young People's League numbered 800 members, and its Junior Young People's League boasted 350 members. Silverman also superintended the congregation's Hebrew and Sunday schools until Emanuel engaged a full-time educational director in 1945. In addition to promoting numerous youth clubs—Bar and Bat Mitzvah clubs, college club, junior congregation— he encouraged adult Jewish study in the Emanuel Literary Circle, Institute for Jewish Studies, and Sisterhood Bible and history classes. When Silverman retired in 1961, he was elected rabbi emeritus.

During his long ministry he was in the forefront of civic work, civil rights, and interfaith endeavors in Hartford. He was president of the Hartford Association of Ministers and Rabbis (1934–35) and chairman of the Connecticut State Commission on Civil Rights. He taught Jewish history at Connecticut State College (1934–36), was recognized by the U.S. Congress for his work in selective service during World War II, and was a member of the boards of trustees of Mt. Sinai Hospital, United Jewish Social Service, and Hartford Yeshiva.

Silverman held a number of positions within the national organizations of Conservatism. He chaired the Rabbinical Assembly's Committee on Ritual (1932), which surveyed for the first time the ritual practices of Conservative congregations. He was president of the Connecticut branch of the United Synagogue (1929–36) and of the Connecticut branch of the Rabbinical Assembly

(1947). He was also chairman of the Rabbinical Committee on Seminary Affairs for Connecticut (1943) and a member of the Board of Overseers of the Seminary (1946).

Silverman's major contribution to American Jewish life was his work as a compiler, editor, and translator of a wide variety of prayer books. Many of these were published by Prayer Book Press, which he founded in Hartford in 1933. In forty years of liturgical endeavor, Silverman published prayer books for almost every Jewish holiday and service for worshippers of all ages. For the most part he retained the traditional Hebrew liturgies, but he met contemporary needs and aspirations by supplementing the texts with explanatory notes, responsive readings, meditations, hymns, prayers for national holidays, and modern—not necessarily literal—translations. In this way he made the traditional concepts of Judaism—God, Israel, and Torah—ensconced in the prayer book "more relevant to modern life and sentiments." Several of his prayer books were published by the United Synagogue. He was a member of the Joint Prayer Book Commission of the United Synagogue and Rabbinical Assembly which prepared the *Sabbath and Festival Prayer Book* (1946), often known as the Silverman prayer book.

Silverman married Althea Osber in 1919; they had four sons. His son Hillel followed him into the Conservative rabbinate. He died on March 4, 1972, in Acapulco, Mexico.

Writings: "Report of Survey on Ritual," *PRA 1932* vol. 4 (1933), pp. 322–48; "Vitalizing Public Worship," *PRA 1940* vol. 7 (1941), pp. 159–79; *Hartford Jews, 1659–1970* (Hartford, Conn., 1970). Comp., ed., and trans., *Junior Prayer Book for Sabbath and Festivals*, 2 vols. (1933; reprint ed., 1937, New York, 1958); *Sabbath and Festival Services* (Hartford, Conn., 1936; rev. 1937); *High Holiday Prayer Book* (1939; reprint ed., New York, 1951; 2d ed. 1970); *Simhat Torah Service* (Hartford, Conn., 1941); *Purim Service* (Hartford, Conn., 1947); *Torah Readings for Festivals* (Hartford, Conn., 1949); *Memorial Service* (Hartford, Conn., 1949); *Prayers of Consolation* (1953; reprint ed., Hartford, Conn., 1959); *Tisha B'Av Service* (Hartford, Conn., 1955); *Weekday Prayer Book* (Hartford, Conn., 1956); *Passover Haggadah* (Hartford, Conn., 1959). With Robert Gordis, *Sabbath and Festival Prayer Book* for the Rabbinical Assembly and United Synagogue of America (New York, 1946); with Hillel Silverman, *Prayer Books for Summer Camps and Institutes* (Hartford, Conn., 1954); *Selihot Service* (Hartford, Conn., 1954); with Sidney Greenberg, *Our Prayer Book* (Hartford, Conn., 1961).

References: *EJ* vol. 14, cols. 1545–46; *PRA 1947* vol. 11 (1948), pp. 219–20; *Recorder* 4, 1 (January 1924), p. 12; *WWWJ* 1965, p. 911.

SIMON, RALPH (1906–   ). Rabbi. The son of Isaac and Yetta Biddelman Simon, Ralph Simon was born on October 19, 1906, in Newark, New Jersey. Educated in the Newark public schools and at Rabbi Isaac Elchanan Yeshiva in New York City, he earned a B.A. from the City College of New York in 1927 and was ordained at the Seminary in 1931.

As the first Conservative rabbi to serve Congregation Rodef Sholom in Johnstown, Pennsylvania (1931–36), Simon introduced adult education classes and worked to unite the community into one center. At his next congregation, the

Jewish Center of Jackson Heights, New York (1937–43), he continued to emphasize education. He developed a large religious school and adult study program, which attracted new members.

In 1943 Simon moved to Chicago to become rabbi of Congregation Rodfei Zedek. There he established an unusually congenial relationship with his predecessor, Rabbi Emeritus Benjamin Daskal, and at the same time worked to infuse new spirit into the congregation. Determined to create a comprehensive educational program at Rodfei Zedek, Simon established a Hebrew high school; revamped the curricula of the nursery, Sunday, and Hebrew schools; upgraded the requirements for Bar Mitzvah and instituted Bat Mitzvah; and created a model adult education institute. His plans to transform Rodfei Zedek into a social center for Jews on Chicago's South Side led the congregation to agree to share facilities and staff with the other Jewish community centers of Chicago. In 1955 Simon oversaw Rodfei Zedek's move to Hyde Park. Demographic trends in the 1960s and 1970s saw much of Chicago Jewry move north and west of the city. Nevertheless, Simon's extraordinary leadership helped preserve Rodfei Zedek, located southeast of Chicago, as a leading Conservative congregation.

Simon's influence extended well beyond his congregation. A leader among metropolitan Chicago Jewry, especially in philanthropy, he was a member of the Board of Directors of the Jewish Federation of Metropolitan Chicago (1954–66), general chairman of Metropolitan Chicago's Israel Bonds Organization (1965–66) and Jewish United Fund Campaign (1967), and president of the Chicago Board of Rabbis (1952–54) and of the Hyde Park-Kenwood Council of Churches and Synagogues (1956). He was the only clergyman to serve on the Illinois Board of Mental Health Commissioners (1955–62). He was also a member of the Chicago Commission on Human Resources (1958–71) and the Chicago Youth Welfare Commission (1956–63).

Simon also played an important role in the development of the Conservative movement. He directed placement for the Seminary (1939) and wrote *The Talmud for Every Jew* (1942) for the National Academy of Adult Jewish Studies. Among his most important contributions, however, was his pivotal role in launching, in 1947 in Wisconsin, the first Camp Ramah. As chairman of the Camp Program and Operations Committee of the Chicago Council of the United Synagogue, Simon joined with the Seminary's Teachers Institute to create a Hebrew-speaking camp designed to prepare the next generation for leadership within the American Jewish community. The Wisconsin summer camp became the progenitor of Conservatism's Camp Ramah movement.

In the Rabbinical Assembly Simon chaired the capital funds campaign and in 1968 was elected president (1968–70). As president, he worked to strengthen ties with Israel, especially to establish Conservative Judaism there on a more secure basis; to build a program for converting the non-Jewish spouses of intermarried couples; and to reduce tensions between the Rabbinical Assembly, Seminary, and United Synagogue. He was also a member of the Board of Directors of the World Council of Synagogues (1974). In 1959 a professorship, the Ralph Simon Chair in Jewish Ethics and Mysticism, was established in his honor at the Seminary.

Simon published *Challenges and Responses* (1985), a collection of his sermons. He married Kelsey Hoffer in 1931; they have three children, including a son Matthew, who was also ordained at the Seminary.

Writings: *The Talmud for Every Jew* (New York, 1942); "Remarks of the President," *PRA 1968* vol. 32 (1968), pp. 156–61; "President's Message," *PRA 1969* vol. 33 (1969), pp. 45–54; "Presidential Address," *PRA 1970* vol. 34 (1971), pp. 1–14; *Challenges and Responses* (Chicago, 1985).

References: Abraham J. Karp, *A History of the United Synagogue of America, 1913–1963* (New York, 1964), pp. 75–76; Carole Krucoff, *Rodfei Zedek: The First One Hundred Years* (Chicago, 1976); *PRA 1970* vol. 34 (1971), pp. 153–58; *PRA 1975* vol. 37 (1976), p. 31; Shuly Schwartz, "Ramah—The Early Years, 1947–52" (M.A. thesis, Jewish Theological Seminary, 1976), pp. 17–19; *WWAJ* 1980, p. 465.

SOLOMON, ELIAS LOUIS (1879–1956). The son of Jacob and Chaye Hinde Frankfurt Solomon, Elias Solomon was born in Vilna, Russia, on April 22, 1879. His family fled Russia in 1881, stopping in England, Cyprus, and Palestine before immigrating to the United States in 1883 (1888?). Solomon earned a B.A. from the City College of New York in 1900, was ordained at the Seminary in 1904, and earned a Doctor of Hebrew Letters from the Seminary in 1910.

After heading the Barnett Memorial Hebrew School in Paterson, New Jersey (1904–5), Solomon served as rabbi at Beth Mordecai, Perth Amboy, New Jersey (1905–7), at Kehillath Israel, Bronx, New York (1907–18), and as associate rabbi at Kehillath Jeshurun, Manhattan (1918–21). Solomon then became rabbi at Congregation Shaare Zedek (1921–56), a synagogue established on New York City's Upper West Side in 1901, where he officiated at more than 6,000 marriages.

An early leader in the Conservative movement, Solomon helped found the United Synagogue of America. During his tenure as its president (1918–24), its auxiliaries, the Women's League and the Young People's League, were established, the *United Synagogue Recorder* was launched, and plans were made to build a synagogue in Palestine. From 1924 to his death, Solomon was honorary president of the United Synagogue. For a brief time, following the retirement of its executive director, Samuel *Cohen, he was acting executive director (1945). Solomon also served as president of the Alumni Association of the Jewish Theological Seminary of America, the forerunner of the Rabbinical Assembly (1914–16).

In addition to his work on behalf of Conservatism, Solomon was treasurer of the Jewish Braille Institute of America, chairman of the America Pro-Falasha Committee, honorary president of the American Biblical Encyclopedia, and president of the New York Board of Rabbis (1929–30) and of the Synagogue Council of America (1930–32), which he helped found. During World War II he served on the Selective Service Panel and was cited for his work by President Truman.

Solomon married Liebe Katz in 1905; they had two daughters. He died in New York City on December 20, 1956.

References: *EJ* vol. 15, cols. 113–14; Abraham J. Karp, *A History of the United Synagogue of America, 1913–1963* (New York, 1964), pp. 37–41; *NYT* 21 December 1956, p. 23; *Recorder* 4, 3 (June-July 1924), p. 15; *WWWJ* 1955, p. 732.

SPEAKER, HENRY M. (1867–1935). Rabbi, educator. The son of Elhanan and Miriam Lewisohn Speaker, Henry Speaker was born on April 6, 1868, (1867?) in Wisowko, Lithuania. He immigrated to America in 1887. Educated in Russian rabbinical academies, at New York University Law School (1894–97), and at Columbia University, Speaker was ordained at the Seminary in 1896. He also served as instructor in Bible and Talmud at the Seminary (1892–98).

In 1898 Speaker became principal and teacher of literature at Gratz College in Philadelphia. At Gratz he helped expand the three-year course of instruction to include a preparatory year, postgraduate work, and instruction in Talmud for students intending to study at the Seminary. During his tenure, Gratz also acquired a library and building. Speaker retired from Gratz in 1933 and was succeeded as principal by Julius *Greenstone.

One of the founders of the Alumni Association of the Jewish Theological Seminary of America, the forerunner of the Rabbinical Assembly, Speaker served as its first president (1901–4). During his tenure, the Alumni Association adopted a constitution and initiated the practice of reading papers at annual conferences.

In 1897 Speaker married Sarah Ginsburg. He died in 1935.

References: *AJYB* vol. 6 (1904–5), p. 192; *The Jewish Exponent* 28 June 1901, p. 7; 24 July 1903, p. 3; *JTS Students' Annual*, vol. 2 (1915), p. 28; Mitchell E. Panzer, "Gratz College: A Community's Involvement in Jewish Education," in *Gratz College: Anniversary Volume*, ed. Isidore D. Passow and Samuel T. Lachs (Philadelphia, 1971), pp. 1–20; *WWAJ* 1926, p. 586.

SPIEGEL, SHALOM (1899–1984). The son of Simon and Regina Schwitz Spiegel, Shalom Spiegel was born in Unter Stanestie, Bukovina, Rumania on January 26, 1899. He received his doctorate at the University of Vienna in 1922. For the next five years he taught in Haifa, Palestine, at the Bet Sefer Reali (1923–28) and at the Technion (1925–28).

In 1928 he immigrated to the United States, where he taught at the Jewish Institute of Religion (lecturer, 1928–29; associate professor, 1930–33; Kohut Professor of Biblical and Post-Biblical Literature, 1933–43; and librarian, 1931–43), the non-denominational rabbinical seminary established by Rabbi Stephen S. Wise in New York City in 1922 (merged with the Reform Hebrew Union College in 1950).

In 1943 Spiegel left the Jewish Institute of Religion to join the faculty of the Seminary as the William Prager Professor of Medieval Hebrew Literature. Al-

though he did not play a leading role in the larger Conservative movement, as
professor at the Seminary for thirty years—he retired from active teaching in
1973—he influenced hundreds of Conservative rabbis. His students fondly re-
called that he made the words and anguish of the prophets come alive and that
he revealed the richness of Jewish liturgy and the grandeur of medieval Hebrew
poetry.

Noted for the breadth of his learning, the originality of his insights, and his
elegant expression, Spiegel—who mastered the art of lecturing without notes—
did not confine his teaching to his Seminary students but lectured widely. Among
his best-known lectures was one on the prophetic concept of justice in a special
course on Talmudic law whose students included former President Harry S.
Truman and former Chief Justice Earl Warren.

Spiegel's scholarship spanned ancient, medieval, and modern Hebrew literatures. He wrote on Jewish legend and the lives of the prophets Hosea, Amos,
Jeremiah, Ezekiel, and Job. In *The Last Trial* (1969), translated from the Hebrew
by Judah *Goldin, he introduced and commented upon a twelfth-century poem
on the theme of the sacrifice of Isaac. Spiegel's major work in the field of modern
Hebrew literature, *Hebrew Reborn* (1930), surveys its development up until the
works of Chaim Nachman Bialik. Spiegel not only made important contributions
to historical and literary research, but his eloquent style marked him as one of
the leading contemporary exponents of Hebrew belles-lettres. His life's work,
never completed, was a study of Eliezar Ha'Kallir.

Spiegel was a fellow of the American Academy for Jewish Research (elected
vice-president, 1959), a trustee of the Israel Matz Foundation, secretary of the
Alexander Kohut Memorial Foundation, and chair of the National Educational
Advisory Committee of Hadassah. In 1983 he was elected to the American
Academy of Arts and Sciences.

He and his wife, Roslein, had one daughter. Spiegel died on May 24, 1984,
in New York City.

Writings: *Hebrew Reborn* (New York, 1930); *Ezekiel or Pseudo-Ezekiel* (New York,
1931); *Noah, Daniel, and Job* (New York, 1945); "*Me-Aggadot ha-Akedah*," in *Alexander Marx Jubilee Volume*, ed. Saul Lieberman (New York, 1950); *Amos versus Amaziah*
(New York, 1958); *The Last Trial: On the Legends and Lore of the Command to Offer
Isaac as a Sacrifice* (New York, 1969).

References: *Directory of American Scholars*, 5th ed. (1969), vol. 3, p. 386; *NYT*
26 May 1984, p. I10; *PRA 1985* vol. 47 (1985), pp. 172–73.

STEINBERG, MILTON (1903–50). Rabbi, author. The son of Samuel and
Fannie Sternberg Steinberg, Milton Steinberg was born on November 25, 1903,
in Rochester, New York. Educated in the Rochester public schools, he completed
high school in New York City following his family's move there in 1919. In
New York he came under the influence of Rabbi Jacob *Kohn. After earning a
B.A. at the City College of New York in 1924, Steinberg entered the Seminary
and was ordained in 1928.

In 1928 he became rabbi of Temple Beth-El Zedeck, Indianapolis, Indiana, a Conservative synagogue founded in 1927 when two existing congregations merged. He united the congregants by concentrating on concerns typical of Conservative synagogues—establishing dignified services, revamping the Sunday school curriculum, introducing Confirmation, and organizing adult education classes, a men's club, and young people's activities. Steinberg, however, missed the intellectual stimulation of New York, and his wife, the former Edith Alpert whom he married in 1929, disliked the Midwest. In 1933 he left Beth-El Zedeck to become rabbi of Park Avenue Synagogue, New York City (1933–50).

At that time Park Avenue Synagogue was affiliated with the Reform movement's Union of American Hebrew Congregations. The congregation of 120 families was greatly overshadowed by its impressive neighbors, Reform's Temple Emanu-El and Central Synagogue and Orthodoxy's Kehillath Jeshurun. Steinberg welcomed the challenge of bringing the congregation into the Conservative movement, and in so doing he transformed Park Avenue into a leading synagogue. He reintroduced traditional practices, requiring all men to cover their heads at services. He attracted new members by organizing study circles and encouraging personal relationships. His eloquent and stimulating preaching on the problems of Jewish survival, on the need for faith, and on social problems viewed through Jewish tradition attracted other congregants. By 1938 the congregation included 350 families, and by 1942 it had reached its capacity of 425 families. Steinberg—a confirmed Zionist active on the educational committees of Hadassah and the Zionist Organization of America and a member of the editorial board of the ZOA's *The New Palestine*—even managed to modify the anti-Zionist tone of the congregation.

He was dismayed, however, by Conservatism's refusal to issue an authoritative statement clarifying its ideology. Consequently, the boldness of Mordecai M. *Kaplan's Reconstructionism, which promised to formulate a theory compatible with tradition and the demands of contemporary life, attracted him. When Kaplan formed the editorial board of the biweekly *Reconstructionist* in 1934, Steinberg joined him. He served as managing editor briefly in 1937. Although for most of his life Steinberg was closely identified with Reconstructionist thought, in his last years he became increasingly critical of Kaplan's theology, especially of his teacher's views on the nature of God.

He nevertheless continued to fight as a member of the left wing of the Rabbinical Assembly for the definition of an ideology for Conservatism. In the 1930s he chaired the RA's Committee on Social Justice, issuing with RA president Elias *Margolis protests against lynchings and the first official Rabbinical Assembly pronouncement on social justice. However, in the 1940s he became increasingly estranged from the national organizations of Conservatism. He resigned from the RA committee preparing the *Sabbath and Festival Prayer Book* (1946) in protest over the timidity of its liturgical modifications. Instead, he joined with Kaplan to work on the Reconstructionist *Sabbath Prayer Book* (1945). Although he had taught homiletics at the Seminary in 1938, Steinberg also became increasingly estranged from the Seminary over its inelastic approach to the adaptation of tradition to meet the demands of contemporary life.

Steinberg was noted for his thoughtful writings on Judaism and his efforts, as he put it, to construct a "total theology of Judaism." His first work, *The Making of the Modern Jew* (1934), analyzed those factors that had enabled Jewish survival in the Middle Ages and showed how they had disintegrated since Jewish emancipation. He followed this with his only published novel, *As a Driven Leaf* (1939), the story of the first-century heretic Elisha ben Abuyah and his conflict between religion and philosophy, which he viewed as analogous to the conflicts posed by the twentieth century. *A Partisan Guide to the Jewish Problem* (1945) was written while he convalesced from a serious illness brought on by overwork and the added burdens he carried during World War II, which included service as divisional chaplain of the New York National Guard. In it he presented a Reconstructionist point of view on the solutions to the numerous problems Jews would face at the end of the war. Steinberg also wrote *Basic Judaism* (1947), a popular work for a general audience that articulated the bases of Jewish civilization.

The Steinbergs had two sons. He died in New York City on March 20, 1950.

Writings: *The Making of the Modern Jew* (1934, reprint ed., New York, 1948); *As a Driven Leaf* (Indianapolis, 1939); *A Partisan Guide to the Jewish Problem* (1945; reprint ed., Indianapolis, 1963); *Basic Judaism* (New York, 1947). Co-ed., with Mordecai M. Kaplan, Eugene Kohn, and Ira Eisenstein, *Sabbath Prayer Book* (New York, 1945). Posthumously, *A Believing Jew: The Selected Writings of Milton Steinberg*, ed. Edith A. Steinberg (1951; reprint ed., New York, 1971); *From the Sermons of Milton Steinberg* (New York, 1954); *Anatomy of Faith* (New York, 1960); *Only Human* (New York, 1963).

References: *EJ* vol. 15, cols. 364–65; Simon Noveck, *Milton Steinberg: Portrait of a Rabbi* (New York, 1978); *NYT* 21 March 1950, p. 29.

SWICHKOW, LOUIS JUDAH (1912–   ). Rabbi. The son of Joseph and Dora Safran Swichkow, Louis Swichkow was born on July 13, 1912, in Chicago, Illinois. He earned a B.S. at DePaul University in 1934, was ordained at Hebrew Theological College in 1937, earned a Doctor of Hebrew Letters at the Seminary in 1956, and earned a Ph.D. at Marquette University in 1973.

As rabbi of Temple Beth El Ner Tamid Synagogue (1937–85; called Beth El Synagogue 1923–49), Swichkow emerged as the leading Conservative rabbi in Milwaukee. Conservatism had first appeared in Milwaukee in 1923 when Beth El was founded as a Conservative congregation. Its early leaders included Seminary rabbis Eugene *Kohn (1923–26) and Philip Kleinman (1926–37). Although not a Seminary graduate, Swichkow, who considered himself within the right wing of the Conservative movement—he joined the Rabbinical Assembly in 1953—followed in 1937 to lead the congregation for the next half century.

Under his leadership, Beth El grew rapidly. In 1945 its 300 families decided to build a larger synagogue and to explore the possibilities of merging with several smaller Orthodox congregations. Although the unions did not materialize as planned, new members—previously Orthodox or unaffiliated—joined Beth El, strengthening Conservatism in Milwaukee. To signify the inclusion of its new members, in 1949 the congregation changed its name to Beth El Ner Tamid Synagogue. Two years later, its members dedicated their new synagogue, which boasted a 1,300–seat sanctuary. Swichkow, who was also education director of the congregation, encouraged the development of the congregational Hebrew school, which during the 1940s came to supplant the Milwaukee communal Hebrew school. When he retired in 1985, he was elected rabbi emeritus.

Active in Milwaukee Jewish communal affairs, Swichkow was chairman of the Milwaukee Zionist Emergency Council (1941–59), which included representatives from local Zionist groups. He was also a member of the Wisconsin Legislative Council Family Law Committee (1957–60), the Milwaukee Commission on Community Relations (1961–65), and the Milwaukee County Family Court Advisory Committee (1963–70), and was vice-chairman of the Milwaukee County Juvenile Court Advisory Committee (1967–70). He also served three terms as president of the Wisconsin Council of Rabbis (1961–63, 1966–68, 1982–84).

Swichkow co-authored *The History of the Jews of Milwaukee* (1963) and published three editions of *Invocations* (1964) for congregational events, which included appropriate prayers for the launching of a building campaign and synagogue groundbreaking ceremonies.

Swichkow married Gertrude Astrachan in 1936; they have four children.

Writings: *Invocations* (New York, 1943; rev. 1951, 1964); with Lloyd P. Gartner, *The History of the Jews of Milwaukee* (Philadelphia, 1963).

Reference: *Who's Who in Religion* 1977, p. 651.

T

TEPLITZ, SAUL I. (1921–). Rabbi. The son of Mendel and Esther Landau Teplitz, Saul Teplitz was born on August 1, 1921, in Vienna, Austria, and brought to the United States in 1922. He earned a B.A. at the University of Pittsburgh in 1941, was ordained at the Seminary in 1945, and earned a Doctor of Hebrew Letters there in 1956.

Teplitz served as rabbi to three congregations: Laurelton Jewish Center, Laurelton, New York (1944–60); Jewish Community Center of Harrison, Harrison, New York (1960–63); and Congregation Sons of Israel, Woodmere, New York (1963–). Keenly aware of the potential frustrations of life in the congregational rabbinate, he has nevertheless remained firmly convinced of the importance of his roles as a teacher and preacher of Torah, for "[w]ith the Torah, we remain a people with purpose."

His sense of purpose and dedication to Torah led Teplitz to leadership in local Jewish communal affairs. He was chairman of the Board of Education of the Hebrew High School of the Five Towns, president of the Commission on Synagogue Relations, and a member of the Executive Committee of the Federation of Jewish Philanthropies of New York. He was also vice-president of the New York Board of Rabbis, chairman of the New York Rabbinic Cabinet of Israel Bonds, and a judge for the Jewish Conciliation Board of America.

Although early in his career he felt that he lived in the shadow of his father-in-law, the distinguished rabbi and Conservative leader Max *Arzt, Teplitz emerged as a leader in the Conservative movement in his own right. As president of the 1,150–member Rabbinical Assembly (1978–80), he strove to make the Rabbinical Assembly "more effectively serve the personal, professional, and communal needs of every member." He represented the Rabbinical Assembly in Washington, Rome, London, and Cairo, as well as New York. He met in Jerusalem with Prime Minister Menachem Begin to protest proposed amendments to the Law of Return that would invalidate in Israel conversions performed by non-Orthodox rabbis elsewhere. His administration saw the publication of several long-awaited Rabbinical Assembly projects, including the *Passover Haggadah: The Feast of Freedom*; the second volume in the series *Emet Ve-Emunah*: Studies in Conservative Jewish Thought; and a *festschrift* honoring RA executive vice-president Wolfe *Kelman. Because Teplitz's presidency coincided with the eightieth anniversary of the founding of the Rabbinical Assembly, he created the Blue Ribbon Committee, a self-study commission authorized to develop a blueprint for the future of the Rabbinical Assembly, and he personally chaired its Task Force on Halachic Guidance and Conservative Ideology. Elsewhere in the Conservative movement, he was a visiting associate professor of homiletics at the Seminary and national chairman of the United Synagogue Youth Commission.

Teplitz's leadership extended beyond the Conservative movement. He was president of the Synagogue Council of America (1977–78) and national vice-chairman of the American Jewish Conference on Soviet Jewry. He has also edited eleven volumes of the series Best Jewish Sermons (1952–   ).

In 1944 Teplitz married Miriam Arzt; they have three sons.

Writings: *PRA 1957* vol. 21 (1958), pp. 225–26; "Preaching for *Shalosh Regalim*," *PRA 1967* vol. 31 (1967), pp. 149–55; "Isaac Leeser: A Spiritual Leader Who Led," *CJ* 23, 1 (Fall 1968), pp. 67–75; *Life is for Living* (New York, 1969); "Presidential Address," *PRA 1979* vol. 41 (1980), pp. 10–17; *PRA 1980* vol. 42 (1981), pp. 7–12.

Reference: *PRA 1978* vol. 40 (1979), pp. 2–3, 178–83.

V

VORSPAN, MAX (1916–   ). Rabbi, administrator. The son of Benjamin and Fanny Swaden Vorspan, Max Vorspan was born on May 22, 1916, in St. Paul, Minnesota. He earned a B.A. from the University of Minnesota in 1937 and was ordained at the Seminary in the fall of 1942 in a special convocation ceremony, held in order to help meet the wartime emergency call for chaplains.

He began his career as assistant director of the Seminary School of Jewish Studies and rabbi of New York's 92nd Street Young Men's Hebrew Association (1943). After being called to the military chaplaincy, Vorspan served in the Pacific.

In 1947 he was appointed to the newly created post of director of youth activities of the United Synagogue. Charged with critiquing the Conservative movement's Young People's League, the organization for young men and women aged eighteen to thirty, and the Junior Young People's League for teens aged fifteen to eighteen, Vorspan concluded that their failures to capture the imagination of more youth stemmed from a lack of well-defined objectives and poor organizational structure. Consequently, he proposed a new blueprint for the clubs that included the establishment of the National Youth Commission to coordinate all youth activities for the Conservative movement.

In 1948 Vorspan left the United Synagogue's New York headquarters for California, where he joined a number of Conservative leaders determined to foster the development of Conservatism in this growing Jewish community. He became rabbi of Temple B'nai Israel, Pasadena, California (1948–53), the only Conservative congregation in Pasadena. There Vorspan was a leader in the creation of the Pasadena Jewish Community, modeled on the East European Jewish communal organization, the *kehilah*.

Vorspan was among the founders of the University of Judaism. Established in Los Angeles in 1947 as the West Coast branch of the Seminary, the University of Judaism was the city's first institution for advanced Jewish study. As registrar

(1954–63), executive dean (1963–65), and associate professor of American Jewish history, Vorspan was one of its first full-time professionals. In 1965 he became provost and later vice-president. An inspiring leader of great depth and imagination, he helped transform the university from its small beginnings as a teachers college and school for adults into a large institution with four degree-granting schools, including a liberal arts college. Vorspan played a pivotal role in establishing the University Institute, the largest adult Jewish education program in the country, and spearheaded the founding of Camp Ramah in California. He also hosts the university's weekly public affairs television program, "Commitment" (1971–   ). In the 1950s he founded and directed the Pacific Southwest Region of the United Synagogue, which claimed 10,000 members by 1985. He was also associate director of the Brandeis-Bardin Camp Institute in Simi Valley.

Vorspan wrote, with Lloyd P. Gartner, *The History of the Jews of Los Angeles* (1970), a volume in the Seminary's American Jewish History Center series on regional Jewish communities.

He married Sylvia Robinson in 1943; they have two children.

Writings: "Principles of Group Work as Applied to Jewish Groups," *PRA 1947* vol. 11 ((1948), pp. 205–16. With Lloyd P. Gartner, *The History of the Jews of Los Angeles* (San Marino, Calif., 1970).

References: *EJ* vol. 16, col. 225; Abraham J. Karp, *A History of the United Synagogue of America, 1913–1963* (New York, 1964), pp. 75, 90; *News of the United Synagogue of America* 2, 5 (October 1946), p. 1; 3, 1 (September 1947), p. 1; *Review* 4, 7 (March 1949), p. 2.

W

WAXMAN, MORDECAI (1917–). Rabbi. The son of Meyer and Sarah Allen Waxman, Mordecai Waxman was ordained at the Seminary in 1941. He has spent the greater part of his career as rabbi of Temple Israel of Great Neck, New York (1947–). His close relations with his congregants have convinced him to call for greater involvement of the laity in shaping the future of the Conservative movement. He believes it essential, in an era of great geographic mobility, for synagogue members to identify themselves with Conservatism as a national movement. And he has called on the Conservative movement to strengthen its organizational structure in order to foster that identification.

Waxman emerged as a leader in the Rabbinical Assembly. In 1958 he edited and wrote the introductory essay to *Tradition and Change*, the Rabbinical Assembly's first anthology of writings on Conservatism. This volume brought together scattered articles and addresses by many of the Conservative movement's early leaders and includes pronouncements by its official bodies, among them the Rabbinical Assembly's Committee on Jewish Law and Standards. The anthology incorporates the diversity of views indicative of Conservatism in its discussion of the movement's origins, philosophies, and attitudes toward prayer, Jewish law, education, the community, and Zionism.

Waxman's next major responsibilities for the Rabbinical Assembly were editing the journal *Conservative Judaism* (1969–74) and chairing the Membership Committee (1966–68) and the Committee on the Study and Reevaluation of the Community Service Program (1969–70). The Community Service Program, adopted in part to encourage more Seminary graduates to enter the military chaplaincy, had required all Seminary rabbis to serve for two years either in the military chaplaincy or in designated alternative "equivalency" positions. Its extreme unpopularity among Seminary students—several had refused to participate altogether—led to its abandonment.

In 1974 Waxman became president of the 1,100–member Rabbinical Assembly (1974–76). As president, he was especially concerned with the Conservative movement's efforts to establish Conservatism in Israel. He worked to strengthen Rabbinical Assembly representation in the World Council of Synagogues, which became the official representative of Conservatism in the World Zionist Organization. He recognized the need for greater coordination of the various Israel programs sponsored by the Seminary, Rabbinical Assembly, and United Synagogue. Because of his leadership in Conservatism's Israel affairs, Waxman was subsequently elected president of the World Council of Synagogues (1981–85).

During his administration, the Rabbinical Assembly also approved the plan to publish a new commentary on the Pentateuch for use in Conservative synagogues to replace *The Pentateuch and the Haftorahs* (1929–36), commonly known as the Hertz *Chumash*, used in virtually every Conservative synagogue. Translated and edited by the Seminary's first graduate, Joseph H. *Hertz, this fifty-year-old edition of the Pentateuch was considered both outmoded and no longer reflective of the Conservative point of view by the majority of the Rabbinical Assembly's members.

Outside of the Conservative movement, Waxman has joined in the annual assemblies on world Jewish affairs convened by the presidents of the state of Israel. He chairs the International Jewish Committee for Interreligious Consultation (1985–   ) and was president of the Synagogue Council of America (1983–85). Deeply concerned about the growing polarity within the American Jewish religious communities and about the possibility that an irreparable schism within world Jewry might occur, Waxman joined with Reform, Orthodox, and Reconstructionist rabbinical colleagues in the "Symposium for Unity," a discussion of the views of the various denominations that took him to Jewish communities across the United States (1986).

Waxman and his wife, Ruth (Bilgray), have a son, Jonathan, who was ordained at the Seminary.

Writings: "Directions for the Conservative Movement," *CJ* 25, 2 (Winter 1971), pp. 1–4; "President's Address," *PRA 1974* vol. 36 (1975), pp. 70–73; "The Rabbinical Assembly at Seventy-Five: Retrospect and Prospect," *CJ* 29, 4 (Summer 1975), pp. 3–13; "President's Address," *PRA 1976* vol. 38 (1977), pp. 68–93. Ed., *Tradition and Change* (New York, 1958).

References: *PRA 1975* vol. 37 (1976), pp. 223–25; *Washington Jewish Week* 9 January 1986, p. 1ff.

WEISS (HALIVNI), DAVID (1927–   ). Scholar. David Weiss was born in 1927 in Polyana Kobelecky, Czechoslovakia, and grew up in Sighet, Rumania in the house of his maternal grandfather, the scholar Isaiah Weiss. He studied at the Yeshivah of Sighet and was ordained at the age of fifteen. Deported to Auschwitz in 1944, Weiss was the only member of his family to survive the Holocaust, spending the war in several concentration and forced labor camps. Later, having learned that German S.S. officers named Weiss worked in the camps and ghettoes, he took the name Halivni, a Biblical word that roughly translates Weiss or white.

In 1947 Weiss arrived in the United States. Anxious to resume his Talmudic studies and to pursue a secular education, he attended Brooklyn's Yeshivah Chaim Berlin at night and studied philosophy at Brooklyn College during the day. But he soon became dissatisfied with the limitations of the *yeshivah*'s traditional methods of Talmudic study. Enticed by Professor Saul *Lieberman, he left the *yeshivah* world for the Seminary, a move his Orthodox teachers viewed as a dangerous betrayal by a scholar of exceptional talent.

Ordained there in 1957, Weiss earned a Ph.D. in 1958 and joined its faculty, first as instructor and later as professor of rabbinics. Seen as the natural successor to Lieberman, he influenced numerous students, particularly those who came to be associated with the Union for Traditional Conservative Judaism. One of the chief opponents of the Seminary's decision to ordain women rabbis, Weiss— since 1968 also an adjunct professor of religion at Columbia University—left the school that had been his home for more than a quarter of a century to join the faculty of Columbia University.

Weiss's major contribution to Jewish scholarship is his projected nine-volume *Meqorot u-Mesorot* (*Sources and Traditions*, 1968, 1975), a page by page commentary on the Talmud. Believing that the Talmudic text became altered first as a result of centuries of oral transmission and later as a result of scribal and typographical errors, his work emphasizes source criticism. By studying earlier texts, their variants, and commentaries, he seeks to restore the Talmud to a more pristine form, one reflecting the original statements of the sages. Vilified by some Orthodox who believe he tampers with a text of divine origin, Weiss nevertheless defends his work for its purging the sacred text of the human errors that accrued in transmission.

Weiss married Tzipora (?) in 1953; they have three sons.

Writings: *Meqorot, u-Mesorot*, 2 vols. (New York, 1968, 1975); *Midrash, Mishnah, and Gemara: The Jewish Predilection for Justified Law* (Cambridge, Mass., 1986).

References: Herman Dicker, *Piety and Perseverance: Jews from the Carpathian Mountains* (New York, 1981), pp. 124–28; Israel Shenker, "A Life in the Talmud," *The New York Times Magazine* 11 September 1977, pp. 44ff.

WIENER, MARVIN S. (1925–). Rabbi, administrator. The son of Max and Rebecca Dodell Wiener, Marvin S. Wiener was born in New York City on March 16, 1925. He earned a B.S. from the City College of New York in 1944, a B.H.L. from the Seminary in 1947, and was ordained at the Seminary in 1951.

Wiener spent his entire career as an administrator within the national organizations of the Conservative movement. Following his ordination, he remained at the Seminary as registrar and secretary of the faculty of the Rabbinical School (1951–57). He subsequently became instructor in liturgy and director of the Cantors Institute-Seminary College of Jewish Music (1954–58); consultant to "Frontiers of Faith" (1951–57), the television series co-produced by the Seminary and NBC; and coordinator of the Seminary School of Jewish Studies and the Women's Institute (1958–64).

In 1958 Wiener turned his efforts to the United Synagogue. He became director of the National Academy for Adult Jewish Studies (1958–78) and editor of the Burning Bush Press (1958–78), the Conservative movement's adult imprint introduced in 1958. The National Academy had been established at the Seminary in 1940 to oversee and to coordinate Conservatism's adult Jewish education programs. Fostering the ancient Jewish tradition of lifelong learning, the National Academy's mission was rooted in the Jewish past, but it borrowed its techniques of publication and dissemination from the contemporary American adult education setting. Directed first by Providence, Rhode Island, rabbi Israel *Goldman, in 1952 the National Academy became affiliated with the United Synagogue under the direction of Simon *Noveck, whom Wiener succeeded. As the head of the National Academy and editor-in-chief of its press, Wiener became one of the chief architects of adult Jewish education in the Conservative synagogue.

While continuing the work of his predecessors, Wiener led the National Academy in new directions. He expanded its publications to include a wide variety of materials—pamphlets, tracts, study guides, small paperbacks, and popular and even scholarly full-length works. Wiener edited many of these, including the Jewish Tract Series (1964–78), booklets covering such topics as the synagogue service and the Conservative approach to Jewish law; the magazine *Adult Jewish Education* and its successor, *National Academy Adult Jewish Studies Bulletin*, with their articles on curricular concerns and developments in adult education in the synagogue; and several full-length volumes, among them a reprint of the works of Seminary professor Israel *Friedlaender. Under his direction, the National Academy distributed the *El Am Talmud*. Published ten times a year with vocalized Hebrew and Aramaic texts, English translation, and modern commentaries, the *El Am Talmud* succeeded in dramatically raising interest in Talmudic study in Conservative congregations across North America. Wiener also led the National Academy to add a number of new programs, including Cavalcades of Conservative Judaism, lectures by key leaders of the Conservative movement, and numerous seminars, consultations, and conferences designed to aid rabbis and adult education committee leaders in shaping their individual congregational programs.

In the 1970s, after an internal reorganization moved the National Academy to the United Synagogue's Department of Education, Wiener assumed other responsibilities for the United Synagogue. He became executive secretary (1976–78) and director of the United Synagogue's Committee on Congregational Standards (1978–86), the committee charged with formulating guidelines for congregational practices and settling disputes between and within congregations. He also edited the *United Synagogue Review* (1978–86) and was a consultant to the United Synagogue's Department of Community Relations/Social Action before his retirement from the United Synagogue in 1986.

Wiener was a trustee and officer of the Joint Retirement Board of the Seminary, Rabbinical Assembly, and United Synagogue (1959–86; chairman, 1982). Outside of the national associations of the Conservative movement, he was co-chairman of the Jewish Bible Association (1960–64), chairman of the Board of Review of the National Council of Jewish Audio-Visual Materials (1968–69), and a member of the executive bodies of the National Council of Adult Jewish Education and the Jewish Book Council. He also led the International Conference on Adult Jewish Education held in Jerusalem in 1972.

Wiener married Sylvia Bodek in 1952; they have two children.

References: *Review* 29, 2 (Fall 1976), p. 20; 31, 1 (Fall 1978), p. 2.

WISE, AARON MEDALIE (1913–   ). Rabbi. The son of Abraham Benjamin and Esther Medalie Wise, Aaron Wise was born in Cincinnati, Ohio, on April 5, 1913. He received his Jewish education from Mesivta Torah Va-Daat, Rabbi Isaac Elchanan Yeshiva, and Yeshiva College. He earned a B.A. from the University of Cincinnati in 1933 and was ordained at the Seminary in 1938.

After serving as rabbi at Nott Torah Synagogue, Schenectady, New York (1938–47), Wise moved to California to become rabbi of the (San Fernando) Valley Jewish Community Center and Temple, later Adat Ari El Congregation, North Hollywood (1947–78). For many years the Conservative movement had a very weak presence in California, with no more than five Conservative rabbis serving the entire state. But beginning in 1947, a concerted effort by the Seminary's Campaign Department to bring Conservative Judaism to California's rapidly growing Jewish community led to a doubling of the number of Conservative rabbis heading congregations there. Wise's move to California was part of this new and deliberate effort to bring Conservative Judaism to the West Coast.

Founded in the 1930s, the Valley Jewish Center had developed slowly until Wise became its rabbi. His skillful leadership, especially his development of the center's Hebrew school, attracted many new members from among the Jews who were settling in this urbanized suburb in the postwar era. By 1957 the Valley Jewish Center boasted 745 families, and they awarded their rabbi life tenure in 1964. Wise developed an extensive adult education program at the center. The *Darshanim* project called upon lay members of the congregation to interpret the weekly Torah readings. By 1964 more than 300 men and women had participated, and the synagogue collected some of their interpretations in *For Love of Torah*.

Wise figured that in his forty years as a rabbi he officiated at 2,400 weddings. Distressed by the growing divorce rate, in the 1960s he created Making Marriage Work, a premarital counseling program at the center. The experiment was so successful that following his retirement in 1978 and election to rabbi emeritus, Wise taught Making Marriage Work at the University of Judaism. His congregation honored his devoted service with a scholarship in his name at the Seminary.

In addition to congregational responsibilities, Wise's many Jewish communal activities included membership on the Board of Directors of the Los Angeles

Bureau of Jewish Education (1952–55, 1964–66) and the Board of Directors of the Community Relations Committee of the Jewish Federation Council of Greater Los Angeles (1966–69). He was also president of the Board of Rabbis of Southern California (1955–56) and lecturer at the Brandeis-Bardin Institute in Simi Valley. Active in interfaith and civil rights affairs, he chaired the Joint Religious Council of Greater Los Angeles (1962–63) and marched in the Montgomery, Alabama, civil-rights protests with the Reverend Martin Luther King, Jr.

In the Conservative movement he was a member of the Executive Committee of the Rabbinical Assembly (1940–43) and the National Advisory Committee of Camp Ramah. In 1969 he led a special committee that studied the possibility of building a Rabbinical Assembly housing facility for rabbis spending sabbaticals in Jerusalem. He was also a member of the faculty and Board of Directors of the University of Judaism since its founding in 1948.

Wise married Miriam Lipson in 1941; they have three children.

Writing: "Making Marriage Work," *PRA 1979* vol. 41 (1979), pp. 95–98.

References: Max Vorspan and Lloyd Gartner, *History of the Jews of Los Angeles* (San Marino, Calif., 1970), p. 261; *WWAJ* 1980, p. 527.

Z

ZEITLIN, JOSEPH (1906–). Rabbi, educator, author. The son of Isaac and Esther Mathilde Levinson Zeitlin, Joseph Zeitlin was born on May 18, 1906, in Brooklyn, New York. He earned a B.A. from the City College of New York in 1926, was ordained at the Seminary in 1930, and earned a Ph.D. from Columbia University in 1943.

Zeitlin served as rabbi at B'nai Jeshurun, Philadelphia, Pennsylvania (1930–32). He then succeeded Jacob *Kohn as rabbi at Temple Ansche Chesed, New York City (1932–50), one of New York's oldest Conservative congregations. Since its founding in 1876 in lower Manhattan, Ansche Chesed had migrated several times as its congregants moved to Yorkville, to Harlem, and finally to New York's Upper West Side, where Zeitlin led the congregation. In 1950 Zeitlin left Ansche Chesed to become rabbi at Riverside Synagogue, New York City (1950–65), where he was elected rabbi emeritus. Following his retirement from the pulpit, Zeitlin was a professor of speech at the University of Bridgeport in Connecticut.

Outside his congregation Zeitlin served the Conservative movement as chairman of the Rabbinical Assembly's Social Justice Committee and of the Speaker's Bureau of the United Synagogue and as a member of the Executive Committee of the Rabbinical Assembly. He was also a member of the Board of Directors of the United Jewish Appeal Federation of Greater New York, grand chaplain of the Free Sons of Israel, and chairman of the Committee on Church and State of the New York Board of Rabbis.

Zeitlin wrote *Disciples of the Wise* (1945), based on his survey, conducted in 1937, of Reform, Conservative, and Orthodox rabbis' views on theological questions, problems in Jewish adjustment, and issues of social and economic life. Their responses enabled him to analyze the differences among the denominations of American Judaism.

Zeitlin married Josephine Cohen Gershaman; they have one daughter.

Writing: *Disciples of the Wise: The Religious and Social Opinions of American Rabbis* (1945; reprint ed., New York, 1970).

References: Jeffrey Gurock, *When Harlem Was Jewish, 1870–1930* (New York, 1979); *WWAJ* 1980, p. 537; *WWWJ* 1978, p. 964.

ZELIZER, NATHAN (1907–   ). Rabbi. The son of Henry and Bashe Kadesh Zelizer, Nathan Zelizer was born on September 22, 1905, in Stavisk, Poland. He immigrated to the United States in 1921. He earned a B.S. from New York University in 1929 and was ordained at the Seminary in 1931.

For more than forty years Zelizer led Tifereth Israel Congregation, the only Conservative congregation in Columbus, Ohio (1932–73). Founded by Hungarian Jewish immigrants in 1901 as the First Hungarian Hebrew Church, Tifereth Israel grew slowly to 200 members, who dedicated a new synagogue in 1927. The onset of the Depression cost the congregation more than half its members and left it unable to meet mortgage payments. When Zelizer arrived in 1932, he knew that renewal of his contract depended upon his ability to spearhead a successful membership drive. Enticing new members proved to be one of his great gifts. Tifereth Israel grew to 168 members by 1936. In 1943 its more than 400 families paid off the mortgage and began planning the addition of an educational center. When Zelizer retired in 1973, the congregation numbered 1,100 families.

Although Zelizer saw little that differentiated Tifereth Israel in its worship from neighboring Orthodox synagogues, with his guidance and the dedicated financial assistance and leadership of philanthropist Samuel M. Melton, Tifereth Israel created one of the leading congregational schools in the Conservative movement. Zelizer was determined to upgrade the standards and curricula of the synagogue's supplementary schools. He discontinued, over opposition, the Sunday school. When Melton endowed the Melton Research Center in Jewish Education at the Jewish Theological Seminary in 1959, he stipulated that the center establish a pilot school at Tifereth Israel. This school became the experimental center for the development of the Melton method of teaching the Bible and a teacher-training center for Jewish educators. Its success affected all areas of the congregation, leading to increased participation in religious services and enhanced Jewish programming for all its members.

Zelizer was active in Columbus Jewish communal and civic affairs. He was president of the Columbus Zionist District (1935–38) and the Columbus Board of Rabbis (1961) and was a chaplain for the American Legion and area hospitals and penal institutions. He was president of the Columbus Recreation Department (1960–65) and Columbus Parks and Recreation Department (1965–68) and a board member of the Franklin County Council of Churches and Ministers.

Elected rabbi emeritus of Tifereth Israel in 1973, Zelizer established a second home in Florida. He did not, however, retire from congregational life. Instead, he put his congregational building experiences to work in this rapidly growing center of American Jewry, helping to found three new congregations. He led

B'nai Torah Congregation, Boca Raton (1973–82). Beginning with thirty families, within a decade B'nai Torah established a Hebrew school, constructed a synagogue, and grew to 300 families. Zelizer then turned to building B'nai Zion Congregation, Royal Palm, Florida (1982–84). In two years the forty-member congregation grew to include 250 families and a school. And in 1985 Zelizer, along with two founding families, turned to building a new congregation, Beth Ami, Boca Raton, Florida (1985–). Within a year it counted 100 members.

Zelizer married Florence Handler in 1947; they had two children. Their son, Gerald, also entered the rabbinate and was national president of United Synagogue Youth (1957–58). In 1983 Zelizer married Jeanette Warshaw.

References: Marc Lee Raphael, *Jews and Judaism in a Midwestern Community: Columbus, Ohio, 1840–1975* (Columbus, Ohio, 1979), pp. 166–68, 183–86; Saul P. Wachs, ''The Impact of the Pilot Educational Project of the Melton Research Center on Congregation Tifereth Israel, 1960–1966,'' in *Studies in Jewish Education and Judaica in Honor of Louis Newman*, ed. Alexander M. Shapiro and Burton I. Cohen (New York, 1984), pp. 57–83; *WWWJ* 1978, p. 965.

THE FOUNTAINHEAD OF A MOVEMENT: THE JEWISH THEOLOGICAL SEMINARY OF AMERICA

On January 31, 1886, "[w]ithout any parade or pretentiousness, twelve earnest representative gentlemen . . . founded a college of instruction in conservative Jewish principles." That college, which became the Jewish Theological Seminary of America, would emerge in the twentieth century as the fountainhead of Conservative Judaism.[1]

Events in American Jewish religious life in the several years preceding the founding of the Seminary had galvanized—perhaps inevitably—the more traditional leaders of American Judaism to establish a rabbinical seminary in New York City, American Jewry's most important center, to provide an alternative to the Reform bastion, Cincinnati's Hebrew Union College (HUC). Sabato *Morais, the future president of the Seminary, had initially supported the fledgling HUC. But the infamous *trefah* banquet, honoring the first class of rabbis to graduate from HUC in July 1883, included an array of foods forbidden to observant Jews and sent shock waves through the traditional Jewish community. As HUC president Isaac Mayer Wise, in the midst of the uproar, railed against those who practiced "kitchen Judaism," the inevitability of the rift between the traditionalists and the Reformers became evident. Within a few months newspapers sympathetic to the traditionalists, including New York's *American Hebrew* and Philadelphia's *Jewish Record*, were calling for the establishment of a second seminary to counter the Reform tendency. Reform's decisive break with Jewish law in the Pittsburgh Platform of November 1885 added a new sense of urgency. It propelled the traditionalist leaders and a group of moderate Reformers, the men historian Moshe *Davis has dubbed the Historical School, the nineteenth-century forerunner of American Conservatism, to act. This diverse group formed a broad coalition determined to win supporters to their cause.[2]

In March 1886 they and several lay leaders formed the Jewish Theological Seminary Association to organize "efforts on the part of the Jews of America faithful to Mosaic law and ancestral tradition" to establish a school for the training of rabbis and teachers: "The purpose of this Association being the preservation in America of the knowledge and practice of historical Judaism as ordained in the Law of Moses and expounded by the prophets and sages of Israel in Biblical and Talmudical writings."[3] Early leaders included Sabato Morais, president of the Seminary's Advisory Board of Ministers (1886–97); Henry Pereira Mendes, acting president of the Seminary (1897–1902); Alexander *Kohut, who modeled the Seminary curriculum on that of his alma mater, the Jewish Theological Seminary of Breslau; Bernard Drachman, the Seminary's first full-time instructor, who later opposed the school; and Joseph Blumenthal, president of the Board of Trustees of the Seminary Association (1886–1901). These leaders of the traditionalist and moderate Reform forces of American Judaism marshalled their congregations and encouraged private philanthropists, including Jacob Schiff, the single largest contributor to the Seminary even in its early years, to raise funds to open the school. On January 3, 1887—after the convening of an Advisory Board of Ministers, whose members agreed to serve as a faculty, the admission of the ten students of the first preparatory class, and the promise by New York's Congregation Shearith Israel that the Seminary could use its vestry rooms for classrooms—the Seminary convened its first class.

The early Seminary, as the school in the years between its founding in 1886 and its reorganization in 1902 has since become known, was not founded as a denominational school promulgating the spirit of Conservative Judaism. Although at its opening exercises Alexander Kohut spoke of Conservative Judaism, and although its founders pledged their allegiance to historical Judaism, one of the pillars of twentieth-century American Conservatism, this rhetoric cannot camouflage the fact that Conservative Judaism, as such, did not yet exist. The neat twentieth-century labels of the denominations of American Judaism do not easily apply to the realities of the nineteenth century. In fact, many of the Seminary's first leaders, including President Morais and Acting President Pereira Mendes, would, if labels must be assigned, more properly be termed Orthodox. The early Seminary was not the spearhead of American Conservatism that its successor would become.[4]

It was a rabbinical school deliberately modeled on the Jewish Theological Seminary of Breslau (Juedisch-Theologisches Seminar), which in the last half of the nineteenth century had produced many of the great rabbis and scholars of European Jewry and whose founding president was Zacharias Frankel. Frankel, who headed the school from 1854 until his death in 1875, developed the concept of Positive-Historical Judaism, which eventually provided much of the ideological basis for American Conservatism.[5] The New York Seminary was directly linked to the Breslau school by two members of its faculty, Alexander Kohut and Bernard Drachman, who had graduated from there. The schools shared a common name and a common curriculum, which stressed not only the classical *yeshivah* subjects of Talmud and Codes but also Bible, Jewish history, philosophy, *midrash*, and homiletics, and which led to ordination. Further evidence of the American school's indebtedness to its European predecessor is its commitment to Frankel's ideology, "to the preservation in America of the knowledge and practice of historical Judaism."

After its first term, the early Seminary held classes at Cooper Union (1887–91). It subsequently moved to 220 East 12th Street (1891–92) before acquiring its first building, a brownstone at 736 Lexington Avenue (1892–1903), which housed the students and their classrooms, library, reading room, lecture hall, and synagogue. Seventeen rabbis and cantors (*hazzanim*) graduated from the early Seminary between 1894 and 1902. Of these first graduates, Joseph H. *Hertz (1894), who became Chief Rabbi of the British Empire, and the philosopher, theologian, and founder of Reconstructionism, Mordecai M. *Kaplan (1902), went on to distinguished careers. Characteristics that became key features of the reorganized Seminary—notably the commitments to English language, secular education, and Zionism, and ambitions for programming beyond the rabbinical curriculum—were hallmarks of the school.[6]

But while the early Seminary managed to send forth a small number of rabbis, it remained plagued throughout its short history by a serious lack of support, especially financial support. Although congregational membership in the Seminary Association numbered between twenty and twenty-five congregations in its first decade, by 1902 only ten congregations were represented at the association's meeting. Efforts to form Seminary branches in various cities throughout the country by and large failed; only the Philadelphia branch managed to raise significant contributions. Many of the Seminary's supporters were young men who could not yet contribute sufficiently to sustain it. Moreover, they were often overextended by their involvement in other new Jewish communal affairs. At the same time that the Seminary required their energies, these same men played leading roles in the founding of the Jewish Publication Society of America in 1888, the American Jewish Historical Society in 1892 (until the early 1960s housed at the Seminary), the Federation of American Zionists in 1897, and Gratz College in 1898, whose funds the Seminary unsuccessfully tried to share.[7]

And while early Seminary leaders had hoped to win support among the immigrants of the Lower East Side, the Seminary's commitment to English for preaching and the school's diversified curriculum of Judaic studies, which distinguished it from the *yeshivah* with its classical curriculum of Talmud and Codes, were indicative of the religious, social, and economic differences between the Seminary and the immigrants. Instead of turning to the Seminary, pious Jews on the Lower East Side rallied around the Yeshivat Etz Chaim (1886) and the Rabbi Isaac Elchanan Theological Seminary (1897), which together would become the nuclei of Yeshiva University, the chief exponent of modern Orthodox Judaism in America. Even efforts by traditionalist Seminary leaders Pereira Mendes, Drachman, and Blumenthal to win support for the Seminary by founding the Union of Orthodox Jewish Congregations (1898) backfired. By 1900 the predominance of the Yiddish speakers and their criticism of the Americanized Seminary and of the moderate reforms of its affiliated congregations were already evident.[8]

With the deaths of the Seminary's mainstays—Alexander Kohut (1894), Sabato Morais (1897), and Joseph Blumenthal (1901), who had on occasion sustained the Seminary out of his own pocket—the Seminary was in serious trouble. Under acting officers Pereira Mendes, president of the faculty, and Adolphus S. Solomons, president of the Seminary Association, the Seminary hovered on the verge of bankruptcy. No students graduated in 1901.[9]

What saved the Seminary from extinction was its reorganization in 1902, which introduced a new group of academic and administrative leaders who succeeded in revitalizing the moribund institution. In his memoir, *I Have Considered the Days*, Cyrus *Adler, later president of the Seminary and then a part-time member of its faculty, recounted how he approached New York's wealthy German Jews and persuaded them to revive the Seminary. Adler considered his role in the Seminary's reorganization one of his major contributions to American Jewry in a long career dedicated to Jewish communal leadership. In 1901 he convinced uptown leaders Jacob Schiff, Louis Marshall, Leonard Lewisohn, and Simon and Daniel Guggenheim—most of them personally committed to Reform Judaism—to endow the Seminary to the then extraordinary sum of $200,000 and to promise to raise that endowment to $500,000 within five years. These men pledged to provide the Seminary with new facilities and to bring to America the renowned Cambridge University scholar and rescuer of the Cairo *genizah*, Solomon *Schechter, as president of its faculty.[10]

In 1900, just a year before Schiff personally donated $100,000 and a new building to the Seminary, and Marshall agreed to join its Board of Directors, both men had favored, following the death of Hebrew Union College president Isaac Mayer Wise and for reasons of economy and efficiency, a merger between HUC and the Seminary. But once it became clear that those closest to the institutions staunchly opposed the proposition on religious and ideological grounds, they and their friends pledged their financial and administrative support to the Seminary. Historians have speculated as to why this elite group, already financially committed to HUC, also undertook sustenance of the Seminary. They have suggested that these laymen saw the Seminary—like other institutions they backed—as an agency for the Americanization of the downtown East European Jewish immigrants. In supporting the Seminary, these men emulated the American philanthropic tradition of establishing schools of higher education under religious auspices. Possibly, their support also revealed their desire to make their hometown, New York City, the center of Jewish institutional life in America at the expense of Cincinnati.[11]

The financial backers of the reorganization made their support contingent upon Schechter's agreeing to become president of the faculty and Adler's and Marshall's willingness to become administrators (Adler was president of the Board of Directors [1902–5] and Marshall chairman of its Executive Committee [1902–5] and chairman of the Board of Directors [1905–29]). In return for guaranteeing the Seminary an income of $24,000 a year (compared to the average $8,000 a year raised by the Seminary Association), these men, to insure continuity and permanence, required the appointment of a group of directors for life. (Directors in 1902 included Adler, Schiff, Marshall, the Guggenheim brothers, Judge Mayer Sulzberger, and Felix M. Warburg.)[12]

In the spring of 1902 the old Seminary Association agreed to merge with the Seminary and to incorporate the school under a new charter. Empowered by New York State to confer degrees of rabbi, *hazzan*, Master and Doctor of Hebrew Literature, and Doctor of Divinity, and to award certificates to those qualified to teach Hebrew school, the Seminary's charter established a school dedicated to "the perpetuation of the tenets of the Jewish religion, the cultivation of Hebrew literature, the pursuit of Biblical and archaeological research, the advancement of Jewish scholarship, the establishment of a library, and for the education and training of Jewish rabbis and teachers." By incorporating the language of Article II of the Association's by-laws, the new charter guaranteed that the Seminary would remain loyal to traditionalism, to "the practice of historical Judaism as ordained in the Laws of Moses and expounded by the prophets and sages of Israel in Biblical and Talmudical writings."[13]

Yet this same reorganization, which not only made possible the Seminary's survival but allowed it to thrive and become the fountainhead of Conservative Judaism in America, also created one of the great dichotomies of American Conservatism. In years to come the Seminary would be stigmatized for "its seeming unrelatedness to the Conservative movement, with a Board dominated by Reform Jews and a faculty dominated by Orthodox Jews."[14]

On April 17, 1902, the new president of the Seminary faculty, Solomon Schechter, landed in New York. Scion of a Hasidic family, Schechter had migrated both physically and intellectually from his Rumanian birthplace to Germany, where he was a student at the Hochschule für die Wissenschaft des Judentums and at the University of Berlin, and then to England, where he became a reader in Talmudics at Cambridge University. There Schechter made his monumental contribution to twentieth-century Jewish scholarship, the reclaiming of the Cairo *genizah*, an extraordinary archive of medieval Hebrew and rabbinic texts languishing in the Ezra Synagogue in Old Cairo. Schechter's bringing of its treasures to Cambridge University won him worldwide fame. His popular writings in the London *Jewish Chronicle* on Jewish tradition marked him as a champion of Jewish traditionalism and demonstrated his talent for speaking to both scholars and laity.[15]

For years Seminary leaders had been wooing Schechter. Both Morais and Blumenthal had tried to bring him to New York as early as 1890. After Morais' death in 1897, these efforts intensified. When the German-Jewish elite contemplated their support for the financial reorganization of the Seminary, Schechter's appointment as president of the faculty was critical to their plans. Eager for disciples to carry his vision of Judaism to American Jewry and for a strong Jewish environment for his family, Schechter decided to abandon Cambridge

University for the challenges of transforming the Seminary into the outstanding center of Jewish scholarship in America.[16]

Although he led the Seminary for but thirteen years, Schechter left so clear an imprint upon the school that it became known, both in his lifetime and afterward, as Schechter's Seminary. The emblem he chose for the revitalized Seminary, the burning bush, and motto, "And the bush was not consumed," symbolized his view, bred in the scholarship of the scientific study of Judaism, of the enduring and evolutionary character of Jewish tradition. Schechter envisioned the Seminary as a great Jewish academy with resources for research and scholarship, not merely a rabbinical school.[17]

Promising to make the Seminary a premier scholastic institution, Schechter assembled a core of gifted scholars for his faculty. As one of his first acts he retained from the early Seminary Bernard Drachman, instructor in Bible and Hebrew grammar (1887–1908), and Joshua Joffe, instructor in Talmud (1893–1917), and persuaded his former Cambridge student B'nai Jeshurun rabbi Joseph Mayor Asher to teach homiletics and philosophy (1902–9). But at the same time Schechter began to scour America and Europe for the scholars of promise he sought. His first appointment was that of Louis *Ginzberg as professor of Talmud (1902–53). Ginzberg, who had a few years earlier immigrated to America, soon became both within and without the walls of the Seminary the *halachic* expert of Conservative Judaism. In the summer of 1903 Schechter and Ginzberg traveled together to Europe in search of additional faculty. There they wooed and won for the Seminary the Semiticist and Jewish communal activist Israel *Friedlaender, who became professor of Biblical literature and exegesis (1903–20), and the bibliographer Alexander *Marx, who became professor of history and Seminary librarian (1903–53). In 1905 the medievalist Israel *Davidson joined the Seminary faculty and subsequently became professor of medieval Hebrew literature (1905–39) and registrar (1913–32). In 1909 Schechter made his last critical appointment when he persuaded the Board of Directors to accept Seminary graduate Mordecai M. Kaplan as principal, later dean, of the newly founded Teachers Institute (1909–46) and, following Asher's death, as professor of homiletics (1910–47; professor of philosophies of religion, 1947–63).[18]

This core of faculty, marked in several cases by extraordinarily long tenure at the Seminary, was responsible for training the first generations of Conservative rabbis in America. Scholars first and foremost, Ginzberg, Marx, and Davidson conveyed to their students the importance of scholarship and their frequent dismay over the reality of the American rabbinate, which, driven by the demands of congregational life, offered so little time for study. The scholastic reputations of the faculty drew large numbers of students to Schechter's Seminary. Whereas a total of seventeen students were ordained between 1894 and 1902 (six of them ordained in 1902 after Schechter's arrival), seventy-four were ordained at Schechter's Seminary between 1903 and 1915 and another eighty-three completed its teachers course (1909–15).[19]

Schechter believed that the Seminary should lead rabbis to return to their traditional function as students and teachers of Torah, dedicated to creative study and serious scholarship. But he also conceived of an American rabbinate that combined Jewish learning and loyalties with a grounding in Western culture. In order to allow for the essential, intensive rabbinical studies he planned, he reshaped the rabbinical program as a tuition-free, four-year, postgraduate course and required all students to have completed a liberal college education (or its equivalent) prior to admission. He hoped thus to avoid the problem, evident in the early Seminary, of students carrying a double burden of secular and rabbinical studies. The revamped rabbinical curriculum continued the early Seminary's emphasis upon both the study of Jewish humanities—philosophy, history, and homiletics—and the traditional rabbinical subjects of Talmud and Codes.

Prospective students had to observe both the Sabbath and the dietary laws of *kashrut*. They were required to pass entrance examinations in Hebrew and Biblical Aramaic grammar; Bible, including translations and interpretations of selections of the Pentateuch and prophets; and rabbinics. They were also expected to be familiar with the prayer book and with Jewish history. Several universities, including Harvard and Columbia, and Philadelphia's Gratz College, indicated that they offered preparatory courses for students seeking admission to the Seminary.[20]

Since there was no division into classes, students entered at any point in the four-year cycle of courses. Both those who had already received intensive Talmudic training in East European *yeshivot* and those who had had limited preparation in American schools sat side by side. There were no courses in Hebrew language or literature or Jewish education, but members of the faculty gathered students together for supplementary instruction. Friedlaender's group read and discussed the lyrical essays of the contemporary writer Ahad Ha-Am, which were important as much for their modern Hebrew prose as for their author's vision of Zionism and its relationship to the Diaspora. Kaplan met regularly with students seeking a philosophy of Jewish life capable of resolving the doubts and difficulties raised by modernity's challenge of tradition. Out of those discussions evolved Kaplan's theory and movement of Reconstructionism.[21]

While Schechter was assembling the faculty, reorganizing the curriculum, and recruiting students, the Board of Directors, led by its president, Cyrus Adler—who commuted between his job at the Smithsonian Museum in Washington, D.C., and his duties at the Seminary—was completing the construction of the new Seminary on Morningside Heights. In the spring of 1903 the Seminary moved to its new headquarters at 531–535 West 123rd Street (1903–29) in the heart of the academic community bounded by Columbia University, Barnard College, and Union Theological Seminary. The spacious facilities of the new fireproof building included a lecture hall, classrooms, offices, student rooms, and a synagogue. The entire top floor was dedicated as a library with space for some 40,000 volumes and separate facilities for a manuscript and rare-book room. Given that the Seminary library at that time consisted of some 5,000 volumes, the new library revealed Schechter's and Adler's dream of building a world-class research facility at the Seminary.[22]

Having established the rabbinical school on a firm footing, in 1905 Schechter became president of the Seminary (president of the faculty, 1902–5; of the Seminary, 1905–15) when the separate office of the president of the Board of Directors, which Adler had held, was abolished. Thereafter all fiscal and administrative affairs as well as curricular and pedagogical matters were within Schechter's purview.

As president of the Seminary, he turned his attention to affairs outside the rabbinical program. From the beginning he had been concerned with the problems of elementary religious education. Schechter considered the supplementary school (Talmud Torah) an essential adjunct of the modern American synagogue. Acutely aware of the need for Hebrew teacher training, in 1903 he had initiated and personally taught in an evening program of Jewish educators courses. But Hebrew teacher training required a more substantial effort. In 1909, thanks to a gift from Jacob Schiff, the Teachers Institute was established. Located at the Uptown Talmud Torah, 134–142 East 111th Street (1909–11), near the homes of its students, its first class (thirty-four students) was taught by Principal Kaplan, Professor Friedlaender, and Seminary rabbi Elias *Solomon.[23]

At the same time, Schechter's plans for Seminary development also focused on the library. Under the guidance of Seminary librarian Alexander Marx it was transformed from a modest library into one of the largest and most valuable collections of Judaica ever owned by Jews, a library of importance for scholars all over the world. Marx's gifts—a phenomenal memory, fluency in many languages, skill as a bibliographer, expertise in paleography, and an extraordinary ability to determine a manuscript's age just by looking at it—made him particularly well suited to his task.[24]

Established in the early days of the old Seminary, the original library, dedicated as the Morais Library in 1893, was intended primarily for the use of the faculty and students. But leaders of Schechter's Seminary envisioned a great library. With the generosity of Judge Mayer Sulzberger, who early in his life recognized the role a first-class library would play in the development of Jewish scholarship in America, Marx set out to build the Seminary collection. In 1903 Sulzberger donated 7,500 books and 750 manuscripts to the Seminary. This magnanimous gift, which included many rare volumes and incunabula, more than doubled the library's holdings of 5,250 books and 3 manuscripts. Over the next fifty years, thanks in large measure to the continued generosity of Sulzberger and the support of patrons Mortimer L. Schiff and Reform rabbi and scholar Hyman Enelow, Marx pursued his vision of a great library in Hebrew and all other relevant languages by constantly seeking new acquisitions, greater funds, and more staff. To enable those who could not support the Seminary on theological grounds to sustain the library, it was incorporated as a separate body in 1924. The result was rapid growth. When Marx died in 1953, the Seminary library contained

165,000 books and over 9,000 Hebrew, Samaritan, Aramaic, and Yiddish manuscripts. It had become Marx's contribution to Jewish scholarship in America.[25]

The purpose of the library was, of course, to facilitate the development of *Wissenschaft des Judentums*, the scientific study of Judaism, in America. Schechter expected the faculty to devote themselves to scholarly research and publication. Books published or begun in Schechter's lifetime include Ginzberg's *Geonica* (1909) and *The Legends of the Jews* (1909–38); Friedlaender's *The Heterodoxies of the Shiites According to Ibn Hazm* (1909); Marx's bibliographical and historical essays, later collected in *Studies in Jewish History and Booklore* (1944); and Davidson's *Thesaurus of Medieval Hebrew Poetry* (1924–38). The appearance of these works marked the emergence of the Seminary as a premier research institution in all fields of Jewish studies.

Schechter's presidency thus charted the future course of the Seminary and established the training of rabbis in the rabbinical school, of teachers in the Teachers Institute, and of scholars in the Seminary library as its foci. Yet despite these considerable achievements, his administration was not without serious turmoil. What historian Herbert Rosenblum called Schechter's honeymoon period, when opponents to the left and to the right of the Seminary desisted from open criticism, was over by 1904.[26]

Schechter's dream, when he arrived in America in 1902, was to transform the Seminary into an institution that would unify the diverse elements of the American Jewish community. But as the Union of Orthodox Rabbis prohibited Orthodox synagogues from hiring Seminary-trained rabbis (because of the critical methodologies of Ginzberg) and as Reform leaders openly expressed criticism, Schechter found the Seminary increasingly distanced from the very forces he had originally hoped to bring together. At the same time, the small group of affluent Seminary directors was increasingly disappointed by his failure to win grass-roots support among the downtown immigrants. These anti- and non-Zionist directors became further alienated after Schechter openly espoused Zionism as a "great bulwark against assimilation" in his Seminary commencement address of 1906. Although Cyrus Adler prevented them from resigning in anger, other projects—the founding of the American Jewish Committee in 1906, Dropsie College in 1908, and the New York *Kehillah* in 1909—siphoned off their enthusiasm and financial aid. Sensing an urgent need to extend his base of support, Schechter began to seriously consider what he had hoped to avoid, founding a third federation of synagogues to support the Seminary and its policies. Joined by Seminary rabbis who felt isolated in their pulpits, Schechter and the Seminary Alumni Association established a union of Conservative congregations, the United Synagogue of America, in 1913.[27]

In November 1915 Schechter died. Although he had led Friedlaender, Ginzberg, and Kaplan to believe—or each came to believe—that one of them would be his successor, the mantle of the presidency fell upon Cyrus Adler.[28] Of the four men, only Adler, born in Van Buren, Arkansas, in 1863, was American born, a significant fact for the Board of Directors as isolationist America watched from the sidelines a Europe sundered by the Great War. Adler's close relationship with his early tutor in Philadelphia, Mikveh Israel's minister-*hazzan* Sabato Morais, the Seminary's founding president, greatly shaped his religious traditionalism. In 1887 at Johns Hopkins University Adler became the first person to receive a Ph.D. in Semitics from an American university. He went on to a distinguished career at the Smithsonian Institution in Washington, D.C. (1888– 1908), where he developed its archaeology and religions collections.[29]

A man of boundless energy and administrative talent, Adler emerged as a leader of American Jewry, the preeminent native-born Jew of his era. President of five major Jewish organizations, he was among the founders of the Jewish Publication Society of America (1888), the American Jewish Historical Society (1892; president 1898–1922), and the American Jewish Committee (1906; president 1929–40). But convinced that the future of American Jewry depended upon its cultural and intellectual creativity, his abiding concern remained Jewish education. In 1908, when Dropsie College was created in Philadelphia as a postgraduate institute for "Hebrew and Cognate Studies," Adler resigned his Smithsonian post in order to become its president (1908–40).

Adler was involved with the Seminary almost from its beginning. He was instructor in Biblical archaeology and advisor to his former teacher, Morais, in the early Seminary. He then played pivotal roles in the reorganization and was for a time president of the Board of Directors. Fearing that the school might falter for lack of support, he joined Schechter in forming its congregational union. Adler's staunch opposition to the use of the word *Conservative*—a term he avoided all his life, even in his autobiography—led to naming it the United Synagogue of America (vice-president, 1913–14; president, 1914–17).

When Schechter died in 1915, the Board of Directors named Adler acting president (1915–24); the temporary appointment became permanent in 1924 (1924–40). It was no secret that the faculty—several of whom had personal ambitions to the presidency—were disturbed by the choice. Adler, a sound executive, was not the gifted scholar they envisioned as Schechter's heir. Instead, the board's decision demonstrated to the faculty the very different conceptions the board and they had of the Seminary. For the board the Seminary was a practical school for training rabbis and teachers to serve American Jewry; for the senior faculty it was first and foremost a bastion of Jewish scholarship in America.[30]

The resentment over the appointment continued to seethe throughout Adler's presidency. First in the hearts of the faculty, the Seminary was but one of Adler's responsibilities in a very public life crowded with other commitments, including the presidency of a rival institution of Jewish scholarship. And as Adler continued to live in Philadelphia, commuting to New York to fulfill his Seminary duties, the faculty concluded that their school was not his primary concern.[31]

The tension was exacerbated by Adler's style of making appointments to the faculty. Historian Herbert Parzen has concluded that his reluctance, even when professorial chairs stood vacant, to hire new faculty whose views differed from his own traditional stance made for serious weaknesses in the Rabbinical Department.[32] For example, Schechter's death left a vacancy in the teaching of theology. Yet even after the members of the Rabbinical Assembly endowed a professorship in his memory, the position was for many years filled only on a part-time basis by Louis *Finkelstein. Finkelstein was the first graduate of the Rabbinical Department to receive from the Seminary, after extended study with Ginzberg, *hatarat horaah*, the classical form of rabbinic ordination that allowed him to judge matters of Jewish law. After teaching for several years as a part-time instructor in Talmud (1920–24), he was appointed Solomon Schechter Lecturer in Theology (1924–30). At the same time he remained the full-time rabbi of Congregation Kehillath Israel in the Bronx. Only after promotion to associate professor (1930) and to professor (1931) was he able to leave the congregational rabbinate to devote all his energies to scholarship and the Seminary.

In other cases Adler's preemptory disposition of new appointments rankled the faculty. In 1920 Friedlaender was murdered on a relief mission to the Ukraine. Without consulting the senior faculty—who, given the chance, would have expressed disapproval—Adler recommended Jacob Hoschander to become the next Sabato Morais Professor of Biblical Literature and Exegesis (1923–1933).[33]

Despite these tensions, several of Adler's appointments ultimately proved as influential as that of Finkelstein for the development of Conservatism and Jewish scholarship. His appointments of Seminary graduates Boaz *Cohen to assist in the library and to teach Talmud (1925–68), Simon *Greenberg to teach education part time (1931–), and Robert *Gordis to teach Bible (1937–) brought to the Seminary men destined to play leading roles in their scholarly fields and in the Conservative movement. In 1936, after Louis Ginzberg advocated the appointment, Adler brought from Palestine the gifted Bible scholar H.L. *Ginsberg to fill the vacancy created by Hoschander's death in 1933. Other appointments Adler made to the Rabbinical Department included the Hebraist Morris D. Levine (1917–36); Seminary graduate Wilfred P. Kotkov (1917–21), who was tragically murdered one evening on his way home from class; Seminary graduate and part-time instructor in *hazzanut* Israel Goldfarb (1921–67); and, with the help of the Emergency Committee in Aid of Displaced German Scholars, the Bible scholar Alexander Sperber (1934–?).[34]

Yet another factor—Adler's opposition to political Zionism—estranged him from both the faculty and the students. Even in the days of the early Seminary, most of the supporters of the school had already embraced the fledgling Zionist program of Theodor Herzl. Early directors and faculty were prominent members of the Federation of American Zionists. In 1899 Seminary students joined in founding the then Zionist fraternity ZBT (*Zion b'mishpat tipodeh*, ''Zion shall be redeemed through justice''). Long before Schechter publicly embraced Zionism off campus in 1905 and on campus in 1906, the Seminary was clearly identified with Zionism. In fact, this early affiliation helped make espousal of

Zionism one of the hallmarks of the Conservative movement at a time when both American Orthodoxy and American Reform were, at best, lukewarm toward the idea. Adler's antagonism to political Zionism was therefore another indication of how ill-matched he was with the Seminary he was to lead for twenty-five years.[35]

Despite the tensions between Adler and the faculty—students rarely saw him— he left a lasting legacy. During his administration, the Seminary consolidated the achievements of the Schechter years and even began to expand in new directions as Adler, the administrator and fund-raiser, brought the Seminary to its fifth home, its present campus at 122nd Street and Broadway.

In the early 1920s the Seminary was once again in serious financial straits. Until the end of World War I, the original endowment, which had grown to $750,000, generated enough funds, about $40,000 a year, to cover the Seminary's expenses. But by 1921 the school needed new resources to provide a belated salary increase, to hire additional faculty, and to offer more student stipends. Projecting a budget of $136,000 for the academic year 1920–21, the Seminary had managed to raise an additional $80,000 in pledges, but only $30,000 actually materialized. Both the amount pledged and the sum donated seem meager when compared with the $47 million American Jews gave to the Joint Distribution Committee between 1919 and 1924 to save the Jews of war-torn Eastern Europe from starvation and death. Surely the failure to collect the pledges and the financial woes that ensued cannot be attributed to a sudden change in the fortunes of American Jewry. Rather, the uncollected pledges may reflect the Seminary's battle to uphold, even at great cost, the principle of academic freedom.[36]

The key test of that principle came then, as it did for most of his career at the Seminary, in the person of Mordecai M. Kaplan. Kaplan, one of the two most famous and influential graduates of the Seminary (the other was Finkelstein), had become "minister" of New York's Orthodox Congregation Kehillath Jeshurun after his ordination. But increasingly unhappy in the pulpit, he had been about to leave the rabbinate to sell life insurance when Schechter invited him, in 1909, to head the newly established Teachers Institute. A few months later, following the death of homiletics professor Asher, Kaplan began teaching in the Rabbinical Department. Now he had the time to develop his own philosophy of Judaism. His elaboration of Reconstructionism in his magnum opus, *Judaism as a Civilization* (1934), would propose a total revolution in Jewish theology, arguing for its reconstruction from supernaturalism to naturalism; rejection of the notion of a supernatural God; and replacement of Jewish laws, which traditional Jews consider divinely ordained, with a system of folkways. Reconstructionism revealed Kaplan as one of the giants of twentieth-century Jewish thought. Before his death in 1983 at the age of 102, his work had influenced virtually every aspect of organized Jewish life and created what eventually became the fourth denomination of American Judaism, Reconstructionism.[37]

Kaplan's first opportunity to test some of his new ideas in the field came in 1915 when he was invited by several men, who were already contributors to the Seminary, to help found a new synagogue, the Jewish Center. At the same time, Kaplan was gradually developing his philosophy of Reconstructionism. In August 1920 he published "A Program for the Reconstruction of Judaism," the first article containing the seeds of Reconstructionism. It so enraged a number of the more traditional members of the Jewish Center that they threatened to withhold their support from the Seminary if Kaplan was not dismissed.[38]

But for some time the principle of academic freedom had been a pillar of the Seminary. During Schechter's presidency, Kaplan had submitted a sampling of his own ideas about the book of Genesis, a study which drew upon the Biblical methodology known as Higher Criticism, which Schechter without hesitation called "Higher Anti-Semitism." While Schechter made certain these ideas were not taught at the Seminary—not by prohibition but by assigning faculty sympathetic to Higher Criticism to courses other than Bible—he did not interfere with Kaplan's writing. Thus, when the leaders of the Jewish Center demanded Kaplan's dismissal, not only did Adler not ask him to resign, but he reassured him that he would be free to continue to work according to his convictions. Throughout his career at the Seminary Kaplan remained a controversial figure, enduring an acrimonious relationship with his colleagues to his ideological right. To give but one public example, in an open letter in the Hebrew weekly *Hadoar* Seminary professors Louis Ginzberg, Alexander Marx, and Saul *Lieberman joined in a vituperative denunciation of Kaplan and his work following the publication of the Reconstructionist *Sabbath Prayer Book* (1945). Yet personal and ideological animosities were never allowed to encroach upon the upholding of academic freedom at the Seminary.[39]

Still the financial crisis remained. In 1921 Chairman of the Board of Directors Louis Marshall donated $14,000 to help pay the Seminary's faculty. As Marshall personally continued to cover the mounting annual deficits, the board in 1923 launched a successful campaign to raise an additional million dollar endowment from among the congregations of the United Synagogue. Shortly thereafter, New York's second major rabbinical seminary, Yeshiva University—the third, the Jewish Institute of Religion, was but a year old in 1923—also launched a campaign. The competition for funds, and the belief by lay leaders of both schools that there was little in the seminaries' outlooks to distinguish one from the other, led to consideration of a merger. But by 1927 the idea had been scrapped. Those closest to the Seminary and Yeshiva University perceived that differences in aims, students' preparation, curricula, religious standards, and faculty theology made merger impossible. Consequently, the Seminary moved forward with a new campaign to raise funds for what had become its most ambitious project to date, the plan to build the new Seminary campus.[40]

The fund-raising was exceedingly and rapidly successful. A large bequest from Louis S. Brush provided over $1.5 million for scholarships and for the construction and maintenance of a dormitory. Israel Unterberg donated funds to build a permanent home for the Teachers Institute, which, after meeting for a time at the Downtown Talmud Torah (1911–16), had moved to the Loeb Memorial Building of Hebrew Technical Institute (1916–30). There its crowded classes often overflowed into the machine shops of its host. From Mortimer Schiff came the funds to endow a library in the memory of his father, Jacob, one of the Seminary's mainstays from its earliest days to his death in 1920.[41]

Dedicated in 1930, the new buildings were grouped around a courtyard, a haven of scholarly refuge from the noise of Broadway. Students and scholars entered the quadrangle through a vaulted passageway and walked under an arched arcade connecting the buildings on the first floor. On one side the Jacob H. Schiff Memorial Library, which incorporated the tower over the entrance, had space for 200,000 books; the Rare Book Room; offices of the United Synagogue, Rabbinical Assembly, and American Jewish Historical Society; and room to display the collection of the Seminary's new Museum of Jewish Ceremonial Objects (1930). The Louis S. Brush Memorial Dormitory, with its dining and lounge rooms, gymanasium, and private study and bedrooms for each student became the center of the Seminary student community. And at last the wandering stepchild, the Teachers Institute, found its own home in the Unterberg Memorial Building.[42]

In addition to the new campus, the Adler years also brought about an expansion of the Seminary's programs as its leaders strove to make the school the "chief institution setting the example and giving tone and direction to the entire conduct of Jewish life" in America.[43] The most striking area of development was in the Teachers Institute, whose faculty then also included the Hebraists Hillel Bavli, Paul Chertoff, and Zvi Scharfstein; the educator Samuel Dinin; and the philologist Abraham S. Halkin. Since 1915 the Teachers Institute had been offering two tracks—one a professional teacher-training curriculum, the other an academic program for students who, having graduated from New York's communal Hebrew High School, wanted to continue to study Judaica for its own sake. Developments in the teacher-training track included offering postgraduate courses for those seeking administrative posts (1920) and upgrading the certificates awarded graduates to the degrees of Bachelor, Master, and Doctor of Jewish Pedagogy (1924). In 1930 the Teachers Institute established a joint program with the Teachers College of Columbia University—the first of the Seminary's many joint programs with Columbia—to enable students to work toward a Bachelor of Science in Education and a Bachelor of Jewish Pedagogy at the same time. Finally, in 1931 the Teachers Institute's academic track was reorganized as the Seminary's undergraduate division, the Seminary College of Jewish Studies, now the Albert A. List College of Jewish Studies.

But perhaps the most influential development in the Teachers Institute—at least in terms of number of students reached—was the Israel Friedlaender Classes. In 1919, after gradually raising standards over the course of its first decade, the Teachers Institute eliminated the elementary courses from the teacher-training division. But these courses had trained Sunday-school teachers, club leaders, and Jewish communal and lay workers. To fill the gap, Kaplan established an Extension Department. Renamed the Israel Friedlaender Classes in 1921, the courses offered young adults—most students were between the ages of seventeen and twenty-three, and eighty percent were women—continuing Jewish education both at the Teachers Institute and in branches throughout the five boroughs and in New Jersey. In the twelve years before 1931, when the courses were absorbed by the Seminary College of Jewish Studies, they enrolled more than 3,200 students.[44]

Changes in the rabbinical program were less striking. Between 1916 and 1939, 231 rabbis were ordained at the Seminary. While the average class size hovered around ten students, classes fluctuated from a high of twenty rabbis ordained in 1931 to only three in 1923.[45]

The subjects studied did not change, although efforts were sporadically made to introduce students to the practical aspects of the rabbinate. Students needed to know the details of synagogue organization and administration, the general problems of the religious school, and the mechanics of community relations. They wanted to learn how to lead services; preside at circumcisions, weddings, and funerals; organize auxiliary associations and study circles; and counsel the distressed. In the early 1920s the United Synagogue sponsored a course in the "practical work of the ministry" to cover these subjects. In the 1930s seniors were to gain practical experience by working with a local congregational rabbi, and Simon Greenberg commuted from Philadelphia to teach Jewish education. But despite the protests of the members of the Rabbinical Assembly, who well knew from personal experience that this was insufficient preparation for the realities of synagogue life and politics, Seminary students were by and large left to learn to be rabbis on their own. Naïvely, they left the Seminary expecting to find that their synagogue boards would raise the money and they would show them how to spend it. But as Rabbi S. Joshua Kohn reminisced, he had discovered that it was his job to raise the money and to have his board show him how to spend it. For more than forty years, members of the Rabbinical Assembly, the rabbis out in the field, would continue to criticize the Seminary for failing to prepare students adequately for the realities of the pulpit rabbinate.[46]

This criticism revealed a fundamental difference in the conceptions Seminary leaders and congregational rabbis had of rabbinic training. As Adler explained in 1931—and surely he spoke here for the faculty—the job of the Seminary was to ground students in the authentic texts of Jewish tradition to shape a rabbi into "another one of the links in the chain of tradition . . . [who] will be able to hand on the fundaments of our religion and to interpret them and to explain the reasons which lie back of them." One could always figure out later how to organize men's clubs or officiate at confirmations. For the years spent at the Seminary were too few and too precious to detour students from the paramount task of mastering the sacred texts of Jewish tradition.[47]

Yet then, as now, the students' need to earn a livelihood took them away from their studies. And in their on-the-job training, students often learned much about the realities of congregational life. A survey of Seminary student occupations in 1923 showed students leading services on the High Holidays, teaching or directing Hebrew schools, and leading youth groups. Some worked in Jewish community centers. A few even organized new synagogues or already had their own congregations.[48]

Perhaps the most significant development in the Rabbinical Department in the Adler years came in the wake of the Depression. By 1931 the Seminary's income from memberships—presumably dues paid through the United Synagogue—had plummeted 60 percent. Because the Seminary could no longer approach its stalwart supporters of the past, Adler appealed to the men of the Rabbinical Assembly to raise funds for the school from within their congregations. But in 1931 those congregations and rabbis were struggling just to stay alive.[49]

The school survived the Depression thanks largely to the Brush Memorial Fund, which provided funds for maintenance and for student scholarships. Tuition and even room and board in the Brush dormitory were free. But the Seminary was forced to curtail many of its programs. The offerings of the Teachers Institute were slashed in lieu of closing down the institute altogether. And with funds precariously low and with no jobs for new rabbis to go to, the Seminary raised admissions standards to keep the rabbinical classes small. The three classes admitted between 1927 and 1929, before the Depression struck, averaged sixteen students. The classes admitted between 1930 and 1935 averaged eight.[50]

In April 1940 Cyrus Adler died. One month later Louis Finkelstein became the Seminary's fourth president (president 1940–51, chancellor 1951–72). Born in Cincinnati in 1895 and raised for much of his youth in the Brownsville section of Brooklyn, where his father, Simon Finkelstein, was rabbi of the Orthodox Congregation Oheb Shalom, Finkelstein was ordained at the Seminary in 1919, a year after completing his Ph.D. at Columbia University. In the 1920s he was both a pulpit rabbi and a part-time lecturer at the Seminary. Only in 1931, after Louis Ginzberg insisted that if Finkelstein were not hired full-time he would encourage his former student to quit the Seminary, did the future president become a full member of the faculty.[51]

When historian Herbert Parzen asserted that Adler had groomed Finkelstein for the presidency and that his succession was widely assumed in advance of Adler's death, Finkelstein vehemently denied that he had been willed the presidency. Whether Parzen's account or Finkelstein's recollection is correct, under Adler Finkelstein had indeed taken on important administrative responsibilities as assistant to the president (1934–37) and then as the Seminary's first provost (1937–40) which surely prepared him for leadership.[52]

Even before assuming the presidency Finkelstein had laid the groundwork for the radical transformation that he would undertake of the Seminary. When he became provost in 1937, the school was in serious financial trouble. The Depression had taken its toll. Mounting budget deficits had seriously depleted the endowment funds. Annual contributions raised a bare $23,000 a year; at the most, 2,000 donors sustained the Seminary. That fall, Finkelstein persuaded Scranton, Pennsylvania, rabbi Max *Arzt to embark upon a three-month tour of Conservative congregations to plead for funds to resolve the crisis. Arzt's personal appeal worked. In the first three months of 1938 he raised $68,000. But a year later another shortfall threatened. This time the Seminary solved the emergency by selling, for $50,000, its old building on 123rd Street, which it could no longer afford to maintain.[53]

Only the creation of a sustaining constituency could permanently resolve the Seminary's financial problems, and in fact those of the entire Conservative movement. The Depression had almost bankrupted the United Synagogue as member congregations failed to pay their dues. The Rabbinical Assembly, operating on a shoestring budget, had no resources. When the Seminary offered its rabbis the chance to acquire the 123rd Street building for their headquarters, they could not afford it. The logical place to seek this sustaining constituency, as Arzt had already shown, was among Conservative Jewry. Therefore, in 1939 the Seminary established a permanent fund-raising division, the Department of Field Service and Activities, later more aptly named the Department of Development, and Finkelstein persuaded his old friend Arzt to head it. Leaving Scranton, he become a rabbi without a pulpit, traveling across North America to convince Conservative Jews of the Seminary's vital role in shaping American Judaism and of their obligation to sustain it in its work.

Arzt's success was soon evident. Contributions rose annually to $70,000 in 1939–40, $97,000 in 1940–41, $117,000 in 1941–42, $206,000 in 1942–43, $307,000 in 1943–44, and $517,000 in 1944–45. Of equal importance, the number of contributors jumped dramatically to 43,000 by 1946.[54]

These Seminary campaigns had major repercussions for the development of Conservative Judaism. As the growing numbers of donors indicate, they helped create a broad base of support among Conservative laity, who came, as Marshall Sklare observed, to identify with Conservatism as a national movement. And since the Seminary conducted the campaigns, sent its officers and speakers out to the congregations, and based its appeal largely on the needs of the Seminary, it was the Seminary that emerged, even to the laity, as the symbol of Conservative Judaism.[55]

But even more importantly, the campaigns decisively determined, just before the movement's explosive growth in the postwar era, that the Seminary would control its purse strings. When the Seminary launched its campaign in 1938, there was concern about what this would mean for the United Synagogue, which historically had been the organization to appeal to Conservative laity in their congregations. Rabbis worried about turning twice to their congregants, seeking funds one month for the Seminary and another for the United Synagogue. Since the Seminary endowment campaign of 1923, the Seminary had not called upon synagogue members en masse, although Adler had apparently considered it in his Depression appeal to the Rabbinical Assembly.[56] The establishment of the Seminary's Department of Field Services and Activities centralized fund-raising for the movement within the Seminary. This arrangement was formalized a few years later when the Seminary campaign was renamed the Joint Campaign for the Seminary, Rabbinical Assembly, and the United Synagogue of America. The cumbersome title in no way implied that the three were equal partners. Instead, the Seminary controlled both the fund-raising and the allocation of monies, setting aside relatively small percentages for the Rabbinical Assembly and the United Synagogue. Finkelstein's achievement, making the Seminary dominant in Conservatism's fiscal affairs, set the stage for the paramount role it would play in directing the movement.

For Finkelstein the essential commandment of Judaism was that only through study would all Jews, not just the scholars, achieve the understanding necessary to apply the norms of Torah to life in a world constantly in flux. Because the primacy of study lay at the heart of his vision of Judaism, the center of Conservatism had to be a school, namely the Seminary. He believed that the Conservative movement could only be as strong as the Seminary, asserting to his colleagues in the Rabbinical Assembly, "Don't deceive yourselves . . . . Your congregations are no stronger than the Seminary."[57] By virtue of its control over the movement's purse strings, and because of Finkelstein's influential personality and the prestige of the faculty, the Seminary led by Finkelstein triumphed as the sovereign power in the Conservative movement and reasserted—after years of stasis under Adler—its status as the fountainhead of Conservative Judaism.

Securing the Seminary's finances allowed Finkelstein to transform it from a tiny school for the training of rabbis and teachers into a major multidimensional institution, nationally and even internationally prominent in Jewish and interfaith affairs. In effect, these plans flowed out of the crisis emanating from a Europe dominated by Hitler. Hitler's campaign against Jewish learning had, by 1940, destroyed the leading rabbinical seminaries of Central and Eastern Europe. As the extent of the Nazi persecution of the Jews unfolded, it became evident that the massacre of 6 million European Jews left American Jewry, by default, the central Jewish community in the world. Finkelstein envisioned the Seminary guiding American Jewry as it responded to the challenges of its new position, and he laid bold plans for the Conservative movement to meet the spiritual crisis of world Judaism.

In a special conference held in 1946 Finkelstein publicly outlined the postwar plans he had forged in his early years as president. First, the Seminary would have to produce large numbers of rabbis for American and even for world Judaism to organize and staff the hundreds of new congregations he expected to spring up in the coming years. Although the Teachers Institute, greatly weakened by the Depression and then by the diversion of young men and women to the war effort, graduated only two students in 1946, he knew these synagogues and their schools would need 2,000 new teachers. Educating large numbers meant the Seminary would have to expand its faculty, add to its library, which had suffered during the Depression, and fund more scholarships. Furthermore, it should educate not only rabbis and teachers but also cantors, scholars, and Jewish social workers. Because the New York school could not possibly do this job alone, the Conservative movement would have to establish new Seminary colleges throughout North America. Now the Seminary must enter fields of service normally outside the purview of a theological school. It must reach out to Jewish laity by enriching their adult education programs, hosting summer retreats, expanding its museum, and producing radio shows. It must engage in interfaith dialogue and assert its moral leadership in ethical affairs to teach a world that had once gone mad never to do so again. What is most remarkable is not the scope of Finkelstein's vision but the fact that he accomplished so much of what he set out to do.[58]

During the war, Conservative rabbis and administrators had come to realize that they were going to have to nurture future leaders from within their own ranks. Until then, most Seminary students had been raised outside Conservative congregations; many were born in Eastern Europe. But the tragedy taking place there meant that the movement could no longer rely upon others to fill its ranks, nor should it. Consequently, in the early postwar period the Conservative movement developed several programs to educate youth and to recruit its elite for the Seminary. Working closely with rabbis and their congregations, the Teachers Institute, led by Moshe *Davis, who became dean (1946–50) following Kaplan's resignation from that post in 1946, turned its attention to high school education. It established the Leadership Training Fellowship (1946), a national Conservative high school that had been Kaplan's idea; the network of Ramah Camps (1947); and the Prozdor High School (1951). In each, faculty, rabbis, and teachers worked with select groups of teens, encouraging the best and the brightest to enter the Seminary, where they would embark upon careers as rabbis, teachers, and leaders of American, and especially of Conservative, Jewry.[59]

So that these students would continue their intensive Jewish education in college, the Seminary College of Jewish Studies established a joint program with Columbia University in 1953. Now students could simultaneously earn two degrees, a Bachelor of Religious Education and a Bachelor of Arts. Later, when the College of Jewish Studies began granting its own baccalaureate degree, the Seminary became a full-fledged American university, with undergraduate, graduate, and professional divisions.

At the same time that Finkelstein was initiating these programs to recruit and educate undergraduates, he was making the Seminary a center for the graduate training of Judaic scholars. Since its early days the Seminary had trained men to be scholars, for after all that was what a rabbi was. Graduates of Schechter's Seminary, such as Jacob *Minkin, had published numerous books. Others—like Charles Eliezer Hillel *Kauvar at the University of Denver and Herman *Halperin at the University of Pittsburgh and Duquesne University—had introduced Jewish studies courses to the university classroom. In fact, since the nineteenth century the introduction of Jewish studies into the university curriculum had been one of the goals of *Wissenschaft des Judentums*, and the Seminary was the American heir to that tradition. Yet by 1940, there were only two full-time faculty teaching Jewish studies in American universities. But Finkelstein recognized that, spurred by the interest in ethnicity and by the influx of Jewish students to the campuses, the time was ripe for the development of Jewish studies in the secular university. He wanted the Seminary to become the chief institution training the first generation of professors of Judaica. Actively recruiting gifted undergraduates in the late 1950s and 1960s, Finkelstein promised them special tracks in the Rabbinical School—the forerunner of the Seminary's Graduate School was established only in 1969—to allow those intending to be academicians, not rabbis, to specialize in Bible, Talmud, or Jewish history. At the same time, many of these men enrolled in Columbia University's graduate programs. The Seminary thus played a major role in training such scholars as the prolific author Jacob Neusner, Brown University Professor of Religious and Judaic Studies, and the future chancellor of the Seminary, the historian Ismar *Schorsch. It even "exported" several Seminary graduates, including Bible scholars Moshe Greenberg, Shalom Paul, and archaeologist and historian Lee Levine, to Israel to teach at Hebrew University. Through their writings and their teaching these and other scholars enhanced the prestige of the Seminary and carried forth Conservatism's—and Finkelstein's—message of the primacy of study and scholarship in Jewish life to tens of thousands whom the Seminary would otherwise never have reached.[60]

In addition, the Seminary established new research centers: the American Jewish History Center (1953), led by Moshe Davis, published a series of Jewish communal histories, and the Melton Research Center for Jewish Education (1960) has striven to improve the quality of Jewish education by developing new curricular materials and teacher-training programs.

Meanwhile, the professional education of Jewish leaders, which included cantors, remained the Seminary's reason for existence. The Seminary's charter had allowed for the awarding of the diploma of *hazzan*, certifying men as cantors. Yet only three graduates of the early school and but one between 1918 and 1939 had been awarded that diploma. With the destruction of the Jewish communities of Europe, the informal settings in which most American cantors had prepared for their careers no longer existed. Moreover, the role of the cantor in the American synagogue had evolved from that of performer to integral member of the staff in charge of all music and many educational programs of the congregation. In 1947 Conservative cantors organized the Cantors Assembly. Aware that Hebrew Union College planned to establish a professional cantorial school, these men encouraged the Seminary to create the Cantors Institute-Seminary College of Jewish Music (1952).[61]

But for Finkelstein the Seminary was more than a school; it was the fountainhead of Conservative Judaism, and as such it was also responsible for the education of Conservative laity. Because lifelong learning is an integral part of what it means to be a Jew, the Seminary sponsored adult education. For decades Conservative rabbis had been working on their own in this field. To coordinate their activities, the National Academy for Adult Jewish Studies was organized at the Seminary in 1941 under the direction of Providence, Rhode Island, rabbi Israel *Goldman. At the same time Seminary leaders, following the tradition of the Women's Institute (1931), which offered New York area women the opportunity to study with faculty and leading rabbis, brought together Men's Club members for the Laymen's Institutes (1944). To reach even wider audiences, Finkelstein, working with representatives of the Reform and Orthodox movements, launched the NBC radio program "The Eternal Light" (1944) and the NBC television program "Frontiers of Faith" (1951). Utilizing a dramatic rather than a documentary format, both series depicted the richness of Jewish tradition. And in 1947 the Museum of Jewish Ceremonial Objects became simply the Jewish Museum when it moved out of the Seminary to its spacious new home in what had been the Warburg Mansion on Fifth Avenue.[62]

But as Conservatism's religious center, the Seminary had an even greater role to play in gathering together scholars and clergy of all faiths to explore the moral, ethical, social, and technological issues confronting moderns. To do this, Finkelstein established several institutes and conferences, including the Institute for Religious and Social Studies (1938); the Conference on Science, Philosophy, and Religion in Their Relation to the Democratic Way of Life (1940), which published several volumes of its proceedings; the World Brotherhood Movement (1955); and the Herbert H. Lehman Institute of Ethics (1958). He also led the Seminary to award a host of medals and honors not just to those who played leading roles in the Conservative movement but also to dignitaries, such as vice-presidents Hubert H. Humphrey and Nelson Rockefeller and Chief Justice Earl Warren. These conferences and awards reflected one of the primary characteristics of Conservatism: its celebration of the American democratic tradition that had made the United States into a haven for American Jewry and a home for Conservative Judaism.

The expansion of the Seminary's mission required a concomitant expansion beyond New York. This led to the creation of the Los Angeles branch of the Seminary, the University of Judaism (1947), the center for Conservative Jewish life in the West. Led first by President Simon Greenberg (1948–63) and since by David *Lieber (1963–), it grew to include an undergraduate college, which graduated eleven students in 1986; preparatory programs for the Seminary's Rabbinical School; several graduate programs, including a Masters of Business Administration for those planning to work in Jewish agencies; and a large department of continuing education. And working through the World Council of Synagogues, the Seminary guided Rabbi Marshall *Meyer in founding the Seminario Rabinico Latino-Americano in Argentina, a preparatory school for training Spanish-speaking rabbis who would conclude their studies in New York.[63]

In addition, the Seminary enhanced its presence in Israel. The school had had a close association with Zionism since its early days. Schechter's public support of Zionism had merely affirmed this stance. Since then, Conservative rabbis and their congregations had put the movement on the map as staunchly Zionist. Two Rabbinical Assembly rabbis, Solomon *Goldman and Israel *Goldstein, were presidents of the Zionist Organization of America. In the 1930s the United Synagogue built the Yeshurun Synagogue in Jerusalem. In the late 1940s Seminary students battled Finkelstein when he refused to allow the playing of *"Hatikvah"* at their graduation because it was the national anthem of a foreign country. But the Seminary's commitment to Zionism and to the new state of Israel was never in question. Although Finkelstein resisted Israeli prime minister Ben Gurion's call to transplant the school to the new state, the Seminary did build the American Student Center at Neve Schechter in Jerusalem. Completed in 1962, it eventually became the home for a year for all rabbinical students and for those engaged, in programs like *Midreshet Yerushalayim*, in intensive study of the classical texts of Jewish tradition.[64]

The extraordinary expansion in Seminary activities, scope, size, and ambitions forced an administrative reorganization that made Finkelstein the chancellor of the Seminary in 1951. His centralization of the forces of Conservatism, at the same time that synagogue affiliations made it the largest denomination of American Judaism, made him more powerful than any single individual in the movement since Solomon Schechter. In the era when sociologist Will Herberg divided American religious society into Protestant, Catholic, and Jew, Finkelstein became one of the most widely known Jewish religious leaders of his day. In 1966 Bernard *Mandelbaum, who had held a variety of Seminary administrative posts since 1946, became president, the first president of the Seminary to serve under the chancellor. His chief responsibility was to win the large donations essential to sustain its leaders' ambitions for the school.[65]

If it seemed that a generation earlier the Seminary existed primarily to train rabbis and that Finkelstein had reshaped it until it came to do almost everything else, its heart nevertheless still remained the rabbinical program. At the student and faculty breakfasts that opened each academic year, Finkelstein told the future rabbis, "If anyone asks you why you came to the Seminary, your answer should be that you 'came to be in the presence of great men.' " The great men of the faculty that Finkelstein assembled included Talmud professor Saul Lieberman (1940–83), also dean of the Rabbinical School and rector and, following Louis Ginzberg's death in 1953, Conservatism's reigning *halachic* expert; and Abraham Joshua *Heschel, professor of Jewish ethics and mysticism (1945–72), philosopher and social activist, whose charismatic personality and teaching were to some extent responsible for the waning of Kaplan's influence among the students until Kaplan's retirement in 1963. Among the other faculty Finkelstein appointed were Professor of Medieval Hebrew Literature Shalom *Spiegel (1943–84) and the future chancellor of the Seminary, the historian Gerson *Cohen (1970–   ). He also persuaded Simon Greenberg, who had been teaching part time for many years, to leave his Philadelphia pulpit to assume a variety of administrative posts, including acting president during Finkelstein's sabbatical (1948–49). A bibliography of faculty publications would confirm that these great men carried forward the Seminary's reputation as a bastion of Jewish scholarship.[66]

Not surprisingly, the composition of the student body changed dramatically during Finkelstein's tenure. By the late 1950s rabbinical students were by and large American born and increasingly came from Conservative homes. These students had good secular educations but were not as well prepared as their predecessors in Jewish studies. As a result, the period of rabbinic training gradually increased from four to five and even six years. In 1958 the rabbinical program was reorganized so that students spent three years in the School of Judaica earning a Masters of Hebrew Literature degree and then three years in the Graduate Rabbinical School prior to ordination. In both schools the texts of Jewish tradition, with Talmud assigned more hours per week than any other subject, remained the core of the curriculum. However, concessions to practical rabbinics led to the introduction of courses in pastoral psychiatry and an internship program.[67]

"A student body without complaints is a student body about which the faculty complains," mused Simon Greenberg, and the Seminary student body, echoing the youth movement of the 1960s, was no exception. In a major essay, "The Training of American Rabbis," which sparked an interdenominational symposium on what many called the crisis in rabbinic training, sociologist Charles Liebman demonstrated that of all the American rabbinical students, Seminary students had the greatest expectations that their studies would lead them to solutions to problems of faith and the meaning and nature of Judaism. Because these students made the highest demands, when the Seminary failed to provide answers, they proved to be the most dissatisfied of their peers.[68]

Finkelstein was not insensitive to their concerns:

A young man comes to the Seminary, having been graduated from college. He spends four or five or sometimes six years in the Seminary. Courses are said to be terrible. According to some the curriculum is awful. It is said that the teachers could not be less interested in their students. I have been told that while they are all very great men, they are very aloof. However, even if all this were so, the fact remains that something happens in these four, five or six years in the Seminary which turns a young man just out of college and quite lost in this world, into a person touched with greatness.[69]

For Finkelstein, the Seminary, despite complaints and perceived crises, fulfilled its mission. Between 1940 and 1972, he presided over the ordination of 662 men, half of all the Conservative rabbis ordained in the Seminary's first century.

However, one key area of student tension was not as easily dispatched. During World War II, the Seminary had accelerated rabbinic training to graduate rabbis for the United States armed forces. A system of eligibility for the chaplaincy was worked out. As many as one-third of the men of the Rabbinical Assembly served during the war. Since then the Seminary, along with the other rabbinical schools, had shared the responsibility for making certain that there were enough Jewish chaplains for the armed forces. But the call to the chaplaincy in the Vietnam War years provoked a very different response reflecting the divisions over the war.

On the one hand there are rabbinical students and recent graduates who see the chaplaincy as a totally discredited part of the military-industrial complex, and who would as soon enter the chaplaincy as commit murder. On the other hand, there are those who think that the army of the United States is the mainstay not only of the Jewish people in particular, but of the entire free world, and that any deviation from previous policies of cooperation is not only an abandonment of the many Jews who are drafted into the services, but an act that smacks of treachery and treason.[70]

When several members of the rabbinical classes of 1968 and 1969 refused to participate in the chaplaincy placement system, they were sanctioned by being barred from full membership in the Rabbinical Assembly.[71]

Not only was there tension between students and Seminary leaders, but the enormous changes Finkelstein wrought brought criticism from other quarters. His critics—many of them leaders of the Rabbinical Assembly—felt the Seminary started too many new projects and diverted too many resources without consulting those outside the school. Some attacked the Seminary for vacillating between the roles of an aloof academy of higher learning and active leader of Conservative Judaism. They argued that if the Seminary was going to lead Conservative Judaism, it should do so in the essential areas of *halachic* development and the evolution of Conservative ideology.[72]

Much of this fault-finding reflected the real ideological polarities of the Conservative movement and the failure of its fountainhead to lead, as it once had, in Conservatism's ideological development. Finkelstein's appointments to the faculty and their general refusal—with few significant exceptions—to work toward or to sanction ideological formulation or *halachic* evolution reflected the Seminary's steady drift toward the ideological right while elsewhere the movement, especially in the decisions of the Rabbinical Assembly's Committee on Jewish Law and Standards, was liberalizing its posture.[73]

Schechter had begun the ideological formulation of Conservatism with his notion of Catholic Israel, one of his most enduring legacies to the movement. Briefly, he believed that the interpretation of the sacred texts of Jewish tradition to meet changing historical circumstances had sustained Jewish life throughout the ages. And he held that the center of authority for the interpretation of tradition rested, not with any corporate priesthood or rabbinate, but rather with "the collective conscience of Catholic Israel as embodied in the Universal Synagogue." The concept of Catholic Israel lies at the heart of Conservatism. It was later refined and limited by Seminary professor Robert Gordis as "the body of men and women within the Jewish people, who accept the authority of Jewish law and are concerned with Jewish observance as a genuine issue."[74]

In the Adler years Seminary leaders and faculty—with the obvious exception of Kaplan—had refrained from further ideological exploration. Adler had opposed ideological development, understanding Conservative Judaism as "a general term . . . applied to those congregations which have departed somewhat in practice from the Orthodox, but not in any great extent in theory."[75]

For Finkelstein, expansion of the Seminary's activities and scope, not ideological definition or *halachic* innovation, was paramount. He had long been a member of the right wing of the movement, and he made certain that the faculty he appointed and increasingly the students admitted shared his traditionalism. When it appeared that Seminary graduates in the Rabbinical Assembly were about to deviate too sharply from an important traditional stance, he saw to it that they were co-opted. The most obvious example was the creation of the Joint Law Conference (1953–68), which effectively ceded to the Seminary control over the Jewish laws of marriage and divorce for the entire movement. The result was a dichotomy within the movement. As Rabbinical Assembly president Aaron *Blumenthal succinctly stated, "The Seminary has remained an Orthodox institution while we have become a Conservative movement."[76]

In September 1971, at the age of seventy-six, Finkelstein announced that he would step down at the end of the academic year. A month later a committee of faculty, executives, and students selected, pending confirmation by the Board of Directors, Bernard Mandelbaum to succeed Finkelstein as chancellor and Gerson Cohen to become the new president of the Seminary. A proposed reorganization of responsibilities meant that, despite the titles, Cohen would be chief executive officer and president of the faculties while, as chancellor, Mandelbaum would retain his previous role as chief fund-raiser. In May 1972 Mandelbaum resigned "for administrative and personal reasons," and Cohen became chancellor (1972–86), the fifth leader of the Seminary since Sabato Morais.[77]

Born in New York City, Cohen was ordained at the Seminary in 1948 and earned a doctorate at Columbia University in 1958. In 1963, after serving as Seminary librarian and teaching Jewish history there (1950–1963), he left to join the faculty of Columbia University, eventually becoming professor of Jewish history and director of the Center of Israel and Jewish Studies.

In 1970 Finkelstein persuaded Cohen to return to the Seminary as Jacob H. Schiff Professor of Jewish History and, as some said, heir apparent. His appointment as chancellor was in keeping with the Seminary's tradition of having a distinguished scholar of Jewish studies at its helm. Moreover, as the second chancellor trained within the Seminary walls, Cohen's election confirmed the Seminary's tradition of producing its own leaders. Although chancellor for only fourteen years, the shortest tenure since Schechter, Cohen made sweeping changes in the Seminary's physical plant, curricula, and faculty.

Cohen inherited a financial crisis that threatened to be worse than that of the 1930s. But once that was resolved, he spearheaded the long-planned expansion and renovation of the Seminary's campus. The Seminary student body and faculty were overflowing the outmoded complex built in 1930 to house fifty men. By 1985 there would be 500 students and 55 full-time faculty. Construction became imperative after the tragic library fire of April 18, 1966. The inferno in its stacks caused an estimated $2 million worth of damage and destroyed 70,000 books. With volunteers working round the clock, some 150,000 water- and smoke-damaged items were salvaged, but tens of thousands of these had to be stored, for lack of space on campus, in warehouses and were inaccessible to scholars. The rest were moved to what unfortunately had become the heart of the Seminary, a quonset hut in the middle of the courtyard.[78]

Finkelstein had planned for the new library and office complex by purchasing adjacent apartment buildings. But the refusal of their few remaining tenants to vacate prevented their razing. For a time Seminary leaders contemplated moving out of New York City altogether. But ultimately the ten-year legal battle with the last tenant was won, funds raised, and construction begun. In 1976 the Mathilde Schechter Residence Hall, a long-dreamed-of gift of the Women's League for Conservative Judaism, became the Seminary's first residence for non-rabbinic students. A few years later Goldsmith Hall offered apartments for graduate students. Meanwhile, the Unterburg Building was renovated. And in 1983 the spacious new library, which completed the 1930 architect's original vision by transforming the courtyard into a quadrangle, brought together under one roof, for the first time since the fire, the entire Seminary collection of 200,000 items. What a few years before seemed like an enclave in the midst of a dying neighborhood of boarded-up buildings had been transformed into a vital community for assembly, study, and prayer.[79]

The physical transformation was matched by sweeping changes in the academic programs that confirmed that the "first-born son," the Rabbinical School, had become "but one child of many." The proliferation of Jewish studies programs throughout North America in the 1960s meant that the Seminary faced staunch competition for students in the Jewish academic world. Recognizing this, Cohen strengthened the Seminary's programs by modeling them on the university. The undergraduate College of Jewish Studies now offered its own Bachelor of Arts degree. And he created the Graduate School, formerly the Institute for Advanced Study in the Humanities, to train scholars in Jewish history, philosophy, literature, and rabbinics. To educate educators, the Teachers Institute was subsumed under the Graduate School's Department of Jewish Education. To prepare social workers and communal servants, a new joint program with Columbia University's School of Social Work offered a degree in Jewish communal service. By 1977, with an international and multireligious student body of 250, the Graduate School had become the Seminary's largest division.[80]

By moving the training of all non-rabbinic professionals to the Graduate School, the Rabbinical School became a training ground for the congregational rabbi. Its curriculum stressed professional preparation and the all-important role of the rabbi as educator in addition to the mastery of the texts of Jewish tradition. In the past, candidates for admission had been expected to be familiar with the languages and classical literatures of Judaism. But now admissions were broadened to open them to those who, having discovered Judaism only in their college years—often in Jewish studies programs staffed by Seminary-trained scholars—were less well prepared. A year of study at the American Student Center in Jerusalem, once optional, became mandatory for rabbinical students.

Without question the most striking change in the Rabbinical School—and one of the most controversial in the history of the movement—was the admission of women. During 1977–78 Cohen, who had initially opposed the ordination of women, presided over the Commission for the Study of the Ordination of Women as Rabbis. The findings of the commission, which concluded by a vote of eleven to three that ethical arguments and the absence of *halachic* counterarguments constituted a strong case for the ordination of women, induced him to become a passionate advocate for women in the rabbinate, a stance his critics charged would split the movement. However, in 1979 the faculty refused to act on the proposal to admit women to the Rabbinical School, largely because of the opposition of the Talmud faculty. In October 1983—after the death of one of the proposal's staunchest opponents, Talmud professor Saul Lieberman—the faculty voted to admit women as candidates for rabbinic ordination. Because Cohen had already opened Rabbinical School classes to all Seminary students, in May 1985 he presided "with great pride" over the ordination of Amy Eilberg, the first woman to become a Conservative rabbi.[81]

Naturally, the Seminary remained a center for scholarship. Cohen brought young men—and women—of promise, trained in American graduate programs, to the faculty. They included historian Paula Hyman, Dean of the College of Jewish Studies (1973–1986), and Judith Hauptman (1974–   ), the first woman to join the Talmud faculty, whose appointment proved that the Seminary had lifted the *halachic* restriction against teaching Oral Law to women. And these faculty were encouraged to share their scholarship to forge closer links with Conservative laity in congregations throughout North America.

Unlike earlier leaders of the Seminary, Cohen did not hesitate to use *Conservative* as a denominational label. While the Seminary, of course, retained its Zionist stance, he actively promoted Conservative Judaism in Israel and battled to protect the rights of non-Orthodox Jews by fighting proposed revisions to the Law of Return. He led in the establishment of the *Masorti* movement to promote Conservative Judaism in Israel and the Foundation for Conservative Judaism in Israel, which raised funds for its development.

In June 1985, ill health forced Cohen to plan his retirement. Eight months later, after an extensive search that included nine finalists, a unanimous decision named Ismar Schorsch the new chancellor (1986–   ). Born in Hanover, Germany, where his father was a rabbi, Schorsch and his family fled Hitler's persecution. In 1940 they settled in Pottstown, Pennsylvania. Schorsch was ordained at the Seminary in 1962 and earned a doctorate at Columbia University in 1969. Since 1964 he had taught at the Seminary and was the first dean of its Graduate School (1975–79) and then provost (1980–84).[82]

The new chancellor, much like his predecessors, faces the challenges of sustaining the Seminary, resolving its most recent financial crisis, recruiting outstanding faculty, and maintaining its commitment to scholarship. Furthermore, he must deal with the realities of the contemporary Conservative movement: keeping open the lines of communication to the Union for Traditional Conservative Judaism, a group of right-wing Conservative rabbis and laity organized in opposition to the movement's liberalization in the sphere of women's rights; and forging a commitment to belief and practice among Conservative laity. In this his challenges remain strikingly similar to those faced by the Seminary's founders one hundred years ago.

In the sermon "The Jewish Theological Seminary," which pleaded for the Seminary's organization in 1886, founding president Sabato Morais declared: "[The] proposed Seminary shall be hallowed to one predominating purpose— the upholding of the principles by which my ancestors lived and for which many have died. From that nursery of learning shall issue forth men whose utterances will kindle enthusiasm for the literature of the Holy Writ." One hundred years later, as the Seminary entered its second century, *A Century of Achievement*, its brief celebratory history, concluded: "Its mission remains to preserve the tradition while revitalizing the community."[83]

As these statements show, for one hundred years the mission of a tiny rabbinical school meeting in rented quarters and its heir, the university with campuses in New York, Los Angeles, and Jerusalem, has remained constant. Believing that a great institution of learning has lain at the heart of every creative Jewish community, the Seminary leaders, Morais, Schechter, Adler, Finkelstein, and Cohen, strove to make the fountainhead of Conservative Judaism the American heir to the eminent Jewish academies of the past. Only a school for the training of rabbis, scholars, and teachers, the fostering of Jewish scholarship, and the education of all could ensure the vitality of this young Jewish community by leading the 1.5 million Jews of the contemporary Conservative movement, and in fact all of American Jewry, to cling to Torah, the tree of life.

NOTES

1. The original name of the Seminary was to have been the Jewish Theological Seminary of New York. The quotation from the *American Hebrew* (5 February 1886, pp. 8–9) is cited in Robert E. Fierstein, "From Foundation to Reorganization: The Jewish Theological Seminary of America, 1886–1902" (D.H.L. diss., Jewish Theological Seminary of America, 1986), p. 66. Forerunners of the Seminary included the Jewish Theological Seminary chartered by New Yorker Sampson Simson in 1852, which never became a reality, and the short-lived Maimonides College (1867–73) of Philadelphia.

2. In addition to Fierstein, pp. 24–86, the chief sources on the founding of the early Seminary are Marc Lee Raphael, *Profiles in American Judaism: The Reform, Conservative, Orthodox, and Reconstructionist Traditions in Historical Perspective* (San Francisco, 1984), pp. 81–88; Herbert Rosenblum, "The Founding of the United Synagogue of America, 1913" (Ph.D. diss., Brandeis University, 1970), pp. 23–34; Moshe Davis, *The Emergence of Conservative Judaism: The Historical School in Nineteenth-Century America* (Philadelphia, 1963), pp. 231–41; Herbert Parzen, *Architects of Conservative Judaism* (New York, 1964), pp. 18–25; and *The American Hebrew* throughout this period. See also John J. Appel, "The Trefa Banquet," *Commentary* (February 1966), pp. 75–78, and Michael A. Meyer, "A Centennial History," in *Hebrew Union College-Jewish*

Institute of Religion at One Hundred Years, ed. Samuel E. Karff (Cincinnati, 1976), pp. 38–43.

3. *Proceedings of the First Biennial Convention of the Jewish Theological Seminary Association* (New York, 1888), pp. 9–10. The citations are from the Preamble and Article II of the Constitution of the Jewish Theological Seminary Association, adopted at its founding convention, May 6, 1886.

4. See, Raphael, *Profiles in American Judaism*, pp. 81–89.

5. Davis discusses the significant ideological connection in *The Emergence of Conservative Judaism*, esp. pp. 13, 139.

6. See also, Julius H. Greenstone, "Reminiscences of Old Seminary Days," *Recorder* 6, 4 (October 1926), pp. 9–10.

7. Fierstein, "From Foundation to Reorganization," pp. 151–76.

8. Davis, *Emergence of Conservative Judaism*, pp. 313–21.

9. Compare Murray Friedman, "The Making of a National Jewish Community," in *Jewish Life in Philadelphia, 1830–1940*, ed. Murray Friedman (Philadelphia, 1983), p. 15.

10. In addition to Adler's *I Have Considered the Days* (Philadelphia, 1941), pp. 243–44, the following discuss the reorganization: Herbert Rosenblum, "The Shaping of an Institution: The 1902 Reorganization of the Seminary," *CJ* 27, 2 (Winter 1973), pp. 35–48, and Parzen, *Architects of Conservative Judaism*, pp. 26–33.

11. On the historiography, see Rosenblum, "Shaping," pp. 39–40.

12. *AJYB* vol. 2 (1900–1901), pp. 136–37; vol. 4 (1902–03), pp. 15–16, 121–24.

13. Charter of the Jewish Theological Seminary of America, 1902.

14. Max Routtenberg, *Decades of Decision* (New York, 1973), p. 153.

15. For bibliography, see the entry on Solomon Schechter.

16. Abraham Karp, "Solomon Schechter Comes to America," *American Jewish Historical Quarterly* 53, 1 (September 1963), pp. 44–62.

17. See, Cyrus Adler, "Semi-Centennial Address," in *Jewish Theological Seminary of America: Semi-Centennial Volume*, ed. Cyrus Adler (New York, 1939), pp. 3–21.

18. On opposition to Kaplan's appointment, see Arthur Hertzberg, "The Changing Rabbinate," *PRA 1975* vol. 37, p. 69. Schechter also appointed Joseph Jacobs registrar and professor of English literature and rhetoric (1906–14) and Moses Hyamson professor of Codes (1915–40).

19. Louis Ginzberg, "The Seminary and Jewish Scholarship," *Recorder* 3, 4 (October 1923), p. 5; Eli Ginzberg, "Address in Honor of Louis Ginzberg," *PRA 1964* vol. 28, pp. 113–14; Seminary Rabbinical Department Lists; *AJYB* vol. 17 (1915–16), p. 308.

20. *AJYB* vol. 5 (1903–04), pp. 145–46.

21. Eugene Kohn, "President's Message," *PRA 1937* vol. 5, pp. 358–60. Since Alexander Marx taught Jewish history in a five-year cycle, students never completed the entire curriculum.

22. *AJYB* vol. 4 (1902–03), pp. 122–23.

23. Mordecai M. Kaplan, "The Teachers Institute and Its Affiliated Departments," in *Semi-Centennial Volume*, pp. 121–43, esp. p. 125.

24. For bibliography, see entry on Marx.

25. Alexander Marx, "The Library of the Jewish Theological Seminary of America," in *Semi-Centennial Volume*, pp. 87–120; A.S. Halkin, in *AJYB* vol. 56 (1955), pp. 580–88.

26. Herbert Rosenblum, *Conservative Judaism: A Contemporary History* (New York, 1983), pp. 17–18.

27. Solomon Schechter, *Seminary Addresses and Other Papers* (New York, 1915; reprinted 1969), p. 93; Mordecai M. Kaplan, "Solomon Schechter and Ethical Nationhood," *PRA 1975* vol. 37, pp. 349–52; Gerson D. Cohen, "On the Eightieth Anniversary of Solomon Schechter's Arrival in the United States," *PRA 1982* vol. 44, pp. 57–68. On the founding, see the essay on the United Synagogue.

28. Baila Round Shargel, *Practical Dreamer: Israel Friedlaender and the Shaping of American Judaism* (New York, 1985), p. 131; Eli Ginzberg, *Keeper of the Law: Louis Ginzberg* (Philadelphia, 1966), p. 132; Kaplan, "Solomon Schechter," p. 351.

29. For bibliography, see Adler entry.

30. Ginzberg, *Keeper of the Law*, p. 133.

31. Eli Ginzberg, "The Seminary Family: A View from My Parents' Home," in *Perspectives on Jews and Judaism: Essays in Honor of Wolfe Kelman*, ed. Arthur A. Chiel (New York, 1978), pp. 117–19.

32. Parzen, *Architects of Conservative Judaism*, p. 96.

33. Ginzberg, "The Seminary Family," pp. 117–19.

34. Israel Davidson, "The Academic Aspect and Growth of the Rabbinical Department—The Seminary Proper," in *Semi-Centennial Volume*, pp. 73–86; on Kotkov, *Jewish Exponent* 4 March 1921, p. 2; on Levine, Israel M. Goldman, "A Giant of the Soul," *CJ* 3, 1 (November 1946), pp. 8–12; see also, "American Jewish Scholarship and the Jewish Theological Seminary," *PRA 1937* vol. 5, pp. 372–87.

35. Fierstien, "From Foundation," pp. 140–41; Robert E. Fierstien, "Solomon Schechter and the Zionist Movement," *CJ* 29, 3 (Spring 1975), pp. 7–8. While Adler opposed political Zionism and its plans for a Jewish state, he strongly supported the physical rehabilitation of Palestine; David G. Dalin, "Cyrus Adler, Non-Zionism, and the Zionist Movement: A Study in Contradictions," *AJS Review* 10, 1 (Spring 1985), pp. 55–86.

36. *JE* 25 March 1921, p. 5; *Recorder* 1, 3 (July 1921), p. 8; Abraham J. Karp, *Haven and Home: A History of the Jews in America* (New York, 1985), p. 246.

37. For bibliography, see the entry on Kaplan, esp. the excellent introductions by Emanuel S. Goldsmith and Mel Scult, eds., *Dynamic Judaism: The Essential Writings of Mordecai M. Kaplan* (New York, 1985).

38. Mordecai M. Kaplan, in *The Menorah Journal* 6, 4 (August 1920), pp. 181–96.

39. Kaplan, "Solomon Schechter," pp. 350–51; Simon Greenberg, "The Jewish Theological Seminary of America," *PRA 1960* vol. 24, pp. 114–153, esp. p. 129.

40. Aaron Rothkoff, *Bernard Revel: Builder of American Jewish Orthodoxy* (Philadelphia, 1972), pp. 94–114.

41. *Recorder* 3, 4 (October 1923), pp. 12–13. Eli Ginzberg claimed not Adler but others—including Kaplan and Marx—drew the funds to the Seminary; "The Seminary Family," p. 118.

42. William Gehron, "The New Great Buildings of the Seminary," *Recorder* 9, 2 (April 1929), pp. 2–3.

43. "The Status of the Seminary," *Recorder* 4, 3 (June-July 1924), p. 1.

44. Israel S. Chipkin, "The Israel Friedlaender Classes," *PRA 1931* vol. 4, pp. 167–78.

45. Rabbinical Department Lists; Davidson, "Academic Aspect," p. 84; *PRA 1938* vol. 5, p. 408.

46. *Recorder* 2, 1 (January 1922); S. Joshua Kohn, "The Rabbi and the Congregational Budget," *PRA 1931* vol. 4, p. 219; see also Elias Charry, "Synagogue Membership: Acquisition and Retention," *PRA 1973* vol. 35, p. 109.

47. Cyrus Adler, "The Seminary Training of the Rabbi—And After," *PRA 1927* vol. 2, pp. 25–31, esp. p. 26.

48. "What Seminary Students Are Doing," *Recorder* 3, 1 (January 1923), p. 24.

49. Cyrus Adler, "Greetings," *PRA 1931* vol. 4, p. 121.

50. Kaplan, "Teachers Institute," p. 135; *PRA 1931* vol. 4, p. 135.

51. For bibliography, see the entry on Finkelstein; Eli Ginzberg, *Keeper*, p. 139.

52. Herbert Parzen, *Architects*, pp. 207–9. The *New York Times* buttressed Parzen's argument (see 2 May 1940, p. 26). The article, written less than a month after Adler died, said Finkelstein was acting president and that at the start of the fall term he would become the Seminary's new president.

53. Max Arzt, "Conservative Judaism Comes of Age," *PRA 1975* vol. 37, pp. 329–30; "Symposium: The Seminary Expansion Program," *PRA 1944* vol. 8, pp. 302–22.

54. Figures, Max D. Klein, "Seminary Campaign Committee," *PRA 1945* vol. 9, pp. 17–18; *PRA 1946* vol. 10, p. 207.

55. Marshall Sklare, *Conservative Judaism* (1955; rev. 1972; reprint ed., Lanham, Md., 1985), p. 260.

56. *PRA 1938* vol. 5, p. 427.

57. Max Arzt, "Our Expansion Program—A Revaluation," *PRA 1946* vol. 10, pp. 205–35, esp. p. 234.

58. "The Spiritual Crisis of World Judaism," *News of the United Synagogue of America* 2, 3 (April 1946), p. 4; Teachers Institute figures, Shuly Rubin Schwartz, "Ramah—The Early Years, 1947–52," (M.A. thesis, Jewish Theological Seminary of America, 1976), p. 5.

59. On the impact of the recruitment programs, see Sylvia Ettenberg, "The Rabbi—A Force in a Program for Recruiting Teachers," *PRA 1956* vol. 20, pp. 223–28; Arthur Hertzberg, "The Conservative Rabbinate: A Sociological Study," in *Essays in Jewish Life and Thought: Presented in Honor of Salo Wittmayer Baron*, ed. Joseph Blau et al. (New York, 1959), pp. 309–32.

60. *PRA 1960* vol. 24, pp. 61–62.

61. Marjorie Wyler, "Cantors Institute: The First Twenty-five Years," *Review* 32, 1 (Fall 1979), p. 6; Fierstien, "From Foundation to Reorganization," p. 124; Rabbinical Department Lists.

62. On the National Academy, see the essay on the United Synagogue; Simon Noveck and Lily Edelman, "The Laymen's Institutes: An Adventure in Jewish Living," in *Roads to Jewish Survival*, ed. Milton Berger et al. (New York, 1967), pp. 270–71; Marjorie G. Wyler, " 'The Eternal Light': Judaism on the Airwaves," *CJ* 39, 2 (Winter 1986–87), pp. 18–22.

63. On the University of Judaism, see its publication *Direction*.

64. On "*Hatikvah*," see Arthur Hertzberg, "The Changing Rabbinate," *PRA 1975* vol. 37, p. 67; on the call to Israel, see Louis Finkelstein, "The Achievement of the Rabbinical Assembly," *PRA 1975* vol. 37, p. 325.

65. Will Herberg, *Protestant—Catholic—Jew* (1955; rev. Garden City, N.Y. 1960).

66. Finkelstein, cited by Bernard Mandelbaum in "Letter to the Editor," *CJ* 39, 2 (Winter 1986–87), pp. 114–15.

67. Eli Ginzberg, "Manpower for Conservative Judaism," *PRA 1960* vol. 24, pp. 19–31; *NYT* 4 December 1958, p. 34.

68. Simon Greenberg, "The Jewish Theological Seminary of America," *PRA 1960* vol. 24, pp. 114–153, esp. p. 149; Charles S. Liebman, in the *AJYB* (1969), pp. 3–112, reprinted in Charles S. Liebman, *Aspects of the Religious Behavior of American Jews* (New York, 1974), pp. 1–110, esp. p. 18; "The Future of Rabbinic Training in America: A Symposium," *Judaism* 18, 4 (Fall 1969), pp. 387–420.

69. Louis Finkelstein, "Spiritual Leadership," *PRA 1970* vol. 34, pp. 147–52, esp. p. 149.

70. Edward M. Gershfield, "On the Seventieth Anniversary of the Rabbinical Assembly," *PRA 1970* vol. 34, pp. 86–95, esp. p. 92.

71. "Membership Committee Report," *PRA 1971* vol. 35, p. 41.

72. Aaron Blumenthal, "Presidential Report," *PRA 1957* vol. 21, p. 43; Edward Sandrow, "President's Report," *PRA 1961* vol. 25, pp. 94–95.

73. On the Committee on Jewish Law and Standards, see the introduction.

74. Solomon Schechter, *Studies in Judaism*, Series One (London and Philadelphia, 1896–1924), p. xviii; Robert Gordis, "Authority in Jewish Law," *PRA 1942* vol. 8, pp. 64–92, esp. p. 79.

75. Cyrus Adler, *Lectures, Selected Papers, Addresses* (Philadelphia, 1933), p. 251.

76. Blumenthal, "Presidential Report," p. 41.

77. *NYT* 28 October 1971, p. 43; 29 October 1971, p. 84; 24 May 1972, p. 51.

78. *Beineinu* 1, 3 (March 1971), p. 19; *NYT* 13 June 1985, p. II3; 19 April 1966, p. 1.

79. *NYT* 18 December 1973, p. 43; 1 February 1975, p. 31.

80. Gerson D. Cohen, "The Conservative Jewish Mission in Our Tenth Decade," *PRA 1977* vol. 39, pp. 37–43.

81. *NYT* 13 June 1985, p. II3.

82. *NYT* 4 March 1986, p. B4.

83. Morais, in Mordecai Waxman, ed., *Tradition and Change* (New York, 1958), pp. 157–61, esp. p. 158; Jewish Theological Seminary of America, *A Century of Achievement* (New York, 1986?), p. 24.

CONSERVATIVE RABBIS IN AMERICA: THE RABBINICAL ASSEMBLY

In 1957 Rabbinical Assembly executive vice-president Wolfe *Kelman told his colleagues:

Some people say that the role of the modern rabbi is entirely new. This is not entirely true. All of the things that the rabbi does today used to be done in the past, but by a number of people; and the rabbi did what a rabbi used to do. He was the *moreh horaah*—which, of course, we hope many of our rabbis still are in their congregations. He was also the final authority in all religious matters,—marriage, divorce, etc. But everything else a rabbi does was done by a *maggid*. The master of ceremonies at weddings was a *badkhan*; arrangements for funerals, for unveilings, and other duties relating to death, were attended to by the *chevreh kadisha*. Education was in the hands of the *melamed*, visiting the sick—*bikkur holim*. . . . A *linat hazedek* stayed with the dying. There were *asarah batlanim* who made up the minyan, and the congregation did not have to depend on the rabbi for that. Now the rabbi is expected to do all these things.[1]

And more.

When students complete their training at the Rabbinical School of the Jewish Theological Seminary of America, they are ordained as rabbis, teachers, and preachers in Israel. But these three titles belie the reality of the lives of the majority of the Seminary rabbis who serve congregations. The list of a rabbi's tasks compiled by Kelman only begins to show the range of duties—ruling on matters of Jewish law, officiating at rites of passage, directing educational programs, and visiting the sick—that engage the modern rabbi. In addition to these tasks, shared by others in the premodern Jewish communities, Conservative rabbis in America took on a host of new responsibilities and roles that grew out of the ways in which immigrant Jews and their descendants accommodated to life in America.

Conservative rabbis found that rabbis in America are preachers. Like the Protestant ministers, whom they meet regularly in their interfaith councils, and like their Reform brethren, with whom they sit on their local boards of rabbis, they preach every Sabbath. As teachers, they have established and administered elementary and secondary congregational schools, created outstanding programs of adult Jewish education, and founded the Conservative Jewish day school movement. As pioneers of the synagogue-center, they directed and shared in the lives of their multifaceted congregations, co-ordinating and planning social activities to serve their congregants from childhood to old age, overseeing million-dollar budgets and building programs, recruiting new members, and raising funds. Because rabbis in America are also priests and pastors, they have arranged and led services; counseled the sick, the dying, the divorcing, and the disenchanted; served as spokesmen to national and international Jewish organizations; and represented the Jewish community at college graduations, on television, in the corridors of Congress, and at the White House.

Obviously, over centuries the rabbinate has undergone significant transformations. Rabbi, the oldest honorific title in continuous use since the first century C.E., literally means "my master," but came to mean sage. As Robert *Gordis, professor at the Jewish Theological Seminary and one of the leading ideologues of the Conservative movement, has shown, what was at first a calling to teaching and preaching later became a livelihood centered chiefly around the study of Jewish law.[2]

In the Talmudic era, rabbis were sages who interpreted and expounded the written and oral laws. Although they taught, preached, and adjudicated matters of law, they earned their livelihoods as tradesmen and laborers, since Torah had to be taught free of charge. In the Middle Ages, however, the rabbinate became a vocation. In addition to interpreting and expounding the law, rabbis were the spiritual heads of their communities. Because they derived their authority from their knowledge of the law, knowledge necessary for the smooth functioning of the community, they were essential to its welfare and were compensated for their efforts. Although rabbis in the Middle Ages taught and preached, the study of and interpretation of Jewish law gradually became their chief activity.

In the premodern Jewish communities of Eastern Europe, the rabbinic preoccupation with study achieved its greatest heights. In his childhood memoir *In My Father's Court*, Yiddish novelist and Nobel Laureate Isaac Bashevis Singer portrayed his father, a rabbi, who from time to time was forced—in order to earn the meagerest of livings—to break his study of the sacred texts to issue a divorce, to rule on the *kashrut* of a chicken, to answer all manner of questions ("Rabbi, may a man sleep with his dead wife?"), to preach to his followers, or to settle a lawsuit.[3]

The majority of the men who comprised the first two generations of Conservative rabbis in America came directly from this world in which rabbis were the arbiters of legal authority. The rabbis ordained at the Seminary in its first decades were overwhelmingly either born in Eastern Europe or the sons of East European immigrants.[4] Many of them were the sons of Old World rabbis who had spent their lives engaged in sacred study and interpretation of the law and preached but twice a year, on the Sabbaths before Yom Kippur and Passover.

Even as they embarked upon the radical step of entering the American, English-speaking rabbinate, they continued to hold before them the image of their fathers, ensconced in their studies, hidden behind towering piles of tomes of Talmud and *responsa*.

But in America the men who became the first Conservative rabbis found other forces at work shaping the modern rabbinate. At the same time that the rabbi as interpreter and judge held sway in Eastern Europe, elsewhere the emancipation of the Jewries of France, England, and later Germany transformed the rabbinate. Emancipation cost the rabbis the jurisdiction they had previously held in most areas of civil law. It forced them to broaden their education in both Jewish and secular fields at the expense of the traditional study of Talmud and Codes in order to gain the consent of the civil authorities to act as rabbis. As the Jewish communities of Western Europe modernized, their rabbis, especially the evolving Reform rabbinate, found new and necessary tasks to engage them. For the first time in the history of the rabbinate, rabbis functioned as priests and pastors.

The forces of emancipation and modernization that transformed the rabbinate in Western and Central Europe had already been at work in America since the seventeenth century. Because European-trained rabbis avoided the cultural waste-land of Jewish America, for more than two centuries the vast majority of Jews in America had functioned rather well, in their eyes, without qualified religious leadership. Emancipated like the Jews of Western Europe, American Jews no longer turned to rabbis to adjudicate civil disputes or to interpret Jewish law. What they did demand, as the pioneer of Reform Judaism in America, Rabbi Isaac Mayer Wise, observed, was less a rabbi than a jack-of-all-trades, a "teacher, butcher, circumciser, [shofar] blower, gravedigger, secretary." When the first European-trained rabbis immigrated to America in the 1840s, they worked deliberately to model American rabbis into the preachers, pastors, and public functionaries that they had been in Europe.[5]

These rabbis fought an uphill battle. Nineteenth-century American rabbis exercised little authority. The difficulties were so widespread that in the very first conference held by the Reform movement's Central Conference of American Rabbis, the problems of the rabbi's role in modern society appeared on the agenda. To their dismay, rabbis serving the more recent East European Jewish immigrants found their flocks quickly adopting the prevailing American Jewish view of the rabbinate as an unnecessary relic of the Old World hindering their rush toward Americanization.

The status of American rabbis in 1901 on the eve of the founding of the Alumni Association of the Jewish Theological Seminary of America, later known simply as the Rabbinical Assembly (RA), was, therefore, dependent primarily upon the power individual rabbis exercised over their congregants and especially upon the goodwill of their synagogue officers. The result was that rabbis in general were treated shamefully. Salaries were dreadfully low; tenure of office, dependent largely upon renewable one-year contracts, was insecure. "The situation turned into a vicious cycle. The less the authority or material rewards, the less the rabbinical office attracted capable men; and the more that mediocrities filled the office, the more the congregations looked down upon their rabbis.''[6]

It was the extraordinary achievement of the men of the RA to play a major role in ameliorating this disastrous state of affairs. The emergence of the American Conservative rabbinate inaugurated a new stage in the two-millenia-old history of the rabbinate. In the eighty-five years since the founding of the RA, the Conservative rabbinate has undertaken the formidable task of amalgamating the roles of the premodern rabbi and the postemancipation rabbi. The new rabbinic ideal draws upon the traditional roles of the rabbi as student, scholar, saint, and interpreter of Jewish law and tradition. But it also expects the American Conservative rabbi to be an educator and administrator, the director and programmer of his synagogue-center, and a spokesman for the local and national Jewish community. The result has been the transformation of the American rabbinate from a lowly calling into a distinguished and respected profession at home in America.

The RA joined with the Seminary in shaping this new archetype, the American Conservative rabbi. Each of its chief spheres of activity reflected the determination of the men of the RA, out in the field and primarily in synagogue pulpits, to adapt the ancient calling to their new American environs. Their outstanding achievements as a group—the development of professional standards for rabbinic placement, the creation of a literature to disseminate the Conservative viewpoint, and even their ''grand obsession'' with the development of *halachah*—all grew out of efforts to reconcile the past with the present. The men of the Rabbinical Assembly retained their commitment to historic Judaism—its leaders and teachers, *halachah* and texts. But they determined to meet head-on the challenges of contemporary American life. In so doing, the Rabbinical Assembly shaped the rabbinate to reflect its unique American context and thus played a critical role in the Americanization of this historic calling.[7]

THE FOUNDING OF THE SEMINARY ALUMNI ASSOCIATION

By 1901 there were but eleven graduates of the Jewish Theological Seminary of America. The first, Rabbi Joseph H. *Hertz, was ordained in 1894. Five of the eleven were rabbis in Philadelphia, where an active branch of the Jewish Theological Seminary Association paved the way for the Seminary rabbis. Fresh out of school, the Seminary alumni found themselves preoccupied with their new rabbinic posts and with the difficult task of injecting their views into already established congregations. The rabbis were loyal to their alma mater, but given their small numbers, they found no need to band together into any kind of formal association. Informal meetings and contacts well served the eleven graduates, who, after all, had lived and studied together in their Seminary school days.

The events of 1901, however, disrupted this status quo. That year the Seminary faced bankruptcy. No students were ordained. The alumni could not yet envision the reorganization of the Seminary, which within a year would revitalize the moribund institution. In June of 1901 it seemed as if the Seminary would indeed fail. Disaster appeared imminent.

At the same time another urgent matter came to the attention of the Seminary alumni. The Reform rabbinic union, the Central Conference of American Rabbis (CCAR), had scheduled its annual conference for July in Philadelphia. Knowing that several Seminary-trained rabbis lived and worked there, its president, Dr. Joseph Silverman, invited the Seminary alumni to join the conference. Rejecting the CCAR's invitation, the Seminary alumni decided to convene a meeting of their own to discuss, among other subjects, "ways and means of improving the status of their alma mater." On June 17, 1901, in Philadelphia at the home of Menachem *Eichler, Seminary alumni Eichler, Henry *Speaker, Leon Elmaleh, and Julius *Greenstone of Philadelphia joined with fellow graduates Morris Mandel of Atlantic City and Michael Fried of Pittsburgh to found the Alumni Association of the Jewish Theological Seminary.[8]

Having chosen a name for their association—one that would subsequently undergo three metamorphoses—the alumni formulated a program, elected officers, and organized committees to write a constitution and to confer with the Board of Trustees of the Seminary. The Philadelphia weekly the *Jewish Exponent* deemed the meeting newsworthy and published the association's platform. The association's goals were:

First, to help in the promotion of a higher spiritual and scholarly status in the Seminary School. Second, to advance the prestige of the Seminary among other theological institutions. Third, to strive earnestly for the establishment of a stronger financial basis for the Seminary. Fourth, to develop the intellectual and spiritual standing of the members. Fifth, to foster feelings of fellowship and mutual helpfulness among the members.

The writer for the *Jewish Exponent* speculated on the association's future.

It is difficult at this early stage of the Alumni Association's conception to foretell just what position it will earn for itself in the Jewish world. It is impossible as yet to gauge the exact character of its development. It may be the nucleus of what some day may be a very powerful organization on which Judaism, especially in this country, will be obliged to count as a mighty factor. On the other hand, it may be the momentary enthusiasm of a few recently graduated young men whose tender sensibilities have been touched and moved by the unhappy plight of their Alma Mater. . . . Time only can show what the Seminary Alumni Association will be.[9]

The Seminary Alumni Association met for the second time on July 3—timed deliberately to coincide with the convention of the CCAR—at the home of its first president, Henry Speaker. The rabbis adopted a constitution and planned to hold annual conventions where they would present papers on Jewish law, religion, and "vital questions in Judaism." Despite the limited objectives of its published agenda—support for the Seminary and enrichment of its members' lives—the Seminary Alumni Association projected from the very beginning the broad agenda that would engage its successor, the Rabbinical Assembly: all areas of Jewish life were to be within its purview.[10]

ORGANIZATIONAL DEVELOPMENT

In June 1904, in order to celebrate the first graduation exercises of the reorganized Seminary, the Alumni Association held its annual reunion there for the first time. Meeting at the Seminary proved popular. Colleagues, eager to visit the haunts of their school days, to see former professors and old friends, came from as far away as Denver and Montreal. For the remainder of this first decade, the alumni returned annually to the Seminary.

In these early years the Alumni Association showed that its mission was promoting Judaism in America. By 1910 the fifty alumni had already discussed the practical work of the rabbinate—the rabbi as student, pastor, and preacher. Frequent sessions on education, the Sunday school, and the development of instructional materials showed that education was and would continue to be an area in which the rabbis would make great strides. A foreshadowing of what later became an overriding preoccupation with Jewish law occurred in 1904, when Julius Greenstone proposed that the alumni spearhead the establishment of a *bet din*—a Jewish court of law—in America. Discussions of relations to the "foreign ministry" indicated that the alumni would try, all too often without success, to work with their Orthodox rabbinical colleagues in their common mission of promoting Judaism as a religious way of life. Rabbi Jacob *Kohn's 1908 address "Zionism in the Pulpit" demonstrated the Seminary alumni's deep commitment to the burgeoning American Zionist movement. Already, the rabbis revealed ambitious plans for liturgical publications and the establishment of a scientific journal. And they were laying the groundwork for the emergence of the union of Conservative synagogues, the United Synagogue of America.[11]

As the Seminary Alumni Association entered its second decade, several new items—rabbinic placement, the position of women in the synagogue (addressed by Seminary professor Louis *Ginzberg), and the Seminary's training of rabbis—were raised for the first time. This ambitious agenda proved that despite small numbers and modest beginnings, the Seminary alumni were already laying the foundations for the transformation of the Alumni Association, a congenial gathering of school chums devoted to their alma mater, into the Rabbinical Assembly, an organization concerned, as rabbis traditionally have been, with every aspect of Jewish life.[12]

If not yet in name, then certainly in fact, the Alumni Association was more than a fraternity of Seminary graduates. In 1903 the association adopted a resolution prohibiting any members from joining "with any existing national conference or union of rabbis." Apparently, the invitation to join the CCAR was still outstanding. In prohibiting members from affiliating with other rabbinic bodies, the nineteen men of the Seminary Alumni Association showed that they had formed their own "union of rabbis," distinguished from other rabbinic groups by their allegiance to the Seminary and its view of traditional Judaism. Although it would be decades before it would make a formal declaration, the Seminary Alumni Association was paving the way for the emergence of "the international organization of Conservative rabbis," the Rabbinical Assembly.[13]

In 1918 the 121 rabbis of the Seminary Alumni Association reorganized as the Rabbinical Assembly of the Jewish Theological Seminary of America. The RA distinguished itself from its predecessor by opening its ranks to "rabbis other than [Seminary] alumni who are in accord with the principles of traditional Judaism and the aims of the Seminary." In welcoming non-Seminary graduates, the RA became—although not in name—the professional association of the Conservative rabbinate.[14]

Although there were reports that the Seminary alumni had earlier adopted a constitution, not until 1928 did rabbi and lawyer Norman *Salit draft a "definite written constitution" for the RA. It set the following goals:

The object of the Assembly shall be to promote traditional Judaism, to advance the cause of Jewish learning and to cooperate with the Jewish Theological Seminary and the United Synagogue of America in the furtherance of these aims, and to foster the spirit of fellowship among the rabbis and other Jewish scholars of America.[15]

Until 1940 the organization officially remained the Rabbinical Assembly of the Jewish Theological Seminary of America. That year, it became the Rabbinical Assembly of America. Actually, Max *Drob had first proposed the change in nomenclature back in 1926, claiming that the Rabbinical Assembly of the Jewish Theological Seminary of America was too cumbersome a title. Perhaps more troubling were the implications of the name. It unduly reflected the reality that as heir to the Seminary Alumni Association, the RA was the junior partner of the Seminary in the Conservative movement. Only after forty years and the coming of age of a new generation of leaders did the men of the RA sever in name, although certainly not in spirit, that formal deference to the Seminary.[16]

At the same time the RA's constitution was reworked to read: "The object of this organization shall be *to conserve* and promote traditional Judaism" [author's emphasis]. The deliberate addition of the words, "to conserve," brought the RA one step closer to formally declaring that it was an organization committed to the furtherance of Conservative Judaism. Only in 1962 did the revised constitution of what was now simply the Rabbinical Assembly acknowledge that "[t]he object of this organization shall be to promote Conservative Judaism." Seventy-five years after the founding of the Seminary Alumni Association, its heirs at last constituted "the international organization of Conservative rabbis."[17]

Beginning with eleven alumni in 1901, the Seminary Alumni Association grew rapidly as each graduating class of newly ordained rabbis joined its ranks. But when the Alumni Association became the Rabbinical Assembly of the Jewish

Theological Seminary of America in 1918, its members, envisioning even greater growth, opened their ranks to non-Seminary graduates. Apparently few clamored for admission, for a decade passed before the RA established firm criteria for the acceptance as members of rabbis trained outside the walls of the Seminary. Non-Seminary graduates were expected to have *semichah* (traditional rabbinic ordination) or to hold a diploma from a recognized rabbinical seminary. They had to have completed secular education equivalent to a college degree and to adhere "to the practices of traditional Judaism."[18]

The onset of the Depression called into question these plans for continued growth from both within and without the ranks of rabbis trained at the Seminary. In 1930 the 200 members of the RA projected a 50 percent increase by the end of the decade. But rabbis, like all Americans, were already facing the specter of unemployment. The Depression took its toll on synagogues, forcing some to demand voluntary salary reductions and others to fail to meet their payrolls entirely. With unemployment looming on the horizon, some members of the RA suggested that there were enough rabbis. Louis *Finkelstein, then president of the RA and later chancellor of the Seminary, turned the problem on its head. The solution, he perceived, was the creation of more positions, not the training of fewer rabbis. Finkelstein won the debate. Despite the difficulty of finding suitable positions for all its men, the ranks of the RA swelled to 300 members by 1938.[19]

In 1940, with America yet isolated from the conflict in Europe, the RA was still trying to deal with the problems of rabbinic placement brought on by the Depression. But the events of December 7, 1941, changed that situation dramatically. Just as America's entry into World War II mobilized American men and women for the war effort, so too it called upon the men of the RA. The result was the opening of extraordinary opportunities for the Conservative rabbinate.

Following the bombing of Pearl Harbor, Conservative leaders adopted plans for expediting the procurement of Jewish chaplains for the armed forces. This led to the formation of the Chaplaincy Availability Board to prioritize RA men for chaplaincy duty. In 1942 three RA men served as chaplains in the armed forces. By 1944 fully one-third of its men were armed forces chaplains.[20]

The mobilizing of RA men for the chaplaincy raised immediate problems for the Conservative rabbinate. Congregations whose rabbis joined the war effort had to be restaffed somehow. In these critical times the Jewish community at home needed religious leaders more than ever—to help congregations mobilize for the war effort, to console mothers and fathers whose sons were sacrificed to the war, and to lead American Jewry in mourning the growing mass destruction of its brethren in Europe. At the same time the call to the chaplaincy raised manifold opportunities for the rabbinate. Within the first year of war work, chaplains were discovering what would soon become a widespread feeling among the men of the RA—the army provided a rich field for winning men back to the synagogue and to Judaism. The chaplains became convinced that through their close contacts with young soldiers far from home, they were laying the groundwork for Jewish religious life in postwar America.[21]

If the chaplains were right—that Jewish servicemen would return both to home and to the synagogues—the Conservative rabbinate would face a severe manpower shortage in the coming years. Already there were not enough rabbis to cope with the wartime emergency. But if these chaplains succeeded in winning soldiers back to Judaism, when the men returned home as civilians and built their own homes and synagogues, they promised significant growth for Conservative Judaism. Where would the Conservative movement find the manpower to meet this projected growth?

Perhaps the most obvious solution was for the Seminary to ordain more rabbis. In the 1930s the Seminary graduated an average of eight rabbis a year. To meet the needs of the wartime emergency, the Seminary increased its class size and stepped up the rabbinic program, so that in the war years as many as nineteen rabbis were ordained in a single class. By the 1950s classes of thirty rabbis were not uncommon.[22]

The men of the RA determined to play an important role in nurturing these future leaders from within their own congregations. These plans led to the establishment of the Leadership Training Fellowship. Conceived of by Seminary professor and dean of the Teachers Institute Mordecai M. *Kaplan and established in 1946, the Leadership Training Fellowship was a national Conservative high school. Kaplan planned that congregational rabbis would work, in conjunction with the Teachers Institute and the Seminary College of Jewish Studies, with select groups of teens, educating them and encouraging them to enter the Seminary and the Teachers Institute. There the students would embark upon careers as rabbis, teachers, and leaders of American, and especially of Conservative, Jewry. In their work with the Leadership Training Fellowship, the men of the RA would play an active role in recruiting the next generation of Conservative leaders.

But ordaining more rabbis at the Seminary and encouraging the youth of their congregations to careers in the Conservative movement were only partial and at best long-range solutions to Conservatism's shortage of rabbis. Admission of more non-Seminary graduates to the ranks of the RA promised an additional source of manpower. The decision to admit non-Seminary graduates to the RA had prompted, in part, the reorganization of the Seminary Alumni in 1918. But in 1944 rabbi and future RA president Max *Davidson guessed that no more than fifteen or twenty members of the RA had been ordained outside the Seminary. The personnel problem led the RA to charge its Membership Committee to revise its processing of applications to avoid the long delays that in the past had deterred non-Seminary graduates from seeking admission. One year later the process was sufficiently streamlined to allow seven rabbis ordained outside the Seminary to join the RA, including one of its most distinguished members, Jacob *Agus. This brought its total membership to 400 rabbis.[23]

Despite these steps, the RA could not keep pace with the demand for congregational rabbis in the postwar era. Of the 132 congregations seeking rabbis in 1949, nearly 100 positions went unfilled. One factor contributing to the manpower shortage was the growing tendency of RA men to seek careers outside the pulpit. Of the 432 members in 1949, 122 or 28 percent did not serve congregations. In 1949 RA vice-president Max *Routtenberg surveyed his colleagues and found more than a quarter of them engaged in work outside the synagogue. While some served the Conservative movement in administration or were members of the Seminary faculty and a dozen men were retired, some eighty rabbis were employed elsewhere. They were Jewish and secular educators, administrators of Jewish organizations, or military and civilian chaplains. Already a handful had immigrated to the new state of Israel. The overwhelming majority of these non-pulpit rabbis was engaged in careers furthering Jewish life. In fact, a survey of the Conservative rabbinate in 1960 found an astonishingly small number of rabbis—some 6 percent—employed in totally unrelated areas. The men of the RA thus remained committed to the ideals of the rabbinate even though they had left congregational life. Nevertheless, this tendency exacerbated the shortage of rabbis available to meet the demands of Conservative congregations.[24]

To help solve the problem, the Membership Committee resolved in 1953 to raise the proportion of non-Seminary graduates in the RA to 25 percent of its total membership. This plan to welcome large numbers of rabbis ordained outside the Seminary was controversial within the RA. Despite the Membership Committee's promise "to ascertain the compatibility of the applicant[s] with the majority of the members of the Rabbinical Assembly," some members feared these "outsiders" would alter the nature of the RA and disrupt its delicate coalition of rabbis representing the right, left, and center of the Conservative movement. But with the member congregations of the United Synagogue growing rapidly—in 1949 there were 365 congregations; in 1956 there were 599—the view prevailed to admit all qualified rabbis who could serve the burgeoning Conservative movement. By 1957 110 or 22 percent of the 619 members of the RA had been ordained at institutions other than the Seminary.[25]

The RA's explosive growth continued throughout the 1960s. Each new class of Seminary rabbis brought on the average twenty-two new members. Increasing numbers of non-Seminary graduates continued to apply for membership, drawn, according to RA executive vice-president Wolfe Kelman, by its superior placement system and active role in fashioning contemporary Jewish life. Between 1950 and 1980, 600 rabbis belonging to other groups applied for membership in the RA. Yet fewer than ten RA rabbis left for other rabbinic conferences. In 1969 the RA admitted its 1,000th member. It counted members in the United States, Canada, Mexico, Venezuela, Argentina, Brazil, Peru, England, Sweden, India, and Japan as well as Israel. By 1980, 100 of the 1,200 RA rabbis had made their home in the Holy Land.[26]

By the early 1970s, however, the era in which a shortage of congregational rabbis had necessitated the expansion of the RA was over. In 1971 Kelman observed that were it not for the sixty RA members who had immigrated to Israel, the more than one hundred rabbis engaged in academic work, or the personnel employed by the national organizations of Conservatism, there would already be an oversupply of rabbis.[27]

Kelman's observations revealed that the RA was no longer predominantly composed of pulpit rabbis. The tendency, first evidenced in the late 1940s, for rabbis to choose related but alternative careers had accelerated. Some 40 percent of its men did not serve congregations. Instead, Conservative rabbis worked as administrators in the national institutions of the Conservative movement, congregational and community school educators, college professors, authors, Hillel directors, military chaplains, Veterans Administration chaplains, counselors, social workers, and executives of Jewish communal agencies. An increasing number had left the world of professional Jewish service entirely, finding employment in the world of business.[28]

If numbers serve as one measure of significance, then "the momentary enthusiasm" of the few young rabbis of the Seminary Alumni Association had indeed sparked the creation of a large, diverse, and potentially powerful organization, more than 1,200 members strong. Over the course of the twentieth century these men would guide the RA to take its rightful place as a leader within the Conservative movement and among American Jewry.

OUTSTANDING ACHIEVEMENT: THE RABBINICAL ASSEMBLY AS A PROFESSIONAL ASSOCIATION

On the eve of the founding of the Seminary Alumni Association, those entering the rabbinate could expect to be jacks-of-all-Jewish-trades—rabbis, teachers, preachers, cantors, synagogue administrators, and Sunday-school principals— poorly paid for their efforts and often at the mercy of the lay leaders of their congregations. Grumblings at RA conventions in the 1920s about the low status of the rabbinate revealed that little had changed for the better since the Seminary Alumni first organized. With rabbinical contracts rarely running more than a year or two, job insecurity was a serious problem. Rabbis sensed that the often frustrating contractual negotiations with their congregants were always just around the corner. Fear that they might soon have to pull up stakes and uproot their families hindered rabbis from undertaking important long-range projects. Rabbis worried about what would happen if they became ill; how their families would manage when they died. Most of all, the undignified, competitive scramble for the few pulpits open to Seminary graduates demeaned everyone involved. When the Seminary Alumni reorganized as the Rabbinical Assembly, it moved to the top of its agenda the amelioration of the status of the rabbinate.

One of the outstanding achievements of the RA was its raising for the Conservative rabbinate and, therefore, to some extent for all American rabbis, the prestige of the rabbinate in America. It did this partly by winning for rabbis the material benefits accorded to members of other professional and trade organizations. As the RA evolved into a professional association, it fought to gain for its members medical, disability, and life insurance policies; to establish a pension fund; to set standards governing rabbi-congregational relations in such sensitive areas as salary, length of tenure, and severance pay; to regularize vacation, sabbatical, and retirement benefits; and to fix guidelines to regulate relationships among rabbis, assistant rabbis, and rabbis emeriti.

The RA battled long and hard to win these benefits of a "trade union," benefits that became a hallmark of the successful Americanization of the rabbinate. Professional organizations in America promote the material welfare of their members. In providing job and economic security, they foster the well-being and effectiveness of their members on the job. In securing material benefits for its men, the RA showed that the American environment not only influenced the RA's interpretations of *halachah*, its educational programs, and its synagogue services, but that it equally shaped the rabbinate as a livelihood. Some members of the RA growled that its concern with job benefits made it "nothing more than an employment agency catering to a restricted clientele." Nevertheless, to a great extent, the men of the RA established Conservative Judaism among American Jewry. Without question, their path was eased by their growing economic and professional security. It is no wonder that whenever the RA invited members to evaluate its past work the observers were unanimous in listing among its achievements the steps taken to promote the material welfare of the rabbinate. What individual rabbis could not do singly—improving their material welfare and raising the status of the Conservative rabbinate in America—the RA as a whole accomplished.[29]

In addition to fighting for "trade union" benefits for its members, the RA set out to seize control of one other aspect of the professional lives of its members—job placement. The RA's determination to regulate rabbinic placements posed one of the greatest challenges of its early years. Traditionally, both in law and in theory, a Jewish community was free to choose its rabbi and to change him at will. Any rabbi could apply for any position. But as Seminary vice-chancellor Simon *Greenberg observed:

The Rabbinical Assembly, in creating its Placement Commission and in instituting its present procedures, and our congregations in submitting by and large to these procedures, have set new precedents in Jewish history. It has made itself an almost indispensable intermediary between the rabbi and the congregation.[30]

Placement was already on the program of the Seminary Alumni Association. Shortly thereafter, the issue moved to the forefront of the RA's agenda. To the delight of many and to the dismay of some, the RA, in partnership with the Jewish Theological Seminary of America, succeeded in regulating for the entire Conservative movement the field of rabbinic placements. This key transformation of the traditional way of matching rabbis and congregations was another change reflective of the adaptation of the rabbinate to America.

As in so many of its other endeavors, the RA began its efforts by establishing the Placement Committee. This grew out of a study undertaken by rabbis Julius Greenstone, Abraham *Neuman and Jacob Kohn in 1922 to investigate ways of standardizing and dignifying the appointment of rabbis to congregations. Previously, the Propaganda Committee of the United Synagogue, in close cooperation with the presidents of the Seminary, served as an intermediary between rabbis seeking congregations and congregations seeking rabbis. By 1927, however, the RA's Placement Committee had become the official employment agency for RA men. But official recognition did not imply that the Placement Committee operated smoothly, nor that it controlled the employment of all Conservative rabbis.[31]

In its early years a volunteer secretary—Louis Finkelstein held that post in the late 1920s—was in charge of placement. But the effectiveness of the Placement Committee was hampered by factors beyond its control. An extraordinary number of rabbis turned to it, looking for advancement. But there were never enough promotional positions for them, in part because the United Synagogue failed to develop new congregations. The committee was so swamped that it needed its own professional, full-time staff, but no money was available. Most importantly, it was powerless before rabbis who deliberately circumvented its authority by contacting congregations on their own in their rush for new and better positions.[32]

In 1929 Louis *Epstein painted a bleak picture of the placement situation. The committee not only had to find jobs for new Seminary graduates each year, but it also bore the burden of dealing with nearly one-quarter of the men of the RA who were annually hunting for new positions. The poor status of many of the congregations willing to welcome Conservative rabbis forced a majority of the men of the RA to accept pulpits that promised, at best, limited futures of a year or two. Some, Epstein observed, were without positions altogether.[33]

As the Depression deepened, ever greater numbers of rabbis turned to the Placement Committee for assistance. In the fourteen months preceding the RA's 1936 convention, 104 rabbis, more than one-third of the RA, applied for new posts. Many of these found themselves at a disadvantage, because the Placement Committee gave priority to finding pulpits for newly ordained rabbis. Since there was no system to reckon with seniority, a beginning rabbi would often start out in a large congregation that had just become vacant. More experienced rabbis, waiting for this kind of promotional position, never even got the chance to compete.[34]

These matters required the attention of a full-time placement director. Since 1925 the RA had been pleading with the Seminary for the appointment of a field secretary. Plans were made at the beginning of the 1930s for the Seminary, RA, and the United Synagogue to share the costs of a field secretary. But although the RA continued to press for the appointment, the financial exigencies of the Depression consumed the funds set aside for the post.[35]

Although the RA was not successful in hiring a placement director during the 1930s, it did strengthen the effectiveness of the Placement Committee. In 1936 the RA adopted rules and regulations for seeking new rabbinic posts. These prohibited members from applying for positions, whether already vacant or not, on their own. All inquiries were to be handled through the Placement Committee, which reserved for itself the sole right to recommend rabbis to congregations. Any member of the RA who violated these procedures was to answer to the newly established Committee on Professional Ethics.[36]

The Placement Committee entered a new phase with the hiring of Rabbi Bernard *Segal as its executive director in 1945. In 1944 rabbi and lawyer Norman Salit had been engaged by the Seminary to serve as the director of the Wartime Emergency Commission for Conservative Judaism. America's entry into World War II had disrupted rabbinic and congregational relationships. As the war dragged on, it became necessary to hire someone—in essence, the field secretary the RA had sought for the past twenty years—to manage the complex affairs of rabbis, chaplains, and their congregations. Salit served as placement director extraordinaire, overseeing the welfare of the chaplains who left pulpits to enter the armed forces and of the men who replaced them for the duration. He began to plan for the postwar era when chaplains would return to the congregations they had left, when their successors would have to make new arrangements, and when the men who went straight from the Seminary into the chaplaincy would have to find congregations to serve. With the end of the war, the Wartime Emergency Commission, which had been funded by the Seminary, was disbanded. Its activities were assigned to the Placement Committee, and Bernard Segal was appointed executive director.[37]

In 1947 a new position, the executive vice-president of the Rabbinical Assembly, was created by adding to Segal's duties as executive director the general administration of the RA. The lack of full-time personnel had hampered the development of the RA—not just its placement work—since its inception, especially in dealing with the Seminary and the United Synagogue, which employed their own staffs. In the meantime, the RA had become a national, even an international, organization of more than 400 members. Yet it was still led by officers who as full-time congregational rabbis could devote only part of their energies to its affairs. Furthermore, since 1925 RA presidents were limited to holding no more than two one-year terms. The result was a serious lack of continuity among administrations. Projects begun by one president often floundered under the next. In addition, an unwritten rule stipulated that the RA choose its chief executive officers from among the men who lived on the East Coast. The RA simply could not conduct business if its presidents were far from Conservatism's New York headquarters. But the growing geographic diffusion of the men of the RA argued against this restriction. Engaging its own personnel would solve these problems. Professional personnel, working full time for the RA, would relieve its overburdened presidents of cumbersome administrative duties and provide the much-needed continuity among administrations. And with its own full-time administrator housed in Seminary headquarters, the RA could turn to men not from the East Coast for its presidents. This executive personnel would strengthen the RA, allowing it to take its rightful place within the national leadership of the Conservative movement.[38]

Although the executive vice-president was responsible for a wide variety of RA activities, in reality those who have held the office—Bernard Segal (executive director, 1945–47, executive vice-president, 1947–49), Max Routtenberg (1949–51), and Wolfe Kelman (1951–)—were first and foremost placement directors. (Kelman was chiefly responsible for placement only until 1965.) In the immediate postwar years, orchestrating the successful return of demobilized chaplains to congregational pulpits engaged the executive vice-presidents. All wartime replacements for chaplains had to leave their posts whether or not a chaplain returned to his original congregation. A seniority system was established that subjected newly ordained rabbis to a two-year assignment immediately following graduation, a policy first suggested a decade before. Segal also continued efforts to strengthen the effectiveness of the Placement Committee, which changed its name to the Placement Commission to reflect the reality that it was a joint venture of the RA and the Seminary. The commission adopted a code of procedure. And after many years of work the RA finally adopted a code of professional conduct. Written in Hebrew, perhaps because earlier English drafts had been rejected by the membership, it mandated that members abide by the placement regulations.[39]

In the year between the conventions of 1949 and 1950, some 225 congregations turned to the RA for rabbis, and 150 men, or more than 40 percent of the rabbis already engaged in congregational work, applied for new posts. This was a dramatic turnaround from the dim employment situation of but a decade before, when thirty-three members were unemployed. And it augured the beginnings of the extraordinary expansion among the member congregations of the United Synagogue. A large number of RA men eagerly sought these new opportunities.[40]

The large volume of placement work made heavy demands upon the executive vice-presidents and the Placement Commission. Already by 1950 Executive Vice-President Max Routtenberg was pleading for additional personnel to help with placement to free him for essential administrative tasks. That plea went unanswered for nearly a decade, even though the RA was the only rabbinic body in America that expected its executive officer to be both the director of placement and the administrator of its affairs. The RA was fortunate that in its busiest years of placement some of its ablest rabbis—Max Davidson, Louis *Levitsky, Edward *Sandrow, David Goldstein, Armond *Cohen, and Judah *Nadich—took on the burdensome job of chairing the Placement Commission. Only in 1959 did the professional staff of the RA expand, when Jules *Harlow joined as Kelman's assistant and later became director of publications. In 1965 Gilbert *Epstein became director of community services, relieving Kelman of many placement chores, a responsibility he had carried since his Seminary school days as director of student placement. The additional personnel enabled the RA under Kelman's strong leadership to expand its activities and to initiate the many new projects that marked its coming of age.

By the mid-1950s there was a strong sense of growing stability and security among Conservative congregational rabbis. Clearly, the work the RA had accomplished in the past decade in establishing a pension fund and pioneering rabbi-congregational relations played an important role in enhancing their security. Moreover, the wanderlust that characterized the Conservative rabbinate of earlier decades was declining. As the Placement Commission observed, a "decreasing number of men ... *actually require* a change of post [original emphasis]."[41]

Different forces motivated rabbis to change congregations in the postwar era. Aware of the expanding opportunities of the Conservative movement, they looked for the refreshing challenges of a new post, or they aspired to larger congregations and their greater material rewards. Rabbis were so eager to live near a large center of Jewish life, preferably New York City with its Jewish educational opportunities for themselves and their families, that they would even take salary cuts for pulpits near there. There was no shortage of rabbis eager to serve metropolitan congregations of 200 or more families, which could afford to hire a cantor or teacher to assist the rabbi. But the Placement Commission had to struggle to find enough rabbis willing to serve the numerous smaller congregations of a hundred families or less, remote from metropolitan centers, where the rabbi would often find himself the only Jewish professional in the community.[42]

The creation of the post of executive vice-president and the joining of Seminary and RA forces in the Placement Commission had at last systematized rabbinic placement for the Conservative movement. The superior placement system was one of the strengths of the RA, drawing increasing numbers of non-Seminary graduates to its ranks. Nevertheless, given the sensitive work of the Commission—matching rabbis with jobs—it was rarely without its critics.[43]

In 1952, 1970, and again in 1980, the workings of the commission were scrutinized by the RA. One complaint, perhaps inevitably, surfaced each time. The commission was accused of favoritism, especially of those rabbis closest to its New York headquarters, who could more easily maintain frequent contact. Other objections were, however, more successfully addressed. Rabbis believed that the Seminary kept tabs on its graduates and that when it disapproved of a rabbi's practices or ideology, it punished him by preventing him from being recommended to a choice pulpit. This prompted in 1953 a modification in the constituency of the Placement Commission to curtail the powers of the Seminary representatives. Hereafter, their role in recommending rabbis to congregations was confined to the most recent graduates of the Seminary—those with less than five years experience in the pulpit. In the early 1950s criticism of the size, scope, and geographic representation of the commission resulted in its restructuring to make it more representative of the RA. And to make it a full joint commission of the Conservative movement, laymen from the United Synagogue were invited to participate. To enhance the commission's authority, the RA revised its Code of Ethics to provide for gradations in violations of the Placement Code and to fix appropriate sanctions accordingly. As a result, a rabbi charged in 1953 with violating placement regulations resigned from the RA. Renewed concerns over seniority led the commission to develop in 1952 a system that took into account the seniority of experienced men in awarding promotional positions.[44]

Despite efforts to address the criticisms leveled against the Placement Commission, discontent with its methods of operation did not abate. A survey of the RA's membership in 1970 found the not unusual, yet nevertheless high, figure of 30 percent of the RA critical of its work. Part of the dissatisfaction stemmed from the inherent paradox in the nature of the Conservative rabbinate. Conservative rabbis, thanks in large measure to the pioneering achievements of the Rabbinical Assembly, are relatively well-rewarded, paid professionals. Nevertheless, the rabbis prefer to think of themselves not as salaried professionals but as devoted to a calling, the heirs to the traditional East European rabbis whose piety, learning, and otherworldliness they to some extent idealize. Consequently, Conservative rabbis walk a fine line between their self-image as salaried professionals—an image born out of the American setting—entitled to the material rewards of their positions, and their self-image as men of calling, spiritual leaders of their congregants. With difficulty they ask—or wish the Placement Commission to ask—their congregations to provide health and disability insurance, pay the entire annual premium on their retirement funds, supply rent-free housing and repair their parsonages, reimburse them for convention expenses, and award tenure. But as spiritual leaders they feel demeaned by the process of negotiating for these worldly necessities. As Rabbi Gilbert Kollin pointedly illustrated, the rabbis sense this paradox, especially when seeking new pulpits:

[The interview] is still very much the old-time *probeh*, in which the candidate is subjected to a detailed examination of his ritual and theological *tsitsis*, trotted through his forensic paces before a critical crowd and then put on the spot to bargain over salary. The rabbi's stature is demolished in front of the very leadership group he must work with.[45]

The impossibility of reconciling the incongruous self-images of paid professional and spiritual leader helps to explain the high level of dissatisfaction with the RA's "trade union" activities. In the past eighty-five years the RA has made enormous strides in raising the material position and enhancing the status of its members, thanks in large measure to its control of rabbinic placement for the Conservative movement and especially to the strengths of its executive vice-president for more than thirty-five years, Wolfe Kelman. Nevertheless, from within the RA the symbol of these accomplishments, the Placement Commission—one of the RA's outstanding achievements—has never been without its critics.

DISSEMINATING THE CONSERVATIVE POINT OF VIEW: THE PUBLICATIONS PROGRAM OF THE RABBINICAL ASSEMBLY

In 1947 RA executive vice-president Bernard Segal reminded his colleagues that until seven years ago they were officially members of the Rabbinical Assembly of the Jewish Theological Seminary of America. He reflected that the change in name heralded the beginning of a new era for the Rabbinical Assembly of America:

And that act, I believe, marked the emergence of the Assembly as a full-grown rabbinical association, professional in character and national in scope. That act also marked the beginning of a clearer understanding on our part concerning the responsibilities which are ours in this national movement which we call Conservative Judaism.

Segal's confidence grew out of the activities of the RA in recent years. Since 1940 the RA had moved forward in directions only hoped for in the past to carry its share of the burden for establishing Conservative Judaism on a national scale across America.[46]

The Conservative rabbinate recognized that by 1940 Conservatism had matured into an independent Jewish denomination. Synagogue membership following the first shocks of the Depression had plummeted in most Conservative congregations in the early 1930s. But by the beginning of World War II, it had risen to new heights, thanks largely to the concerted efforts of many RA rabbis who zealously led membership drives. The majority of Conservative synagogues emerged from the Depression, according to a survey conducted by the RA Prayer Book Commission, as securely established congregations, a quarter of a century old.[47]

Moreover, in the early 1940s the Conservative movement's financial picture brightened considerably, thanks to the success of the Seminary Campaign, later called the Joint Campaign for the Seminary, United Synagogue, and Rabbinical Assembly. This large-scale fund-raising project led to substantial increases in the financial fortunes of the Conservative movement. The RA shared in the newfound prosperity. In 1940 the RA had a budget of $2,500, which covered the erratic publication of its *Proceedings*, the activities of its Committee on Jewish Law, and some secretarial assistance. By 1946 the RA had an institutional budget of over $15,000, two-thirds of which came from the Seminary Campaign. And an additional $10,000 in personnel expenses were carried directly by the Seminary. Since the RA received a percentage of the proceeds of the campaign, as the latter's revenues increased, so did those of the RA.[48]

The dramatic budgetary growth also signified greater acceptance among American Jewry of Conservatism. The rabbis were already encouraged by growth within their own congregations and by the improving economic base of the movement. Now, as World War II progressed, they were also heartened by the warm reception they received as chaplains among Jewish servicemen in the U.S. armed forces. Sensing that war-weary American Jews welcomed their philosophy of "historic continuity" and that Conservative Judaism was an established movement with national appeal, the RA ambitiously planned to move forward on projects that in the past had seen much debate but little action.

RA president Robert Gordis (1944–46) understood that Conservatism's expanding ambitions and activities raised three challenges for the movement: to strengthen its organizational structure, to ameliorate its comparative failure in the field of education, and to develop a philosophy and literature. He called for the RA to take the lead in launching this agenda, whose key items remained priorities for the RA over the next decades. As indicated above, during Gordis' administration the RA began strengthening its organizational structure, laying the foundations for its transformation into a professional association. In the field of Jewish education the rabbis responded with innovative programs and new directions that were joint ventures of the men of the RA and the United Synagogue. Finally, the RA wasted no time in launching a bold publications program and restructuring its Committee on Jewish Law, actions which were seen as significant steps toward evolving a philosophy for the movement.[49]

Even in the early years of the Seminary Alumni Association, the rabbis made plans for a publications program. A modest one started in the 1920s when the RA began issuing a monthly newsletter, edited by Rabbi Abraham *Burstein. In the early 1920s the RA also planned to publish the *Proceedings* of its annual conventions. But the funds earmarked for this project were initially diverted to establish the Solomon Schechter Memorial Chair at the Seminary. Only in 1928 did the RA produce its first volume of *Proceedings*, a collection of the most important papers and reports presented at its annual convention the year before.[50]

During the Depression the RA managed to maintain these publications irregularly. Not until the 1940s, however, did the RA begin to fulfill those early dreams of a substantial and influential publications program. In the wake of World War II, the men of the RA, many of whom believed that their alma mater had failed to develop a strong ideological base for Conservatism, determined to take the lead in publishing works reflective of Conservative Jewish thought.

As World War II drew to a close, the RA regularized its existing publications. With the end of the war the *Proceedings* began appearing, for the first time, on an annual basis. Now the RA considered other forums for evolving, articulating, and disseminating its view of Conservatism. This led to the launching of the journal *Conservative Judaism* (1945–   ) and the publication of the *Sabbath and Festival Prayer Book* by the Rabbinical Assembly and the United Synagogue (1946). Gordis anticipated that these new publications, along with a series of pronouncements his administration issued on topics such as "Goals and Objectives of Jewish Education," were the beginnings of the creation of a literature necessary to clarify the philosophy of the Conservative movement.

The RA launched *Conservative Judaism* in January 1945 as "clear-cut evidence of the serious desire of our most creative spirits to produce a forum of discussion and research for the crystallization of our philosophy." Its editors promised that all aspects of Jewish life and thought—religious ideas, Jewish law, the changing social and economic scene, Zionism, Jewish education, and especially contemporary Jewish life—would occupy its pages. The journal, generally a quarterly publication, had a rocky early history. Its editor, Leon *Lang (1945–52), had to resort to printing an appeal inviting submissions. Still he had difficulty finding enough suitable articles. Because circulation was poor and expenses high, the project was abandoned in 1952 in favor of diverting funds to a new project—an anthology of readings on Conservative Judaism that the RA ambitiously hoped would become an annual publication.[51]

But some rabbis still felt that the RA needed a continuing, public forum "to clarify and enunciate for ourselves and for the American Jewish community what Conservative Judaism means." Three years later, therefore, *Conservative Judaism* was revived with Samuel *Dresner (1955–64) as editor. The unstinting efforts of a small group of men—Dresner and his editorial board—kept *Conservative Judaism* going over the next decade. But it still remained plagued by inadequate support. With Jack Riemer as editor (1964–65) and the appointment of Jules Harlow as associate editor (1964–80; managing editor, 1962–64), *Conservative Judaism* was redesigned in the hope of increasing circulation and stabilizing the journal. Sensing that the Conservative movement stretched itself by publishing several poorly funded periodicals, the RA also began exploring the possibility of sharing publication of *Conservative Judaism* with the Seminary. In 1968 the journal, then edited by S. Gershon *Levi (1965–69), received a new infusion of funds and source of contributors when it became a joint venture of the RA and the Seminary.[52]

Under the direction of its editors since then, Mordecai *Waxman (1969–74), Stephen C. Lerner (1974–77), Myron Fenster (1977–79), Arthur A. *Chiel (1979–80), Harold *Kushner (1980–84), and David Wolf Silverman (1984–   ), *Conservative Judaism* has established itself as a journal of "serious, critical inquiry of Jewish texts and traditions, legacy, and law; further[ing] the quest for a Conservative theology and ideology; and explor[ing] today's changing Jewish community." Its scholarly articles on Jewish law and literature, the changing roles of women in the synagogue, educational curricula, and the state of the fields of Jewish research—generally, but not exclusively, written by Conservative rabbis and Seminary professors—continue to explore the key themes articulated when it was first founded. Although the RA sensed that the Conservative movement should publish a popular magazine for its laity, it never intended *Conservative Judaism* to become that forum. Instead, the quarterly was designed for the elite—Conservative leaders and readers learned in Judaica. With a paid subscription of 1,600 in 1984, including the 1,200 members of the RA, *Conservative Judaism* has remained influential chiefly among the leadership of the Conservative movement.[53]

The RA's other publications project of the postwar era was its first venture into the field of liturgy. The idea of publishing prayer books for use in the synagogues led by the alumni of the Jewish Theological Seminary was not new. As early as 1909, Rabbi Herman *Rubenovitz, one of the principal movers in the formation of the United Synagogue of America, called for the publication of a revised prayer book as one of the main tasks awaiting the union that he proposed. In 1918 Seminary professors Alexander *Marx and Louis Ginzberg and Rabbi Jacob Kohn began work on a festival prayer book for the United Synagogue. Published in 1927, the *Festival Prayer Book* presented for the first time the three pilgrimage holiday services with English translations in a single volume. Reflecting the very traditional nature of the Conservative movement at this time, it appeared in two editions, one with the traditional text intact and one in which Kohn introduced liturgical emendations for use in more liberal Conservative congregations. The editors presumed that this was merely "the first of a series [of prayer books] planned by the United Synagogue of America to meet the needs of congregations affiliated with it and of American congregations in general."[54]

But the United Synagogue dragged its feet in issuing other prayer books. In the meantime, Conservative rabbis and their congregations were caught in a bind. By the 1920s the rabbis were aware that existing traditional prayer books were inadequate for contemporary Americanized, English-speaking congregants. Consequently, individual rabbis, among them Jacob *Bosniak and Morris *Silverman, turned to publishing their own prayer books as alternatives. Generally, these retained the traditional Hebrew prayers, but they offered higher quality editions, superior English translations, supplementary readings, and songs for congregational singing. In 1933 Silverman founded the Prayer Book Press in Hartford, Connecticut, to publish the large variety of prayer books contemporary worshippers of all ages required. Conservative congregations bought these prayer books for their synagogues. The organized and decorous services afforded by congregants using a single prayer book became a hallmark of Conservative synagogues.[55]

But because the United Synagogue failed to continue to publish or to endorse prayer books for the movement, Conservative synagogues employed a variety of different texts in their services. This had serious implications for the national unity of Conservatism. As worshippers moved from one synagogue to the next, they had to accommodate to different prayer books and to somewhat different services. From a survey conducted in 1942 the members of the RA learned that their congregations used a dozen different texts just on the Sabbath. Similarly, a number of different prayer books were in use on the High Holidays. Moreover, less than one-quarter of the congregations responding to the survey used the *Festival Prayer Book* of the United Synagogue. Surely, the diversity of prayer books was indicative of the disunity within the movement at large, a disunity that the rabbis determined to combat.[56]

As Marshall Sklare has suggested, "Prior to the 1950s the emerging strength of Conservative Judaism on the local level was not reflected on the national scene. The only group that visualized Conservatism in national terms was the rabbis, organized as the Rabbinical Assembly of America."[57] One reflection of this national vision was the decision of the RA to go ahead with its plans to create a prayer book for the movement. The publication of a Sabbath and festival prayer book, to be used by the majority of United Synagogue congregations, would go a long way toward fostering a greater sense of identification among the laity with this "national movement which we call Conservative Judaism." By the early 1940s the RA was convinced that one of its chief responsibilities for directing the future development of Conservative Judaism was the compilation, editing, translation, and creation of prayer books for use in Conservative synagogues.

In the 1930s Morris Silverman had published for the United Synagogue the *Junior Prayer Book* (2 volumes, 1933) and *High Holiday Prayer Book* (1939). Neither the former, intended for junior congregations and instruction, nor the latter, which had yet to gain wide acceptance, obviated the problem of the lack of prayer books for the movement. Moreover, the men of the RA believed that it was their responsibility as "the collective rabbi of the Conservative movement" to create prayer books reflective of the philosophy of Conservatism, prayer books that could win consensus among the movement's rabbis and congregations. The ideological and theological decisions inherent in publishing a Conservative prayer book, they felt, had to be made by a group of experts—the luminaries of the Seminary or the RA—not by an individual or the lay leaders in the United Synagogue.

In the past the Seminary's president, Cyrus *Adler, had unequivocally opposed Conservative prayer books. Determined not to create a new wing within American Judaism, he refused to sanction any steps that unnecessarily marked Conservative Judaism as a separate denomination. The publication of a prayer book, emended to reflect the Conservative viewpoint, fell into the realm of just such interdicted projects. Adler believed that faith, language, and the prayer book had united Israel throughout the ages: "Speaking for myself, I may say without qualifications that the old prayer book and the old service without any innovation whatsoever are entirely satisfactory to me and that I do not feel at home anywhere else." He would not be the one to lead in overthrowing what he understood to have been preserved for four thousand years.[58]

After Adler's death in 1940, the Seminary, under its new president, Louis Finkelstein, showed no signs of departing from this stance and leading the way in liturgical creativity. Meanwhile, the venture of the Reconstructionists, at that time still the left wing of the RA, into prayer book publication spurred the rest of their colleagues. In 1942 the Reconstructionist Foundation published *The New Haggadah*, and three years later it published the *Sabbath Prayer Book*. This activity reflected growing attempts among all wings of the Conservative movement to build a liturgical literature reflective of their particular philosophies.[59]

The RA thus determined that it would take the lead in publishing a Sabbath and festival prayer book for the broad base of the movement. It charged its Prayer Book Commission to research religious ideology, formulate appropriate new prayers, arrange the service, and publish a prayer book "*in keeping with the desired practice of the majority of our congregations*" [original emphasis]. With Robert *Gordis as chairman and Morris Silverman as editor, the Commission began working on revising Silverman's *Sabbath and Festival Services* (Hartford, Conn., 1936) for publication by the RA. In 1944, after three years of activity on the part of the RA's Prayer Book Commission, the United Synagogue—presumptuously in the eyes of the RA—announced plans to issue its own prayer book. Subsequently, the RA joined with the United Synagogue to see if the two bodies could work together on the *Sabbath and Festival Prayer Book*. In so doing, the leadership of the RA retained effective control over its content. Seven of the nine members of the Joint Prayer Book Commission had been presidents of the RA. All were rabbis. But at the same time cooperation with the United Synagogue promised that both the leadership and the laity would accept this prayer book. The 1927 United Synagogue *Festival Prayer Book* was used by only 24 percent of the Conservative congregations. Neither the RA nor the United Synagogue wanted that to be the rate of acceptance for their *Sabbath and Festival Prayer Book*.[60]

When the *Sabbath and Festival Prayer Book* appeared in 1946, Gordis wrote: ''The future chronicler of our movement will probably rank as the most significant single achievement in the direction of a philosophy for Conservative Judaism, the publication of our *Sabbath and Festival Prayer Book*.'' This was, in his estimation, the first effort ''to give expression to the spirit and the approach of our movement, by embodying them in a recognizable pattern of worship, identifiable with our convictions and accessible to the gaze of all, both within and without our ranks.'' Scholars of liturgy have debated the significance of the changes incorporated into the Conservative prayer book. What is not debatable, however, is that the *Sabbath and Festival Prayer Book* played a role in the sharp change that Sklare noted in Conservatism in the 1950s and 1960s. He saw the emergence of a sense on the part of the laity that Conservative Judaism constituted a national movement. By 1949, over 300 of the 365 congregations of the United Synagogue had adopted the *Sabbath and Festival Prayer Book*, enabling Conservative congregants to make themselves at home in almost any Conservative synagogue in America. Clearly, the publication of the *Sabbath and Festival Prayer Book* was a contributing factor in the laity's ''transmut[ing] their loyalty to local congregations into attachment to a national movement.''[61]

The RA's efforts to foster unity and to develop Conservative Judaism on a national scale by publishing a prayer book for the movement rank among its most important successes. In the overwhelming majority of Conservative synagogues in America, the use of the *Sabbath and Festival Prayer Book* symbolized that Conservative Judaism was indeed a national movement, that it had come of age. This prayer book, with its prayers for ''our country'' and the national anthem, also symbolized the continuing evolution of Conservative Judaism as a distinctly American version of Judaism. Its wide acceptance strengthened the RA as a professional association, for the RA earmarked the considerable revenue from its sales to personnel and pension funds—and to the future publication of more prayer books. The rabbis recognized that ''[a] congregation which adopts *our prayer books* is by that very act putting a distinctive stamp upon itself and forging ties of unity and cooperation with the movement as a whole'' [emphasis added].[62]

The rabbis knew that Conservative congregants needed all sorts of specialized prayer books and services—for weekdays, for High Holidays, for the home, for houses of mourning, for joyous celebrations, for junior congregations, for summer camps, and even for Conservative synagogues in Israel. They envisioned the *Sabbath and Festival Prayer Book* as but their first step in the RA's creation of a liturgy for the movement. Therefore, as soon as it appeared, the RA immediately began working on its next venture into the field of liturgy—the weekday prayer book.

Many—including Gordis—thought that with the basic principles and techniques already established and the bulk of the translation work already done for the *Sabbath and Festival Prayer Book*, the weekday prayer book would appear in no time. But fifteen years passed before the RA published the *Weekday Prayer Book* (1961). Several factors caused the unanticipated delay. First and foremost, the thorny issues of content—the translation and, when essential, emendation of the classical prayers to bring them into consonance with modern thought—remained difficult stumbling blocks. Although the Prayer Book Committee could have endorsed existing prayer books in the name of the RA or edited to its satisfaction someone else's text, it refused to do so. Instead, because it saw its work as a critical part of the RA's role in creating a literature and philosophy for Conservatism, it determined to fashion the prayer book by committee—"a return to the noble example of cooperative thinking in our sacred literature of the past." But with almost all committee members holding primary responsibilities elsewhere as pulpit rabbis, the project could scarcely merit their undivided attention. Finally, the RA's long-standing problem of insufficient staff, especially in the era of Conservatism's rapid physical growth, meant that no one in RA headquarters had the time to oversee the project.[63]

In 1946 the Joint Prayer Book Commission of the RA and the United Synagogue, led now by Rabbi Max *Arzt, who was also director of the Seminary's Field Service and Activities and later vice-chancellor of the Seminary, began working on the weekday prayer book. As it had done with the *Sabbath and Festival Prayer Book*, the commission originally planned to edit another of Morris Silverman's manuscripts. But several years into the project, the RA backed out of the Joint Commission. Although the RA enjoyed the cooperation of the United Synagogue in selling the prayer books to member congregations, the rabbis had never liked sharing responsibility for liturgical creativity with Conservatism's lay branch. The Prayer Book Committee, reorganized solely as an agency of the RA, with Baltimore rabbi Jacob Agus as chairman, abandoned Silverman's text in order to start from scratch "to make [the weekday prayer book] truly the work of a movement as a whole." Agus' committee produced a manuscript, but the RA Executive Council raised objections to its content and translations. Next, rabbis Jack Riemer and Max Arzt and Hebrew literary scholar Arnold Band prepared alternative readings. Still the prayer book failed to win a consensus. Finally, in November 1957, Kansas City rabbi Gershon Hadas agreed to take charge of the project and to begin working on new translations. In 1959, fresh out of the Seminary, Rabbi Jules Harlow joined the RA as its second executive officer. Appointed secretary of the Prayer Book Committee, he was charged with getting the weekday prayer book to press. Published solely under the auspices of the RA, the *Weekday Prayer Book* appeared in 1961. Its first edition immediately sold out. By 1965 it had sold over 20,000 copies.[64]

Since then, the RA has published a number of other "official" prayer books and services for the movement: a pamphlet for the midnight service, *Selichot* (1964); *Yearnings* (1968) and *Yearnings II* (1974), supplementary readings and meditations for the Days of Awe; the landmark *Mahzor for Rosh Hashanah and Yom Kippur* (1972), graced by Harlow's moving mourner's prayer—interspersed among the lines of the *kaddish* are the names of the death camps; *The Feast of Freedom: A Passover Haggadah* (1982); and most recently, the lovely *Siddur Sim Shalom* (1985), a new prayer book for Sabbath, festivals, and weekdays, published once again jointly by the RA and the United Synagogue. Much of this creativity has been the work of the chief liturgist of Conservatism, Jules Harlow. As RA director of publications, he has played a major role as editor and translator in nearly all of the liturgical publications of the RA over the past quarter century. His prayer books, especially *Siddur Sim Shalom*, reveal a command of and sensitivity for the traditional and contemporary sources of Jewish creativity; a vision that the participation of women, remembrance of the Holocaust, and the reality of the state of Israel belong in modern Jewish liturgy; and a concern for aesthetics that make these volumes a delight to behold. Harlow helped put the RA on the map—along with the Reform movement's Central Conference of American Rabbis—as one of the leaders in American Jewish liturgical creativity.[65]

The prayer books and *Conservative Judaism* were not the only literary activities of the RA's publications program. The RA's third literary project to disseminate Conservative philosophy dates to the publication of *Tradition and Change* (1958). Edited and with an introductory survey of the Conservative movement by Rabbi Mordecai Waxman, *Tradition and Change* was the anthology that the RA had planned in 1952—and been proposing since 1930—when it temporarily suspended publication of *Conservative Judaism*. When the volume appeared—again after the usual delays—it brought together scattered articles and addresses by representative figures of Conservatism—Solomon *Schechter, Mordecai Kaplan, Cyrus Adler, Louis Finkelstein, Robert Gordis, Simon Greenberg—and pronouncements by its official bodies, including the RA's Committee on Jewish Law and Standards. The anthology incorporated the diversity of views within the Conservative movement under the broad rubrics of the origins of Conservatism, its philosophies, and its attitudes toward prayer, Jewish law, education, the community, and Zionism. Without ever explicitly acknowledging Marshall Sklare's sociological study, *Conservative Judaism* (1955), the RA used the anthology to set forth its opposing view "that there is a clearly defined Conservative movement, that it has an ideology, and that it is considerably more than the product of American sociological forces."[66]

Although the RA ambitiously planned annual anthologies of the best of Conservative thought, Waxman's volume remained the sole work in this genre for two decades. In 1977 the RA revived the scheme with the series *Emet Ve-*

Emunah: Studies in Conservative Jewish Thought. It continues the work of what Gordis called the two principal items on the agenda of Conservative Judaism—"crystallizing and articulating a philosophy of Jewish faith and practice for the movement" and building a committed laity. To date, three volumes have appeared in the series. Each contains essays and addresses by men primarily but not exclusively identified with the Jewish Theological Seminary or the RA's right and left wings. The first, *Conservative Judaism and Jewish Law* (1977), surveyed the common denominators and the wide range of views of *halachah* in the Conservative movement. The second, *Understanding Conservative Judaism* (1978), gathered diverse articles and addresses of one of its chief spokesmen, Robert Gordis, explaining Conservative thought on a variety of issues including prayer, day schools, the rabbinate, and the Conservative movement in Israel. Most recently, *God in the Teachings of Conservative Judaism* (1985) explored Conservative leaders' responses to the age-old questions of the knowledge of the existence of the Divinity and the persistence of evil in the Creator's world.[67]

For nearly a century the men of the RA tried time and again to articulate Conservatism's ideology and repeatedly bemoaned their inability and that of the movement at large to do so. Just as Reform Judaism, in its platforms of 1885, 1937, and 1976, had defined the parameters of its thought, so too Conservative leaders, led by Robert Gordis, chariman of the Commission on the Philosophy of Conservative Judaism, have at last reached a consensus upon what prevails in their ranks. In 1988 they joined together to publish the first *Statement of Principles of Conservative Judaism*. In the past the RA's publications program—*Conservative Judaism*, the prayer books, and anthologies—along with the work of its Committee on Jewish Law and Standards presented to committed laity just what Conservative Judaism stands for. Now the *Statement* marks the culmination of decades of effort to articulate Conservative ideology. Distributed in many synagogues to every congregant, it synthesized Conservative philosophy. Meant to spark a public discourse among Conservative Jews, it is designed to guide them to live their lives according to its vision of what it means to be a Conservative Jew at home in America.[68]

NOTES

1. Wolfe Kelman, "Report of the Executive Vice-President," *PRA 1957* vol. 21, p. 22.

2. Robert Gordis, "The Rabbinate: Its History, Functions, and Future," (1957), reprinted in his *Understanding Conservative Judaism* (New York, 1978), pp. 168–90.

3. Isaac Bashevis Singer, *In My Father's Court* (1962; reprint ed., New York, 1983). The question appears on page 29.

4. On the familial background of the Conservative rabbinate, see Arthur Hertzberg, "The Conservative Rabbinate: A Sociological Study," in *Essays on Jewish Life and Thought*, ed. Joseph Blau (New York, 1959), pp. 309–32.

5. Naomi Cohen, *Encounter with Emancipation* (Philadelphia, 1984), pp. 190–94;

Wise quoted in Cohen, p. 191; on the development of a new rabbinic type in America, see Leon Jick, *The Americanization of the Synagogue, 1820–1870* (Hanover, New Hampshire, 1976), pp. 8–10, 58–78.

6. Cohen, *Encounter*, p. 192.

7. On *halachah*, see the introduction.

8. *JE* 21 June 1901, p. 10; Max Routtenberg, "The Conservative Rabbinate," *PRA 1960*, reprinted in Max Routtenberg, *Decades of Decision* (New York, 1973), pp. 118–19.

9. *JE* 28 June 1901, p. 7.

10. *JE* 12 July 1901, p. 3.

11. *JE* 31 July 1903, p. 3; 10 June 1904, p. 7; 16 June 1905, p. 2; 7 June 1907, p. 1ff.; 12 June 1908, p. 8ff.; 11 June 1909, p. 8; 3 June 1910, p. 2.

12. *JE* 9 June 1911, p. 9; 14 July 1911, p. 8ff; 28 June 1912, p. 6; 5 July 1912, p. 6; 27 March 1914, p. 2; 29 June 1917, p. 9; 6 July 1917, p. 2; 28 June 1918, p. 2.

13. *JE* 31 July 1903, p. 3; "The Revised Constitution of the Rabbinical Assembly," *PRA 1977* vol. 39, p. 153.

14. *JE* 28 June 1918, p. 2; on the development of the RA, see also Abraham J. Karp, "The Conservative Rabbinate—Dissatisfied But Not Unhappy," *AJA* 35, 2 (November 1983), pp. 188–262.

15. *PRA 1928* vol. 2, pp. 18, 187–90; *Recorder* 3, 2 (April 1923), p. 9. The author has been unable to locate copies of the 1901 and 1923 constitutions.

16. *PRA 1940* vol. 7, pp. 17–23; Max Drob, "For a Militant Assembly," *Recorder* 6, 4 (October 1926), p. 26. On the deference of the alumni to the Seminary, see Marshall Sklare, *Conservative Judaism* (1955; reprint ed., Lanham, Md., 1985), pp. 186–88.

17. "Revised Constitution of the Rabbinical Assembly," *PRA 1962* vol. 26, pp. 246–51; *PRA 1977* vol. 39, pp. 153–59.

18. *PRA 1928* vol. 2, pp. 10–11, 187–90.

19. Louis Finkelstein, "Presidential Address," *PRA 1930* vol. 4, pp. 13–19; Simon Greenberg, "The President's Message," *PRA 1938* vol. 5, p. 423.

20. *PRA 1942* vol. 8, pp. 56–60; *PRA 1943* vol. 8, p. 164; *PRA 1944* vol. 8, p. 282.

21. Harry Nelson, "A Chaplain's Pulpit," *PRA 1943*, pp. 200–206; Isaac Klein, *The Anguish and the Ecstasy of a Jewish Chaplain* (New York, 1974), esp. pp. 40–48.

22. JTS Rabbinical Department Lists.

23. *PRA 1945* vol. 9, pp. 16, 29–30; Robert Gordis, "Annual Report of the President," *PRA 1945* vol. 9, pp. 32–43.

24. Max Routtenberg, "Report of Executive Vice-President," *PRA 1949* vol. 13, pp. 27–38; Eli Ginzberg, "Manpower for Conservative Judaism," *PRA 1960* vol. 24, pp. 19–30.

25. *PRA 1953* vol. 17, p. 87; *PRA 1956* vol. 20, pp. 37–38; *PRA 1957* vol. 21, pp. 29–31.

26. "Reports of the Membership Committee," *PRA 1960–1969* vols. 24–33; Wolfe Kelman, "Report of the Executive Vice-President," *PRA 1980* vol. 42, p. 14.

27. Wolfe Kelman, "The American Synagogue: Present and Prospects," *CJ* 26, 1 (Fall 1971), p. 23.

28. *PRA 1975* vol. 37, p. 259. Rabbi Howard Singer claims that the loss to non-related fields is between 20 and 40 percent; Singer's response to "Letters from Readers," *Commentary* 80, 3 (September 1985), p. 23.

29. Aaron Blumenthal, "The Status of the Rabbinical Assembly in the Conservative

Movement,'' *PRA 1955* vol. 19, p. 126; Robert Gordis, "The Rabbinical Assembly and Conservative Judaism: Retrospect and Prospect," *PRA 1965* vol. 29, pp. 88–89.

30. Simon Greenberg, "The Role of the Rabbinical Assembly," *PRA 1955* vol. 19, p. 146.

31. *Recorder* 2, 2 (April 1922), p. 13; *PRA 1927* vol. 1, p. 21.

32. *PRA 1928* vol. 2, pp. 19–20.

33. "Report on the Proposed Reorganization of the Placement Committee," *PRA 1929* vol. 3, pp. 119–25.

34. Eugene Kohn, "President's Message," *PRA 1936* vol. 5, pp. 263–64; *PRA 1936* vol. 5, pp. 244–45.

35. *Recorder* 5, 1 (January 1925), p. 21; *PRA 1931* vol. 4, p. 134.

36. "Rules and Regulations for the Guidance of the Rabbinical Assembly of America as adopted by the Executive Council, May 13, 1936 and amended May 13, 1946," *PRA 1945* vol. 10, pp. 314–15; "Report of the Committee on Professional Ethics," *PRA 1937* vol. 5, pp. 342–49.

37. *PRA 1945* vol. 9, p. 11–13; *PRA 1946* vol. 10, p. 52.

38. Israel M. Goldman, "The Rabbinical Assembly of America in the Contemporary World: Presidential Message," *PRA 1947* vol. 11, pp. 141–42.

39. Max Davidson, "Report of the Placement Committee," *PRA 1946* vol. 10, pp. 316–17; Bernard Segal, "Report of the Executive Vice-President," *PRA 1947* vol. 11, p. 31; *PRA 1937* vol. 5, p. 344.

40. *PRA 1950* vol. 14, p. 35; *PRA 1940* vol. 7, p. 26.

41. "Report of the Placement Commission," *PRA 1954* vol. 18, pp. 95–97.

42. Wolfe Kelman, "Report of the Executive Vice-President," *PRA 1961* vol. 25, pp. 123–24.

43. Wolfe Kelman, "Report of the Executive Director," *PRA 1955* vol. 19, pp. 20–21.

44. *PRA 1952* vol. 16, pp. 80–86; *PRA 1970* vol. 34, pp. 216–17; *PRA 1980* vol. 42, pp. 260–67; Simon Greenberg, "The Jewish Theological Seminary of America," *PRA 1960* vol. 24, p. 150; Ira Eisenstein, "President's Message", *PRA 1953* vol. 17, p. 140.

45. Harry Gersh, "The Survey on Rabbinic Status," *Beineinu* 1, 3 (March 1971), p. 63–64; *Beineinu* 3, 1 (January 1973), pp. 24–26; Gilbert Kollin, "Placement," *Beineinu* 1, 2 (January 1971), pp. 3–8.

46. Bernard Segal, "The Rabbinical Assembly: Expanding Its Organizational Structure," *PRA 1947* vol. 11, p. 363.

47. "Report of the Prayer Book Commission," *PRA 1942* vol. 8, pp. 155–56.

48. Max Arzt, "Our Expansion Program: A Revaluation," *PRA 1946* vol. 10, pp. 206–30.

49. Robert Gordis, "President's Address: New Vistas for Conservative Judaism" *PRA 1946* vol. 10, pp. 59–60; on developments in education, see the essay on the United Synagogue; on the Law Committee, see the introduction.

50. *Recorder* 4, 3 (June-July 1924), p. 28; Drob, "Militant Assembly," p. 26.

51. Robert Gordis, "The Tasks Before Us," *CJ* 1, 1 (January 1945), pp. 5–6; "An Appeal to our Colleagues and Readers," *CJ* 4, 2 (Fall 1948), pp. 24–26; *PRA 1953* vol. 17, pp. 145–46.

52. *CJ* 10, 1 (Fall 1955), p. 1; *PRA 1962* vol. 26, pp. 129, 136.

53. *CJ* 37, 2 (Winter 1983–84), pp. 1, 80.

54. Herman and Mignon Rubenovitz, *The Waking Heart* (Cambridge, Mass., 1967), pp. 82–83, 139–40, 148–53; United Synagogue of America, *Festival Prayer Book*, ed. Alexander Marx et al. (New York, 1927), p. iii.

55. Jacob Bosniak, *Prayers of Israel: For the Sabbath and the Festivals* (Brooklyn, 1925; rev. 1937); Morris Silverman, *Sabbath and Festival Services* (Hartford, Conn., 1936); *PRA 1942* vol. 8, p. 147.

56. "Report of the Prayer Book Commission," *PRA 1942* vol. 8, pp. 148–50.

57. Sklare, *Conservative Judaism*, p. 257.

58. Adler quoted by Herbert Parzen in *Architects of Conservative Judaism* (New York, 1964), pp. 98–100.

59. Mordecai Kaplan, Eugene Kohn, and Ira Eisenstein, eds., *The New Haggadah for the Pesach Seder* (New York, 1942; rev. 1972); Mordecai M. Kaplan, Eugene Kohn, Ira Eisenstein, and Milton Steinberg, eds., *Sabbath Prayer Book* (New York, 1945).

60. *PRA 1941* vol. 8, pp. 4–25; *PRA 1942* vol. 8, pp. 155–56; *PRA 1944* vol. 8, pp. 278–87; Robert Gordis, "Introduction to the Sabbath and Festival Prayer Book," (New York, 1946), reprinted in Mordecai Waxman, *Tradition and Change* (New York, 1958), p. 335.

61. Robert Gordis, "New Vistas," *PRA 1946* vol. 10, p. 63; Robert Gordis, "Reinterpretation—Its Canons and Limits," *CJ* 13, 4 (Summer 1959), p. 21; *CJ* 5, 1–2, (October-January, 1948–49), back cover; Sklare, *Conservative Judaism*, p. 260.

62. Aaron Blumenthal, "Presidential Address," *PRA 1958* vol. 22, pp. 49–50.

63. Robert Gordis, "Message," *PRA 1945* vol. 9, p. 48; Jacob Agus, "Report of the Prayer Book Committee," *PRA 1953* vol. 17, p. 98; *PRA 1959* vol. 23, p. 125.

64. *Weekday Prayer Book* (New York, 1961; 2d ed., 1962; 3rd ed., 1974); *PRA 1965* vol. 29, p. 15.

65. *Selichot* (New York, 1964); Jules Harlow, ed. and trans., *Yearnings* (New York, 1968), *Mahzor for Rosh Hashanah and Yom Kippur* (New York, 1972), *Yearnings II* (New York, 1974), *Siddur Sim Shalom* (New York, 1985); Rachel Anne Rabinowicz, *The Feast of Freedom: A Passover Haggadah* (New York, 1982).

66. Waxman, *Tradition and Change*, pp. 3–4; *PRA 1930* vol. 4, pp. 10–11.

67. Seymour Siegel with Elliot Gertel, eds., *Conservative Judaism and Jewish Law* (New York, 1977); Robert Gordis, *Understanding Conservative Judaism* (New York, 1978), p. xi; Seymour Siegel and Elliot Gertel, eds., *God in the Teachings of Conservative Judaism* (New York, 1985). Other publications of the RA in the postwar period were intended exclusively for the rabbis. These included the *Rabbinical Assembly Manual*, a collection of benedictions, prayers, and services for all occasions, from the naming of a newborn to the synagogue's mortgage-burning ceremony, edited by Isidore Signer (New York, 1952) and revised by Jules Harlow (New York, 1965); *Beineinu* (1971–), a journal, which temporarily replaced the *Proceedings of the Rabbinical Assembly* in 1971 and 1972 and became an open forum for the 1,200- member-plus Assembly; and the newsletter, *Rabbinical Assembly News* (1983–).

68. Jewish Theological Seminary of America, Rabbinical Assembly, United Synagogue of America, Women's League for Conservative Judaism, Federation of Jewish Men's Clubs, *Emet Ve-Emunah: Statement of Principles of Conservative Judaism* (New York, n.d.).

A UNION OF CONSERVATIVE CONGREGATIONS: THE UNITED SYNAGOGUE OF AMERICA

THE FOUNDING OF THE UNITED SYNAGOGUE OF AMERICA

More than a quarter of a century after the establishment of the Jewish Theological Seminary of America and more than a decade after the Seminary alumni organized their association, the third central institution of American Conservatism, the United Synagogue of America, was launched in 1913. For some time the leaders of the Seminary had assumed that the Union of Orthodox Jewish Congregations of America would attract the traditional forces of American Jewry to stand behind the Seminary. In 1898 the founders of the early Seminary had helped bring the union into being to provide just such support. But within a few short years the leaders of the newly reorganized Seminary recognized that even though young Seminary rabbis and their congregations continued their activity in the union, large social and cultural differences, as well as ideological divisions, had moved the union away from the Seminary. The Seminary group discovered that it was the only school of American Judaism without a congregational union.[1]

At the same time Seminary president Solomon Schechter recognized that support for his school was waning. His espousal of Zionism had alienated the mostly non-Zionist Seminary directors. The founding of the American Jewish Committee in 1906 by largely these same men, the establishment of Dropsie College in Philadelphia as an institute for advanced Jewish study, and the creation of the New York *Kehillah* in 1909 had siphoned off support for the Seminary. The foundering of the Seminary branches established in various cities to help sustain the school made it clear that the Seminary lacked a strong constituency. With these events ominously paralleling the conditions that had caused the old Seminary to falter, Schechter was forced to conclude that he must do what he had so long avoided, establish a third federation of synagogues to champion the Seminary and its policies.

In 1909 Schechter conveyed his scheme for building a following for the Seminary to friends, colleagues, and the Alumni Association. By this time he was not the only Conservative leader concerned with the narrow base of support. Seminary rabbis in synagogues in Boston, Denver, and Louisville, Kentucky, felt isolated. They were struggling valiantly in the field, trying to guide congregations whose members included older immigrants, their acculturated immigrant children, and the latter's American-born children, as each group asserted a different view as to what was and was not proper in a traditional synagogue. The rabbis wanted institutional backing to relieve their isolation and to help them introduce to their congregations the synthesis of modernity and tradition that was the cornerstone of their Seminary training. They were made keenly aware of the urgency of the problem, watching with frustration as many congregants, alienated by the East European traditionalism of their synagogues, turned away to Reform temples. The rabbis knew that a union of Conservative congregations could become their springboard for shaping the American Conservative synagogue and stopping the exodus.

In the fall of 1909 Rabbi Herman *Rubenovitz suggested to Seminary alumni president Charles I. *Hoffman that the graduates of the Seminary take the lead in forming "a union of conservative forces in America." The proposal was a key item on the agenda of the 1910 annual alumni meeting. Along with Jacob *Kohn and Mordecai M. *Kaplan, Hoffman and Rubenovitz, as chairman, formed the Committee on Conservative Union to plan for its establishment. Soon Schechter agreed to lead the committee to mediate the differences that had arisen between Cyrus *Adler and the alumni leaders over the mission of the organization. Although Adler's opposition to an aggressive platform and the use of the word *conservative* in the organization's title prevailed, the organization of the United Synagogue of America may rightly be considered the first major achievement of the Seminary Alumni Association.[2]

On February 23, 1913, representatives from twenty-two congregations and four academic institutions and invited rabbis met at the Seminary and founded the United Synagogue of America. Although the provisional name Agudath Jeshurun had been proposed, the organization emerged as the United Synagogue of America, a Union for Promoting Traditional Judaism. Most likely, this title reflected the participation of Seminary alumnus Joseph *Hertz, who had just been elected Chief Rabbi of the United Synagogue of the British Empire. Schechter was elected the first president of the United Synagogue of America (1913–14), and a board of twenty-one was chosen to work with him. Congregational affiliation was the chief unit of membership, although, until the bylaws were changed in 1918, institutions of higher learning, members of their faculties, and individual laymen and rabbis could also join.

The preamble to the constitution of the United Synagogue committed it to "embrac[ing] all elements essentially loyal to traditional Judaism." Its goals were to advance Jewish life in America, specifically the observance of the Sabbath and dietary laws; to promote Jewish religious life in the home; and to foster

Jewish education. It was committed to maintaining the traditional character of worship with Hebrew as the language of prayer and to upholding "loyalty to the Torah and its historical exposition." But while the United Synagogue did not endorse ritual and ceremonial innovation, neither did it commit itself to a blanket acceptance of *halachah*.[3]

In addressing the founding meeting, Schechter presented his vision of the organization and proposed its early agenda. The speech, which was never published in his lifetime, gave the Seminary rabbis the support they so sorely needed. In order to make traditional Judaism viable on the North American continent, in order for the Conservative synagogue to become a bulwark against assimilation, it would have to embrace Schechter's program. It included maintaining decorous behavior in worship; employing rabbis and teachers trained in scientific research; establishing educational programs consonant with modern pedagogy; and introducing English-language sermons, since "in our days [the sermon is] the only means of making the public acquainted with the word of God, the tenets of Judaism, and the history of Israel's heroic sufferings."[4]

Schechter's vision of the United Synagogue was a broad one. He claimed that he was not founding a new party but rather consolidating an old one. The United Synagogue would therefore welcome all congregations that were not avowedly Reform, that is, congregations that neither used the *Union Prayer Book* nor worshipped with uncovered heads. But he recognized that the United Synagogue could learn from both those who stood to its right and those who stood to its left. He hoped that it would emulate the "enthusiasm and intensiveness" of Orthodoxy and borrow the structural organization essential to accomplish its goals from Reform.

Finally, Schechter enumerated the key items of what emerged as the broad agenda of the United Synagogue: field work to lay the foundations for the development of new congregations, whose membership would strengthen the association; organizational work to enlist the support of all those, especially Jewish women, who could help the United Synagogue achieve its goals; and educational work to guide the next generation to Judaism as a religious life, the key to Jewish survival in America. Schechter never spelled out the details of these activities, but his agenda established the chief priorities of the United Synagogue and directed its development.

ORGANIZATIONAL DEVELOPMENT

When the United Synagogue was created in 1913, its twenty-two member congregations hardly constituted Conservative Judaism as a viable force in America. Instead, the United Synagogue was meant to become a tool for promoting the triumph of historical Judaism in America. Because Conservatism was a fledgling movement, the leaders of the United Synagogue saw its mission as laying the foundations for the future by pioneering new congregations and drawing established ones into a loose confederation of synagogues. Its very existence would constitute the movement. The goal thus became first and foremost greater numbers. Other issues—among them embracing a program for the synagogue that epitomized Conservative ideology and setting appropriate congregational standards—would have to wait. Consequently, the United Synagogue emerged initially as an institution chiefly concerned with expansion—with the field and organizational work necessary to attract Jewish men, women, and their congregations to affiliate with what came to be known as Conservative Judaism.

The early triumph of the proponents of "extensity" set the scene for these developments. Extensity was championed by the United Synagogue's second president, Cyrus Adler (1914–17). Adler, who was also president of the Seminary (1916–40), succeeded Schechter at the United Synagogue when ill health forced the latter's resignation. The new president decided that the major focus of the United Synagogue should be to affiliate large numbers of congregations. Because Schechter had left broad guidelines for the inclusion of all congregations except those that were openly Reform, the result was great diversity among its members. Of the three founding congregations that later seceded from the United Synagogue, Denver's Beth HaMedrosh Hagadol and Philadelphia's Mikveh Israel joined the Union of Orthodox Jewish Congregations, and Newark, later Livingston, New Jersey's Temple B'nai Abraham, in 1986 unaffiliated with any congregational union, considered itself the best of both the Reform and Conservative movements.[5]

The opponents of extensity, a minority led by Seminary homiletics professor Mordecai M. Kaplan, urged "intensity" to develop an organization with esprit de corps. They wanted to lead those congregations already affiliated with the United Synagogue to unite around a defined program and ideology. The results of the triumph of the extensists were twofold: the United Synagogue did grow rapidly in its early years, but its desire to embrace all possible members prevented it from forging solidarity and intercongregational cooperation. Instead, a loose confederacy of independent congregations emerged that failed to project a national vision of Conservative Judaism. It became, as observers of Conservatism noted, largely a "paper organization."[6]

During the formative period of the United Synagogue, more pressing items sapped the creative forces of American Jewry. The ravages of World War I, relief to beleaguered brethren in Eastern Europe, the extraordinary developments in the Zionist movement, the controversy over the American Jewish Congress, and the ongoing struggle between the dominant German Jews of the old guard and the new East European immigrants vying for the leadership of American Jewry—all took precedence over the less spectacular development of but another American Jewish organization. Against this larger background, the rapid growth of the United Synagogue, which expanded as new congregations responded to its outreach and affiliated with the federation, stands as a notable achievement of its early years. While it did not become the organization its critics wished, this loose confederacy of synagogues became a base for the future growth of Conservative Judaism in America.

The keys to its development were the field and extension work its leaders conducted, with the United Synagogue Committee on Propaganda paving the way. Chaired by Newark, New Jersey, rabbi Charles I. Hoffman (United Synagogue corresponding secretary, 1913–43), the Committee on Propaganda secured the cooperation of rabbis throughout the country, sent its advocates on pastoral tours, issued press releases, and even served as an early placement bureau for Seminary rabbis. Meanwhile, representatives of the United Synagogue, most often Seminary-trained rabbis, negotiated with individual congregations for affiliations. In the twelve months preceding the 1915 annual convention, the United Synagogue explored with sixty-six synagogues the possibility of membership.[7]

By 1917 the United Synagogue required and was able to hire a chief executive. Seminary rabbi Samuel M. *Cohen left the pulpit of Congregation Beth Sholom, Kansas City, Missouri, to return to New York to accept the post of supervising director, later executive director, of the United Synagogue. From 1917 until shortly before his death in 1945, Cohen devoted his energies exclusively to building the United Synagogue. Primarily interested in field work and extension, he personally helped establish more than 150 congregations.[8]

The founding of Providence, Rhode Island's Temple Emanu-El is a typical example of Cohen's role in the United Synagogue's extension and field work. In 1924 he learned that a segment of Providence's Jewish community had relocated to the city's east side. Its members lived too far away to join Temple Beth Israel, Providence's only Conservative synagogue. These upwardly mobile east-side Jews were typical of those who joined Conservative congregations: they had already turned away from the Yiddish-speaking rabbis of the Orthodoxy of their past but found the ritual and ideological innovations of Reform Judaism unappealing. Cohen took the lead in establishing the new Conservative congregation by contacting a prominent lay leader of the community, Philip C. Joslin, speaker of the Rhode Island House of Representatives, to persuade him to convene a meeting of those interested in founding a new congregation, one dedicated to preserving traditional Judaism but in a fashion amenable to contemporary American Jews. The establishment in 1924 of Providence's Temple Emanu-El was the result.[9]

Senior rabbinical student Israel *Goldman was hired to conduct Emanu-El's first High Holiday services. He returned following his ordination in 1926 as the congregation's first rabbi. He quickly introduced programs typical of Conservative synagogues—late Friday night services, a Sunday school, a Hebrew school, and adult education classes—and in 1927 dedicated the congregation's first synagogue. All aspects of his leadership shaped the synagogue as a model Conservative congregation.

Marshall Sklare, the leading sociologist of Conservatism, sees the evolution of the Conservative synagogue guided by the laity, not the Conservative leaders. Unquestionably, the laity played the major role in the founding of Conservative congregations. There is simply no congregation without the congregants. Yet the United Synagogue's role in pioneering the establishment of Conservative congregations and in matching them with Seminary graduates and Rabbinical Assembly rabbis suggests that the establishment of many of the synagogues founded specifically as Conservative synagogues in the post–World War I period—as well as older synagogues that evolved toward Conservatism—resulted from a joint effort. Conservative leaders trained at the Seminary, men like Cohen and Goldman, brought to their tasks a specific vision of Conservatism as they cooperated with and led local lay leaders in establishing the Conservative synagogue in America.[10]

The efforts at extension were successful. The United Synagogue numbered 50 congregations in 1916, 156 in 1922, and 220 by 1927. At the same time that the United Synagogue expanded its membership, it also organized affiliated associations for the men, women, and youth of the United Synagogue "to enroll under its banner all the members of the family." Solomon Schechter had envisioned enlisting the support of all those, especially Jewish women, who could help the United Synagogue achieve its goals of advancing Jewish life in America. The United Synagogue implemented Schechter's mandate for extending its influence by creating subsidiary bodies. In essence, the United Synagogue developed into the umbrella organization of the various lay constituencies of the Conservative movement. In so doing, it followed the lead, sometimes deliberately, of the Reform movement's Union of American Hebrew Congregations, which had earlier organized its first affiliated lay societies. The subsidiary associations were knit together under United Synagogue auspices for the promotion of Judaism in America, but they preserved their separate identities in order to better meet the needs of their members. This pattern of association was established in the early years of the United Synagogue's development when its first affiliated bodies were founded. They grouped together by age (Young People's League, 1921) or by gender (National Women's League of the United Synagogue of America, 1918; National Federation of Jewish Men's Clubs, 1929). Eventually, the United Synagogue also took the lead in organizing professional associations of those serving its member congregations: Conservative cantors, educators, and synagogue administrators. The United Synagogue thus became both a loose confederation of Conservative congregations and of the lay organizations of the Conservative movement.[11]

During its first period of rapid growth, three affiliates of the United Synagogue were formed. In 1918, in response to her late husband's call that the United Synagogue "assign a certain portion of its work to women and give them a regular share in its activities," Mathilde Roth *Schechter founded the National Women's League of the United Synagogue of America. As founding president, she drafted the blueprint for its work as the coordinating body of Conservative synagogue sisterhoods. She led the Women's League to set an agenda that included service to the home, synagogue, and community with special concern for youth and adult education, the blind, and the welfare of the students at the Seminary. By 1925 the Women's League had grown from the founding 26 sisterhoods to 230 with a membership of 20,000 women. By its jubilee convention in 1968, the Women's League, whose membership was then and has since stabilized at 800 sisterhoods with 200,000 women, had matured as an independent organization within the Conservative movement. Among its most significant achievements was the raising of funds to build the Mathilde Schechter Residence Hall, which opened at the Seminary in 1976. In 1972 the association formally changed its name to the Women's League for Conservative Judaism, signifying that it was no longer a subsidiary of the United Synagogue; at the same time its executives moved out of their old Seminary complex headquarters to new offices on 74th Street.[12]

The second United Synagogue affiliate, the Young People's League (YPL), was organized in 1921. United Synagogue leaders recognized that the survival of the synagogue as a viable institution in America was directly tied to the interest of the youth in its affairs, in this case young men and women over the age of eighteen. They launched the YPL to coordinate the activities of the various young people's societies, both those affiliated with United Synagogue congregations and independent groups willing to join. Led by President Pro Tem Eugene *Kohn and then by founding President Israel *Goldstein, a Seminary graduate and rabbi of New York's Congregation B'nai Jeshurun, the YPL worked to interest its members, those between the ages of eighteen and thirty-five (Junior YPLs were for fifteen to eighteen year olds), in the synagogue, in Jewish education and culture, and in forming new societies. Its first convention drew representatives from 32 societies in twenty cities across North America. By 1927 the YPL included 127 societies with nearly 15,000 members. In the late 1940s Rabbi Max *Vorspan worked to strengthen the YPL, but attendance at its annual conventions declined rapidly from a high of 900 in 1950 to 200 in 1955, partly because YPL was unable to attract the growing numbers of Conservative youth on college campuses. As a result, the United Synagogue abandoned the YPL organization in the late 1950s in favor of building up its new teenage movement, United Synagogue Youth (1951), and *Atid* (1961), a college-based organization whose first executive director, Paul *Freedman, was founding president of USY.[13]

In 1929 the United Synagogue established its third affiliate, the National Federation of Jewish Men's Clubs (FJMC), to coordinate the religious, cultural, social, and recreational activities of its congregations' men's clubs. This time the United Synagogue was responding directly to the Union of American Hebrew Congregations, which had already organized its National Federation of Temple Brotherhoods in 1923. In 1924 Rabbi Joseph Miller called for the United Synagogue to create a separate body for the fifty men's clubs within its member congregations. He warned that if the United Synagogue hesitated, the Conservative men's clubs would affiliate with the Reform association—certainly a possibility at a time when the lines of demarcation within American Judaism were not firmly fixed. Once that occurred, he imagined it would be but a short time before their parent congregations also defected to the Reform union. Miller argued that the opportunity for organizing the men of the United Synagogue, just like its women and youth, should not be missed. The FJMC would provide its members with a uniform program and enable them to enhance their activities by strengthening the Jewish content. By 1934 the FJMC counted 10,000 members in 100 societies. In 1986 the FJMC, which in the early 1980s dropped the word *national* out of deference to its Canadian members, included 38,000 men in some 350 societies. Adult education and lay leadership training have remained its priorities. Its projects have included the Laymen's Institutes, retreats for Jewish study begun in 1944; sponsorship of the Leadership Training Fellowship, a national Hebrew high school directed by the Teachers Institute; the Hebrew Literacy Campaign, launched in 1978, which had 50,000 students by 1986; and the publication of The Art of Jewish Living series, whose first volume on *Shabbat* taught members the rites and rituals essential to conducting the traditional Friday night meal at home.[14]

In each case the formation and the development of the lay associations worked to foster Jewish religious life among their members. Each national association achieved this chiefly by sponsoring publications, conventions, and even radio broadcasts aimed at enhancing their members' knowledge of Judaism, its history, traditions, rites, and rituals. In this way they educated their members in a greater awareness of their responsibilities to live a full Jewish life at home and in the synagogue. The Women's League, youth movements, and FJMC provided their sisterhoods, youth groups, and men's clubs with appropriate materials and programs. Their guidance of their local affiliates thus helped lay the foundations for their members' growing identification with Conservative Judaism as a national movement.

Organizational work brought congregations and their congregants into the Conservative fold, but the chief work of the United Synagogue remained "promoting traditional Judaism" in America—in essence forging a synthesis of the Jewish past and the present by Americanizing Judaism. The Seminary trained an Americanized rabbinate; the Rabbinical Assembly furthered the process of adaptation to America, especially by adjusting Jewish law to the contemporary environment. It remained for the United Synagogue to take the lead in providing traditional synagogues with the programs and services essential to make them a bulwark against the assimilation that appeared to threaten the survival of Jewish religious life in America. The goals—as Leon Jick suggested in his study of nineteenth-century American synagogues—remained respectability and Americanization. The means became a wide range of services—publications, conferences, lobbying, broadcasting, consultations, and all manner of assistance—to member congregations. The result was the emergence of the Conservative synagogue in America.[15]

In its early years the United Synagogue, concerned with the large task of making traditional Judaism viable in America, carried many of its activities beyond its member congregations. It promoted the manufacture of kosher bread and was involved in *kashrut* supervision. It placed prayer books on ocean liners and arranged for the posting of schedules of religious services on hotel bulletin boards. It published a directory of 300 kosher dining places, a list of kosher food products, and a Jewish travelers' guide listing the names and addresses of rabbis in major American cities. The United Synagogue distributed to schools and public institutions a calendar listing Jewish holidays and supported legislation allowing *Shabbat* observers to work on Sundays. It joined with other Jewish religious bodies in issuing a prayer book for distribution to Jewish soldiers and sailors. And when it launched its radio broadcasting program in 1923, which in advance of every holiday and festival aired appropriate sermons, music, and tales, the United Synagogue established itself as a pioneer in religious radio broadcasting. By showing that one could travel, take a vacation, and learn Torah from the radio, the United Synagogue was demonstrating to American Jewry that it was possible to synthesize a modern American life-style with Jewish traditional observance.

But at the same time the United Synagogue developed its paramount focus of guiding member congregations to espouse its vision of the modern American synagogue. In 1920 the United Synagogue launched its first quarterly, *The United Synagogue Recorder* (1920–29). Edited by Charles I. Hoffman and with a circulation of 13,000 in 1926, the *Recorder* and its successors, the *Synagogue Center* (1943–45), *News of the United Synagogue of America* (1945–48) and the *United Synagogue Review* (1948–   ), were "to spread the knowledge of our principles and purposes: Sabbath, dietary laws, Hebrew, Jewish observances, the practice of the Torah."[16]

But the *United Synagogue Recorder* accomplished a larger purpose. It communicated to member congregations the developing patterns of Conservative synagogue life. In its pages the *Recorder* regularly carried reports of individual congregational activities—school programs, youth work, adult education topics, late Friday night services, sisterhood and men's club activities, fund-raising, and synagogue building plans. The dissemination of this information helped guide member synagogues and influenced emerging congregations to reflect the broad program of what came to be known as the Conservative synagogue-center or institutional synagogue. Given its theoretical justification by Seminary professor Mordecai M. Kaplan, the synagogue-center became the focal point for the neighborhood, a place where Jews could gather for worship, fellowship, study, social service, and recreation. Kaplan organized New York's Jewish Center in 1917 as the first such synagogue-center, but Sklare has shown that Conservative laity had earlier pioneered the concept—albeit without such an articulate rationale—as these men and women established synagogues in their new neighborhoods of second settlement. In publicizing the ongoing activities of its congregations, the United Synagogue communicated to the Conservative movement at large its vision of the modern synagogue-center. Similarly, United Synagogue conventions, with their discussions of issues important to synagogue life—organization, financing, management, education, and youth work—helped shape United Synagogue congregations into a recognizable pattern. And United

Synagogue officers supplemented these efforts by consulting individually with congregational leaders, giving them advice on synagogue building and fund-raising, budgeting, school construction, and even on how to choose a rabbi.[17]

As a result, the typical Conservative congregation evolved into a major urban and later a major suburban community institution. With its broad program of schools, men's and women's organizations, youth activities, adult education, social action, and sometimes even health club facilities, the Conservative syn-agogue-center, as historian Deborah Dash Moore has shown, was a response to Americanization designed to ensure ethnic group survival. Fostering this devel-opment became one of the chief priorities and great successes of the early United Synagogue. In fact, its role in fashioning the model modern synagogue-center led the United Synagogue, in 1925, to launch an ambitious project to transplant its vision of the modern synagogue to Palestine. After conducting a successful fund-raising campaign, the United Synagogue built, in Jerusalem, the Yeshurun Synagogue, a modern house of prayer, study, and gathering which it deeded to the Jewish National Fund in 1946.[18]

The promising expansion within the United Synagogue in the growth of mem-ber congregations, in the creation of affiliated associations, and in the devel-opment of new projects came to a grinding halt with the onset of the Depression. By 1934 the United Synagogue was sunk in a mire of debts, its future extremely precarious. With many of its member congregations in dire straits in the heart of the Depression, often unable to meet their own obligations, dues owed to the United Synagogue surely fell into arrears. Unable to raise its annual budget of $12,000—even as late as 1945 token payments of dues totaled only $8,296— the United Synagogue could scarcely keep its offices operating. It left numerous bills unpaid and owed its executive and secretarial personnel back pay.[19]

Not only did the expansion work of the 1920s cease, but much of the progress that had characterized the formative period of the United Synagogue was undone as the United Synagogue sharply curtailed many of its publications and outreach programs. At the same time, far more pressing issues—the ominous situation of world Jewry, the struggles of the Depression, and the concerns of a world moving toward war—occupied American, and of course Conservative, Jews. The rise of Hitler in Germany, the increasing viciousness of anti-Semitism in Poland and elsewhere in Europe, and the fate of the *yishuv* under British rule in Palestine emerged unquestionably as the major items on the public agenda of American Jewry. While the United Synagogue continued to hold its biennial conventions in the 1930s, devoting considerable attention to such matters as social and economic justice and the plight of the *agunah*, and even celebrating its silver jubilee in 1938, the years of the Depression were years of stasis for the development of the United Synagogue and much of the Conservative movement.[20]

In the late 1930s the leaders of the Seminary implemented new plans to resolve the financial crisis that had engulfed the entire movement, not just the United

Synagogue. Anticipating that the hegemony of world Jewry was shifting from European to American Jewry, then Seminary provost Louis *Finkelstein charted a course to make Conservatism a leading force in shaping the future of American Jewry. His ambitious plans for the movement required first a resolution of the existing financial crisis and then the raising of large amounts of money for a host of new projects. In 1939 Finkelstein invited Scranton, Pennsylvania, rabbi Max *Arzt, later vice-chancellor of the Seminary, to head the Seminary's fund-raising campaign as director of the Seminary's new Department of Field Service and Activities. Within a few short years the Seminary campaigns, soon renamed the Joint Campaign for the Seminary, Rabbinical Assembly, and the United Synagogue, had transformed the fortunes of the Conservative movement. By 1946 the United Synagogue, which received a percentage of the campaign proceeds, had an annual budget of well over $100,000. The dramatic financial turnaround enabled the United Synagogue to recover lost ground and to launch once again an ambitious program.

Already in the spring of 1941, the United Synagogue projected new efforts to strengthen Jewish religious life by renewing and expanding its programs of youth work, education, leadership development, and outreach to unaffiliated synagogues. These plans, of course, remained dependent upon resolution of the fiscal crisis. But this ambitious program was temporarily halted as the United Synagogue "mobilized for victory" following America's entry into World War II in December 1941. For the next several years the far more pressing issues of the war effort and the contributions Conservative men, women, and youth could make at home in their synagogues as civilian workers and away at the front as soldiers and chaplains took precedence over United Synagogue internal ambitions and concerns.

The end of the war coincided with a transition in the leadership of the United Synagogue. At the end of 1944 the United Synagogue's first executive director, Samuel Cohen, retired. His promising leadership of the United Synagogue in the 1920s had unfortunately been undermined by the financial problems and stasis brought on by the Depression. For nearly two years, partly as a result of the Conservative movement's severe manpower shortage brought on by the need to send the overwhelming majority of its rabbis to the military chaplaincy, the United Synagogue was led by acting executive directors, first former United Synagogue president Elias *Solomon and then recent Seminary graduate Stanley *Rabinowitz. In 1946 a new executive director, Albert I. *Gordon (1946–49), a congregational rabbi ordained at the Seminary in 1929, took over the helm of the United Synagogue. Gordon, who was also an early student of American Jewish sociology, combined personal commitment to Conservatism with his knowledge of the social forces of American Jewish life. The combination of his approaches made him a particularly effective leader as the United Synagogue once again entered into a period of growth and expansion.

Shortly before Gordon's arrival, the United Synagogue moved to new headquarters in the Seminary complex. The move from its old basement offices to rooms in the library building symbolized the possibility that the United Synagogue might emerge as a more influential force in the Conservative movement. Gordon determined to reorganize the United Synagogue to secure greater lay participation and to provide those services indispensable to member congregations. As a result, he believed, members would feel greater identification with Conservatism as a national movement. Under his leadership the United Synagogue dramatically expanded its activities. New departments—music, youth activities, and programs—appeared. The United Synagogue organized registries of teachers, cantors, and synagogue administrators to serve as placement bureaus for its members. In order to strengthen the commitment of these professionals to the Conservative movement, the United Synagogue took the lead in organizing the Cantors Assembly in 1947, the National Association of Synagogue Administrators in 1948, and the Jewish Educators Assembly in 1951. It created the National Youth Commission in 1948 to oversee its growing programs of youth services, including the premier Conservative camping movement, Camp Ramah. It inaugurated a book service to provide books and ceremonial objects to synagogue gift shops and planned ambitious publications programs of educational materials and synagogue administrative aids.[21]

With the United Synagogue providing substantive services to member congregations and with a war-weary generation turning in record numbers to the synagogue, the ranks of the United Synagogue began to swell. Gordon, like Cohen before him, traveled extensively throughout the United States to establish new congregations. To aid his efforts, the United Synagogue revitalized its regional offices, which were first established in 1926; by 1949 there were seventeen regions. Gordon relied upon regional directors, many of whom were field officers for both the Seminary and the United Synagogue, to pave his way. In 1948 the United Synagogue launched a campaign to add 100 new congregations to its rosters. Its rapid growth was strikingly impressive. In 1945 the ranks of the United Synagogue had shrunk to 190. But the postwar era brought new members. As Jewish soldiers returned from the war, married, began their families, and joined the urban exodus, they and their wives founded synagogues in new neighborhoods. By 1949 the United Synagogue had grown to 365 congregations. The nearly 100 percent increase in just four years was remarkable given the stasis of the preceding period. The United Synagogue's newfound confidence even led to an increase in the dues assessed its congregations to fifty cents per synagogue member, the first increase since its founding in 1913.

At the end of 1949 Gordon resigned from the United Synagogue. While he had accomplished much in expanding its activities, he had been frustrated in his efforts to shape it as an organization that was more than a service agency to member congregations. He believed that to strengthen the United Synagogue it was necessary to clarify Conservative ideology, but his plans for the United Synagogue to take the lead in this area had fallen far short of his goals. This failure and other frustrations persuaded him to return to the congregational rabbinate.

After an interim period under the acting directorship of Dr. Emil Lehman, Rabbi Simon *Greenberg became the executive director of the United Synagogue (1950–53). Greenberg had been rabbi of Har Zion Congregation, Philadelphia, Pennsylvania. In 1946 he left Har Zion for a full-time career at the Seminary. At the same time that he was executive director of the United Synagogue, Greenberg also held positions at the Seminary as provost, vice-chancellor, and president of the faculties. In 1953 Greenberg returned to the Seminary full time and was succeeded at the United Synagogue by Rabbi Bernard *Segal (executive director, 1953–70; executive vice-president, 1970–76). Ordained at the Seminary in 1933, Segal had served, since his discharge from the army in 1945, first the Rabbinical Assembly and then the Seminary as executive vice-president. For more than a quarter of a century he led the United Synagogue. The expansion of United Synagogue activities during his leadership led to an administrative reorganization in 1970 that elevated Segal to a new post, executive vice-president.

United Synagogue professional leaders Cohen, Gordon, Greenberg, Segal, and since 1976 Benjamin Z. *Kreitman, a rabbi ordained at the Seminary in 1942 and former chairman of the Rabbinical Assembly's Committee on Jewish Law and Standards, illustrate the fact that the United Synagogue has remained throughout its history an institution dominated by Seminary faculty and rabbis. All of its early presidents were Seminary men. Seminary Talmud professor Louis *Ginzberg succeeded Seminary presidents Solomon Schechter and Cyrus Adler in the presidency of the United Synagogue (1917–18) after Adler resigned in protest over the United Synagogue's participation in the American Jewish Congress. Then Seminary rabbis Elias L. Solomon (1918–26) and Montreal's Herman *Abramowitz (1926–27) followed. It was not until 1927, with the election of S. Herbert Golden, that the first lay leader was elected president of the United Synagogue. But by that time Seminary rabbi Cohen was firmly entrenched at its helm as chief executive. Since then lay leaders have held the presidency, fostering the impression of the United Synagogue as Conservatism's lay institution. Some of them, notably Maxwell Abbell (1950–53), have been quite influential, especially because they retain the power of the purse. But United Synagogue chief executive officers, and therefore policy makers, remained Seminary faculty and rabbis. As a result, while the United Synagogue conducted numerous activities under its own auspices, its guiding lights remained in or closely connected to the Seminary. The United Synagogue thus helped establish the precedent that the Seminary was the chief institution of American Conservatism. The United Synagogue created a constituency for the Seminary, for its interpretation of Judaism, and for its rabbis. But despite its important services to member congregations, it remained the subordinate institution of the movement, following first the lead of the Seminary and then, as the Rabbinical Assembly became influential in its own right, of both the Seminary and the Rabbinical Assembly. The United Synagogue—which did not move out of the Seminary complex until the late 1970s—thus helped foster the image of Conservatism as a movement in which the rabbis led and the people followed.

In the 1950s and the 1960s, first under Greenberg and then under Segal, the United Synagogue continued to expand the services it provided member congregations. With the transfer of the National Academy for Adult Jewish Study from the Seminary to the United Synagogue in 1951, the United Synagogue emerged as the chief agency for all educational activities in the Conservative synagogue. Its organization, in 1964, of the Solomon Schechter Day School Association signified the success of this new educational venture. The various divisions of the United Synagogue consulted with congregations and offered advice on synagogue management, budget, personnel, programming, youth work, publicity, and even supplied speakers. With the establishment in 1950 of the Solomon Schechter awards for outstanding congregational leadership in a variety of areas—elementary, high school, day school, and adult education; youth activities; synagogue programming; creative arts; libraries; music; publications; worship and ritual; social action; and community service—the United Synagogue became an indispensable clearinghouse for successful synagogue programs. It moved into the arena of social action by establishing, with the Rabbinical Assembly, the Joint Social Actions Commission (1953). To lay the foundations for future loyalty to the synagogue and the Conservative movement among Conservative youth, the United Synagogue took the lead in establishing new youth movements, United Synagogue Youth (1951, for teens), the college-age *Atid* (1961), and *Kadima* (formerly pre-USY, reorganized in 1968 for preteens). To bring Conservatism to Jewish communities throughout the world, especially to South America, Segal led the United Synagogue in establishing the World Council of Synagogues in 1957. The gift of a building in Jerusalem in 1972 enabled the United Synagogue to strengthen its presence in Israel and to maintain close ties to the thirty-five member synagogues that it counted in its Israel region.

Increasing services brought new congregations to the fold, especially as the United Synagogue stepped up its outreach to embryonic congregations. It added 130 new affiliates in 1956–57, the largest single increase in United Synagogue membership in a two-year period, bringing the total membership to 628 congregations. By 1964 there were 778 members. By 1971 it numbered 832 congregations, comprising some 350,000 families with an estimated 1.5 million members. The United Synagogue budget grew correspondingly. In 1959 its budget was over $300,000 a year, derived from the $2 per capita dues from congregations and the 10 percent allocation from the Joint Campaign of the Seminary, United Synagogue, and Rabbinical Assembly. And with numerical strength came the ability to do that which several of its early founders had anticipated—to adopt and to enforce standards for synagogue practice that would go a long way toward unifying its member congregations. In ratifying these standards in 1957, standards that were subsequently revised in 1961, 1969, 1971, and 1975, the United Synagogue demonstrated the public adherence to Jewish law and ritual that became a hallmark of Conservatism.[22]

But as Rabbinical Assembly executive vice-president Wolfe *Kelman noted in an address in 1971, by 1968—with the war in Vietnam raging, the youth rebellion in full swing, and the end of the "baby boom" that had caused the founding of so many new congregations in the suburbs to which young parents had fled—the United Synagogue had ended its period of explosive growth. United Synagogue membership stabilized at just over 800 congregations; in 1986, 826 synagogues in North America were affiliated with the United Synagogue. In the 1970s and the 1980s the United Synagogue continued to do that which it had learned to do well in the past: to provide Conservative congregations with materials and programs, especially in its chief areas of education and youth work essential for the development of religious life in America.

The stabilization in the United Synagogue raised new concerns. Financial problems plagued it throughout the 1970s, leading to a significant dues increase in 1980. Serious concerns were also raised during these years about the future of the Conservative movement. Some of the grand old synagogue-centers—such as Brooklyn's Jewish Center—built in the 1920s, which had survived earlier population shifts to the suburbs, were in decline. The suburban congregations built in the 1950s and 1960s faced aging buildings and rising costs. Some were making hard choices about refurbishing or building new additions in the hope of attracting new members. Their leaders watched as the children, for whom these synagogues and their schools had first been built, grew up and had children of their own. They anticipated that soon these young men and women of the post-World War II population boom, many of whom had rebelled so strenuously against institutional synagogues in their youth, would find themselves turning back to the synagogue, just as their parents a generation before had done when they needed support in bringing up Jewish children in America. By the mid-1980s there were even signs of new Conservative congregations emerging in the new neighborhoods to which young Jewish families moved in search of affordable housing. The impressionistic data suggests that the prospects for the future of the Conservative movement, despite some widely publicized studies to the contrary, hold some promise. If so, the United Synagogue will continue to fulfill, as it has during its first three-quarters of a century, its mandate to promote Jewish religious life among the men, women, and youth of the Conservative synagogues in America.[23]

EDUCATION AND YOUTH WORK

From inception the Conservative movement saw as critical to its mission the fulfillment of the commandment "And you shall teach them diligently unto your children" (Deuteronomy 6:7). The goal of educating American Jewish men, women, and children in their responsibilities as Jews at home and in the synagogue became one of the overarching themes of the Conservative movement. Every one of the national bodies of Conservatism made education a priority. The Seminary's mission was to train rabbis, teachers, and cantors to be educational leaders in their communities. The Rabbinical Assembly had from its earliest years as the Seminary Alumni Association considered Jewish education—

in particular the desperate need to develop textbooks and curricula for the schools housed within its members' congregations—one of its primary concerns. When the United Synagogue was founded in 1913, it too, heeding Solomon Schechter's inaugural charge, determined to foster Jewish education. Eventually each of the groups that it established, including the Women's League, the Federation of Jewish Men's Clubs, and the United Synagogue Youth, made education of its members a goal.

At first, the chief mode of education in the Conservative synagogue was the Sunday school. But by the 1980s Conservative Jewish education included a wide network of three-day-a-week congregational schools, Sunday schools, weekday kindergartens, Solomon Schechter day schools, and numerous kinds of adult education as well as the informal and formal education carried on in Conservatism's youth and camping movements. Conservative rabbis and educators established goals for each of these, creating textbooks, programs, curricula, and syllabi, and training teachers pedagogically and ideologically able to prepare the next generation of Conservative Jews. True to their charge as "teachers in Israel," the leaders of Conservatism struggled within their local congregations and within their national organizations to establish decent educational standards, to build budgets and physical facilities, and to encourage young men and women to follow in their footsteps as educators.

Each of the national organizations of Conservatism undertook education and youth work. In their synagogues the men of the Rabbinical Assembly were the leading educators; there they forged the system of congregational Conservative Jewish education. As in the movement's other endeavors, Seminary personnel and professors—especially those associated with its Teachers Institute, established in 1909—carefully monitored and guided from behind the scenes the development of Conservative educational policies. But while the Seminary took direct charge of educating the movement's elite, training all its personnel and preparing selected youth for future leadership in the Leadership Training Fellowship and Camp Ramah, it allowed the United Synagogue to emerge as the movement's chief clearinghouse and coordinator of educational and youth programs in the Conservative synagogue.

The main underpinning of the Conservative system of elementary Jewish education became the three-day-a-week afternoon congregational school, the Hebrew school. Prior to the emergence of congregational schools on a national scale, communal Hebrew schools taught most American Jewish boys the rudiments necessary to perform the rites of Bar Mitzvah. But Conservative leaders were convinced "that a congregation without an educational network was a hollow institution, and that Jewish education undirected by the religious impulse was somehow just not fully Jewish." The spiritual education of the next generation was too important a task to leave to others.[24]

Although traditional synagogues had been "houses of study," these congregational schools were an American innovation. In 1914 Mordecai M. Kaplan, then chair of the Education Committee of the newly founded United Synagogue and dean of the Teachers Institute, surveyed Conservative Jewish education. He found a variety of educational programs in the United Synagogue's member congregations. Most synagogues held Sunday school and Hebrew school to meet the needs of congregants requesting "more Judaism" or "less Judaism." The textbooks were "beneath criticism," the preparation of teachers little better. There were no uniform curricula and few advanced classes. Only one-third of the children attended class more than once a week. Apparently, twentieth-century congregational schools had progressed little beyond those observed by Leon Jick in his study of nineteenth-century synagogues: untrained teachers, students' failure to learn anything, and ribald classrooms were still serious problems.[25]

For Conservative leaders this system of Jewish education was disastrously inadequate to transmit Judaism's spiritual heritage to the next generation. While others, like Samson Benderly, director of New York City's Bureau of Jewish Education, worked to transform Jewish education outside the synagogue, Conservative rabbis determined to reverse the deterioration of American Jewish education by moving it into a position of centrality in the synagogue. They planned to develop curricula and materials to raise educational standards and to wage a battle for intensification that would make Jewish learning a lifelong experience. Not only would this program allow them to fulfill their mission as educators, but it would also strengthen their synagogues. As Conservative rabbis quickly realized, the synagogue school became the nucleus of a family-centered congregation that drew parents and children together to the synagogue. The congregational school thus became one of the great strengths and one of the mainstays of the Conservative synagogue.

While individual rabbis worked within their congregations to upgrade the standards of their schools, the Education Committee of the United Synagogue, chaired next by Philadelphia rabbi and author Julius H. *Greenstone (1920–25) and then by Rabbi Alter F. *Landesman (1925–40), executive director of the Hebrew Education Society of Brownsville, began the not inconsiderable task of supporting and supervising the preparation of educational materials suitable for the movement's schools. Because the Education Committee had neither the finances nor personnel to prepare a complete set of texts for Conservative classrooms, it confined itself to publishing those educational materials that the rabbis felt were most sorely needed and were unavailable elsewhere. In an early effort to systematize what children learned in the movement's schools, Landesman prepared for the committee four separate curricula—for the school meeting daily, for the three-day-a-week school, for the Sunday school, and a special two-year course for children beginning their schooling at age eleven—to standardize the diverse educational tracks in United Synagogue congregations.[26]

The Conservative synagogue-centers built in the 1920s reflected this growing emphasis upon congregational education. Educational facilities—classrooms for Hebrew and Sunday schools, auditoriums and lecture halls for adult education forums—became integral components of the new structures. By the end of the 1920s congregational Hebrew schools had begun to supplant communal Hebrew schools in importance.[27]

The financial exigencies of the Depression temporarily halted developments in Conservative education. During the 1930s the United Synagogue's Education Committee and its counterpart in the Rabbinical Assembly considered dividing their responsibilities to curb unnecessary duplication. Several years later, in 1940, the two committees agreed to merge to form the body that became the movement's central agency for elementary Jewish education, the Joint Commission on Education. Consisting of equal representatives from the Rabbinical Assembly and the United Synagogue and co-chaired by rabbis Morris *Goodblatt and Alter Landesman, the commission planned to pool the movement's resources to improve the quality of congregational schools, to promote a more intensive program of Jewish education in the synagogue, and to foster standardization of curricula and programs in Conservative schools. One of its primary goals was to publish materials reflecting the spirit and ideology of Conservatism. Its first publications included Simon Greenberg's five-volume Hebrew language instruction series, Harishon (1940–43), which sold over 100,000 textbooks, workbooks, and teachers' guides in five years, and the commission's first magazine, The Jewish School and Democracy.[28]

But even these substantial efforts could not possibly remedy what Robert *Gordis called in his leading article in the premiere issue of Conservative Judaism (1945) "our widespread lack of success in the field of Jewish education." In 1945 most children in Conservative synagogues still received their Jewish education in Sunday schools. Although the quality of teachers had been raised beyond what Professor Max Margolis had once called "an ignorant female, oozing religion," low salaries and status made it difficult to train and retain teachers. And, as Gordis observed, even superior teachers could not erase the fundamental problems of the Sunday school: its limited hours of instruction and the general disregard for this supplemental education. Conservative leaders agreed that these Sunday schools were grossly inadequate to transmit to the next generation the values and skills essential to perpetuate Jewish tradition in America. The solution, they felt, lay in making the three-day-a-week Hebrew school the cornerstone of Conservative elementary education.[29]

In the wake of World War II Conservative leaders determined to shift the bulk of their educational resources from the Sunday school to the Hebrew school. Sadly cognizant of the new responsibilities of American Jewry, they urgently mobilized resources to make the afternoon congregational Hebrew school the standard vehicle of American Jewish education. These plans for "Reshaping the Structure of Jewish Education in America," as the Rabbinical Assembly called its first conference on Jewish education, held in 1946, were aided by a demographic shift of American Jewry that brought to an end most urban communal Hebrew schools. As Jews left the cities for the suburbs in the early postwar period, they founded hundreds of new Conservative congregations. In each one the rabbis fought to make the Hebrew school one of the pillars of their new synagogues.

These rabbis were aided by the *Statement on the Objectives and Standards for the Congregational Schools* published by the Joint Commission on Jewish Education in 1946, the first attempt since the 1920s to formulate a philosophy and program for Jewish education in the Conservative synagogue. The statement followed several studies of congregational schools conducted by a committee headed by educator and Seminary officer Rabbi Simon Greenberg. Published as a pamphlet for convenient distribution to synagogue boards of education, the *Statement* reflected the consensus of Conservative leadership to make the three-day-a-week school the medium by which a child would acquire the knowledge and skills necessary to fit into congregational life: knowledge of synagogue rituals, worship, and the rudiments of Hebrew; familiarity with the Bible, prayer book, Jewish history, literature, and culture; an appreciation of the centrality of the land of Israel to Jews and Judaism; and indoctrination in Jewish values and ethics. Because no less than six hours a week were required for this instruction, all Jewish children above the age of eight were to attend Hebrew school three times a week; the Hebrew school thus incorporated the Sunday session.[30]

The success of the drive to reshape Conservative education hinged upon Conservatism's national headquarters providing greater guidance and assistance to rabbis and congregants developing education programs in the synagogue. Greater ambitions mandated greater resources for the Joint Commission on Jewish Education to enable it to fulfill its task. Consequently, the United Synagogue, in accord with the Seminary, agreed to furnish the commission with a budget and to employ a full-time educational director, and the commission was restructured to include representatives from the Teachers Institute. Since it had become Conservative practice to house joint commissions within one of the national associations to indicate which agency had primary responsibility for its work, the commission was also renamed the United Synagogue Commission on Jewish Education. The new title signified the United Synagogue's fiscal responsibility for the commission as well as an overall plan to enhance the standing of the United Synagogue within the Conservative movement. As Robert Gordis, then president of the Rabbinical Assembly, explained to his colleagues, responsibility for the Commission on Jewish Education was meant to win for the United Synagogue "the prestige and sense of achievement which this important agency has to offer."[31]

With Rabbi Abraham Ezra *Millgram as its first director (1946–61), followed by educators Walter I. Ackerman (1961–64) and Morton *Siegel (1964–   ), the commission accelerated its efforts to intensify elementary Jewish education. It expanded its publication plans to include textbooks in Hebrew and English, songsters, programs for all-school assemblies, preschool (at one time called foundation school) materials, and parent education handbooks. It developed administrative aids, record and report cards, Bar and Bat Mitzvah certificates, and audio-visual materials. It inaugurated a series of national curricular guides—

the first appeared in 1949—to provide fully integrated educational programs for every class from the nursery through the junior high school. Within a few years, these publications would change the entire complexion of education in Conservative congregational schools. The commission also worked, in cooperation with the Teachers Institute, to professionalize the field of Hebrew teaching. It sought to improve teacher qualifications, hosted regional conferences to stimulate higher educational standards, helped establish a summer Hebrew day camp for the training of kindergarten teachers, organized a teacher's placement bureau, and in 1951 spearheaded the founding of the Jewish Educators Assembly as the professional association of Conservative teachers, principals, and educational directors. These programs enabled the rabbis to win their battle to make the Hebrew school the pillar of elementary education in the Conservative synagogue. By the end of the 1950s, Sunday schools had virtually disappeared except for the very young.[32]

At the same time that Conservative leaders worked to strengthen the Hebrew school, they developed new educational endeavors—the Leadership Training Fellowship, Solomon Schechter day schools, Ramah camps, and United Synagogue Youth—all designed to win the next generation for Conservative Judaism. In the wake of the ravages of World War II, Conservative officials realized that they could no longer rely, as they had in the past, upon Europe to produce the next generation of leaders for the movement. Once it became evident that future Conservative rabbis, scholars, and teachers would, almost exclusively, be American born, a deliberate decision was made to recruit the youth in Conservative synagogues to become Conservatism's future leaders. This decision led, in 1946, to the establishment of the Leadership Training Fellowship (LTF), a national high school conceived of by Seminary professor Mordecai M. Kaplan. Conducted under the auspices of the Teachers Institute, the LTF enlisted congregational rabbis to prepare selected young men and women in their synagogues for advanced study at the Seminary. But even a special high-school curriculum could not compensate adequately for the minimum Jewish education provided by the elementary Hebrew schools. Although Conservative teachers planned to intensify these schools to better educate the next generation of Conservative laity, they did not expect congregational schools to be adequate to train the next generation of Conservative elite. The solution, some felt, lay in day schools.

Free, nondenominational public education in the United States had led to the virtual eradication of separate Jewish day schools by the mid-nineteenth century. Even the massive migration of Jews from Eastern Europe had barely stemmed this tide. In the early twentieth century, only the largest American Jewish communities, like New York City and Chicago, maintained Jewish day schools. But as Orthodox Judaism gained strength, its leaders began to reverse this trend. By 1945 there were some one hundred Jewish day schools in America, all Orthodox. Many of the rabbis ordained at the Seminary had received their early training in these schools modeled on European *yeshivot*. Now as rabbis in new suburban Jewish communities, they found themselves and even some of their congregants involved in efforts to establish day schools, albeit Orthodox ones, for their own children. Chafing under the dominance of Orthodox educators, who made all pedagogical decisions, individual Conservative rabbis began exploring alternatives.[33]

In the early postwar period, several of Conservatism's most distinguished rabbis, including orator and author Solomon *Goldman and Seminary professor Robert Gordis, established day schools in their synagogues. Goldman's Anshe Emet Day School (Chicago, 1946) and Temple Beth El Day School, later the Robert Gordis Day School of Temple Beth El (Rockaway Park, New York, 1950), became the models for those to follow. By 1958 there were fourteen Conservative day schools. Eager to encourage these exciting developments, the United Synagogue's Commission on Jewish Education sponsored its first conference on day school education (1957) and launched the Solomon Schechter Day School system. The commission published materials and curricula for the schools, organized additional conferences, created the Solomon Schechter Day School Association, and adopted standards for accreditation and affiliation with the association. These standards mandated that Solomon Schechter Day Schools—most, but not all, of which bear this name—devote twelve hours a week or 40 percent of the total classroom time, whichever was greater, to Judaic studies.[34]

As urban schools and neighborhoods declined and a long-standing American Jewish prejudice against parochial schools gave way, Conservative Jews, at first in small numbers, turned to the day school as an alternative. By 1968 there were twenty-eight schools with some 5,000 students. But in the 1970s and 1980s a growing disaffection with the afternoon Hebrew school and with changing public schools and the greater affluence of American Jewry, which made private school tuitions affordable, won for the Solomon Schechter Day School movement greater adherents and sponsors. By 1987 the Solomon Schechter Day School Association had sixty-nine schools, including seven high schools, throughout the United States and Canada and an enrollment of just under 14,000 students.[35]

For Conservative leaders no opportunities to foster Jewish education were to be missed. This conviction led to the establishment of two of the movement's most successful endeavors: the national camping movement, Camp Ramah, and the teenage youth movement, United Synagogue Youth. The first Camp Ramah opened in Conover, Wisconsin, in 1947 with nearly one hundred campers. Although the United Synagogue had a long-standing interest in Jewish camping— in its early years it had supervised *kashrut* and religious programming at several private camps—the Conservative movement had never before invested resources in its own camping movement.[36]

The local impetus to found the first Camp Ramah came from Chicago rabbi Ralph *Simon. He had seen firsthand in a Protestant camp the promises such a setting offered for youth education and intensive religious life. Simon persuaded the Chicago Council of Conservative Synagogues and the Midwest branch of the United Synagogue to sponsor the first Camp Ramah.[37]

These plans coincided with new directions being explored at the Teachers Institute. Two of its leaders had extensive experience with Jewish educational camping. Both Dean Moshe *Davis and Administrative Secretary Sylvia Ettenberg (later Seminary dean of educational development) had been among the founders of Massad, a Hebrew-speaking camp for students with more intensive Jewish and Hebrew educations than those produced by Conservative congregational schools. Davis also worked closely with the LTF, several of whose students had spent the summer of 1946 in intensive study at the Teachers Institute. It became obvious to Davis and Ettenberg that a camp setting—rather than summers in the city—would better foster the kind of intensive education essential to prepare adolescents to become Conservative leaders. Accordingly, they worked out an arrangement with Simon to give the Teachers Institute responsibility for hiring and supervising Ramah's first staff. They thus set the precedent for control from Seminary headquarters of the Ramah program, curriculum, and ideology. That ideology called for a Hebrew-speaking camp to immerse campers in Jewish living—daily worship, Sabbath observance, and *kashrut*—and to teach them the basics of Judaism and Hebrew language, knowledge that was the prerequisite to future leadership. This experience, Ramah founders believed, would prove so powerful that it would propel Conservative youth to commit themselves to lives filled with Judaism, observance, and study.[38]

Camp Ramah in Wisconsin, run for its first two summers by LTF director Henry Goldberg, was an immediate success. Although a second camp opened in Maine in 1948, it lasted only two seasons, largely because of difficulties with its owner. A third camp was established in the Poconos (Pennsylvania) in 1950. The organization in the winter of 1950–51 of the National Ramah Commission, with representatives from the Seminary, Rabbinical Assembly, and United Synagogue, marked an end to the pattern of local and ad hoc organization of new camps. In 1953 the National Ramah Commission acquired its first camp, in Connecticut, signaling the evolution of the network of Ramah camps. The Ramah program was also enhanced by the involvement of educator Louis Newman, who, as director of Ramah in Wisconsin (1951–53), reshaped Ramah ideology to include progressive thought designed to strengthen the character of campers and staff.[39]

Since then, the Camp Ramah movement has grown to include six overnight camps and one day camp in North America (in addition to those mentioned above, they are California, 1955; Canada, 1960; New York, 1961; and Palmer, Massachusetts, 1965, closed in 1971 after radical experiments with youth culture in the summers of 1969 and 1970). A camp in Argentina was opened in 1960, and the Ramah Israel Seminar, a summer-long program in Israel, was inaugurated in 1962. From some one hundred youth in its first summer, Ramah grew to host several thousand campers each year. The camps rapidly and handsomely paid back Conservatism's investment. Not only did they propel thousands of teens to become committed members of Conservative congregations as they reached the age of maturity, but they also yielded numerous "Ramah marriages." Most importantly, Ramah produced the elite that its founders had been seeking. Many of its campers went on to the Seminary to advance—one never completes—their Jewish education. According to Seminary vice-chancellor Max Arzt, by 1975 some 300 former Ramah campers had graduated to become the rabbis, educators, and scholars of Jewish studies, the leaders of American Jewish life that Conservative rabbis were determined to train.[40]

The other major endeavor to capture the hearts and minds of Conservative youth was the establishment of United Synagogue Youth (USY) in 1951. Previously, the United Synagogue's major "youth" organization had been the Young People's League (YPL), established in 1921 for eighteen to thirty-five year olds. Although some synagogues sponsored Junior YPL chapters for teens fifteen to eighteen, the Junior YPLs, neither numerous nor very successful, had too often degenerated into social organizations; they were not the models of educational youth work Conservative leaders desired. In the postwar era, local Conservative rabbis, particularly in the Midwest, and national officials—in this case Simon Greenberg, then executive director of the United Synagogue—became increasingly concerned over the defection of post–Bar and Bat Mitzvah youth from the synagogue. Simultaneously, they abandoned the Junior YPL to create the nucleus of the USY. Developed for teens aged thirteen to seventeen, USY became within a few short years an enormously successful youth movement and a training ground for future Hebrew teachers, synagogue officers, sisterhood presidents, and rabbis; five of its national presidents went on to be ordained at the Seminary.[41]

Directed first by Morton Siegel (1951–64) and since by his successor, USY's first national president, Rabbi Paul Freedman, USY grew rapidly. From 500 delegates representing 68 chapters at its charter convention in 1951, within a decade it numbered 25,000 members in 500 chapters. Its success lay in its variety of attractive programs. USYers committed themselves to maintain a reading knowledge of Hebrew, attend some services, and undertake some Jewish study— at one time that meant four hours per month. In return they were eligible not only to participate in their local chapters but also in regional *kinnusim*; summer encampments; the Israel (inaugurated 1956) and European (1969) pilgrimages; USY-on-Wheels (1961), a summer bus tour across America; and *Nativ*, a year-long program in Israel. USYers raised funds for special projects to further Conservative Judaism, helping to establish the Seminary Center in Jerusalem and to buy Camp USY in Glen Spey, New York (1966). To repair the world by fulfilling the commandment of *tzedakah* (charity), they raised monies for *Tikkun Olam*. Guided by the United Synagogue's Youth Department (which published materials and program guides), the National Youth Commission (composed of representatives from Conservatism's constituent bodies), and local Conservative rabbis and educators, USYers found that their programs blended religious observance, study, and socializing in a seamless fashion. USY's regional, national, and even international activities—it added an Israel chapter, NOAM, in 1968—gave members a network of friendships and an extended social circle. The annual calendar of events led members to plan their high school recreational time and summers around these activities and promised Conservative leaders a sizeable audience for their ongoing, informal educational programs.

Building upon the success of USY, the United Synagogue launched two spin-offs. *Atid*, formed in 1961 and first directed by Paul Freedman, was a college-age youth group that drew mostly USY graduates and former members of the LTF. Its limited success eventually led to its abandonment in favor of another college youth organization, *Ometz* (1982). *Kadima*, a preteenage youth movement formalized in 1968, was meant to prepare fifth through eighth graders to join USY.[42]

Conservative leaders used these youth organizations, especially USY, to demonstrate to youth that Judaism mandated higher standards of observance than they were accustomed to, especially in the area of Sabbath observance. In 1964 the Rabbinical Assembly's Committee on Jewish Law and Standards (CJLS) asked USY, in scheduling its conventions, to avoid the necessity of automobile travel on the Sabbath "to teach USYers that there is something offensive in Sabbath travel." This ruling, a strict construction of Jewish law, sharply contradicted an earlier CJLS pronouncement (1950) permitting such travel for the purposes of public worship. While protests over the difficulties of adhering to this position eventually led to a more lenient ruling (1967), the rabbis still encouraged USYers to avoid such travel whenever possible. The youth organizations thus became tools both for fostering the Jewish education of Conservative youth and for guiding them to live fuller Jewish lives.[43]

And if they were to live full Jewish lives, then Conservative youth, when they became adults, were to commit themselves to a life of Jewish study. The development of rich, synagogue-based adult education programs became one of the hallmarks of the Conservative synagogue. In the early decades of the Conservative movement, individual rabbis had developed their own adult education programs. But in 1941, thanks largely to his pioneering efforts at Temple Emanuel, Providence, Rhode Island, Rabbi Israel Goldman was invited by the Seminary to establish the National Academy for Adult Jewish Studies. Fostering the ancient Jewish tradition of lifelong learning, the National Academy's mission was rooted in the Jewish past, but it borrowed its techniques of publication and dissemination from the contemporary American adult education setting. In 1952, as part of the directive to make the United Synagogue the headquarters of all synagogue-based education from cradle to grave, the National Academy became its affiliate. Directed next by Simon*Noveck (1952–58) and then by Marvin *Wiener (1958–78), the National Academy orchestrated adult education in the Conservative synagogue. While Orthodox adult education classes focused largely on rabbinics, and Reform adult students confronted the social issues of the day, the Conservative adult education program took its broad view of religious education for the adult from the wide range of Jewish culture and civilization of the past. Under Wiener, the National Academy developed Conservatism's adult education imprint, Burning Bush Press, to publish a wide variety of materials—pamphlets, tracts, study guides, small paperbacks, and popular and even scholarly full-length works. Its Jewish Tract Series included booklets on the synagogue service and the Conservative approach to Jewish law. Among its full-length volumes were reprints of the works of early Seminary leaders and Mordecai *Waxman's *Tradition and Change* (1958), the first full-length collection of articles and essays on Conservatism. To encourage study of the Talmud, the National Academy distributed the *El Am Talmud*. Many of these publications were subsidized by the United Synagogue to make them readily available to adult learners. Although a structural reorganization of the United Synagogue in 1973, which placed adult education under the Department of Jewish Education, led to the abandonment of the National Academy as a separate division, fostering lifelong learning remains a priority of the Conservative movement.

While the postwar developments of stronger Hebrew schools, day school education, youth work, and adult education made the program of Conservative Jewish education appear extremely successful, by the early 1960s Conservative rabbis and educators were asking themselves, "Now that we have been so successful, why are we such failures?" Their dismay grew in part out of the *Report on Jewish Education in the United States*, published by the American Association for Jewish Education, which concluded that "Jewish education in America is a mile wide and an inch deep." Former Rabbinical Assembly executive vice-president Max *Routtenberg joined in the criticism that focused primarily on the congregational school. He saw that while three-fourths of its class time was devoted to Hebrew language and to reading the Bible and prayer book, "[n]one of the thousands of children that have been put in our care learned to use Hebrew functionally." Instead, they are

ill-at-ease in the synagogue, unfamiliar with the service, find the prayers irrelevant and boring, and Judaism as a whole a meaningless collection of rites and rituals. . . . Except for the climactic experience of Bar or Bat Mitzvah, we have given them nothing that remains memorable or pleasurable in their Jewish lives, only negative attitudes which later experiences may somehow overcome.

The problem with the congregational schools, according to Routtenberg, was that their goals were "unattainable" and "unrealistic." He called for a revamping of the afternoon Hebrew school to limit the curricular objectives to preparing children to participate in basic Jewish rituals and ceremonies in the synagogue and the home and to inculcate the rudiments of Judaism.[44]

Over the course of the 1960s Routtenberg's criticisms were echoed, this time by Jewish youth, who in challenging establishments of all kinds challenged the synagogues and Hebrew schools in which they had been raised. In 1969 the Rabbinical Assembly reexamined the Hebrew school. Rabbinical Assembly executive vice-president Wolfe Kelman called for "radical solutions, radical reevaluations, a radical reconsideration of our curriculum" to alleviate the dissatisfaction with the system. But he urged his colleagues not to belittle the very real accomplishments of the congregational schools. After all, it was a mark of achievement that Jewish youth, educated in those schools and Conservative youth movements, knew enough and were sufficiently committed to the Jewish way of life to demand more from these same institutions.[45]

Despite Kelman's balanced perspective, the consensus was that serious problems remained in the congregational schools. Rabbi Raphael Arzt believed that the educational system did not realistically address the plurality of viable options Jewish youth faced. The schools were "intellectually stale and emotionally arid" and could not attract and keep the next generation of Conservative Jews. Mordecai M. Kaplan believed that the essential problem was a lack of motivation, that Conservative leadership had failed to "create a sense of need for Jewish education."[46]

In the 1970s a new concern was added to the criticism of the congregational schools. In his presidential address to the Rabbinical Assembly in 1976, Mordecai Waxman observed the frightening decline in the number of students receiving an education in Conservative Hebrew schools. In 1962 there were 550,000 students enrolled in congregational schools; by 1976 there were only 330,000. True, Jewish day schools and the declining birthrate that followed the boom of 1947–60 accounted for some of the loss. Still, the conclusion was unmistakably clear. The Conservative congregational schools were no longer attracting parents and children the way they had in the past.[47]

The solution to these problems, some felt, was to develop new curricula and materials for the afternoon congregational school. The Seminary tried to address the problem with the establishment of the Melton Research Center for Jewish Education (1960), a research institute funded by Columbus, Ohio, philanthropist Samuel M. Melton. With a broad charge of helping teachers and students in Conservative afternoon schools, the Melton Center emphasized the centrality of teacher education and the development of new and exciting methods and materials for bringing classical Jewish texts to the classroom. Its first and best-known project was the development of the Melton Bible Method. Meanwhile, in the mid-1970s the United Synagogue Commission on Jewish Education experimented with the Menorah Curriculum, an ambitious program that promised schools and students a choice of studies, like the branches on a menorah (prayer-commandments, literature, language, or history) after completion of a minimum two-year core of basic educational requirements.[48]

Still, by the 1980s it was not clear that a solution to the problems of the Conservative congregational school had been found. Certainly, a list of Conservatism's educational achievements—the congregational schools, Leadership Training Fellowship, Solomon Schechter Day Schools, Camp Ramah, United Synagogue Youth, and the work in adult education—reflects well on the Conservative movement. They buttress Kelman's assertion: "I think I can say unequivocally that today more Jewish children on every level, from the nursery through the college years, are receiving a better Jewish education than in any time in Jewish history, certainly on this continent." Yet as Edward *Sandrow observed in his presidential address to the Rabbinical Assembly in 1961, many of the problems within the Conservative movement centered "about the still unsolved critical problems of Jewish education." Despite an impressive list of accomplishments in the field of education and youth work, that statement rings as true today as it did a quarter of a century ago.[49]

NOTES

1. The chief work on the United Synagogue of America is Abraham J. Karp, *A History of the United Synagogue of America, 1913–1963* (New York, 1964); on its founding and early years, see Herbert Rosenblum, "The Founding of the United Synagogue of America, 1913" (Ph.D. diss., Brandeis University, 1970); Rosenblum's *Conservative Judaism: A Contemporary History* (New York, 1983) has data; Herbert Parzen, *Architects of Conservative Judaism* (New York, 1964) also contains essential materials, esp. ch. 4; on the early need for a congregational union, see Moshe Davis, *The Emergence of Conservative Judaism* (New York, 1963), pp. 314–21.

2. Herman H. and Mignon L. Rubenovitz, *The Waking Heart* (Cambridge, Mass., 1967), pp. 35–54, 82.

3. "Preamble to the Constitution of the United Synagogue," in Mordecai Waxman, ed., *Tradition and Change* (New York, 1958), p. 173.

4. Solomon Schechter, "The Work of Heaven: An Address," in Waxman, *Tradition and Change*, pp. 163–72.

5. On the debate over extensity, see Parzen, *Architects*, pp. 106–9.

6. Marshall Sklare, *Conservative Judaism* (1955; rev. 1972; reprint ed., Lanham, Md., 1985), pp. 218–19, 257.

7. On field work and propaganda, see *United Synagogue Third Annual Report*, 1915, pp. 20–22; *Recorder* 1, 1 (January 1921), pp. 4–5. Denver rabbi Charles Eliezer Hillel Kauvar was typical of the early Conservative rabbis who traveled to neighboring states on behalf of the United Synagogue; see, for example, Bernard Shuman, *A History of the Sioux City Jewish Community* (Sioux City, 1969), pp. 47–56.

8. *NYT* 30 August 1945, p. 21.

9. *Temple Emanu-El: The First Fifty Years, 1924–1975* (Providence, Rhode Island, n.d.), pp. 24–30.

10. Sklare, *Conservative Judaism*, pp. 66–82.

11. Quotation from Max Drob, "The Achievements of the United Synagogue Convention," *Recorder* 1, 2 (April 1921), p. 3; on the lead of the UAHC, see Joseph Miller, "Organizing Men's Clubs," *Recorder* 8, 2 (April 1928), p. 8.

12. The Women's League has published two histories, *They Dared to Dream: A History of National Women's League, 1918–1968* (New York, 1967) and *The Sixth Decade: 1968–78* (New York, 1978), a *Handbook for Jewish Women's Organizations* (New York, 1924), and the magazine *Women's League Outlook* (1930–   ).

13. Eugene Kohn, "Our Young People and the Synagogue," *Recorder* 1, 2 (April 1921), pp. 16–17; Israel Goldstein, "A Message to the Jewish Youth of America," *Recorder* 2, 1 (January 1922), p. 18; *Recorder* 6, 4 (October 1926), p. 27; *Review* 8, 5 (March 1955), p. 4.

14. Among its publications are Samuel M. Cohen, *The Men's Club: A Manual* (New York, 1930); the magazines *The Torch* (1942–76) and *The Torchlight* (1976–   ); and *Roads to Jewish Survival*, a volume of selections from the first twenty-five years of *The*

Torch edited by Milton Berger, Joel S. Geffen, and M. David Hoffman (New York, 1967).

15. Leon Jick, *The Americanization of the Synagogue, 1820–1870* (Hanover, N.H., 1976), p. 183.

16. "Salutory," *Recorder* 1, 1 (July 1920), p. 1.

17. See, for example, "Congregational Activities," *Recorder* 5, 1 (January 1925), pp. 29–30; Sklare, *Conservative Judaism*, pp. 75–82, 130–44.

18. Deborah Dash Moore, *At Home in America: Second Generation New York Jews* (New York, 1981), pp. 123–47.

19. *PRA 1934* vol. 5, p. 66; *PRA 1946* vol. 10, pp. 206–7; *PRA 1955* vol. 19, p. 200; on the impact of the Depression on synagogues, see community and synagogue histories, for example, Marc Lee Raphael, *Jews and Judaism in a Midwestern Community: Columbus, Ohio, 1840–1975* (Columbus, Ohio, 1979), pp. 266–67, and *The Anshe Emet Synagogue, 1873–1973* (Chicago, n.d.), p. 16. Lucy Dawidowicz describes how the Jackson Heights Jewish Center paid a token $25 annual dues to the United Synagogue rather than the $250 assessed; see "Middle-Class Judaism," in her *The Jewish Presence: Essays in Identity and History* (New York, 1977), p. 79.

20. The year-in-review essays that appeared in the *American Jewish Year Book* in the 1930s, written for the most part by Harry Schneiderman, chronicled developments in the Orthodox, Conservative, and Reform religious organizations. They show quite well the changing concerns of American Jewry; see, for example, *AJYB* vol. 38 (1936–37), pp. 175–394.

21. Albert I. Gordon, "The United Synagogue: A Vision for the Future," *PRA 1947* vol. 11, pp. 356–62; these developments are chronicled in the *News of the United Synagogue of America*, vols. 1–4, (June 1945–Sept. 1948) and the *United Synagogue Review* (irregularly numbered, October 1948–1950). The *United Synagogue Review*, numbered consecutively starting with vol. 3, 7 (March 1950), remains the principal journal of the United Synagogue. In its more than thirty-five-year history it has been published as often as ten times a year and as infrequently as once a year. Most recently, it has appeared twice a year, in magazine format, edited by former National Women's League president Ruth Perry.

22. The standards are printed in United Synagogue of America, *1986 Yearbook, Directory and Buyer's Guide* (New York), pp. 64–67. In accordance with a ruling of the Rabbinical Assembly's Committee on Jewish Law and Standards, which found that games of chance should not be played in a synagogue, the standards originally prohibited bingo games for fund-raising. In the 1960s some fifteen congregations were suspended for violating this standard; *Review* 24, 4 (Winter 1972), p. 7. In 1967 the Committee on Jewish Law and Standards reconsidered its decision and allowed for, while it did not encourage, games of chance for fund-raising; *PRA 1967* vol. 31, pp. 192, 209–19. The standards were subsequently amended.

23. Wolfe Kelman, "The American Synagogue: Present and Prospects," *CJ* 26, 1 (Fall 1971), pp. 3–24. The negative predictions for the future of Conservative Judaism stem primarily from the studies of Charles Liebman, including a private report made to Seminary chancellor Gerson Cohen in 1979; see Charles S. Liebman and Saul Shapiro, "A Survey of the Conservative Movement and Some of Its Religious Attitudes," an unpublished report submitted to the Chancellor and the Faculty of the Jewish Theological Seminary of America (1979); Charles Liebman, "The Future of Conservative Judaism in the United States," *Jerusalem Letter: Viewpoints* 11, 31 March 1980.

24. Quotation from Rosenblum, *Conservative Judaism*, p. 70.

25. Report cited by Karp, *A History*, pp. 15–16; Jick, *Americanization*, pp. 148–50.

26. Julius H. Greenstone, Chairman of the United Synagogue Education Committee, "The Forward Work for Jewish Education," *Recorder* 1, 1 (July 1920), p. 2; Julius H. Greenstone, "Text Books for Our Religious Schools," *Recorder* 4, 1 (January 1924), p. 8. The Education Committee's first publications included Eugene Kohn, *A Manual for Teaching Biblical History* (New York, 1917) and *The Bible Story Told by Sulamith Ish-Kishor* (New York, 1921).

27. "The United Synagogue Convention Reviewed," *Recorder* 9, 3 (July 1929), pp. 5–6.

28. Morris Goodblatt, "Report of the Commission on Jewish Education," *PRA 1943* vol. 8, pp. 253–55; "Joint Commission on Jewish Education," *PRA 1945* vol. 9, pp. 11–12.

29. Robert Gordis, "The Tasks Before Us," *CJ* 1, 1 (January 1945), pp. 4–5; see also, Simon Greenberg, "Educational Content in Terms of Contemporary Needs," *PRA 1943* vol. 8, pp. 182–90.

30. "Statement on the Objectives and Standards for the Congregational School," *CJ* 2, 3 (April 1946), pp. 24–31. In addition to this paper, the following three articles form the blueprints for Jewish education in the congregational schools: Simon Greenberg, "Basic Premises of a Proposed Structure for Jewish Education in America," *CJ* 3, 1 (Fall 1947), pp. 5–13; Moshe Davis, "Ladder of Jewish Education," *CJ* 4, 4 (May 1948), pp. 1–14; Abraham E. Millgram, "Implementing a Program of Intensive Jewish Education in the Congregational School," *CJ* 5, 4 (June 1949), pp. 1–9.

31. Morris Goodblatt, "A Report on the Joint Commission on Education," *PRA 1946* vol. 10, pp. 317–19; Robert Gordis, "Presidential Address: New Vistas for Conservative Judaism," *PRA 1946* vol. 10, p. 65.

32. Abraham E. Millgram, "Report of the United Synagogue Commission on Jewish Education," *PRA 1947* vol. 11, pp. 87–93; *PRA 1949* vol. 13, pp. 72–73. In 1985 the commission listed more than 140 publications.

33. Davis, *Emergence*, pp. 34–64; Max Gelb, "The Day School: Making It an Effective Enterprise," *PRA 1974* vol. 36, pp. 114–21.

34. *Review* 11, 3 (Autumn 1958), p. 3; "Solomon Schechter Day School Association Statement of Requirements," United Synagogue, *1986 Yearbook*, pp. 84–87.

35. *Review* 21, 1 (April 1968), p. 22; United Synagogue Commission on Jewish Education, "Solomon Schechter Day School Association Student Enrollment Survey, 1985–87" (mimeo).

36. Norman Salit, "Intensifying the Jewish Nature of Summer Camps," *Recorder* 4, 2 (April 1924), pp. 14–15.

37. Shuly Rubin Schwartz, "Ramah—The Early Years, 1947–1952" (M.A. thesis, Jewish Theological Seminary of America, 1976).

38. Ibid., esp. p. 22.

39. See Burton I. Cohen, "Louis Newman's Wisconsin Innovations and Their Effect upon the Ramah Camping Movement," in *Studies in Jewish Education and Judaica in Honor of Louis Newman*, ed. Alexander M. Shapiro and Burton I. Cohen (New York, 1984), pp. 23–38.

40. Max Arzt, "Conservative Judaism Comes of Age," *PRA 1975* vol. 37, p. 341.

41. Simon Greenberg, "Strengthening the Weakest Link," *Review* 4, 6 (February

1951), p. 6; Helen Mintz, "The Youth Challenge," *Review* 15, 4 (Winter 1963), pp. 10–13.

42. *Review* 36, 1 (Fall 1983), p. 7.

43. Ben Zion Bokser, "Report of the Committee on Jewish Law and Standards," *PRA 1964* vol. 28, pp. 240–41; Seymour Siegel, "United Synagogue Youth Kinnusim," *PRA 1967* vol. 31, pp. 229–30.

44. Max Routtenberg, "The Crisis in the Congregational School" (1963), reprinted in Max Routtenberg, *Decades of Decision* (New York, 1973), pp. 30–41.

45. Wolfe Kelman, "The Introspective Overview," *PRA 1969* vol. 33, pp. 5–6; Wolfe Kelman, "New Directions in Jewish Education," *PRA 1969* vol. 33, pp. 86–87.

46. Raphael Arzt, *PRA 1969* vol. 33, pp. 108–9; Mordecai M. Kaplan, "Discussion," *PRA 1969* vol. 33, p. 106.

47. Mordecai Waxman, "President's Address," *PRA 1976* vol. 38, p. 87; see David Lieber, "The Conservative Congregational School" *CJ* 27, 4 (Summer 1973), pp. 24–34.

48. "New Materials from the Melton Research Center," *PRA 1980* vol. 42, pp. 144–46; Joel H. Zaiman, "On Educating Our Children," *CJ* 31, 2, (Winter 1977), pp. 80–81; Jay B. Stern, "The Menorah Curriculum," *CJ* 31, 2 (Winter 1977), p. 85.

49. Kelman, "Introspective," p. 5; Edward Sandrow, "President's Report," *PRA 1961* vol. 25, p. 97.

APPENDICES

APPENDICES

1. JEWISH THEOLOGICAL SEMINARY OF AMERICA

PRESIDENTS/CHANCELLORS (1886; the title chancellor was introduced in 1951)

1886–1897	Sabato Morais
1897–1902	Henry Pereira Mendes (Acting President)
1902–1915	Solomon Schechter
1916–1940	Cyrus Adler (Acting 1915–1924)
1940–1972	Louis Finkelstein
1972–1986	Gerson Cohen
1986–	Ismar Schorsch

PRESIDENTS OF THE UNIVERSITY OF JUDAISM (1947)

1948–1963	Simon Greenberg
1963–	David Lieber

PRESIDENTS OF THE JEWISH THEOLOGICAL SEMINARY ASSOCIATION

1886–1901	Joseph Blumenthal
1901–1902	Adolphus S. Solomons

CHAIRMEN OF THE BOARD OF DIRECTORS

1902–1905	Cyrus Adler
1905–1929	Louis Marshall
1929–1941	Sol M. Stroock
1942–1943	Henry S. Hendricks
1943–1963	Alan M. Stroock
1964–1966	Simon H. Rifkind
1966–1973	Stanley H. Fuld
1974–1979	Sol M. Linowitz
1979–1983	Alan M. Stroock

1983–1986   Howard M. Holtzman
1986–   Stephen M. Peck

CHAIRMEN OF THE BOARD OF OVERSEERS

1946–1963   Herbert H. Lehman
1963–1969   Arthur J. Goldberg
1969–1974   Sol M. Linowitz
1974–1978   Newton N. Minow
1979–1983   Lester Crown
1983–   George A. Strichman

2. THE RABBINICAL ASSEMBLY

PRESIDENTS OF THE ALUMNI ASSOCIATION OF THE JEWISH THEOLOGICAL SEMINARY OF AMERICA

1901–1904	Henry Speaker
1904–1907	Menahem Max Eichler
1907–1912	Charles I. Hoffman
1912–1914	Jacob Kohn
1914–1916	Elias Solomon
1916–1918	Max D. Klein

PRESIDENTS OF THE RABBINICAL ASSEMBLY

1918–1922	Max D. Klein
1922–1925	Louis M. Epstein
1925–1928	Max Drob
1928–1930	Louis Finkelstein
1930–1932	Israel Levinthal
1932–1933	Mordecai M. Kaplan
1933–1935	Elias Margolis
1935–1937	Eugene Kohn
1937–1939	Simon Greenberg
1939–1940	Max Arzt
1940–1942	Leon Lang
1942–1944	Louis Levitsky
1944–1946	Robert Gordis
1946–1948	Israel Goldman
1948–1950	David Aronson
1950–1952	Max D. Davidson
1952–1954	Ira Eisenstein
1954–1956	Harry Halpern
1956–1958	Aaron H. Blumenthal
1958–1960	Isaac Klein

1960–1962 Edward Sandrow
1962–1964 Theodore Friedman
1964–1966 Max J. Routtenberg
1966–1968 Eli A. Bohnen
1968–1970 Ralph Simon
1970–1972 S. Gershon Levi
1972–1974 Judah Nadich
1974–1976 Mordecai Waxman
1976–1978 Stanley Rabinowitz
1978–1980 Saul I. Teplitz
1980–1982 Seymour J. Cohen
1982–1984 Arnold M. Goodman
1984–1986 Alexander Shapiro
1986– Kassel Abelson

EXECUTIVE VICE-PRESIDENTS OF THE RABBINICAL ASSEMBLY

1945–1949 Bernard Segal (Executive Director, 1945–1947)
1949–1951 Max Routtenberg
1951– Wolfe Kelman

3. THE CANTORS ASSEMBLY

PRESIDENTS OF THE CANTORS ASSEMBLY (founded 1947)

1947–1948	Abraham J. Rose
1948–1951	Max Wohlberg
1951–1954	Nathan Mendelson
1954–1956	Charles Sudock
1956–1959	Samuel Rosenbaum
1959–1961	Isaac Wall
1961–1964	Moses J. Silverman
1964–1967	Saul Meisels
1967–1969	Arthur Koret
1969–1971	David J. Leon
1971–1973	Yehudah L. Mandel
1973–1975	Gregor Shelkan
1975–1977	Michael Hammerman
1977–1979	Kurt Silbermann
1979–1981	Morton Shames
1981–1983	Abraham Shapiro
1983–1985	Ivan Perlman
1985–1987	Saul Hammerman
1987–	Solomon Mendelson

EXECUTIVE VICE-PRESIDENTS OF THE CANTORS ASSEMBLY

1947–1959	David J. Putterman
1959–	Samuel Rosenbaum

4. JEWISH EDUCATORS ASSEMBLY

PRESIDENTS OF JEWISH EDUCATORS ASSEMBLY (founded 1951)

1951–1955	Henry Goldberg
1955–1957	Harry Malin
1957–1959	William B. Lakritz
1959–1961	Alfred Weisel
1961–1963	Martin Goldstein
1963–1965	Hyman Pomerantz
1965–1967	Norman Schanin
1967–1969	Nathan Winter
1969–1971	Gabriel Cohen
1971–1973	Shimon Frost
1973–1975	Aryeh Rohn
1975–1977	Hyman Campeas
1977–1979	Jay Stern
1979–1981	Solomon Goldman
1981–1983	Irving H. Skolnick
1983–1985	Aaron M. Nussbaum
1985–1987	Michael Korman
1987–	Marim Charry

5. THE UNITED SYNAGOGUE OF AMERICA

PRESIDENTS

1913–1914	Solomon Schechter
1914–1917	Cyrus Adler
1917–1918	Louis Ginzberg
1918–1926	Elias L. Solomon
1926–1927	Herman Abramowitz
1927–1929	S. Herbert Golden
1929–1931	Nathan Levy
1931	Jacob Kohn
1931–1944	Louis J. Moss
1944–1950	Samuel Rothstein
1950–1953	Maxwell Abbell
1953–1957	Charles Rosengarten
1957–1961	Bernath L. Jacobs
1961–1965	George Maislen
1965–1969	Henry N. Rapaport
1969–1973	Jacob Stein
1973–1977	Arthur J. Levine
1977–1981	Simon Schwartz
1981–1985	Marshall Wolke
1985–	Franklin D. Kreutzer

EXECUTIVE DIRECTORS

1917–1944	Samuel M. Cohen
1945	Elias Solomon (Acting)
1946	Stanley Rabinowitz (Acting)
1946–1949	Albert I. Gordon
1950	Emil Lehman (Acting)
1950–1953	Simon Greenberg
1953–1970	Bernard Segal

EXECUTIVE VICE-PRESIDENTS

1970–1976   Bernard Segal
1976–   Benjamin Z. Kreitman

DIRECTORS OF THE NATIONAL ACADEMY FOR ADULT JEWISH STUDIES (1941)

1941–1951   Israel Goldman
1952–1957   Simon Noveck
1958–1978   Marvin Wiener

DIRECTORS OF THE UNITED SYNAGOGUE COMMISSION ON JEWISH EDUCATION (1946)

1946–1961   Abraham Ezra Millgram
1961–1964   Walter I. Ackerman
1964–   Morton Siegel

6. WORLD COUNCIL OF SYNAGOGUES (organized 1957, chartered 1959)

PRESIDENTS

1959–1964	Charles Rosengarten
1964–1968	Emanuel Scoblionko
1968–1972	Morris Speizman
1972–1976	Samuel Rothstein
1976–1981	David Zucker
1981–1985	Mordecai Waxman
1985–	Marshall Wolke

EXECUTIVE DIRECTORS

1959–1976	Morris Laub
1976–1980	Muriel Bermar
1980–1986	Zipporah Liben
1986–	Barbara Kessel

7. MERCAZ: THE MOVEMENT TO REAFFIRM CONSERVATIVE ZIONISM (1978)

PRESIDENTS

1978–1983 Stanley Rabinowitz
1983–   Simon Schwartz

8. FOUNDATION FOR CONSERVATIVE *(MASORTI)* JUDAISM IN ISRAEL (1982)

PRESIDENTS

1984–1987	Louis Winer (National Lay Chairman)
1987–	Neil Norry

EXECUTIVE DIRECTORS

1982–1984	David Gordis
1984–1986	Simon Greenberg
1986–1987	Lee Levine
1987–	Michael Monson

9. WOMEN'S LEAGUE FOR CONSERVATIVE JUDAISM (NATIONAL WOMEN'S LEAGUE OF THE UNITED SYNAGOGUE OF AMERICA, 1918–1972)

PRESIDENTS

1918–1919	Mathilde Schechter
1919–1928	Fanny Hoffman
1928–1944	Dora Spiegel
1944–1950	Sarah Kopelman
1950–1954	Marion Siner Gordon
1954–1958	Helen Sussman
1958–1962	Syd Rossman
1962–1966	Helen Fried
1966–1970	Evelyn Henkind
1970–1974	Selma Rapaport
1974–1978	Ruth Perry
1978–1982	Goldie Kweller
1982–1986	Selma Weintraub
1986–	Evelyn Auerbach

10. THE FEDERATION OF JEWISH MEN'S CLUBS (NATIONAL FEDERATION OF JEWISH MEN'S CLUBS, 1929–1982)

PRESIDENTS

1929–1933	Edwin C. Weinrib
1933–1937	Theodore Charnas
1937–1941	Louis J. Schwartz
1941–1943	Abraham J. Leonard
1943–1945	Milton Berger
1945–1947	Stanley Garten
1947–1949	Arthur S. Bruckman
1949–1950	Barnet Lieberman
1950–1952	Milton Nevins
1952–1954	Albert H. Jacobson
1954–1956	Albert Kaufman
1956–1958	Abraham Satovsky
1958–1960	Bernard Rackmil
1960–1961	Morris Spelfogel
1961–1963	Philip Goldstein
1963–1965	S. David Rosenzweig
1965–1967	Mannye London
1967–1969	Herman Rothenberg
1969–1971	Morton Tabas
1971–1973	Max M. Goldberg
1973–1975	I. Murray Jacobs
1975–1977	Abraham A. Silver
1977–1979	Morton R. Lang
1979–1981	Sam Berlin
1981–1983	Jacob C. Lish
1983–1985	Joseph Gurmankin
1985–1987	Jules Porter
1987–	Jerome Agrest

11. UNITED SYNAGOGUE YOUTH
(founded 1951)

PRESIDENTS

1951–1953	Rabbi Paul Freedman
1953–1955	Arthur Podell
1955–1957	Arthur Pescoe
1957–1958	Rabbi Gerald Zelizer
1958–1959	Alan Kaplan
1959–1960	Martin Dank
1960–1961	Rabbi James Lebeau
1961–1962	David Lissy
1962–1963	Danny Siegel
1963–1964	Peter Geffen
1964–1965	Richard Hoffman
1965–1966	Alan Mintz
1966–1967	Rabbi Stephen Garfinkel
1967–1968	Oscar Fruchtman
1968–1969	Richie Finkelstein
1969–1970	David Schwartz
1970–1971	Marc Gary
1971–1972	Larry Burrows
1972–1973	James Kaufman
1973–1974	Richard Moline
1974–1975	Robert Lennick
1975–1976	Rabbi Jeff Segelman
1976–1977	David Yolen
1977–1978	Jeff Schoenberg
1978–1979	David Marcus
1979–1980	Jeremy J. Fingerman
1980–1981	Bruce Gordon
1981–1982	Mark Davis
1982–1983	Shraga Sherman

1983–1984   Eric Weinstock
1984–1985   David Israel
1985–1986   David Stern
1986–1987   David Kaye
1987–1988   Hillary Buff

12. RECONSTRUCTIONIST ORGANIZATIONS

PRESIDENTS OF THE RECONSTRUCTIONIST RABBINICAL COLLEGE (1968)

1968–1981   Ira Eisenstein
1981–1986   Ira Silverman
1986–   Arthur Green (Acting, 1986–87)

PRESIDENTS OF THE FEDERATION OF RECONSTRUCTIONIST CONGREGATIONS AND HAVUROT (1954)

1960–1962   Benjamin W. Mehlman
1962–1966   Arthur C. Kellman
1966–1972   Lavy M. Becker
1972–1974   Herman Levin
1974–1976   Leroy C. Shuster
1976–1978   Leonard Leveton
1978–1980   Herbert I. Winer
1980–1982   Jacob M. Snyder
1982–1984   Samuel Blumenthal
1984–   Lillian Kaplan

PRESIDENTS OF THE RECONSTRUCTIONIST RABBINICAL ASSOCIATION (1975)

1975–1977   David Brusin
1977–1979   Arnold Rachlis
1979–1981   Dennis Sasso
1981–1983   Elliot Skiddell
1983–1985   Steven Sager
1985–1987   Ira J. Schiffer
1987–   Joy Levitt

GLOSSARY

In general, spelling of Hebrew terms has been standardized according to Werner Weinberg's *How Do You Spell Chanukah?* (Cincinnati: Hebrew Union College Press, 1976). However, where variant spellings have been employed extensively in Conservative publications, they have been retained.

agadah: a generic term for the non-*halachic* materials of rabbinic literature, i.e., non-legal materials; contains explications of the narrative, historical, ethical, and prophetic portions of the Bible and includes stories, legends, folklore, anecdotes, and maxims

agunah: a woman unable to remarry according to Jewish law because of desertion by her husband or because his death cannot be certified; a deserted wife

aliyah, pl. *aliyot*: being called up to the Torah; a symbolic reading of the Torah by the members of the congregation; the person who has the *aliyah* usually recites only the appropriate blessings while a cantor or reader chants the actual Torah portion

baraita, pl. *beraitot*: rabbinic statements not found in the Mishnah

bar mitzvah, bat mitzvah: a ceremony at which a young boy (*bar mitzvah*) or a young girl (*bat mitzvah*), usually at the age of thirteen, participates in the synagogue service, signifying that he/she has reached the age of religious maturity; an occasion for celebration

bet din: Jewish court of law

bet din hagadol: supreme court of Jewish law

blood libel: allegation, dating from the Middle Ages, that Jews murder Christians in order to obtain blood for ritual purposes

cheder: lit. room; old-fashioned elementary school

chevrah kadisha: society whose members fulfill the commandment to bury the dead according to the dictates of Jewish law

confirmation: originally a nineteenth-century German Reform ceremony substituting for *bar mitzvah*; more commonly in Conservative congregations, a ceremony, often held at Shavuot, in which sixteen and seventeen year olds who continued their Jewish education beyond the *bar/bat mitzvah* affirm their devotion to Judaism

diaspora: Jewish settlement outside the land of Israel

Eretz Yisrael: Hebrew for the land of Israel

gaon, pl. *geonim*: formal title of the heads of the academies of Sura and Pumbedita in Babylonia, ca. sixth to eleventh centuries

genizah: place, often a room in a synagogue, where worn-out books and ritual objects which may no longer be used are stored

get, pl. *gittin*: Jewish bill of divorcement

halachah, adj. *halachic*: the legal material of rabbinic literature; a generic term for the whole legal system of Judaism with its laws, practices, and observances; also a specific ruling within Jewish law

hatarat horaah: the classical formula of rabbinic ordination

hazzan, pl. *hazzanim*: a cantor in the synagogue; the one who leads the congregation in worship

Hatikvah: lit. the hope; the national anthem of Israel

kaddish: doxology recited during worship; doxology recited by close relatives of the deceased during a set period of mourning

kallah, pl. *kallot*: summer adult study sessions; also retreats

kasher: lit. to make fit or proper; generally to prepare foods according to Jewish dietary laws; to make kosher

kashrut: Jewish dietary laws

kehilah: congregation or communal organization

ketubah: Jewish marriage contract

kinnusim: conventions

Klal Yisrael: the Jewish people

maggid: popular, often itinerant preacher

mahzor: High Holiday prayer book

mara d'atra: lit. the master of the locality; refers to the concept that a rabbi is the supreme legal authority for his congregation

mechizah: a partition separating men and women during worship in the synagogue

megillah: lit. scroll; commonly refers to the scroll of the Biblical book of Esther

melamed: elementary teacher

midrash, pl. *midrashim*: a form of rabbinic literature that expands and explicates the Biblical text to bring out lessons through stories or homiletics

mikveh: ritual bath

minchah: daily afternoon service

minyan: quorum of ten, traditionally adult males, required for public worship

Mishnah: a code of Jewish law redacted and arranged by Rabbi Judah ha-Nasi, ca. 200 C.E.

mitzvah, pl. *mitzvot*: commandment; good deed

responsa: a form of rabbinic literature consisting of legal opinions written in response to questions about actual cases

rosh yeshivah: head of the *yeshivah* or Talmudical academy

selichot: special prayers recited from before Rosh Hashanah until Yom Kippur

semichah: rabbinic ordination

Shabbat: Sabbath

shtetl, pl. *shtetlakh*: small-town Jewish communities in Eastern Europe; note that their size varied greatly

Shulchan Aruch: lit. the prepared table; the code of Jewish law compiled by Joseph Caro in the sixteenth century

siddur: prayer book

takanah, pl. *takanot*: rabbinic legislation in the post-Talmudic period that can alter or amend a law

Talmud: lit. study or learning; most commonly, the body of rabbinic literature comprising the commentary and discussions on the Mishnah; one version was codified in Babylonia ca. 500 C.E.; a Palestinian version, known as the Jerusalem Talmud, was codified a century earlier

tanna, pl. *tannaim*: sages from the period of Hillel to the compilation of the Mishnah, ca. 20–200 C.E.

tevilah: immersion in a ritual bath

t'nai b'kiddushin: a conditional agreement to the marriage

Torah: lit. teaching; commonly, the Pentateuch or the scroll of the Five Books of Moses read in the synagogue

trefah: not kosher

tsedakah: charity; also justice

tsitsis: a fringed garment worn by strictly observant Jewish men

Wissenschaft des Judentums: lit. science of Judaism; a nineteenth-century movement advocating the scientific study of Judaism using modern scholastic methods

yeshivah, pl. *yeshivot*: Talmudical academies

Yishuv: Jewish community in the land of Israel before the establishment of the state of Israel

yom tov sheni: second day of festivals

BIBLIOGRAPHY

ANNUAL REPORTS, PROCEEDINGS, ORGANIZATION MAGAZINES, AND JOURNALS

Beineinu. New York: 1970–   .(Rabbinical Assembly.)

The Biennial Reports, The Jewish Theological Seminary Association. New York: 1888–1902.

Conservative Judaism. New York: 1945–   .

Direction. Los Angeles: 1969–   . (University of Judaism.)

Jewish Theological Seminary Association. *Constitution and By-Laws*. New York: 1886.

———. *Proceedings* (of the Biennial Conventions). New York: 1888–1902.

Jewish Theological Seminary of America. *Academic Bulletin*. New York: 1902–   . (Previously called *Annual Register*.)

———. *Chancellor's Report*. New York: ?–

———. *Documents, Charter and By-Laws*. New York: 1903.

———. *Preliminary Announcement*. New York: 1902.

———. *Report for the Board of Overseers*. New York: 1962–   .

Jewish Theological Seminary Students Annual. Vols. 1–3. New York: 1914–16.

The Melton Journal. New York: 1966–   . (Melton Research Center for Jewish Education.)

News of the United Synagogue of America. New York: 1945–48.

Proceedings of the Rabbinical Assembly. New York: 1927–   .

Raayonot. Wyncote, Pa.: 1981–   . (Reconstructionist Rabbinical Association.)

Rabbinical Assembly News. New York: 1983–   .

Reconstructionist. New York: 1935–   .

SAJ Review. New York: 1922–29. (Society for the Advancement of Judaism, called *SAJ Bulletin*, 1922–25.)

The Synagogue Center. New York: 1943–45. (United Synagogue of America.)

Torch. New York: 1942–76. (National Federation of Jewish Men's Clubs.)

Torchlight. New York: 1977–   . (Federation of Jewish Men's Clubs.)

United Synagogue of America Annual Reports. New York 1913–   . (Later *Biennial Reports.*)

United Synagogue Recorder. New York: 1921–29.

United Synagogue Review. New York: 1948–   .

Women's League Outlook. New York: 1930–   .

SELECTED WRITINGS BY KEY LEADERS OF THE CONSERVATIVE AND RECONSTRUCTIONIST MOVEMENTS

Adler, Cyrus. *Lectures, Selected Papers, Addresses.* Philadelphia: 1933.

————. *Selected Letters of Cyrus Adler.* Edited by Ira Robinson. 2 vols. Philadelphia: 1985.

————, ed. *Jewish Theological Seminary of America: Semi-Centennial Volume.* New York: 1939.

Agus, Jacob. *Guideposts in Modern Judaism.* New York: 1954.

————. *Jewish Identity in an Age of Ideologies.* New York: 1978.

————. *The Jewish Quest: Essays on Basic Concepts of Jewish Theology.* New York: 1983.

————. *Modern Philosophies of Judaism.* New York: 1941.

Berger, Milton; Geffen, Joel; and Hoffman, M. David, eds. *Roads to Jewish Survival.* New York: 1967.

Bokser, Ben Zion. *Jewish Law: A Conservative Approach.* New York: 1964.

————. *Judaism and Modern Man: Essays in Jewish Theology.* New York: 1957.

————. *Judaism: Profile of a Faith.* New York: 1963.

Cohen, Gerson D. "The Present State of Conservative Judaism." *Judaism* 26 (Summer 1977): 268–74.

Cohen, Jack J. *The Case for Religious Naturalism: A Philosophy for the Modern Jew.* New York: 1958.

————. *Jewish Education in Democratic Society.* New York: 1964.

Dorff, Elliot N. *Conservative Judaism: Our Ancestors to Our Descendants.* New York: 1977.

Dresner, Samuel. *The Jewish Dietary Laws: Their Meaning for Our Time.* New York: 1959.

————. *Prayer, Humility and Compassion.* New York: 1957.

————. *The Sabbath.* New York: 1970.

Eisenstein, Ira. *Creative Judaism.* New York: 1936; rev. 1953.

————. *Judaism under Freedom.* New York: 1956.

————. *Varieties of Jewish Belief.* New York: 1966.

————. *What We Mean by Religion: A Modern Interpretation of the Sabbath and Festivals.* New York: 1938; rev. 1958.

Epstein, Louis. *Li-Shealat Ha-Agunah.* New York: 1940.

————. *A Solution to the Agunah Problem.* New York: 1936.

Finkelstein, Louis. *Tradition in the Making.* New York: 1937.

————. "The Underlying Concepts of Conservative Judaism." *CJ* 26, 4 (Summer 1972): 2–12.

Friedlaender, Israel. *Past and Present: Selected Essays.* 1919. Reprint, New York: 1961.

Friedman, Theodore. "Jewish Tradition in Twentieth Century America—The Conservative Approach." *Judaism* 3 (1954): 310–21.

———, ed. *What Is Conservative Judaism?* New York: N.D.

Gertel, Elliot. "Is Conservative Judaism—Conservative?" *Judaism* 28 (Spring 1979): 202–15.

Ginzberg, Louis. *On Jewish Law and Lore.* Philadelphia: 1955.

———. *Students, Scholars, and Saints.* Philadelphia: 1928.

Goldman, Solomon. *Crisis and Decision.* New York: 1938.

———. *A Rabbi Takes Stock.* New York: 1931.

Gordis, Robert. *Conservative Judaism: An American Philosophy.* New York: 1945.

———. *Conservative Judaism: A Modern Approach.* New York: 1956.

———. *A Faith for Moderns.* New York: 1960.

———. *The Jew Faces a New World.* New York: 1941.

———. *Judaism for the Modern Age.* New York: 1955.

———. "The Ordination of Women." *Midstream* 26, 7 (August/September 1980): 25–32.

———. "Reinterpretation—Its Canons and Limits." *CJ* 13, 4 (Summer 1959): 21–26.

———. "The Tasks Before Us: A Preface to Our Journal." *CJ* 1, 1 (January 1945): 1–8.

———. *Understanding Conservative Judaism.* Edited by Max Gelb. New York: 1978.

——— et al. "Conservative Judaism on Its Ninetieth Birthday: An Evaluation by Leaders in Conservatism, Orthodoxy, Reform, Reconstructionsim." *Judaism* 26, 3 (Summer 1977): 261–325.

——— et al. "The Issue of Patrilineal Descent—A Symposium." *Judaism* 34, 1 (Winter 1985): 3–135.

——— et al. "Women as Rabbis: A Many-Sided Examination of All Aspects—Halakhic, Ethical, Pragmatic." *Judaism* 33 (Winter 1984): 3–121.

Greenberg, Simon. *The Conservative Movement in Judaism: An Introduction.* New York: 1955.

———. *The Ethical in the Jewish and American Heritage.* New York: 1977.

———. *Foundations of Faith.* New York: 1967.

———. *The Ideals of the Jewish Prayer Book.* New York: 1940.

———. *A Jewish Philosophy and Pattern of Life.* New York: 1981.

Hertzberg, Arthur. *Being Jewish in America.* New York: 1979.

———. *Essays on Jewish Life and Thought.* New York: 1959.

Heschel, Abraham Joshua. *God in Search of Man: A Philosophy of Judaism.* New York: 1955.

———. *Man is Not Alone: A Philosophy of Religion.* New York: 1951.

———. *Sabbath: Its Meaning for Modern Man.* New York: 1951.

———. *Torah min Hashamayim b'Aspeklarya shel Hadorot.* 2 vols. New York: 1962–65.

Jacobs, Louis. *A Jewish Theology.* New York: 1973.

———. *Principles of the Jewish Faith: An Analytical Study.* New York: 1964.

———. *We Have Reason to Believe.* London: 1962.

Jewish Theological Seminary of America et al. *Emet Ve-Emunah: Statement of Principles of Conservative Judaism.* New York: n.d.

Kaplan, Mordecai M. *Dynamic Judaism: The Essential Writings of Mordecai M. Kaplan.* Edited by Emanuel S. Goldsmith and Mel Scult. New York: 1985.

———. *The Future of the American Jew*. New York: 1949.

———. *The Greater Judaism in the Making: A Study of the Modern Evolution of Judaism*. New York: 1960.

———. *Judaism as a Civilization: Toward a Reconstruction of American-Jewish Life*. New York: 1934.

———. *Judaism in Transition*. New York: 1936.

———. *Judaism Without Supernaturalism: The Only Alternative to Orthodoxy and Secularism*. New York: 1958.

———. *Know How to Answer: A Guide to Reconstructionism*. New York: 1951.

———. *The Meaning of God in Modern Jewish Religion*. New York: 1936.

———. *A New Approach to the Problem of Judaism*. New York: 1924.

———, ed. *The Reconstructionist Papers*. New York: 1936.

Karp, Abraham J., ed. *Conservative Judaism: The Legacy of Solomon Schechter*. 1963. Reprint, New York: 1975.

Kelman, Wolfe. "The American Synagogue: Present and Prospects." *CJ* 26, 1 (Fall 1971): 3–24.

Klein, Isaac. *A Guide to Jewish Religious Practice*. New York: 1979.

———. *Responsa and Halakhic Studies*. New York: 1975.

Kohn, Eugene. "Conservative Judaism—A Review." *CJ* 2 (June 1946): 17–28.

———. *The Future of Judaism in America*. New Rochelle, N.Y.: 1934.

———. *Religious Humanism: A Jewish Interpretation*. New York: 1953.

Kushner, Harold. *When Bad Things Happen to Good People*. New York: 1981.

———. *When All You Ever Wanted Isn't Enough*. New York: 1986.

Lerner, Stephen et al. "The Congregational Rabbi and the Conservative Synagogue: A Symposium." *CJ* 29, 2 (Winter 1975): 3–96.

Litvin, Baruch, and Hoenig, Sidney B., eds. *Jewish Identity: Modern Responsa and Opinions on the Registration of Children of Mixed Marriages*. New York: 1965. Contributors include Louis Finkelstein, Abraham Joshua Heschel, Mordecai M. Kaplan, and Saul Lieberman.

Mandelbaum, Bernard. *The Maturing of the Conservative Movement*. New York: 1968.

———. "The Meaning of the Conservative Movement." *CJ* 21 (Spring 1967): 54–64.

———. *The Wisdom of Solomon Schechter*. New York: 1963.

National Women's League of the United Synagogue of America. *They Dared to Dream: A History of the National Women's League*. New York: 1967.

Novak, David. "The Distinctiveness of Conservative Judaism." *Judaism* 26 (Summer 1977): 305–9.

———. *Law and Theology in Judaism*. 2 vols. New York: 1974–76.

Plotkin, Paul; Schulweis, Harold M.; Price, Ronald D.; and Nadich, Judah. "I Love Conservative Judaism But . . . " *Sh'ma* 17 (29 May 1987): 113–17.

Rabbinical Assembly. *Final Report of the Commission for the Study of the Ordination of Women as Rabbis*. Typescript, JTSA library, 30 January 1979.

Roth, Joel. *The Halakhic Process: A Systemic Analysis*. New York: 1987.

Routtenberg, Max. *Decades of Decision*. New York: 1973.

Schechter, Solomon. *Some Aspects of Rabbinic Theology*. New York: 1909.

———. *Seminary Addresses and Other Papers*. Cincinnati: 1915.

———. *Studies in Judaism*. 3 vols. London and Philadelphia: 1896–1924.

Schorsch, Ismar. "Emancipation and the Crisis of Religious Authority: The Emergence of the Modern Rabbinate." In *Revolution and Evolution: 1848 in German-Jewish History*, edited by Werner E. Mosse et al., Tubingen: 1981, pp. 205–48.

————. *Thoughts From 3080: Selected Addresses and Writings*. New York: n.d.

————. "Zacharias Frankel and the European Origins of Conservative Judaism." *Judaism* 30 (1981): 344–54.

Schulweis, Harold. *Evil and the Morality of God*. New York: 1984.

Siegel, Seymour. *The Jewish Dietary Laws: Contemporary Issues in Jewish Ethics*. New York: 1980.

————. "The Sabbath and Conservative Judaism." *Judaism*, 31 (Winter 1982): 45–54.

———— with Elliot Gertel, eds. *Conservative Judaism and Jewish Law*. New York: 1977.

———— with Elliot Gertel, eds. *God in the Teachings of Conservative Judaism*. New York: 1985.

Silver, Daniel Jeremy et al. "The Future of Rabbinic Training in America: A Symposium." *Judaism* 18 (1969): 387–420.

Steinberg, Milton. *Anatomy of Faith*. Edited by Arthur A. Cohen. New York: 1966.

————. *Basic Judaism*. New York: 1947.

————. *A Believing Jew: The Selected Writings of Milton Steinberg*. Edited by Edith A. Steinberg. New York: 1951.

————. *The Making of the Modern Jew*. 1934. Reprint, New York: 1948.

————. *A Partisan Guide to the Jewish Problem*. Indianapolis: 1945.

Tabory, Ephraim et al. "Reform and Conservative Judaism: Today and Tomorrow, A Symposium." *Judaism*, 31 (Fall 1982): 387–458.

Waxman, Mordecai, ed. *Tradition and Change*. New York: 1958.

Women's League for Conservative Judaism. *The Sixth Decade, 1968–1978*. New York: 1978.

MEMOIRS, AUTOBIOGRAPHIES, BIOGRAPHIES, COLLECTIONS OF SERMONS

Only a handful of biographical studies of the leaders of American Conservatism have been written, a situation that future historians of the movement must surely address. By and large the movement's leaders have been reticent in writing their own memoirs or intellectual histories, preferring instead to devote themselves to classical Jewish scholarship. Pulpit rabbis have also published numerous volumes of their sermons, addresses, and even their synagogue bulletin columns. A careful reading of these shows the range of the pulpit rabbis' exhortatory concerns and occasionally elicits biographical materials.

"Abraham Joshua Heschel: A Yahrzeit Tribute." *CJ* 28, 1 (Fall 1973): 3–96.

Adler, Cyrus. *I Have Considered the Days*. Philadelphia: 1943.

Adler, Morris. *May I Have a Word with You?* Edited by Goldie Adler and Lily Edelman. N.p.: 1967.

————. *The Voice Still Speaks: Message of the Torah for Contemporary Man*. Edited by Jacob Chinitz. New York: 1969.

Bentwich, Norman. *Solomon Schechter: A Biography*. Philadelphia: 1948.

Berger, Julius. *The Weekly Sermon*. New York: 1931.

Blumenthal, Aaron H. *And Bring Them Closer to Torah: The Life and Work of Rabbi Aaron H. Blumenthal*. Edited by David R. Blumenthal. Hoboken, N.J.: 1986.

Bosniak, Jacob. *Interpreting Jewish Life: The Sermons and Addresses of Jacob Bosniak.* New York: 1944.

Brauner, Ronald A., ed. *Shiv'im: Essays and Studies in Honor of Ira Eisenstein.* Philadelphia and New York: 1977.

Burstein, Abraham. *The Books of Moses: Sermons by American Rabbis.* New York: 1932.

Cohen, Armond. *All God's Children: A Jew Speaks.* New York: 1945.

Cohen, Boaz. *Professor Alexander Marx.* New York: 1928.

Cohen, Gerson D. "Wolfe Kelman—A Personal Tribute." In *Perspectives on Jews and Judaism: Essays in Honor of Wolfe Kelman,* edited by Arthur A. Chiel, pp. 1–6. New York: 1978.

Cohen, Helen, and Davis, Patricia Talbot. *Together They Built a Mountain.* Elkins Park, Pa.: 1969. (On Mortimer J. Cohen.)

Cohen, Seymour. *Affirming Life.* New York: 1987.

———. *Form, Fire, and Ashes.* New York: 1978.

———. *A Time to Speak.* New York: 1968.

Corre, Allen D. "Sabato Morais and Social Justice in Philadelphia, 1858–1897." *Shofar* 4, 1 (Fall 1985): 28–45.

Dalin, David G. "Cyrus Adler, Non-Zionism, and the Zionist Movement: A Study in Contradictions." *AJS Review* 10, 1 (Spring 1985): 55–86.

Davidson, Carrie. *Out of Endless Yearnings: A Memoir of Israel Davidson.* New York: 1946.

Druck, David. *Reb Levi Ginzberg.* New York: 1933.

Eisenstein, Ira. *Reconstructing Judaism: An Autobiography.* New York: 1986.

———, and Kohn, Eugene. *Mordecai M. Kaplan: An Evaluation.* New York: 1952.

Faber, Solomon. "Robert Gordis: A Tribute on the Occasion of His Seventy-fifth Birthday." *Jewish Book Annual* 40 (1982–83): 139–44.

Feinberg, Louis. *The Spiritual Foundations of Judaism and Other Essays, Selected Addresses, and Writings.* Cincinnati: 1951.

Friedman, Theodore. *Judgment and Destiny: Sermons for the Modern Jew.* New York: 1965.

———. *Letters to Jewish College Students.* New York: 1965.

Ginzberg, Eli. *Keeper of the Law: Louis Ginzberg.* Philadelphia: 1966.

Goldstein, Israel. *Israel at Home and Abroad (1962–1972).* Jerusalem: 1973.

———. *My World as a Jew: The Memoirs of Israel Goldstein.* 2 vols. New York: 1984.

———. *To Serve My People.* New York: 1983.

———. *Toward a Solution.* New York: 1940.

———. *Transition Years: New York-Jerusalem, 1960–62.* Jerusalem: 1962.

Greenberg, Sidney. *Adding Life to Our Years.* New York: 1959.

———. *Say Yes to Life.* New York: 1982.

Greenberg, Sidney et al. "Mordecai M. Kaplan: On His Centennial." *CJ* 34, 4 (March/April 1981): 3–41.

Greenstone, Julius. *Jewish Feasts and Fasts.* New York: 1945.

Gutstein, Morris. *Frontiers of Faith: Sermonic Discourses on the Weekly Biblical Readings.* New York: 1967.

Hailperin, Herman. *A Rabbi Teaches: A Collection of Addresses and Sermons.* New York: 1939.

Halpern, Harry. *From Where I Stand.* New York: 1974.

Heller, Abraham M. *Jewish Survival: Sermons and Addresses.* New York: 1939.

Hertz, Joseph Herman. *Early and Late: Addresses, Messages, and Prayers*. Hindhead, Surrey: 1943.

————. *Sermons, Addresses, and Studies*. 3 vols. London: 1938.

Hoffman, M. David. "Charles Isaiah Hoffman: One Hundredth Anniversary (1864–1964)." *American Jewish Historical Quarterly* 55 (1965–66): 212–34.

Klein, Isaac. *The Anguish and Ecstasy of a Jewish Chaplain*. New York: 1974.

————. *Spiritual Legacies: Sermons*. New York: 1981.

Levinthal, Israel H. *Judaism: An Analysis and Interpretation*. New York: 1935.

————. *Judaism Speaks to the Modern World*. London: 1963.

————. *The Message of Israel: Sermons, Addresses, Memoirs*. New York: 1973.

————. *Point of View: An Analysis of American Judaism*. New York: 1958.

————. *Steering or Drifting—Which?: Sermons and Discourses*. New York: 1928.

Libowitz, Richard. *Mordecai M. Kaplan and the Development of Reconstructionism*. New York and Toronto: 1983.

LoCicero, T.V. *Murder in the Synagogue*. Englewood Cliffs, N.J.: 1970. (On Morris Adler.)

Mandelbaum, Bernard, and Ratner, Victor M. *Choose Life*. New York: 1968.

Minkin, Fanny R. "Jacob Minkin: An Appreciation." In *The Shaping of the Modern Mind: The Life and Thought of the Great Jewish Philosophers*, edited by Jacob Minkin, pp. 9–35. New York and London: 1963.

Modlinger, Joshua. *Michael Higger: Idealist, Systematizer of the Talmud, and Progressive-Traditionalist Interpreter of Its Laws*. New York: 1947.

Mowshowitz, Israel. *A Rabbi's Rovings*. Hoboken, N.J.: 1985.

Nadich, Judah. *Eisenhower and the Jews*. New York: 1953.

Neuman, Abraham A. *Cyrus Adler: A Biographical Sketch*. Philadelphia: 1942.

Noveck, Simon. *Milton Steinberg: Portrait of a Rabbi*. New York: 1977.

Parzen, Herbert. *Architects of Conservative Judaism*. New York: 1964.

Rabinowitz, Hyman Reuven. *Bene Binah*. Jerusalem: 1972.

Reznikoff, Charles, ed. *Louis Marshall: Champion of Liberty*. Philadelphia: 1957.

Rosenberg, Stuart E. *The Real Jewish World: A Rabbi's Second Thoughts*. New York, 1984.

Routtenberg, Max. *Seedtime and Harvest*. New York: 1969.

Rubenovitz, Herman H., and Rubenovitz, Mignon L. *The Waking Heart*. Cambridge, Mass.: 1967.

Salit, Norman. *The Worlds of Norman Salit: Sermons, Papers, Addresses*. Edited by Abraham Burstein. New York: 1966.

Shargel, Baila Round. *Practical Dreamer: Israel Friedlaender and the Shaping of American Judaism*. New York: 1985.

Shohet, David M. *Preacher and Thinker: A Collection of Jewish Sermons for the Holidays and Other Occasions*. New York: 1933.

Simon, Ralph. *Challenges and Responses*. Chicago: 1985.

Steinberg, Milton. *From the Sermons of Rabbi Milton Steinberg*. Edited by Bernard Mandelbaum. 2 vols. New York: 1954–63.

Steinberg, Theodore. "Max Kadushin: An Appreciation." *CJ* 35, 4 (Summer 1982): 3–16.

Teplitz, Saul I., ed. *Best Jewish Sermons*. 11 vols. New York: 1952– .

Weinstein, Jacob L. *Solomon Goldman: A Rabbi's Rabbi*. New York: 1973.

Wigoder, Geoffrey, ed. *Contemporary Jewry: Studies in Honor of Moshe Davis*. Jerusalem: 1984.

SYNAGOGUE HISTORIES

Many Conservative congregations have published works commemorating significant events in the history of the congregation—celebrating a rabbi's anniversary or a milestone in the life of the synagogue. These works range from small pamphlets to lengthy, hardcover volumes filled with reprints of congratulatory letters and photos of confirmation classes and sisterhood musical revues. Almost all include an historical overview of the development of the synagogue and its leading lay and professional personnel. Buried within these volumes are a wealth of materials about the social history of Conservative congregations. Unfortunately, locating these histories is in and of itself not an easy task. The library of the Jewish Theological Seminary has but a handful of these volumes on its shelves; the catalogue of the Library of Congress lists some forty such volumes for all denominations of American Judaism. As a genre, synagogue histories have infrequently engaged the professional historian. Carole Kruckoff's *Rodfei Zedek: The First Hundred Years (1874–1974)* is an exemplary model. For further discussion of the genre, see Elliot Gertel's review essay, "From Beth Tefillah to Beth Midrash: Learning from Synagogue Histories," *American Jewish History*, 74, 3 (March 1985): 312–22.

Because many congregations have the same name, these histories are listed by city.

Bayonne, New Jersey. *Thy Goodly Tent: The First Fifty Years of Temple Emanu-el.* By Henry R. Schnitzer. 1961.

Chattanooga, Tennessee. *The Golden Book of B'nai Zion Congregation, 1888–1938.* 1938.

Chestnut Hill, Massachusetts. *Congregation Mishkan Tefila.* N.D.

Chicago, Illinois. *The Anshe Emet Synagogue, 1873–1973.* N.D.

Chicago, Illinois. *Rodfei Zedek: The First Hundred Years.* By Carole Kruckoff. 1976.

Dallas, Texas. *Centennial Journal Congregation Shearith Israel, Dallas, Texas, 1884–1984.* 1983.

Dallas, Texas. *Golden Book of Congregation Shearith Israel.* 1934.

Elkins Park, Pennsylvania. *Beth Shalom Synagogue: A Description and Interpretation.* By Mortimer J. Cohen. 1959.

Elkins Park, Pennsylvania. *The Beth Sholom Story, 1919–1969.* 1969.

Elkins Park, Pennsylvania. *To Commemorate 125 Years: Congregation Adath Jeshurun, 1858–1983, 5619–5744.* 1983.

Flint, Michigan. *Congregation Beth Israel: Dedication Volume.* 1972.

Hamilton, Ontario. *History of the Congregation (Beth Jacob).* By Marjorie Campbell. 1969.

Harrisburg, Pennsylvania. *Fiftieth Anniversary: Temple Beth El, 1926–1976.* N.D.

Los Angeles, California. *The Pressman Chronicles in the Jubilee Year of Temple Beth Am, 1935–1985.* 1985.

Montreal, Quebec. *One Hundred Years of Spiritual Growth.* By Herman Abramowitz. 1948. (On Shaar Hashomayim Congregation.)

New Haven, Connecticut. *Congregation Beth El-Kesher Israel: Twenty-Fifth Anniversary, May 30–June 2, 1985.* 1985.

New Haven, Connecticut. *The George Street Synagogue of Congregation B'nai Jacob.* Edited by Harvey N. Ladin. 1961.

New Haven, Connecticut. *The George Street Synagogue of Congregation B'nai Jacob.* By Nahum Zilberberg. 1961.

New Rochelle, New York. *Let Them Make Me a Sanctuary: A Contemporary American Synagogue Inspired by the Art of Ancient Israel.* By Stanley Irving Batkin. New York: Behrman House, 1978. (On Congregation Beth El.)

New York, New York. *A Century of Judaism in New York: B'nai Jeshurun, 1825–1925: New York's Oldest Ashkenazic Congregation.* By Israel Goldstein. 1930.

New York, New York. *Silver Jubilee Celebration of the Ministry of Rabbi Israel Goldstein to Congregation B'nai Jeshurun.* 1944.

New York, New York. *Story of Shaarey Zedek: One Hundredth Anniversary of Congregation Shaarey Zedek.* By Elias L. Solomon. 1937.

New York, New York. "The Synagogue in American Judaism: A Study of Congregation B'nai Jeshurun, New York City." By Moshe Davis. In *Two Generations in Perspective: Notable Events and Trends, 1896–1956.* Edited by Harry Schneiderman, pp. 210–35. New York: Monde Publishers, 1957.

New York, New York. *Within the Gates.* By Jacob Monsky. 1964. (On Congregation Shaare Zedek.)

Oklahoma City, Oklahoma. *Emanuel, 1904–1984: 80 Years of Faith.* N.D.

Philadelphia, Pennsylvania. *The Har Zion Temple, 1924–1949.* Edited by Samuel Sussman. 1949.

Providence, Rhode Island. *Temple Emanu-El: The First Fifty Years, 1924–1975.* By Louis B. Rubinstein. 1976.

Richmond, Virginia. *The Beth-El-Lite.* 1944.

Richmond, Virginia. *Our Jubilee Year—A Commemoration of the Founding and Growth of Temple Beth-El, 1931–1981.* By Myron Berman. N.D.

San Francisco, California. "A Merger of Synagogues in San Francisco." By C.L. Wiener. *Jewish Journal of Sociology,* 14 (December 1972): 167–96.

Southfield, Michigan. *Congregation Shaarey Zedek, 1861–1981.* By Eli Grad and Bette Roth. 1982.

St. Louis, Missouri. *B'nai Amoona for All Generations.* By Rosalind Mae Bronsen. 1984.

Troy, New York. *Our First Fifty Years: Temple Beth El, 1929–1979.* N.D.

Wilmington, Delaware. *Temple Beth Shalom: Fifty Year Historical Record, 1922–1972.* 1972.

Woodbridge, Connecticut. *B'nai Jacob: One Hundred Years, 1882–1982.* N.D.

PRAYER BOOKS

In addition to the prayer books officially published by the national associations of the Conservative and Reconstructionist movements, numerous rabbis arranged, translated, and compiled their own liturgies for their synagogues. Some of these were used widely; others were used only in the rabbi's own congregation.

Bokser, Ben Zion, ed. *The High Holy Day Prayer Book.* New York: 1959.

———, ed. *The Prayer Book: Weekday, Sabbath, and Festival.* New York: 1957.

———, ed. *Selihot Service.* New York: 1955.

Bosniak, Jacob, ed. *Prayers of Israel.* 2 vols. New York: 1925.

————, ed. *Anthology of Prayer*. New York: 1958.

Chanover, Hyman. *A Book of Prayers for Junior Congregations*. New York: 1959.

————. *A Haggadah for the School*. New York: 1964.

————. *My Book of Prayers*. 2 vols. New York: 1959.

Goldfarb, Israel, and Levinthal, Israel H., eds. *Songs and Praise for Sabbath Eve*. New York: 1920.

Greenberg, Sidney, ed. *Likrat Shabbat*. Bridgeport, Conn.: 1973.

————, and Sugarman, S. Allan, eds. *Sabbath and Festival Services for Children*. Hartford, Conn.: 1970.

————, and Levine, Jonathan, eds. *The New Mahzor*. Bridgeport, Conn.: 1977.

Guthman, Sidney S. *Sabbath Eve Services and Hymns*. New York: 1944.

Harlow, Jules, ed. *Mahzor for Rosh Hashanah and Yom Kippur*. New York: 1972.

————, ed. *Siddur Sim Shalom*. New York: 1985.

————, ed. *Yearnings: Prayer and Meditation for the Days of Awe*. New York: 1968.

————, ed. *Yearnings II*. New York: 1974.

Hertz, Joseph Herman, ed. *The Authorized Daily Prayer Book of the United Hebrew Congregations of the British Empire*. London: 1942.

————, ed. *The Pentateuch and the Haftorahs*. London: 1929–36.

Kaplan, Mordecai M. et al., eds. *The Daily Prayer Book*. New York: 1963.

———— et al., eds. *The Festival Prayer Book*. New York: 1958.

———— et al., eds. *High Holiday Prayer Book*. 2 vols. New York: 1948.

———— et al., eds. *The New Haggadah for the Pesah Seder*. New York: 1941; rev. 1942.

———— et al., eds. *Sabbath Prayer Book*. New York: 1945.

Klein, Max D. *Seder Avodah for Rosh Hashannah and Yom Kippur*. Philadelphia: 1960.

————. *Seder Avodah for Sabbath, Festivals, and Weekdays*. Philadelphia: 1951.

Kohn, Eugene, ed. *Shir Hadash*. New York: 1939.

Levinthal, Israel H. *Sabbath Eve Services*. New York: 1916.

Millgram, Abraham E., ed. *Beth Israel Hymnal*. Philadelphia: 1937.

Rabbinical Assembly of America and the United Synagogue of America. *Sabbath and Festival Prayer Book*. Edited by Robert Gordis et al. New York: 1946.

Silverman, Morris, ed. *High Holiday Prayer Book*. New York: 1939.

————, ed. *Junior Prayer Book for Sabbath and Festivals*. 2 vols. New York: 1933.

————, ed. *Purim Service*. Hartford, Conn.: 1947.

————, ed. *Sabbath and Festival Services*. Hartford, Conn.: 1936.

————, ed. *Simhat Torah Service*. Hartford, Conn.: 1941.

————, ed. *Weekday Prayer Book*. Hartford, Conn.: 1956.

————, and Greenberg, Sidney, eds. *Our Prayer Book*. Hartford, Conn.: 1961.

United Synagogue of America. *Festival Prayer Book*. Edited by Alexander Marx et al. New York: 1927.

SECONDARY SOURCES

Ackerman, Walter I. "Toward a History of the Curriculum of the Conservative Congregational School." *Jewish Education* 48 (Summer 1980): 12–20.

Agus, Jacob. *Modern Philosophies of Judaism*. New York: 1941.

Ahlstrom, Sydney E. *A Religious History of the American People*. New Haven: 1972.

Alpert, Rebecca T. "The Making of a Rabbi: The Reconstructionist Approach." *Encyclopedia Judaica Year Book*. Jerusalem: 1985.

————, and Staub, Jacob J. *Exploring Judaism: A Reconstructionist Approach.* New York: 1985.

Appel, John J. "The Trefa Banquet." *Commentary* (February 1966): 75–78.

Baron, Salo. "The Image of a Rabbi Formerly and Today." In his *Steeled by Adversity*, pp. 147–57. Philadelphia: 1971.

Blau, Joseph. *Judaism in America: From Curiosity to Third Faith.* Chicago: 1976.

————. *Modern Varieties of Judaism.* New York: 1966.

Brauner, Ronald A., ed. *Jewish Civilization: Essays and Studies.* Philadelphia: 1981.

Bubis, Gerald B. and Wasserman, Harry. *Synagogue Havurot: A Comparative Study.* Washington, D.C.: 1983.

Carlin, Jerome E., and Mendolovitz, Saul H. "The American Rabbi: A Religious Specialist Responds to Loss of Authority." In *The Jews: Social Structure of an American Group*, edited by Marshall Sklare. New York: 1958.

Davis, Moshe. *The Emergence of Conservative Judaism: The Historical School in Nineteenth-Century America.* Philadelphia: 1963.

————. "Jewish Religious Life and Institutions in America." In *The Jews: Their History, Culture, and Religion*, edited by Louis Finkelstein, vol. 2, pp. 274–379. New York: 1971.

————. *Yahadut Amerika Be-hitpathutah (Toldot Haescola Hahistorit Bimayah Hateshaesray).* New York: 1951.

Dorff, Elliot N. "The Ideology of Conservative Judaism: Sklare After Thirty Years." *American Jewish History* 74 (December 1984): 102–117.

Eisen, Arnold. *The Chosen People in America: A Study in Jewish Religious Ideology.* Bloomington, Ind.: 1983.

Elazar, Daniel J. *Community and Polity: The Organizational Dynamics of American Jewry.* Philadelphia: 1976.

————. "The Development of the American Synagogue." *Modern Judaism* 4 (October 1984): 255–73.

————and Monson, Rela Geffen. "The Evolving Roles of American Congregational Rabbis." *Modern Judaism* 2 (February 1982): 73–89.

————. "Women in the Synagogue Today." *Midstream*, (April 1979): 25–30.

Ellenson, David. "Liberal Judaism in Israel: Problems and Prospects." *Journal of Reform Judaism*, 31 (Winter 1984): 60–70.

Engleman, Uriah Z. "Jewish Statistics in the United States Census of Religious Bodies, 1850–1936." *Jewish Social Studies*, 9 (1947): 127–74.

Fierstien, Robert E. "Solomon Schechter and the Zionist Movement." *CJ*, 29 (Spring 1975): 3–13.

Friedman, Theodore. "Halakhah: The Attitude of Conservative Judaism." In *Encyclopedia Judaica Year Book 1975–76*, pp. 145–55. Jerusalem: 1976.

Gal, Allon. "The Mission Motif in American Zionism." *American Jewish History*, 75 (June 1986): 363–85.

Gelber, Sholome Michael. *The Failure of the American Rabbi: A Program for the Revitalization of the Rabbinate in America.* New York: 1961.

Glazer, Nathan. *American Judaism.* 2d ed. Chicago: 1972.

Graetz, Heinrich. *The Structure of Jewish History and Other Essays.* Translated by Ismar Schorsch. New York: 1975.

Grobman, Alex. "American Jewish Chaplains and the Shearit Hapletah: April-June 1945." *Simon Wiesenthal Center Annual* 1 (1984): 89–111.

Gurock, Jeffrey S. "Resisters and Accommodators: Varieties of Orthodox Rabbis in America, 1886–1983." *American Jewish Archives* 35 (November 1983): 100–187.

———. "The Winnowing of American Orthodoxy." In *Approaches to Modern Judaism*, edited by Marc Lee Raphael, vol. 2. Chico, Calif.: 1984.

Hammer, Reuven. "The Dilemma of the Conservative Rabbi." *CJ* 27 (Summer 1973): 79–82.

Handlin, Oscar. *Adventure in Freedom—Three Hundred Years of Jewish Life in America.* New York: 1954.

Herberg, Will. *Judaism and Modern Man*. Philadelphia: 1951.

———. *Protestant—Catholic—Jew: An Essay in American Religious Sociology*. 1955; rev. Garden City, N.Y., 1960.

Hertzberg, Arthur. "The Changing American Rabbinate." *Midstream* (January 1966): 16–30.

———. "The Conservative Rabbinate: A Sociological Study." In *Essays on Jewish Life and Thought*, edited by Joseph Blau, pp. 309–32. New York: 1959.

Jick, Leon. *The Americanization of the Synagogue, 1820–1870*. Hanover, N.H.: 1976.

Joselit, Jenna Weissman. "Modern Orthodox Jews and the Ordeal of Civility." *American Jewish History*, 74 (December 1984): 133–42.

Kaplan, Lawrence J. "The Dilemma of Conservative Judaism." *Commentary* (November 1976): 44–54.

Karp, Abraham J. "A Century of Conservative Judaism in the United States." *American Jewish Year Book* 86 (1986): 3–61.

———. "The Conservative Rabbi." *American Jewish Archives* 25 (November 1983): 188–262.

———. *A History of the United Synagogue of America, 1913–1963*. New York: 1964.

———. "The Origins of Conservative Judaism." *CJ*, 19, 4 (Summer 1965): 33–48.

Katzoff, Louis. *Issues in Jewish Education: A Study of the Philosophy of the Conservative Congregational School*. New York: 1949.

Kertzer, Morris N. "Synagogue Surveys—Conservative Trends." *American Jewish Year Book* 53 (1952): 155ff.

Klagsbrun, Francine. "3080 Broadway." *Moment* 12, 4 (June 1987): 11–18.

Lazar, M.M. "The Role of Women in Synagogue Ritual in Canadian Conservative Congregations." *Jewish Journal of Sociology* 20 (December 1978): 165–71.

Leiser, Joseph. *American Judaism: Religion and Religious Institutions of the Jewish People in the United States*. New York: 1925.

Liebman, Charles S. *The Ambivalent American Jew*. Philadelphia: 1973.

———. *Aspects of the Religious Behavior of American Jews*. New York: 1974.

———. "Changing Social Characteristics of Orthodox, Conservative and Reform Jews." *Sociological Analysis* 27 (Winter 1966): 210–22.

———. "The Future of Conservative Judaism in the United States." *Jerusalem Newsletter: Viewpoints* 11, 31 March 1980.

———. "Reconstructionism in American Jewish Life." *American Jewish Year Book* 71 (1970): 3–99.

———. "The Training of American Rabbis." *American Jewish Year Book* 69 (1968): 3–114.

Linzer, Norman, ed. *Jewish Communal Services in the United States, 1960–1970, A Selected Bibliography*. New York: 1972.

Martin, Bernard. "Conservative Judaism and Reconstructionism." In his *Movements and Issues in American Judaism (since 1945)*, pp. 103–157. Westport, Conn.: 1978.

Meyer, Michael M. "A Centennial History." In *Hebrew Union College-Jewish Institute of Religion at One Hundred Years*, edited by Samuel E. Karff, pp. 3–283. Cincinnati: 1976.

Neusner, Jacob. "Conservative Judaism in a Divided Community." *CJ* 20, 4 (Summer 1966): 1–19.

———. *The Way of Torah: An Introduction to Judaism*. Belmont, Calif.: 1970.

———, ed. *Understanding American Judaism*. 2 vols. New York: 1975.

Olan, Levi A. "A New Prayer Book: Conservative Judaism Defines Itself." *Judaism*, 22 (Fall 1973): 418–25.

Polner, Murray. *Rabbi: The American Experience*. New York: 1977.

Rakeffet-Rothkoff, Aaron. "The Attempt to Merge the Jewish Theological Seminary and Yeshiva College, 1926–27." *Michael* 3 (1975).

Raphael, Marc Lee. *Profiles in American Judaism: The Reform, Conservative, Orthodox, and Reconstructionist Traditions in Historical Perspective*. San Francisco: 1984.

Rischin, Moses. *The Promised City: New York's Jews, 1870–1914*. Cambridge, Mass.: 1962.

Rosenblum, Herbert. *Conservative Judaism: A Contemporary History*. New York: 1983.

———. "Ideology and Compromise: The Evolution of the United Synagogue Constitutional Preamble." *Jewish Social Studies* 35 (January 1973): 18–31.

———. "The Shaping of an Institution: The 1902 Reorganization of the Seminary." *CJ* 27, 2 (Winter 1973): 35–48.

Rosenthal, Gilbert S. *Contemporary Judaism: Patterns of Survival*. 2d ed. New York: 1986.

Rothkoff, Aaron. *Bernard Revel: Builder of American Jewish Orthodoxy*. Philadelphia: 1972.

Rubinoff, Michael W. "Crisis in Conservative Judaism, Denver, 1949–1958." *Western States Jewish History* 12 (July 1980): 326–40.

Rudavsky, David. *Modern Jewish Religious Movements: A History of Emancipation and Adjustment*. New York: 1967; rev. 1979.

Schneiderman, Harry. *Two Generations in Perspective: Notable Events and Trends, 1896–1956*. New York: 1957.

Schwarz, Sidney H. "Conservative Judaism's 'Ideology' Problem." *American Jewish History* 74, 2 (December 1984): 143–57.

———. "Reconstructionism and Conservative Judaism." *Judaism* 33 (Spring 1984): 171–78.

Scult, Mel. "Mordecai M. Kaplan: Challenges and Conflicts in the Twenties." *American Jewish Historical Quarterly* 66 (March 1977): 401–16.

———. "The Teachers Institute and the Foundations of Jewish Education in America." *American Jewish Archives* 38 (April 1986): 57–84.

Shankman, Jacob K. "The Changing Role of the Rabbi." In *Retrospect and Prospect*, edited by Bertram W. Korn, pp. 230–51. New York: 1965.

Shapiro, Alexander M., and Cohen, Burton I., eds. *Studies in Jewish Education and Judaica in Honor of Louis Newman*. New York: 1984.

Singer, Howard. "Rabbis & Their Discontents," *Commentary* 79, 5 (May 1985): 55–58.

Sklare, Marshall. *Conservative Judaism: An American Religious Movement*. 1955. Rev., 1972; Reprint, Lanham, Md., 1985.

———. "Recent Developments in Conservative Judaism." *Midstream* 18, 1 (January 1972): 3–19.

———. "Response." *American Jewish History* 74 (December 1984): 158–168.

Tabak, Robert. "Orthodox Judaism in Transition." In *Jewish Life in Philadelphia, 1830–1940*, edited by Murray Friedman, pp. 48–63. Philadelphia: 1983.

Trachtenberg, Joshua. "Books on Conservative Judaism." *American Jewish Year Book* 50 (1948): 164–75.

Waxman, Chaim I. *America's Jews in Transition*. Philadelphia: 1983.

Weiss-Rosmarin, Trude. "Women in Conservative Synagogues." *Jewish Spectator* 38 (October 1973): 5–6.

Wertheimer, Jack. "The Conservative Synagogue Revisited." *American Jewish History* 74 (Dec. 1984): 118–132.

———, ed. *The History of the Synagogue in America*. New York: 1987.

"What Kind of Job is that for a Nice Jewish Person?: A Moment Conversation with Six New Rabbis." *Moment* 10, 7 (July-August 1985): 30–34ff.

Whiteman, Maxwell. "The Philadelphia Group." In *Jewish Life in Philadelphia, 1830–1940*, edited by Murray Friedman, pp. 163–78. Philadelphia: 1983.

Zeitlin, Joseph. *Disciples of the Wise: The Religious and Social Opinions of American Rabbis*. New York: 1945.

COMMUNITY HISTORIES

Many Jewish communal histories, scholarly studies, and personal accounts written by those born and bred within the community often include materials about local Conservative synagogues and their rabbis. For an insightful discussion of the genre, see Jonathan Sarna's review essay, "Jewish Community Histories: Recent Non-Academic Contributions," *Journal of American Ethnic History* 6, 1 (Fall 1986): 62–70.

Abelow, Samuel Phillip. *History of Brooklyn Jewry*. New York: 1937.

Adler, Selig, and Connolly, Thomas. *From Ararat to Suburbia: The History of the Jewish Community of Buffalo*. Philadelphia: 1960.

Berman, Myron. *Richmond's Jewry, 1769–1976: Shabbat in Shockoe*. Charlottesville, Va.: 1979.

Breck, Alan DuPont. *The Centennial History of the Jews of Colorado, 1859–1959*. Denver: 1960.

Chiel, Arthur A. *The Jews in Manitoba*. Toronto: 1961.

Dawidowicz, Lucy. "Middle-Class Judaism." In her *The Jewish Presence: Essays on Identity and History*. New York: 1977. (On Jackson Heights, New York.)

Endelman, Judith E. *The Jewish Community of Indianapolis: 1849 to the Present*. Bloomington: 1984.

Fein, Isaac. *The Making of an American Jewish Community*. Philadelphia: 1971.

Friedman, Murray, ed. *Jewish Life in Philadelphia, 1830–1940*. Philadelphia: 1983.

Gartner, Lloyd P. *The History of the Jews of Cleveland*. Cleveland: 1978.

Gartner, Lloyd P., and Swichkow, Louis J. *The History of the Jews of Milwaukee*. Philadelphia: 1963.

Goldstein, Sidney, and Goldscheider, Calvin. *Jewish Americans: Three Generations in a Jewish Community*. Englewood Cliffs, N.J.: 1968. (On Providence, Rhode Island.)

Gordon, Albert. *Jews in Transition*. Minneapolis: 1949. (On Minneapolis, Minnesota.)

Gurock, Jeffrey. *When Harlem Was Jewish, 1870–1930*. New York: 1979.

Gutstein, Morris A. *A Priceless Heritage: The Epic Growth of Nineteenth-Century Chicago Jewry*. New York: 1953.

———. *The Story of the Jews of Newport: 1658–1908*. New York: 1936.

Landesman, Alter F. *Brownsville: The Birth, Development, and Passing of a Jewish Community in New York*. New York: 1969.

Meites, Hyman L. *History of the Jews of Chicago*. Chicago: 1924.

Moore, Deborah Dash. *At Home in America: Second Generation New York Jews*. New York: 1981.

Plaut, W. Gunther. *The Jews of Minnesota*. New York: 1959.

Raphael, Marc Lee. *Jews and Judaism in a Midwestern Community: Columbus, Ohio 1840–1975*. Columbus: 1979.

Rosenberg, Stuart E. *The Jewish Community in Canada*. 2 vols. Toronto and Montreal: 1970.

———. *The Jewish Community of Rochester, 1843–1925*. New York: 1954.

Sarna, Jonathan D., ed. *Jews in New Haven*. New Haven: 1978.

Schultz, Joseph P., ed. *Mid-America's Promise: A Profile of Kansas City Jewry*. Kansas City: 1982.

Shuman, Bernard. *A History of the Sioux City Jewish Community, 1869–1969*. Sioux City, Iowa: 1969.

Silverman, Morris. *Hartford Jews, 1959–1970*. Hartford, Conn.: 1970.

Toll, William. *The Making of an Ethnic Middle Class: Portland Jewry over Four Generations*. Albany: 1982.

Vincent, Sidney Z., and Rubinstein, Judah. *Merging Traditions: Jewish Life in Cleveland*. Cleveland: 1978.

Vorspan, Max, and Gartner, Lloyd P. *History of the Jews of Los Angeles*. San Marino, Calif.: 1970.

UNPUBLISHED THESES, DISSERTATIONS, AND PAPERS

Bauman, Mark K. "Harry Hyman Epstein and the Rabbinate as the Conduit for Change." Unpublished Paper, Atlanta Junior College, 1987.

Bekerman, Zvi. "The Social Construction of Jewishness: An Anthropological Interactional Study of a Camp [Ramah] System." Ph.d. dissertation, Jewish Theological Seminary of America, 1986.

Berman, Howard Allen. "His Majesty's Loyal Opponents." Rabbinical dissertation, Hebrew Union College-Jewish Institute of Religion, Cincinnati, 1974.

Elster, Sheldon Ephraim. "*Kiddushin*: Values in the Jewish Wedding Ceremony and Their Use in Pre-Marital Counseling by Conservative Rabbis." D. Min. dissertation, Wesley Theological Seminary, 1973.

Farago, Uri. "The Influence of a Jewish Summer Camp's Social Climate on the Camper's Identity." Ph.D. dissertation, Brandeis University, 1972. (On Camp Ramah at Palmer.)

Fierstein, Robert E. "From Foundation to Reorganization: The Jewish Theological Seminary of America, 1886–1902." D.H.L. dissertation, Jewish Theological Seminary of America, 1986.

Gertel, Elliot B. "The Sermons and Other Writings of Rabbi Israel H. Levinthal." Unpublished paper.

Gordon, Rebecca. "The Religious Ideology of Conservative Jews." M.A. thesis, Hebrew Union College, Los Angeles, 1981.

Kandel, Andrea C. "Processes of Jewish American Identity Development: Perceptions of Conservative Jewish Women." Ph.D. dissertation, University of Massachusetts, 1986.

Liebman, Charles S., and Shapiro, Saul. "A Survey of the Conservative Movement and Some of Its Religious Attitudes." An unpublished report presented to the Chancellor and the Faculty of the Jewish Theological Seminary of America, 11 November 1979.

Markovitz, Eugene. "Henry Pereira Mendes." D.H.L. dissertation, Yeshiva University, 1961.

Nussenbaum, Max Samuel. "Champion of Orthodox Judaism: A Biography of the Reverend Sabato Morais." D.H.L. dissertation, Yeshiva University, 1964.

Rosenblum, Herbert. "The Founding of the United Synagogue of America, 1913." Ph.D. dissertation, Brandeis University, 1970.

Rosenthal, Jerome C. "The Public Life of Louis Marshall." Ph.D. dissertation, University of Cincinnati, 1983.

Rubinoff, Michael Wayne. "Rabbi Charles Eliezer Hillel Kauvar of Denver: The Life of a Rabbi in the American West." Ph.D. dissertation, University of Denver, 1978.

Sasso, Dennis C. "A Case Study in Congregational Pluralism and Vitality." D. Min. dissertation, Christian Theological Seminary, 1985. (On Congregation Beth El-Zedeck, Indianapolis, Indiana.)

Schwartz, Shuly Rubin. "Ramah—The Early Years, 1947–1952." M.A. thesis, Jewish Theological Seminary of America, 1976.

Schwarz, Sidney Howard. "Law and Legitimacy: An Intellectual History of Conservative Judaism, 1902–1973." Ph.D. dissertation, Temple University, 1982.

Solomon, Sidney. "The Conservative Congregational School as a Response to the American Scene." D.H.L. dissertation, Jewish Theological Seminary of America, 1982.

Steinberg, Theodore. "Max Kadushin, Scholar of Rabbinic Judaism: A Study of His Life, World, and Theory of Valuational Thought." Ph.D. dissertation, New York University, 1980.

Wachs, Saul P. "An Application of Inquiry-Teaching to the Siddur." Ph.D. dissertation, The Ohio State University, 1970. (On the educational approach of the Melton Research Center.)

———. "The Impact of a Pilot Project in Religious Education upon a Midwestern Conservative Jewish Congregation." M.A. thesis, The Ohio State University, 1966. (On Congregation Tifereth Israel, Columbus, Ohio.)

INDEX

Bold face numbers refer to the bibliographical sketch

Aaronson, Grace Avis, 104
Aaron (St. Paul, MN), 201
Abbell, Maxwell, 337
Abeles, Ray Steinhardt, 125
Abelson, Kassel Elijah, **25–26**
Abramowitz, Herman, **26–27**, 173, 233, 337
Abramowitz, Miriam Burros, 26
Academy for Judaism, 111
Achavah Club, 91
Ackerman, Walter I., 235, 343
Adas Israel (Chicago), 126
Adas Israel (Washington, DC), 206, 207
Adat Ari El (North Hollywood, CA), 257
Adath Israel (Bronx), 35, 146, 217
Adath Israel (Cincinnati), 83, 102–3
Adath Jeshuron (Syracuse, NY), 164
Adath Jeshurun (Louisville, KY), 214
Adath Jeshurun (Minneapolis), 112, 116–17, 186, 206
Adath Jeshurun (Philadelphia), 41, 161
Adath Yeshurun (Syracuse, NY), 72, 135
Adler, Cyrus, **27–31**, 84, 89, 99–100, 109, 121, 151, 164, 192, 198, 201, 223, 224, 225, 226, 266, 267, 269–70, 271–74, 275, 277, 278, 286, 290, 316, 319, 326, 328, 337
Adler, Hermann, 135
Adler, Jennie Resnick, 31
Adler, Joseph, 31
Adler, Morris, 10, **31–32**, 33
Adler, Samuel, 27

Adler, Sarah Sulzberger, 27
Adult School of Jewish Studies of the Five Towns, 219
Agadah, 101
Agassi, Hadassa, 211
Agudas Achim North Shore (Chicago), 33
Agudat ha-Rabbanim, 7, 174
Agunah, 7, 10, 11, 14, 36, 54, 80, 92, 212–13
Agudath Jeshurun, 326
Agus, Jacob Bernard, 8, 10–11, **32–35**, 303, 318
Agushewitz, Bela Devorah Bereznitzky, 32
Agushewitz, Judah, 32
Ahavai Shalom (Portland, OR), 201, 219
Ahavath Achim (Atlanta), 79, 112
Ahavath Chesed (NYC), 166, 167
Ahavath Israel (Philadelphia), 49, 136
Aliyot, 41
Allied Jewish Appeal, 161
Alpert, Edith, 245
Alstat, Fannie Reis, 35
Alstat, Mendel, 35
Alstat, Philip R., **35**
America-Holy Land Studies Program, 69
American Academy for Jewish Research, 98, 101, 180, 185, 244
American Academy of Arts and Sciences, 244
American Association of Jewish Education, 49, 71, 349
American-Israel Cultural Foundation, 182

Chertoff, Paul, 276
Chiel, Arthur Abraham, **50–51**, 314
Chiel, Frieda, 50
Chiel, Solomon, 50
Chizuk Amuno (Baltimore), 106, 163
Chodos, Israel, 124, 164
Clark, Hattie, 231
Cleveland Jewish Center, 52, 58, 107
Cohen, Armond E., **51–53**, 58, 309
Cohen, Boaz, 6, 8, **53–55**, 273, 288–89, 290, 330, 336, 337
Cohen, Duscoff, 61
Cohen, Gerson David, 16, **55–58**, 227, 232, 284, 287
Cohen, Goldie L., 62
Cohen, Helen Grossman, 58
Cohen, Hermann, 33
Cohen, Isidor, 58
Cohen, Jack Joseph, **58–59**
Cohen, Jacob, 53
Cohen, Joseph, 59
Cohen, Meyer, 55
Cohen, Mortimer Joseph, **59–61**
Cohen, Nehama Goldin, 55
Cohen, Philip J., 62
Cohen, Rachel Harriet Levine, 59
Cohen, Rachmiel, 61
Cohen, Rebecca Lipkowitz, 51
Cohen, Rose Cohen, 62
Cohen, Samuel C., 51
Cohen, Samuel Meir, 42, **61–62**, 104, 129, 206, 242, 335, 329
Cohen, Seymour J., **62–64**
Cohn, Stella, 47
College of Jewish Studies, 63
Columbian Exposition (Chicago, 1893), 28
Commission for the Study of the Ordination of Women as Rabbis, 289
Commission of Community Service (RA), 196
Commission on Public Relief and Assistance for the Commonwealth of Pennsylvania, 37
Commission on Social Action, 231
Communidat Bet El (Buenos Aires), 187
Concourse Center of Israel (Bronx), 72, 181
Conference in Memory of the Six Million, 34
Conference of Presidents of Major American Jewish Organizations, 78, 213
Conference on Jewish Social Studies, 137
Conference on Science, Philosophy, and Religion in Their Relation to the Democratic Way of Life, 43, 86, 283
Congregation Emanuel (Mount Vernon, NY), 40

Congress of Jewish Notables, 166
Conservative Judaism, 70–71
Conservative Judaism, definition of, 1
Conservative Synagogue of Fifth Avenue (NYC), 77
Council of Conservative Synagogues of Chicago, 206

Daskal, Benjamin, 241
Davidowitz, Harry S., 5
Davidson, Bessie Stern, 67
Davidson, Charles, 67
Davidson, Israel, **65–66**, 224, 268, 271
Davidson, Max David, 12, **67–68**, 303, 309
Davis, Betty, 123
Davis, Dorothy Etta, 118
Davis, Ida Schenker, 68
Davis, Moshe, **68–70**, 122, 151, 167, 263, 281, 282, 346
Davis, William, 68
Dawidowitz, Harry, 52
Denver Hebrew School, 156
Denver Jewish Welfare Board, 156
Depth Theology, 140
Detroit Round Table of Catholics, Protestants and Jews, 31
Diaspora Jewry, 19–20, 152–53
Dinn, Samuel, 276
"Directions," 213
Dirnfield, Kinneret, 51
Drachman, Bernard, 167, 264, 268
Dresner, Julius, 70
Dresner, Maude Handmacher, 70
Dresner, Samuel H., **70–72**, 140, 314
Dreyfuss, Carrie, 66
Drob, Etta Schwartz, 72
Drob, Judah Idel, 72
Drob, Max, 5, **72–73**, 75, 301
Dropsie College, 29, 198, 226, 272, 325
Dubnow, Simon, 89, 90
Durkheim, Emile, 19, 152
Dushkin, Alexander, 145

East Midwood Jewish Center (Brooklyn), 132
Ehrlich, Arnold, 147
Eibeschuetz, Jonathan, 60
Eichler, Menahem Max, **75–76**, 299
Eilberg, Amy, 16, 56, 232, 289
Eisenhower, Dwight D., 86, 195
Eisenstein, Ira, 21, 58, 62, **76–77**, 149, 151, 152
Eisenstein, Isaac, 76

About the Author

PAMELA S. NADELL is Associate Professor of Jewish Studies and History at American University. She specializes in American Jewish History from 1881 to the present day and Jewish immigration. She has published articles in *American Jewish History* and *Studies in the American Jewish Experience*.